T0254262

Learning Kernel Classifiers

Adaptive Computation and Machine Learning

Thomas G. Dietterich, Editor

Christopher Bishop, David Heckerman, Michael Jordan, and Michael Kearns, Associate Editors

Bioinformatics: The Machine Learning Approach, Pierre Baldi and Søren Brunak

Reinforcement Learning: An Introduction, Richard S. Sutton and Andrew G. Barto

Graphical Models for Machine Learning and Digital Communication, Brendan J. Frey

Learning in Graphical Models, Michael I. Jordan

Causation, Prediction, and Search, second edition, Peter Spirtes, Clark Glymour, and Richard Scheines

Principles of Data Mining, David Hand, Heikki Mannilla, and Padhraic Smyth

Bioinformatics: The Machine Learning Approach, second edition, Pierre Baldi and Søren Brunak

Learning Kernel Classifiers: Theory and Algorithms, Ralf Herbrich

Learning with Kernels: Support Vector Machines, Regularization, Optimization, and Beyond, Bernhard Schölkopf and Alexander J. Smola

Learning Kernel Classifiers
Theory and Algorithms

Ralf Herbrich

The MIT Press
Cambridge, Massachusetts
London, England

©2002 Massachusetts Institute of Technology

All rights reserved. No part of this book may be reproduced in any form by any electronic or mechanical means (including photocopying, recording, or information storage and retrieval) without permission in writing from the publisher.

This book was set in Times Roman by the author using the LaTeX document preparation system.

Library of Congress Cataloging-in-Publication Data

Herbrich, Ralf.
Learning kernel classifiers : theory and algorithms / Ralf Herbrich.
p. cm. — (Adaptive computation and machine learning)
Includes bibliographical references and index.
ISBN 978-0-262-08306-5 (hc. : alk. paper), 978-0-262-54659-1 (pb.)
1. Machine learning. 2. Algorithms. I. Title. II. Series.

Q325.5 .H48 2001
006.3′1—dc21

2001044445

To my wife, Jeannette

There are many branches of learning theory that have not yet been analyzed and that are important both for understanding the phenomenon of learning and for practical applications. They are waiting for their researchers.
—Vladimir Vapnik

Geometry is illuminating; probability theory is powerful.
—Pál Ruján

Contents

Series Foreword

One of the most exciting recent developments in machine learning is the discovery and elaboration of kernel methods for classification and regression. These algorithms combine three important ideas into a very successful whole. From mathematical programming, they exploit quadratic programming algorithms for convex optimization; from mathematical analysis, they borrow the idea of kernel representations; and from machine learning theory, they adopt the objective of finding the maximum-margin classifier. After the initial development of support vector machines, there has been an explosion of kernel-based methods. Ralf Herbrich's *Learning Kernel Classifiers* is an authoritative treatment of support vector machines and related kernel classification and regression methods. The book examines these methods both from an algorithmic perspective and from the point of view of learning theory. The book's extensive appendices provide pseudo-code for all of the algorithms and proofs for all of the theoretical results. The outcome is a volume that will be a valuable classroom textbook as well as a reference for researchers in this exciting area.

The goal of building systems that can adapt to their environment and learn from their experience has attracted researchers from many fields, including computer science, engineering, mathematics, physics, neuroscience, and cognitive science. Out of this research has come a wide variety of learning techniques that have the potential to transform many scientific and industrial fields. Recently, several research communities have begun to converge on a common set of issues surrounding supervised, unsupervised, and reinforcement learning problems. The MIT Press series on Adaptive Computation and Machine Learning seeks to unify the many diverse strands of machine learning research and to foster high quality research and innovative applications.

Thomas Dietterich

Preface

Machine learning has witnessed a resurgence of interest over the last few years, which is a consequence of the rapid development of the information industry. Data is no longer a scarce resource—it is abundant. Methods for "intelligent" data analysis to extract relevant information are needed. The goal of this book is to give a self-contained overview of machine learning, particularly of kernel classifiers—both from an algorithmic and a theoretical perspective. Although there exist many excellent textbooks on learning algorithms (see Duda and Hart (1973), Bishop (1995), Vapnik (1995), Mitchell (1997) and Cristianini and Shawe-Taylor (2000)) and on learning theory (see Vapnik (1982), Kearns and Vazirani (1994), Wolpert (1995), Vidyasagar (1997) and Anthony and Bartlett (1999)), there is no single book which presents both aspects together in reasonable depth. Instead, these monographs often cover much larger areas of function classes, e.g., neural networks, decision trees or rule sets, or learning tasks (for example regression estimation or unsupervised learning). My motivation in writing this book is to summarize the enormous amount of work that has been done in the specific field of kernel classification over the last years. It is my aim to show how all the work is related to each other. To some extent, I also try to demystify some of the recent developments, particularly in learning theory, and to make them accessible to a larger audience. In the course of reading it will become apparent that many already known results are proven again, and in detail, instead of simply referring to them. The motivation for doing this is to have all these different results together in one place—in particular to see their similarities and (conceptual) differences.

The book is structured into a general introduction (Chapter 1) and two parts, which can be read independently. The material is emphasized through many examples and remarks. The book finishes with a comprehensive appendix containing mathematical background and proofs of the main theorems. It is my hope that the level of detail chosen makes this book a useful reference for many researchers working in this field. Since the book uses a very rigorous notation system, it is perhaps advisable to have a quick look at the background material and list of symbols on page 333.

The first part of the book is devoted to the study of algorithms for learning kernel classifiers. This part starts with a chapter introducing the basic concepts of learning from a machine learning point of view. The chapter will elucidate the basic concepts involved in learning kernel classifiers—in particular the kernel technique. It introduces the support vector machine learning algorithm as one of the most prominent examples of a learning algorithm for kernel classifiers. The second chapter presents the Bayesian view of learning. In particular, it covers Gaussian processes, the relevance vector machine algorithm and the classical Fisher discriminant. The first part is complemented by Appendix D, which gives all the pseudo code for the presented algorithms. In order to enhance the understandability of the algorithms presented, all algorithms are implemented in *R*—a statistical language similar to *S-PLUS*. The source code is publicly available at `http://www.kernel-machines.org/`. At this web site the interested reader will also find additional software packages and many related publications.

The second part of the book is devoted to the theoretical study of learning algorithms, with a focus on kernel classifiers. This part can be read rather independently of the first part, although I refer back to specific algorithms at some stages. The first chapter of this part introduces many seemingly different models of learning. It was my objective to give easy-to-follow "proving arguments" for their main results, sometimes presented in a "vanilla" version. In order to unburden the main body, all technical details are relegated to Appendix B and C. The classical PAC and VC frameworks are introduced as the most prominent examples of mathematical models for the learning task. It turns out that, despite their unquestionable generality, they only justify training error minimization and thus do not fully use the training sample to get better estimates for the generalization error. The following section introduces a very general framework for learning—the *luckiness* framework. This chapter concludes with a PAC-style analysis for the particular class of real-valued (linear) functions, which qualitatively justifies the support vector machine learning algorithm. Whereas the first chapter was concerned with bounds which hold uniformly for all classifiers, the methods presented in the second chapter provide bounds for specific learning algorithms. I start with the PAC-Bayesian framework for learning, which studies the generalization error of Bayesian learning algorithms. Subsequently, I demonstrate that for all learning algorithms that can be expressed as compression schemes, we can upper bound the generalization error by the fraction of training examples used—a quantity which can be viewed as a compression coefficient. The last section of this chapter contains a very recent development known as algorithmic stability bounds. These results apply to all algorithms for which an additional training example has only limited influence.

As with every book, this monograph has (almost surely) typing errors as well as other mistakes. Therefore, whenever you find a mistake in this book, I would be very grateful to receive an email at `herbrich@kernel-machines.org`. The list of errata will be publicly available at `http://www.kernel-machines.org`.

This book is the result of two years' work of a computer scientist with a strong interest in mathematics who stumbled onto the secrets of statistics rather innocently. Being originally fascinated by the the field of artificial intelligence, I started programming different learning algorithms, finally ending up with a giant learning system that was completely unable to generalize. At this stage my interest in learning theory was born—highly motivated by the seminal book by Vapnik (1995). In recent times, my focus has shifted toward theoretical aspects. Taking that into account, this book might at some stages look mathematically overloaded (from a practitioner's point of view) or too focused on algorithmical aspects (from a theoretician's point of view). As it presents a snapshot of the state-of-the-art, the book may be difficult to access for people from a completely different field. As complementary texts, I highly recommend the books by Cristianini and Shawe-Taylor (2000) and Vapnik (1995).

This book is partly based on my doctoral thesis (Herbrich 2000), which I wrote at the Technical University of Berlin. I would like to thank the whole statistics group at the Technical University of Berlin with whom I had the pleasure of carrying out research in an excellent environment. In particular, the discussions with Peter Bollmann-Sdorra, Matthias Burger, Jörg Betzin and Jürgen Schweiger were very inspiring. I am particularly grateful to my supervisor, Professor Ulrich Kockelkorn, whose help was invaluable. Discussions with him were always very delightful, and I would like to thank him particularly for the inspiring environment he provided. I am also indebted to my second supervisor, Professor John Shawe-Taylor, who made my short visit at the Royal Holloway College a total success. His support went far beyond the short period at the college, and during the many discussions we had, I easily understood most of the recent developments in learning theory. His "anytime availability" was of uncountable value while writing this book. Thank you very much! Furthermore, I had the opportunity to visit the Department of Engineering at the Australian National University in Canberra. I would like to thank Bob Williamson for this opportunity, for his great hospitality and for the many fruitful discussions. This book would not be as it is without the many suggestions he had. Finally, I would like to thank Chris Bishop for giving all the support I needed to complete the book during my first few months at Microsoft Research Cambridge.

During the last three years I have had the good fortune to receive help from many people all over the world. Their views and comments on my work were very influential in leading to the current publication. Some of the many people I am particularly indebted to are David McAllester, Peter Bartlett, Jonathan Baxter, Shai Ben-David, Colin Campbell, Nello Cristianini, Denver Dash, Thomas Hofmann, Neil Lawrence, Jens Matthias, Manfred Opper, Patrick Pérez, Gunnar Rätsch, Craig Saunders, Bernhard Schölkopf, Matthias Seeger, Alex Smola, Peter Sollich, Mike Tipping, Jaco Vermaak, Jason Weston and Hugo Zaragoza. In the course of writing the book I highly appreciated the help of many people who proofread previous manuscripts. David McAllester, Jörg Betzin, Peter Bollmann-Sdorra, Matthias Burger, Thore Graepel, Ulrich Kockelkorn, John Krumm, Gary Lee, Craig Saunders, Bernhard Schölkopf, Jürgen Schweiger, John Shawe-Taylor, Jason Weston, Bob Williamson and Hugo Zaragoza gave helpful comments on the book and found many errors. I am greatly indebted to Simon Hill, whose help in proofreading the final manuscript was invaluable. Thanks to all of you for your enormous help!

Special thanks goes to one person—Thore Graepel. We became very good friends far beyond the level of scientific cooperation. I will never forget the many enlightening discussions we had in several pubs in Berlin and the few excellent conference and research trips we made together, in particular our trip to Australia. Our collaboration and friendship was—and still is—of uncountable value for me. Finally, I would like to thank my wife, Jeannette, and my parents for their patience and moral support during the whole time. I could not have done this work without my wife's enduring love and support. I am very grateful for her patience and reassurance at all times.

Finally, I would like to thank Mel Goldsipe, Bob Prior, Katherine Innis and Sharon Deacon Warne at The MIT Press for their continuing support and help during the completion of the book.

Second Reprint

I am greatly indebted to all readers of the first print of this book who found (and corrected) errors. In particular, I would like to thank Dongwei Cao, Arthur Gretton, Vu Ha, Matthias Heiler, Jaz Kandola, Malte Kuss, Petra Philips, Vikas Sindhwani and Mingrui Wu. All of your comments have greatly enhanced this second reprint. Thank you!

1 Introduction

This chapter introduces the general problem of machine learning and how it relates to statistical inference. It gives a short, example-based overview about supervised, unsupervised and reinforcement learning. The discussion of how to design a learning system for the problem of handwritten digit recognition shows that kernel classifiers offer some great advantages for practical machine learning. Not only are they fast and simple to implement, but they are also closely related to one of the most simple but effective classification algorithms—the nearest neighbor classifier. Finally, the chapter discusses which theoretical questions are of particular, and practical, importance.

1.1 The Learning Problem and (Statistical) Inference

It was only a few years after the introduction of the first computer that one of man's greatest dreams seemed to be realizable—artificial intelligence. It was envisaged that machines would perform intelligent tasks such as vision, recognition and automatic data analysis. One of the first steps toward intelligent machines is machine learning.

The *learning problem* can be described as finding a general rule that explains data given only a sample of limited size. The difficulty of this task is best compared to the problem of children learning to speak and see from the continuous flow of sounds and pictures emerging in everyday life. Bearing in mind that in the early days the most powerful computers had much less computational power than a cell phone today, it comes as no surprise that much theoretical research on the potential of machines' capabilities to learn took place at this time. One of the most influential works was the textbook by Minsky and Papert (1969) in which they investigate whether or not it is realistic to expect machines to learn complex tasks. They found that simple, biologically motivated learning systems called *perceptrons* were incapable of learning an arbitrarily complex problem. This negative result virtually stopped active research in the field for the next ten years. Almost twenty years later, the work by Rumelhart et al. (1986) reignited interest in the problem of machine learning. The paper presented an efficient, locally optimal learning algorithm for the class of neural networks, a direct generalization of perceptrons. Since then, an enormous number of papers and books have been published about extensions and empirically successful applications of neural networks. Among them, the most notable modification is the so-called support vector machine—a learning algorithm for perceptrons that is motivated by theoretical results from statistical learning theory. The introduction of this algorithm by Vapnik and coworkers (see Vapnik (1995) and Cortes (1995)) led many researchers to focus on learning theory and its potential for the design of new learning algorithms.

The learning problem can be stated as follows: Given a sample of limited size, find a concise description of the data. If the data is a sample of input-output patterns, a concise description of the data is a function that can produce the output, given the input. This problem is also known as the supervised learning problem because the objects under considerations are already associated with target values (classes, real-values). Examples of this learning task include classification of handwritten letters and digits, prediction of the stock market share values, weather forecasting, and the classification of news in a news agency.

If the data is only a sample of objects without associated target values, the problem is known as unsupervised learning. A concise description of the data could be a set of clusters or a probability density stating how likely it is to observe a certain object in the future. Typical examples of unsupervised learning tasks include the problem of image and text segmentation and the task of novelty detection in process control.

Finally, one branch of learning does not fully fit into the above definitions: reinforcement learning. This problem, having its roots in control theory, considers the scenario of a dynamic environment that results in state-action-reward triples as the data. The difference between reinforcement and supervised learning is that in reinforcement learning no optimal action exists in a given state, but the learning algorithm must identify an action so as to maximize the expected reward over time. The concise description of the data is in the form of a strategy that maximizes the reward. Subsequent subsections discuss these three different learning problems.

Viewed from a statistical perspective, the problem of machine learning is far from new. In fact, it can be related to the general problem of inference, i.e., going from particular observations to general descriptions. The only difference between the machine learning and the statistical approach is that the latter considers description of the data in terms of a probability measure rather than a deterministic function (e.g., prediction functions, cluster assignments). Thus, the tasks to be solved are virtually equivalent. In this field, learning methods are known as estimation methods. Researchers long have recognized that the general philosophy of machine learning is closely related to nonparametric estimation. The statistical approach to estimation differs from the learning framework insofar as the latter does not require a probabilistic model of the data. Instead, it assumes that the only interest is in further prediction on new instances—a less ambitious task, which hopefully requires many fewer examples to achieve a certain performance.

The past few years have shown that these two conceptually different approaches converge. Expressing machine learning methods in a probabilistic framework is often possible (and vice versa), and the theoretical study of the performances of the methods is based on similar assumptions and is studied in terms of probability theory. One of the aims of this book is to elucidate the similarities (and differences) between algorithms resulting from these seemingly different approaches.

1.1.1 Supervised Learning

In the problem of supervised learning we are given a sample of input-output pairs (also called the *training sample*), and the task is to find a deterministic function that maps *any* input to an output such that disagreement with future input-output observations is minimized. Clearly, whenever asked for the target value of an object present in the training sample, it is possible to return the value that appeared the highest number of times together with this object in the training sample. However, generalizing to new objects not present in the training sample is difficult. Depending on the type of the outputs, classification learning, preference learning and function learning are distinguished.

Classification Learning

If the output space has no structure except whether two elements of the output space are equal or not, this is called the problem of *classification learning*. Each element of the output space is called a *class*. This problem emerges in virtually any pattern recognition task. For example, the classification of images to the classes "image depicts the digit x" where x ranges from "zero" to "nine" or the classification of image elements (pixels) into the classes "pixel is a part of a cancer tissue" are standard benchmark problems for classification learning algorithms (see

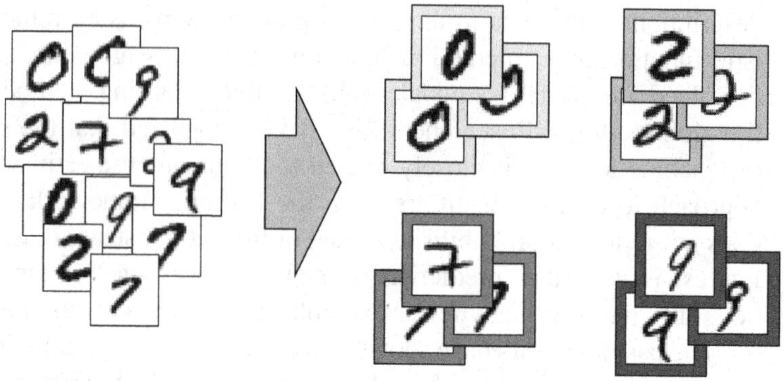

Figure 1.1 Classification learning of handwritten digits. Given a sample of images from the four different classes "zero", "two", "seven" and "nine" the task is to find a function which maps images to their corresponding class (indicated by different colors of the border). Note that there is no ordering between the four different classes.

also Figure 1.1). Of particular importance is the problem of binary classification, i.e., the output space contains only two elements, one of which is understood as the positive class and the other as the negative class. Although conceptually very simple, the binary setting can be extended to multiclass classification by considering a series of binary classifications.

Preference Learning

If the output space is an order space—that is, we can compare whether two elements are equal or, if not, which one is to be preferred—then the problem of supervised learning is also called the problem of *preference learning*. The elements of the output space are called *ranks*. As an example, consider the problem of learning to arrange Web pages such that the most relevant pages (according to a query) are ranked highest (see also Figure 1.2). Although it is impossible to observe the relevance of Web pages directly, the user would always be able to rank any pair of documents. The mappings to be learned can either be functions from the objects (Web pages) to the ranks, or functions that classify two documents into one of three classes: "first object is more relevant than second object", "objects are equivalent" and "second object is more relevant than first object". One is tempted to think that we could use any classification of pairs, but the nature of ranks shows that the represented relation on objects has to be asymmetric and transitive. That means, if "object b is more relevant than object a" and "object c is more relevant than object

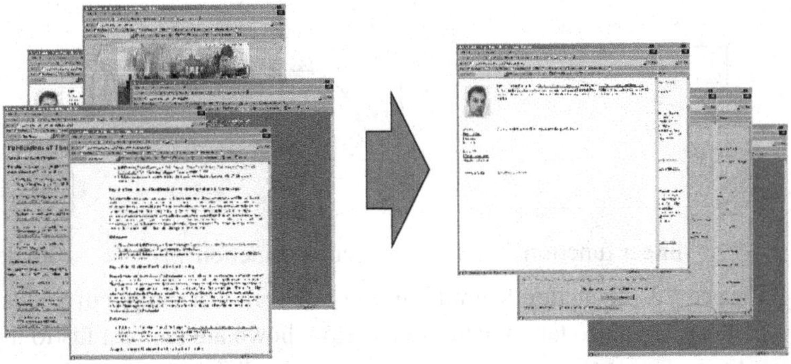

Figure 1.2 Preference learning of Web pages. Given a sample of pages with different relevances (indicated by different background colors), the task is to find an ordering of the pages such that the most relevant pages are mapped to the highest rank.

b", then it must follow that "object c is more relevant than object a". Bearing this requirement in mind, relating classification and preference learning is possible.

Function Learning

If the output space is a metric space such as the real numbers then the learning task is known as the problem of *function learning* (see Figure 1.3). One of the greatest advantages of function learning is that by the metric on the output space it is possible to use gradient descent techniques whenever the functions value $f(x)$ is a differentiable function of the object x itself. This idea underlies the *back-propagation algorithm* (Rumelhart et al. 1986), which guarantees the finding of a local optimum. An interesting relationship exists between function learning and classification learning when a probabilistic perspective is taken. Considering a binary classification problem, it suffices to consider only the probability that a given object belongs to the positive class. Thus, whenever we are able to learn the function from objects to $[0, 1]$ (representing the probability that the object is from the positive class), we have learned implicitly a classification function by thresholding the real-valued output at $\frac{1}{2}$. Such an approach is known as *logistic regression* in the field of statistics, and it underlies the support vector machine classification learning algorithm. In fact, it is common practice to use the real-valued output before thresholding as a measure of confidence even when there is no probabilistic model used in the learning process.

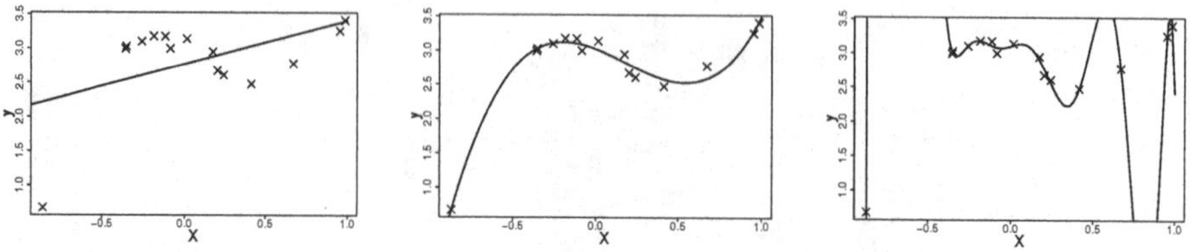

linear function cubic function . 10th degree polynomial

Figure 1.3 Function learning in action. Given is a sample of points together with associated real-valued target values (crosses). Shown are the best fits to the set of points using a linear function (left), a cubic function (middle) and a 10th degree polynomial (right). Intuitively, the cubic function class seems to be most appropriate; using linear functions the points are under-fitted whereas the 10th degree polynomial over-fits the given sample.

1.1.2 Unsupervised Learning

In addition to supervised learning there exists the task of unsupervised learning. In unsupervised learning we are given a training sample of objects, for example images or pixels, with the aim of extracting some "structure" from them—e.g., identifying indoor or outdoor images, or differentiating between face and background pixels. This is a very vague statement of the problem that should be rephrased better as learning a concise representation of the data. This is justified by the following reasoning: If some structure exists in the training objects, it is possible to take advantage of this redundancy and find a short description of the data. One of the most general ways to represent data is to specify a similarity between any pairs of objects. If two objects share much structure, it should be possible to reproduce the data from the same "prototype". This idea underlies *clustering algorithms*: Given a fixed number of clusters, we aim to find a grouping of the objects such that similar objects belong to the same cluster. We view all objects within one cluster as being similar to each other. If it is possible to find a clustering such that the similarities of the objects in one cluster are much greater than the similarities among objects from different clusters, we have extracted structure from the training sample insofar as that the whole cluster can be represented by one representative. From a statistical point of view, the idea of finding a concise representation of the data is closely related to the idea of *mixture models*, where the overlap of high-density regions of the individual mixture components is as small as possible (see Figure 1.4). Since we do not observe the mixture component that generated a particular training object, we have to treat the assignment of training examples to the mixture components as

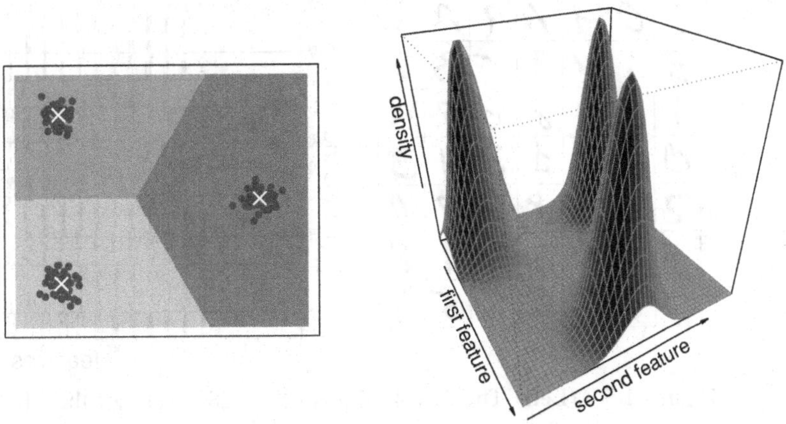

Figure 1.4 **(Left)** Clustering of 150 training points (black dots) into three clusters (white crosses). Each color depicts a region of points belonging to one cluster. **(Right)** Probability density of the estimated mixture model.

hidden variables—a fact that makes estimation of the unknown probability measure quite intricate. Most of the estimation procedures used in practice fall into the realm of *expectation-maximization (EM) algorithms* (Dempster et al. 1977).

1.1.3 Reinforcement Learning

The problem of reinforcement learning is to learn what to do—how to map situations to actions—so as to maximize a given reward. In contrast to the supervised learning task, the learning algorithm is not told which actions to take in a given situation. Instead, the learner is assumed to gain information about the actions taken by some reward not necessarily arriving immediately after the action is taken. One example of such a problem is learning to play chess. Each board configuration, i.e., the position of all figures on the 8×8 board, is a given state; the actions are the possible moves in a given position. The reward for a given action (chess move) is winning the game, losing it or achieving a draw. Note that this reward is delayed which is very typical for reinforcement learning. Since a given state has no "optimal" action, one of the biggest challenges of a reinforcement learning algorithm is to find a trade-off between exploration and exploitation. In order to maximize reward a learning algorithm must choose actions which have been tried out in the past and found to be effective in producing reward—it must exploit its current

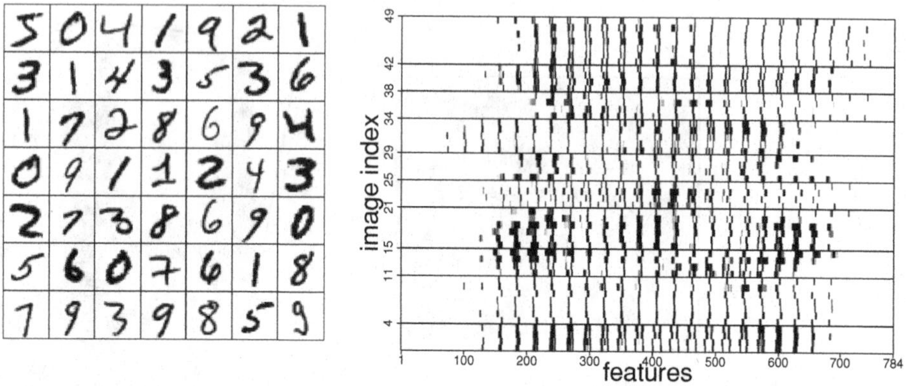

Figure 1.5 **(Left)** The first 49 digits (28 × 28 pixels) of the MNIST dataset. **(Right)** The 49 images in a data matrix obtained by concatenation of the 28 rows thus resulting in $28 \cdot 28 = 784$–dimensional data vectors. Note that we sorted the images such that the four images of "zero" are the first, then the 7 images of "one" and so on.

knowledge. On the other hand, to discover those actions the learning algorithm has to choose actions not tried in the past and thus explore the state space. There is no general solution to this dilemma, but that neither of the two options can lead exclusively to an optimal strategy is clear. As this learning problem is only of partial relevance to this book, the interested reader is referred to Sutton and Barto (1998) for an excellent introduction to this problem.

1.2 Learning Kernel Classifiers

Here is a typical classification learning problem. Suppose we want to design a system that is able to recognize handwritten zip codes on mail envelopes. Initially, we use a scanning device to obtain images of the single digits in digital form. In the design of the underlying software system we have to decide whether we "hardwire" the recognition function into our program or allow the program to learn its recognition function. Besides being the more flexible approach, the idea of learning the recognition function offers the additional advantage that any change involving the scanning can be incorporated automatically; in the "hardwired" approach we would have to reprogram the recognition function whenever we change the scanning device. This flexibility requires that we provide the learning

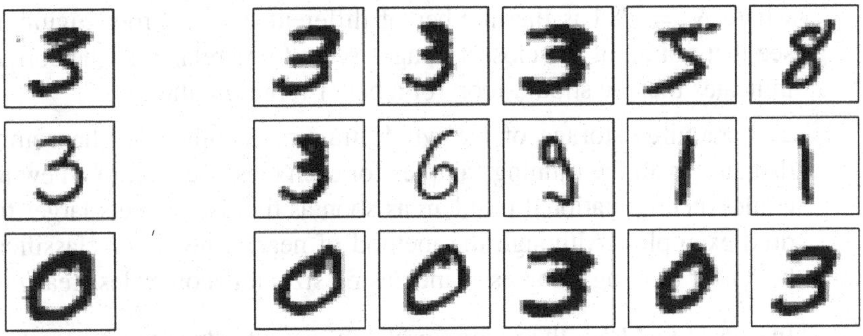

Figure 1.6 Classification of three new images (leftmost column) by finding the five images from Figure 1.5 which are closest to it using the Euclidean distance.

algorithm with some example classifications of typical digits. In this particular case it is relatively easy to acquire at least 100–1000 images and label them manually (see Figure 1.5 (left)).

Our next decision involves the *representation* of the images in the computer. Since the scanning device supplies us with an image matrix of intensity values at fixed positions, it seems natural to use this representation directly, i.e., concatenate the rows of the image matrix to obtain a long data vector for each image. As a consequence, the data can be represented by a matrix $\mathbf{X}$ with as many rows as number of training samples and as many columns are there are pixels per image (see Figure 1.5 (right)). Each row $\mathbf{x}_i$ of the data matrix $\mathbf{X}$ represents one image of a digit by the intensity values at the fixed pixel positions.

Now consider a very simple learning algorithm where we just store the training examples. In order to classify a new test image, we assign it to the class of the training image closest to it. This surprisingly easy learning algorithm is also known as the *nearest-neighbor classifier* and has almost optimal performance in the limit of a large number of training images. In our example we see that nearest neighbor classification seems to perform very well (see Figure 1.6). However, this simple and intuitive algorithm suffers two major problems:

1. It requires a distance measure which must be small between images depicting the same digit and large between images showing different digits. In the example shown in Figure 1.6 we use the Euclidean distance

$$\|\mathbf{x} - \tilde{\mathbf{x}}\| \stackrel{\text{def}}{=} \sqrt{\sum_{j=1}^{N} \left(x_j - \tilde{x}_j\right)^2},$$

where $N = 784$ is the number of different pixels. From Figure 1.6 we already see that not all of the closest images seem to be related to the correct class, which indicates that we should look for a better representation.

2. It requires storage of the whole training sample and the computation of the distance to all the training samples for each classification of a new image. This becomes a computational problem as soon as the dataset gets larger than a few hundred examples. Although the method of nearest neighbor classification performs better for training samples of increasing size, it becomes less realizable in practice.

In order to address the second problem, we introduce ten parameterized functions $f_0, \ldots, f_9$ that map image vectors to real numbers. A positive number $f_i(\mathbf{x})$ indicates belief that the image vector is showing the digit i; its magnitude should be related to the degree with which the image is believed to depict the digit i. The interesting question is: Which functions should we consider? Clearly, as computational time is the only reason to deviate from nearest-neighbor classification, we should only consider functions whose value can quickly be evaluated. On the other hand, the functions should be powerful enough to approximate the classification as carried out by the nearest neighbor classifier. Consider a linear function, i.e.,

$$f_i(\mathbf{x}) = \sum_{j=1}^{N} w_j \cdot x_j\,, \tag{1.1}$$

which is simple and quickly computable. We summarize all the images showing the same digit in the training sample into one parameter vector $\mathbf{w}$ for the function f_i. Further, by the Cauchy-Schwarz inequality, we know that the difference of this function evaluated at two image vectors $\mathbf{x}$ and $\tilde{\mathbf{x}}$ is bounded from above by $\|\mathbf{w}\| \cdot \|\mathbf{x} - \tilde{\mathbf{x}}\|$. Hence, if we only consider parameter vectors $\mathbf{w}$ with a constant norm $\|\mathbf{w}\|$, it follows that *whenever two points are close to each other*, any linear function would assign similar real-values to them as well. These two properties make linear functions perfect candidates for designing the handwritten digit recognizer.

In order to address the first problem, we consider a generalized notion of a distance measure as given by

$$\|\mathbf{x} - \tilde{\mathbf{x}}\| = \sqrt{\sum_{j=1}^{n} \left(\phi_j(\mathbf{x}) - \phi_j(\tilde{\mathbf{x}})\right)^2}\,. \tag{1.2}$$

Here, $\boldsymbol{\phi} = (\phi_1, \ldots, \phi_n)$ is known as the feature mapping and allows us to change the representation of the digitized images. For example, we could consider all products of intensity values at two different positions, i.e. $\boldsymbol{\phi}(\mathbf{x}) = (x_1x_1, \ldots, x_1x_N, x_2x_1, \ldots, x_Nx_N)$, which allows us to exploit correlations in the image. The advantage of choosing a distance measure as given in equation (1.2) becomes apparent when considering that for all parameter vectors $\mathbf{w}$ that can be represented as a linear combination of the mapped training examples $\boldsymbol{\phi}(\mathbf{x}_1), \ldots, \boldsymbol{\phi}(\mathbf{x}_m)$,

$$\mathbf{w} = \sum_{i=1}^{m} \alpha_i \boldsymbol{\phi}(\mathbf{x}_i) ,$$

the resulting linear function in equation (1.1) can be written purely in terms of a linear combination of inner product functions in feature space, i.e.,

$$f(\mathbf{x}) = \sum_{i=1}^{m} \alpha_i \underbrace{\sum_{j=1}^{n} \phi_j(\mathbf{x}_i) \cdot \phi_j(\mathbf{x})}_{k(\mathbf{x}_i,\mathbf{x})} = \sum_{i=1}^{m} \alpha_i k(\mathbf{x}_i, \mathbf{x}) .$$

In contrast to standard linear models, we need never explicitly construct the parameter vector $\mathbf{w}$. Specifying the inner product function k, which is called the *kernel*, is sufficient. The linear function involving a kernel is known as *kernel classifier* and is parameterized by the vector $\boldsymbol{\alpha} \in \mathbb{R}^m$ of expansion coefficients. What has not yet been addressed is the question of which parameter vector $\mathbf{w}$ or $\boldsymbol{\alpha}$ to choose when given a training sample. This is the topic of the first part of this book.

1.3 The Purposes of Learning Theory

The first part of this book may lead the reader to wonder—after learning so many different learning algorithms—which one to use for a particular problem. This legitimate question is one that the results from learning theory try to answer. Learning theory is concerned with the study of learning algorithms' performance. By casting the learning problem into the powerful framework of probability theory, we aim to answer the following questions:

1. How many training examples do we need to ensure a certain performance?

2. Given a fixed training sample, e.g., the forty-nine images in Figure 1.5, what performance of the function learned can be guaranteed?

3. Given two different learning algorithms, which one should we choose for a given training sample so as to maximize the performance of the resulting learning algorithm?

I should point out that all these questions must be followed by the additional phrase "with high probability over the random draw of the training sample". This requirement is unavoidable and reflects the fact that we model the training sample as a random sample. Thus, in any of the statements about the performance of learning algorithms we have the inherent duality between precision and confidence: The more precise the statement on the algorithm's performance is, e.g., the prediction error is not larger than 5%, the less confident it is. In the extreme case, we can say that the prediction error is exactly 5%, but we have absolutely no (mathematical) confidence in this statement. The performance measure is most easily defined when considering supervised learning tasks. Since we are given a target value for each object, we need only to measure by how much the learned function deviates from the target value at all objects—in particular for the unseen objects. This quantity is modeled by the expected loss of a function over the random draw of object-target pairs. As a consequence our ultimate interest is in (probabilistic) upper bounds on the expected loss of the function learned from the random training sample, i.e.,

$$\mathsf{P}\left(\text{training samples s.t. the expected loss of the function learned } \leq \varepsilon\left(\delta\right)\right) \geq 1-\delta\,.$$

The function ε is called a bound on the generalization error because it quantifies how much we are mislead in choosing the optimal function when using a learning algorithm, i.e., when generalizing from a given training sample to a general prediction function. Having such a bound at our disposal allows us to answer the three questions directly:

1. Since the function ε is dependent on the size of the training sample[1], we fix ε and solve for the training sample size.

2. This is exactly the question answered by the generalization error bound. Note that the ultimate interest is in bounds that depend on the particular training sample observed; a bound independent of the training sample would give a guarantee ex-ante which therefore cannot take advantage of some "simplicity" in the training sample.

3. If we evaluate the two generalization errors for the two different learning algorithms, we should choose the algorithm with the smaller generalization error

1 In fact, it will be inversely related because with increasing size of the training sample the expected loss will be non-increasing due to results from large deviation theory (see Appendix A.5.2).

bound. Note that the resulting bound would no longer hold for the selection algorithm. Nonetheless, Part II of this book shows that this can be achieved with a slight modification.

It comes as no surprise that learning theory needs assumptions to hold. In contrast to parametric statistics, which assumes that the training data is generated from a distribution out of a given set, the main interest in learning theory is in bounds that hold for all possible data distributions. The only way this can be achieved is to constrain the class of functions used. In this book, this is done by considering linear functions only. A practical advantage of having results that are valid for all possible probability measures is that we are able to check whether the assumptions imposed by the theory are valid in practice. The price we have to pay for this generality is that most results of learning theory are more an indication than a good estimate of the real generalization error. Although recent efforts in this field aim to tighten generalization error bound as much as possible, it will always be the case that any distribution-dependent generalization error bound is superior in terms of precision.

Apart from enhancing our understanding of the learning phenomenon, learning theory is supposed to serve another purpose as well—to suggest new algorithms. Depending on the assumption we make about the learning algorithms, we will arrive at generalization error bounds involving different measures of (data-dependent) complexity terms. Although these complexity terms give only upper bounds on the generalization error, they provide us with ideas as to which quantities should be optimized. This is the topic of the second part of the book.

I Learning Algorithms

2 Kernel Classifiers from a Machine Learning Perspective

This chapter presents the machine learning approach to learning kernel classifiers. After a short introduction to the problem of learning a linear classifier, it shows how learning can be viewed as an optimization task. As an example, the classical perceptron algorithm is presented. This algorithm is an implementation of a more general principle known as *empirical risk minimization.* The chapter also presents a descendant of this principle, known as *regularized (structural) risk minimization.* Both these principles can be applied in the primal or dual space of variables. It is shown that the latter is computationally less demanding if the method is extended to nonlinear classifiers in input space. Here, the *kernel technique* is the essential method used to invoke the nonlinearity in input space. The chapter presents several families of kernels that allow linear classification methods to be applicable even if no vectorial representation is given, e.g., strings. Following this, the *support vector* method for classification learning is introduced. This method elegantly combines the kernel technique and the principle of structural risk minimization. The chapter finishes with a presentation of a more recent kernel algorithm called *adaptive margin machines.* In contrast to the support vector method, the latter aims at minimizing a leave-one-out error bound rather than a structural risk.

2.1 The Basic Setting

The task of classification learning is the problem of finding a good strategy to assign class labels to objects based on past observations of object-class pairs. We shall only assume that all objects x are contained in the set $\mathcal{X}$, often referred to as the *input space.* Let $\mathcal{Y}$ be a finite set of classes called the *output space.* If not otherwise stated, we will only consider the two-element output space $\{-1, +1\}$, in which case the learning problem is called a *binary classification* learning task. Suppose we are given a sample of m training objects,

$$\boldsymbol{x} = (x_1, \ldots, x_m) \in \mathcal{X}^m ,$$

together with a sample of corresponding class labels,

$$\boldsymbol{y} = (y_1, \ldots, y_m) \in \mathcal{Y}^m .$$

We will often consider the labeled training sample,[1]

$$\boldsymbol{z} = (\boldsymbol{x}, \boldsymbol{y}) = ((x_1, y_1), \ldots, (x_m, y_m)) \in (\mathcal{X} \times \mathcal{Y})^m = \mathcal{Z}^m ,$$

and assume that $\boldsymbol{z}$ is a sample drawn identically and independently distributed (iid) according to some unknown probability measure $\mathbf{P}_\mathsf{Z}$.

Definition 2.1 (Learning problem) *The* learning problem *is to find the unknown (functional) relationship $h \in \mathcal{Y}^\mathcal{X}$ between objects $x \in \mathcal{X}$ and targets $y \in \mathcal{Y}$ based solely on a sample $\boldsymbol{z} = (\boldsymbol{x}, \boldsymbol{y}) = ((x_1, y_1), \ldots, (x_m, y_m)) \in (\mathcal{X} \times \mathcal{Y})^m$ of size $m \in \mathbb{N}$ drawn iid from an unknown distribution $\mathbf{P}_\mathsf{XY}$. If the output space $\mathcal{Y}$ contains a finite number $|\mathcal{Y}|$ of elements then the task is called a* classification learning problem.

Of course, having knowledge of $\mathbf{P}_\mathsf{XY} = \mathbf{P}_\mathsf{Z}$ is sufficient for identifying this relationship as for all objects x,

$$\mathbf{P}_{\mathsf{Y}|\mathsf{X}=x}(y) = \frac{\mathbf{P}_\mathsf{Z}((x, y))}{\mathbf{P}_\mathsf{X}(x)} = \frac{\mathbf{P}_\mathsf{Z}((x, y))}{\sum_{\tilde{y} \in \mathcal{Y}} \mathbf{P}_\mathsf{Z}((x, \tilde{y}))} . \tag{2.1}$$

Thus, for a given object $x \in \mathcal{X}$ we could evaluate the distribution $\mathbf{P}_{\mathsf{Y}|\mathsf{X}=x}$ over class labels and decide on the class label $\hat{y} \in \mathcal{Y}$ with the largest probability $\mathbf{P}_{\mathsf{Y}|\mathsf{X}=x}(\hat{y})$. Estimating $\mathbf{P}_\mathsf{Z}$ based on the given sample $\boldsymbol{z}$, however, poses a nontrivial problem. In the (unconstrained) class of all probability measures, the *empirical measure*

$$\mathbf{v}_{\boldsymbol{z}}((x, y)) = \frac{|\{i \in \{1, \ldots, m\} \mid z_i = (x, y)\}|}{m} \tag{2.2}$$

1 Though mathematically the training sample is a *sequence* of iid drawn object-class pairs (x, y) we sometimes take the liberty of calling the training sample a *training set*. The notation $z \in \boldsymbol{z}$ then refers to the fact that there exists an element z_i in the sequence $\boldsymbol{z}$ such that $z_i = z$.

is among the "most plausible" ones, because

$$\mathbf{v}_z(\{z_1,\ldots,z_m\}) = \sum_{i=1}^{m} \mathbf{v}_z(z_i) = 1\,.$$

However, the corresponding "identified" relationship $h_{\mathbf{v}_z} \in \mathcal{Y}^{\mathcal{X}}$ is unsatisfactory because

$$h_{\mathbf{v}_z}(x) = \sum_{x_i \in \boldsymbol{x}} y_i \cdot \mathbf{I}_{x=x_i}$$

assigns zero probability to all unseen objects-class pairs and thus cannot be used for predicting a class label given a new object $x \in \mathcal{X}$. In order to resolve this difficulty, we need to constrain the set $\mathcal{Y}^{\mathcal{X}}$ of possible mappings from objects $x \in \mathcal{X}$ to class labels $y \in \mathcal{Y}$. Often, such a restriction is imposed by assuming a given *hypothesis space* $\mathcal{H} \subseteq \mathcal{Y}^{\mathcal{X}}$ of functions[2] $h : \mathcal{X} \to \mathcal{Y}$. Intuitively, similar objects x_i should be mapped to the same class y_i. This is a very reasonable assumption if we wish to infer class labels on unseen objects x *based on a given training sample* z *only.*

A convenient way to model *similarity* between objects is through an inner product function $\langle\cdot,\cdot\rangle$ which has the appealing property that its value is maximal whenever its arguments are equal. In order to employ inner products to measure similarity between objects we need to represent them in an inner product space which we assume to be ℓ_2^n (see Definition A.39).

Definition 2.2 (Features and feature space) *A function* $\phi_i : \mathcal{X} \to \mathbb{R}$ *that maps each object* $x \in \mathcal{X}$ *to a real value* $\phi_i(x)$ *is called a* feature. *Combining n features* $\phi_1,\ldots,\phi_n$ *results in a* feature mapping $\boldsymbol{\phi} : \mathcal{X} \to \mathcal{K} \subseteq \ell_2^n$ *and the space* $\mathcal{K}$ *is called a* feature space.

In order to avoid an unnecessarily complicated notation we will abbreviate $\boldsymbol{\phi}(x)$ by $\mathbf{x}$ for the rest of the book. The vector $\mathbf{x} \in \mathcal{K}$ is also called the *representation* of $x \in \mathcal{X}$. This should not be confused with the training sequence $\boldsymbol{x}$ which results in an $m \times n$ matrix $\mathbf{X} = \left(\mathbf{x}_1'; \ldots; \mathbf{x}_m'\right)$ when applying $\boldsymbol{\phi}$ to it.

Example 2.3 (Handwritten digit recognition) *The important task of classifying handwritten digits is one of the most prominent examples of the application of learning algorithms. Suppose we want to automatically construct a procedure*

2 Since each h is a hypothetical mapping to class labels, we synonymously use *classifier, hypothesis* and *function* to refer to h.

which can assign digital images to the classes "image is a picture of 1" *and "image is not a picture of* 1"*. Typically, each feature* $\phi_i : \mathcal{X} \to \mathbb{R}$ *is the intensity of ink at a fixed picture element, or* pixel, *of the image. Hence, after digitalization at* $N \times N$ *pixel positions, we can represent each image as a high dimensional vector* $\mathbf{x}$ *(to be precise,* N^2*–dimensional). Obviously, only a small subset of the* N^2*–dimensional space is occupied by handwritten digits*[3]*, and, due to noise in the digitization, we might have the same picture* x *mapped to different vectors* $\mathbf{x}_i, \mathbf{x}_j$*. This is assumed encapsulated in the probability measure* P_X*. Moreover, for small* N*, similar pictures* $x_i \approx x_j$ *are mapped to the same data vector* $\mathbf{x}$ *because the single pixel positions are too coarse a representation of a single image. Thus, it seems reasonable to assume that one could hardly find a deterministic mapping from* N^2*–dimensional vectors to the class "picture of* 1"*. This gives rise to a probability measure* $\mathsf{P}_{\mathsf{Y}|\mathsf{X}=\mathbf{x}}$*. Both these uncertainties—which in fact constitute the basis of the learning problem—are expressed via the unknown probability measure* P_Z *(see equation (2.1)).*

In this book, we will be concerned with linear functions or classifiers only. Let us formally define what we mean when speaking about linear classifiers.

Definition 2.4 (Linear function and linear classifier) *Given a feature mapping* $\boldsymbol{\phi} : \mathcal{X} \to \mathcal{K} \subseteq \ell_2^n$*, the function* $f : \mathcal{X} \to \mathbb{R}$ *of the form*[4]

$$f_\mathbf{w}(x) = \langle \boldsymbol{\phi}(x), \mathbf{w} \rangle = \langle \mathbf{x}, \mathbf{w} \rangle$$

is called a linear function *and the* n*–dimensional vector* $\mathbf{w} \in \mathcal{K}$ *is called a* weight vector. *A* linear classifier *is obtained by thresholding a linear function,*

$$h_\mathbf{w}(x) = \operatorname{sign}(\langle \mathbf{x}, \mathbf{w} \rangle) \; . \tag{2.3}$$

Clearly, the intuition that similar objects are mapped to similar class labels is satisfied by such a model because, by the Cauchy-Schwarz inequality (see Theorem A.106), we know that

$$\left| \langle \mathbf{w}, \mathbf{x}_i \rangle - \langle \mathbf{w}, \mathbf{x}_j \rangle \right| = \left| \langle \mathbf{w}, \mathbf{x}_i - \mathbf{x}_j \rangle \right| \le \|\mathbf{w}\| \cdot \left\| \mathbf{x}_i - \mathbf{x}_j \right\| \; ;$$

3 To see this, imagine that we generate an image by tossing a coin N^2 times and mark a black dot in a $N \times N$ array, if the coin shows head. Then, it is very unlikely that we will obtain an image of a digit. This outcome is expected as digits presumably have a pictorial structure in common.

4 In order to highlight the dependence of f on $\mathbf{w}$, we use $f_\mathbf{w}$ when necessary.

that is, whenever two data points are close in feature space (small $\left\|\mathbf{x}_i - \mathbf{x}_j\right\|$), their difference in the real-valued output of a hypothesis with weight vector $\mathbf{w} \in \mathcal{K}$ is also small. It is important to note that the classification $h_{\mathbf{w}}(x)$ remains unaffected if we rescale the weight $\mathbf{w}$ by some positive constant,

$$\forall \lambda > 0 : \forall x \in \mathcal{X} : \quad \operatorname{sign}(\langle \mathbf{x}, \lambda \mathbf{w} \rangle) = \operatorname{sign}(\lambda \langle \mathbf{x}, \mathbf{w} \rangle) = \operatorname{sign}(\langle \mathbf{x}, \mathbf{w} \rangle) . \tag{2.4}$$

Thus, if not stated otherwise, we assume the weight vector $\mathbf{w}$ to be of unit length,

$$\mathcal{F} = \{x \mapsto \langle \mathbf{x}, \mathbf{w} \rangle \mid \mathbf{w} \in \mathcal{W}\} \subseteq \mathbb{R}^{\mathcal{X}} , \tag{2.5}$$

$$\mathcal{W} = \{\mathbf{w} \in \mathcal{K} \mid \quad \|\mathbf{w}\| = 1\} \subset \mathcal{K} , \tag{2.6}$$

$$\mathcal{H} = \left\{h_{\mathbf{w}} \stackrel{\text{def}}{=} \operatorname{sign}(f_{\mathbf{w}}) \mid f_{\mathbf{w}} \in \mathcal{F}\right\} \subseteq \mathcal{Y}^{\mathcal{X}} . \tag{2.7}$$

Ergo, the set $\mathcal{F}$, also referred to as the *hypothesis space*, is isomorphic to the unit hypersphere $\mathcal{W}$ in $\mathbb{R}^n$ (see Figure 2.1).

The task of learning reduces to finding the "best" classifier f^* in the hypothesis space $\mathcal{F}$. The most difficult question at this point is: "How can we measure the goodness of a classifier f? We would like the goodness of a classifier to be

- strongly dependent on the unknown measure $\mathbf{P}_\mathsf{Z}$; otherwise, we would not have a learning problem because f^* could be determined without knowledge of the underlying relationship between objects and classes expressed via $\mathbf{P}_\mathsf{Z}$.
- pointwise w.r.t. the object-class pairs (x, y) due to the independence assumption made for z.
- a positive, real-valued function, making the maximization task computationally easier.

All these requirements can be encapsulated in a fixed *loss function* $l : \mathbb{R} \times \mathcal{Y} \to \mathbb{R}$. Here $l(f(x), y)$ measures how costly it is when the prediction at the data point x is $f(x)$ but the true class is y. It is natural to assume that $l(+\infty, +1) = l(-\infty, -1) = 0$, that is, the greater $y \cdot f(x)$ the better the prediction of $f(x)$ was. Based on the loss l it is assumed that the goodness of f is the expected loss $\mathbf{E}_{\mathsf{XY}}\left[l(f(\mathsf{X}), \mathsf{Y})\right]$, sometimes referred to as the expected risk. In summary, the ultimate goal of learning can be described as:

> Based on the training sample $z \in \mathcal{Z}^m$, a hypothesis space $\mathcal{F} \subseteq \mathbb{R}^{\mathcal{X}}$ and a loss function $l : \mathbb{R} \times \mathcal{Y} \to \mathbb{R}$ find the function
>
> $$f^* = \operatorname*{argmin}_{f \in \mathcal{F}} \mathbf{E}_{\mathsf{XY}}\left[l(f(\mathsf{X}), \mathsf{Y})\right] .$$

Assuming an unknown, but fixed, measure $\mathbf{P}_\mathsf{Z}$ over the object-class space $\mathcal{Z}$ we can view the expectation value $\mathbf{E}_{\mathsf{XY}}\left[l\left(f\left(\mathsf{X}\right),\mathsf{Y}\right)\right]$ of the loss as an *expected risk functional* over $\mathcal{F}$.

Definition 2.5 (Expected risk) *Given a loss* $l : \mathbb{R}\times\mathcal{Y}\to\mathbb{R}$ *and a measure* $\mathbf{P}_{\mathsf{XY}}$*, the functional*

$$R\left[f\right]\stackrel{\text{def}}{=}\mathbf{E}_{\mathsf{XY}}\left[l\left(f\left(\mathsf{X}\right),\mathsf{Y}\right)\right], \tag{2.8}$$

is called expected risk *or* expected loss *of a function* $f\in\mathcal{F}\subseteq\mathbb{R}^{\mathcal{X}}$*, respectively. If the loss function* $l:\mathcal{Y}\times\mathcal{Y}\to\mathbb{R}$ *maps from the predicted and true class labels to the reals, the expected risk is also defined by (2.8) but this time w.r.t.* $h\in\mathcal{H}\subseteq\mathcal{Y}^{\mathcal{X}}$*.*

Example 2.6 (Classification loss) *In the case of classification learning, a natural measure of goodness of a classifier* $h\in\mathcal{H}$ *is the probability of assigning a new object to the wrong class, i.e.,* $\mathbf{P}_{\mathsf{XY}}\left(h\left(\mathsf{X}\right)\neq\mathsf{Y}\right)$*. In order to cast this into a loss-based framework we exploit the basic fact that* $\mathbf{P}\left(A\right)=\mathbf{E}\left[\mathbf{I}_A\right]$ *for some A. As a consequence, using the* zero-one loss $l_{0-1}:\mathbb{R}\times\mathcal{Y}\to\mathbb{R}$ *for real-valued functions*

$$l_{0-1}\left(f\left(x\right),y\right)\stackrel{\text{def}}{=}\mathbf{I}_{yf(x)\leq 0}, \tag{2.9}$$

renders the task of finding the classifier with minimal misclassification probability as a risk minimization task. Note that, due to the fact that $y\in\{-1,+1\}$*, the zero-one loss in equation (2.9) is a special case of the more general loss function* $l_{0-1}:\mathcal{Y}\times\mathcal{Y}\to\mathbb{R}$

$$l_{0-1}\left(h\left(x\right),y\right)\stackrel{\text{def}}{=}\mathbf{I}_{h(x)\neq y}. \tag{2.10}$$

Example 2.7 (Cost matrices) *Returning to Example 2.3 we see that the loss given by equation (2.9) is inappropriate for the task at hand. This is due to the fact that there are approximately ten times more "no pictures of* 1*" than "pictures of* 1*". Therefore, a classifier assigning each image to the class "no picture of* 1*" (this classifier is also known as the* default classifierf*) would have an expected risk of about 10%. In contrast, a classifier assigning each image to the class "picture of* 1*" would have an expected risk of about 90%. To correct this imbalance of prior probabilities* $\mathbf{P}_\mathsf{Y}(+1)$ *and* $\mathbf{P}_\mathsf{Y}(-1)$ *one could define a* 2×2 *cost matrix*

$$\mathbf{C}=\begin{pmatrix}0 & c_{12}\\ c_{21} & 0\end{pmatrix}.$$

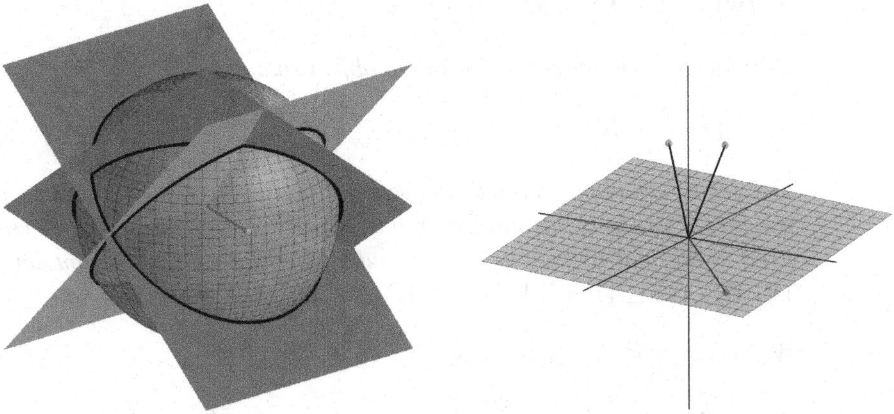

Figure 2.1 **(Left)** The hypothesis space $\mathcal{W}$ for linear classifiers in $\mathbb{R}^3$. Each single point x defines a plane in $\mathbb{R}^3$ and thus incurs a grand circle $\{\mathbf{w} \in \mathcal{W} \mid \langle \mathbf{x}, \mathbf{w} \rangle = 0\}$ in hypothesis space (black lines). The three data points in the right picture induce the three planes in the left picture. **(Right)** Considering a fixed classifier $\mathbf{w}$ (single dot on the left) the decision plane $\left\{\mathbf{x} \in \mathbb{R}^3 \mid \langle \mathbf{x}, \mathbf{w} \rangle = 0\right\}$ is shown.

Let $\mathbf{1}_y$ *and* $\mathbf{1}_{\text{sign}(f(x))}$ *denote the* 2×1 *indicator vectors of the true class and the classification made by* $f \in \mathcal{F}$ *at* $x \in \mathcal{X}$. *Then we have a* cost matrix classification loss l_{C} *by*

$$l_{\text{C}}(f(x), y) \stackrel{\text{def}}{=} \mathbf{1}_y' \mathbf{C} \mathbf{1}_{\text{sign}(f(x))} = \begin{cases} c_{12} & y = +1 \text{ and } f(x) < 0 \\ c_{21} & y = -1 \text{ and } f(x) > 0 \\ 0 & \text{otherwise}. \end{cases}$$

Obviously, setting $c_{12} = \mathbf{P}_{\mathsf{Y}}(-1)$ *and* $c_{21} = \mathbf{P}_{\mathsf{Y}}(+1)$ *leads to equal risks for both default classifiers and thus allows the incorporation of prior knowledge on the probabilities* $\mathbf{P}_{\mathsf{Y}}(+1)$ *and* $\mathbf{P}_{\mathsf{Y}}(-1)$.

Remark 2.8 (Geometrical picture) *Linear classifiers, parameterized by a weight vector* $\mathbf{w}$, *are hyperplanes passing through the origin in feature space* $\mathcal{K}$. *Each classifier divides the feature space into two open half spaces,* $X_{+1}(\mathbf{w}) \subset \mathcal{K}$, $X_{-1}(\mathbf{w}) \subset$

$\mathcal{K}$ by the hyperplane[5] $X_0(\mathbf{w}) \subset \mathcal{K}$ *using the following rule,*

$$X_y(\mathbf{w}) = \{\mathbf{x} \in \mathcal{K} \mid \operatorname{sign}(\langle \mathbf{x}, \mathbf{w} \rangle) = y\} .$$

Considering the images of $X_0(\mathbf{w})$ *in object space* $\mathcal{X}$

$$\widetilde{X}_0(\mathbf{w}) = \{x \in \mathcal{X} \mid \langle \mathbf{x}, \mathbf{w} \rangle = 0\} ,$$

this set is sometimes called the decision surface. *Our hypothesis space* $\mathcal{W}$ *for weight vectors* $\mathbf{w}$ *is the unit hypersphere in* $\mathbb{R}^n$ *(see equation (2.6)). Hence, having fixed* $\mathbf{x}$*, the unit hypersphere* $\mathcal{W}$ *is subdivided into three disjoint sets* $W_{+1}(\mathbf{x}) \subset \mathcal{W}$, $W_{-1}(\mathbf{x}) \subset \mathcal{W}$ *and* $W_0(\mathbf{x}) \subset \mathcal{W}$ *by exactly the same rule, i.e.,*

$$W_y(\mathbf{x}) = \{\mathbf{w} \in \mathcal{W} \mid \operatorname{sign}(\langle \mathbf{x}, \mathbf{w} \rangle) = y\} .$$

As can be seen in Figure 2.1 (left), for a finite sample $\mathbf{x} = (x_1, \ldots, x_m)$ *of training objects and any vector* $\mathbf{y} = (y_1, \ldots, y_m) \in \{-1, +1\}^m$ *of labelings the resulting* equivalence classes

$$W_z = \bigcap_{i=1}^{m} W_{y_i}(\mathbf{x}_i)$$

are (open) convex polyhedra. Clearly, the labeling of the x_i *determines the training error of each equivalence class*

$$W_z = \{\mathbf{w} \in \mathcal{W} \mid \forall i \in \{1, \ldots, m\} : \operatorname{sign}(\langle \mathbf{x}_i, \mathbf{w} \rangle) = y_i\} .$$

2.2 Learning by Risk Minimization

Apart from algorithmical problems, as soon as we have a fixed object space $\mathcal{X}$, a fixed set (or space) $\mathcal{F}$ of hypotheses and a fixed loss function l, learning reduces to a pure optimization task on the functional $R[f]$.

Definition 2.9 (Learning algorithm) *Given an object space* $\mathcal{X}$*, an output space* $\mathcal{Y}$ *and a fixed set* $\mathcal{F} \subseteq \mathbb{R}^{\mathcal{X}}$ *of functions mapping* $\mathcal{X}$ *to* $\mathbb{R}$*, a* learning algorithm $\mathcal{A}$

5 With a slight abuse of notation, we use $\operatorname{sign}(0) = 0$.

for the hypothesis space $\mathcal{F}$ *is a mapping*[6]

$$\mathcal{A} : \bigcup_{m=1}^{\infty} (\mathcal{X} \times \mathcal{Y})^m \rightarrow \mathcal{F} .$$

The biggest difficulty so far is that we have no knowledge of the function to be optimized, i.e., we are only given an iid sample z instead of the full measure $\mathbf{P}_\mathsf{Z}$. Thus, it is impossible to solve the learning problem exactly. Nevertheless, for any learning method we shall require its performance to improve with increasing training sample size, i.e., the probability of drawing a training sample z such that the generalization error is large will decrease with increasing m. Here, the generalization error is defined as follows.

Definition 2.10 (Generalization error) *Given a learning algorithm* $\mathcal{A}$ *and a loss* $l : \mathbb{R} \times \mathcal{Y} \rightarrow \mathbb{R}$ *the* generalization error of $\mathcal{A}$ *is defined as*

$$R[\mathcal{A}, z] \stackrel{\text{def}}{=} R[\mathcal{A}(z)] - \inf_{f \in \mathcal{F}} R[f] .$$

In other words, the generalization error measures the deviation of the expected risk of the function learned from the minimum expected risk.

The most well known learning principle is the *empirical risk minimization* (ERM) principle. Here, we replace $\mathbf{P}_\mathsf{Z}$ by $\mathbf{v}_z$, which contains all knowledge that can be drawn from the training sample z. As a consequence the expected risk becomes an empirically computable quantity known as the empirical risk.

Definition 2.11 (Empirical risk) *Given a training sample* $z \in (\mathcal{X} \times \mathcal{Y})^m$ *the functional*

$$R_{\text{emp}}[f, z] \stackrel{\text{def}}{=} \frac{1}{m} \sum_{i=1}^{m} l(f(x_i), y_i) , \tag{2.11}$$

is called the empirical risk functional *over* $f \in \mathcal{F} \subseteq \mathbb{R}^{\mathcal{X}}$ *or* training error *of* f, *respectively.*

6 The definition for the case of hypotheses $h \in \mathcal{H} \subseteq \mathcal{Y}^{\mathcal{X}}$ is equivalent.

By construction, R_{emp} can be minimized solely on the basis of the training sample z. We can write any ERM algorithm in the form,

$$\mathcal{A}_{\text{ERM}}(z) \stackrel{\text{def}}{=} \operatorname*{argmin}_{f \in \mathcal{F}} R_{\text{emp}}[f, z] . \tag{2.12}$$

In order to be a consistent learning principle, the expected risk $R[\mathcal{A}_{\text{ERM}}(z)]$ must converge to the minimum expected risk $R[f^*]$, i.e.,

$$\forall \varepsilon > 0: \qquad \lim_{m \to \infty} \mathbf{P}_{\mathsf{Z}^m}\left(R\left[\mathcal{A}_{\text{ERM}}(\mathbf{Z})\right] - R\left[f^*\right] > \varepsilon\right) = 0 , \tag{2.13}$$

where the randomness is due to the random choice of the training sample z.

It is known that the empirical risk $R_{\text{emp}}[f, z]$ of a *fixed* function f converges toward $R[f]$ at an exponential rate w.r.t. m for any probability measure $\mathbf{P}_{\mathsf{Z}}$ (see Subsection A.5.2). Nonetheless, it is not clear whether this holds when we consider the empirical risk minimizer $\mathcal{A}_{\text{ERM}}(z)$ given by equation (2.12) because this function changes over the random choice of training samples z. We shall see in Chapter 4 that the finiteness of the number n of feature space dimensions completely determines the consistency of the ERM principle.

2.2.1 The (Primal) Perceptron Algorithm

The first iterative procedure for learning linear classifiers presented is the *perceptron learning algorithm* proposed by F. Rosenblatt. The learning algorithm is given on page 323 and operates as follows:

1. At the start the weight vector $\mathbf{w}$ is set to $\mathbf{0}$.
2. For each training example (x_i, y_i) it is checked whether the current hypothesis correctly classifies or not. This can be achieved by evaluating the sign of $y_i \langle \mathbf{x}_i, \mathbf{w} \rangle$. If the ith training sample is not correctly classified then the misclassified pattern $\mathbf{x}_i$ is added to or subtracted from the current weight vector depending on the correct class label y_i. In summary, the weight vector $\mathbf{w}$ is updated to $\mathbf{w} + y_i \mathbf{x}_i$.
3. If no mistakes occur during an iteration through the training sample z the algorithm stops and outputs $\mathbf{w}$.

The optimization algorithm is a mistake-driven procedure, and it assumes the existence of a version space $V(z) \subseteq \mathcal{W}$, i.e., it assumes that there exists at least one classifier f such that $R_{\text{emp}}[f, z] = 0$.

Definition 2.12 (Version space) *Given the training sample* $z = (x, y) \in (\mathcal{X} \times \mathcal{Y})^m$ *and a hypothesis space* $\mathcal{H} \subseteq \mathcal{Y}^{\mathcal{X}}$, *we call*

$$V_{\mathcal{H}}(z) \stackrel{\text{def}}{=} \{h \in \mathcal{H} \mid \forall i \in \{1, \ldots, m\} : h(x_i) = y_i\} \subseteq \mathcal{H}$$

the version space, *i.e., the set of all classifiers consistent with the training sample. In particular, for linear classifiers given by (2.5)–(2.7) we synonymously call the set of consistent weight vectors*

$$V(z) \stackrel{\text{def}}{=} \{\mathbf{w} \in \mathcal{W} \mid \forall i \in \{1, \ldots, m\} : y_i \langle \mathbf{x}_i, \mathbf{w} \rangle > 0\} \subseteq \mathcal{W}$$

the version space.

Since our classifiers are linear in feature space, such training samples are called *linearly separable*. In order that the perceptron learning algorithm works for *any* training sample it must be ensured that the unknown probability measure $\mathbf{P}_{\mathsf{Z}}$ satisfies $R[f^*] = 0$. Viewed differently, this means that $\mathbf{P}_{\mathsf{Y}|\mathsf{X}=x}(y) = \mathbf{I}_{y=h^*(x)}$, $h^* \in \mathcal{H}$, where h^* is sometimes known as the *teacher perceptron*. It should be noticed that the number of parameters learned by the perceptron algorithm is n, i.e., the dimensionality of the feature space $\mathcal{K}$. We shall call this space of parameters the *primal space*, and the corresponding algorithm the *primal perceptron learning algorithm*. As depicted in Figure 2.2, perceptron learning is best viewed as starting from an arbitrary[7] point $\mathbf{w}_0$ on the hypersphere $\mathcal{W}$, and each time we observe a misclassification with a training example (x_i, y_i), we update $\mathbf{w}_t$ toward the misclassified training object $y_i\mathbf{x}_i$ (see also Figure 2.1 (left)). Thus, geometrically, the perceptron learning algorithm performs a walk through the primal parameter space with each step made in the direction of decreasing training error. Note, however, that in the formulation of the algorithm given on page 323 we do not normalize the weight vector $\mathbf{w}$ after each update.

2.2.2 Regularized Risk Functionals

One possible method of overcoming the lack of knowledge about $\mathbf{P}_{\mathsf{Z}}$ is to replace it by its empirical estimate $\mathbf{v}_z$. This principle, discussed in the previous section, justifies the perceptron learning algorithm. However, minimizing the empirical risk, as done by the perceptron learning algorithm, has several drawbacks:

7 Although in algorithm 1 on page 323 we start at $\mathbf{w}_0 = \mathbf{0}$ it is not necessary to do so.

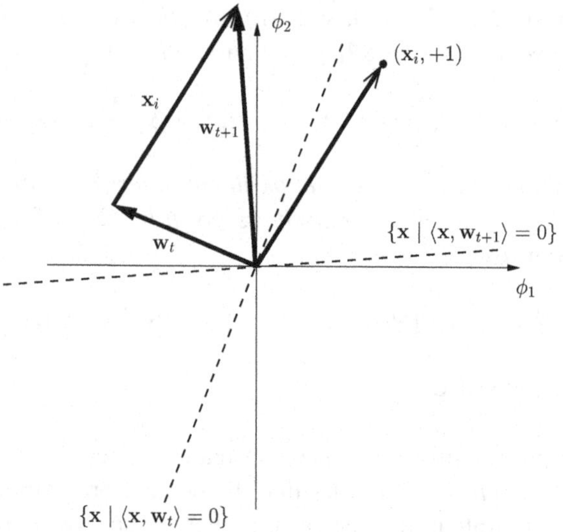

Figure 2.2 A geometrical picture of the update step in the perceptron learning algorithm in $\mathbb{R}^2$. Evidently, $\mathbf{x}_i \in \mathbb{R}^2$ is misclassified by the linear classifier (dashed line) having normal $\mathbf{w}_t$ (solid line with arrow). Then, the update step amounts to changing $\mathbf{w}_t$ into $\mathbf{w}_{t+1} = \mathbf{w}_t + y_i \mathbf{x}_i$ and thus $y_i \mathbf{x}_i$ "attracts" the hyperplane. After this step, the misclassified point $\mathbf{x}_i$ is correctly classified.

1. Many examples are required to ensure a small generalization error $R[\mathcal{A}_{\mathrm{ERM}}, z]$ with high probability taken over the random choice of z.
2. There is no unique minimum, i.e., each weight vector $\mathbf{w} \in V(z)$ in version space parameterizes a classifier $f_{\mathbf{w}}$ that has $R_{\mathrm{emp}}[f_{\mathbf{w}}, z] = 0$.
3. Without any further assumptions on $\mathbf{P}_{\mathsf{Z}}$ the number of steps until convergence of the perceptron learning algorithm is not bounded.

- A training sample $z \in \mathcal{Z}^m$ that is linearly separable in feature space is required.

The second point in particular shows that ERM learning makes the learning task an *ill-posed* one (see Appendix A.4): A slight variation $\tilde{z}$ in the training sample z might lead to a large deviation between the expected risks of the classifiers learned using the ERM principle, $\left|R[\mathcal{A}_{\mathrm{ERM}}(z)] - R\left[\mathcal{A}_{\mathrm{ERM}}\left(\tilde{z}\right)\right]\right|$. As will be seen in Part II of this book, a very influential factor in this deviation is the possibility of the hypothesis space $\mathcal{F}$ adopting different labelings $\boldsymbol{y}$ for randomly drawn objects $\boldsymbol{x}$. The more diverse the set of functions a hypothesis space contains, the more easily it can produce a given labeling $\mathbf{y}$ regardless of how bad the subsequent prediction might be on new, as yet unseen, data points $z = (x, y)$. This effect is also known as *overfitting*, i.e., the empirical risk as given by equation (2.11) is much smaller than the expected risk (2.8) we originally aimed at minimizing.

One way to overcome this problem is the method of *regularization*. In our example this amounts to introducing a regularizer a-priori, that is, a functional $\Omega : \mathcal{F} \to \mathbb{R}^+$, and defining the solution to the learning problem to be

$$\mathcal{A}_\Omega(z) \stackrel{\text{def}}{=} \underset{f \in \mathcal{F}}{\operatorname{argmin}} \underbrace{R_{\text{emp}}[f, z] + \lambda \Omega[f]}_{R_{\text{reg}}[f,z]} . \tag{2.14}$$

The idea of regularization is to restrict the space of solutions to compact subsets of the (originally overly large) space $\mathcal{F}$. This can be achieved by requiring the set $F_\varepsilon = \{f \mid \Omega[f] \le \varepsilon\} \subseteq \mathcal{F}$ to be compact for each positive number $\varepsilon > 0$. This, in fact, is the essential requirement for any regularizer Ω. Then, if we decrease λ for increasing training sample sizes in the right way, it can be shown that the regularization method leads to f^* as $m \to \infty$ (see equation (2.13)). Clearly, $0 \le \lambda < \infty$ controls the amount of regularization. Setting $\lambda = 0$ is equivalent to minimizing only the empirical risk. In the other extreme, considering $\lambda \to \infty$ amounts to discounting the sample and returning the classifier which minimizes Ω alone. The regularizer Ω can be thought of as a penalization term for the "complexity" of particular classifiers.

Another view of the regularization method can be obtained from the statistical study of learning algorithms. This will be discussed in greater detail in Part II of this book but we shall put forward the main idea here. We shall see that there exist several measures of "complexity" of hypothesis spaces, the VC dimension being the most prominent thereof. V. Vapnik suggested a learning principle which he called *structural risk minimization* (SRM). The idea behind SRM is to, a-priori, define a structuring of the hypothesis space $\mathcal{F}$ into nested subsets $\mathcal{F}_0 \subset \mathcal{F}_1 \subset \cdots \subseteq \mathcal{F}$ of increasing complexity. Then, in each of the hypothesis spaces $\mathcal{F}_i$ empirical risk minimization is performed. Based on results from statistical learning theory, an SRM algorithm returns the classifier with the smallest *guaranteed risk*[8]. This can be related to the algorithm (2.14), if $\Omega[f]$ is the complexity value of f given by the used bound for the guaranteed risk.

From a Bayesian perspective, however, the method of regularization is closely related to *maximum-a-posteriori* (MAP) estimation. To see this, it suffices to

8 This is a misnomer as it refers to the value of an upper bound at a fixed confidence level and can in no way be guaranteed.

express the empirical risk as the negative log-probability of the training sample z, given a classifier f. In general, this can be achieved by

$$\mathbf{P}_{\mathsf{Z}^m|\mathsf{F}=f}(z) = \prod_{i=1}^{m} \mathbf{P}_{\mathsf{Y}|\mathsf{X}=x_i,\mathsf{F}=f}(y_i)\, \mathbf{P}_{\mathsf{X}|\mathsf{F}=f}(x_i)\,,$$

$$\mathbf{P}_{\mathsf{Y}|\mathsf{X}=x,\mathsf{F}=f}(y) = \frac{\exp\left(-l\left(f(x), y\right)\right)}{\sum_{\tilde{y}\in\mathcal{Y}} \exp\left(-l\left(f(x), \tilde{y}\right)\right)} = \frac{1}{C(x)} \exp\left(-l\left(f(x), y\right)\right).$$

Assuming a prior density $\mathbf{f}_{\mathsf{F}}(f) = \exp(-\lambda m \Omega[f])$, by Bayes' theorem we have the posterior density

$$\mathbf{f}_{\mathsf{F}|\mathsf{Z}^m=z}(f) \propto \exp\left(-\sum_{i=1}^{m} l\left(f(x_i), y_i\right)\right) \exp\left(-\lambda m \Omega[f]\right) \propto \exp\left(-R_{\mathrm{emp}}[f, z] - \lambda \Omega[f]\right).$$

The MAP estimate is that classifier f_{MAP} which maximizes the last expression, i.e., the mode of the posterior density. Taking the logarithm we see that the choice of a regularizer is comparable to the choice of the prior probability in the Bayesian framework and therefore reflects prior knowledge.

2.3 Kernels and Linear Classifiers

In practice we are often given a vectorial representation $x = \vec{x}$ of the objects. Using the identity feature mapping, i.e., $\mathbf{x} = \boldsymbol{\phi}(x) = \vec{x}$, results in classifiers linear in input space. Theoretically, however, any mapping into a high-dimensional feature space is conceivable. Hence, we call a classifier *nonlinear* in input space whenever a feature mapping different from the identity map is used.

Example 2.13 (Nonlinear classifiers) *Let $\mathcal{X} = \mathbb{R}^2$ and let the mapping $\boldsymbol{\phi} : \mathcal{X} \to \mathcal{K}$ be given by*

$$\boldsymbol{\phi}(\vec{x}) = \left((\vec{x})_1, (\vec{x})_2^2, (\vec{x})_1 (\vec{x})_2\right)'. \tag{2.15}$$

In Figure 2.3 (left) the mapping is applied to the unit square $[0, 1]^2$ and the resulting manifold in $\mathbb{R}^3$ is shown. Note that in this case the decision surface $\widetilde{X}_0(\mathbf{w})$

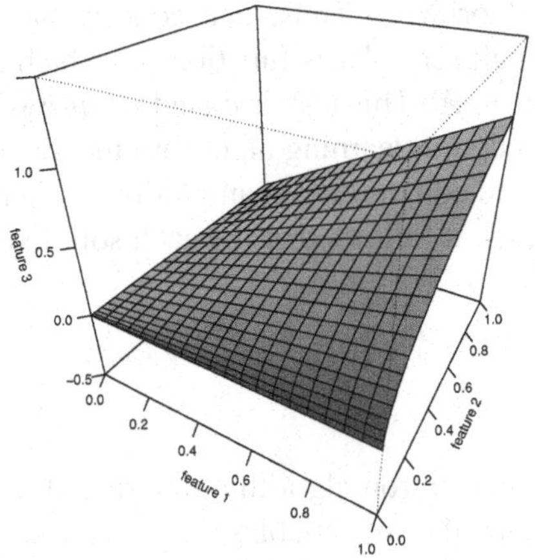

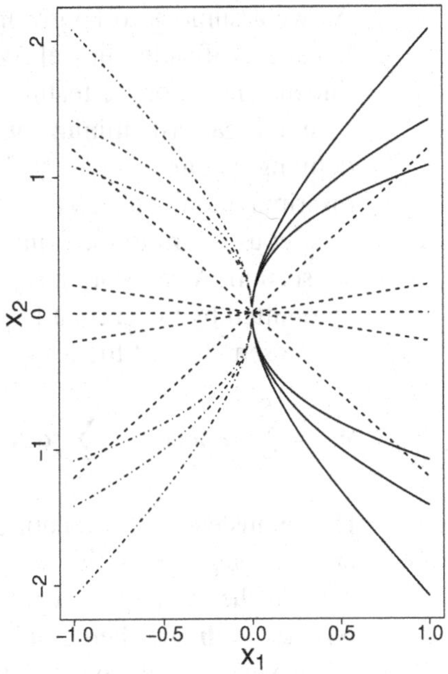

Figure 2.3 **(Left)** Mapping of the unit square $[0, 1]^2 \subset \mathbb{R}^2$ to the feature space $\mathcal{K} \subseteq \ell_2^3$ by equation (2.15). The mapped unit square forms a two-dimensional sub-manifold in $\mathbb{R}^3$ though $\dim(\mathcal{K}) = 3$. **(Right)** Nine different decision surfaces obtained by varying w_1 and w_3 in equation (2.16). The solid, dashed and dot-dashed lines result from varying w_3 for different values of $w_1 = -1, 0$ and $+1$, respectively.

in input space is given by

$$\widetilde{X}_0(\mathbf{w}) = \left\{ \vec{x} \in \mathbb{R}^2 \;\middle|\; w_1 (\vec{x})_1 + w_2 (\vec{x})_2^2 + w_3 (\vec{x})_1 (\vec{x})_2 = 0 \right\}, \tag{2.16}$$

whose solution is given by

$$(\vec{x})_2 = -\frac{w_3}{2w_2} \cdot (\vec{x})_1 \pm \frac{\sqrt{(\vec{x})_1 \left(w_3^2 (\vec{x})_1 - 4 w_1 w_2 \right)}}{2w_2}.$$

In Figure 2.3 (right) we have depicted the resulting decision surfaces for various choices of w_1 and w_3. Clearly, the decision surfaces are nonlinear functions although in feature space we are still dealing with linear functions.

As we assume $\boldsymbol{\phi}$ to be given we will call this the *explicit* way to non-linearize a linear classification model. We already mentioned in Section 2.2 that the number of dimensions, n, of the feature space has a great impact on the generalization ability of empirical risk minimization algorithms. Thus, one conceivable criterion for defining features ϕ_i is to seek a small set of basis functions ϕ_i which allow perfect discrimination between the classes in $\mathcal{X}$. This task is called *feature selection.*

Let us return to the primal perceptron learning algorithm mentioned in the last subsection. As we start at $\mathbf{w}_0 = \mathbf{0}$ and add training examples only when a mistake is committed by the current hypothesis, it follows that the each solution has to admit a representation of the form,

$$\mathbf{w}_t = \sum_{i=1}^{m} \alpha_i \boldsymbol{\phi}(x_i) = \sum_{i=1}^{m} \alpha_i \mathbf{x}_i \,. \tag{2.17}$$

Hence, instead of formulating the perceptron algorithm in terms of the n variables $(w_1, \ldots, w_n)' = \mathbf{w}$ we could learn the m variables $(\alpha_1, \ldots, \alpha_m)' = \boldsymbol{\alpha}$ which we call the *dual space* of variables. In the case of perceptron learning we start with $\boldsymbol{\alpha}_0 = \mathbf{0}$ and then employ the representation of equation (2.17) to update $\boldsymbol{\alpha}_t$ whenever a mistake occurs. To this end, we need to evaluate

$$y_j \langle \mathbf{x}_j, \mathbf{w}_t \rangle = y_j \left\langle \mathbf{x}_j, \sum_{i=1}^{m} \alpha_i \mathbf{x}_i \right\rangle = y_j \sum_{i=1}^{m} \alpha_i \langle \mathbf{x}_j, \mathbf{x}_i \rangle$$

which requires only knowledge of the inner product function $\langle \cdot, \cdot \rangle$ between the mapped training objects $\mathbf{x}$. Further, for the classification of a novel test object x it suffices to know the solution vector $\boldsymbol{\alpha}_t$ as well as the inner product function, because

$$\langle \mathbf{x}, \mathbf{w}_t \rangle = \left\langle \mathbf{x}, \sum_{i=1}^{m} \alpha_i \mathbf{x}_i \right\rangle = \sum_{i=1}^{m} \alpha_i \langle \mathbf{x}, \mathbf{x}_i \rangle \,.$$

Definition 2.14 (Kernel) *Suppose we are given a feature mapping* $\boldsymbol{\phi} : \mathcal{X} \to \mathcal{K} \subseteq \ell_2^n$. *The* kernel *is the inner product function* $k : \mathcal{X} \times \mathcal{X} \to \mathbb{R}$ *in* $\mathcal{K}$, *i.e., for all* $x_i, x_j \in \mathcal{X}$,

$$k(x_i, x_j) \stackrel{\text{def}}{=} \langle \boldsymbol{\phi}(x_i), \boldsymbol{\phi}(x_j) \rangle = \langle \mathbf{x}_i, \mathbf{x}_j \rangle \,.$$

Using the notion of a kernel k we can therefore formulate the *kernel perceptron* or *dual perceptron algorithm* as presented on page 324. Note that we can benefit from the fact that, in each update step, we only increase the jth component of the expansion vector $\boldsymbol{\alpha}$ (assuming that the mistake occurred at the jth training point). This can change the real-valued output $\langle \mathbf{x}_i, \mathbf{w}_t \rangle$ at each mapped training object $\mathbf{x}_i$ by only one summand $y_j \langle \mathbf{x}_j, \mathbf{x}_i \rangle$ which requires just one evaluation of the kernel function with all training objects. Hence, by caching the real-valued outputs $\mathbf{o} \in \mathbb{R}^m$ at all training objects we see that the kernel perceptron algorithm requires exactly $2m$ memory units (for the storage of the vectors $\boldsymbol{\alpha}$ and $\mathbf{o}$) and is thus suited for large scale problems, i.e., $m \gg 1000$.

Definition 2.15 (Gram matrix) *Given a kernel $k : \mathcal{X} \times \mathcal{X} \to \mathbb{R}$ and a set $\boldsymbol{x} = (x_1, \ldots, x_m) \in \mathcal{X}^m$ of m objects in $\mathcal{X}$ we call the $m \times m$ matrix* $\mathbf{G}$ *with*

$$\mathbf{G}_{ij} \stackrel{\text{def}}{=} k\left(x_i, x_j\right) = \left\langle \mathbf{x}_i, \mathbf{x}_j \right\rangle \tag{2.18}$$

the Gram matrix *of k at $\boldsymbol{x}$.*

By the above reasoning we see that the Gram matrix (2.18) and the m–dimensional vector of kernel evaluations between the training objects x_i and a new test object $x \in \mathcal{X}$ suffice for learning and classification, respectively. It is worth also mentioning that the Gram matrix and feature space are called the *kernel matrix* and *kernel space*, respectively, as well.

2.3.1 The Kernel Technique

The key idea of the kernel technique is to invert the chain of arguments, i.e., choose a kernel k rather than a mapping *before* applying a learning algorithm. Of course, not any symmetric function k can serve as a kernel. The necessary and sufficient conditions of $k : \mathcal{X} \times \mathcal{X} \to \mathbb{R}$ to be a kernel are given by Mercer's theorem. Before we rephrase the original theorem we give a more intuitive characterization of Mercer kernels.

Example 2.16 (Mercer's theorem) *Suppose our input space $\mathcal{X}$ has a finite number of elements, i.e., $\mathcal{X} = \{x_1, \ldots, x_r\}$. Then, the $r \times r$ kernel matrix* $\mathbf{K}$ *with $\mathbf{K}_{ij} = k\left(x_i, x_j\right)$ is by definition a symmetric matrix. Consider the eigenvalue decomposition of $\mathbf{K} = \mathbf{U}\boldsymbol{\Lambda}\mathbf{U}'$, where $\mathbf{U} = (\mathbf{u}_1, \ldots, \mathbf{u}_n) = \left(\mathbf{v}'_1; \ldots; \mathbf{v}'_r\right)$ is an $r \times n$ matrix such that $\mathbf{U}'\mathbf{U} = \mathbf{I}_n$, $\boldsymbol{\Lambda} = \operatorname{diag}(\lambda_1, \ldots, \lambda_n)$, $\lambda_1 \geq \lambda_2 \geq \cdots \geq \lambda_n > 0$ and $n \leq r$ being known as the rank of the matrix* $\mathbf{K}$ *(see also Theorem A.83 and*

Definition A.62). Now the mapping $\boldsymbol{\phi} : \mathcal{X} \to \mathcal{K} \subseteq \ell_2^n$,

$$\boldsymbol{\phi}(x_i) = \boldsymbol{\Lambda}^{\frac{1}{2}} \mathbf{v}_i ,$$

leads to a Gram matrix $\mathbf{G}$ *given by*

$$\mathbf{G}_{ij} = \langle \boldsymbol{\phi}(x_i), \boldsymbol{\phi}(x_j) \rangle_{\mathcal{K}} = \left(\boldsymbol{\Lambda}^{\frac{1}{2}} \mathbf{v}_i\right)' \left(\boldsymbol{\Lambda}^{\frac{1}{2}} \mathbf{v}_j\right) = \mathbf{v}_i' \boldsymbol{\Lambda} \mathbf{v}_j = \mathbf{K}_{ij} .$$

We have constructed a feature space $\mathcal{K}$ *and a mapping* $\boldsymbol{\phi}$ *into it purely from the kernel* k. *Note that* $\lambda_n > 0$ *is equivalent to assuming that* $\mathbf{K}$ *is positive semidefinite denoted by* $\mathbf{K} \geq 0$ *(see Definition A.40). In order to show that* $\mathbf{K} \geq 0$ *is also necessary for* k *to be a kernel, we assume that* $\lambda_n < 0$. *Then, the squared length of the point* $\sum_{i=1}^{r} \mathbf{U}_{in} \boldsymbol{\phi}(x_i) = \boldsymbol{\Lambda}^{\frac{1}{2}} \mathbf{U}' \mathbf{u}_n$ *is*

$$\left\| \boldsymbol{\Lambda}^{\frac{1}{2}} \mathbf{U}' \mathbf{u}_n \right\|^2 = \mathbf{u}_n' \mathbf{U} \boldsymbol{\Lambda} \mathbf{U}' \mathbf{u}_n = \mathbf{e}_n' \boldsymbol{\Lambda} \mathbf{e}_n = \lambda_n < 0 ,$$

which contradicts the geometry in an inner product space.

Mercer's theorem is an extension of this property, mainly achieved by studying the eigenvalue problem for integral equations of the form

$$\int_{\mathcal{X}} k(x, \tilde{x}) f(\tilde{x}) \, d\tilde{x} = \lambda f(x) ,$$

where k is a bounded, symmetric and positive semidefinite function.

Theorem 2.17 (Mercer's theorem) *Suppose* $k \in L_\infty(\mathcal{X} \times \mathcal{X})$ *is a symmetric function, i.e.,* $k(x, \tilde{x}) = k(\tilde{x}, x)$, *such that the integral operator* $T_k : L_2(\mathcal{X}) \to L_2(\mathcal{X})$ *given by*

$$(T_k f)(\cdot) = \int_{\mathcal{X}} k(\cdot, x) f(x) \, dx$$

is positive semidefinite, that is,

$$\int_{\mathcal{X}} \int_{\mathcal{X}} k(\tilde{x}, x) f(x) f(\tilde{x}) \, dx d\tilde{x} \geq 0 , \tag{2.19}$$

for all $f \in L_2(\mathcal{X})$. *Let* $\psi_i \in L_2(\mathcal{X})$ *be the eigenfunction of* T_k *associated with the eigenvalue* $\lambda_i \geq 0$ *and normalized such that* $\|\psi_i\|_2 = \int_{\mathcal{X}} \psi_i^2(x) \, dx = 1$, *i.e.,*

$$\forall x \in \mathcal{X} : \qquad \int_{\mathcal{X}} k(x, \tilde{x}) \psi_i(\tilde{x}) \, d\tilde{x} = \lambda_i \psi_i(x) .$$

Then

1. $(\lambda_i)_{i\in\mathbb{N}} \in \ell_1$,
2. $\psi_i \in L_\infty(\mathcal{X})$,
3. k can be expanded in a uniformly convergent series, i.e.,

$$k(x,\tilde{x}) = \sum_{i=1}^{\infty} \lambda_i \psi_i(x)\psi_i(\tilde{x}) \tag{2.20}$$

holds for all $x, \tilde{x} \in \mathcal{X}$.

The positivity condition (2.19) is equivalent to the positive semidefiniteness of $\mathbf{K}$ in Example 2.16. This has been made more precise in the following proposition.

Proposition 2.18 (Mercer Kernels) *The function* $k : \mathcal{X} \times \mathcal{X} \to \mathbb{R}$ *is a* Mercer kernel *if, and only if, for each* $r \in \mathbb{N}$ *and* $\mathbf{x} = (x_1, \ldots, x_r) \in \mathcal{X}^r$, *the* $r \times r$ *matrix* $\mathbf{K} = \left(k\left(x_i, x_j\right)\right)_{i,j=1}^{r}$ *is positive semidefinite.*

Remarkably, Mercer's theorem not only gives necessary and sufficient conditions for k to be a kernel, but also suggests a constructive way of obtaining features ϕ_i from a given kernel k. To see this, consider the mapping $\boldsymbol{\phi}$ from $\mathcal{X}$ into ℓ_2

$$\boldsymbol{\phi}(x) = \left(\sqrt{\lambda_1}\psi_1(x), \sqrt{\lambda_2}\psi_2(x), \ldots\right)'. \tag{2.21}$$

By equation (2.20) we have for each $x, \tilde{x} \in \mathcal{X}$

$$k(x,\tilde{x}) = \sum_{i=1}^{\infty} \lambda_i \psi_i(x)\psi_i(\tilde{x}) = \sum_{i=1}^{\infty} \phi_i(x)\phi_i(\tilde{x}) = \langle \boldsymbol{\phi}(x), \boldsymbol{\phi}(\tilde{x}) \rangle .$$

The features ψ_i are called *Mercer features;* the mapping

$$\boldsymbol{\psi}(x) = (\psi_1(x), \psi_2(x), \ldots)'$$

is known as the *Mercer map*; the image $\mathcal{M}$ of $\boldsymbol{\psi}$ is termed *Mercer space.*

Remark 2.19 (Mahalanobis metric) *Consider kernels* k *such that* $\dim(\mathcal{K}) = \dim(\mathcal{M}) < \infty$. *In order to have equal inner products in feature space* $\mathcal{K}$ *and Mercer space* $\mathcal{M}$, *we need to redefine the inner product in* $\mathcal{M}$, *i.e.,*

$$\langle \mathbf{a}, \mathbf{b} \rangle_{\mathcal{M}} = \mathbf{a}'\boldsymbol{\Lambda}\mathbf{b},$$

where $\mathbf{\Lambda} = \operatorname{diag}(\lambda_1, \ldots, \lambda_n)$. *This metric appears in the study of covariances of multidimensional Gaussians and is also known as the* Mahalanobis metric. *In fact, there is a very close connection between covariance functions for Gaussian processes and kernels which we will discuss in more depth in Chapter 3.*

2.3.2 Kernel Families

So far we have seen that there are two ways of making linear classifiers nonlinear in input space:

1. Choose a mapping $\boldsymbol{\phi}$ which *explicitly* gives us a (Mercer) kernel k, or
2. Choose a Mercer kernel k which *implicitly* corresponds to a fixed mapping $\boldsymbol{\phi}$.

Though mathematically equivalent, kernels are often much easier to define and have the intuitive meaning of serving as a similarity measure between objects $x, \tilde{x} \in \mathcal{X}$. Moreover, there exist simple rules for designing kernels on the basis of given kernel functions.

Theorem 2.20 (Functions of kernels) *Let* $k_1 : \mathcal{X} \times \mathcal{X} \to \mathbb{R}$ *and* $k_2 : \mathcal{X} \times \mathcal{X} \to \mathbb{R}$ *be any two Mercer kernels. Then, the functions* $k : \mathcal{X} \times \mathcal{X} \to \mathbb{R}$ *given by*

1. $k(x, \tilde{x}) = k_1(x, \tilde{x}) + k_2(x, \tilde{x})$,
2. $k(x, \tilde{x}) = c \cdot k_1(x, \tilde{x})$, *for all* $c \in \mathbb{R}^+$,
3. $k(x, \tilde{x}) = k_1(x, \tilde{x}) + c$, *for all* $c \in \mathbb{R}^+$,
4. $k(x, \tilde{x}) = k_1(x, \tilde{x}) \cdot k_2(x, \tilde{x})$,
5. $k(x, \tilde{x}) = f(x) \cdot f(\tilde{x})$, *for any function* $f : \mathcal{X} \to \mathbb{R}$

are also Mercer kernels.

The proofs can be found in Appendix B.1. The real impact of these design rules becomes apparent when we consider the following corollary (for a proof see Appendix B.1).

Corollary 2.21 (Functions of kernels) *Let* $k_1 : \mathcal{X} \times \mathcal{X} \to \mathbb{R}$ *be any Mercer kernel. Then, the functions* $k : \mathcal{X} \times \mathcal{X} \to \mathbb{R}$ *given by*

1. $k(x, \tilde{x}) = (k_1(x, \tilde{x}) + \theta_1)^{\theta_2}$, *for all* $\theta_1 \in \mathbb{R}^+$ *and* $\theta_2 \in \mathbb{N}$,
2. $k(x, \tilde{x}) = \exp\left(\frac{k_1(x, \tilde{x})}{\sigma^2}\right)$, *for all* $\sigma \in \mathbb{R}^+$,

3. $k(x,\tilde{x}) = \exp\left(-\frac{k_1(x,x)-2k_1(x,\tilde{x})+k_1(\tilde{x},\tilde{x})}{2\sigma^2}\right)$, *for all* $\sigma \in \mathbb{R}^+$
4. $k(x,\tilde{x}) = \frac{k_1(x,\tilde{x})}{\sqrt{k_1(x,x)\cdot k_1(\tilde{x},\tilde{x})}}$

are also Mercer kernels.

It is worth mentioning that, by virtue of the fourth proposition of this corollary, it is possible to normalize data in feature space without performing the explicit mapping because, for the inner product after normalization, it holds that

$$k_{\text{norm}}(x,\tilde{x}) \stackrel{\text{def}}{=} \frac{k(x,\tilde{x})}{\sqrt{k(x,x)\cdot k(\tilde{x},\tilde{x})}} = \frac{1}{\sqrt{\|\mathbf{x}\|^2\cdot\|\tilde{\mathbf{x}}\|^2}}\langle\mathbf{x},\tilde{\mathbf{x}}\rangle = \left\langle\frac{\mathbf{x}}{\|\mathbf{x}\|},\frac{\tilde{\mathbf{x}}}{\|\tilde{\mathbf{x}}\|}\right\rangle. \quad (2.22)$$

Kernels on Inner Product Spaces—Polynomial and RBF Kernels

If the input space $\mathcal{X}$ is already an N–dimensional inner product space ℓ_2^N we can use Corollary 2.21 to construct new kernels because, according to Example A.41 at page 219, the inner product function $\langle\cdot,\cdot\rangle_{\mathcal{X}}$ in $\mathcal{X}$ is already a Mercer kernel. In Table 2.1 some commonly used families of kernels on ℓ_2^N are presented. The last column gives the number of linearly independent features ϕ_i in the induced feature space $\mathcal{K}$.

The *radial basis function* (RBF) kernel has the appealing property that each linear combination of kernel functions of the training objects[9] $\boldsymbol{x} = (\vec{x}_1,\ldots,\vec{x}_m)$

$$f(\vec{x}) = \sum_{i=1}^{m}\alpha_i k(\vec{x},\vec{x}_i) = \sum_{i=1}^{m}\alpha_i \exp\left(-\frac{\|\vec{x}-\vec{x}_i\|_{\mathcal{X}}^2}{2\sigma^2}\right), \quad (2.23)$$

can also be viewed as a density estimator in input space $\mathcal{X}$ because it effectively puts a Gaussian on each $\vec{x}_i$ and weights its contribution to the final density by α_i. Interestingly, by the third proposition of Corollary 2.21, the weighting coefficients α_i correspond directly to the expansion coefficients for a weight vector $\mathbf{w}$ in a classical linear model $f(\vec{x}) = \langle\boldsymbol{\phi}(\vec{x}),\mathbf{w}\rangle$. The parameter σ controls the amount of smoothing, i.e., big values of σ lead to very flat and smooth functions f—hence it defines the unit on which distances $\|\vec{x}-\vec{x}_i\|$ are measured (see Figure 2.4). The *Mahalanobis* kernel differs from the standard RBF kernel insofar as each axis of the input space $\mathcal{X} \subseteq \ell_2^N$ has a separate smoothing parameter, i.e., a

9 In this subsection we use $\vec{x}$ to denote the N–dimensional vectors in input space. Note that $\mathbf{x} := \boldsymbol{\phi}(\vec{x})$ denotes a mapped input object (vector) $\vec{x}$ in feature space $\mathcal{K}$.

Name	Kernel function	dim $(\mathcal{K})$
pth degree polynomial	$k(\vec{u},\vec{v}) = (\langle\vec{u},\vec{v}\rangle_{\mathcal{X}})^p$ $p \in \mathbb{N}^+$	$\binom{N+p-1}{p}$
complete polynomial	$k(\vec{u},\vec{v}) = (\langle\vec{u},\vec{v}\rangle_{\mathcal{X}} + c)^p$ $c \in \mathbb{R}^+,\ p \in \mathbb{N}^+$	$\binom{N+p}{p}$
RBF kernel	$k(\vec{u},\vec{v}) = \exp\left(-\frac{\lVert\vec{u}-\vec{v}\rVert_{\mathcal{X}}^2}{2\sigma^2}\right)$ $\sigma \in \mathbb{R}^+$	∞
Mahalanobis kernel	$k(\vec{u},\vec{v}) = \exp\left(-(\vec{u}-\vec{v})'\,\mathbf{\Sigma}\,(\vec{u}-\vec{v})\right)$ $\mathbf{\Sigma} = \operatorname{diag}\left(\sigma_1^{-2},\ldots,\sigma_N^{-2}\right)$, $\sigma_1,\ldots,\sigma_N \in \mathbb{R}^+$	∞

Table 2.1 List of kernel functions over ℓ_2^N. The dimensionality of the input space is N.

separate scale onto which differences on this axis are viewed. By setting $\sigma_i \to \infty$ we are able to eliminate the influence of the ith feature in input space. We shall see in Section 3.2 that inference over these parameters is made in the context of *automatic relevance determination* (ARD) of the features in input space (see also Example 3.12). It is worth mentioning that RBF kernels map the input space onto the surface of an infinite dimensional hypersphere because by construction $\lVert\boldsymbol{\phi}(\vec{x})\rVert = \sqrt{k(\vec{x},\vec{x})} = 1$ for all $\vec{x} \in \mathcal{X}$. Finally, by using RBF kernels we have automatically chosen a classification model which is shift invariant, i.e., translating the whole input space $\mathcal{X}$ by some fixed vector $\vec{a}$ does not change anything because

$$\forall \vec{a} \in \mathcal{X}: \quad \lVert(\vec{x}+\vec{a}) - (\vec{x}_i+\vec{a})\rVert^2 = \lVert\vec{x}+\vec{a}-\vec{x}_i-\vec{a}\rVert^2 = \lVert\vec{x}-\vec{x}_i\rVert^2 .$$

The most remarkable advantage in using these kernels is the saving in computational effort, e.g., to calculate the inner product for pth degree complete polynomial kernels we need $\mathcal{O}(N+p)$ operations whereas an explicit mapping would require calculations of order $\mathcal{O}(\exp(p\ln(N/p)))$. Further, for radial basis function kernels, it is very difficult to perform the explicit mapping.

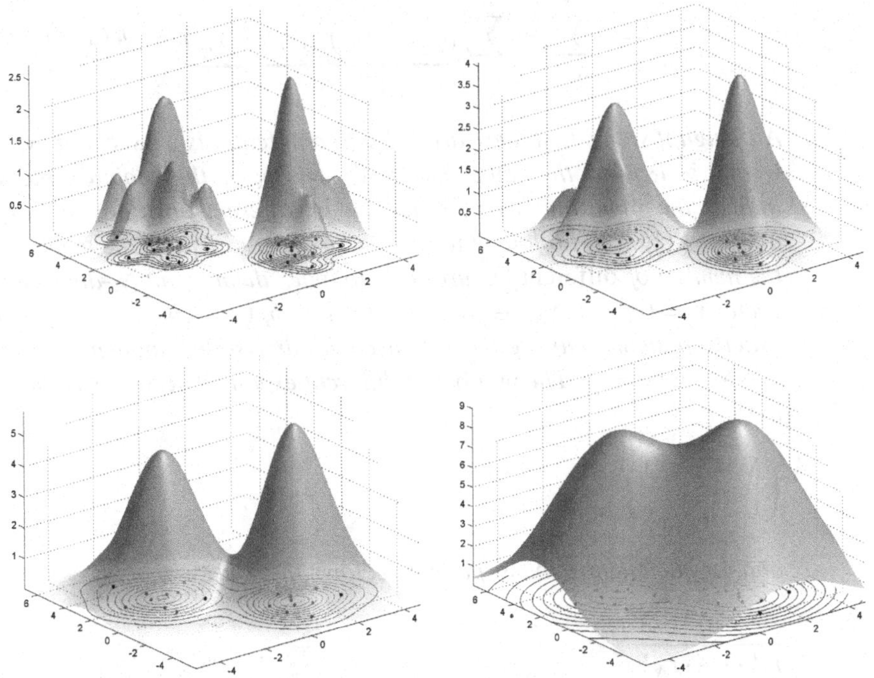

Figure 2.4 The real-valued function $f(\vec{x})$ for $m = 20$ training points $\vec{x} \in \mathbb{R}^2$ with $\boldsymbol{\alpha} = \mathbf{1}$ (see equation (2.23)) for varying values of σ (from upper left to lower right $\sigma = 0.5$, $\sigma = 0.7$, $\sigma = 1.0$ and $\sigma = 2.0$). From the contour plot it can be seen that by increasing σ the contribution of single points to the final density vanishes. Further, for bigger values of σ the resulting surface is smoother. For visualization purposes the surface $\{\vec{x} \mid f(\vec{x}) = 0\}$ is made transparent.

Example 2.22 (Polynomial kernel) *Consider the pth degree polynomial kernel as given in Table 2.1. In order to obtain explicit features $\phi : \mathcal{X} \to \mathbb{R}$ let us expand the kernel function as follows*[10]

$$(\langle \vec{u}, \vec{v} \rangle_{\mathcal{X}})^p = \left(\sum_{i=1}^{N} u_i v_i\right)^p = \left(\sum_{i_1=1}^{N} u_{i_1} v_{i_1}\right) \cdots \left(\sum_{i_p=1}^{N} u_{i_p} v_{i_p}\right)$$

10 For notational brevity, in this example we denote the i–th component of the vector $\vec{u} \in \mathcal{X}$ and $\vec{v} \in \mathcal{X}$ by u_i and v_i, respectively.

$$= \sum_{i_1=1}^{N} \cdots \sum_{i_p=1}^{N} \underbrace{\left(u_{i_1} \cdots u_{i_p}\right)}_{\phi_{\mathbf{i}}(\vec{u})} \cdot \underbrace{\left(v_{i_1} \cdots v_{i_p}\right)}_{\phi_{\mathbf{i}}(\vec{v})} = \langle \boldsymbol{\phi}(\vec{u}), \boldsymbol{\phi}(\vec{v}) \rangle .$$

Although it seems that there are N^p different features we see that two index vectors $\mathbf{i}_1$ and $\mathbf{i}_2$ lead to the same feature $\phi_{\mathbf{i}_1} = \phi_{\mathbf{i}_2}$ if they contain the same distinct indices the same number of times but at different positions, e.g., $\mathbf{i}_1 = (1, 1, 3)$ and $\mathbf{i}_2 = (1, 3, 1)$ both lead to $\phi(\vec{u}) = u_1 u_1 u_3 = u_1^2 u_3$. One method of computing the number of different *features ϕ is to index them by an N–dimensional exponent vector $\mathbf{r} = (r_1, \ldots, r_N) \in \{0, \ldots, p\}^N$, i.e., $\phi_{\mathbf{r}}(\vec{u}) = u_1^{r_1} \cdot \cdots \cdot u_N^{r_N}$. Since there are exactly p summands we know that each admissible exponent vector $\mathbf{r}$ must obey $r_1 + \cdots + r_N = p$. The* number *of different exponent vectors $\mathbf{r}$ is thus exactly given by*[11]

$$\binom{N+p-1}{p},$$

and for each admissible exponent vector $\mathbf{r}$ there are exactly[12]

$$\frac{p!}{r_1! \cdot \cdots \cdot r_N!}$$

different index vectors $\mathbf{i} \in \{1, \ldots, N\}^p$ leading to $\mathbf{r}$. Hence the $\mathbf{r}$th feature is given by

$$\phi_{\mathbf{r}}(\vec{u}) = \sqrt{\frac{p!}{r_1! \cdot \cdots \cdot r_N!}} \cdot u_1^{r_1} \cdot \cdots \cdot u_N^{r_N} .$$

Finally note that the complete polynomial kernel in Table 2.1 is a pth degree polynomial kernel in an $N+1$–dimensional input space by the following identity

$$\left(\langle \vec{u}, \vec{v} \rangle + c\right)^p = \left(\left\langle \left(\vec{u}, \sqrt{c}\right), \left(\vec{v}, \sqrt{c}\right) \right\rangle\right)^p ,$$

11 This problem is known as the *occupancy problem*: Given p balls and N cells, how many different configurations of occupancy numbers $r_1, \ldots, r_N$ whose sum is exactly p exist? (see Feller (1950) for results).

12 To see this note that we have first to select r_1 indices $j_1, \ldots, j_{r_1}$ and set $i_{j_1} = \cdots = i_{j_{r_1}} = 1$. From the remaining $p - r_1$ indices select r_2 indices and set them all to 2, etc. Thus, the total number of different index vectors $\mathbf{i}$ leading to the same exponent vector $\mathbf{r}$ equals

$$\binom{p}{r_1}\binom{p-r_1}{r_2} \cdot \cdots \cdot \binom{p-r_1-\cdots-r_{N-2}}{r_{N-1}} = \frac{p!}{r_1! \cdot \cdots \cdot r_N!},$$

which is valid because $r_1 + \cdots + r_N = p$ (taken from Feller (1950)).

where we use the fact that $c \geq 0$. This justifies the number of dimensions of feature space given in the third column of Table 2.1.

Kernels on Strings

One of the greatest advantages of kernels is that they are not limited to vectorial objects $\vec{x} \in \mathcal{X}$ but that they are applicable to virtually any kind of object representation. In this subsection we will demonstrate that it is possible to efficiently formulate computable kernels on strings. An application of string kernels is in the analysis of DNA sequences which are given as strings composed of the symbols[13] A, T, G, C. Another interesting use of kernels on strings is in the field of text categorization and classification. Here we treat each document as a sequence or string of letters. Let us start by formalizing the notion of a string.

Definition 2.23 (Strings and alphabets) *An* alphabet Σ *is a finite collection of symbols called characters. A* string *is a finite sequence* $\boldsymbol{u} = (u_1, \ldots, u_r)$ *of characters from an alphabet* Σ. *The symbol* Σ^* *denotes the set of all strings of any length, i.e.,* $\Sigma^* \stackrel{\text{def}}{=} \cup_{i=0}^{\infty} \Sigma^i$. *The number* $|\boldsymbol{u}|$ *of symbols in a string* $\boldsymbol{u} \in \Sigma^*$ *is called the* length *of the string. Given two strings* $\boldsymbol{u} \in \Sigma^*$ *and* $\boldsymbol{v} \in \Sigma^*$, *the symbol* $\boldsymbol{uv} \stackrel{\text{def}}{=} \left(u_1, \ldots, u_{|\boldsymbol{u}|}, v_1, \ldots, v_{|\boldsymbol{v}|}\right)$ *denotes the* concatenation *of the two strings.*

Definition 2.24 (Subsequences and substrings) *Given a string* $\boldsymbol{u} \in \Sigma^*$ *and an index vector* $\mathbf{i} = (i_1, \ldots, i_r)$ *such that* $1 \leq i_1 < \cdots < i_r \leq |\boldsymbol{u}|$, *we denote by* $\boldsymbol{u}[\mathbf{i}]$ *the* subsequence $\left(u_{i_1}, \ldots, u_{i_r}\right)$. *The index vector* $(1, \ldots, r)$ *is abbreviated by* $1 : r$. *Given two strings* $\boldsymbol{v} \in \Sigma^*$ *and* $\boldsymbol{u} \in \Sigma^*$ *where* $|\boldsymbol{u}| \geq |\boldsymbol{v}|$ *we define the index set* $I_{\boldsymbol{v},\boldsymbol{u}} \stackrel{\text{def}}{=} \{i : (i + |\boldsymbol{v}| - 1) \mid i \in \{1, \ldots, |\boldsymbol{u}| - |\boldsymbol{v}| + 1\}\}$, *i.e., the set of all consecutive sequences of length* $|\boldsymbol{v}|$ *in* $|\boldsymbol{u}|$. *Then the string* $\boldsymbol{v}$ *is said to be a* substring *of* $\boldsymbol{u}$ *if there exists an index vector* $\mathbf{i} \in I_{\boldsymbol{v},\boldsymbol{u}}$ *such that* $\boldsymbol{v} = \boldsymbol{u}[\mathbf{i}]$. *The* length $l(\mathbf{i})$ *of an index vector is defined by* $i_{|\boldsymbol{v}|} - i_1 + 1$, *i.e., the total extent of the subsequence (substring)* $\boldsymbol{v}$ *in the string* $\boldsymbol{u}$.

In order to derive kernels on strings, it is advantageous to start with the explicit mapping $\boldsymbol{\phi} : \Sigma^* \to \mathcal{K}$ and then make sure that the resulting inner product function $\langle \boldsymbol{\phi}(\cdot), \boldsymbol{\phi}(\cdot) \rangle$ is easy to compute. By the finiteness of the alphabet Σ, the set Σ^* is countable and we can therefore use it to index the features $\boldsymbol{\phi}$.

---

13 These letters correspond to the four bases *Adenine, Thymine, Guanine* and *Cytosine*.

The most trivial feature set and corresponding kernel are obtained if we consider binary features $\phi_{\boldsymbol{u}}$ that indicate whether the given string matches $\boldsymbol{u}$ or not,

$$\phi_{\boldsymbol{u}}(\boldsymbol{v}) = \mathbf{I}_{\boldsymbol{u}=\boldsymbol{v}} \quad \Leftrightarrow \quad k(\boldsymbol{u}, \boldsymbol{v}) = \begin{cases} 1 & \text{if } \boldsymbol{u} = \boldsymbol{v} \\ 0 & \text{otherwise} \end{cases},$$

Though easy to compute, this kernel is unable to measure the similarity to any object (string) not in the training sample and hence would not be useful for learning.

A more commonly used feature set is obtained if we assume that we are given a *lexicon* $B = \{\boldsymbol{b}_1, \ldots, \boldsymbol{b}_n\} \subset \Sigma^*$ of possible substrings which we will call *words*. We compute the number of times the ith substring $\boldsymbol{b}_i$ appears within a given string (document). Hence, the so-called *bag-of-words kernel* is given by

$$\phi_{\boldsymbol{b}}(\boldsymbol{v}) = \beta_{\boldsymbol{b}} \cdot \sum_{\mathbf{i} \in I_{\boldsymbol{b},\boldsymbol{v}}} \mathbf{I}_{\boldsymbol{b}=\boldsymbol{v}[\mathbf{i}]} \quad \Leftrightarrow \quad k_B(\boldsymbol{u}, \boldsymbol{v}) = \sum_{\boldsymbol{b} \in B} \beta_{\boldsymbol{b}}^2 \sum_{\mathbf{i} \in I_{\boldsymbol{b},\boldsymbol{u}}} \sum_{\mathbf{j} \in I_{\boldsymbol{b},\boldsymbol{v}}} \mathbf{I}_{\boldsymbol{b}=\boldsymbol{u}[\mathbf{i}]=\boldsymbol{v}[\mathbf{j}]}, \tag{2.24}$$

which can be efficiently computed if we assume that the data is preprocessed such that only the indices of the words occurring in a given string are stored. The coefficients $\beta_{\boldsymbol{b}}$ allow the weighting of the importance of words $\boldsymbol{b} \in B$ to differ. A commonly used heuristic for the determination of the $\beta_{\boldsymbol{b}}$ is the use of the *inverse-document-frequency* (IDF) which is given by the logarithm of the inverse probability that the substring (word) $\boldsymbol{b}$ appears in a randomly chosen string (document).

The kernel given in equation (2.24) has the disadvantage of requiring a fixed lexicon $B \subset \Sigma^*$ which is often difficult to define *a-priori*. This is particularly true when dealing with strings *not* originating from natural languages. If we fix the maximum length, r, of substrings considered and weight the feature $\phi_{\boldsymbol{b}}$ by $\lambda^{|\boldsymbol{b}|}$, i.e., for $\lambda \in (0, 1)$ we emphasize short substrings whereas for $\lambda > 1$ the weight of longer substrings increases, we obtain

$$\phi_{\boldsymbol{b}}(\boldsymbol{v}) = \lambda^{|\boldsymbol{b}|} \sum_{\mathbf{i} \in I_{\boldsymbol{b},\boldsymbol{v}}} \mathbf{I}_{\boldsymbol{b}=\boldsymbol{v}[\mathbf{i}]} \Leftrightarrow k_r(\boldsymbol{u}, \boldsymbol{v}) = \sum_{s=1}^{r} \lambda^{2s} \sum_{\boldsymbol{b} \in \Sigma^s} \sum_{\mathbf{i} \in I_{\boldsymbol{b},\boldsymbol{u}}} \sum_{\mathbf{j} \in I_{\boldsymbol{b},\boldsymbol{v}}} \mathbf{I}_{\boldsymbol{b}=\boldsymbol{u}[\mathbf{i}]=\boldsymbol{v}[\mathbf{j}]}, \tag{2.25}$$

which can be computed using the following recursion (see Appendix B.2)

$$k_r(u_1\boldsymbol{u}, \boldsymbol{v}) = \begin{cases} 0 & \text{if } |u_1\boldsymbol{u}| = 0 \\ k_r(\boldsymbol{u}, \boldsymbol{v}) + \sum_{j=1}^{|\boldsymbol{v}|} \lambda^2 \cdot k_r'(u_1\boldsymbol{u}, \boldsymbol{v}) & \text{otherwise} \end{cases}, \tag{2.26}$$

$$k'_r(u_1\boldsymbol{u}, v_1\boldsymbol{v}) = \begin{cases} 0 & \text{if } r = 0 \\ 0 & \text{if } |u_1\boldsymbol{u}| = 0 \text{ or } |v_1\boldsymbol{v}| = 0 \\ 0 & \text{if } u_1 \neq v_1 \\ \left(1 + \lambda^2 \cdot k'_{r-1}(\boldsymbol{u}, \boldsymbol{v})\right) & \text{otherwise} \end{cases} . \quad (2.27)$$

Since the recursion over k_r invokes at most $|\boldsymbol{v}|$ times the recursion over k'_r (which terminates after at most r steps) and is invoked itself exactly $|\boldsymbol{u}|$ times, the computational complexity of this string kernel is $\mathcal{O}(r \cdot |\boldsymbol{u}| \cdot |\boldsymbol{v}|)$.

One of the disadvantages of the kernels given in equations (2.24) and (2.25) is that each feature requires a perfect match of the substring $\boldsymbol{b}$ in the given string $\boldsymbol{v} \in \Sigma^*$. In general, strings can suffer from deletion and insertion of symbols, e.g., for DNA sequences it can happen that a few bases are inserted somewhere in a given substring $\boldsymbol{b}$. Hence, rather than requiring $\boldsymbol{b}$ to be a substring we assume that $\phi_{\boldsymbol{b}}(\boldsymbol{v})$ only measures how often $\boldsymbol{b}$ is a subsequence of $\boldsymbol{v}$ and penalizes the non-contiguity of $\boldsymbol{b}$ in $\boldsymbol{v}$ by using the length $l(\mathbf{i})$ of the corresponding index vector $\mathbf{i}$, i.e.,

$$\phi_{\boldsymbol{b}}(\boldsymbol{v}) = \sum_{\{\mathbf{i} \mid \boldsymbol{b}=\boldsymbol{v}[\mathbf{i}]\}} \lambda^{l(\mathbf{i})} \quad \Leftrightarrow \quad k_r(\boldsymbol{u}, \boldsymbol{v}) = \sum_{\boldsymbol{b} \in \Sigma^r} \sum_{\{\mathbf{i} \mid \boldsymbol{b}=\boldsymbol{u}[\mathbf{i}]\}} \sum_{\{\mathbf{j} \mid \boldsymbol{b}=\boldsymbol{v}[\mathbf{j}]\}} \lambda^{l(\mathbf{i})+l(\mathbf{j})} \quad (2.28)$$

This kernel can efficiently be computed by applying the the following recursion formula (see Appendix B.2)

$$k_r(\boldsymbol{u}u_s, \boldsymbol{v}) = \begin{cases} 0 & \text{if } \min(|\boldsymbol{u}u_s|, |\boldsymbol{v}|) < r \\ k_r(\boldsymbol{u}, \boldsymbol{v}) + \lambda^2 \sum_{\{t \mid v_t = u_s\}} k'_{r-1}(\boldsymbol{u}, \boldsymbol{v}[1:(t-1)]) & \end{cases} \quad (2.29)$$

$$k'_r(\boldsymbol{u}u_s, \boldsymbol{v}) = \begin{cases} 0 & \text{if } \min(|\boldsymbol{u}u_s|, |\boldsymbol{v}|) < r \\ 1 & \text{if } r = 0 \\ \lambda \cdot k'_r(\boldsymbol{u}, \boldsymbol{v}) + \lambda^2 \sum_{\{t \mid v_t = u_s\}} \lambda^{|\boldsymbol{v}|-t} k'_{r-1}(\boldsymbol{u}, \boldsymbol{v}[1:(t-1)]) & \end{cases} \quad (2.30)$$

Clearly, the recursion for k_r is invoked exactly $|\boldsymbol{u}|$ times by itself and each time invokes at most $|\boldsymbol{v}|$ times the recursive evaluation of k'_r. The recursion over k'_r is invoked at most r times itself and invokes at most $|\boldsymbol{v}|$ times the recursion over k'_{r-1}. As a consequence the computational complexity of this algorithm is $\mathcal{O}\left(r \cdot |\boldsymbol{u}| \cdot |\boldsymbol{v}|^2\right)$. It can be shown, however, that with simple caching it is possible to reduce the complexity further to $\mathcal{O}(r \cdot |\boldsymbol{u}| \cdot |\boldsymbol{v}|)$.

Remark 2.25 (Ridge Problem) *The kernels (2.25) and (2.28) lead to the so-called* ridge problem *when applied to natural language documents, i.e., different documents $\boldsymbol{u} \in \Sigma^*$ and $\boldsymbol{v} \in \Sigma^*$ map to almost orthogonal features $\boldsymbol{\phi}(\boldsymbol{u})$ and $\boldsymbol{\phi}(\boldsymbol{v})$. Thus, the Gram matrix has a dominant diagonal (see Figure 2.5) which is prob-*

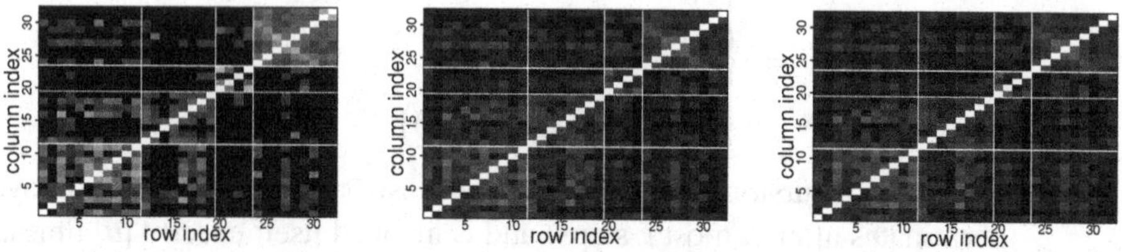

Figure 2.5 Intensity plots of the normalized Gram matrices when applying the string kernels (2.24), (2.25) and (2.28) (from left to right) to 32 sentences taken from this chapter with $n = 5$ and $\lambda = 0.5$. 11, 8, 4 and 9 sentences were taken from Section 2.2, Subsection 2.2.2, Section 2.3 and Subsection 2.3.1, respectively. For the sake of clarity, white lines are inserted to indicate the change from one section to another section.

lematic because each new test document x is likely to have a kernel value $k(x, x_i)$ close to zero. In order to explain this we notice that a document $\boldsymbol{u} \in \Sigma^*$ has at least $|\boldsymbol{u}| - r + 1$ matches of contiguous substrings with itself, i.e., all substrings $\boldsymbol{u}[i : (i + r - 1)]$ for all $i \in \{1, \ldots, |\boldsymbol{u}| - r + 1\}$. However, even if two documents $\boldsymbol{u} \in \Sigma^*$ and $\boldsymbol{v} \in \Sigma^*$ share all words $\boldsymbol{b} \in \Sigma^r$ of length r (on average) but in different orders, we have approximately $\frac{|\boldsymbol{u}|}{r}$ matches (assuming $|\boldsymbol{u}| \approx |\boldsymbol{v}|$). Therefore the difference $\left((|\boldsymbol{u}| - r) - \frac{|\boldsymbol{u}|}{r}\right) \cdot \lambda^r$ between diagonal and off-diagonal elements of the Gram matrix becomes systematically larger with increasing subsequence length r.

Kernels from Probabilistic Models of the Data

A major disadvantage of the two kernel families presented so far is that they are limited to a fixed representation of objects, x, i.e., vectorial data or strings. In order to overcome this limitation, Jaakkola and Haussler introduced the so-called Fisher kernel. The idea of the Fisher kernel is to use a probabilistic model of the input data, x, to derive a similarity measure between two data items. In order to achieve this, let us assume that the object generating probability measure $\mathbf{P}_{\mathsf{X}}$ can be written as a mixture, i.e., there exists a vector $\boldsymbol{\theta} = (\boldsymbol{\theta}_1; \ldots; \boldsymbol{\theta}_r; \boldsymbol{\pi})$ such that[14]

$$\mathbf{P}_{\mathsf{X}}(x) = \mathbf{P}_{\mathsf{X}}^{\boldsymbol{\theta}}(x) = \sum_{i=1}^{r} \mathbf{P}_{\mathsf{X}|\mathsf{M}=i}^{\boldsymbol{\theta}_i}(x) \cdot \underbrace{\mathbf{P}_{\mathsf{M}}(i)}_{\pi_i} = \sum_{i=1}^{r} \pi_i \cdot \mathbf{P}_{\mathsf{X}|\mathsf{M}=i}^{\boldsymbol{\theta}_i}(x) , \tag{2.31}$$

14 With a slight abuse of notation, we always use $\mathbf{P}_{\mathsf{X}}$ even if X is a continuous random variable possessing a density $\mathbf{f}_{\mathsf{X}}$. In this case we have to replace $\mathbf{P}_{\mathsf{X}}$ by $\mathbf{f}_{\mathsf{X}}$ and $\mathbf{P}_{\mathsf{X}|\mathsf{M}=i}$ by $\mathbf{f}_{\mathsf{X}|\mathsf{M}=i}$ but the argument would not change.

where the measure $\mathbf{P}^{\boldsymbol{\theta}_i}_{\mathsf{X}|\mathsf{M}=i}$ is parameterized by $\boldsymbol{\theta}_i$ only. In the search for the most plausible mixture components $\boldsymbol{\theta}_{\mathrm{ML}}$ (given a set $\boldsymbol{x} \in \mathcal{X}^m$ of m training objects) the Fisher score and the Fisher information matrix play a major role.

Definition 2.26 (Fisher score and Fisher information matrix) *Given a parameterized family $\mathcal{P}_{\mathcal{Q}}$ of probability measures $\mathbf{P}^{\boldsymbol{\theta}}_{\mathsf{X}}$ over the space $\mathcal{X}$ and a parameter vector $\tilde{\boldsymbol{\theta}} \in \mathcal{Q}$ the function*

$$\mathbf{f}_{\tilde{\boldsymbol{\theta}}}(x) \stackrel{\text{def}}{=} \left. \frac{\partial \ln \left(\mathbf{P}^{\boldsymbol{\theta}}_{\mathsf{X}}(x)\right)}{\partial \boldsymbol{\theta}} \right|_{\boldsymbol{\theta}=\tilde{\boldsymbol{\theta}}}$$

is called the Fisher score *of x at $\tilde{\boldsymbol{\theta}}$. Further, the matrix*

$$\boldsymbol{I}_{\tilde{\boldsymbol{\theta}}} \stackrel{\text{def}}{=} \mathbf{E}_{\mathsf{X}}\left[\mathbf{f}_{\tilde{\boldsymbol{\theta}}}(\mathsf{X}) \left(\mathbf{f}_{\tilde{\boldsymbol{\theta}}}(\mathsf{X})\right)'\right] \tag{2.32}$$

is called Fisher information matrix *at $\tilde{\boldsymbol{\theta}}$. Note that the expectation in equation (2.32) is w.r.t. $\mathbf{P}^{\tilde{\boldsymbol{\theta}}}_{\mathsf{X}}$.*

Now, given an estimate $\hat{\boldsymbol{\theta}} \in \mathcal{Q}$ of the parameter vector $\boldsymbol{\theta}$—probably obtained by using unlabeled data $\{x_1, \ldots, x_M\}$, where $M \gg m$—let us consider the *Fisher score mapping* in the $|\boldsymbol{\theta}|$–dimensional feature space $\mathcal{K}$, i.e.,

$$\boldsymbol{\phi}_{\hat{\boldsymbol{\theta}}}(x) = \mathbf{f}_{\hat{\boldsymbol{\theta}}}(x) \,. \tag{2.33}$$

Interestingly, we see that the features ϕ associated with π_i measure the amount by which the ith mixture component $\mathbf{P}_{\mathsf{X}|\mathsf{M}=i}$ contributes to the generation of the pattern x, i.e.,

$$\frac{\partial \ln \left(\mathbf{P}^{\boldsymbol{\theta}}_{\mathsf{X}}(x)\right)}{\partial \pi_j} = \frac{\partial \ln \left(\sum_{i=1}^{r} \pi_i \mathbf{P}^{\boldsymbol{\theta}_i}_{\mathsf{X}|\mathsf{M}=i}(x)\right)}{\partial \pi_j} = \frac{\mathbf{P}^{\boldsymbol{\theta}_j}_{\mathsf{X}|\mathsf{M}=j}(x)}{\sum_{i=1}^{r} \pi_i \mathbf{P}^{\boldsymbol{\theta}_i}_{\mathsf{X}|\mathsf{M}=i}(x)} = \frac{\mathbf{P}^{\boldsymbol{\theta}_j}_{\mathsf{X}|\mathsf{M}=j}(x)}{\mathbf{P}^{\boldsymbol{\theta}}_{\mathsf{X}}(x)} \,.$$

As a consequence, these features allow a good separation of all regions of the input space $\mathcal{X}$ in which the mixture measure (2.31) is high for exactly one component only. Hence, using the Fisher score $\mathbf{f}_{\boldsymbol{\theta}}(x)$ as a vectorial representation of x provides a principled way of obtaining kernels from a generative probabilistic model of the data.

Definition 2.27 (Fisher kernel) *Given a parameterized family $\mathcal{P}$ of probability measures $\mathbf{P}_{\mathsf{X}}^{\boldsymbol{\theta}}$ over the input space $\mathcal{X}$ and a parameter vector $\boldsymbol{\theta} \in \mathcal{Q}$ the function*

$$k(x, \tilde{x}) = (\mathbf{f}_{\boldsymbol{\theta}}(x))' \boldsymbol{I}_{\boldsymbol{\theta}}^{-1} \mathbf{f}_{\boldsymbol{\theta}}(\tilde{x})$$

is called the Fisher kernel. *The* naive Fisher kernel *is the simplified function*

$$k(x, \tilde{x}) = (\mathbf{f}_{\boldsymbol{\theta}}(x))' \mathbf{f}_{\boldsymbol{\theta}}(\tilde{x}) .$$

This assumes that the Fisher information matrix $\boldsymbol{I}_{\boldsymbol{\theta}}$ is the identity matrix $\mathbf{I}$.

The naive Fisher kernel is practically more relevant because the computation of the Fisher information matrix is very time consuming and sometimes not even analytically possible. Note, however, that not only do we need a probability model $\mathbf{P}_{\mathsf{X}}^{\boldsymbol{\theta}}$ of the data but also the model $\mathcal{P} \supset \mathbf{P}_{\mathsf{X}}^{\boldsymbol{\theta}}$ of probability measures.

Example 2.28 (Fisher kernel) *Let us assume that the measures $\mathbf{P}_{\mathsf{X}|\mathsf{M}=i}$ belong to the exponential family, i.e., their density can be written as*

$$\mathbf{f}_{\mathsf{X}|\mathsf{M}=i}^{\boldsymbol{\theta}_i}(x) = a_i(\boldsymbol{\theta}_i) \cdot c_i(x) \cdot \exp\left(\boldsymbol{\theta}_i' \boldsymbol{\tau}_i(x)\right) ,$$

where $c_i : \mathcal{X} \to \mathbb{R}$ is a fixed function, $\boldsymbol{\tau}_i : \mathcal{X} \to \mathbb{R}^{n_i}$ is known as a sufficient statistic *of x and $a_i : \mathbb{R}^{n_i} \to \mathbb{R}$ is a normalization constant. Then the value of the features $\boldsymbol{\phi}_{\boldsymbol{\theta}_j}$ associated with the jth parameter vector $\boldsymbol{\theta}_j$ are given by*

$$\frac{\partial \ln\left(\mathbf{f}_{\mathsf{X}}^{\boldsymbol{\theta}}(x)\right)}{\partial \boldsymbol{\theta}_j} = \frac{1}{\mathbf{f}_{\mathsf{X}}^{\boldsymbol{\theta}}(x)} \cdot \frac{\partial \left(\sum_{i=1}^{r} \mathbf{P}_{\mathsf{M}}(i) \cdot a_i(\boldsymbol{\theta}_i) \cdot c_i(x) \cdot \exp\left(\boldsymbol{\theta}_i' \boldsymbol{\tau}_i(x)\right)\right)}{\partial \boldsymbol{\theta}_j}$$

$$= \frac{\mathbf{f}_{\mathsf{X}|\mathsf{M}=j}^{\boldsymbol{\theta}_j}(x) \, \mathbf{P}_{\mathsf{M}}(j)}{\mathbf{f}_{\mathsf{X}}^{\boldsymbol{\theta}}(x)} \left(\underbrace{\frac{\frac{\partial a_j(\boldsymbol{\theta}_j)}{\partial \boldsymbol{\theta}_j}}{a_j(\boldsymbol{\theta}_j)}}_{\text{independent of } x} + \boldsymbol{\tau}_j(x) \right) .$$

Let us consider the contribution of the features $\boldsymbol{\phi}_{\boldsymbol{\theta}_j}$ at objects $x, \tilde{x} \in \mathcal{X}$ for which[15]

$$\frac{\mathbf{f}_{\mathsf{X}|\mathsf{M}=j}^{\boldsymbol{\theta}_j}(x)}{\mathbf{f}_{\mathsf{X}}^{\boldsymbol{\theta}}(x)} \approx \frac{\mathbf{f}_{\mathsf{X}|\mathsf{M}=j}^{\boldsymbol{\theta}_j}(\tilde{x})}{\mathbf{f}_{\mathsf{X}}^{\boldsymbol{\theta}}(\tilde{x})}$$

15 If this relation does not hold then the features associated with π_j already allow good discrimination.

and, additionally, assume that P_M *is the uniform measure. We see that*

$$\left\langle \boldsymbol{\phi}_{\boldsymbol{\theta}_j}(x), \boldsymbol{\phi}_{\boldsymbol{\theta}_j}(\tilde{x}) \right\rangle \propto \left(\boldsymbol{\tau}_j(x)\right)' \boldsymbol{\tau}_j(\tilde{x}),$$

that is, we effectively consider the sufficient statistic $\boldsymbol{\tau}_j(x)$ *of the* j*th mixture component measure as a vectorial representation of our data.*

2.3.3 The Representer Theorem

We have seen that kernels are a powerful tool that enrich the applicability of linear classifiers by a large extent. Nonetheless, apart from the solution of the perceptron learning algorithm it is not yet clear when this method can successfully be applied, i.e., for which learning algorithms $\mathcal{A} : \cup_{m=1}^{\infty} \mathcal{Z}^m \to \mathcal{F}$ the solution $\mathcal{A}(z)$ admits a representation of the form

$$(\mathcal{A}(z))(\cdot) = \sum_{i=1}^{m} \alpha_i k(x_i, \cdot) . \tag{2.34}$$

Before identifying this class of learning algorithms we introduce a purely functional analytic point of view on kernels. We will show that each Mercer kernel automatically defines a *reproducing kernel Hilbert space* (RKHS) of functions as given by equation (2.34). Finally, we identify the class of cost functions whose solution has the form (2.34).

Reproducing Kernel Hilbert Spaces

Suppose we are given a Mercer kernel $k : \mathcal{X} \times \mathcal{X} \to \mathbb{R}$. Then let $\mathcal{F}_0$ be the linear space of real-valued functions on $\mathcal{X}$ generated by the functions $\{k(x, \cdot) \mid x \in \mathcal{X}\}$. Consider any two functions $f(\cdot) = \sum_{i=1}^{r} \alpha_i k(x_i, \cdot)$ and $g(\cdot) = \sum_{j=1}^{s} \beta_j k(\tilde{x}_j, \cdot)$ in $\mathcal{F}_0$ where $\boldsymbol{\alpha} \in \mathbb{R}^r$, $\boldsymbol{\beta} \in \mathbb{R}^s$ and $x_i, \tilde{x}_j \in \mathcal{X}$. Define the inner product $\langle f, g \rangle$ between f and g in $\mathcal{F}_0$ as

$$\langle f, g \rangle \stackrel{\text{def}}{=} \sum_{i=1}^{r} \sum_{j=1}^{s} \alpha_i \beta_j k(x_i, \tilde{x}_j) = \sum_{j=1}^{s} \beta_j f(\tilde{x}_j) = \sum_{i=1}^{r} \alpha_i g(x_i), \tag{2.35}$$

where the last equality follows from the symmetry of the kernel k. Note that this inner product $\langle \cdot, \cdot \rangle$ is independent of the representation of the function f and g because changing the representation of f, i.e., changing r, $\boldsymbol{\alpha}$ and $\{x_1, \ldots, x_r\}$, would not change $\sum_{j=1}^{s} \beta_j f(\tilde{x}_j)$ (similarly for g). Moreover, we see that

1. $\langle f, g\rangle = \langle g, f\rangle$ for all functions $f, g \in \mathcal{F}_0$,
2. $\langle cf + dg, h\rangle = c\langle f, h\rangle + d\langle g, h\rangle$ for all functions $f, g, h \in \mathcal{F}_0$ and all $c, d \in \mathbb{R}$,
3. $\langle f, f\rangle = \sum_{i=1}^{r}\sum_{j=1}^{r}\alpha_i\alpha_j k\left(x_i, x_j\right) \geq 0$ for all functions $f \in \mathcal{F}_0$ because k is a Mercer kernel.

It still remains to established that $\langle f, f\rangle = 0$ implies that $f = 0$. To show this we need first the following important *reproducing property*: For all functions $f \in \mathcal{F}_0$ and all $x \in \mathcal{X}$

$$\langle f, k(x, \cdot)\rangle = f(x) , \tag{2.36}$$

which follows directly from choosing $s = 1$, $\beta_1 = 1$ and $\tilde{x}_1 = x$ in (2.35)—hence $g(\cdot) = k(x, \cdot)$. Now using the Cauchy-Schwarz inequality (see Theorem A.106 and preceding comments) we know that

$$0 \leq (f(x))^2 = (\langle f, k(x, \cdot)\rangle)^2 \leq \langle f, f\rangle \underbrace{\langle k(x, \cdot), k(x, \cdot)\rangle}_{k(x,x)} , \tag{2.37}$$

which shows that $\langle f, f\rangle = 0$ only if $f(x) = 0$ for all $x \in \mathcal{X}$, i.e., $f = 0$.

Finally, let us consider any Cauchy sequence $(f_r)_{r\in\mathbb{N}}$ of functions in $\mathcal{F}_0$. Then, by virtue of equation (2.37), we know that, for all $r, s \in \mathbb{N}$, $(f_r(x) - f_s(x))^2 \leq \|f_r - f_s\|^2 k(x, x)$ and hence $(f_r)_{r\in\mathbb{N}}$ converges toward some real-valued function f on $\mathcal{X}$. It is possible to complete $\mathcal{F}_0$ by adding the limits of all Cauchy sequences to it, extending it and its inner product to a slightly larger class $\mathcal{F} \subseteq \mathbb{R}^{\mathcal{X}}$. Thus, we have shown that each kernel $k : \mathcal{X} \times \mathcal{X} \to \mathbb{R}$ defines a Hilbert space $\mathcal{F}$ of real-valued functions over $\mathcal{X}$ which has the reproducing property (2.36), i.e., the value of the function f at x is "reproduced" by the inner product of f with $k(x, \cdot)$. The full power of this consideration is expressed in the following theorem.

Theorem 2.29 (Representer theorem) *Let k be a Mercer kernel on $\mathcal{X}$, $z \in (\mathcal{X} \times \mathcal{Y})^m$ be a training sample and $g_{\text{emp}} : (\mathcal{X} \times \mathcal{Y} \times \mathbb{R})^m \to \mathbb{R} \cup \{\infty\}$ be any arbitrary but fixed function. Let $g_{\text{reg}} : \mathbb{R} \to [0, \infty)$ be any strictly monotonically increasing function. Define $\mathcal{F}$ as the RKHS induced by k. Then any $f \in \mathcal{F}$ minimizing the regularized risk*

$$R_{\text{reg}}[f, z] = g_{\text{emp}}\left(((x_i, y_i, f(x_i)))_{i\in\{1,\ldots,m\}}\right) + g_{\text{reg}}(\|f\|) , \tag{2.38}$$

admits a representation of the form

$$f(\cdot) = \sum_{i=1}^{m} \alpha_i k(x_i, \cdot) \qquad \boldsymbol{\alpha} \in \mathbb{R}^m . \tag{2.39}$$

The proof is given in Appendix B.3. It elucidates once more the advantage of kernels: Apart from limiting the computational effort in application, they allow for a quite general class of learning algorithms (characterized by the minimization of a functional of the form (2.38)) to be applied in dual variables $\boldsymbol{\alpha} \in \mathbb{R}^m$.

2.4 Support Vector Classification Learning

The methods presented in the last two sections, namely the idea of regularization, and the kernel technique, are elegantly combined in a learning algorithm known as *support vector learning* (SV learning).[16] In the study of SV learning the notion of *margins* is of particular importance. We shall see that the *support vector machine* (SVM) is an implementation of a more general regularization principle known as the *large margin principle*. The greatest drawback of SVMs, that is, the need for zero training error, is resolved by the introduction of *soft margins*. We will demonstrate how both large margin and soft margin algorithms can be viewed in the geometrical picture given in Figure 2.1 on page 23. Finally, we discuss several extensions of the classical SVM algorithm achieved by reparameterization.

2.4.1 Maximizing the Margin

Let us begin by defining what we mean by the margin of a classifier. In Figure 2.6 a training sample z in $\mathbb{R}^2$ together with a classifier (illustrated by the incurred decision surface) is shown. The classifier $f_{\mathbf{w}}$ in Figure 2.6 (a) has a "dead zone" (gray area) separating the two sets of points which is larger than the classifier $f_{\tilde{\mathbf{w}}}$ chosen in Figure 2.6 (b). In both pictures the "dead zone" is the tube around the (linear) decision surface which does not contains any training example $(x_i, y_i) \in z$. To measure the extent of such a tube we can use the norm of the weight vector $\mathbf{w}$ parameterizing the classifier $f_{\mathbf{w}}$. In fact, the size of this tube must be inversely proportional to the minimum real-valued output $y_i \langle \mathbf{x}_i, \mathbf{w} \rangle$ of a classifier $\mathbf{w}$ on a

16 Vapnik also introduced the term *support vector machines* (SVMs) for learning algorithms of the "support vector" type.

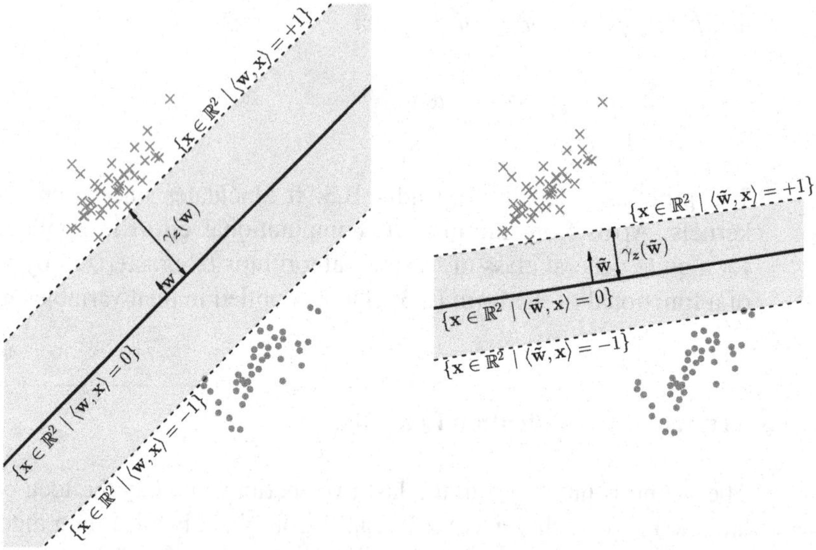

Figure 2.6 Geometrical margins of a plane (thick solid line) in $\mathbb{R}^2$. The crosses ($y_i = +1$) and dots ($y_i = -1$) represent labeled examples $\mathbf{x}_i$. **(Left)** The classifier $f_{\mathbf{w}}$ with the largest geometrical margin $\gamma_z(\mathbf{w})$. Note that this quantity is invariant under rescaling of the weight vector. **(Right)** A classifier $f_{\tilde{\mathbf{w}}}$ with a smaller geometrical margin $\gamma_z(\tilde{\mathbf{w}})$. Since $\min_{(x_i,y_i)\in z} y_i \langle \mathbf{x}_i, \tilde{\mathbf{w}} \rangle = 1$, $\|\tilde{\mathbf{w}}\|$ can be used to measure the extent of the gray zone tube by $\gamma_z(\tilde{\mathbf{w}}) = 1/\|\tilde{\mathbf{w}}\|$.

given training sample z. This quantity is also known as the functional margin on the training sample z and needs to be normalized to be useful for comparison across different weight vectors $\mathbf{w}$ not necessarily of unit length. More precisely, when normalizing the real-valued outputs by the norm of the weight vector $\mathbf{w}$ (which is equivalent to considering the real-valued outputs of normalized weight vectors $\mathbf{w}/\|\mathbf{w}\|$ only) we obtain a confidence measure comparable across different hyperplanes. The following definition introduces the different notions of margins more formally.

Definition 2.30 (Margins) *Suppose we are given a training sample* $z = (\boldsymbol{x}, \boldsymbol{y}) \in \mathcal{Z}^m$, *a mapping* $\boldsymbol{\phi} : \mathcal{X} \to \mathcal{K} \subseteq \ell_2^n$ *and a vector* $\mathbf{w} \in \mathcal{K}$. *For the hyperplane having normal* $\mathbf{w}$ *we define the*

- functional margin $\tilde{\gamma}_i(\mathbf{w})$ *on an example* $(x_i, y_i) \in z$ *to be* $\tilde{\gamma}_i(\mathbf{w}) \stackrel{\text{def}}{=} y_i \langle \mathbf{x}_i, \mathbf{w} \rangle$,

- functional margin $\tilde{\gamma}_z(\mathbf{w})$ *on a training sample* z *to be* $\tilde{\gamma}_z(\mathbf{w}) \stackrel{\text{def}}{=} \min_{(x_i,y_i)\in z} \tilde{\gamma}_i(\mathbf{w})$,
- geometrical margin $\gamma_i(\mathbf{w})$ *on an example* $(x_i, y_i) \in z$ *to be* $\gamma_i(\mathbf{w}) \stackrel{\text{def}}{=} \tilde{\gamma}_i(\mathbf{w}) / \|\mathbf{w}\|$,
- geometrical margin $\gamma_z(\mathbf{w})$ *on a training sample* z *to be* $\gamma_z(\mathbf{w}) \stackrel{\text{def}}{=} \tilde{\gamma}_z(\mathbf{w}) / \|\mathbf{w}\|$.

Note that $\tilde{\gamma}_i(\mathbf{w}) > 0$ *implies correct classification of* $(x_i, y_i) \in z$. *Furthermore, for* $\mathbf{w} \in \mathcal{W}$ *the functional and geometrical margin coincide.*

In 1962 Novikoff proved a theorem for perceptrons which was, in 1964, extended to linear classifiers in kernel space. The theorem shows that the number of corrections in the perceptron learning algorithm is provably decreasing for training samples which admit a large margin.

Theorem 2.31 (Perceptron convergence theorem) *Let* $z = (\boldsymbol{x}, \boldsymbol{y}) \in \mathcal{Z}^m$ *be a training sample, let* $\boldsymbol{\phi} : \mathcal{X} \to \mathcal{K} \subseteq \ell_2^n$ *be a fixed feature map, and let* $\varsigma = \max_{x_i \in \boldsymbol{x}} \|\boldsymbol{\phi}(x_i)\|$ *be the smallest radius of a sphere enclosing all the mapped training objects* $\boldsymbol{x}$. *Suppose that there exists a vector* $\mathbf{w}^* \in \mathcal{W}$ *such that* $\tilde{\gamma}_z(\mathbf{w}^*) = \gamma_z(\mathbf{w}^*) > 0$. *Then the number of mistakes made by the perceptron learning algorithm on* z *is at most*

$$\left(\frac{\varsigma}{\gamma_z(\mathbf{w}^*)}\right)^2 .$$

The proof is given in Appendix B.4. This theorem answers one of the questions associated with perceptron learning, that is, the number of steps until convergence. The theorem was one of the first theoretical justifications of the idea that large margins yield better classifiers; here in terms of mistakes during learning. We shall see in Part II that large margins indeed yield better classifiers in terms of expected risk.

Let $\mathcal{F}$ and $\mathcal{K}$ be the RKHS and feature space connected with the Mercer kernel k, respectively. The classifier $\mathbf{w}$ with the largest margin $\gamma_z(\mathbf{w})$ on a given training sample can be written as

$$\mathbf{w}_{\mathrm{SVM}} \stackrel{\text{def}}{=} \operatorname*{argmax}_{\mathbf{w}\in\mathcal{W}} \gamma_z(\mathbf{w}) = \operatorname*{argmax}_{\mathbf{w}\in\mathcal{K}} \frac{1}{\|\mathbf{w}\|}\tilde{\gamma}_z(\mathbf{w}) . \tag{2.40}$$

Two methods of casting the problem of finding this classifier into a regularization framework are conceivable. One method is to refine the (coarse) l_{0-1} loss function given in equation (2.9) by exploiting the minimum real-valued output $\gamma_z(\mathbf{w})$ of each classifier $\mathbf{w} \in \mathcal{W}$. A second option is to fix the minimum real-valued output $\tilde{\gamma}_z(\mathbf{w})$ of the classifier $\mathbf{w} \in \mathcal{K}$ and to use the norm $\|\mathbf{w}\|$ of each classifier to measure its complexity. Though the latter is better known in the SV community we shall present both formulations.

1. Fix the norm of the classifiers to unity (as done in Novikoff's theorem), then we must maximize the geometrical margin. More formally, in terms of equation (2.38) we have

$$\mathbf{w}_{\mathrm{SVM}} = \underset{\mathbf{w} \in \mathcal{W}}{\operatorname{argmin}} \; l_{\mathrm{margin}}(\gamma_z(\mathbf{w})) \,, \tag{2.41}$$

where

$$l_{\mathrm{margin}}(t) \stackrel{\mathrm{def}}{=} -t \,. \tag{2.42}$$

A more convenient notation of this minimization problem is

$$\begin{array}{ll} \text{maximize} & \min\left(f_{\mathbf{w}}(x_1), \ldots, f_{\mathbf{w}}(x_m)\right) = \gamma_z(\mathbf{w}) \\ \text{subject to} & \|f_{\mathbf{w}}\|^2 = \|\mathbf{w}\|^2 = 1 \,. \end{array}$$

This optimization problem has several difficulties associated with it. First, the objective function is neither linear nor quadratic. Further, the constraints are nonlinear. Hence, from an algorithmic viewpoint this optimization problem is difficult to solve. Nonetheless, due to the independence of the hypothesis space from the training sample it is very useful in the study of the generalization error.

2. Fix the functional margin to unity and minimize the norm $\|\mathbf{w}\|$ of the weight vector. More formally, the set of all classifiers considered for learning is

$$\mathcal{W}(z) \stackrel{\mathrm{def}}{=} \left\{\mathbf{w} \in \mathcal{K} \mid \tilde{\gamma}_z(\mathbf{w}) = 1\right\} \,, \tag{2.43}$$

which are known as *canonical hyperplanes*. Clearly, this definition of the hypothesis space is data dependent which makes a theoretical analysis quite intricate[17]. The advantage of this formulation becomes apparent if we consider the corresponding risk functional:

$$\mathbf{w}_{\mathrm{SVM}} \propto \underset{\mathbf{w} \in \mathcal{W}(z)}{\operatorname{argmin}} \; \|f_{\mathbf{w}}\|^2 = \underset{\mathbf{w} \in \mathcal{W}(z)}{\operatorname{argmin}} \; \|\mathbf{w}\|^2 \,. \tag{2.44}$$

17 In general, the hypothesis space must be independent of the training sample. The training sample dependence on the hypothesis space for Mercer kernels is resolved in Theorem 2.29. Note, however, that this theorem does not apply to canonical hyperplanes.

The risk functional seems to imply that we minimize a complexity or structural risk, but this is wrong. In fact, the lack of any empirical term in the risk functional is merely due to the formulation which uses a data dependent hypothesis space (2.43). If we cast the minimization of this risk functional in a convex programming framework we obtain

$$\begin{array}{lll} \text{minimize} & \|\mathbf{w}\|^2 = \|f_{\mathbf{w}}\|^2 & \\ \text{subject to} & y_i \langle \mathbf{x}_i, \mathbf{w} \rangle \geq 1 & i = 1, \ldots, m\,. \end{array} \tag{2.45}$$

This optimization problem is much more computationally amenable. Here, the objective function is quadratic and the constraints are linear. As a consequence, the solution must be expressible in its dual form. Introducing m Lagrangian multipliers α_i for the linear constraints (which turn out to be the expansion coefficients of the weight vector $\mathbf{w}$ in terms of the mapped training objects), taking the derivative w.r.t. $\mathbf{w}$ and back-inserting into the Lagrangian, we obtain the following *Wolfe dual* (for details see Section B.5)

$$W(\boldsymbol{\alpha}) = \boldsymbol{\alpha}'\mathbf{1} - \frac{1}{2}\boldsymbol{\alpha}'\mathbf{YGY}\boldsymbol{\alpha}\,, \tag{2.46}$$

which needs to be maximized in the positive quadrant $\mathbf{0} \leq \boldsymbol{\alpha}$,

$$\hat{\boldsymbol{\alpha}} = \underset{\mathbf{0}\leq\boldsymbol{\alpha}}{\operatorname{argmax}}\; W(\boldsymbol{\alpha})\,.$$

Here, $\mathbf{G}$ is the $m \times m$ Gram matrix defined by equation (2.18) and $\mathbf{Y} \stackrel{\text{def}}{=} \operatorname{diag}(y_1, \ldots, y_m)$. Note, however, that the solution

$$\mathbf{w}_{\text{SVM}} = \sum_{i=1}^{m} \hat{\alpha}_i y_i \mathbf{x}_i$$

is equivalent to the solution of optimization problem (2.41) up to a scaling factor. Using decomposition techniques to solve the problem, the computational effort is roughly of order $\mathcal{O}(m^2)$.

2.4.2 Soft Margins—Learning with Training Error

The algorithm presented in the last subsection is clearly restricted to training samples which are linearly separable. One way to deal with this insufficiency is to use "powerful" kernels (like an RBF kernel with very small σ) which makes each training sample separable in feature space. Although this would not cause any computational difficulties, the "large expressive" power of the classifiers in feature space may lead to overfitting, that is, a large discrepancy between empirical risk (which was previously zero) and true risk of a classifier. Moreover, the above algorithm is "nonrobust" in the sense that one outlier (a training point $(x_i, y_i) \in z$ whose removal would lead to a large increase in margin) can cause the learning algorithm to converge very slowly or, even worse, make it impossible to apply at all (if $\gamma_i(\mathbf{w}) < 0$ for all $\mathbf{w} \in \mathcal{W}$).

In order to overcome this insufficiency we introduce a heuristic which has become known as the *soft margin SVM*. The idea exploited is to upper bound the zero-one loss l_{0-1} as given in equation (2.9) by a linear or quadratic function (see Figure 2.7),

$$\begin{aligned} l_{0-1}(f(x), y) = \mathbf{I}_{-yf(x)>0} &\leq \max\{1 - yf(x), 0\} = l_{\text{lin}}(f(x), y), \\ l_{0-1}(f(x), y) = \mathbf{I}_{-yf(x)>0} &\leq \max\{1 - yf(x), 0\}^2 = l_{\text{quad}}(f(x), y). \end{aligned} \tag{2.47}$$

It is worth mentioning that, due to the cut off at a real-valued output of one (on the correct side of the decision surface), the norm $\|f\|$ can still serve as a regularizer. Viewed this way, the idea is in the spirit of the second parameterization of the optimization problem of large margins (see equation (2.40)).

Linear Approximation

Let us consider the case of a linear approximation. Given a tradeoff parameter $\lambda > 0$, the regularization functional becomes

$$R_{\text{reg}}[f_{\mathbf{w}}, z] = \frac{1}{m}\sum_{i=1}^{m} l_{\text{lin}}(f_{\mathbf{w}}(x_i), y_i) + \lambda \|f_{\mathbf{w}}\|^2,$$

or equivalently

$$\begin{aligned} &\text{minimize} && \sum_{i=1}^{m} \xi_i + \lambda m \|\mathbf{w}\|^2 \\ &\text{subject to} && y_i \langle \mathbf{x}_i, \mathbf{w} \rangle \geq 1 - \xi_i \qquad i = 1, \ldots, m, \\ &&& \boldsymbol{\xi} \geq \mathbf{0}. \end{aligned} \tag{2.48}$$

Transforming this into an optimization problem involving the corresponding Wolfe dual we must maximize an equation of the form (2.46), but this time in the "box" $\mathbf{0} \leq \boldsymbol{\alpha} \leq \frac{1}{2\lambda m}\mathbf{1}$ (see Section B.5). In the limit $\lambda \to 0$ we obtain the "hard margin" SVM because there is no upper bound on $\boldsymbol{\alpha}$. Another explanation of

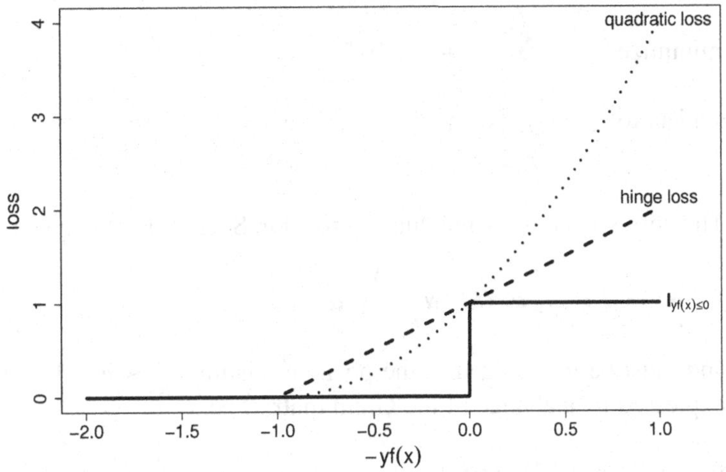

Figure 2.7 Approximation to the Heaviside step function $\mathbf{I}_{yf(x)\leq 0}$ (solid line) by the so-called "hinge loss" (dashed line) and a quadratic margin loss (dotted line). The x–axis contains the negative real-valued output $-yf(\mathbf{x})$ which is positive in the case of misclassification of x by f.

this equivalence is given by the fact that the objective function is proportional to $\frac{1}{\lambda m}\sum_{i=1}^{m}\xi_i + \|\mathbf{w}\|^2$. Thus, in the limit of $\lambda \to 0$, any $\mathbf{w}$ for which $\boldsymbol{\xi} \neq \mathbf{0}$ incurs an infinitely large value of the objective function and therefore in the optimum $\sum_{i=1}^{m}\xi_i = 0$. Note that by virtue of this formulation the "box" is decreased with increasing training sample size.

Quadratic Approximation

Though not as popular in the SV community, the quadratic approximation has proven to be successful in real world applications. Formally, the regularization functional becomes

$$R_{\text{reg}}[f_{\mathbf{w}}, z] = \frac{1}{m}\sum_{i=1}^{m} l_{\text{quad}}(f_{\mathbf{w}}(x_i), y_i) + \lambda \|f_{\mathbf{w}}\|^2 ,$$

which in its equivalent form is

$$
\begin{aligned}
\text{minimize} \quad & \sum_{i=1}^{m} \xi_i^2 + \lambda m \|\mathbf{w}\|^2 \\
\text{subject to} \quad & y_i \langle \mathbf{x}_i, \mathbf{w} \rangle \geq 1 - \xi_i \qquad i = 1, \ldots, m\,, \\
& \boldsymbol{\xi} \geq \mathbf{0}\,.
\end{aligned}
\tag{2.49}
$$

The corresponding Wolfe dual (derived in Section B.5) is given by

$$
W(\boldsymbol{\alpha}) = \boldsymbol{\alpha}'\mathbf{1} - \frac{1}{2}\boldsymbol{\alpha}'\mathbf{YGY}\boldsymbol{\alpha} - \frac{\lambda m}{2}\boldsymbol{\alpha}'\boldsymbol{\alpha}\,,
$$

and must be maximized in the positive quadrant $\mathbf{0} \leq \boldsymbol{\alpha}$. This can equivalently be expressed by a change of the Gram matrix, i.e.,

$$
W(\boldsymbol{\alpha}) = \boldsymbol{\alpha}'\mathbf{1} - \frac{1}{2}\boldsymbol{\alpha}'\mathbf{Y}\widetilde{\mathbf{G}}\mathbf{Y}\boldsymbol{\alpha}\,, \qquad \widetilde{\mathbf{G}} = \mathbf{G} + \lambda m \mathbf{I}\,.
\tag{2.50}
$$

Remark 2.32 (Data independent hypothesis spaces) *The two algorithms presented in this subsection use the idea of fixing the functional margin to unity. This allows the geometrical margin to be controlled by the norm $\|\mathbf{w}\|$ of the weight vector $\mathbf{w}$. As we have seen in the previous subsection there also exists a "data independent" formulation. In the case of a quadratic soft margin loss the formulation is apparent from the change of the Gram matrix: The quadratic soft margin SVM is equivalent to a hard margin SVM if we change the Gram matrix $\mathbf{G}$ to $\mathbf{G} + \lambda m\mathbf{I}$. Furthermore, in the hard margin case, we could alternatively have the hypothesis space being the unit hypersphere in feature space. As a consequence thereof, all we need to consider is the change in the feature space, if we* penalize the diagonal of the Gram matrix *by λm.*

Remark 2.33 (Cost matrices) *In Example 2.7 we showed how different a-priori class probabilities $\mathbf{P}_{\mathsf{Y}}(-1)$ and $\mathbf{P}_{\mathsf{Y}}(+1)$ can be incorporated through the use of a cost matrix loss function. In the case of soft margin loss this can be approximately achieved by using different values $\lambda_+ \in \mathbb{R}^+$ and $\lambda_- \in \mathbb{R}^+$ at the constraints for the training points of class $+1$ and -1, respectively. As the (general) regularizer is inversely related to the allowed violation of constraints it follows that the underrepresented class having smaller prior probability should have the larger λ value.*

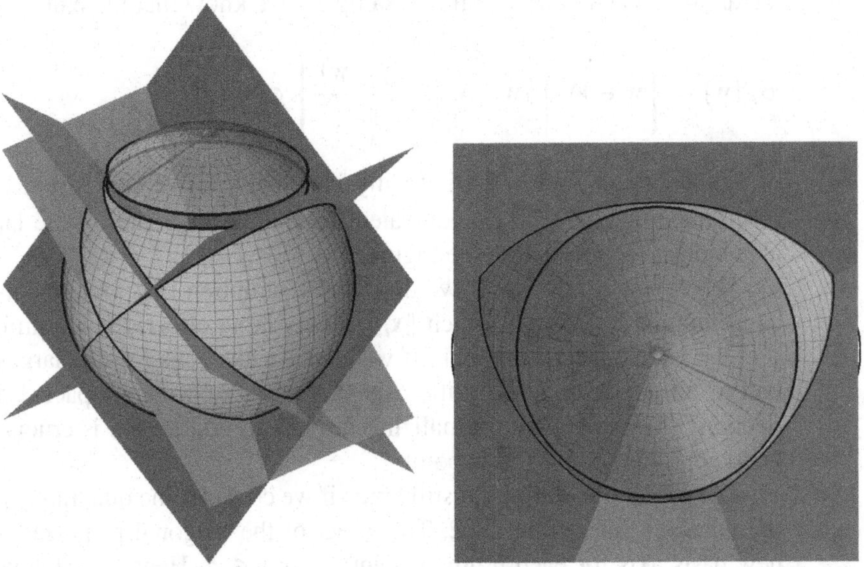

Figure 2.8 Finding the center of the largest inscribable ball in version space. **(Left)** In this example four training points were given which incur the depicted four planes. Let us assume that the labeling of the training sample was such that the polyhedra on top of the sphere is the version space. Then, the SV learning algorithm finds the (weight) vector $\mathbf{w}$ on top of the sphere as the center of the largest inscribable ball $\mathcal{B}_\tau(\mathbf{w})$ (transparent cap). Here, we assumed $\|y_i \mathbf{x}_i\| = \|\mathbf{x}_i\|$ to be constant. The distance of the $\mathbf{w}$ from the hyperplanes (dark line) is proportional to the margin $\gamma_z(\mathbf{w})$ (see text). **(Right)** Viewed from top we see that the version space $V(z)$ is a bended convex body into which we can fully inscribe a circle of radius proportional to $\gamma_z(\mathbf{w})$.

2.4.3 Geometrical Viewpoints on Margin Maximization

In the previous two subsections the SV learning algorithms were introduced purely from a margin maximization perspective. In order to associate these algorithms with the geometrical picture given in Figure 2.1 on page 23 we note that, for a fixed point $(x_i, y_i) \in z$, the geometrical margin $\gamma_i(\tilde{\mathbf{w}})$ can be read as the distance of the linear classifier having normal $\tilde{\mathbf{w}}$ to the hyperplane $\{\mathbf{w} \in \mathcal{K} \mid y_i \langle \mathbf{x}_i, \mathbf{w} \rangle = 0\}$. In fact, the Euclidean distance of the point $\tilde{\mathbf{w}}$ from the hyperplane having normal $y_i \mathbf{x}_i$ is $y_i \langle \mathbf{x}_i, \tilde{\mathbf{w}} \rangle / \|y_i \mathbf{x}_i\| = \gamma_i(\tilde{\mathbf{w}}) / \|\mathbf{x}_i\|$. For the moment let us assume that $\|\mathbf{x}_i\|$ is constant for all x_i in the training objects $\boldsymbol{x} \in \mathcal{X}^m$. Then, if a classifier $f_{\tilde{\mathbf{w}}}$ achieves a margin of $\gamma_z(\tilde{\mathbf{w}})$ on the training sample z we know that the ball,

$$\mathcal{B}_\tau(\tilde{\mathbf{w}}) = \left\{ \mathbf{w} \in \mathcal{W} \;\middle|\; \|\mathbf{w} - \tilde{\mathbf{w}}\| < \frac{\gamma_z(\tilde{\mathbf{w}})}{\|\mathbf{x}_i\|} \right\} \subset V(z)$$

of radius $\tau = \gamma_z(\tilde{\mathbf{w}}) / \|\mathbf{x}_i\|$ is totally inscribable in version space $V(z)$. Henceforth, maximizing $\gamma_z(\tilde{\mathbf{w}})$ is equivalent to finding the center of the largest inscribable ball in version space (see Figure 2.8).

The situation changes if we drop the assumption that $\|\mathbf{x}_i\|$ is constant. In this case, training objects for which $\|\mathbf{x}_i\|$ is very large effectively minimize the radius τ of the largest inscribable ball. If we consider the center of the largest inscribable ball as an approximation to the center of mass of version space $V(z)$ (see also Section 3.4) we see that normalizing the $\mathbf{x}_i$'s to unit length is crucial to finding a good approximation for this point.

The geometrical intuition still holds if we consider the quadratic approximation presented in Subsection 2.4.2. The effect of the diagonal penalization is to add a new basis axis for each training point $(x_i, y_i) \in z$. Hence, in this new space the quadratic SVM tries to find the center of the largest inscribable ball. Needless to say that we again assume the $\mathbf{x}_i$'s to be of constant length $\|\mathbf{x}_i\|$. We shall see in Section 5.1 that the margin $\gamma_z(\tilde{\mathbf{w}})$ is too coarse a measure to be used for bounds on the expected risk if $\|\mathbf{x}_i\| \neq$ const.—especially if we apply the kernel technique.

2.4.4 The ν–Trick and Other Variants

The SV algorithms presented so far constitute the basis of the standard SV tool box. There exist, however, several (heuristic) extensions for the case of multiple classes ($2 < |\mathcal{Y}| < \infty$), regression estimation ($\mathcal{Y} = \mathbb{R}$) and reparameterizations in terms of the assumed noise level $\mathbf{E}_\mathsf{X}\left[1 - \max_{y \in \mathcal{Y}}\left(\mathbf{P}_{\mathsf{Y}|\mathsf{X}=x}(y)\right)\right]$ which we present here.

Multiclass Support Vector Machines

In order to extend the SV learning algorithm to $K = |\mathcal{Y}| > 2$ classes two different strategies have been suggested.

1. The first method is to learn K SV classifiers f_j by labeling all training points having $y_i = j$ with $+1$ and $y_i \neq j$ with -1 during the training of the jth classifier.

In the test stage, the final decision is obtained by

$$f_{\text{multiple}}(x) = \operatorname*{argmax}_{y \in \mathcal{Y}} \ f_y(x) .$$

Clearly, this method learns one classifier for each of the K classes against all the other classes and is hence known as the *one-versus-rest* (o-v-r) method. It can be shown that it is possible to solve the K optimization problems at once. Note that the computational effort is of order $\mathcal{O}\left(Km^2\right)$.

2. The second method is to learn $K(K-1)/2$ SV classifiers. If $1 \le i < j \le K$ the classifiers $f_{i,j}$ is learned using only the training samples from the class i and j, labeling them $+1$ and -1, respectively. This method has become known as the *one-versus-one* (o-v-o) method. Given a new test object $x \in \mathcal{X}$, the frequency n_i of "wins" for class i is computed by applying $f_{i,j}$ for all j. This results in a vector $\mathbf{n} = (n_1; \ldots; n_K)$ of frequencies of "wins" of each class. The final decision is made for the most frequent class, i.e.,

$$f_{\text{multiple}}(x) = \operatorname*{argmax}_{y \in \mathcal{Y}} \ n_y .$$

Using a probabilistic model for the frequencies $\mathbf{n}$, different prior probabilities of the classes $y \in \mathcal{Y}$ can be incorporated, resulting in better generalization ability. Instead of solving $K(K-1)/2$ separate optimization problems, it is again possible to combine them in a single optimization problem. If the prior probabilities $\mathbf{P}_{\mathsf{Y}}(j)$ for the K classes are roughly $\frac{1}{K}$, the method scales as $\mathcal{O}\left(m^2\right)$ and is independent of the number of classes.

Recently, a different method for combining the single pairwise decisions has been suggested. By specifying a *directed acyclic graph* (DAG) of consecutive pairwise classifications, it is possible to introduce a class hierarchy. The leaves of such a DAG contain the final decisions which are obtained by exclusion rather than by voting. This method compares favorably with the o-v-o and o-v-r methods.

Support Vector Regression Estimation

In the regression estimation problem we are given a sample of m real target values $t = (t_1, \ldots, t_m) \in \mathbb{R}^m$, rather than m class labels $y = (y_1, \ldots, y_m) \in \mathcal{Y}^m$. In order to extend the SV learning algorithm to this task, we note that an "inversion" of the linear loss l_{lin} suffices in order to use the SV machinery for real-valued outputs t_i. In classification the linear loss $l_{\text{lin}}(f(x), \cdot)$ adds to the total cost, if the real-valued output of $|f(x)|$ is smaller than 1. For regression estimation it is desirable to have the opposite true, i.e., incurred costs result if $|t - f(x)|$ is very large instead of small. This requirement is formally captured by the *ε–insensitive* loss

$$l_\varepsilon(f(x), t) = \begin{cases} 0 & \text{if } |t - f(x)| \leq \varepsilon \\ |t - f(x)| - \varepsilon & \text{if } |t - f(x)| > \varepsilon \end{cases} . \tag{2.51}$$

Then, one obtains a quadratic programming problem similar to (2.46), this time in $2m$ dual variables α_i and $\tilde{\alpha}_i$—two corresponding to each training point constraint. This is simply due to the fact that f can fail to attain a deviation less than ε on both sides of the given real-valued output t_i, i.e., $t_i - \varepsilon$ and $t_i + \varepsilon$. An appealing feature of this loss is that it leads to sparse solutions, i.e., only a few of the α_i (or $\tilde{\alpha}_i$) are non-zero. For further references that cover the regression estimation problem the interested reader is referred to Section 2.6.

ν–Support Vector Machines for Classification

A major drawback of the soft margin SV learning algorithm given in the form (2.48) is the lack of control over how many training points will be considered as margin errors or "outliers", that is, how many have $\tilde{\gamma}_i(\mathbf{w}_{\mathrm{SVM}}) < 1$. This is essentially due to the fact that we fixed the functional margin to one. By a simple reparameterization it is possible to make the functional margin itself a variable of the optimization problem. One can show that the solution of the following optimization problem has the property that the new parameter ν bounds the fraction of *margin errors* $\frac{1}{m}\left|\{(x_i, y_i) \in z \mid \tilde{\gamma}_i(\mathbf{w}_{\mathrm{SVM}}) < \rho\}\right|$ from above:

$$\begin{aligned} &\text{minimize} && \frac{1}{m}\sum_{i=1}^{m} \xi_i - \nu\rho + \frac{1}{2}\|\mathbf{w}\|^2 \\ &\text{subject to} && y_i \langle \mathbf{x}_i, \mathbf{w} \rangle \geq \rho - \xi_i \qquad i = 1, \ldots, m, \\ &&& \boldsymbol{\xi} \geq \mathbf{0}, \ \rho \geq 0 . \end{aligned} \tag{2.52}$$

It can be shown that, for each value of $\nu \in [0, 1]$, there exists a value of $\lambda \in \mathbb{R}^+$ such that the solution $\mathbf{w}_\nu$ and $\mathbf{w}_\lambda$ found by solving (2.52) and (2.48) have the same geometrical margins $\gamma_z(\mathbf{w}_\nu) = \gamma_z(\mathbf{w}_\lambda)$. Thus we could try different values of λ in the standard linear soft margin SVM to obtain a required fraction of margin errors. The appealing property of the problem (2.52) is that this adjustment is done within the one optimization problem (see Section B.5). Another property which can be proved is that, for all probability models where neither $\mathbf{P}_{\mathsf{X}}(\{\mathsf{X}, 1\})$ nor

$\mathbf{P_X}(\{X, -1\})$ contains any discrete component, ν asymptotically equals the fraction of margin errors. Hence, we can incorporate prior knowledge of the noise level $\mathbf{E_X}\left[1 - \max_{y \in \mathcal{Y}}\left(\mathbf{P_{Y|X=x}}(y)\right)\right]$ via ν. Excluding all training points for which the real-valued output is less than ρ in absolute value, the geometrical margin of the solution on the remaining training points is $\rho / \|\mathbf{w}\|$.

2.5 Adaptive Margin Machines

In this last section we will introduce an algorithm which is based on a conceptually different principle. Our new approach is motivated by a recently derived leave-one-out bound on the generalization error of kernel classifiers. Let us start by introducing the concept of the leave-one-out error.

2.5.1 Assessment of Learning Algorithms

Whilst the mathematical model of learning to be introduced in Part II of this book gives some motivation for the algorithms introduced so far, the derived bounds are often too loose to be useful in practical applications. A completely different approach can be taken if we study the expected risk of *a learning algorithm* $\mathcal{A}$ rather than any hypothesis.

Definition 2.34 (Expected risk of a learning algorithm) *Given an algorithm* $\mathcal{A} : \cup_{m=1}^{\infty} \mathcal{Z}^m \to \mathcal{F}$*, a loss function* $l : \mathbb{R} \times \mathcal{Y} \to \mathbb{R}$ *and a training sample size* $m \in \mathbb{N}$*, the* expected risk $R[\mathcal{A}, m]$ of the learning algorithm $\mathcal{A}$ *is defined by*

$$R[\mathcal{A}, m] \stackrel{\text{def}}{=} \mathbf{E}_{\mathbf{Z}^m}\left[R\left[\mathcal{A}(\mathbf{Z})\right]\right] .$$

Note that this quantity does not bound the expected risk of the *one* classifier learned from a training sample z but the *average expected risk performance* of the algorithm $\mathcal{A}$. For any training sample z, an almost unbiased estimator of this quantity is given by the *leave-one-out error* $R_{\text{loo}}[\mathcal{A}, z]$ of $\mathcal{A}$.

Definition 2.35 (Leave-one-out error) *Given an algorithm* $\mathcal{A} : \cup_{m=1}^{\infty} \mathcal{Z}^m \to \mathcal{F}$*, a loss function* $l : \mathbb{R} \times \mathcal{Y} \to \mathbb{R}$ *and a training sample* $z \in \mathcal{Z}^m$*, the* leave-one-out error *is defined by*

$$R_{\text{loo}}[\mathcal{A}, z] \stackrel{\text{def}}{=} \frac{1}{m}\sum_{i=1}^{m} l\left(\mathcal{A}\left(\left(z_1, \ldots, z_{i-1}, z_{i+1}, \ldots, z_m\right)\right)(x_i), y_i\right).$$

This measure counts the fraction of examples that are misclassified if we leave them out for learning when using the algorithm $\mathcal{A}$. The unbiasedness of the estimator is made more precise in the following proposition.

Theorem 2.36 (Unbiasedness of the leave-one-out error) *Given a fixed measure* $\mathbf{P}_{\mathsf{Z}}$*, a fixed hypothesis space* $\mathcal{F}$*, a fixed loss* l *and a fixed learning algorithm* $\mathcal{A} : \bigcup_{m=1}^{\infty} \mathcal{Z}^m \to \mathcal{F}$*, the leave-one-out error is almost unbiased, that is,*

$$\mathbf{E}_{\mathsf{Z}^m}\left[R_{\text{loo}}\left[\mathcal{A}, \mathbf{Z}\right]\right] = R\left[\mathcal{A}, m-1\right].$$

Proof In order to prove the result we note that

$$\begin{aligned}
\mathbf{E}_{\mathsf{Z}^m}\left[R_{\text{loo}}\left[\mathcal{A}, \mathbf{Z}\right]\right] &= \mathbf{E}_{\mathsf{Z}^m}\left[\frac{1}{m}\sum_{i=1}^{m} l\left(\mathcal{A}\left(\left(\mathsf{Z}_1, \ldots, \mathsf{Z}_{i-1}, \mathsf{Z}_{i+1}, \ldots, \mathsf{Z}_m\right)\right)(\mathsf{X}_i), \mathsf{Y}_i\right)\right] \\
&= \frac{1}{m}\sum_{i=1}^{m} \mathbf{E}_{\mathsf{Z}^m}\left[l\left(\mathcal{A}\left(\left(\mathsf{Z}_1, \ldots, \mathsf{Z}_{i-1}, \mathsf{Z}_{i+1}, \ldots, \mathsf{Z}_m\right)\right)(\mathsf{X}_i), \mathsf{Y}_i\right)\right] \\
&= \frac{1}{m}\sum_{i=1}^{m} \mathbf{E}_{\mathsf{Z}^{m-1}}\left[\mathbf{E}_{\mathsf{XY}|\mathsf{Z}^{m-1}=z}\left[l\left(\mathcal{A}(z)(\mathsf{X}), \mathsf{Y}\right)\right]\right] \\
&= \mathbf{E}_{\mathsf{Z}^{m-1}}\left[R\left[\mathcal{A}(\mathbf{Z})\right]\right] = R\left[\mathcal{A}, m-1\right].
\end{aligned}$$

The theorem is proved. ∎

Despite the fact that this result allows us to obtain a precise estimate of the expected risk of the learning algorithm, its computation is very time consuming as the learning algorithm must be invoked m times. Therefore, it is desirable to have a bound on this quantity which can be computed solely on the basis of the training sample z and the learned hypothesis $\mathcal{A}(z)$. As demonstrated in Section 2.4, a rather powerful class of learning algorithms is given by

$$\hat{\boldsymbol{\alpha}} = \underset{\mathbf{0} \le \boldsymbol{\alpha} \le \mathbf{u}}{\operatorname{argmax}}\ W(\boldsymbol{\alpha})$$

$$W(\boldsymbol{\alpha}) = -\frac{1}{2}\boldsymbol{\alpha}'\mathbf{YGY}\boldsymbol{\alpha} + \sum_{i=1}^{m} J(\alpha_i) , \tag{2.53}$$

where $J : \mathbb{R} \to \mathbb{R}$ is a fixed function, $\mathbf{u}$ is an $m \times 1$ vector of positive real numbers, $\mathbf{Y} \stackrel{\text{def}}{=} \text{diag}(y_1, \ldots, y_m)$ and $\mathbf{G}$ is the $m \times m$ Gram matrix given by equation (2.18). Based on the vector $\hat{\boldsymbol{\alpha}} \in \mathbb{R}^m$, the linear classifier f is then given by

$$f(x) = \langle \hat{\mathbf{w}}, \mathbf{x} \rangle = \sum_{i=1}^{m} \hat{\alpha}_i y_i k(x_i, x) \quad \Leftrightarrow \quad \hat{\mathbf{w}} = \sum_{i=1}^{m} \hat{\alpha}_i y_i \mathbf{x}_i . \tag{2.54}$$

We can give the following bound on the leave-one-out error $R_{\text{loo}}[\mathcal{A}_W, z]$.

Theorem 2.37 (Leave-One-Out Bound) *Suppose we are given a training sample $z \in \mathcal{Z}^m$ and a Mercer kernel k. Let $\hat{\boldsymbol{\alpha}}$ be the maximizing coefficients of (2.53). Then an upper bound on the leave-one-out error of $\mathcal{A}_W$ is given by*

$$R_{\text{loo}}[\mathcal{A}_W, z] \leq \frac{1}{m}\sum_{i=1}^{m} \Theta\left(-y_i \sum_{\substack{j=1 \\ j \neq i}}^{m} \hat{\alpha}_j y_j k(x_i, x_j) \right) , \tag{2.55}$$

where $\Theta(t) = \mathbf{I}_{t \geq 0}$ is the Heaviside step function.

The proof is given in Appendix B.6. For support vector machines V. Vapnik has shown that the leave-one-out error is bounded by the ratio of the number of non-zero coefficients $\hat{\alpha}_i$ to the number m of training examples. The bound given in Theorem 2.37 is slightly tighter than Vapnik's leave-one-out bound. This is easy to see because all training points that have $\hat{\alpha}_i = 0$ cannot be leave-one-out errors in either bound. Vapnik's bound assumes all support vectors (all training points with $\hat{\alpha}_i > 0$) are leave-one-out errors, whereas they only contribute as errors in equation (2.55) if $y_i \sum_{\substack{j=1 \\ j \neq i}}^{m} \hat{\alpha}_j y_j k(x_i, x_j) \leq 0$. In practice this means that the bound (2.55) is tighter for less sparse solutions.

2.5.2 Leave-One-Out Machines

Theorem 2.37 suggests an algorithm which directly minimizes the expression in the bound. The difficulty is that the resulting objective function will contain the step function $\mathbf{I}_{t \geq 0}$. The idea we exploit is similar to the idea of soft margins in

SVMs, where the step function is upper bounded by a piecewise linear function, also known as the hinge loss (see Figure 2.7). Hence, introducing slack variables, gives the following optimization problem:

$$\begin{aligned}
&\text{minimize} && \sum_{i=1}^{m} \xi_i \\
&\text{subject to} && y_i \sum_{\substack{j=1 \\ j \neq i}}^{m} \alpha_j y_j k\left(x_i, x_j\right) \geq 1 - \xi_i \qquad i = 1, \ldots, m\,, \\
& && \boldsymbol{\alpha} \geq \mathbf{0}\,, \boldsymbol{\xi} \geq \mathbf{0}\,.
\end{aligned} \tag{2.56}$$

For further classification of new test objects we use the decision rule given in equation (2.54). Let us study the resulting method which we call a *leave-one-out machine* (LOOM).

First, the technique appears to have no free regularization parameter. This should be compared with support vector machines, which control the amount of regularization through the free parameter λ. For SVMs, in the case of $\lambda \to 0$ one obtains a hard margin classifier with no training errors. In the case of linearly inseparable datasets in feature space (through noise, outliers or class overlap) one must admit some training errors (by constructing soft margins). To find the best choice of training error/margin tradeoff one must choose the appropriate value of λ. In leave-one-out machines a soft margin is automatically constructed. This happens because the algorithm does not attempt to minimize the number of training errors—it minimizes the number of training points that are classified incorrectly even when they are removed from the linear combination which forms the decision rule. However, if one can classify a training point correctly when it is removed from the linear combination, then it will always be classified correctly when it is placed back into the rule. This can be seen as $\alpha_i y_i k(x_i, x_i)$ always has the same sign as y_i; any training point is pushed further from the decision boundary by its own component of the linear combination. Note also that summing for all $j \neq i$ in the constraint (2.56) is equivalent to setting the diagonal of the Gram matrix $\mathbf{G}$ to zero and instead summing for all j. Thus, the regularization employed by leave-one-out machines disregards the values $k(x_i, x_i)$ for all i.

Second, as for support vector machines, the solutions $\hat{\boldsymbol{\alpha}} \in \mathbb{R}^m$ can be sparse in terms of the expansion vector; that is, only some of the coefficients $\hat{\alpha}_i$ are non-zero. As the coefficient of a training point does not contribute to its leave-one-out error in constraint (2.56), the algorithm does not assign a non-zero value to the coefficient of a training point in order to correctly classify it. A training point has to be classified correctly by the training points of the same label that are close to it, but the point itself makes no contribution to its own classification in training.

2.5.3 Pitfalls of Minimizing a Leave-One-Out Bound

The core idea of the presented algorithm is to directly minimize the leave-one-out bound. Thus, it seems that we are able to control the generalization ability of an algorithm disregarding quantities like the margin. This is not true in general[18] and in particular the presented algorithm is not able to achieve this goal. There are some pitfalls associated with minimizing a leave-one-out bound:

1. In order to get a bound on the leave-one-out error we must specify the algorithm $\mathcal{A}$ *beforehand*. This is often done by specifying the form of the objective function which is to be maximized (or minimized) during learning. In our particular case we see that Theorem 2.37 only considers algorithms defined by the maximization of $W(\boldsymbol{\alpha})$ with the "box" constraint $\mathbf{0} \leq \boldsymbol{\alpha} \leq \mathbf{u}$. By changing the learning algorithm to minimize the bound itself we may well develop an optimization algorithm which is no longer compatible with the assumptions of the theorem. This is true in particular for leave-one-out machines which are no longer in the class of algorithms considered by Theorem 2.37—whose bound they are aimed at minimizing. Further, instead of minimizing the bound directly we are using the hinge loss as an upper bound on the Heaviside step function.

2. The leave-one-out bound does not provide any guarantee about the generalization error $R[\mathcal{A}, z]$ (see Definition 2.10). Nonetheless, if the leave-one-out error is small then we know that, for most training samples $z \in \mathcal{Z}^m$, the resulting classifier has to have an expected risk close to that given by the bound. This is due to Hoeffding's bound which says that for bounded loss (the expected risk of a hypothesis f is bounded to the interval $[0, 1]$) the expected risk $R[\mathcal{A}(z)]$ of the learned classifier $\mathcal{A}(z)$ is close to the expectation of the expected risk (bounded by the leave-one-out bound) with high probability over the random choice of the training sample.[19] Note, however, that the leave-one-out estimate does not provide any information about the variance of the expected risk. Such information would allow the application of tighter bounds, for example, Chebyshev's bound.

18 Part II, Section 4.3, shows that there are models of learning which allow an algorithm to *directly* minimize a *bound* on its generalization error. This should not be confused with the possibility of controlling the generalization error of the algorithm itself.

19 We shall exploit this idea further in Part II, Section 5.3.

3. The original motivation behind the use of the leave-one-out error was to measure the goodness of the hypothesis space $\mathcal{F}$ and of the learning algorithm $\mathcal{A}$ for the learning problem given by the unknown probability measure $\mathbf{P}_{\mathsf{Z}}$. Commonly, the leave-one-out error is used to select among different models $\mathcal{F}_1, \mathcal{F}_2, \ldots$ for a given learning algorithm $\mathcal{A}$. In this sense, minimizing the leave-one-out error is more a model selection strategy than a learning paradigm within a fixed model.

Definition 2.38 (Model selection) *Suppose we are given $r \in \mathbb{N}$ fixed learning algorithms $\mathcal{A}_i : \cup_{m=1}^{\infty} \mathcal{Z}^m \to \mathcal{Y}^{\mathcal{X}}$ which map training samples z to classifiers $h \in \mathcal{Y}^{\mathcal{X}}$. Then, given a training sample $z \in \mathcal{Z}^m$, the problem of* model selection *is to identify the learning algorithm $\mathcal{A}_i$ which would lead to a classifier $\mathcal{A}_i(z)$ possessing the smallest expected risk, i.e., find the algorithm $\mathcal{A}_z$ such that*

$$\mathcal{A}_z = \operatorname*{argmin}_{\mathcal{A}_i} R\left[\mathcal{A}_i(z)\right] .$$

If we have a fixed learning procedure $\mathcal{A}_\chi : \cup_{m=1}^{\infty} \mathcal{Z}^m \to \mathcal{Y}^{\mathcal{X}}$ which is parameterized by χ then the model selection problem reduces to finding the the best parameter $\chi(z)$ for a given training sample $z \in \mathcal{Z}^m$.

A typical model selection task which arises in the case of kernel classifiers is the selection of parameters of the kernel function used, for example, choosing the optimal value of σ for RBF kernels (see Table 2.1).

2.5.4 Adaptive Margin Machines

In order to generalize leave-one-out machines we see that the m constraints in equation (2.56) can be rewritten as

$$y_i \sum_{\substack{j=1\\ j\neq i}}^{m} \alpha_j y_j k\left(x_i, x_j\right) + \alpha_i k\left(x_i, x_i\right) \;\geq\; 1 - \xi_i + \alpha_i k\left(x_i, x_i\right) \qquad i = 1, \ldots, m ,$$

$$y_i f\left(x_i\right) \;\geq\; 1 - \xi_i + \alpha_i k\left(x_i, x_i\right) \qquad i = 1, \ldots, m .$$

Now, it is easy to see that a training point $(x_i, y_i) \in z$ is linearly penalized for failing to obtain a functional margin of $\tilde{\gamma}_i(\mathbf{w}) \geq 1 + \alpha_i k(x_i, x_i)$. In other words, the larger the contribution the training point makes to the decision rule (the larger the value of α_i), the larger its functional margin must be. Thus, the algorithm controls the margin for each training point *adaptively*. From this formulation one can generalize the algorithm to control regularization through the margin loss. To make the margin at each training point a controlling variable we propose the following learning algorithm:

$$\text{minimize} \quad \sum_{i=1}^{m} \xi_i \tag{2.57}$$

$$\text{subject to} \quad y_i \sum_{j=1}^{m} \alpha_j y_j k\left(x_i, x_j\right) \geq 1 - \xi_i + \lambda \alpha_i k\left(x_i, x_i\right), \quad i = 1, \ldots, m.$$

$$\boldsymbol{\alpha} \geq \mathbf{0}, \boldsymbol{\xi} \geq \mathbf{0}. \tag{2.58}$$

This algorithm—which we call *adaptive margin machines*—can also be viewed in the following way: If an object $x_o \in \boldsymbol{x}$ is an outlier (the kernel values w.r.t. points in its class are small and w.r.t. points in the other class are large), α_o in equation (2.58) must be large in order to classify x_o correctly. Whilst support vector machines use the same functional margin of one for such an outlier, they attempt to classify x_o correctly. In adaptive margin machines the functional margin is automatically increased to $1 + \lambda \alpha_o k\left(x_o, x_o\right)$ for x_o and thus less effort is made to change the decision function because each increase in α_o would lead to an even larger increase in ξ_o and can therefore not be optimal.

Remark 2.39 (Clustering in feature space) *In adaptive margin machines the objects $x_r \in \boldsymbol{x}$, which are representatives of clusters (centers) in feature space $\mathcal{K}$, i.e., those which have large kernel values w.r.t. objects from its class and small kernel values w.r.t. objects from the other class, will have non-zero α_r. In order to see this we consider two objects, $x_r \in \boldsymbol{x}$ and $x_s \in \boldsymbol{x}$, of the same class. Let us assume that x_r with $\xi_r > 0$ is the center of a cluster (w.r.t. the metric in feature space $\mathcal{K}$ induced by the kernel k) and s with $\xi_s > 0$ lies at the boundary of the cluster. Hence we subdivide the set of all objects into*

$$\begin{aligned}
x_i \in C^+ &: \quad \xi_i = 0,\, y_i = y_r,\, i \neq r,\, i \neq s\,, \\
x_i \in C^- &: \quad \xi_i = 0,\, y_i \neq y_r\,, \\
x_i \in I^+ &: \quad \xi_i > 0,\, y_i = y_r,\, i \neq r,\, i \neq s\,, \\
x_i \in I^- &: \quad \xi_i > 0,\, y_i \neq y_r\,.
\end{aligned}$$

We consider the change in $\boldsymbol{\xi}$ if we increase α_r by $\Delta > 0$ (giving $\boldsymbol{\xi}'$) and simultaneously decrease α_s by Δ (giving $\boldsymbol{\xi}''$). From equations (2.57)–(2.58) we know *that*

$$\begin{array}{rlcllcl} x_i \in C^+: & \xi_i' & = & \xi_i\,, & \xi_i'' & \leq & \Delta k(x_i, x_s)\,, \\ x_i \in C^-: & \xi_i' & \leq & \Delta k(x_i, x_r)\,, & \xi_i'' & = & \xi_i\,, \\ x_i \in I^+: & \xi_i' & \geq & \xi_i - \Delta k(x_i, x_r)\,, & \xi_i'' & = & \xi_i + \Delta k(x_i, x_s)\,, \\ x_i \in I^-: & \xi_i' & = & \xi_i + \Delta k(x_i, x_r)\,, & \xi_i'' & \geq & \xi_i - \Delta k(x_i, x_s)\,, \\ x_r: & \xi_r' & \geq & \xi_r - \Delta(1-\lambda)\,k(x_r, x_r)\,, & \xi_r'' & = & \xi_r + \Delta k(x_r, x_s)\,, \\ x_s: & \xi_s' & \geq & \xi_s - \Delta k(x_s, x_r)\,, & \xi_s'' & \geq & \xi_s + \Delta(1-\lambda)\,k(x_s, x_s)\,. \end{array}$$

Now we choose the biggest Δ *such that all inequalities for* $x_i \in \{I^+, I^-, r, r'\}$ *become equalities and for* $x_i \in \{C^+, C^-\}$ *the r.h.s. equals zero. Then, the relative change in the objective function is given by*

$$\frac{1}{\Delta}\sum_{i=1}^{m}\left(\xi_i' + \xi_i'' - \xi_i\right) = \underbrace{\sum_{i\in I^+}\left(k(x_i, x_s) - k(x_i, x_r)\right)}_{\text{change of intra-class distance}} - \underbrace{\sum_{i\in I^-}\left(k(x_i, x_s) - k(x_i, x_r)\right)}_{\text{change of inter-class distance}},$$

where we assume that $k(x_r, x_r) = k(x_s, x_s)$*. Since the cluster centers in feature space* $\mathcal{K}$ *minimize the intra-class distance whilst maximizing the inter-class distances it becomes apparent that their* α_r *will be higher. Taking into account that the maximum* Δ *considerable for this analysis is decreasing as* λ *increases we see that, for suitable small* λ*, adaptive margin machines tend to only associate cluster centers in feature space* $\mathcal{K}$ *with non-zero* α*'s.*

2.6 Bibliographical Remarks

Linear functions have been investigated for several hundred years and it is virtually impossible to identity their first appearance in scientific literature. In the field of artificial intelligence, however, the first studies of linear classifiers go back to the early works of Rosenblatt (1958), Rosenblatt (1962) and Minsky and Papert (1969). These w

orks also contains the first account of the perceptron learning algorithm which was originally developed without any notion of kernels. The more general ERM principle underpinning perceptron learning was first formulated in Vapnik and Chervonenkis (1974). In this book we introduce perceptron learning using the notion of version space. This somewhat misleading name comes from Mitchell (1977), Mitchell (1982), Mitchell (1997) and refers to the fact that all classifiers

$h \in V(z)$ are different "versions" of consistent classifiers. Originally, T. Mitchell considered the hypothesis space of logic formulas only.

The method of regularization introduced in Section 2.2 was originally developed in Tikhonov and Arsenin (1977) and introduced into the machine learning framework in Vapnik (1982). The adaptation of ill-posed problems to machine learning can be found in Vapnik (1982) where they are termed *stochastic ill-posed problems*. In a nutshell, the difference to classical ill-posed problems is that the solution $\mathbf{y}$ is a random variable of which we can only observe one specific sample. As a means to solving these stochastic ill-posed problems, Vapnik suggested *structural risk minimization*.

The original paper which proved Mercer's theorem is by Mercer (1909); the version presented in this book can be found in König (1986). Regarding Remark 2.19, the work by Wahba (1990) gives an excellent overview of covariance functions of Gaussian processes and kernel functions (see also Wahba (1999)). The detailed derivation of the feature space for polynomial kernels was first published in Poggio (1975). In the subsection on string kernels we mentioned the possibility of using kernels in the field of Bioinformatics; first approaches can be found in Jaakkola and Haussler (1999b) and Karchin (2000). For a more detailed treatment of machine learning approaches in the field of Bioinformatics see Baldi and Brunak (1998). The notion of string kernels was independently introduced and developed by T. Jaakkola, C. Watkins and D. Haussler in Watkins (2000) and Haussler (1999). A detailed study of support vector machines using these kernels can be found in Joachims (1998) and Lodhi et al. (2001). For more traditional methods in information retrieval see Salton (1968). The Fisher kernel was originally introduced in Jaakkola and Haussler (1999a) and later applied to the problem of detecting remote protein homologizes (Jaakkola et al. 1999). The motivation of Fisher kernels in these works is much different to the one given in this book and relies on the notion of Riemannian manifolds of probability measures.

The consideration of RKHS introduced in Subsection 2.3.3 presents another interesting aspect of kernels, that is, that they can be viewed as regularization operators in function approximation. By noticing that kernels are the Green's functions of the corresponding regularization operator we can directly go from kernels to regularization operators and vice versa (see Smola and Schölkopf (1998), Smola et al. (1998), Smola (1998) and Girosi (1998) for details). The original proof of the representer theorem can be found in Schölkopf et al. (2001). A simpler version of this theorem was already proven in Kimeldorf and Wahba (1970) and Kivinen et al. (1997).

In Section 2.4 we introduced the support vector algorithm as a combination of structural risk minimization techniques with the kernel trick. The first appearance of this algorithm—which has its roots in the early 1960s (Vapnik and Lerner 1963)—is in Boser et al. (1992). The notion of functional and geometrical margins is due to Cristianini and Shawe-Taylor (1999). For recent developments in kernel methods and large margin classifiers the interested reader is referred to Schölkopf et al. (1998) and Smola et al. (2000). The original perceptron convergence theorem (without using kernels) is due to Novikoff (1962) and was independently proved by Block (1962). The extension to general kernels was presented in Aizerman et al. (1964).

In the derivation of the support vector algorithm we used the notion of canonical hyperplanes which is due to Vapnik (1995); for more detailed derivations of the algorithm see also Vapnik (1998), Burges (1998) and Osuna et al. (1997). An extensive study of the computational complexity of the support vector algorithm can be found in Joachims (1999). In the five years an array of different implementations have been presented, e.g., SVM^{light} (Joachims 1998; Osuna et al. 1997), SMO (Platt 1999; Keerthi et al. 1999a; Shevade et al. 1999) and NPA (Keerthi et al. 1999b).

It was noted that without the introduction of soft margins, classifiers found by the support vector algorithm tend to overfit. This was already observed in practice (Cortes 1995; Schölkopf et al. 1995; Osuna et al. 1997; Joachims 1999; Bennett 1998). This tendency is called the *nonrobustness* of the hard margin SVM algorithm—a term which is due to Shawe-Taylor and Cristianini (2000). In order to introduce soft margins we used the hinge loss (due to Gentile and Warmuth (1999)) whose relation to support vector machines was shown in Sollich (2000). The seminal paper, which introduced the linear soft margin algorithm is Cortes and Vapnik (1995); it also mentions the possibility of quadratically penalizing the slacks. The empirical success of quadratic soft margin support vector machines has been demonstrated in Veropoulos et al. (1999) and Brown et al. (2000). The former paper also noted that different values of λ for training points from different classes can be used to compensate for unequal class probabilities (see also Osuna et al. (1997) for details). Experimental evidence of the advantage of normalizing training data in feature space before applying the support vector algorithm can be found in Schölkopf et al. (1995), Joachims (1998) and Joachims (1999); theoretical evidence is given in Herbrich and Graepel (2001b).

It is interesting to remark that the research on linear classifiers has run rather parallel in the computer science and the statistical physics community (see Guyon and Storck (2000) for a recent overview). One of the earliest works about support vector machines (which are called *maximal stability perceptrons*) is by Lambert (1969). After this work, many statistical physicists got involved in neural networks (Gardner 1988; Gardner and Derrida 1988). As a consequence, several large margin alternative of the perceptron learning algorithm were devised, for example, the *minimal overlap* (MinOver) algorithm (Krauth and Mézard 1987) or the *adatron* (Anlauf and Biehl 1989). Finally, a fast primal-dual method for solving the maximum margin problem has been published in Ruján (1993).

In Subsection 2.4.4 several extensions of the original support vector algorithm are presented. For more details on the extension to multiple classes see Weston and Watkins (1998), Platt et al. (2000), Hastie and Tibshirani (1998), Guermeur et al. (2000) and Allwein et al. (2000). There exits a vast literature on support vector regression estimation; for an excellent overview see Smola and Schölkopf (2001), Smola (1996), Smola (1998) and Smola and Schölkopf (1998). It has also been shown that support vector machines can be applied to the problem of density estimation (Weston et al. 1999; Vapnik and Mukherjee 2000). The reparameterization of the support vector algorithm in terms of ν, the fraction of margin errors, was first published in Schölkopf et al. (2000) where it was also applied to the support vector algorithm for regression estimation.

Finally, in Section 2.5, we introduce the leave-one-out error of algorithms which motivate an algorithm called adaptive margin machines (Weston and Herbrich 2000). The proof of the unbiasedness of the leave-one-out error can be found in Lunts and Brailovsky (1969) and also in Vapnik (1998, p. 417). The bound on the leave-one-out error for kernel classifiers presented in Theorem 2.37 was proven in Jaakkola and Haussler (1999b).

3 Kernel Classifiers from a Bayesian Perspective

This chapter presents the probabilistic, or *Bayesian* approach to learning kernel classifiers. It starts by introducing the main principles underlying Bayesian inference both for the problem of learning within a fixed model and across models. The first two sections present two learning algorithms, *Gaussian processes* and *relevance vector machines*, which were originally developed for the problem of regression estimation. In regression estimation, one is given a sample of real-valued outputs rather than class labels. In order to adapt these methods to the problem of classification we introduce the concept of *latent variables* which, in the current context, are used to model the probability of the class labels. The chapter shows that the principle underlying *relevance vector machines* is an application of Bayesian model selection to classical Bayesian linear regression. In the third section we present a method which *directly* models the observed class labels by imposing prior knowledge only on weight vectors of unit length. In general, it is impossible to analytically compute the solution to this algorithm. The section presents a Markov chain Monte Carlo algorithm to approximately solve this problem, which is also known as *Bayes point learning*. Finally, we discuss one of the earliest approaches to the problem of classification learning—the *Fisher linear discriminant*. There are ways to apply the kernel trick to all these algorithms thus rendering them powerful tools in the application of kernel methods to the problem of classification learning.

3.1 The Bayesian Framework

In the last chapter we saw that a learning problem is given by the identification of an unknown relationship $h \in \mathcal{Y}^{\mathcal{X}}$ between objects $x \in \mathcal{X}$ and class labels $y \in \mathcal{Y}$ solely on the basis of a given iid sample $z = (\boldsymbol{x}, \boldsymbol{y}) = ((x_1, y_1), \ldots, (x_m, y_m)) \in (\mathcal{X} \times \mathcal{Y})^m = \mathcal{Z}^m$ (see Definition 2.1). Any approach that deals with this problem starts by choosing a hypothesis space[1] $\mathcal{H} \subseteq \mathcal{Y}^{\mathcal{X}}$ and a loss function $l : \mathcal{Y} \times \mathcal{Y} \to \mathbb{R}$ appropriate for the task at hand. Then a learning algorithm $\mathcal{A} : \cup_{m=1}^{\infty} \mathcal{Z}^m \to \mathcal{H}$ aims to find the *one* particular hypothesis $h^* \in \mathcal{H}$ which minimizes a pre-defined risk determined on the basis of the loss function only, e.g., the expected risk $R[h]$ of the hypothesis h or the empirical risk $R_{\text{emp}}[h, z]$ of $h \in \mathcal{H}$ on the given training sample $z \in \mathcal{Z}^m$ (see Definition 2.5 and 2.11). Once we have *learned* a classifier $\mathcal{A}(z) \in \mathcal{H}$ it is used for further classification on new test objects. Thus, all the information contained in the given training sample is summarized in the single hypothesis learned.

The Bayesian approach is conceptually different insofar as it starts with a measure $\mathbf{P}_{\mathsf{H}}$ over the hypotheses—also known as the *prior measure*—which expresses the *belief* that $h \in \mathcal{H}$ is the relationship that underlies the data. The notion of belief is central to Bayesian analysis and should not be confused with more frequentistic interpretations of the probability $\mathbf{P}_{\mathsf{H}}(h)$. In a frequentistic interpretation, $\mathbf{P}_{\mathsf{H}}(h)$ is the relative frequency with which h underlies the data, i.e., $\mathbf{P}_{\mathsf{Y}|\mathsf{X}=x}(y) = \mathbf{I}_{h(x)=y}$, over an infinite number of different (randomly drawn) learning problems. As an example consider the problem of learning to classify images of Kanji symbols always using the same set $\mathcal{H}$ of classifiers on the images. Then $\mathbf{P}_{\mathsf{H}}(h)$ is the relative frequency of Kanji symbols (and therefore learning tasks) for which h is the best classifier in $\mathcal{H}$. Clearly, this number is difficult to determine and meaningless when given exactly one learning problem. In contrast, a Bayesian interpretation sees the number $\mathbf{P}_{\mathsf{H}}(h)$ as expressing the *subjective belief* that $h \in \mathcal{H}$ models the unknown relationship between objects and classes. As such the term "belief" is dependent on the observer and unquestionably the "truth"—or at least the best knowledge about the truth—for that particular observer. The link between frequentistic probabilities and subjective beliefs is that, under quite general assumptions of rational behavior on the basis of beliefs, both measures have to satisfy the Kolmogorov axioms, i.e., the same mathematical operations apply to them.

Learning in the Bayesian framework is the incorporation of the observed training sample $z \in \mathcal{Z}^m$ in the belief expression $\mathbf{P}_{\mathsf{H}}$. This results in a so-called *posterior measure* $\mathbf{P}_{\mathsf{H}|\mathsf{Z}^m=z}$. Compared to the single summary $h^* \in \mathcal{H}$ obtained through the machine learning approach, the Bayesian posterior $\mathbf{P}_{\mathsf{H}|\mathsf{Z}^m=z}$ is a much richer representation of the information contained in the training sample z about the unknown object-class relationship. As mentioned earlier, the Bayesian posterior $\mathbf{P}_{\mathsf{H}|\mathsf{Z}^m=z}$ is

1 In order to unburden the main text we again take the liberty of synonymously referring to $\mathcal{H}$, $\mathcal{F}$ and $\mathcal{W}$ as the *hypothesis space* and to $h \in \mathcal{H}$, $f \in \mathcal{F}$ and $\mathbf{w} \in \mathcal{W}$ as *hypothesis*, *classifier* or just *function* (see also Section 2.1 and footnotes therein).

obtained by applying the rules of probability theory (see Theorem A.22), i.e.,

$$\forall h \in \mathcal{H}: \quad \mathbf{P}_{\mathsf{H}|\mathsf{Z}^m=z}(h) = \frac{\mathbf{P}_{\mathsf{Z}^m|\mathsf{H}=h}(z)\,\mathbf{P}_{\mathsf{H}}(h)}{\mathbf{E}_{\mathsf{H}}\left[\mathbf{P}_{\mathsf{Z}^m|\mathsf{H}=h}(z)\right]} = \underbrace{\frac{\overbrace{\mathbf{P}_{\mathsf{Y}^m|\mathsf{X}^m=x,\mathsf{H}=h}(y)}^{\text{likelihood of } h}\,\overbrace{\mathbf{P}_{\mathsf{H}}(h)}^{\text{prior of } h}}{\mathbf{E}_{\mathsf{H}}\left[\mathbf{P}_{\mathsf{Y}^m|\mathsf{X}^m=x,\mathsf{H}=h}(y)\right]}}_{\text{evidence of } \mathcal{H}}, \tag{3.1}$$

where we have used the fact that $\mathbf{P}_{\mathsf{Z}^m|\mathsf{H}=h}(z) = \mathbf{P}_{\mathsf{Y}^m|\mathsf{X}^m=x,\mathsf{H}=h}(y)\,\mathbf{P}_{\mathsf{X}^m}(x)$ because hypotheses $h \in \mathcal{Y}^{\mathcal{X}}$ only influence the generation of class labels $y \in \mathcal{Y}^m$ but not objects $x \in \mathcal{X}^m$. Due to the central importance of this formula—which constitutes the main inference principle in the Bayesian framework—the three terms in equation (3.1) deserve some discussion.

The Likelihood Let us start with the training data dependent term. Interpreted as a function of $h \in \mathcal{H}$ this term expresses how "likely" it is to observe the label sequence y if we are given m objects x and the true relationship is $h \in \mathcal{H}$. Without any further prior knowledge, the likelihood contains all information that can be obtained from the training sample z about the unknown relationship[2]. In the case of learning, the notion of likelihood is defined as follows.

Definition 3.1 (Likelihood) *Given a family $\mathcal{P}$ of models $\mathbf{P}_{\mathsf{Y}|\mathsf{X}=x,\mathsf{H}=h}$ over the space $\mathcal{Y}$ together with an observation $z = (x, y) \in \mathcal{Z}$ the function $\mathcal{L} : \mathcal{H} \times \mathcal{Z} \to \mathbb{R}^+$ is called the* likelihood of h *and is defined by*

$$\mathcal{L}(h, z) \stackrel{\text{def}}{=} \mathbf{P}_{\mathsf{Y}|\mathsf{X}=x,\mathsf{H}=h}(y),$$

that is, the probability of observing y under the probability measure $\mathbf{P}_{\mathsf{Y}|\mathsf{X}=x,\mathsf{H}=h}$.

In order to relate this definition to the likelihood expression given in equation (3.1) we note that, due to the independence assumption made, it holds that

$$\mathcal{L}(h, z) = \mathbf{P}_{\mathsf{Y}^m|\mathsf{X}^m=x,\mathsf{H}=h}(y) = \prod_{i=1}^{m} \mathbf{P}_{\mathsf{Y}|\mathsf{X}=x_i,\mathsf{H}=h}(y_i).$$

Given an appropriately chosen loss function $l : \mathcal{Y} \times \mathcal{Y} \to \mathbb{R}$ it is reasonable to assume that the smaller the loss incurred by the hypothesis $h \in \mathcal{H}$ on a given

2 In fact, among statisticians there is a school of thought which adheres to the so-called *likelihood principle*: Any inference about hypothesis $h \in \mathcal{H}$ for a given training sample $z \in \mathcal{Z}^m$ should only be done on the basis of the likelihood function $\mathcal{L} : \mathcal{H} \to \mathbb{R}^+$.

training sample $z \in \mathcal{Z}$, the more likely it is that the function h underlies the data. This has been made more precise in the following likelihood model.

Definition 3.2 (Inverse loss likelihood) *Given a fixed loss function* $l : \mathcal{Y}\times\mathcal{Y} \to \mathbb{R}$ *the* inverse loss likelihood *for a fixed* $z = (x, y) \in \mathcal{Z}$ *is defined by*

$$\mathcal{L}_l(h, z) \stackrel{\text{def}}{=} \frac{\exp\left(-\beta^{-1} \cdot l(h(x), y)\right)}{\sum_{\hat{y}\in\mathcal{Y}} \exp\left(-\beta^{-1} \cdot l\left(h(x), \hat{y}\right)\right)}, \tag{3.2}$$

where $\beta \in [0, \infty)$ *is known as the noise level.*

In the limiting case $\beta \to \infty$ the inverse loss likelihood is a constant function, i.e., $\mathcal{L}_l(h, z) = \frac{1}{|\mathcal{Y}|}$ regardless of the hypothesis h considered. In this case no additional information is conveyed by the training sample. The likelihood obtained in the no-noise case, i.e., $\beta = 0$, is of particular importance to us and we shall call it the PAC-likelihood.[3]

Definition 3.3 (PAC-likelihood) *Assume* $\mathcal{Y}$ *to be a finite set of classes. Then the* PAC likelihood *is defined by*

$$\mathcal{L}_{\mathrm{PAC}}(h, (x, y)) \stackrel{\text{def}}{=} \mathbf{I}_{h(x)=y}.$$

The Prior The prior measure (or belief) $\mathbf{P}_{\mathsf{H}}$ is the crucial quantity in a Bayesian analysis—it is all the knowledge about the relationship between objects and classes *before training data has arrived*, encapsulated in a probability measure. Of course, there is no general rule for determining particular priors. At the time when computational power was a scarce resource, practitioners suggested conjugate priors.

Definition 3.4 (Conjugate prior) *Given a set* $\mathcal{P}_{\mathcal{Y}} = \{\mathbf{P}_{\mathsf{Y}|\mathsf{X}=x,\mathsf{H}=h} \mid h \in \mathcal{H}\}$ *of measures over the sample space* $\mathcal{Y}$*, a set* $\mathcal{P}_{\mathcal{H}} = \{\mathbf{P}^{\boldsymbol{\theta}}_{\mathsf{H}} \mid \boldsymbol{\theta} \in \mathcal{Q}\}$ *of probability measures over the hypothesis space* $\mathcal{H}$ *is called a* conjugate prior family to $\mathcal{P}_{\mathcal{Y}}$ *if, for any prior* $\mathbf{P}_{\mathsf{H}} \in \mathcal{P}_{\mathcal{H}}$*, the corresponding posterior* $\mathbf{P}_{\mathsf{H}|\mathsf{Z}=z}$ *is still in the set* $\mathcal{P}_{\mathcal{H}}$ *for all values of* z*, i.e.,*

$$\forall \mathbf{P}_{\mathsf{H}} \in \mathcal{P}_{\mathcal{H}} : \forall (x, y) \in \mathcal{Z} : \qquad \mathbf{P}_{\mathsf{H}|\mathsf{Z}=(x,y)} \propto \left(\mathbf{P}_{\mathsf{Y}|\mathsf{X}=x,\mathsf{H}=h}\mathbf{P}_{\mathsf{H}}\right) \in \mathcal{P}_{\mathcal{H}},$$

where the measure $\mathbf{P}_{\mathsf{H}|\mathsf{Z}=z}$ *is defined in (3.1).*

---

3 The abbreviation PAC is introduced in Part II, Section 4.2.

The advantage of conjugate priors becomes apparent if we additionally assume that the conjugate family $\mathcal{P}_{\mathcal{H}}$ is parameterized by a small number of parameters. Then, inference on the basis of the data, $z \in \mathcal{Z}^m$, simplifies to the computation of a few new parameter values.

Example 3.5 (Conjugate prior) *A popular example of a conjugate prior family is the family of Beta distributions over the success probability p for the binomially distributed random variables (see also Table A.1), i.e., for* $\mathbf{P}_\mathsf{P} = \text{Beta}(\alpha, \beta)$ *and* $\mathbf{P}_{\mathsf{X}|\mathsf{P}=p} = \text{Binomial}(n, p)$ *we know that* $\mathbf{P}_{\mathsf{P}|\mathsf{X}=i} = \text{Beta}(\alpha + i, \beta + n - i)$ *because*

$$
\begin{aligned}
\mathbf{f}_{\mathsf{P}|\mathsf{X}=i}(p) &= \frac{\mathbf{P}_{\mathsf{X}|\mathsf{P}=p}(i)\,\mathbf{f}_\mathsf{P}(p)}{\int_0^1 \mathbf{P}_{\mathsf{X}|\mathsf{P}=\hat{p}}(i)\,\mathbf{f}_\mathsf{P}(\hat{p})\,d\hat{p}} \\
&= \frac{\binom{n}{i} p^i (1-p)^{n-i} \frac{\Gamma(\alpha+\beta)}{\Gamma(\alpha)\Gamma(\beta)} p^{\alpha-1}(1-p)^{\beta-1}}{\int_0^1 \binom{n}{i} \hat{p}^i (1-\hat{p})^{n-i} \frac{\Gamma(\alpha+\beta)}{\Gamma(\alpha)\Gamma(\beta)} \hat{p}^{\alpha-1}(1-\hat{p})^{\beta-1}\,d\hat{p}} \\
&= \frac{p^{\alpha+i-1}(1-p)^{n+\beta-i-1}}{\int_0^1 \hat{p}^{\alpha+i-1}(1-\hat{p})^{n+\beta-i-1}\,d\hat{p}}\,.
\end{aligned}
$$

Another example of a conjugate prior family is the family of Gaussian measures over the mean $\boldsymbol{\mu}$ *of another Gaussian measure, which will be discussed at more length in Section 3.2.*

It is worth mentioning that, apart from computational reasons, there is no motivation for favoring conjugate priors over other prior measures $\mathbf{P}_\mathsf{H}$. As a general guideline, one should try to model the prior knowledge with a family of probability measures that is quite flexible but which leaves inference still computationally feasible. Examples of such prior families are given in the subsequent sections.

Evidence of $\mathcal{H}$ The denominator of equation (3.1) is called the *evidence* of the model (or hypothesis space) $\mathcal{H}$. It expresses how likely the observation of the label sequence $\boldsymbol{y} \in \mathcal{Y}^m$ is, in conjunction with the m training objects $\boldsymbol{x} \in \mathcal{X}^m$ under all different hypotheses $h \in \mathcal{Y}^\mathcal{X}$ contained in $\mathcal{H}$, weighted by their prior belief $\mathbf{P}_\mathsf{H}(h)$. Hence, this quantity is a function of the label sequence $\boldsymbol{y} \in \mathcal{Y}^m$ for a fixed hypothesis space $\mathcal{H}$ and for the object sample $\boldsymbol{x} \in \mathcal{X}^m$. In fact, when viewed as a function of the class labels the evidence is merely a probability measure over the space of all classifications at the m training objects $\boldsymbol{x}$. As every probability measure has the property that it must sum to one, we see that high values of the

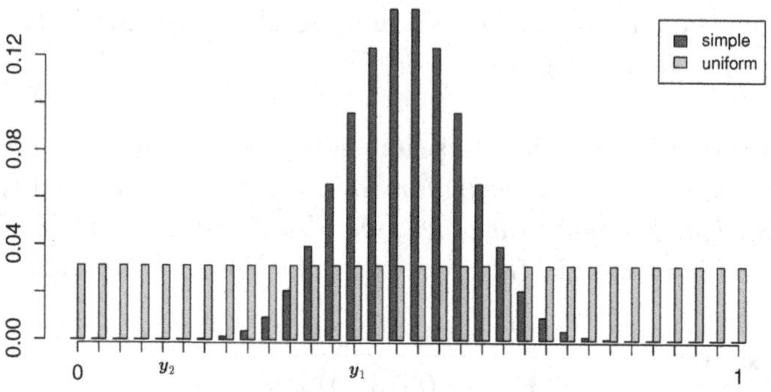

Figure 3.1 Effect of evidence maximization. For a training set size of $m = 5$ we have arranged all possible classifications $\mathbf{y} \in \{-1, +1\}^5$ on the interval $[0, 1]$ by $g(\mathbf{y}) = \sum_{i=1}^{5} 2^{-i+1} \mathbf{I}_{y_i=+1}$ and depicted two different distributions $\mathbf{E}_{\mathsf{H}_i}\left[\mathbf{P}_{\mathsf{Y}^5|\mathsf{X}^5=\mathbf{x},\mathsf{H}_i=h}(\mathbf{y})\right]$ over the space of all classifications on the 5 training objects $\mathbf{x} \in \mathcal{X}^5$ (gray and white bars). Since both probability mass functions sum up to one there must exist classifications $\mathbf{y}$, e.g., $\mathbf{y}_1$, for which the more simple model $\mathcal{H}_1$ (because it explains only a small number of classifications) has a higher evidence than the more complex model $\mathcal{H}_2$. Nonetheless, if we *really* observe a complex classification, e.g., $\mathbf{y}_2$, then the maximization of the evidence leads to the "correct" model $\mathcal{H}_2$.

evidence for some classifications $\mathbf{y}$ must imply that other classifications, $\tilde{\mathbf{y}}$, lead to a small evidence of the fixed model $\mathcal{H}$. Hence every hypothesis space has some "preferred" classifications for which its evidence is high but, necessarily, also other "non-preferred" classifications of the observed object sequence $\mathbf{x} \in \mathcal{X}^m$.

This reasoning motivates the usage of the evidence for the purpose of model selection. We can view the choice of the hypothesis space $\mathcal{H}$ out of a given set $\{\mathcal{H}_1, \ldots, \mathcal{H}_r\}$ a as model selection problem because it directly influences the Bayesian inference given in equation (3.1). Using the evidence would lead to the following model selection algorithm:

> Given a training sample $z = (\mathbf{x}, \mathbf{y})$ and r hypothesis spaces $\mathcal{H}_1, \ldots, \mathcal{H}_r$ choose the hypothesis space $\mathcal{H}$ such that $\mathbf{E}_{\mathsf{H}_i}\left[\mathbf{P}_{\mathsf{Y}^m|\mathsf{X}^m=\mathbf{x},\mathsf{H}_i=h}(\mathbf{y})\right]$ is maximized.

By the above reasoning we see that overly complex models $\mathcal{H}$, which fit almost any possible classification $\mathbf{y} \in \mathcal{Y}^m$ of a given sequence $\mathbf{x} \in \mathcal{X}^m$ of training objects, are automatically penalized. This is because the more classifications a hypothesis space is capable of describing[4], the smaller the probability of a single classification under the fixed model. If, however, we *really* observe a classification $\mathbf{y}$ that cannot be accommodated by any of the simple models, the evidence of the complex model $\mathcal{H}$ is largest. This is also illustrated in Figure 3.1.

The evidence as a measure of the quality of a hypothesis space can also be derived if we additionally consider the space $\mathcal{D} = \{\mathcal{H}_1, \ldots, \mathcal{H}_r\}$ of all possible hypothesis spaces considered. First, equation (3.1) can be rewritten as

$$\begin{aligned}\mathbf{P}_{\mathsf{H}|\mathsf{Z}^m=\mathbf{z},\mathsf{D}=\mathcal{H}_i}(h) &= \frac{\mathbf{P}_{\mathsf{Y}^m|\mathsf{X}^m=\mathbf{x},\mathsf{H}=h,\mathsf{D}=\mathcal{H}_i}(\mathbf{y})\,\mathbf{P}_{\mathsf{H}|\mathsf{D}=\mathcal{H}_i}(h)}{\mathbf{E}_{\mathsf{H}|\mathsf{D}=\mathcal{H}_i}\left[\mathbf{P}_{\mathsf{Y}^m|\mathsf{X}^m=\mathbf{x},\mathsf{H}=h,\mathsf{D}=\mathcal{H}_i}(\mathbf{y})\right]} \\ &= \frac{\mathbf{P}_{\mathsf{Y}^m|\mathsf{X}^m=\mathbf{x},\mathsf{H}=h,\mathsf{D}=\mathcal{H}_i}(\mathbf{y})\,\mathbf{P}_{\mathsf{H}|\mathsf{D}=\mathcal{H}_i}(h)}{\mathbf{P}_{\mathsf{Y}^m|\mathsf{X}^m=\mathbf{x},\mathsf{D}=\mathcal{H}_i}(\mathbf{y})},\end{aligned}$$

where we have included the conditioning on the fixed hypothesis space $\mathcal{H}_i$. Now, using Theorem A.22 to compute the posterior belief in the hypothesis space $\mathcal{H}_i$ after having seen the training sample $\mathbf{z}$ we see that

$$\mathbf{P}_{\mathsf{D}|\mathsf{Z}^m=\mathbf{z}}(\mathcal{H}_i) = \frac{\mathbf{P}_{\mathsf{Z}^m|\mathsf{D}=\mathcal{H}_i}(\mathbf{z})\,\mathbf{P}_{\mathsf{D}}(\mathcal{H}_i)}{\mathbf{E}_{\mathsf{D}}\left[\mathbf{P}_{\mathsf{Z}^m|\mathsf{D}=\mathcal{H}_i}(\mathbf{z})\right]} \propto \mathbf{P}_{\mathsf{Y}^m|\mathsf{X}^m=\mathbf{x},\mathsf{D}=\mathcal{H}_i}(\mathbf{y})\,\mathbf{P}_{\mathsf{D}}(\mathcal{H}_i)\,, \tag{3.3}$$

because the denominator of equation (3.3) does not depend on $\mathcal{H}_i$. Without any prior knowledge, i.e., with a uniform measure $\mathbf{P}_{\mathsf{D}}$, we see that the posterior belief is directly proportional to the evidence $\mathbf{P}_{\mathsf{Y}^m|\mathsf{X}^m=\mathbf{x},\mathsf{D}=\mathcal{H}_i}(\mathbf{y})$ of the model $\mathcal{H}_i$. As a consequence, maximizing the evidence in the course of model selection is equivalent to choosing the model with the highest posterior belief.

3.1.1 The Power of Conditioning on Data

From a purely Bayesian point of view, for the task of learning we are finished as soon as we have updated our prior belief $\mathbf{P}_{\mathsf{H}}$ into the posterior belief $\mathbf{P}_{\mathsf{H}|\mathsf{Z}^m=\mathbf{z}}$ using equation (3.1). Nonetheless, our ultimate goal is to find *one* (deterministic) function $h \in \mathcal{Y}^{\mathcal{X}}$ that best describes the relationship objects and classes, which is implicitly

---

4 We say that the hypothesis space $\mathcal{H}$ *describes* the classification $\mathbf{y}$ at some given training points $\mathbf{x}$ if there exists at least one hypothesis $h \in \mathcal{H}$ which leads to a high likelihood $\mathcal{L}(h, (\mathbf{x}, \mathbf{y}))$. Using the notion of an inverse loss likelihood this means that there exists a hypothesis $h \in \mathcal{H}$ that has a small empirical risk or training error $R_{\text{emp}}[h, (\mathbf{x}, \mathbf{y})]$ (see also Definition 2.11).

expressed by the unknown measure $\mathbf{P}_{\mathsf{Z}} = \mathbf{P}_{\mathsf{Y}|\mathsf{X}}\mathbf{P}_{\mathsf{X}}$. In order to achieve this goal, Bayesian analysis suggests strategies based on the posterior belief $\mathbf{P}_{\mathsf{H}|\mathsf{Z}^m=z}$:

- If we are restricted to returning a function $h \in \mathcal{H}$ from a pre-specified hypothesis space $\mathcal{H} \subseteq \mathcal{Y}^{\mathcal{X}}$ and assume that $\mathbf{P}_{\mathsf{H}|\mathsf{Z}^m=z}$ is highly peaked around one particular function then we determine the classifier with the maximum posterior belief.

Definition 3.6 (Maximum-a-posteriori estimator) *For a given posterior belief $\mathbf{P}_{\mathsf{H}|\mathsf{Z}^m=z}$ over a hypothesis space $\mathcal{H} \subseteq \mathcal{Y}^{\mathcal{X}}$, the* maximum-a-posteriori estimator *is defined by*[5]

$$\mathcal{A}_{\text{MAP}}(z) \stackrel{\text{def}}{=} \underset{h \in \mathcal{H}}{\operatorname{argmax}} \ \mathbf{P}_{\mathsf{H}|\mathsf{Z}^m=z}(h) . \tag{3.4}$$

If we use the inverse loss likelihood and note that the posterior $\mathbf{P}_{\mathsf{H}|\mathsf{Z}^m=z}$ is given by the product of the likelihood and the prior we see that this scheme returns the minimizer of the training error and our prior belief, which can be thought of as a regularizer (see also Subsection 2.2.2). The drawback of the MAP estimator is that it is very sensitive to the training sample if the posterior measure is multi modal. Even worse, the classifier $\mathcal{A}_{\text{MAP}}(z) \in \mathcal{H}$ is, in general, not unique, for example if the posterior measure is uniform.

- If we are not confined to returning a function from the original hypothesis space $\mathcal{H}$ then we can use the posterior measure $\mathbf{P}_{\mathsf{H}|\mathsf{Z}^m=z}$ to induce a measure $\mathbf{P}_{\mathsf{Y}|\mathsf{X}=x,\mathsf{Z}^m=z}$ over class labels $y \in \mathcal{Y}$ at a novel object $x \in \mathcal{X}$ by

$$\mathbf{P}_{\mathsf{Y}|\mathsf{X}=x,\mathsf{Z}^m=z}(y) = \mathbf{P}_{\mathsf{H}|\mathsf{Z}^m=z}(\{h \in \mathcal{H} \mid h(x) = y\}) .$$

This measure can then be used to determine the class label y which incurs the smallest loss at a given object x.

Definition 3.7 (Bayes classification strategy) *Given a posterior belief $\mathbf{P}_{\mathsf{H}|\mathsf{Z}^m=z}$ over a hypothesis space $\mathcal{H}$ and a loss function $l : \mathcal{Y} \times \mathcal{Y} \to \mathbb{R}$ the* Bayes classification strategy *$Bayes_z$ implements the following classification*

$$Bayes_z(x) \stackrel{\text{def}}{=} \underset{y \in \mathcal{Y}}{\operatorname{argmin}} \ \mathbf{E}_{\mathsf{H}|\mathsf{Z}^m=z}\left[l(y, \mathsf{H}(x))\right] . \tag{3.5}$$

5 If we have an infinite number of hypotheses the quantity $\mathbf{P}_{\mathsf{H}|\mathsf{Z}^m=z}(h)$ is replaced by the corresponding value of the density, i.e., $\mathbf{f}_{\mathsf{H}|\mathsf{Z}^m=z}(h)$.

Assuming the zero-one loss l_{0-1} given in equation (2.10) we see that the Bayes optimal decision *at x is given by*

$$Bayes_z(x) \stackrel{\text{def}}{=} \underset{y \in \mathcal{Y}}{\operatorname{argmax}} \mathbf{P}_{\mathsf{H}|\mathsf{Z}^m=z}(\{h \in \mathcal{H} \mid h(x) = y\}) . \tag{3.6}$$

It is interesting to note that, in the special case of the two-classes $\mathcal{Y} = \{-1, +1\}$, we can write $Bayes_z$ as a thresholded real-valued function, i.e.,

$$Bayes_z(x) = \operatorname{sign}\left(\mathbf{E}_{\mathsf{H}|\mathsf{Z}^m=z}\left[\mathsf{H}(x)\right]\right) . \tag{3.7}$$

▪ If we are not restricted to returning a *deterministic* function $h \in \mathcal{Y}^{\mathcal{X}}$ we can consider the so-called Gibbs classification strategy.

Definition 3.8 (Gibbs classification strategy) *Given a posterior belief $\mathbf{P}_{\mathsf{H}|\mathsf{Z}^m=z}$ over a hypothesis space $\mathcal{H} \subseteq \mathcal{Y}^{\mathcal{X}}$, the* Gibbs classification strategy *$Gibbs_z$ is given by*

$$Gibbs_z(x) \stackrel{\text{def}}{=} h(x), \qquad h \sim \mathbf{P}_{\mathsf{H}|\mathsf{Z}^m=z},$$

that is, for a novel test object $x \in \mathcal{X}$ we randomly draw a function h according to $\mathbf{P}_{\mathsf{H}|\mathsf{Z}^m=z}$ and use this function to label x.

Although this classifier is used less often in practice we will explore the full power of this classification scheme later in Section 5.1.

In the following three sections we consider specific instances of the Bayesian principle which result in new learning algorithms for linear classifiers. It is worth mentioning that the Bayesian method is not limited to the task of binary classification learning, but can also be applied if the output space is the set of real numbers. In this case, the learning problem is called the problem of *regression estimation.* We shall see that in many cases, the regression estimation algorithm is the starting point to obtain a classification algorithm.

3.2 Gaussian Processes

In this section we are going to consider Gaussian processes both for the purpose of regression and for classification. Gaussian processes, which were initially developed for the regression estimation case, are extended to classification by using the concept of latent variables and marginalization. In this sense, the regression estimation case is much more fundamental.

3.2.1 Bayesian Linear Regression

In the regression estimation problem we are given a sequence $\boldsymbol{x} = (x_1, \ldots, x_m) \in \mathcal{X}^m$ of m objects together with a sequence $\boldsymbol{t} = (t_1, \ldots, t_m) \in \mathbb{R}^m$ of m real-valued outcomes forming the training sample $z = (\boldsymbol{x}, \boldsymbol{t})$. Our aim is to find a functional relationship $f \in \mathbb{R}^{\mathcal{X}}$ between objects x and target values t. In accordance with Chapter 2 we will again consider a linear model $\mathcal{F}$

$$\mathcal{F} = \{x \mapsto \langle \mathbf{x}, \mathbf{w} \rangle \mid \mathbf{w} \in \mathcal{K}\} \ ,$$

where we assume that $\mathbf{x} \stackrel{\text{def}}{=} \boldsymbol{\phi}(x)$ and $\boldsymbol{\phi} : \mathcal{X} \to \mathcal{K} \subseteq \ell_2^n$ is a given feature mapping (see also Definition 2.2). Note that $\mathbf{x} \in \mathcal{K}$ should not be confused with the training sequence $\boldsymbol{x} \in \mathcal{X}^m$ which results in an $m \times n$ matrix $\mathbf{X} = \left(\mathbf{x}_1'; \ldots; \mathbf{x}_m'\right)$ when $\boldsymbol{\phi}$ is applied to it.

First, we need to specify a prior over the function space $\mathcal{F}$. Since each function $f_{\mathbf{w}}$ is uniquely parameterized by its weight vector $\mathbf{w} \in \mathcal{K}$ it suffices to consider a prior distribution on weight vectors. For algorithmic convenience let the prior distribution over weights be a Gaussian measure with mean $\mathbf{0}$ and covariance $\mathbf{I}_n$, i.e.,

$$\mathbf{P}_{\mathsf{W}} = \text{Normal}\left(\mathbf{0}, \mathbf{I}_n\right) \ . \tag{3.8}$$

Apart from algorithmical reasons such a prior favors weight vectors $\mathbf{w} \in \mathcal{K}$ with small coefficients w_i because the log-density is proportional to $-\|\mathbf{w}\|^2 = -\sum_{i=1}^n w_i^2$ (see Definition A.26). In fact, the weight vector with the highest a-priori density is $\mathbf{w} = \mathbf{0}$.

Second, we must specify the likelihood model $\mathbf{P}_{\mathsf{T}^m|\mathsf{X}^m=\boldsymbol{x},\mathsf{W}=\mathbf{w}}$. Let us assume that, for a given function $f_{\mathbf{w}}$ and a given training object $x \in \mathcal{X}$, the real-valued output T is normally distributed with mean $f_{\mathbf{w}}(x)$ and variance σ_t^2. Using the notion of an inverse loss likelihood such an assumption corresponds to using the *squared loss*, i.e., $l_2(f(x), t) = (f(x) - t)^2$ when considering the prediction task under a machine learning perspective. Further, it shall be assumed that the real-valued outputs T_1 and T_2 at x_1 and $x_2 \neq x_1$ are independent. Combining these two requirements results in the following likelihood model:

$$\mathbf{P}_{\mathsf{T}^m|\mathsf{X}^m=\boldsymbol{x},\mathsf{W}=\mathbf{w}}(\boldsymbol{t}) = \text{Normal}\left(\mathbf{X}\mathbf{w}, \sigma_t^2 \mathbf{I}_m\right) \ . \tag{3.9}$$

A straightforward application of Bayes' theorem then reveals that the posterior measure $\mathbf{P}_{\mathsf{W}|\mathsf{X}^m=x,\mathsf{T}^m=t}$ is also a Gaussian measure (see Theorem A.28), i.e.,

$$\begin{aligned}\mathbf{P}_{\mathsf{W}|\mathsf{X}^m=x,\mathsf{T}^m=t} &= \text{Normal}\left(\sigma_t^{-2}\left(\sigma_t^{-2}\mathbf{X}'\mathbf{X}+\mathbf{I}_n\right)^{-1}\mathbf{X}'\boldsymbol{t},\left(\sigma_t^{-2}\mathbf{X}'\mathbf{X}+\mathbf{I}_n\right)^{-1}\right)\\ &= \text{Normal}\left(\left(\mathbf{X}'\mathbf{X}+\sigma_t^2\mathbf{I}_n\right)^{-1}\mathbf{X}'\boldsymbol{t},\left(\sigma_t^{-2}\mathbf{X}'\mathbf{X}+\mathbf{I}_n\right)^{-1}\right).\end{aligned}$$

In order to predict at a new test object $x \in \mathcal{X}$ using the Bayes prediction strategy we take into account that, by the choice of our likelihood model, we look for the minimizer of squared loss, i.e.,

$$\begin{aligned}Bayes_z(x) &= \underset{t\in\mathbb{R}}{\operatorname{argmin}}\ \mathbf{E}_{\mathsf{W}|\mathsf{X}^m=x,\mathsf{T}^m=t}\left[l_2\left(f_{\mathsf{W}}(x),t\right)\right]\\ &= \underset{t\in\mathbb{R}}{\operatorname{argmin}}\ \mathbf{E}_{\mathsf{W}|\mathsf{X}^m=x,\mathsf{T}^m=t}\left[\left(\langle\mathbf{x},\mathbf{W}\rangle-t\right)^2\right]\\ &= \mathbf{E}_{\mathsf{W}|\mathsf{X}^m=x,\mathsf{T}^m=t}\left[\langle\mathbf{x},\mathbf{W}\rangle\right]=\left\langle\mathbf{x},\mathbf{E}_{\mathsf{W}|\mathsf{X}^m=x,\mathsf{T}^m=t}\left[\mathbf{W}\right]\right\rangle, \qquad (3.10)\\ &= \left\langle\mathbf{x},\left(\mathbf{X}'\mathbf{X}+\sigma_t^2\mathbf{I}_n\right)^{-1}\mathbf{X}'\boldsymbol{t}\right\rangle,\end{aligned}$$

where the third line follows from the fact that $(\langle\mathbf{x},\mathbf{w}\rangle-t)^2$ is minimized at $t = \langle\mathbf{x},\mathbf{w}\rangle$. In the current form the prediction at x involves the inversion of the $n \times n$ matrix $\mathbf{X}'\mathbf{X}+\sigma_t^2\mathbf{I}_n$ which is the empirical covariance matrix of the training objects in feature space $\mathcal{K}$. This is an unfavorable property as it requires explicit evaluation of the feature mapping $\boldsymbol{\phi} : \mathcal{X} \to \mathcal{K}$. In order to simplify this expression we apply the Woodbury formula (see Theorem A.79) to the inverse of this matrix, i.e.,

$$\begin{aligned}\left(\mathbf{X}'\mathbf{X}+\sigma_t^2\mathbf{I}_n\right)^{-1} &= \sigma_t^{-2}\mathbf{I}_n-\sigma_t^{-4}\mathbf{X}'\left(\mathbf{I}_m+\sigma_t^{-2}\mathbf{X}\mathbf{X}'\right)^{-1}\mathbf{X}\\ &= \sigma_t^{-2}\left(\mathbf{I}_n-\mathbf{X}'\left(\mathbf{X}\mathbf{X}'+\sigma_t^2\mathbf{I}_m\right)^{-1}\mathbf{X}\right).\end{aligned}$$

Thus, the Bayesian prediction strategy at a given object $x \in \mathcal{X}$ can be written as,

$$\begin{aligned}\mathbf{x}'\left(\mathbf{X}'\mathbf{X}+\sigma_t^2\mathbf{I}_n\right)^{-1}\mathbf{X}'\boldsymbol{t} &= \sigma_t^{-2}\left(\mathbf{x}'\mathbf{X}'-\mathbf{x}'\mathbf{X}'\left(\mathbf{X}\mathbf{X}'+\sigma_t^2\mathbf{I}_m\right)^{-1}\mathbf{X}\mathbf{X}'\right)\boldsymbol{t}\\ &= \sigma_t^{-2}\mathbf{x}'\mathbf{X}'\left(\mathbf{X}\mathbf{X}'+\sigma_t^2\mathbf{I}_m\right)^{-1}\left(\left(\mathbf{X}\mathbf{X}'+\sigma_t^2\mathbf{I}_m\right)-\mathbf{X}\mathbf{X}'\right)\boldsymbol{t}\\ &= \mathbf{x}'\mathbf{X}'\left(\mathbf{X}\mathbf{X}'+\sigma_t^2\mathbf{I}_m\right)^{-1}\boldsymbol{t}. \qquad (3.11)\end{aligned}$$

Note that this modification only requires us to invert a $m \times m$ matrix rather than the $n \times n$ matrix $\mathbf{X}'\mathbf{X}+\sigma_t^2\mathbf{I}_n$. As a consequence, all that is needed for the prediction at individual objects is the inner product function $k(x,\tilde{x}) = \langle\mathbf{x},\tilde{\mathbf{x}}\rangle = \langle\boldsymbol{\phi}(x),\boldsymbol{\phi}(\tilde{x})\rangle$

also known as the kernel for the mapping $\boldsymbol{\phi} : \mathcal{X} \to \mathcal{K} \subseteq \ell_2^n$ (see also Definition 2.14). Exploiting the notions of kernels the prediction at any $x \in \mathcal{X}$ can be written as

$$f(x) = \sum_{i=1}^{m} \hat{\alpha}_i k(x, x_i), \qquad \hat{\boldsymbol{\alpha}} = \left(\mathbf{G} + \sigma_t^2 \mathbf{I}_m\right)^{-1} \boldsymbol{t}, \tag{3.12}$$

where the $m \times m$ matrix $\mathbf{G} = \mathbf{X}\mathbf{X}'$ is defined by $\mathbf{G}_{ij} = k\left(x_i, x_j\right)$ and is called the Gram matrix. From this expression we see that the computational effort involved in finding the linear function from a given training sample is $\mathcal{O}\left(m^3\right)$ since it involves the inversion of the $m \times m$ matrix $\mathbf{G} + \sigma_t^2 \mathbf{I}_m$. However, by exploiting the fact that, for many kernels, the matrix $\mathbf{G}$ has eigenvalues $\boldsymbol{\lambda} = (\lambda_1, \ldots, \lambda_m)'$ that decay quickly toward zero, it is possible to approximate the inversion of the matrix $\mathbf{G} + \sigma_t^2 \mathbf{I}_m$ with $\mathcal{O}\left(m^2\right)$ computations.

In order to understand why this method is also called *Gaussian process regression* we note that, under the assumptions made, the probability model of the data $\mathbf{P}_{\mathsf{T}^m|\mathsf{X}^m=x}(\boldsymbol{t})$ is a Gaussian measure with mean vector $\mathbf{0}$ and covariance $\mathbf{X}\mathbf{X}' + \sigma_t^2 \mathbf{I} = \mathbf{G} + \sigma_t^2 \mathbf{I}$ (see Theorem A.28 and equations (3.8) and (3.9)). This is the defining property of a Gaussian process.

Definition 3.9 (Stochastic and Gaussian processes) *A* stochastic process $\mathsf{T} : \mathcal{X} \to (\mathbb{R}, \mathfrak{B}_1, \mathbf{P}_\mathsf{T})$ *is a collection of random variables indexed by* $x \in \mathcal{X}$ *and is fully defined by the probability distribution of any finite sequence* $\mathbf{T} = (\mathsf{T}(x_1), \ldots, \mathsf{T}(x_m))$. Gaussian processes *are a subset of stochastic processes that can be specified by giving only the mean vector* $\mathbf{E}_\mathsf{T}\left[\mathbf{T}\right]$ *and the covariance matrix* $\mathbf{Cov}(\mathbf{T})$ *for any finite sample* $\boldsymbol{x} \in \mathcal{X}^m$.

As can be seen, Bayesian regression involving linear functions and the prior and likelihood given in equations (3.8) and (3.9), respectively, is equivalent to modeling the outputs as a Gaussian process having mean $\mathbf{0}$ and covariance function $C(x, \tilde{x}) = \left\langle \mathbf{x}, \tilde{\mathbf{x}} \right\rangle + \sigma_t^2 \mathbf{I}_{x=\tilde{x}} = k(x, \tilde{x}) + \sigma_t^2 \mathbf{I}_{x=\tilde{x}}$. The advantage of the Gaussian process viewpoint is that weight vectors are avoided—we simply model the data $z = (\boldsymbol{x}, \boldsymbol{t})$ directly. In order to derive the prediction $f_{\mathrm{GP}}(x)$ of a Gaussian process at a new object $x \in \mathcal{X}$ we exploit the fact that every conditional measure of a Gaussian measure is again Gaussian (see Theorem A.29). According to equation (A.12) this yields $\mathbf{P}_{\mathsf{T}|\mathsf{T}^m=t,\mathsf{X}^m=x,\mathsf{X}=x} = \text{Normal}\left(\mu_t, \upsilon_t^2\right)$ with

$$\mu_t = \mathbf{x}'\mathbf{X}'\left(\mathbf{G}+\sigma_t^2\mathbf{I}\right)^{-1}\boldsymbol{t} = \sum_{i=1}^{m}\left(\left(\mathbf{G}+\sigma_t^2\mathbf{I}\right)^{-1}\boldsymbol{t}\right)_i k\left(x_i, x\right), \tag{3.13}$$

$$\begin{aligned}\upsilon_t^2 &= \mathbf{x}'\mathbf{x}+\sigma_t^2-\mathbf{x}'\mathbf{X}'\left(\mathbf{G}+\sigma_t^2\mathbf{I}\right)^{-1}\mathbf{X}\mathbf{x} \qquad (3.14)\\ &= k(x,x)+\sigma_t^2-\sum_{i=1}^{m}\sum_{j=1}^{m}k\left(x_i,x\right)\cdot k\left(x_j,x\right)\cdot\left(\left(\mathbf{G}+\sigma_t^2\mathbf{I}\right)^{-1}\right)_{ij},\end{aligned}$$

by considering the joint probability of the real-valued outputs $(\boldsymbol{t}; t)$ at the training points $\boldsymbol{x} \in \mathcal{X}^m$ and the new test object $x \in \mathcal{X}$ with covariance matrix

$$\begin{pmatrix} \mathbf{G}+\sigma_t^2\mathbf{I} & \mathbf{X}\mathbf{x} \\ \mathbf{x}'\mathbf{X}' & \mathbf{x}'\mathbf{x}+\sigma_t^2 \end{pmatrix}.$$

Note that the expression given in equation (3.13) equals the Bayesian prediction strategy given in equation (3.11) or (3.12) when using a kernel. Additionally, the Gaussian process viewpoint offers an analytical expression for the variance of the prediction at the new test point, as given in equation (3.14). Hence, under the assumption made, we cannot only predict the new target value at a test object but, also judge the reliability of that prediction. It is though important to recognize that such error bars on the prediction are meaningless if we cannot guarantee that our Gaussian process model is appropriate for the learning problem at hand.

Remark 3.10 (Covariance functions and kernels) *It is interesting to compare equation (3.12) with the expression for the change of the Gram matrix* $\mathbf{G}$ *when considering quadratic soft margin support vector machines (see equation (2.50) and Remark 2.32). We can either treat the feature space mapping* $\boldsymbol{\phi}: \mathcal{X} \to \mathcal{K}$ *and the variance on the outputs* $t \in \mathbb{R}$ *separately or incorporate the latter directly into the kernel* $k: \mathcal{X} \times \mathcal{X} \to \mathbb{R}$ *by changing the Gram matrix* $\mathbf{G}$ *into* $\widetilde{\mathbf{G}}$

$$\widetilde{\mathbf{G}} = \mathbf{G}+\sigma_t^2\mathbf{I} \quad \Leftrightarrow \quad k_{\sigma_t^2}(x,\tilde{x}) = k(x,\tilde{x})+\sigma_t^2\mathbf{I}_{x=\tilde{x}}. \tag{3.15}$$

This equivalence allows us to view the parameter λ *in the support vector classification case as an assumed noise level on the real-valued output* $y_i\langle\mathbf{w},\mathbf{x}_i\rangle$ *at all the training points* $z_i = (x_i, y_i)$*. Note that the difference in the classification case is the thresholding of the target* $t \in \mathbb{R}$ *to obtain a binary decision* $y \in \{-1,+1\}$*.*

Under the Gaussian process consideration we see that all prior knowledge has been incorporated in the choice of a particular kernel $k : \mathcal{X} \times \mathcal{X} \to \mathbb{R}$ and variance $\sigma_t^2 \in \mathbb{R}^+$. In order to choose between different kernels and variances we employ the evidence maximization principle. For a given training sample $z = (\boldsymbol{x}, \boldsymbol{t})$ of object-target pairs we maximize the expression $\mathbf{P}_{\mathsf{T}^m|\mathsf{X}^m=\boldsymbol{x}}(\boldsymbol{t})$ w.r.t. the kernel parameters and variance σ_t^2. The appealing feature of the Gaussian process model is that this expression is given in an analytical form. It is the value of the m–dimensional Gaussian density with mean $\mathbf{0}$ and covariance matrix $\mathbf{G} + \sigma_t^2\mathbf{I}$ at $\boldsymbol{t} \in \mathbb{R}^m$. If we consider the log-evidence given by

$$\ln\left(\mathbf{P}_{\mathsf{T}^m|\mathsf{X}^m=\boldsymbol{x}}(\boldsymbol{t})\right) = -\frac{1}{2}\left(m\ln(2\pi) + \ln\left(\left|\mathbf{G} + \sigma_t^2\mathbf{I}\right|\right) + \boldsymbol{t}'\left(\mathbf{G} + \sigma_t^2\mathbf{I}\right)^{-1}\boldsymbol{t}\right),$$

we see that, in the case of a differentiable kernel function k, the gradient of the log-evidence can be computed analytically and thus standard optimization methods can be used to find the most probable kernel parameters.

Example 3.11 (Evidence maximization with Gaussian processes) *In Figure 3.2 we have shown an application of the maximization of the evidence for a simple regression problem on the real line $\mathcal{X} = \mathbb{R}$. As can be seen from this example, the evidence is often multi-modal which can make its maximization very difficult—a few observations $x_1, \ldots, x_r$ as well as initial parameters $\boldsymbol{\theta}_0$ and σ_0 in the search for the most probable parameter can have a large influence on the local maximum found. One way to overcome this problem is to integrate over all possible parameters $\boldsymbol{\theta}$ and variances σ_t^2 and weight each prediction by its evidence.*

Another interesting observation to be drawn from Figure 3.2 is the ability of the method to provide error bars on the prediction $t \in \mathbb{R}$ (dotted lines in the middle and left plot). If we have chosen a model which assumes almost no variance on the outputs then we have a small variance for test points which are near the training sample $\boldsymbol{x}$ (in the metric induced by the kernel). This is in accordance with the intuitive notion of the variability of the target values for all test points having high correlation with the training sample.

Example 3.12 (Automatic relevance determination) *An interesting application of the analytical maximization of the evidence in Gaussian processes is for the determination of* relevant dimensions *in the case of an N–dimensional input space*

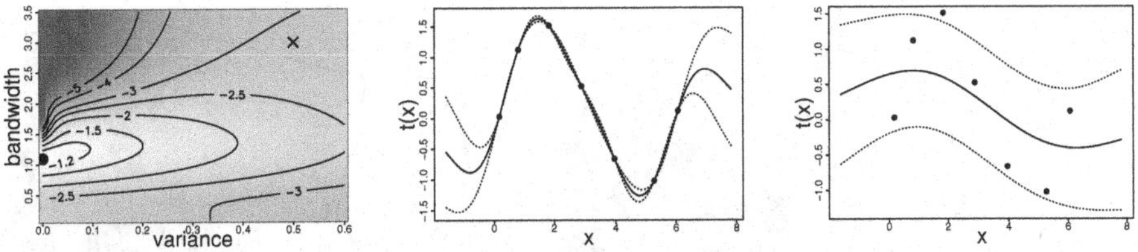

Figure 3.2 **(Left)** The log-evidence for a simple regression problem on the real line $\mathcal{X} = \mathbb{R}$. The x–axis varies over different values of the assumed variance σ_t^2 whereas the y–axis ranges over different values for the bandwidth σ in an RBF kernel (see Table 2.1). The training sample consists of the 7 observations shown in the middle plot (dots). The dot ($\bullet$) and cross ($\times$) depict two values at which the gradient vanishes, i.e., local maxima of the evidence. **(Middle)** The estimated function corresponding to the kernel bandwidth $\sigma = 1.1$ and variance $\sigma_t^2 = 0$ ($\bullet$ in the left picture). The dotted line shows the error bars of one standard deviation computed according to equation (3.14). Note that the variance increases in regions where no training data is available. **(Right)** The estimated function corresponding to the kernel bandwidth $\sigma = 3$ and variance $\sigma_t^2 = 0.5$ ($\times$ in the left picture). This local maximum is attained because all observations are assumed to be generated by the variance component σ_t^2 only.

$\mathcal{X} \subseteq \mathbb{R}^N$. If we use the Mahalanobis kernel (see also Table 2.1) given by

$$k(\vec{u}, \vec{v}) = \exp\left(-\sum_{i=1}^{N} \frac{(u_i - v_i)^2}{\sigma_i^2}\right)$$

we see that, for the case of $\sigma_i \to \infty$, the ith input dimension is neglected in the computation of the kernel and can therefore be removed from the dataset (see also Figure 3.3). The appealing feature of using such a kernel is that the log-evidence $\ln\left(\mathbf{P}_{\mathsf{T}^m|\mathsf{X}^m=x}(\boldsymbol{t})\right)$ can be written as a differentiable function in the parameters $\boldsymbol{\sigma} \in \left(\mathbb{R}^+\right)^N$ and thus standard maximization methods such as gradient ascent, Newton-Raphson and conjugate gradients can be applied. Moreover, in a Bayesian spirit it is also possible to additionally favor large values of the parameters σ_i by placing an exponential prior on σ_i^{-2}.

3.2.2 From Regression to Classification

We shall now return to our primary problem, which is classification. We are given m class labels $\boldsymbol{y} = (y_1, \ldots, y_m) \in \mathcal{Y}^m = \{-1, +1\}^m$ rather than m real-valued

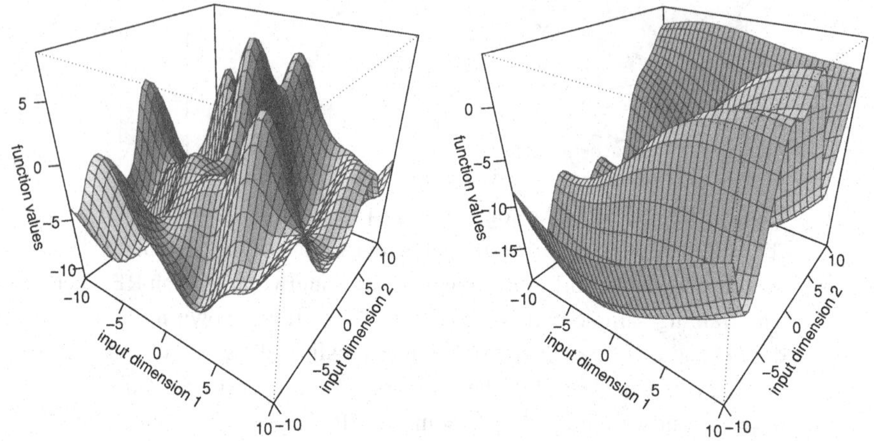

Figure 3.3 **(Left)** A function $f_{\mathbf{w}}$ sampled from the ARD prior with $\sigma_1 = \sigma_2 = \sqrt{5}$ where $\mathcal{X} = \mathbb{R}^2$. Considering the 1–D functions over the second input dimension for fixed values of the first input dimension, we see that the functions change slowly only for nearby values of the first input dimension. The size of the neighborhood is determined by the choice of σ_1 and σ_2. **(Right)** A function $f_{\mathbf{w}}$ sampled from the ARD prior with $\sigma_1 = 20\sigma_2$. As can be seen the function is only changing very slowly over the first input dimension. In the limiting case $\sigma_1 \to \infty$ any sample $f_{\mathbf{w}}$ is a function of the second input dimension only.

outputs $\boldsymbol{t} = (t_1, \ldots, t_m) \in \mathbb{R}^m$. In order to use Gaussian processes for this purpose we are faced with the following problem: Given a model for m real-valued outputs $\boldsymbol{t} \in \mathbb{R}^m$ how can we model 2^m different binary vectors $\boldsymbol{y} \in \mathcal{Y}^m$?

In order to solve this problem we note that, for the purpose of classification, we need to know the *predictive distribution* $\mathbf{P}_{\mathsf{Y}|\mathsf{X}=x,\mathsf{Z}^m=z}(y)$ where $z = (\boldsymbol{x}, \boldsymbol{y})$ is the full training sample of object-class pairs. Given the predictive distribution at a new test object $x \in \mathcal{X}$ we decide on the class label y with maximum probability $\mathbf{P}_{\mathsf{Y}|\mathsf{X}=x,\mathsf{Z}^m=z}(y)$. The trick which enables the use of a regression estimation method such as Gaussian processes is the introduction of a *latent random variable* T which has influence on the conditional class probability $\mathbf{P}_{\mathsf{Y}|\mathsf{X}=x}$. As we saw in the last subsection, each prediction $f_{\mathrm{GP}}(x)$ of a Gaussian process at some test object $x \in \mathcal{X}$ can be viewed as the real-valued output of a mean weight vector $\mathbf{w}_{\mathrm{cm}} = \mathbf{E}_{\mathsf{W}|\mathsf{X}^m=\boldsymbol{x},\mathsf{T}^m=\boldsymbol{t}}[\mathsf{W}]$ in some fixed feature space $\mathcal{K}$ (see equation (3.10)), i.e., the distance to the hyperplane with the normal vector $\mathbf{w}_{\mathrm{cm}}$. Intuitively, the further away a test object $x \in \mathcal{X}$ is from the hyperplane (the larger the value of t), the

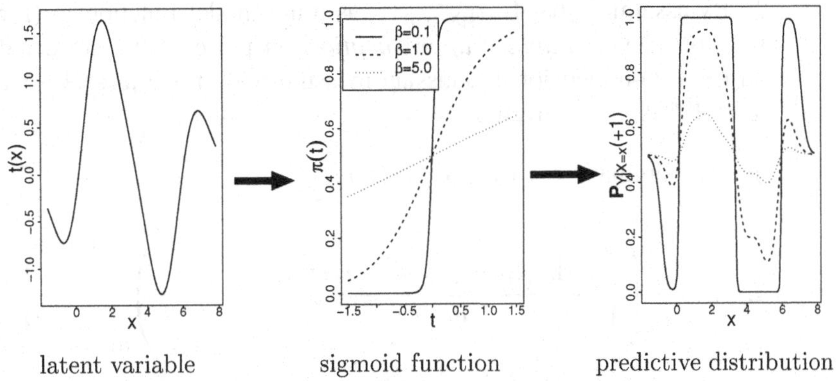

Figure 3.4 Latent variable model for classification with Gaussian processes. Each real-valued function (left) is "transfered" through a *sigmoid* given by equation (3.16) (middle plot). As a result we obtain the predictive distribution $\mathbf{P}_{\mathsf{Y}|\mathsf{X}=x,\mathsf{T}=t}(+1)$ for the class $+1$ as a function of the inputs (right). By increasing the noise parameter β we get smoother functions $g(x) = \mathbf{P}_{\mathsf{Y}|\mathsf{X}=x,\mathsf{T}=t}(+1)$. In the limit of $\beta \to 0$ the predictive distribution becomes a zero-one valued function.

more likely it is that the object is from the class $y = \text{sign}(t)$. One way to model this intuitive notion is by

$$\mathbf{P}_{\mathsf{Y}|\mathsf{T}=t}(y) = \frac{\exp\left(\beta^{-1} \cdot yt\right)}{\exp\left(\beta^{-1} \cdot yt\right) + \exp\left(-\beta^{-1} \cdot yt\right)} = \frac{\exp\left(2\beta^{-1} \cdot yt\right)}{1 + \exp\left(2\beta^{-1} \cdot yt\right)}, \tag{3.16}$$

where β can be viewed as a noise level, i.e., for $\lim_{\beta \to 0} \mathbf{P}_{\mathsf{Y}|\mathsf{T}=t}(y) = \mathbf{I}_{yt \geq 0}$ (see also Definition 3.2 and Figure 3.4). In order to exploit the latent random variables we marginalize over all their possible values $(\boldsymbol{t}, t) \in \mathbb{R}^{m+1}$ at the m training objects $\boldsymbol{x} \in \mathcal{X}^m$ and the test object $x \in \mathcal{X}$, i.e.,

$$\begin{aligned}
\mathbf{P}_{\mathsf{Y}|\mathsf{X}=x,\mathsf{Z}^m=z}(y) &= \mathbf{E}_{\mathsf{T}^{m+1}|\mathsf{X}=x,\mathsf{Z}^m=z}\left[\mathbf{P}_{\mathsf{Y}|\mathsf{X}=x,\mathsf{Z}^m=z,\mathsf{T}^{m+1}=(\boldsymbol{t},t)}\right] \\
&= \int_{\mathbb{R}} \int_{\mathbb{R}^m} \mathbf{P}_{\mathsf{Y}|\mathsf{T}=t}(y)\, \mathbf{f}_{\mathsf{T}^{m+1}|\mathsf{X}=x,\mathsf{Z}^m=z}((\boldsymbol{t}, t))\, d\boldsymbol{t}\, dt\,.
\end{aligned} \tag{3.17}$$

A problem arises with this integral due to the non-Gaussianity of the term $\mathbf{P}_{\mathsf{Y}|\mathsf{T}=t}(y)$ meaning that the integrand $\mathbf{f}_{\mathsf{T}^{m+1}|\mathsf{X}=x,\mathsf{Z}^m=z}$ is no longer a Gaussian density and, thus, it becomes analytically intractable. There are several routes we can take:

1. By assuming that $\mathbf{f}_{\mathsf{T}^{m+1}|\mathsf{X}=x,\mathsf{Z}^m=z}$ is a uni-modal function in $(\boldsymbol{t}, t) \in \mathbb{R}^{m+1}$ we can consider its *Laplace approximation*. In place of the correct density we use an $(m+1)$-dimensional Gaussian measure with mode $\boldsymbol{\mu} \in \mathbb{R}^{m+1}$ and covariance $\boldsymbol{\Sigma} \in \mathbb{R}^{(m+1)\times(m+1)}$ given by

$$\boldsymbol{\mu} = \operatorname*{argmax}_{(\boldsymbol{t},t)\in\mathbb{R}^{m+1}} \mathbf{f}_{\mathsf{T}^{m+1}|\mathsf{X}=x,\mathsf{Z}^m=z}((\boldsymbol{t}, t)) \tag{3.18}$$

$$\boldsymbol{\Sigma} = -\left(\left(\left.\frac{\partial^2 \ln\left(\mathbf{f}_{\mathsf{T}^{m+1}|\mathsf{X}=x,\mathsf{Z}^m=z}((\boldsymbol{t}, t))\right)}{\partial t_i \partial t_j}\right|_{t_i=\mu_i, t_j=\mu_j}\right)_{i,j=1}^{m+1,m+1}\right)^{-1}. \tag{3.19}$$

2. We can use a Markov chain to sample from $\mathbf{P}_{\mathsf{T}^{m+1}|\mathsf{X}=x,\mathsf{Z}^m=z}$ and use a Monte Carlo approximation to the integral. So, given K samples $(\boldsymbol{t}_1, t_1), \ldots, (\boldsymbol{t}_K, t_K)$ we approximate the predictive distribution by averaging over the samples

$$\mathbf{P}_{\mathsf{Y}|\mathsf{X}=x,\mathsf{Z}^m=z}(y) \approx \frac{1}{K}\sum_{i=1}^{K} \mathbf{P}_{\mathsf{Y}|\mathsf{T}=t_i}(y) .$$

Note that in order to generate samples $t_i \in \mathbb{R}$ we also have to sample $\boldsymbol{t}_i \in \mathbb{R}^m$ although these are not used in the final approximation.

Let us pursue the first idea and determine the maximizer $\boldsymbol{\mu} = \left(\hat{\boldsymbol{t}}, \hat{t}\right)$ of $\mathbf{f}_{\mathsf{T}^{m+1}|\mathsf{X}=x,\mathsf{Z}^m=z}$. In Appendix B.7 we show that the maximization can be decomposed into a maximization over the real-valued outputs $\boldsymbol{t} \in \mathbb{R}^m$ of the latent variables corresponding to the m training objects and a maximization of the real-valued output $t \in \mathbb{R}$ at the new test object. We prove that the value $\hat{\boldsymbol{t}} \in \mathbb{R}^m$ is formally given by

$$\hat{\boldsymbol{t}} = \operatorname*{argmax}_{\boldsymbol{t}\in\mathbb{R}^m} \sum_{i=1}^{m} \ln\left(\mathbf{P}_{\mathsf{Y}|\mathsf{T}=t_i}(y_i)\right) - \boldsymbol{t}'\mathbf{G}^{-1}\boldsymbol{t} . \tag{3.20}$$

Having found this vector using an iterative Newton-Raphson update we can then compute $\hat{t}$ directly using $\hat{t} = \hat{\boldsymbol{t}}'\mathbf{G}^{-1}\mathbf{X}\mathbf{x}$. As a consequence, by Theorem A.29, and the results from Appendix B.7, it follows that

$$\mathbf{P}_{\mathsf{T}|\mathsf{X}=x,\mathsf{Z}^m=z} = \text{Normal}\left(\hat{\boldsymbol{t}}'\mathbf{G}^{-1}\mathbf{X}\mathbf{x}, \mathbf{x}'\mathbf{x} - \mathbf{x}'\mathbf{X}'(\mathbf{I}+\mathbf{P}\mathbf{G})^{-1}\mathbf{P}\mathbf{X}\mathbf{x}\right) = \text{Normal}\left(\hat{t}, \upsilon^2\right),$$

where $\mathbf{P}$ is a $m \times m$ diagonal matrix with entries $\beta^{-1} \cdot \mathbf{P}_{\mathsf{Y}|\mathsf{T}=\hat{t}_i}(1)\left(1 - \mathbf{P}_{\mathsf{Y}|\mathsf{T}=\hat{t}_i}(1)\right)$. The benefit of this consideration is that the problem of determining the predictive distribution (3.17) reduces to computing

$$\mathbf{P}_{\mathsf{Y}|\mathsf{X}=x,\mathsf{Z}^m=z}(y) = \int_{\mathbb{R}} \mathbf{P}_{\mathsf{Y}|\mathsf{T}=t}(y)\,\mathbf{f}_{\mathsf{T}|\mathsf{X}=x,\mathsf{Z}^m=z}(t)\,dt\,, \tag{3.21}$$

which is now computationally feasible because $\mathbf{f}_{\mathsf{T}|\mathsf{X}=x,\mathsf{Z}^m=z}$ is a normal density only depending on the two parameters $\hat{t}$ and υ^2. In practice, we would approximate the function $\mathbf{P}_{\mathsf{Y}|\mathsf{T}=t}$ by Gaussian densities to be able to evaluate this expression numerically. However, if all we need is the classification, we exploit the fact that $\text{sign}(\hat{t})$ always equals the class $y \in \{-1, +1\}$ with the larger probability $\mathbf{P}_{\mathsf{Y}|\mathsf{X}=x,\mathsf{Z}^m=z}(y)$ (see Appendix B.7). In this case it suffices to compute the vector $\hat{\mathbf{t}} \in \mathbb{R}^m$ using equation (3.20) and to classify a new point according to

$$h_{\text{GPC}}(x) = \text{sign}\left(\sum_{i=1}^{m} \hat{\alpha}_i k(x_i, x)\right), \qquad \hat{\boldsymbol{\alpha}} = \mathbf{G}^{-1}\hat{\mathbf{t}}\,. \tag{3.22}$$

In Appendix B.7 we derive a stable algorithm to compute the vector $\hat{\boldsymbol{\alpha}} \in \mathbb{R}^m$ of expansion coefficients[6]. The pseudocode of the algorithm can be found on page 328.

Remark 3.13 (Support vector classification learning) *A closer look at equation (3.16) reveals that this likelihood is equivalent to the inverse loss likelihood for the margin loss given in equation (2.42). This equivalence allows us to directly relate linear soft margin support vector machines and Gaussian process classification when using a Laplace approximation:*

1. *Since we only require the maximizing vector* $\hat{\mathbf{t}} \in \mathbb{R}^m$ *of latent real-valued outputs at the training objects* $\mathbf{x} \in \mathcal{X}^m$ *to be found, we know that we effectively search for one weight vector* $\hat{\mathbf{w}} = \sum_{i=1}^m \hat{\alpha}_i \mathbf{x}_i = \mathbf{X}'\hat{\boldsymbol{\alpha}}$. *In particular, using the linear expansion of the weight vector in the mapped training objects, we see that*

$$\hat{\mathbf{t}} = \mathbf{X}\hat{\mathbf{w}} = \mathbf{X}\mathbf{X}'\hat{\boldsymbol{\alpha}} = \mathbf{G}\hat{\boldsymbol{\alpha}}\,, \quad \Leftrightarrow \quad \hat{\boldsymbol{\alpha}} = \mathbf{G}^{-1}\hat{\mathbf{t}}\,.$$

2. *By the same argument we know that the term* $\mathbf{t}'\mathbf{G}^{-1}\mathbf{t}$ *equals* $\boldsymbol{\alpha}'\mathbf{G}\boldsymbol{\alpha} = \|\mathbf{w}\|^2$ *(assuming that* $\mathbf{w} = \mathbf{X}'\boldsymbol{\alpha}$ *exists in the linear span of the mapped training inputs).*

---

6 Basically, a closer look at equation (3.22) and (3.20) shows that, in order to obtain $\hat{\mathbf{t}}$, we need to invert the Gram matrix $\mathbf{G} \in \mathbb{R}^{m\times m}$ which is then used *again* to compute $\hat{\boldsymbol{\alpha}}$. If the Gram matrix is badly conditioned, i.e., the ratio between the largest and smallest eigenvector of $\mathbf{G}$ is significantly large, then the error in computing $\hat{\boldsymbol{\alpha}}$ by (3.22) can be very large although we may have found a good estimate $\hat{\mathbf{t}} \in \mathbb{R}^m$. Therefore, the algorithm presented avoids the "detour" via $\hat{\mathbf{t}}$ but *directly* optimizes w.r.t. $\boldsymbol{\alpha}$. The more general difficulty is that inverting a matrix is an ill-posed problem (see also Appendix A.4).

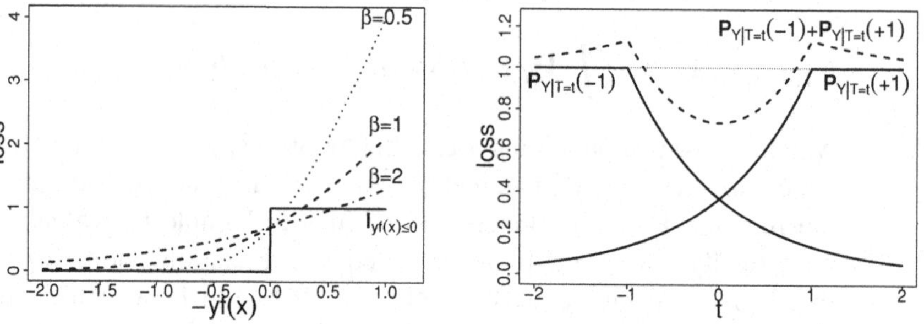

Figure 3.5 **(Left)** Approximation of the zero-one loss function $\mathbf{I}_{yt\leq 0}$ (solid line) by the sigmoidal loss given by $l_{\text{sigmoid}}(t, y) = \ln\left(1 + \exp\left(2\beta^{-1} \cdot yt\right)\right) - 2\beta^{-1}yt$ (dashed and dotted lines). Note that these loss functions are no longer upper bounds except when $\beta \to 0$. In this case, however, the loss becomes infinitely large whenever $yf(x) < 0$. **(Right)** Likelihood model induced by the hinge loss $l_{\text{lin}}(t, y) = \max\{1 - yt, 0\}$. Note that in contrast to the model given in equation (3.16), this likelihood is not normalizable.

Now, if we consider an inverse loss likelihood $\mathbf{P}_{\mathsf{Y}|\mathsf{T}=t}$ for the loss $l : \mathbb{R} \times \mathcal{Y} \to \mathbb{R}$ the maximizer $\hat{\mathbf{t}} \in \mathbb{R}^m$, of equation (3.20) must equal the minimizer $\hat{\mathbf{w}} \in \mathcal{K}$ of

$$-\sum_{i=1}^{m} \ln\left(\mathbf{P}_{\mathsf{Y}|\mathsf{T}=t_i}(y_i)\right) + \|\mathbf{w}\|^2 = \sum_{i=1}^{m} l_{\text{sigmoid}}\left(\langle \mathbf{x}_i, \mathbf{w}\rangle, y_i\right) + \|\mathbf{w}\|^2 , \qquad (3.23)$$

where $l_{\text{sigmoid}}(t, y) = \ln\left(1 + \exp\left(2\beta^{-1} \cdot yt\right)\right) - 2\beta^{-1}yt$. Note that $l_{\text{sigmoid}} : \mathbb{R} \times \mathcal{Y} \to \mathbb{R}$ is another approximation of the zero-one loss l_{0-1} (see Figure 3.5 (left) and equation (2.9)). In this sense, Gaussian processes for classification are another implementation of soft margin support vector machines.

3. *Using the identity (3.23) we could also try to find an interpretation of support vector machines as Gaussian process classification with a different likelihood model $\mathbf{P}_{\mathsf{Y}|\mathsf{T}=t}$. In fact, the likelihood model can easily be derived from (3.23) and (2.47) and is given by*

$$\mathbf{P}_{\mathsf{Y}|\mathsf{T}=t}(y) = \exp\left(-l_{\text{lin}}(t, y)\right) = \exp\left(-\max\{1 - yt, 0\}\right) .$$

In Figure 3.5 (right) we have plotted this likelihood model for varying values of $t \in \mathbb{R}$. As can be seen from the plots the problem with this loss-function induced likelihood model is that it cannot be normalized independently of the value $t = \langle \mathbf{x}, \mathbf{w}\rangle$. Hence, it is not directly possible to cast support vector machines into a probabilistic framework by relating them to a particular likelihood model.

3.3 The Relevance Vector Machine

In the last section we saw that a direct application of Bayesian ideas to the problem of regression estimation yields efficient algorithms known as Gaussian processes. In this section we will carry out the same analysis with a slightly refined prior $\mathbf{P_W}$ on linear functions $f_{\mathbf{w}}$ in terms of their weight vectors $\mathbf{w} \in \mathcal{K} \subseteq \ell_2^n$. As we will see in Section 5.2 an important quantity in the study of the generalization error is the sparsity $\|\mathbf{w}\|_0 = \sum_{i=1}^{n} \mathbf{I}_{w_i \neq 0}$ or $\|\boldsymbol{\alpha}\|_0$ of the weight vector or the vector of expansion coefficients, respectively. In particular, it is shown that the expected risk of the classifier $f_{\mathbf{w}}$ learned from a training sample $z \in \mathcal{Z}^m$ is, with high probability over the random draw of z, as small as $\approx \frac{\|\mathbf{w}\|_0}{n}$ or $\frac{\|\boldsymbol{\alpha}\|_0}{m}$, where n is the dimensionality of the feature space $\mathcal{K}$ and $\mathbf{w} = \sum_{i=1}^{m} \alpha_i \mathbf{x}_i = \mathbf{X}'\boldsymbol{\alpha}$. These results suggest favoring weight vectors with a small number of non-zero coefficients. One way to achieve this is to modify the prior in equation (3.8), giving

$$\mathbf{P_W} = \text{Normal}\left(\mathbf{0}, \boldsymbol{\Theta}\right) ,$$

where $\boldsymbol{\Theta} = \text{diag}\left(\boldsymbol{\theta}\right)$ and $\boldsymbol{\theta} = (\theta_1, \ldots, \theta_n)' \in \left(\mathbb{R}^+\right)^n$ is assumed known. The idea behind this prior is similar to the idea of automatic relevance determination given in Example 3.12. By considering $\theta_i \to 0$ we see that the only possible value for the ith component of the weight vector $\mathbf{w}$ is 0 and, therefore, even when considering the Bayesian prediction $Bayes_z$ the ith component is set to zero. In order to make inference we consider the likelihood model given in equation (3.9), that is, we assume that the target values $\boldsymbol{t} = (t_1, \ldots, t_m) \in \mathbb{R}^m$ are normally distributed with mean $\langle \mathbf{x}_i, \mathbf{w} \rangle$ and variance σ_t^2. Using Theorem A.28 it follows that the posterior measure over weight vectors $\mathbf{w}$ is again Gaussian, i.e.,

$$\mathbf{P_{W|X^m=x,T^m=t}} = \text{Normal}\left(\boldsymbol{\mu}, \boldsymbol{\Sigma}\right) ,$$

where the posterior covariance $\boldsymbol{\Sigma} \in \mathbb{R}^{n\times n}$ and mean $\boldsymbol{\mu} \in \mathbb{R}^n$ are given by

$$\boldsymbol{\Sigma} = \left(\sigma_t^{-2}\mathbf{X}'\mathbf{X} + \boldsymbol{\Theta}^{-1}\right)^{-1} , \qquad \boldsymbol{\mu} = \sigma_t^{-2}\boldsymbol{\Sigma}\mathbf{X}'\boldsymbol{t} = \left(\mathbf{X}'\mathbf{X} + \sigma_t^2\boldsymbol{\Theta}^{-1}\right)^{-1}\mathbf{X}'\boldsymbol{t} . \quad (3.24)$$

As described in the last section, the Bayesian prediction at a new test object $x \in \mathcal{X}$ is given by $Bayes_z(x) = \langle \mathbf{x}, \boldsymbol{\mu} \rangle$. Since we assumed that many of the θ_i are zero, i.e., the effective number $n_{\text{eff}} = \|\boldsymbol{\theta}\|_0$ of features $\phi_i : \mathcal{X} \to \mathbb{R}$ is small, it follows that $\boldsymbol{\Sigma}$ and $\boldsymbol{\mu}$ are easy to calculate[7]. The interesting question is: Given a

7 In practice, we delete all features $\phi_i : \mathcal{X} \to \mathbb{R}$ corresponding to small $\boldsymbol{\theta}$–values and fix the associated $\boldsymbol{\mu}$–values to zero.

training sample $z = (\boldsymbol{x}, \boldsymbol{t}) \in (\mathcal{X} \times \mathbb{R})^m$, how can we "learn" the sparse vector $\boldsymbol{\theta} = (\theta_1, \ldots, \theta_n)'$?

In the current formulation, the vector $\boldsymbol{\theta}$ is a model parameter and thus we shall employ evidence maximization to find the value $\hat{\boldsymbol{\theta}}$ that is best supported by the given training data $z = (\boldsymbol{x}, \boldsymbol{t})$. One of the greatest advantages is that we know the evidence $\mathbf{f}_{\mathsf{T}^m|\mathsf{X}^m=\boldsymbol{x}}(\boldsymbol{t})$ explicitly (see Theorem A.28),

$$\begin{aligned} \mathbf{f}_{\mathsf{T}^m|\mathsf{X}^m=\boldsymbol{x}}(\boldsymbol{t}) &= \mathbf{E}_{\mathsf{W}}\left[\mathbf{f}_{\mathsf{T}^m|\mathsf{X}^m=\boldsymbol{x},\mathsf{W}=\mathbf{w}}(\boldsymbol{t})\right] \\ &= (2\pi)^{-\frac{m}{2}} \left|\sigma_t^2\mathbf{I} + \mathbf{X}\boldsymbol{\Theta}\mathbf{X}'\right|^{-\frac{1}{2}} \exp\left(-\frac{\boldsymbol{t}'\left(\sigma_t^2\mathbf{I} + \mathbf{X}\boldsymbol{\Theta}\mathbf{X}'\right)^{-1}\boldsymbol{t}}{2}\right). \end{aligned} \tag{3.25}$$

In Appendix B.8 we derive explicit update rules for $\boldsymbol{\theta}$ and σ_t^2 which, in case of convergence, are guaranteed to find a local maximum of the evidence (3.25). The update rules are given by

$$\theta_i^{(\text{new})} = \frac{\mu_i^2}{\zeta_i}, \qquad \left(\sigma_t^2\right)^{(\text{new})} = \frac{\|\boldsymbol{t} - \mathbf{X}\boldsymbol{\mu}\|^2}{m - \sum_{i=1}^n \zeta_i}, \qquad \zeta_i = 1 - \theta_i^{-1}\Sigma_{ii}.$$

Interestingly, during application of these update rules, it turns out that many of the θ_i decrease quickly toward zero which leads to a high sparsity in the mean weight vector $\boldsymbol{\mu}$. Note that, whenever θ_i falls below a pre-specified threshold, we delete the ith column from $\mathbf{X}$ as well as θ_i itself which reduces the number of features used by one. This leads to a faster convergence of the algorithm as it progresses because the necessary inversion of the matrix $\sigma_t^{-2}\mathbf{X}'\mathbf{X} + \boldsymbol{\Theta}^{-1}$ in (3.24) is computationally less demanding. After termination, all components $\hat{w}_i$ of the learned weight vector $\hat{\mathbf{w}} \in \mathbb{R}^n$, for which θ_i is below the threshold, are set to exactly 0; the remaining coefficients $\hat{w}_i$ are set equal to corresponding values in $\boldsymbol{\mu} = \sigma_t^{-2}\boldsymbol{\Sigma}\mathbf{X}'\boldsymbol{t}$.

In order to apply this algorithm (which has so far been developed for the case of regression estimation only) to our initial problem of classification learning (recall, are given a sample $z = (\boldsymbol{x}, \boldsymbol{y}) \in (\mathcal{X} \times \{-1, +1\})^m$ of object-class pairs), we use the idea outlined in the previous subsection. In particular, when computing the predictive distribution $\mathbf{P}_{\mathsf{Y}|\mathsf{X}=x,\mathsf{Z}^m=z}$ of the class $y \in \{-1, +1\}$ at a new test object $x \in \mathcal{X}$, we consider $m + 1$ latent variables $\mathsf{T}_1, \ldots, \mathsf{T}_m, \mathsf{T}_{m+1}$ at all the m training objects $\boldsymbol{x} \in \mathcal{X}^m$ and at the test object $x \in \mathcal{X}$, computed by applying a latent weight vector W to all the $m + 1$ mapped objects $(\boldsymbol{x}, x) \in \mathcal{X}^{m+1}$. By marginalizing over all the possible values $\mathbf{w} \in \mathbb{R}^n$ of W we obtain

$$\mathbf{P}_{\mathsf{Y}|\mathsf{X}=x,\mathsf{Z}^m=z}(y) = \mathbf{E}_{\mathsf{W}|\mathsf{X}=x,\mathsf{Z}^m=z}\left[\mathbf{P}_{\mathsf{Y}|\mathsf{X}=x,\mathsf{Z}^m=z,\mathsf{W}=\mathbf{w}}(y)\right]$$

$$= \int_{\mathbb{R}^n} \mathbf{P}_{\mathsf{Y}|\mathsf{X}=x,\mathbf{W}=\mathbf{w}}(y) \cdot \mathbf{f}_{\mathbf{W}|\mathsf{Z}^m=z}(\mathbf{w})\, d\mathbf{w}\,.$$

Note that $\mathbf{P}_{\mathsf{Y}|\mathsf{X}=x,\mathbf{W}=\mathbf{w}}(y) = \mathbf{P}_{\mathsf{Y}|\mathsf{T}=\langle \mathbf{x},\mathbf{w}\rangle}(y)$ where $\mathbf{P}_{\mathsf{Y}|\mathsf{T}=t}$ is given by equation (3.16). Similarly to the Gaussian process case, the problem with this integral is that it cannot be performed analytically because the integrand $\mathbf{f}_{\mathbf{W}|\mathsf{Z}^m=z}(\mathbf{w})$ is no longer Gaussian. We shall therefore exploit the idea of using a Laplace approximation to it, i.e., approximating this density by a Gaussian density with the mean $\boldsymbol{\mu} \in \mathbb{R}^n$ and the covariance $\boldsymbol{\Sigma} \in \mathbb{R}^{n \times n}$ given by

$$\boldsymbol{\mu} = \operatorname*{argmax}_{\mathbf{w} \in \mathbb{R}^n} \mathbf{f}_{\mathbf{W}|\mathsf{Z}^m=z}(\mathbf{w})\,, \tag{3.26}$$

$$\boldsymbol{\Sigma} = \left(\left(-\left. \frac{\partial^2 \ln\left(\mathbf{f}_{\mathbf{W}|\mathsf{Z}^m=z}(\mathbf{w})\right)}{\partial w_i \partial w_j} \right|_{w_i=\mu_i, w_j=\mu_j} \right)_{i,j=1}^{n,n} \right)^{-1}. \tag{3.27}$$

As we essentially aim to finding $\hat{\boldsymbol{\theta}} \in \left(\mathbb{R}^+\right)^n$ it turns out that the Laplacian approximation is a perfect choice because it allows us to estimate $\hat{\boldsymbol{\theta}}$ by iterating the following scheme:

1. For a fixed valued $\boldsymbol{\theta} \in \left(\mathbb{R}^+\right)^n$ we compute the Laplacian approximation to $\mathbf{f}_{\mathbf{W}|\mathsf{Z}^m=z}$ yielding $\boldsymbol{\mu}$ and a covariance matrix $\boldsymbol{\Sigma}$.
2. Using the current values of $\boldsymbol{\mu}$ and $\boldsymbol{\Sigma}$ we make one update step on $\boldsymbol{\theta}$. Note that in the classification case we omit a variance $\sigma_t^2 \in \mathbb{R}^+$ on the latent variables T_i.

It is worth mentioning that we formulate the Laplacian approximation in terms of the weight vectors $\mathbf{w}$ rather than the real-valued outputs $\boldsymbol{t} \in \mathbb{R}^m$. This is because, for classification, whenever $\|\boldsymbol{\theta}\|_0 < m$ (we identify fewer features than training examples), the covariance matrix of $\boldsymbol{t}$ cannot have full rank, which would cause numerical instabilities in the resulting algorithm. The two algorithms for regression estimation and classification are given on pages 329 and 330, respectively.

In order to understand why this algorithm is called a *relevance vector machine* we note that it is also possible to use a kernel function $k : \mathcal{X} \times \mathcal{X} \to \mathbb{R}$ evaluated at the training objects $\boldsymbol{x} \in \mathcal{X}^m$ as m features $\phi_i = k(x_i, \cdot)$. In this case the weight vector $\mathbf{w}$ becomes the vector $\boldsymbol{\alpha} \in \mathbb{R}^m$ of expansion coefficients and the data matrix $\mathbf{X} \in \mathbb{R}^{m \times n}$ is given by the Gram matrix $\mathbf{G} \in \mathbb{R}^{m \times m}$. The algorithm aims to find the smallest subset of training objects such that the target values $\boldsymbol{t} \in \mathbb{R}^m$ (regression estimation) or the class labels $\boldsymbol{y} \in \{-1, +1\}^m$ (classification) can be well explained

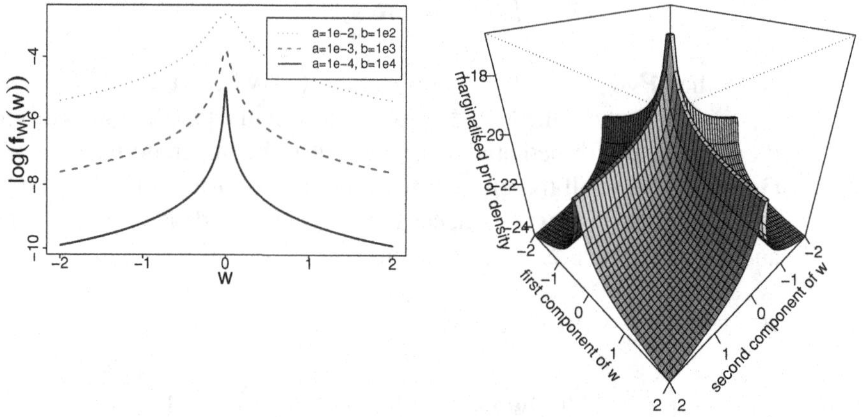

Figure 3.6 **(Left)** Marginalized log-prior densities $\mathbf{f}_{\mathsf{W}_i}$ over single weight vector components $\mathbf{w}_i$ implicitly considered in relevance vector machines. Relevance vector machines are recovered for the case of $a \to 0$ and $b \to \infty$ in which the prior is indefinitely peaked at $w = 0$. **(Right)** Surface plot for the special case of $n = 2$ and $b = a^{-1} = 1\,000$. Note that this prior favors one zero weight vector component $w_1 = 0$ much more that two very small values $|w_1|$ and $|w_2|$ and is sometimes called a *sparsity* prior.

by

$$f(\cdot) = \sum_{i=1}^{m} \alpha_i k(x_i, \cdot) , \qquad h(\cdot) = \operatorname{sign}\left(\sum_{i=1}^{m} \alpha_i k(x_i, \cdot)\right) . \tag{3.28}$$

All the training objects $x_i \in \boldsymbol{x}$ which have a non-zero coefficient α_i are termed *relevance vectors* because they appear the most relevant for the correct prediction of the whole training sample.[8] The appealing feature when using models of the form (3.28) is that we still learn a linear classifier (function) in some feature space $\mathcal{K}$. Not only does it allow us to apply all the theoretical results we shall obtain in Part II of this book but the geometrical picture given in Section 2.1 is also still valid for this algorithm.

Remark 3.14 (Sparsity in relevance vector machines) *In a fully Bayesian treatment, rather than using just one value $\hat{\boldsymbol{\theta}}$ of the parameters $\boldsymbol{\theta}$ we should define a*

8 Another reason for terming them relevance vectors is that the idea underlying the algorithm is motivated by automatic relevance determination, introduced in Example 3.12 (personal communication with M. Tipping).

prior $\mathbf{P_Q}$ *over all possible values of* $\boldsymbol{\theta} \in \mathbb{R}^n$ *and then marginalize, i.e.,*

$$\mathbf{f}_{\mathsf{T}|\mathsf{X}=x,\mathsf{X}^m=x,\mathsf{T}^m=t}(t) = \frac{\mathbf{E_Q}\left[\mathbf{E}_{\mathsf{W}|\mathsf{Q}=\boldsymbol{\theta}}\left[\mathbf{f}_{\mathsf{T}^{m+1}|\mathsf{X}=x,\mathsf{X}^m=x,\mathsf{W}=\mathbf{w}}((t,t))\right]\right]}{\mathbf{E_Q}\left[\mathbf{E}_{\mathsf{W}|\mathsf{Q}=\boldsymbol{\theta}}\left[\mathbf{f}_{\mathsf{T}^m|\mathsf{X}^m=x,\mathsf{W}=\mathbf{w}}(t)\right]\right]}$$
$$= \frac{\mathbf{E_Q}\left[\mathbf{f}_{\mathsf{T}^{m+1}|\mathsf{X}=x,\mathsf{X}^m=x,\mathsf{Q}=\boldsymbol{\theta}}((t,t))\right]}{\mathbf{E_Q}\left[\mathbf{f}_{\mathsf{T}^m|\mathsf{X}^m=x,\mathsf{Q}=\boldsymbol{\theta}}(t)\right]}\,.$$

The problem with the latter expression is that we cannot analytically compute the final integral. Although we get a closed form expression for the density $\mathbf{f}_{\mathsf{T}^m|\mathsf{X}^m=x,\mathsf{Q}=\boldsymbol{\theta}}$ *(a Gaussian measure derived in equation (3.25)) we cannot perform the expectation analytically regardless of the prior distribution chosen. When using a product of Gamma distributions for* $\mathbf{P_Q}$*, i.e.,* $\mathbf{f_Q}(\boldsymbol{\theta}) = \prod_{i=1}^{n} \mathrm{Gamma}(a,b)\left(\theta_i^{-1}\right)$*, it can be shown, however, that, in the limit of* $a \to 0$ *and* $b \to \infty$*, the mode of the joint distribution* $\mathbf{f}_{\mathsf{QT}^m|\mathsf{X}^m=x}(\boldsymbol{\theta}, \mathbf{t})$ *equals the vector* $\hat{\boldsymbol{\theta}}$ *and* $\hat{\mathbf{t}} = \mathbf{X}\boldsymbol{\mu}$ *(see equation (3.24)) as computed by the relevance vector machine algorithm. Hence, the relevance vector machine—which performs evidence maximization over the hyperparameters* $\boldsymbol{\theta} \in \mathbb{R}^n$*—can also be viewed as a maximum-a-posteriori estimator of* $\mathbf{P}_{\mathsf{WQ}|\mathsf{X}^m=x,\mathsf{T}^m=t}$ *because* $\mathbf{t} = \mathbf{Xw}$*. As such it is interesting to investigate the* marginalized prior $\mathbf{P_W} = \mathbf{E_Q}\left[\mathbf{P}_{\mathsf{W}|\mathsf{Q}=\boldsymbol{\theta}}\right]$. *In Figure 3.6 we have depicted the form of this marginalized prior for a single component (left) and for the special case of a two-dimensional feature space (right). It can be seen from these plots that, by the implicit choice of this prior, the relevance vector machine looks for a mode* $\hat{\boldsymbol{\theta}}$ *in a posterior density which has almost all a-priori probability mass on sparse solutions. This somewhat explains why the relevance vector machine algorithm tends to find very sparse solutions.*

3.4 Bayes Point Machines

The algorithms introduced in the last two sections solve the classification learning problem by taking a "detour" via the regression estimation problem. For each training object it is assumed that we have prior knowledge $\mathbf{P_W}$ about the latent variables T_i corresponding to the logit transformation of the probability of x_i being from the observed class y_i. This is a quite cumbersome assumption as we are unable to directly express prior knowledge on observed quantities such as the class labels $\mathbf{y} \in \mathcal{Y}^m = \{-1, +1\}^m$. In this section we are going to consider an algorithm which results from a direct modeling of the classes.

Let us start by defining the prior $\mathbf{P_W}$. In the classification case we note that, for any $\lambda > 0$, the weight vectors $\mathbf{w}$ and $\lambda\mathbf{w}$ perform the same classification because $\operatorname{sign}(\langle\mathbf{x},\mathbf{w}\rangle) = \operatorname{sign}(\langle\mathbf{x},\lambda\mathbf{w}\rangle)$. As a consequence we consider only weight vectors of unit length, i.e., $\mathbf{w} \in \mathcal{W}$, $\mathcal{W} = \{\mathbf{w} \in \mathcal{K} \mid \|\mathbf{w}\| = 1\}$ (see also Section 2.1). In the absence of any prior knowledge we assume a uniform prior measure $\mathbf{P_W}$ over the unit hypersphere $\mathcal{W}$. An argument in favor of the uniform prior is that the belief in the weight vector $\mathbf{w}$ should be equal to the belief in the weight vector $-\mathbf{w}$ under the assumption of equal class probabilities $\mathbf{P_Y}(-1)$ and $\mathbf{P_Y}(+1)$. Since the classification $\mathbf{y}_{-\mathbf{w}} = (\operatorname{sign}(\langle\mathbf{x}_1,-\mathbf{w}\rangle),\ldots,\operatorname{sign}(\langle\mathbf{x}_m,-\mathbf{w}\rangle))$ of the weight vector $-\mathbf{w}$ at the training sample $z \in \mathcal{Z}^m$ equals the negated classification $-\mathbf{y}_\mathbf{w} = -(\operatorname{sign}(\langle\mathbf{x}_1,\mathbf{w}\rangle),\ldots,\operatorname{sign}(\langle\mathbf{x}_m,\mathbf{w}\rangle))$ of $\mathbf{w}$ it follows that the assumption of equal belief in $\mathbf{w}$ and $-\mathbf{w}$ corresponds to assuming that $\mathbf{P_Y}(-1) = \mathbf{P_Y}(+1) = \frac{1}{2}$.

In order to derive an appropriate likelihood model, let us assume that there is no noise on the classifications, that is, we shall use the PAC-likelihood l_{PAC} as given in Definition 3.3. Note that such a likelihood model corresponds to using the zero-one loss l_{0-1} in the machine learning scenario (see equations (2.10) and (3.2)). According to Bayes' theorem it follows that the posterior belief in weight vectors (and therefore in classifiers) is given by

$$\begin{aligned} \mathbf{f}_{\mathbf{W}|\mathbf{Z}^m=z}(\mathbf{w}) &= \frac{\mathbf{P}_{\mathbf{Y}^m|\mathbf{X}^m=x,\mathbf{W}=\mathbf{w}}(y)\,\mathbf{f_W}(\mathbf{w})}{\mathbf{P}_{\mathbf{Y}^m|\mathbf{X}^m=x}(y)} \\ &= \begin{cases} \frac{1}{\mathbf{P_W}(V(z))} & \text{if } \mathbf{w} \in V(z) \\ 0 & \text{otherwise} \end{cases}. \end{aligned} \tag{3.29}$$

The set $V(z) \subseteq \mathcal{W}$ is called version space and is the set of all weight vectors that parameterize classifiers which classify all the training objects correctly (see also Definition 2.12). Due to the PAC-likelihood, any weight vector $\mathbf{w}$ which does not have this property is "cut-off" resulting in a uniform posterior measure $\mathbf{P}_{\mathbf{W}|\mathbf{Z}^m=z}$ over version space. Given a new test object $x \in \mathcal{X}$ we can compute the predictive distribution $\mathbf{P}_{\mathbf{Y}|\mathbf{X}=x,\mathbf{Z}^m=z}$ of the class label y at $x \in \mathcal{X}$ by

$$\mathbf{P}_{\mathbf{Y}|\mathbf{X}=x,\mathbf{Z}^m=z}(y) = \mathbf{P}_{\mathbf{W}|\mathbf{Z}^m=z}(\operatorname{sign}(\langle\mathbf{x},\mathbf{W}\rangle) = y)\,.$$

The Bayes classification strategy based on $\mathbf{P}_{\mathbf{Y}|\mathbf{X}=x,\mathbf{Z}^m=z}$ decides on the class label with the larger probability. An appealing feature of the two class case $\mathcal{Y} = \{-1,+1\}$ is that this decision can also be written as

$$Bayes_z(x) = \operatorname{sign}\left(\mathbf{E}_{\mathbf{W}|\mathbf{Z}^m=z}\left[\operatorname{sign}(\langle\mathbf{x},\mathbf{W}\rangle)\right]\right), \tag{3.30}$$

that is, the Bayes classification strategy effectively performs majority voting involving all version space classifiers. The difficulty with the latter expression is that we cannot analytically compute the expectation as this requires efficient integration of a convex body on a hypersphere (see also Figure 2.1 and 2.8). Hence, we approximate the Bayes classification strategy by a *single* classifier.

Definition 3.15 (Bayes point) *Given a training sample* z *and a posterior measure* $\mathbf{P}_{\mathsf{W}|\mathsf{Z}^m=z}$ *over the unit hypersphere* $\mathcal{W}$*, the* Bayes point $\mathbf{w}_{\text{bp}} \in \mathcal{W}$ *is defined*

$$\mathbf{w}_{\text{bp}} = \underset{\mathbf{w}\in\mathcal{W}}{\operatorname{argmin}} \ \mathbf{E}_{\mathsf{X}}\left[l_{0-1}\left(Bayes_z\left(\mathsf{X}\right), \operatorname{sign}\left(\left\langle \boldsymbol{\phi}\left(\mathsf{X}\right), \mathbf{w}\right\rangle\right)\right)\right],$$

that is, the Bayes point is the optimal projection of the Bayes classification strategy to a single classifier $\mathbf{w}_{\text{bp}}$ *w.r.t. generalization error.*

Although the Bayes point is easily defined its computation is much more difficult because it requires complete knowledge of the input distribution $\mathbf{P}_{\mathsf{X}}$. Moreover, it requires a minimisation process w.r.t. the Bayes classification strategy which involves the posterior measure $\mathbf{P}_{\mathsf{W}|\mathsf{Z}^m=z}$—a computationally difficult task. A closer look at equation (3.30), however, shows that a another reasonable approximation to the Bayes classification strategy is given by exchanging sign $(\cdot)$ and expectation, i.e.,

$$h_{\text{cm}}(x) = \operatorname{sign}\left(\operatorname{sign}\left(\mathbf{E}_{\mathsf{W}|\mathsf{Z}^m=z}\left[\langle \mathbf{x}, \mathbf{W}\rangle\right]\right)\right) = \operatorname{sign}\left(\left\langle \mathbf{x}, \underbrace{\mathbf{E}_{\mathsf{W}|\mathsf{Z}^m=z}\left[\mathbf{W}\right]}_{\mathbf{w}_{\text{cm}}}\right\rangle\right).$$

The idea behind this "trick" is that, if the version space $V(z)$ is almost point-symmetric w.r.t. $\mathbf{w}_{\text{cm}}$ then, for each weight vector $\mathbf{w} \in V(z)$ in version space, there exists another weight vector $\tilde{\mathbf{w}} = 2\mathbf{w}_{\text{cm}} - \mathbf{w} \in V(z)$ also in version space and, thus,

$$\operatorname{sign}\left(\langle \mathbf{x}, \mathbf{w}\rangle\right) + \operatorname{sign}\left(\langle \mathbf{x}, \tilde{\mathbf{w}}\rangle\right) = \begin{cases} 2 \cdot \operatorname{sign}\left(\langle \mathbf{x}, \mathbf{w}_{\text{cm}}\rangle\right) & \text{if } \left|\langle \mathbf{x}, \mathbf{w}\rangle\right| < \left|\langle \mathbf{x}, \mathbf{w}_{\text{cm}}\rangle\right| \\ 0 & \text{otherwise} \end{cases},$$

that is, the Bayes classification of a new test object equals the classification carried out by the single weight vector $\mathbf{w}_{\text{cm}}$. The advantage of the classifier $\mathbf{w}_{\text{cm}}$—which is also the center of mass of version space $V(z)$—is that it can be computed or estimated without any extra knowledge about the data distribution. Since the center of mass is another approximation to the Bayes classification we call every algorithm that computes $\mathbf{w}_{\text{cm}}$ a *Bayes point algorithm*, although the formal definition of the Bayes point approximation is slightly different. In the following subsection we present one possible algorithm for estimating the center of mass.

3.4.1 Estimating the Bayes Point

The main idea in computing the center of mass of version space is to replace the analytical integral by a sum over randomly drawn classifiers, i.e.,

$$\mathbf{w}_{\text{cm}} = \mathbf{E}_{\mathsf{W}|\mathsf{Z}^m=z}\left[\mathsf{W}\right] \approx \frac{1}{K}\sum_{i=1}^{K}\mathbf{w}_i \qquad \mathbf{w}_i \sim \mathbf{P}_{\mathsf{W}|\mathsf{Z}^m=z}\,.$$

Such methods are known as *Monte-Carlo* methods and have proven to be successful in practice. A difficulty we encounter with this approach is in obtaining samples $\mathbf{w}_i$ drawn according to the distribution $\mathbf{P}_{\mathsf{W}|\mathsf{Z}^m=z}$. Recalling that $\mathbf{P}_{\mathsf{W}|\mathsf{Z}^m=z}$ is uniform in a convex polyhedra on the surface of hypersphere in feature space we see that it is quite difficult to directly sample from it. A commonly used approach to this problem is to approximate the sampling distribution $\mathbf{P}_{\mathsf{W}|\mathsf{Z}^m=z}$ by a Markov chain. A *Markov chain* is fully specified by a probability distribution $\mathbf{P}_{\mathsf{W}_1\mathsf{W}_2}$ where $\mathbf{f}_{\mathsf{W}_1\mathsf{W}_2}((\mathbf{w}_1, \mathbf{w}_2))$ is the "transition" probability for progressing from a randomly drawn weight vector $\mathbf{w}_1$ to another weight vector $\mathbf{w}_2$. Sampling from the Markov chain involves iteratively drawing a new weight vector $\mathbf{w}_{i+1}$ by sampling from $\mathbf{P}_{\mathsf{W}_2|\mathsf{W}_1=\mathbf{w}_i}$. The Markov chain is called *ergodic w.r.t.* $\mathbf{P}_{\mathsf{W}|\mathsf{Z}^m=z}$ if the limiting distribution of this sampling process is $\mathbf{P}_{\mathsf{W}|\mathsf{Z}^m=z}$ regardless of our choice of $\mathbf{w}_0$. Then, it suffices to start with a random weight vector $\mathbf{w}_0 \in \mathcal{W}$ and at each step, to obtain a new sample $\mathbf{w}_i \in \mathcal{W}$ drawn according to $\mathbf{P}_{\mathsf{W}_2|\mathsf{W}_1=\mathbf{w}_{i-1}}$. The combination of these two techniques has become known as the Markov-Chain-Monte-Carlo (MCMC) method for estimating the expectation $\mathbf{E}_{\mathsf{W}|\mathsf{Z}^m=z}\left[\mathsf{W}\right]$.

We now outline an MCMC algorithm for approximating the Bayes point by the center of mass of version space $V(z)$ (the whole pseudo code is given on page 332). Since it is difficult to generate weight vectors that parameterize classifiers consistent with the whole training sample $z \in \mathcal{Z}^m$ we average over the trajectory of a ball which is placed inside version space and bounced like a billiard ball. As a consequence we call this MCMC method the kernel billiard. We express each position $\mathbf{b} \in \mathcal{W}$ of the ball and each estimate $\mathbf{w}_i \in \mathcal{W}$ of the center of mass of $V(z)$ as a linear combination of the mapped training objects, i.e.,

$$\mathbf{w} = \sum_{i=1}^{m}\alpha_i\mathbf{x}_i\,, \quad \mathbf{b} = \sum_{i=1}^{m}\gamma_i\mathbf{x}_i\,, \qquad \boldsymbol{\alpha} \in \mathbb{R}^m\,, \quad \boldsymbol{\gamma} \in \mathbb{R}^m\,.$$

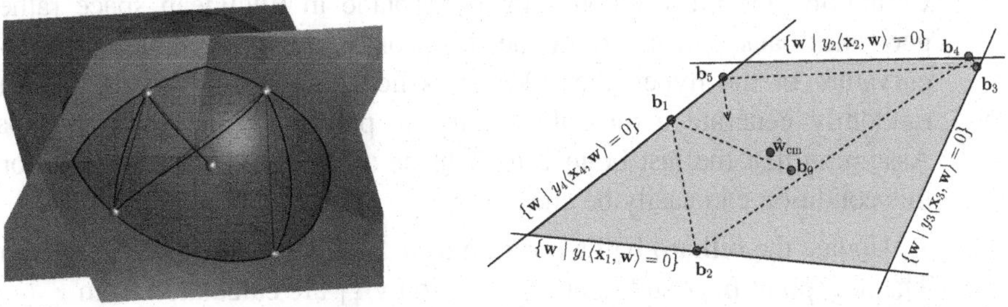

Figure 3.7 **(Left)** 5 samples $\mathbf{b}_1, \ldots, \mathbf{b}_5$ (white dots) obtained by playing billiards on the sphere in the special case of $\mathcal{W} \subseteq \mathbb{R}^3$. In the update step, only the chord length (gray lines) are taken into consideration. **(Right)** Schematic view of the kernel billiard algorithm. Starting at $\mathbf{w}_0 \in V(z)$ a trajectory of billiard bounces $\mathbf{b}_1, \ldots, \mathbf{b}_5, \ldots$ is computed and then averaged over so as to obtain an estimate $\hat{\mathbf{w}}_{\mathrm{cm}}$ of the center of mass of version space.

Without loss of generality we can make the following assumption about the needed direction vector $\mathbf{v}$

$$\mathbf{v} = \sum_{i=1}^{m} \beta_i \mathbf{x}_i\,, \qquad \boldsymbol{\beta} \in \mathbb{R}^m\,.$$

To begin we assume that $\mathbf{w}_0 = \mathbf{0} \Leftrightarrow \boldsymbol{\alpha} = \mathbf{0}$. Before generating a billiard trajectory in version space $V(z)$ we first run a learning algorithm to find an initial starting point $\mathbf{b}_0$ inside version space (e.g., kernel perceptron or support vector learning (see Algorithm 2 and Section D.2)). The *kernel billiard* algorithm then consists of three steps (see also Figure 3.7):

1. Determine the closest boundary starting from the position $\mathbf{b}_i$ in direction $\mathbf{v}_i$.
Since it is computationally very demanding to calculate the flight time of the billiard ball *on* geodesics of the hypersphere $\mathcal{W}$ we make use of the fact that the shortest distance in Euclidean space (if it exists) is also the shortest distance on the hypersphere $\mathcal{W}$. Thus, for the flight time τ_j of the billiard ball from position $\mathbf{b}_i$ in direction $\mathbf{v}_i$ to the hyperplane with normal vector $y_j\mathbf{x}_j$ we have

$$\tau_j = -\frac{\left\langle \mathbf{b}_i, \mathbf{x}_j \right\rangle}{\left\langle \mathbf{v}_i, \mathbf{x}_j \right\rangle}\,. \tag{3.31}$$

After computing all m flight times, we look for the smallest positive one,

$$c = \operatorname*{argmin}_{j:\tau_j > 0} \tau_j\,.$$

Computing the closest bounding hyperplane in Euclidean space rather than on geodesics causes problems if the direction vector $\mathbf{v}_i$ is almost orthogonal to the curvature of the hypersphere $\mathcal{W}$, in which case $\tau_c \to \infty$. If this happens we randomly generate a direction vector $\mathbf{v}_i$ pointing *toward* version space $V(z)$. Assuming that the last bounce took place at the hyperplane having normal $y_{c'}\mathbf{x}_{c'}$ this condition can easily be checked by $y_{c'} \langle \mathbf{v}_i, \mathbf{x}_{c'} \rangle > 0$.

2. Update the billiard ball's position to $\mathbf{b}_{i+1}$ and the new direction vector to $\mathbf{v}_{i+1}$. The new point $\mathbf{b}_{i+1}$ and the new direction $\mathbf{v}_{i+1}$ are calculated from

$$\mathbf{b}_{i+1} = \mathbf{b}_i + \tau_c \mathbf{v}_i \,, \tag{3.32}$$

$$\mathbf{v}_{i+1} = \mathbf{v}_i - 2\frac{\langle \mathbf{v}_i, \mathbf{x}_c \rangle}{\|\mathbf{x}_c\|^2}\mathbf{x}_c \,. \tag{3.33}$$

Afterwards, the position $\mathbf{b}_{i+1}$ must be normalized.

3. Update the center of mass $\mathbf{w}_i$ of the whole trajectory by the new line segment from $\mathbf{b}_i$ to $\mathbf{b}_{i+1}$ calculated on the hypersphere $\mathcal{W}$.

Since the solution $\mathbf{w}_\infty$ lies on the hypersphere $\mathcal{W}$ we cannot simply update the center of mass using weighted vector addition. Instead we use the operation $\oplus_\mu : \mathcal{W} \times \mathcal{W} \to \mathcal{W}$ acting on vectors of unit length and having the property that

$$\left\| \mathbf{m} - \left(\mathbf{w}_i \oplus_\mu \mathbf{m} \right) \right\| = \mu \cdot \| \mathbf{m} - \mathbf{w}_i \| \,,$$

that is, μ is the fraction between the resulting chord length $\left\| \mathbf{m} - \left(\mathbf{w}_i \oplus_\mu \mathbf{m} \right) \right\|$ and the total chord length $\| \mathbf{m} - \mathbf{w}_i \|$. It can be shown that

$$\mathbf{w}_i \oplus_\mu \mathbf{m} = \rho_1 \left(\langle \mathbf{w}_i, \mathbf{m} \rangle , \mu \right) \mathbf{w}_i + \rho_2 \left(\langle \mathbf{w}_i, \mathbf{m} \rangle , \mu \right) \mathbf{m}$$

where the explicit formulas for ρ_1 and ρ_2 can be found in Appendix B.9. Since the posterior density is uniform in version space, the whole line between $\mathbf{b}_i$ and $\mathbf{b}_{i+1}$ can be represented by the midpoint $\mathbf{m} \in V(z)$, given by

$$\mathbf{m} = \frac{\mathbf{b}_i + \mathbf{b}_{i+1}}{\|\mathbf{b}_i + \mathbf{b}_{i+1}\|} \,.$$

Thus, we can update the center of mass of the trajectory by

$$\mathbf{w}_{i+1} = \rho_1 \left(\langle \mathbf{w}_i, \mathbf{m} \rangle , \frac{\Xi_i}{\Xi_i + \xi_i} \right) \mathbf{w}_i + \rho_2 \left(\langle \mathbf{w}_i, \mathbf{m} \rangle , \frac{\Xi_i}{\Xi_i + \xi_i} \right) \mathbf{m} \,,$$

where $\xi_i = \|\mathbf{b}_i - \mathbf{b}_{i+1}\|$ is the length of the trajectory in the ith step and $\Xi_i = \sum_{j=1}^{i} \xi_j$ is the accumulated length up to the ith step. Note that the operation $\oplus_\mu$ is only an approximation to the addition operation we sought because an exact weighting would require arc lengths rather than chord lengths.

As a stopping criterion we compute an upper bound on ρ_2, the weighting factor of the new part of the trajectory. If this value falls below a prespecified threshold we stop the algorithm. Note that an increase in Ξ_i will always lead to termination.

3.5 Fisher Discriminants

In this last section we are going to consider one of the earliest approaches to the problem of classification learning. The idea underlying this approach is slightly different from the ideas outlined so far. Rather than using the decomposition $\mathbf{P}_{\mathsf{XY}} = \mathbf{P}_{\mathsf{Y}|\mathsf{X}}\mathbf{P}_{\mathsf{X}}$ we now decompose the unknown probability measure $\mathbf{P}_{\mathsf{XY}} = \mathbf{P}_{\mathsf{Z}}$ constituting the learning problem as $\mathbf{P}_{\mathsf{XY}} = \mathbf{P}_{\mathsf{X}|\mathsf{Y}}\mathbf{P}_{\mathsf{Y}}$. The essential difference between these two formal expressions becomes apparent when considering the model choices:

1. In the case of $\mathbf{P}_{\mathsf{XY}} = \mathbf{P}_{\mathsf{Y}|\mathsf{X}}\mathbf{P}_{\mathsf{X}}$ we use hypotheses $h \in \mathcal{H} \subseteq \mathcal{Y}^{\mathcal{X}}$ to model the conditional measure $\mathbf{P}_{\mathsf{Y}|\mathsf{X}}$ of class labels $y \in \mathcal{Y}$ given objects $x \in \mathcal{X}$ and marginalize over $\mathbf{P}_{\mathsf{X}}$. In the noise-free case, each hypothesis defines such a model by $\mathbf{P}_{\mathsf{Y}|\mathsf{X}=x,\mathsf{H}=h}(y) = \mathbf{I}_{h(x)=y}$. Since our model for learning contains only *predictors* $h : \mathcal{X} \to \mathcal{Y}$ that *discriminate* between objects, this approach is sometimes called the *predictive* or *discriminative* approach.

2. In the case of $\mathbf{P}_{\mathsf{XY}} = \mathbf{P}_{\mathsf{X}|\mathsf{Y}}\mathbf{P}_{\mathsf{Y}}$ we model the generation of objects $x \in \mathcal{X}$ given the class label $y \in \mathcal{Y} = \{-1, +1\}$ by some assumed probability model $\mathbf{P}_{\mathsf{X}|\mathsf{Y}=y,\mathsf{Q}=\boldsymbol{\theta}}$ where $\boldsymbol{\theta} = (\boldsymbol{\theta}_{+1}, \boldsymbol{\theta}_{-1}, p) \in \mathcal{Q}$ parameterizes this generation process. We have the additional parameter $p \in [0, 1]$ to describe the probability $\mathbf{P}_{\mathsf{Y}|\mathsf{Q}=\boldsymbol{\theta}}(y)$ by $p \cdot \mathbf{I}_{y=+1} + (1-p) \cdot \mathbf{I}_{y=-1}$. As the model $\mathcal{Q}$ contains probability measures from which the *generated* training sample $\boldsymbol{x} \in \mathcal{X}$ is *sampled*, this approach is sometimes called the *generative* or *sampling* approach.

In order to classify a new test object $x \in \mathcal{X}$ with a model $\boldsymbol{\theta} \in \mathcal{Q}$ in the generative approach we make use of Bayes' theorem, i.e.,

$$\mathbf{P}_{\mathsf{Y}|\mathsf{X}=x,\mathsf{Q}=\boldsymbol{\theta}}(y) = \frac{\mathbf{P}_{\mathsf{X}|\mathsf{Y}=y,\mathsf{Q}=\boldsymbol{\theta}}(x)\,\mathbf{P}_{\mathsf{Y}|\mathsf{Q}=\boldsymbol{\theta}}(y)}{\sum_{\tilde{y}\in\mathcal{Y}} \mathbf{P}_{\mathsf{X}|\mathsf{Y}=\tilde{y},\mathsf{Q}=\boldsymbol{\theta}}(x)\,\mathbf{P}_{\mathsf{Y}|\mathsf{Q}=\boldsymbol{\theta}}(\tilde{y})}\,.$$

In the case of two classes $\mathcal{Y} = \{-1, +1\}$ and the zero-one loss, as given in equation (2.10), we obtain for the Bayes optimal classification at a novel test object $x \in \mathcal{X}$,

$$
\begin{aligned}
h_{\boldsymbol{\theta}}(x) &= \underset{y \in \{-1,+1\}}{\operatorname{argmax}} \; \mathbf{P}_{\mathsf{Y}|\mathsf{X}=x}(y) \\
&= \operatorname{sign}\left(\ln\left(\frac{\mathbf{P}_{\mathsf{X}|\mathsf{Y}=+1,\mathbf{Q}=\boldsymbol{\theta}}(x) \cdot p}{\mathbf{P}_{\mathsf{X}|\mathsf{Y}=-1,\mathbf{Q}=\boldsymbol{\theta}}(x) \cdot (1-p)}\right)\right),
\end{aligned}
\tag{3.34}
$$

as the fraction in this expression is greater than one if, and only, if $\mathbf{P}_{\mathsf{XY}|\mathbf{Q}=\boldsymbol{\theta}}((x, +1))$ is greater than $\mathbf{P}_{\mathsf{XY}|\mathbf{Q}=\boldsymbol{\theta}}((x, -1))$. In the generative approach the task of learning amounts to finding the parameters $\boldsymbol{\theta}^* \in \mathcal{Q}$ or measures $\mathbf{P}_{\mathsf{X}|\mathsf{Y}=y,\mathbf{Q}=\boldsymbol{\theta}^*}$ and $\mathbf{P}_{\mathsf{Y}|\mathbf{Q}=\boldsymbol{\theta}^*}$ which incur the smallest expected risk $R[h_{\boldsymbol{\theta}^*}]$ by virtue of equation (3.34). Again, we are faced with the problem that, without restrictions on the measure $\mathbf{P}_{\mathsf{X}|\mathsf{Y}=y}$, the best model is the empirical measure $\mathbf{v}_{\boldsymbol{x}_y}(x)$, where $\boldsymbol{x}_y \subseteq \boldsymbol{x}$ is the sample of all training objects of class y. Obviously, this is a bad model because $\mathbf{v}_{\boldsymbol{x}_y}(x)$ assigns zero probability to all test objects not present in the training sample and thus $h_{\boldsymbol{\theta}}(x) = 0$, i.e., we are unable to make predictions on unseen objects. Similarly to the choice of the hypothesis space in the discriminative model we must constrain the possible generative models $\mathbf{P}_{\mathsf{X}|\mathsf{Y}=y}$.

Let us consider the class of probability measures from the exponential family

$$
\mathbf{f}_{\mathsf{X}|\mathsf{Y}=y,\mathbf{Q}=\boldsymbol{\theta}}(x) = a_0\left(\boldsymbol{\theta}_y\right) \tau_0(x) \exp\left(\boldsymbol{\theta}_y'(\boldsymbol{\tau}(x))\right),
$$

for some fixed function $a_0 : \mathcal{Q}_y \to \mathbb{R}$, $\tau_0 : \mathcal{X} \to \mathbb{R}$ and $\boldsymbol{\tau} : \mathcal{X} \to \mathcal{K}$. Using this functional form of the density we see that each decision function $h_{\boldsymbol{\theta}}$ must be of the following form

$$
\begin{aligned}
h_{\boldsymbol{\theta}}(x) &= \operatorname{sign}\left(\ln\left(\frac{a_0(\boldsymbol{\theta}_{+1}) \tau_0(x) \exp\left(\boldsymbol{\theta}_{+1}'(\boldsymbol{\tau}(x))\right) \cdot p}{a_0(\boldsymbol{\theta}_{-1}) \tau_0(x) \exp\left(\boldsymbol{\theta}_{-1}'(\boldsymbol{\tau}(x))\right)(1-p)}\right)\right) \\
&= \operatorname{sign}\left(\underbrace{(\boldsymbol{\theta}_{+1} - \boldsymbol{\theta}_{-1})}_{\mathbf{w}}(\boldsymbol{\tau}(x)) + \underbrace{\ln\left(\frac{a_0(\boldsymbol{\theta}_{+1}) \cdot p}{a_0(\boldsymbol{\theta}_{-1})(1-p)}\right)}_{b}\right) \\
&= \operatorname{sign}\left(\langle \mathbf{w}, \boldsymbol{\tau}(x) \rangle + b\right).
\end{aligned}
\tag{3.35}
$$

This result is very interesting as it shows that, for a rather large class of generative models, the final classification function is a linear function in the model parameters $\boldsymbol{\theta} = (\boldsymbol{\theta}_{-1}, \boldsymbol{\theta}_{+1}, p)$. Now, consider the special case that the distribution $\mathbf{P}_{\mathsf{X}|\mathsf{Y}=y,\mathbf{Q}=\boldsymbol{\theta}}$ of objects $x \in \mathcal{X}$ given class labels $y \in \{-1, +1\}$ is a multidimensional Gaussian

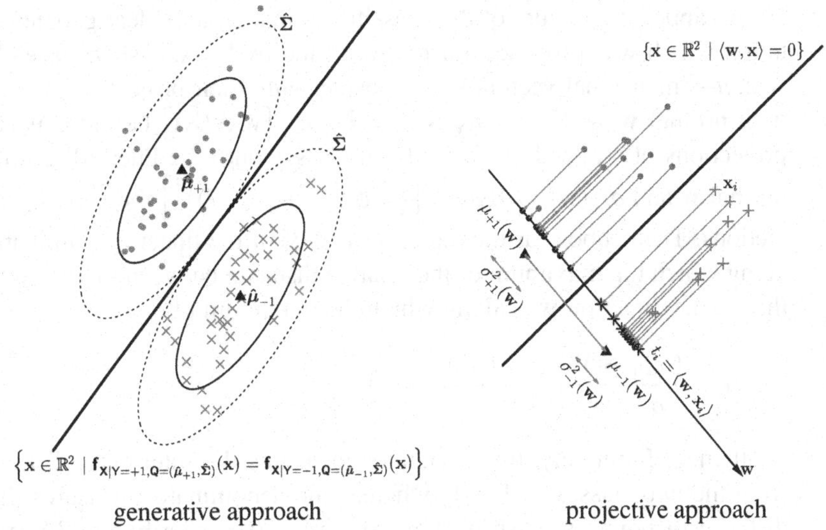

Figure 3.8 **(Left)** The Fisher discriminant estimated from 80 data points in $\mathbb{R}^2$. The black line represents the decision boundary. This must always be a linear function because both models use the same (estimated) covariance matrix $\hat{\boldsymbol{\Sigma}}$ (ellipses). **(Right)** A geometrical interpretation of the Fisher discriminant objective function (3.38). Given a weight vector $\mathbf{w} \in \mathcal{K}$, each mapped training object $\mathbf{x}$ is projected onto $\mathbf{w}$ by virtue of $t = \langle \mathbf{x}, \mathbf{w} \rangle$. The objective function measures the ratio of the inter-class distance $(\mu_{+1}(\mathbf{w}) - \mu_{-1}(\mathbf{w}))^2$ and the intra-class distance $\sigma^2_{+1}(\mathbf{w}) + \sigma^2_{-1}(\mathbf{w})$.

in some feature space $\mathcal{K} \subseteq \ell_2^n$ mapped into by some given feature map $\boldsymbol{\phi} : \mathcal{X} \to \mathcal{K}$,

$$\mathbf{f}_{\mathsf{X}|\mathsf{Y}=y,\mathsf{Q}=\boldsymbol{\theta}}(x) = (2\pi)^{-\frac{n}{2}} |\boldsymbol{\Sigma}|^{-\frac{1}{2}} \exp\left(-\frac{1}{2}\left(\mathbf{x} - \boldsymbol{\mu}_{\mu}\right)' \boldsymbol{\Sigma}^{-1}\left(\mathbf{x} - \boldsymbol{\mu}_y\right)\right), \tag{3.36}$$

where the parameters $\boldsymbol{\theta}_y$ are the mean vector $\boldsymbol{\mu}_y \in \mathbb{R}^n$ and the covariance matrix $\boldsymbol{\Sigma}_y \in \mathbb{R}^{n \times n}$, respectively. Making the additional assumptions that the covariance matrix $\boldsymbol{\Sigma}$ is the same for both models $\boldsymbol{\theta}_{+1}$ and $\boldsymbol{\theta}_{-1}$ and $p = \mathbf{P}_{\mathsf{Y}|\mathsf{Q}=\boldsymbol{\theta}}(+1) = \mathbf{P}_{\mathsf{Y}|\mathsf{Q}=\boldsymbol{\theta}}(-1) = \frac{1}{2}$ we see that, according to equations (A.16)–(A.17) and (3.35),

$$\boldsymbol{\tau}(x) = \mathbf{x}, \quad \mathbf{w} = \boldsymbol{\Sigma}^{-1}\left(\boldsymbol{\mu}_{+1} - \boldsymbol{\mu}_{-1}\right), \quad b = \frac{1}{2}\left(\boldsymbol{\mu}'_{-1}\boldsymbol{\Sigma}^{-1}\boldsymbol{\mu}_{-1} - \boldsymbol{\mu}'_{+1}\boldsymbol{\Sigma}^{-1}\boldsymbol{\mu}_{+1}\right). \tag{3.37}$$

This results also follows from substituting (3.36) directly into equation (3.34) (see Figure 3.8 (left)).

An appealing feature of this classifier is that it has a clear geometrical interpretation which was proposed for the first time by R. A. Fisher. Instead of working with n–dimensional vectors $\mathbf{x}$ we consider only their projection onto a hyperplane with normal $\mathbf{w} \in \mathcal{K}$. Let $\mu_y(\mathbf{w}) = \mathbf{E}_{\mathsf{X}|\mathsf{Y}=y}\left[\mathbf{w}'\boldsymbol{\phi}(\mathsf{X})\right]$ be the expectation of the projections of mapped objects $\mathbf{x}$ from class y onto the linear discriminant having normal $\mathbf{w}$ and $\sigma_y^2(\mathbf{w}) = \mathbf{E}_{\mathsf{X}|\mathsf{Y}=y}\left[\left(\mathbf{w}'\boldsymbol{\phi}(\mathsf{X}) - \mu_y(\mathbf{w})\right)^2\right]$ the variance of these projections. Then choose as the direction $\mathbf{w} \in \mathcal{K}$ of the linear discriminant a direction along which the maximum of the relative distance between the $\mu_y(\mathbf{w})$ is obtained, that is, the direction $\mathbf{w}_{\mathrm{FD}}$ along which the maximum of

$$J(\mathbf{w}) = \frac{\left(\mu_{+1}(\mathbf{w}) - \mu_{-1}(\mathbf{w})\right)^2}{\sigma_{+1}^2(\mathbf{w}) + \sigma_{-1}^2(\mathbf{w})} \tag{3.38}$$

is attained. Intuitively, the numerator measures the inter-class distance of points from the two classes $\{-1, +1\}$ whereas the denominator measures the intra-class distance of points in each of the two classes (see also Figure 3.8 (right)). Thus, the function J is maximized if the inter-class distance is large and the intra-class distance is small. In general, the Fisher linear discriminant $\mathbf{w}_{\mathrm{FD}}$ suffers from the problem that its determination is a very difficult mathematical and algorithmical problem. However, in the particular case of[9] $\mathbf{P}_{\mathsf{X}|\mathsf{Y}=y,\mathsf{Q}=\boldsymbol{\theta}} = \mathrm{Normal}\left(\boldsymbol{\mu}_y, \boldsymbol{\Sigma}\right)$, a closed form solution to this problem is obtained by noticing that $\mathsf{T} = \mathbf{w}'\boldsymbol{\phi}(\mathsf{X})$ is also normally distributed with $\mathbf{P}_{\mathsf{T}|\mathsf{Y}=y,\mathsf{Q}=\boldsymbol{\theta}} = \mathrm{Normal}\left(\mathbf{w}'\boldsymbol{\mu}_y, \mathbf{w}'\boldsymbol{\Sigma}\mathbf{w}\right)$. Thus, the objective function given in equation (3.38) can be written as

$$J(\mathbf{w}) = \frac{\left(\mathbf{w}'\left(\boldsymbol{\mu}_{+1} - \boldsymbol{\mu}_{-1}\right)\right)^2}{\mathbf{w}'\boldsymbol{\Sigma}\mathbf{w} + \mathbf{w}'\boldsymbol{\Sigma}\mathbf{w}} = \frac{1}{2} \cdot \frac{\mathbf{w}'\left(\boldsymbol{\mu}_{+1} - \boldsymbol{\mu}_{-1}\right)\left(\boldsymbol{\mu}_{+1} - \boldsymbol{\mu}_{-1}\right)'\mathbf{w}}{\mathbf{w}'\boldsymbol{\Sigma}\mathbf{w}},$$

which is known as the generalized Rayleigh quotient having the maximizer $\mathbf{w}_{\mathrm{FD}}$

$$\mathbf{w}_{\mathrm{FD}} = \boldsymbol{\Sigma}^{-1}\left(\boldsymbol{\mu}_{+1} - \boldsymbol{\mu}_{-1}\right).$$

This expression equals the weight vector $\mathbf{w}$ found by considering the optimal classification under the assumption of a multidimensional Gaussian measure for the class conditional distributions $\mathbf{P}_{\mathsf{X}|\mathsf{Y}=y}$.

Unfortunately, as with the discriminative approach, we do not know the parameters $\boldsymbol{\theta} = \left(\boldsymbol{\mu}_{+1}, \boldsymbol{\mu}_{-1}, \boldsymbol{\Sigma}\right) \in \mathcal{Q}$ but have to "learn" them from the given training sample $z = (\boldsymbol{x}, \boldsymbol{y}) \in \mathcal{Z}^m$. We shall employ the Bayesian idea of expressing our prior belief in certain parameters via some prior measure $\mathbf{P}_{\mathsf{Q}}$. After having seen the

9 Note that $\mu_y(\mathbf{w}) \in \mathbb{R}$ is a real number whereas $\boldsymbol{\mu}_y \in \mathcal{K}$ is an n–dimensional vector in feature space.

training sample z we update our prior belief $\mathbf{P_Q}$, giving a posterior belief $\mathbf{P}_{\mathbf{Q}|\mathbf{Z}^m=z}$. Since we need one particular parameter value we compute the MAP estimate $\hat{\boldsymbol{\theta}}$, that is, we choose the value of $\boldsymbol{\theta}$ which attains the maximum a-posteriori belief $\mathbf{P}_{\mathbf{Q}|\mathbf{Z}^m=z}$ (see also Definition 3.6). If we choose a (improper) uniform prior $\mathbf{P_Q}$ then the parameter $\hat{\boldsymbol{\theta}}$ equals the parameter vector which maximizes the likelihood and is therefore also known as the *maximum likelihood estimator.* In Appendix B.10 it is shown that these estimates are given by

$$\hat{\boldsymbol{\mu}}_y = \frac{1}{m_y}\sum_{(x_i,y)\in z}\mathbf{x}_i\,, \qquad \hat{\boldsymbol{\Sigma}} = \frac{1}{m}\sum_{y\in\{-1,+1\}}\sum_{(x_i,y)\in z}\left(\mathbf{x}_i-\hat{\boldsymbol{\mu}}_y\right)\left(\mathbf{x}_i-\hat{\boldsymbol{\mu}}_y\right)' \tag{3.39}$$

$$= \frac{1}{m}\left(\mathbf{X}'\mathbf{X}-\sum_{y\in\{-1,+1\}} m_y\hat{\boldsymbol{\mu}}_y\hat{\boldsymbol{\mu}}_y'\right),$$

where $\mathbf{X}\in\mathbb{R}^{m\times n}$ is the data matrix obtained by applying $\boldsymbol{\phi}:\mathcal{X}\to\mathcal{K}$ to each training object $x\in\boldsymbol{x}$ and m_y equals the number of training examples of class y. Substituting the estimates into the equations (3.37) results in the so-called *Fisher linear discriminant* $\mathbf{w}_{\mathrm{FD}}$. The pseudocode of this algorithm is given at page 331.

In an attempt to "kernelize" this algorithm we note that a crucial requirement is that $\hat{\boldsymbol{\Sigma}}\in\mathbb{R}^{n\times n}$ has full rank which is impossible if $\dim(\mathcal{K})=n\gg m$. Since the idea of using kernels only reduces computational complexity in these cases we see that it is impossible to apply the kernel trick *directly* to this algorithm. Therefore, let us proceed along the following route: Given the data matrix $\mathbf{X}\in\mathbb{R}^{m\times n}$ we project the m data vectors $\mathbf{x}_i\in\mathbb{R}^n$ into the m–dimensional space spanned by the mapped training objects using $\mathbf{x}\mapsto\mathbf{X}\mathbf{x}$ and then estimate the mean vector and the covariance matrix in $\mathbb{R}^m$ using equation (3.39). The problem with this approach is that $\hat{\boldsymbol{\Sigma}}$ is at most of rank $m-2$ because it is an outer product matrix of two centered vectors. In order to remedy this situation we apply the technique of regularization to the resulting $m\times m$ covariance matrix, i.e., we penalize the diagonal of this matrix by adding $\lambda\mathbf{I}$ to it where large values of λ correspond to increased penalization. As a consequence, the projected m–dimensional mean vector $\mathbf{k}_y\in\mathbb{R}^m$ and covariance matrix $\mathbf{S}\in\mathbb{R}^{m\times m}$ are given by

$$\mathbf{k}_y = \frac{1}{m_y}\sum_{(x_i,y)\in z}\mathbf{X}\mathbf{x}_i = \frac{1}{m_y}\mathbf{G}\left(\mathbf{I}_{y_1=y},\ldots,\mathbf{I}_{y_m=y}\right)',$$

$$\begin{aligned}\mathbf{S} &= \frac{1}{m}\left(\mathbf{XX}'\mathbf{XX}' - \sum_{y\in\{-1,+1\}} m_y \mathbf{k}_y \mathbf{k}_y'\right) + \lambda\mathbf{I} \\ &= \frac{1}{m}\left(\mathbf{GG} - \sum_{y\in\{-1,+1\}} m_y \mathbf{k}_y \mathbf{k}_y'\right) + \lambda\mathbf{I}\,,\end{aligned}$$

where the $m \times m$ matrix $\mathbf{G}$ with $\mathbf{G}_{ij} = \langle \mathbf{x}_i, \mathbf{x}_j \rangle = k(x_i, x_j)$ is the Gram matrix. Using $\mathbf{k}_y$ and $\mathbf{S}$ in place of $\boldsymbol{\mu}_y$ and $\boldsymbol{\Sigma}$ in the equations (3.37) results in the so-called *kernel Fisher discriminant*. Note that the m–dimensional vector computed corresponds to the linear expansion coefficients $\hat{\boldsymbol{\alpha}} \in \mathbb{R}^m$ of a weight vector $\mathbf{w}_{\text{KFD}}$ in feature space because the classification of a novel test object $x \in \mathcal{X}$ by the kernel Fisher discriminant is carried out on the projected data point $\mathbf{Xx}$, i.e

$$\begin{aligned} h(x) &= \operatorname{sign}\left(\langle \hat{\boldsymbol{\alpha}}, \mathbf{Xx}\rangle + \hat{b}\right) = \operatorname{sign}\left(\sum_{i=1}^{m} \hat{\alpha}_i k(x_i, x) + \hat{b}\right), \\ \hat{\boldsymbol{\alpha}} &= \mathbf{S}^{-1}(\mathbf{k}_{+1} - \mathbf{k}_{-1})\,, \quad \hat{b} = \frac{1}{2}\left(\mathbf{k}_{-1}'\mathbf{S}^{-1}\mathbf{k}_{-1} - \mathbf{k}_{+1}'\mathbf{S}^{-1}\mathbf{k}_{+1}\right). \end{aligned} \tag{3.40}$$

It is worth mentioning that we would have obtained the same solution by exploiting the fact that the objective function (3.38) depends only on inner products between mapped training objects $\mathbf{x}_i$ and the unknown weight vector $\mathbf{w}$. By virtue of Theorem 2.29 the solution $\mathbf{w}_{\text{FD}}$ can be written as $\mathbf{w}_{\text{FD}} = \sum_{i=1}^{m} \hat{\alpha}_i \mathbf{x}_i$ which, inserted into (3.38), yields a function in $\boldsymbol{\alpha}$ whose maximizer is given by equation (3.40). The pseudocode of this algorithm is given on page 331.

Remark 3.16 (Least squares regression and Fisher discriminant) *An additional insight into the Fisher discriminant can be obtained by exploiting its relationship with standard* least squares regression. *In least squares regression we aim to find the weight vector* $\mathbf{w} \in \mathcal{K}$ *which minimizes* $\|\mathbf{Xw} - \mathbf{t}\|^2 = (\mathbf{Xw} - \mathbf{t})'(\mathbf{Xw} - \mathbf{t})$, *where* $\mathbf{t} \in \mathbb{R}^m$ *is a given vector of* m *real values. Maximizing this expression w.r.t.* $\mathbf{w}$ *gives*

$$\left.\frac{\partial \|\mathbf{Xw} - \mathbf{t}\|^2}{\partial \mathbf{w}}\right|_{\mathbf{w}=\hat{\mathbf{w}}} = 2\mathbf{X}'\mathbf{X}\hat{\mathbf{w}} - 2\mathbf{X}'\mathbf{t} = \mathbf{0}, \Leftrightarrow \hat{\mathbf{w}} = \left(\mathbf{X}'\mathbf{X}\right)^{-1}\mathbf{X}'\mathbf{t}\,.$$

In order to reveal the relation between this algorithm and the Fisher linear discriminant we assume that $\widetilde{\mathbf{X}} \in \mathbb{R}^{m\times(n+1)}$ *is a new data matrix constructed from* $\mathbf{X}$ *by adding a column of ones, i.e.,* $\widetilde{\mathbf{X}} = (\mathbf{X}, \mathbf{1})$. *Our new weight vector* $\tilde{\mathbf{w}} = (\mathbf{w}; b) \in \mathbb{R}^{n+1}$ *already contains the offset* b. *By choosing*

$$\mathbf{t} = m \cdot (y_1/m_{y_1}, \ldots, y_m/m_{y_m}) \,,$$

where m_{+1} *and* m_{-1} *are the number of positively and negatively labeled examples in the training sample, we see that the maximum condition* $\widetilde{\mathbf{X}}'\widetilde{\mathbf{X}}\widehat{\tilde{\mathbf{w}}} = \widetilde{\mathbf{X}}'\mathbf{t}$ *can also be written*

$$\begin{pmatrix} \mathbf{X}' \\ \mathbf{1}' \end{pmatrix} \begin{pmatrix} \mathbf{X} & \mathbf{1} \end{pmatrix} \begin{pmatrix} \hat{\mathbf{w}} \\ \hat{b} \end{pmatrix} = \begin{pmatrix} \mathbf{X}' \\ \mathbf{1}' \end{pmatrix} \mathbf{t} \Leftrightarrow \begin{pmatrix} \mathbf{X}'\mathbf{X} & \mathbf{X}'\mathbf{1} \\ \mathbf{1}'\mathbf{X} & \mathbf{1}'\mathbf{1} \end{pmatrix} \begin{pmatrix} \hat{\mathbf{w}} \\ \hat{b} \end{pmatrix} = \begin{pmatrix} \mathbf{X}'\mathbf{t} \\ \mathbf{1}'\mathbf{t} \end{pmatrix} .$$

By construction $\mathbf{1}'\mathbf{t} = m\left(\frac{m_{+1}}{m_{+1}} - \frac{m_{-1}}{m_{-1}}\right) = 0$ *and, thus, the last equation gives*

$$\mathbf{1}'\mathbf{X}\hat{\mathbf{w}} + \hat{b} \cdot \mathbf{1}'\mathbf{1} = 0 \,, \quad \Leftrightarrow \quad \hat{b} = -\frac{1}{m}\mathbf{1}'\mathbf{X}\hat{\mathbf{w}} \,. \tag{3.41}$$

Inserting this expression into the first equation and noticing that by virtue of equation (3.39)

$$\mathbf{X}'\mathbf{t} = m \cdot \left(\hat{\boldsymbol{\mu}}_{+1} - \hat{\boldsymbol{\mu}}_{+1}\right) \,,$$

we see that

$$\mathbf{X}'\mathbf{X}\hat{\mathbf{w}} + \mathbf{X}'\mathbf{1} \cdot \hat{b} = \left(\mathbf{X}'\mathbf{X} - \frac{1}{m}\mathbf{X}'\mathbf{1}\mathbf{1}'\mathbf{X}\right)\hat{\mathbf{w}} = m \cdot \left(\hat{\boldsymbol{\mu}}_{+1} - \hat{\boldsymbol{\mu}}_{+1}\right) . \tag{3.42}$$

A straightforward calculation shows that

$$\frac{1}{m}\mathbf{X}'\mathbf{1}\mathbf{1}'\mathbf{X} = m_{+1}\hat{\boldsymbol{\mu}}_{+1}\hat{\boldsymbol{\mu}}_{+1}' + m_{-1}\hat{\boldsymbol{\mu}}_{-1}\hat{\boldsymbol{\mu}}_{-1}' - \frac{m_{+1}m_{-1}}{m}\left(\hat{\boldsymbol{\mu}}_{+1} - \hat{\boldsymbol{\mu}}_{-1}\right)\left(\hat{\boldsymbol{\mu}}_{+1} - \hat{\boldsymbol{\mu}}_{-1}\right)' .$$

Combining this expression with equation (3.42) results in

$$\left(\hat{\boldsymbol{\Sigma}} + \frac{m_{+1}m_{-1}}{m}\left(\hat{\boldsymbol{\mu}}_{+1} - \hat{\boldsymbol{\mu}}_{-1}\right)\left(\hat{\boldsymbol{\mu}}_{+1} - \hat{\boldsymbol{\mu}}_{-1}\right)'\right)\hat{\mathbf{w}} = m \cdot \left(\hat{\boldsymbol{\mu}}_{+1} - \hat{\boldsymbol{\mu}}_{+1}.\right)$$

where we used the definition of $\hat{\boldsymbol{\Sigma}}$ *given in equation (3.39). Finally, noticing that*

$$\frac{m_{+1}m_{-1}}{m}\left(\hat{\boldsymbol{\mu}}_{+1} - \hat{\boldsymbol{\mu}}_{-1}\right)\left(\hat{\boldsymbol{\mu}}_{+1} - \hat{\boldsymbol{\mu}}_{-1}\right)'\mathbf{w} = (1 - c)\left(\hat{\boldsymbol{\mu}}_{+1} - \hat{\boldsymbol{\mu}}_{-1}\right)$$

for some $c \in \mathbb{R}$ *the latter expression implies that*

$$\hat{\mathbf{w}} = m \cdot c \cdot \hat{\boldsymbol{\Sigma}}^{-1}\left(\hat{\boldsymbol{\mu}}_{+1} - \hat{\boldsymbol{\mu}}_{-1}\right) ,$$

that is, up to a scaling factor (which is immaterial in classification) the weight vector $\hat{\mathbf{w}} \in \mathcal{K}$ *obtained by least square regression on* $\mathbf{t} \propto \mathbf{y}$ *equals the Fisher discriminant. The value of the threshold* $\hat{b}$ *is given by equation (3.41).*

3.6 Bibliographical Remarks

In the first section of this chapter we introduced the Bayesian inference principle whose basis is given by Bayes' theorem (see equation (3.1)). Excellent monographs introducing this principle in more detail are by Bernardo and Smith (1994) and by Robert (1994); for a more applied treatment of ideas to the problem of learning see MacKay (1991) and MacKay (1999). It was mentioned that the philosophy underlying Bayesian inference is based on the notion of belief. The link between belief and probability is established in the seminal paper Cox (1946) where a minimal number of axioms regarding belief are given. Broadly speaking, these axioms formalize rational behavior on the basis of belief. A major concept in Bayesian analysis is the concept of prior belief. In the book we have only introduced the idea of conjugate priors. As the prior is the crux of Bayesian inference there exist, of course, many different approaches to defining a prior, for example on the basis of invariances w.r.t. parameterization of the likelihood (Jeffreys 1946; Jaynes 1968). In the context of learning, the model selection principle of evidence maximization was formulated for the first time in MacKay (1992). In Subsection 3.1.1 we introduced several prediction strategies on the basis of posterior belief in hypotheses. Note that the term *Bayes classification strategy* (see Definition 3.7) should not be confused with the term *Bayes (optimal) classifier* which is used to denote the strategy which decides on the class y that incurs minimal loss on the prediction of x (see Devroye et al. (1996)). The latter strategy is based on complete knowledge of the data distribution $\mathbf{P}_{\mathsf{Z}}$ and therefore achieves minimal error (sometimes also called *Bayes error*) for a particular learning problem.

Section 3.2 introduced Bayesian linear regression (see Box and Tiao (1973)) and revealed its relation to certain stochastic processes known as Gaussian processes (Feller 1966); the presentation closely follows MacKay (1998) and Williams (1998). In order to relate this algorithm to neural networks (see Bishop (1995)) it was shown in Neal (1996) that a Gaussian process on the targets emerges in the limiting case of an infinite number of hidden neurons and Gaussian priors on the individual weights. The extension to classification using the Laplace approximation was done for the first time in Barber and Williams (1997) and Williams and

Barber (1998). It was noted that there also exists a Markov chain approximation (see Neal (1997b)) and an approximation known as the mean field approximation (see Opper and Winther (2000)). It should be noted that Gaussian processes for regression estimation are far from new; historical details dating back to 1880 can be found in Lauritzen (1981). Within the geostatistics field, Matheron proposed a framework of regression identical to Gaussian processes which he called "kriging" after D. G. Krige, a South African mining engineer (Matheron 1963). However, the geostatistics approach has concentrated mainly on low-dimensional problems. The algorithmical problem of inverting the Gram matrix has been investigated by Gibbs and Mackay (1997) who also proposes a variational approximation to Gaussian processes; for other approaches to speeding Gaussian process regression and classification see Trecate et al. (1999), Williams and Seeger (2001) and Smola and Bartlett (2001). Finally, the reasoning in Remark 3.13 is mainly taken from Sollich (2000).

The relevance vector machine algorithm presented in Section 3.3 can be found in Tipping (2000) and Tipping (2001). This algorithm is motivated by automatic relevance determination (ARD) priors which have been suggested in MacKay (1994) and Neal (1996) and empirically investigated in Neal (1998). There exists a variational approximation to this method found in Bishop and Tipping (2000).

In Section 3.4 we presented the Bayes point machine which is also known as the *optimal perceptron* (Watkin 1993). This algorithm has received a lot of attention in the statistical mechanics community (Opper et al. 1990; Opper and Haussler 1991; Biehl and Opper 1995; Opper and Kinzel 1995; Dietrich et al. 2000). There it has been shown that the optimal perceptron is the classifier which achieves best generalization error on average and in the so-called thermodynamical limit, i.e., the number of features n and the number samples m tend to infinity although their ratio $m/n = \beta$ stays constant. The idea of using a billiard on the unit hypersphere is due to Ruján (1997); its "kernelization" was done independently by Ruján and Marchand (2000) and Herbrich et al. (2001). For an extensive overview of other applications of Markov Chain Monte Carlo methods the interested reader is referred to Neal (1997a). There exist several extension to this algorithm which aim to reduce the computational complexity (see Herbrich and Graepel (2001a) and Rychetsky et al. (2000)). A promising approach has been presented in Minka (2001) where the uniform posterior measure over version space is approximated by a multidimensional Gaussian measure. This work also presents a modification of the billiard algorithm which is guaranteed to converge (Minka 2001, Section 5.8).

The algorithm presented in the last section, that is, Fisher linear discriminants, has its roots in the first half of the last century (Fisher 1936). It became part of the standard toolbox for classification learning (also called discriminant analysis when considered from a purely statistical perspective). The most appealing feature of Fisher discriminants is that the direction vector found is the maximizer of a function which approximately measures the inter-class distance vs. the inner-class distance after projection. The difficulty in determining this maximizer in general has been noticed in several places, e.g., Vapnik (1982, p. 48). The idea of kernelizing this algorithm has been considered by several researchers independently yet at the same time (see Baudat and Anouar (2000), Mika et al. (1999) and Roth and Steinhage (2000)). Finally, the equivalence of Fisher discriminants and least squares regression, demonstrated in Remark 3.16, can also be found in Duda et al. (2001).

It is worth mentioning that, beside the four algorithms presented, an interesting and conceptually different learning approach has been put forward in Jaakkola et al. (2000) and Jebara and Jaakkola (2000). The algorithm presented there employs the principle of *maximum entropy* (see Levin and Tribus (1978)). Rather than specifying a prior distribution over hypotheses together with a likelihood model $\mathbf{P}_{\mathsf{Z}|\mathsf{H}=h}$ for the objects and classes, given a hypothesis h, which, by Bayes' theorem, result in the Bayesian posterior, we consider any measure $\mathbf{P}_{\mathsf{H}}$ which satisfies certain constraints on the given training sample z as a potential candidate for the posterior belief. The principle then chooses the measure $\mathbf{P}_{\mathsf{H}}^{\mathrm{ME}}$ which maximizes the entropy $\mathbf{E}_{\mathsf{H}}\left[\ln\left(\mathbf{P}_{\mathsf{H}}\left(\mathsf{H}\right)\right)\right]$. The idea behind this principle is to use as little prior knowledge or information as possible in the construction of $\mathbf{P}_{\mathsf{H}}^{\mathrm{ME}}$. Implementing this formal principle for the special case of linear classifiers results in an algorithm very similar to the support vector algorithm (see Section 2.4). The essential difference is given by the choice of the cost function on the margin slack variables. A similar observation has already been made in Remark 3.13.

II Learning Theory

4 Mathematical Models of Learning

This chapter introduces different mathematical models of learning. A mathematical model of learning has the advantage that it provides bounds on the generalization ability of a learning algorithm. It also indicates which quantities are responsible for generalization. As such, the theory motivates new learning algorithms. After a short introduction into the classical parametric statistics approach to learning, the chapter introduces the PAC and VC models. These models directly study the convergence of expected risks rather than taking a detour over the convergence of the underlying probability measure. The fundamental quantity in this framework is the growth function which can be upper bounded by a one integer summary called the VC dimension. With classical *structural risk minimization*, where the VC dimension must be known before the training data arrives, we obtain *a-priori* bounds, that is, bounds whose values are the same for a fixed training error.

In order to explain the generalization behavior of algorithms minimizing a regularized risk we will introduce the luckiness framework. This framework is based on the assumption that the growth function will be estimated on the basis of a sample. Thus, it provides *a-posteriori* bounds; bounds which can only be evaluated *after* the training data has been seen. Finally, the chapter presents a PAC analysis for real-valued functions. Here, we take advantage of the fact that, in the case of linear classifiers, the classification is carried out by thresholding a real-valued function. The real-valued output, also referred to as the margin, allows us to define a scale sensitive version of the VC dimension which leads to tighter bounds on the expected risk. An appealing feature of the margin bound is that we can obtain nontrivial bounds even if the number of training samples is significantly less than the number of dimensions of feature space. Using a technique, which is known as the robustness trick, it will be demonstrated that the margin bound is also applicable if one allows for training error via a quadratic penalization of the diagonal of the Gram matrix.

4.1 Generative vs. Discriminative Models

In Chapter 2 it was shown that a learning problem is given by a training sample $z = (\boldsymbol{x}, \boldsymbol{y}) = ((x_1, y_1), \ldots, (x_m, y_m)) \in (\mathcal{X} \times \mathcal{Y})^m = \mathcal{Z}^m$, drawn iid according to some (unknown) probability measure $\mathbf{P}_{\mathsf{Z}} = \mathbf{P}_{\mathsf{XY}}$, and a loss $l : \mathcal{Y} \times \mathcal{Y} \to \mathbb{R}$, which defines how costly the prediction $h(x)$ is if the true output is y. Then, the goal is to find a deterministic function $h \in \mathcal{Y}^{\mathcal{X}}$ which expresses the dependency implicitly expressed by $\mathbf{P}_{\mathsf{Z}}$ with minimal expected loss (risk) $R[h] = \mathbf{E}_{\mathsf{XY}}\left[l(h(\mathsf{X}), \mathsf{Y})\right]$ while only using the given training sample z. We have already seen in the first part of this book that there exist two different algorithmical approaches to tackling this problem. We shall now try to study the two approaches more generally to see in what respect they are similar and in which aspects they differ.

1. In the *generative* (or parametric) statistics approach we restrict ourselves to a parameterized space $\mathcal{P}$ of measures for the space $\mathcal{Z}$, i.e., we model the data generation process. Hence, our model is given by[1] $\mathcal{P} = \left\{\mathbf{P}_{\mathsf{Z}|\mathsf{Q}=\boldsymbol{\theta}} \mid \boldsymbol{\theta} \in \mathcal{Q}\right\}$, where $\boldsymbol{\theta}$ should be understood as the parametric description of the measure $\mathbf{P}_{\mathsf{Z}|\mathsf{Q}=\boldsymbol{\theta}}$. With a fixed loss l each measure $\mathbf{P}_{\mathsf{Z}|\mathsf{Q}=\boldsymbol{\theta}}$ implicitly defines a decision function $h_{\boldsymbol{\theta}}$,

$$h_{\boldsymbol{\theta}}(x) = \underset{y \in \mathcal{Y}}{\operatorname{argmin}} \; \mathbf{E}_{\mathsf{Y}|\mathsf{X}=x,\mathsf{Q}=\boldsymbol{\theta}}\left[l(y, \mathsf{Y})\right] . \tag{4.1}$$

In order to see that this function has minimal expected risk we note that

$$R_{\boldsymbol{\theta}}[h] \stackrel{\text{def}}{=} \mathbf{E}_{\mathsf{XY}|\mathsf{Q}=\boldsymbol{\theta}}\left[l(h(\mathsf{X}), \mathsf{Y})\right] = \mathbf{E}_{\mathsf{X}|\mathsf{Q}=\boldsymbol{\theta}}\left[\mathbf{E}_{\mathsf{Y}|\mathsf{X}=x,\mathsf{Q}=\boldsymbol{\theta}}\left[l(h(x), \mathsf{Y})\right]\right] , \tag{4.2}$$

where $h_{\boldsymbol{\theta}}$ minimizes the expression in the innermost brackets. For the case of zero-one loss $l_{0-1}(h(x), y) = \mathbf{I}_{h(x) \neq y}$ also defined in equation (2.10), the function $h_{\boldsymbol{\theta}}$ reduces to

$$h_{\boldsymbol{\theta}}(x) = \underset{y \in \mathcal{Y}}{\operatorname{argmin}} \left(1 - \mathbf{P}_{\mathsf{Y}|\mathsf{X}=x,\mathsf{Q}=\boldsymbol{\theta}}(y)\right) = \underset{y \in \mathcal{Y}}{\operatorname{argmax}} \; \mathbf{P}_{\mathsf{Y}|\mathsf{X}=x,\mathsf{Q}=\boldsymbol{\theta}}(y) ,$$

which is known as the Bayes optimal decision based on $\mathbf{P}_{\mathsf{Z}|\mathsf{Q}=\boldsymbol{\theta}}$.

2. In the *discriminative*, or machine learning, approach we restrict ourselves to a parameterized space $\mathcal{H} \subseteq \mathcal{Y}^{\mathcal{X}}$ of deterministic mappings h from $\mathcal{X}$ to $\mathcal{Y}$. As a consequence, the model is given by $\mathcal{H} = \{h_{\mathbf{w}} : \mathcal{X} \to \mathcal{Y} \mid \mathbf{w} \in \mathcal{W}\}$, where $\mathbf{w}$ is the parameterization of single hypotheses $h_{\mathbf{w}}$. Note that this can also be interpreted as

1 We use the notation $\mathbf{P}_{\mathsf{Z}|\mathsf{Q}=\boldsymbol{\theta}}$ to index different measures over $\mathcal{Z}$ by some parameters $\boldsymbol{\theta}$. Note that it is neither assumed nor true that the unknown data distribution $\mathbf{P}_{\mathsf{Z}}$ fulfills $\mathbf{P}_{\mathsf{Z}} = \mathbf{E}_{\mathsf{Q}}[\mathbf{P}_{\mathsf{Z}|\mathsf{Q}=\boldsymbol{\theta}}]$ because this requires *a measure* $\mathbf{P}_{\mathsf{Q}}$. Further, this would not take into account that we conditioned on the parameter space $\mathcal{Q}$.

a model of the conditional distribution of class labels $y \in \mathcal{Y}$ given objects $x \in \mathcal{X}$ by assuming that $\mathbf{P}_{\mathsf{Y}|\mathsf{X}=x,\mathsf{H}=h} = \mathbf{I}_{y=h(x)}$. Viewed this way, the model $\mathcal{H}$ is a subset of the more general model $\mathcal{P}$ used in classical statistics.

The term *generative* refers to the fact that the model $\mathcal{P}$ contains different descriptions of the *generation* of the training sample z (in terms of a probability measure). Similarly, the term *discriminative* refers to the fact that the model $\mathcal{H}$ consists of different descriptions of the *discrimination* of the sample z. We already know that a machine learning method selects one hypothesis $\mathcal{A}(z) \in \mathcal{H}$ given a training sample $z \in \mathcal{Z}^m$. The corresponding selection mechanism of a probability measure $\mathbf{P}_{\mathsf{Z}|\mathsf{Q}=\boldsymbol{\theta}}$ given the training sample z is called an estimator.

Definition 4.1 (Estimator) *Given a set $\mathcal{P}$ of probability measures $\mathbf{P}_\mathsf{Z}$ over $\mathcal{Z}$, a mapping $\mathcal{E} : \bigcup_{m=1}^{\infty} \mathcal{Z}^m \to \mathcal{P}$ is called an* estimator. *If the set $\mathcal{P}$ is parameterized by $\boldsymbol{\theta} \in \mathcal{Q}$ then $\hat{\boldsymbol{\theta}}_z \in \mathcal{Q}$ is defined by*

$$\hat{\boldsymbol{\theta}}_z = \boldsymbol{\theta} \Leftrightarrow \mathcal{E}(z) = \mathbf{P}_{\mathsf{Z}|\mathsf{Q}=\boldsymbol{\theta}} ,$$

that is, $\hat{\boldsymbol{\theta}}_z$ returns the parameters of the measure estimated using $\mathcal{E}$.

If we view a given hypothesis space $\mathcal{H}$ as the set of parameters h for the conditional distribution $\mathbf{P}_{\mathsf{Y}|\mathsf{X}=x,\mathsf{H}=h}$ then we see that each learning algorithm $\mathcal{A} : \cup_{m=1}^{\infty} \mathcal{Z}^m \to \mathcal{H}$ is a special estimator $\mathcal{E}$ for only the class-conditional distribution $\mathbf{P}_{\mathsf{Y}|\mathsf{X}=x}$. However, the conceptual difference becomes apparent when we consider the type of convergence results that have been studied for the two different models:

1. In the parametric statistics framework we are concerned with the convergence of the estimated measure $\mathcal{E}(z) \in \mathcal{P}$ to the unknown measure $\mathbf{P}_\mathsf{Z}$ where it is often assumed that the model is correct, that is, there exists a $\boldsymbol{\theta}^*$ such that $\mathbf{P}_\mathsf{Z} = \mathbf{P}_{\mathsf{Z}|\mathsf{Q}=\boldsymbol{\theta}^*} \in \mathcal{P}$. Hence, a theoretical result in the statistics framework often has the form

$$\mathbf{P}_{\mathsf{Z}^m}\left(\rho\left(\mathcal{E}(\mathbf{Z}), \mathbf{P}_{\mathsf{Z}|\mathsf{Q}=\boldsymbol{\theta}^*}\right) > \varepsilon\right) < \delta(\varepsilon, m) , \tag{4.3}$$

where ρ is a metric in the space $\mathcal{P}$ of measures, for example the ℓ_2 norm $\left\|\hat{\boldsymbol{\theta}}_z - \boldsymbol{\theta}^*\right\|_2$ of the difference vector of the parameters $\boldsymbol{\theta}$.

2. In the machine learning framework we are concerned with the convergence of the expected risk $R[\mathcal{A}(z)]$ of the learned function $\mathcal{A}(z)$ to the minimum expected

risk $\inf_{h\in\mathcal{H}} R[h] = R[h^*]$. A theoretical result in this framework has the form

$$\mathbf{P}_{\mathsf{Z}^m}\left(R\left[\mathcal{A}(\mathbf{Z})\right] - R\left[h^*\right] > \varepsilon\right) < \delta(\varepsilon, m) , \tag{4.4}$$

where the expression in the parenthesis is also known as the *generalization error* (see also Definition 2.10). In case $R[h^*] = 0$ the generalization error equals the expected risk. Note that each hypothesis $h \in \mathcal{H}$ is reduced to a scalar $R[h]$ so that the question of an appropriate metric ρ is meaningless[2]. Since $\mathbf{P}_{\mathsf{Z}}$ is assumed to be unknown, the above inequality has to hold for *all probability measures* $\mathbf{P}_{\mathsf{Z}}$. This is often referred to as the *worst case* property of the machine learning framework. The price we have to pay for this generality is that our choice of the predictive model $\mathcal{H}$ might be totally wrong (e.g., $R[h^*] = 0.5$ in the case of zero-one loss l_{0-1}) so that learning $\mathcal{A}(z) \in \mathcal{H}$ is useless.

For the task of learning—where finding the best discriminative description of the data is assumed to be the ultimate goal—the convergence (4.4) of risks appears the most appropriate. We note, however, that this convergence is a special case of the convergence (4.3) of probability measures when identifying $\mathcal{H}$ and $\mathcal{Q}$ and using $\rho\left(\mathbf{P}_{\mathsf{Z}|\mathsf{H}=h}, \mathbf{P}_{\mathsf{Z}|\mathsf{H}=h^*}\right) = R[h] - R[h^*]$. The interesting question is:

> Does the convergence of probability measures always imply a convergence of risks when using equation (4.1) regardless of ρ?

If this were the case than there would be no need to study the convergence of risk but we could use the plethora of results known from statistics about the convergence of probability measures. If, on the other hand, this is not the case then it also follows that (in general) the common practice of interpreting the parameters $\mathbf{w}$ (or $\boldsymbol{\theta}$) of the hypothesis learned is theoretically not justified on the basis of convergence results of the form (4.4). Let us consider the following example.

Example 4.2 (Convergence of probability measures[3]) *Let us consider the zero-one loss l_{0-1}. Suppose $\mathcal{Y} = \{1, 2\}$, $\mathcal{X} = \mathbb{R}$, $\mathcal{Q} = \mathbb{R}^2$, $\mathbf{P}_{\mathsf{X}|\mathsf{Y}=y,\mathbf{Q}=(\theta_1,\theta_2)}$ uniform in $\left[-\theta_y, 0\right]$ if $\theta_y \neq 1$ and uniform in $\left[0, \theta_y\right]$ if $\theta_y = 1$, and $\mathbf{P}_{\mathsf{Y}}(1) = \mathbf{P}_{\mathsf{Y}}(2) = \frac{1}{2}$. Let us assume that the underlying probability measure is given by $\boldsymbol{\theta}^* = (1, 2)$. Given a training sample $z \in (\mathcal{X} \times \mathcal{Y})^m$, a reasonable estimate $\hat{\boldsymbol{\theta}}_z$ of θ_1 and θ_2 would be*

2 All norms on the real line $\mathbb{R}^1$ are equivalent (see Barner and Flohr (1989, p. 15)).

3 This example is taken from Devroye et al. (1996, p. 267).

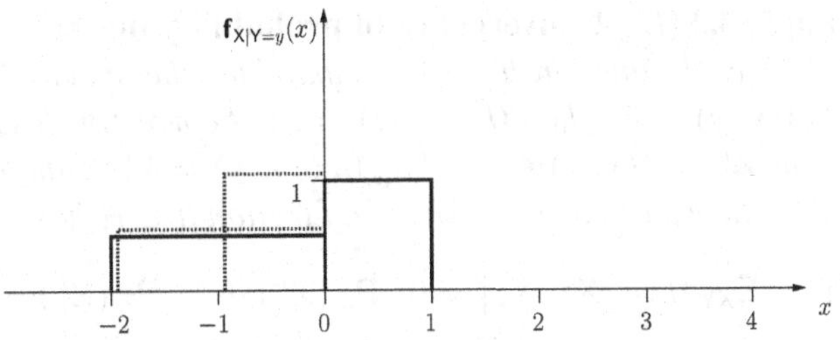

Figure 4.1 True densities $\mathbf{f}_{X|Y=y}$ underlying the data in Example 4.2. The uniform densities (solid lines) on $[0, 1]$ and $[-2, 0]$ apply for $Y = 1$ and $Y = 2$, respectively. Although with probability one the parameter $\theta_1^* = 1$ will be estimated to arbitrary precision, the probability that a sample point falls at exactly $x = 1$ is zero, whence $(\hat{\boldsymbol{\theta}}_{\mathbf{Z}})_1 \neq 1$. Since the model $\mathcal{P}$ is noncontinuous in its parameters $\boldsymbol{\theta}$, for almost all training samples the estimated densities are uniform on $[-(\hat{\boldsymbol{\theta}}_{\mathbf{Z}})_2, 0]$ and $[-(\hat{\boldsymbol{\theta}}_{\mathbf{Z}})_1, 0]$ (dashed lines). Thus, for all $x > 0$ the prediction based on $\hat{\boldsymbol{\theta}}_{\mathbf{Z}}$ is wrong.

$\left(\hat{\boldsymbol{\theta}}_z\right)_i = \max_{(x,i)\in z} |x|$ *for* $i \in \{1, 2\}$ *because*

$$\forall \varepsilon > 0 : \qquad \lim_{m\to\infty} \mathbf{P}_{\mathbf{Z}^m}\left(\left\|\hat{\boldsymbol{\theta}}_{\mathbf{Z}} - \boldsymbol{\theta}^*\right\|_2 > \varepsilon\right) = 0 ,$$

or $\hat{\boldsymbol{\theta}}_z$ converges to $\boldsymbol{\theta}^*$ in probability. *However, as the class conditional measures* $\mathbf{P}_{X|Y=y}$ *are densities, we know that for both classes* $y \in \{1, 2\}$,

$$\mathbf{P}_{\mathbf{Z}^m}\left(\left(\hat{\boldsymbol{\theta}}_{\mathbf{Z}}\right)_y \neq 1\right) = 1 .$$

As a consequence, with probability one over the random choice of a training sample z, the expected risk $R\left[h_{\hat{\boldsymbol{\theta}}_{\mathbf{Z}}}\right]$ *equals* $\frac{1}{2}$ *(see also Figure 4.1).*

This simple example shows that the convergence of probability measures is not necessarily a guarantee of convergence of associated risks. It should be noted, however, that this example used the noncontinuity of the parameterization $\boldsymbol{\theta}$ of the probability measure $\mathbf{P}_{\mathbf{Z}|\mathbf{Q}=\boldsymbol{\theta}}$ as well as one specific metric ρ on probability measures. The following example shows that along with the difference $R\left[h_{\hat{\boldsymbol{\theta}}_z}\right] - R\left[h_{\boldsymbol{\theta}^*}\right]$ in expected risks there exists another "natural" metric on probability measures which leads to a convergence of risks.

Example 4.3 **(L_1–Convergence of probability measures)** *In case of zero-one loss l_{0-1} each function $h \in \mathcal{Y}^{\mathcal{X}}$ subdivides the space $\mathcal{Z}$ into two classes: A set $Z_h^c = \{(x, y) \in \mathcal{Z} \mid l_{0-1}(h(x), y) = 0\}$ of correctly classified points and its complement $Z_h^i = \{(x, y) \in \mathcal{Z} \mid l_{0-1}(h(x), y) = 1\}$ of incorrectly classified points. Clearly, the expected risk $R[h]$ of a function $h \in \mathcal{H}$ has the property*

$$R[h] = \mathbf{E}_{\mathsf{XY}}\left[l(h(\mathsf{X}), \mathsf{Y})\right] = 0 \cdot \mathbf{P}_{\mathsf{Z}}\left(Z_h^c\right) + 1 \cdot \mathbf{P}_{\mathsf{Z}}\left(Z_h^i\right) = \mathbf{P}_{\mathsf{Z}}\left(Z_h^i\right) . \tag{4.5}$$

Let us assume that our generative model $\mathcal{P}$ only consists of measures $\mathbf{P}_{\mathsf{Z}|\mathsf{Q}=\boldsymbol{\theta}}$ that possess a density $\mathbf{f}_{\mathsf{Z}|\mathsf{Q}=\boldsymbol{\theta}}$ over the σ–algebra $\mathfrak{B}_n$ of Borel sets in $\mathbb{R}^n$. The theorem of Scheffé states that

$$\rho\left(\mathbf{P}_{\mathsf{Z}|\mathsf{Q}=\boldsymbol{\theta}}, \mathbf{P}_{\mathsf{Z}|\mathsf{Q}=\boldsymbol{\theta}^*}\right) \stackrel{\text{def}}{=} \left\|\mathbf{f}_{\mathsf{Z}|\mathsf{Q}=\boldsymbol{\theta}} - \mathbf{f}_{\mathsf{Z}|\mathsf{Q}=\boldsymbol{\theta}^*}\right\|_1 = 2 \sup_{A \in \mathfrak{B}_n} \left|\mathbf{P}_{\mathsf{Z}|\mathsf{Q}=\boldsymbol{\theta}}(A) - \mathbf{P}_{\mathsf{Z}|\mathsf{Q}=\boldsymbol{\theta}^*}(A)\right| .$$

Utilizing equation (4.5) and the fact that each measure $\mathbf{P}_{\mathsf{Z}|\mathsf{Q}=\boldsymbol{\theta}}$ defines a Bayes optimal classifier $h_{\boldsymbol{\theta}}$ by equation (4.1) we conclude

$$\begin{aligned}
\left\|\mathbf{f}_{\mathsf{Z}|\mathsf{Q}=\boldsymbol{\theta}} - \mathbf{f}_{\mathsf{Z}|\mathsf{Q}=\boldsymbol{\theta}^*}\right\|_1 &= 2 \sup_{A \in \mathfrak{B}_n} \left|\mathbf{P}_{\mathsf{Z}|\mathsf{Q}=\boldsymbol{\theta}}(A) - \mathbf{P}_{\mathsf{Z}|\mathsf{Q}=\boldsymbol{\theta}^*}(A)\right| \\
&\geq 2 \sup_{\tilde{\boldsymbol{\theta}} \in \mathcal{Q}} \left|R_{\boldsymbol{\theta}}\left[h_{\tilde{\boldsymbol{\theta}}}\right] - R_{\boldsymbol{\theta}^*}\left[h_{\tilde{\boldsymbol{\theta}}}\right]\right| \\
&\geq \left|R_{\boldsymbol{\theta}}[h_{\boldsymbol{\theta}}] - R_{\boldsymbol{\theta}^*}[h_{\boldsymbol{\theta}}]\right| + \left|R_{\boldsymbol{\theta}}[h_{\boldsymbol{\theta}^*}] - R_{\boldsymbol{\theta}^*}[h_{\boldsymbol{\theta}^*}]\right| \\
&= \left|R_{\boldsymbol{\theta}^*}[h_{\boldsymbol{\theta}}] - R_{\boldsymbol{\theta}}[h_{\boldsymbol{\theta}}]\right| + \left|R_{\boldsymbol{\theta}}[h_{\boldsymbol{\theta}^*}] - R_{\boldsymbol{\theta}^*}[h_{\boldsymbol{\theta}^*}]\right| \\
&\geq \left|R_{\boldsymbol{\theta}^*}[h_{\boldsymbol{\theta}}] - R_{\boldsymbol{\theta}}[h_{\boldsymbol{\theta}}] + R_{\boldsymbol{\theta}}[h_{\boldsymbol{\theta}^*}] - R_{\boldsymbol{\theta}^*}[h_{\boldsymbol{\theta}^*}]\right| \\
&= \left|\underbrace{R_{\boldsymbol{\theta}^*}[h_{\boldsymbol{\theta}}] - R_{\boldsymbol{\theta}^*}[h_{\boldsymbol{\theta}^*}]}_{\geq 0} + \underbrace{R_{\boldsymbol{\theta}}[h_{\boldsymbol{\theta}^*}] - R_{\boldsymbol{\theta}}[h_{\boldsymbol{\theta}}]}_{\geq 0}\right| \\
&\geq R_{\boldsymbol{\theta}^*}[h_{\boldsymbol{\theta}}] - R_{\boldsymbol{\theta}^*}[h_{\boldsymbol{\theta}^*}] \\
&= R[h_{\boldsymbol{\theta}}] - R[h_{\boldsymbol{\theta}^*}] ,
\end{aligned}$$

where we use the triangle inequality in the fifth line and assume $\mathbf{P}_{\mathsf{Z}} = \mathbf{P}_{\mathsf{Z}|\mathsf{Q}=\boldsymbol{\theta}^*}$ in the last line. Thus we see that the convergence of the densities in L_1 implies the convergence (4.4) of the expected risks for the associated decision functions because each upper bound on $\left\|\mathbf{f}_{\mathsf{Z}|\mathsf{Q}=\boldsymbol{\theta}} - \mathbf{f}_{\mathsf{Z}|\mathsf{Q}=\boldsymbol{\theta}^*}\right\|_1$ is also an upper bound on $R[h_{\boldsymbol{\theta}}] - R[h_{\boldsymbol{\theta}^*}]$.

As a consequence, bounding the L_1–distance of densities underlying the training sample implies that we are able to bound the difference in expected risks, too.

Note, however, that the convergence in expected risks could be much faster and thus we lose some tightness of the potential results when studying the convergence of probability measures.

The main problem in the last two examples is summarized in the following statement made in Vapnik (1995): *When solving a given problem one should avoid solving a more general problem as an intermediate step*. In our particular case this means that if we are interested in the convergence of the expected risks we should not resort to the convergence of probability measures because the latter might not imply the former or might be a weaker convergence than required. Those who first estimate $\mathbf{P}_\mathsf{Z}$ by $\mathcal{E}(z) \in \mathcal{P}$ and then construct rules based on the loss l do themselves a disservice.

4.2 PAC and VC Frameworks

As a starting point let us consider the huge class of empirical risk minimization algorithms $\mathcal{A}_{\mathrm{ERM}}$ formally defined in equation (2.12). To obtain upper bounds on the deviation between the expected risk of the function $\mathcal{A}_{\mathrm{ERM}}(z)$ (which minimizes the training error $R_{\mathrm{emp}}[h, z]$) and the best function $h^* = \operatorname{arginf}_{h \in \mathcal{H}} R[h]$, the general idea is to make use of the following relation

$$R_{\mathrm{emp}}\left[h^*, z\right] \geq R_{\mathrm{emp}}\left[\mathcal{A}_{\mathrm{ERM}}(z), z\right] \Leftrightarrow R_{\mathrm{emp}}\left[h^*, z\right] - R_{\mathrm{emp}}\left[\mathcal{A}_{\mathrm{ERM}}(z), z\right] \geq 0,$$

which clearly holds by definition of $h_z \stackrel{\mathrm{def}}{=} \mathcal{A}_{\mathrm{ERM}}(z)$. Then it follows that

$$\begin{aligned} R\left[\mathcal{A}_{\mathrm{ERM}}(z)\right] - R\left[h^*\right] &\leq R\left[h_z\right] - R\left[h^*\right] + \underbrace{\left(R_{\mathrm{emp}}\left[h^*, z\right] - R_{\mathrm{emp}}\left[h_z, z\right]\right)}_{\geq 0} \\ &= \left|\left(R\left[h_z\right] - R_{\mathrm{emp}}\left[h_z, z\right]\right) + \left(R_{\mathrm{emp}}\left[h^*, z\right] - R\left[h^*\right]\right)\right| \\ &\leq \left|R\left[h_z\right] - R_{\mathrm{emp}}\left[h_z, z\right]\right| + \left|R\left[h^*\right] - R_{\mathrm{emp}}\left[h^*, z\right]\right| \\ &\leq 2 \sup_{h \in \mathcal{H}} \left|R[h] - R_{\mathrm{emp}}[h, z]\right|, \end{aligned} \tag{4.6}$$

where we have made use of the triangle inequality in the third line and bounded the uncertainty about $\mathcal{A}_{\mathrm{ERM}}(z) \in \mathcal{H}$ and $h^* \in \mathcal{H}$ by the worst case assumption of $\sup_{h \in \mathcal{H}} \left|R[h] - R_{\mathrm{emp}}[h, z]\right|$ from above. We see that, rather than studying the generalization error of an empirical risk minimization algorithm directly, it suffices to consider the *uniform convergence of training errors to expected errors* over all hypotheses $h \in \mathcal{H}$ contained in the hypothesis space $\mathcal{H}$ because any upper bound on the deviation $\sup_{h\in\mathcal{H}} \left|R[h] - R_{\text{emp}}[h, z]\right|$ is also an upper bound on the generalization error $R[\mathcal{A}_{\text{ERM}}(z)] - R[h^*]$ by virtue of equation (4.6). The framework which studies this convergence is called the *VC* (Vapnik-Chervonenkis) or *PAC* (Probably Approximately Correct) framework due to their different origins (see Section 4.5 for a detailed discussion about their origins and connections). Broadly speaking, the difference between the PAC framework and the VC framework is that the former considers only data distributions $\mathbf{P}_{\mathsf{Z}}$ where $\mathbf{P}_{\mathsf{Y}|\mathsf{X}=x}(y) = \mathbf{I}_{h^*(x)=y}$, for some $h^* \in \mathcal{H}$, which immediately implies that $R[h^*] = 0$ and $R_{\text{emp}}[\mathcal{A}_{\text{ERM}}(z), z] = 0$. Thus, it follows that

$$R[\mathcal{A}_{\text{ERM}}(z)] - R\left[h^*\right] = R[\mathcal{A}_{\text{ERM}}(z)] \leq \sup_{\left\{h\in\mathcal{H} \mid R_{\text{emp}}[h,z]=0\right\}} R[h] , \tag{4.7}$$

because $\mathcal{A}_{\text{ERM}}(z) \in \left\{h \in \mathcal{H} \mid R_{\text{emp}}[h, z] = 0\right\} \subseteq \mathcal{H}$.

Definition 4.4 (VC and PAC generalization error bounds) *Suppose we are given a hypothesis space $\mathcal{H} \subseteq \mathcal{Y}^{\mathcal{X}}$ and a loss function $l : \mathcal{Y} \times \mathcal{Y} \to \mathbb{R}$. Then the function $\varepsilon_{\text{VC}} : \mathbb{N} \times (0, 1] \to \mathbb{R}$ is called a* VC generalization error bound *if, and only if, for all training sample sizes $m \in \mathbb{N}$, all $\delta \in (0, 1]$ and all $\mathbf{P}_{\mathsf{Z}}$*

$$\mathbf{P}_{\mathsf{Z}^m}\left(\forall h \in \mathcal{H} : \left|R[h] - R_{\text{emp}}\left[h, \mathbf{Z}\right]\right| \leq \varepsilon_{\text{VC}}(m, \delta)\right) \geq 1 - \delta .$$

Similarly, a function $\varepsilon_{\text{PAC}} : \mathbb{N} \times (0, 1] \to \mathbb{R}$ is called a PAC generalization error bound *if, and only if,*

$$\mathbf{P}_{\mathsf{Z}^m}(\forall h \in V_{\mathcal{H}}(\mathbf{Z}) : R[h] \leq \varepsilon_{\text{PAC}}(m, \delta)) \geq 1 - \delta ,$$

for all samples sizes $m \in \mathbb{N}$, all $\delta \in (0, 1]$ and all $\mathbf{P}_{\mathsf{Z}}$.

Example 4.5 (Uniform convergence of frequencies to probabilities) *There exists an interesting relationship between VC generalization error bounds and the more classical problem of uniform convergence of frequencies to probabilities in the special case of the zero-one loss l_{0-1} given in equation (2.10). As shown in Example 4.3, in this case the expected risk $R[h]$ of a single hypothesis $h \in \mathcal{H}$ is the probability of the set $Z_h^i = \{(x, y) \in \mathcal{Z} \mid l_{0-1}(h(x), y) = 1\} \subseteq \mathcal{Z}$ whereas the training error $R_{\text{emp}}[h, z]$ equals the empirical measure $\mathbf{v}_z\left(Z_h^i\right)$. Hence we see that*

$$R[\mathcal{A}_{\text{ERM}}(z)] - R\left[h^*\right] \leq 2 \sup_{Z_h^i \in \mathfrak{Z}} \left|\mathbf{P}_{\mathsf{Z}}\left(Z_h^i\right) - \mathbf{v}_z\left(Z_h^i\right)\right| ,$$

which inevitably shows that all we are concerned with is the uniform convergence of frequencies $\mathbf{v}_{\mathbf{z}}\left(Z_h^i\right)$ *to probabilities* $\mathbf{P}_{\mathsf{Z}}\left(Z_h^i\right)$ *over the fixed set* $\mathfrak{Z} = \left\{Z_h^i \subseteq \mathcal{Z} \mid h \in \mathcal{H}\right\}$ *of events. Note, however, that up to this point we have only shown that the uniform convergence of frequencies to probabilities provides a sufficient condition for the convergence of the generalization error of an empirical risk minimization algorithm. If we restrict ourselves to "non trivial" hypothesis spaces and the one-sided uniform convergence, it can be shown that this is also a necessary condition.*

4.2.1 Classical PAC and VC Analysis

In the following three subsections we will only be concerned with the zero-one loss l_{0-1} given by equation (2.10). It should be noted that the results we will obtain can readily be generalized to loss function taking only a finite number values; the generalization to the case of real-valued loss functions is conceptually similar but will not be discussed in this book (see Section 4.5 for further references).

The general idea is to bound the probability of "bad training samples", i.e., training samples $z \in \mathcal{Z}^m$ for which there exists a hypothesis $h \in \mathcal{H}$ where the deviation between the empirical risk $R_{\text{emp}}[h, z]$ and the expected risk $R[h]$ is larger than some prespecified $\varepsilon \in [0, 1]$. Setting the probability of this to δ and solving for ε gives the required generalization error bound. If we are only given a finite number $|\mathcal{H}|$ of hypotheses h then such a bound is very easily obtained by a combination of Hoeffding's inequality and the union bound.

Theorem 4.6 (VC bound for finite hypothesis spaces) *Suppose we are given a hypothesis space* $\mathcal{H}$ *having a finite number of hypotheses, i.e.,* $|\mathcal{H}| < \infty$. *Then, for any measure* $\mathbf{P}_{\mathsf{Z}}$, *for the zero-one loss* l_{0-1} *given by equation (2.10) and all* $\varepsilon > 0$ *we have*

$$\mathbf{P}_{\mathsf{Z}^m}\left(\exists h \in \mathcal{H} : \left|R[h] - R_{\text{emp}}\left[h, \mathbf{Z}\right]\right| > \varepsilon\right) < 2 \cdot |\mathcal{H}| \cdot \exp\left(-2m\varepsilon^2\right) . \tag{4.8}$$

Proof Let $\mathcal{H} = \left\{h_1, \ldots, h_{|\mathcal{H}|}\right\}$. By an application of the union bound given in Theorem A.107 we know that $\mathbf{P}_{\mathsf{Z}^m}\left(\exists h \in \mathcal{H} : \left|R[h] - R_{\text{emp}}\left[h, \mathbf{Z}\right]\right| > \varepsilon\right)$ is given by

$$\mathbf{P}_{\mathsf{Z}^m}\left(\bigvee_{i=1}^{|\mathcal{H}|}\left(\left|R[h_i] - R_{\text{emp}}\left[h_i, \mathbf{Z}\right]\right| > \varepsilon\right)\right) \leq \sum_{i=1}^{|\mathcal{H}|} \mathbf{P}_{\mathsf{Z}^m}\left(\left|R[h_i] - R_{\text{emp}}\left[h_i, \mathbf{Z}\right]\right| > \varepsilon\right) .$$

Since, for any fixed h, $R[h]$ and $R_{\text{emp}}[h, z]$ are the expectation and mean of a random variable between 0 and 1, the result follows by Hoeffding's inequality. ■

In order to generalize this proof to an infinite number $|\mathcal{H}|$ of hypotheses we use a very similar technique which, however, requires some preparatory work to reduce the analysis to a finite number of hypotheses. Basically, the approach can be decomposed into three steps:

1. First, consider a double sample $z\tilde{z} \in \mathcal{Z}^{2m}$ drawn iid where $\tilde{z}$ is sometimes referred to as a *ghost sample*. We upper bound the probability that there exists a hypothesis $h \in \mathcal{H}$ such that $R_{\text{emp}}[h, z]$ is more than ε apart from $R[h]$ by twice the probability that there exists $h' \in \mathcal{H}$ such that $R_{\text{emp}}\left[h', z\right]$ is more than $\varepsilon/2$ apart from $R_{\text{emp}}\left[h', \tilde{z}\right]$. This lemma has become known as the *basic lemma* and the technique is often referred to as *symmetrization by a ghost sample*. The idea is intuitive—it takes into account that it is very likely that the mean of a random variable is close to its expectation (see Subsection A.5.2). If it is likely that two means estimated on iid samples $z \in \mathcal{Z}^m$ and $\tilde{z} \in \mathcal{Z}^m$ are very close then it appears very probable that a single random mean is close to its expectation otherwise we would likely have observed a large deviation between the two means.

2. Since we assume the sample (and ghost sample) to be an iid sample it holds that, for any permutation $\pi : \{1, \ldots, 2m\} \to \{1, \ldots, 2m\}$,

$$\mathbf{P}_{\mathsf{Z}^{2m}}\left(\Upsilon\left(\mathsf{Z}_1, \ldots, \mathsf{Z}_{2m}\right)\right) = \mathbf{P}_{\mathsf{Z}^{2m}}\left(\Upsilon\left(\mathsf{Z}_{\pi(1)}, \ldots, \mathsf{Z}_{\pi(2m)}\right)\right),$$

whatever the logical formula $\Upsilon : \mathcal{Z}^{2m} \to \{\text{true}, \text{false}\}$ stands for. As a consequence, for any set Π_{2m} of permutations it follows that

$$\begin{aligned}
\mathbf{P}_{\mathsf{Z}^{2m}}\left(\Upsilon\left(\mathsf{Z}_1, \ldots, \mathsf{Z}_{2m}\right)\right) &= \frac{1}{|\Pi_{2m}|} \sum_{\pi \in \Pi_{2m}} \mathbf{P}_{\mathsf{Z}^{2m}}\left(\Upsilon\left(\mathsf{Z}_{\pi(1)}, \ldots, \mathsf{Z}_{\pi(2m)}\right)\right) \qquad (4.9)\\
&= \int_{\mathcal{Z}^{2m}} \left(\frac{1}{|\Pi_{2m}|} \sum_{\pi \in \Pi_{2m}} \mathbf{I}_{\Upsilon\left(z_{\pi(1)}, \ldots, z_{\pi(2m)}\right)}\right) d\mathbf{F}_{\mathsf{Z}^{2m}}(z)\\
&\le \max_{z \in \mathcal{Z}^{2m}} \left(\frac{1}{|\Pi_{2m}|} \sum_{\pi \in \Pi_{2m}} \mathbf{I}_{\Upsilon\left(z_{\pi(1)}, \ldots, z_{\pi(2m)}\right)}\right). \qquad (4.10)
\end{aligned}$$

The appealing feature of this step is that we have reduced the problem of bounding the probability over $\mathcal{Z}^{2m}$ to a counting of permutations $\pi \in \Pi_{2m}$ *for a fixed* $z \in \mathcal{Z}^{2m}$. This step is also known as *symmetrization by permutation* or *conditioning*.

3. It remains to bound the number of permutations $\pi \in \Pi_{2m}$ such that there exists a hypothesis $h' \in \mathcal{H}$ on which the deviation of two empirical risks (on the training sample z and the ghost sample $\tilde{z}$) exceeds $\varepsilon/2$. Since we considered the zero-one loss l_{0-1} we know that there are at most 2^{2m} different hypotheses w.r.t. the empirical risks $R_{\text{emp}}\left[h', z\right]$ and $R_{\text{emp}}\left[h', \tilde{z}\right]$. If we denote the maximum number of such equivalence classes by $\mathcal{N}_{\mathcal{H}}(2m)$ then we can again use a combination of the union bound and Hoeffding's inequality to bound the generalization error. Note that the cardinality $|\mathcal{H}|$ of the hypothesis space in the finite case has been replaced by the number $\mathcal{N}_{\mathcal{H}}(2m)$.

Following these three steps we obtain the main VC and PAC bounds.

Theorem 4.7 (VC and PAC generalization error bound) *For all probability measures* $\mathbf{P}_{\mathsf{Z}}$*, any hypothesis space* $\mathcal{H}$*, the zero-one loss* l_{0-1} *given by equation (2.10) and all* $\varepsilon > 0$

$$\mathbf{P}_{\mathsf{Z}^m}\left(\exists h \in \mathcal{H} : \left|R[h] - R_{\text{emp}}\left[h, \mathbf{Z}\right]\right| > \varepsilon\right) < 4\mathcal{N}_{\mathcal{H}}(2m)\exp\left(-\frac{m\varepsilon^2}{8}\right), \quad (4.11)$$

$$\mathbf{P}_{\mathsf{Z}^m}\left(\exists h \in V(\mathbf{Z}) : R[h] > \varepsilon\right) < 2\mathcal{N}_{\mathcal{H}}(2m)\exp\left(-\frac{m\varepsilon}{4}\right), \quad (4.12)$$

$$\mathbf{P}_{\mathsf{Z}^m}\left(R\left[\mathcal{A}_{\text{ERM}}(\mathbf{Z})\right] - R\left[h^*\right] > \varepsilon\right) < 4\mathcal{N}_{\mathcal{H}}(2m)\exp\left(-\frac{m\varepsilon^2}{32}\right). \quad (4.13)$$

Proof The first two results are proven in Appendix C.1. The final result follows from equation (4.6) using the fact that

$$\left(2\sup_{h\in\mathcal{H}}\left|R[h] - R_{\text{emp}}[h,z]\right| \le \varepsilon \Rightarrow R\left[\mathcal{A}_{\text{ERM}}(z)\right] - R\left[h^*\right] \le \varepsilon\right) \Leftrightarrow$$
$$\left(R\left[\mathcal{A}_{\text{ERM}}(z)\right] - R\left[h^*\right] > \varepsilon \Rightarrow \sup_{h\in\mathcal{H}}\left|R[h] - R_{\text{emp}}[h,z]\right| > \frac{\varepsilon}{2}\right),$$

which proves the assertion. ■

Confidence Intervals

Disregarding the fact that $\mathcal{N}_{\mathcal{H}}$ is unknown up to this point we see that, from these assertions, we can construct *confidence intervals* for the expected risk $R[h]$ of the function h by setting the r.h.s. of equations (4.11) and (4.12) to δ. Assuming that the event (violation of the bound) has taken place (which will happen with probability not more than δ over the random draw of training sample z) then with probability at least $1-\delta$ over the random draw of the training sample z for all probability measures $\mathbf{P}_{\mathsf{Z}}$, and simultaneously for all functions $h \in \mathcal{H}$

$$R[h] \leq R_{\text{emp}}[h, z] + \underbrace{\sqrt{\frac{8}{m}\left(\ln\left(\frac{4}{\delta}\right) + \ln\left(\mathcal{N}_{\mathcal{H}}(2m)\right)\right)}}_{\varepsilon_{\text{VC}}(m,\delta)} . \tag{4.14}$$

Also, for all functions having zero training error $R_{\text{emp}}[h, z] = 0$

$$R[h] \leq \underbrace{\frac{4}{m}\left(\ln\left(\frac{2}{\delta}\right) + \ln\left(\mathcal{N}_{\mathcal{H}}(2m)\right)\right)}_{\varepsilon_{\text{PAC}}(m,\delta)} . \tag{4.15}$$

These two bounds constitute the basis results obtained in the VC and PAC framework. There are some interesting conclusions we can draw:

1. If the function $\mathcal{N}_{\mathcal{H}}$ fulfills $\mathcal{N}_{\mathcal{H}}(2m) = 2^{2m}$ then both bounds are trivial because $\ln\left(2^{2m}\right) = m\ln(4) > m$ whence the r.h.s. of both inequalities is always greater than one. Note this is a meaningless bound as $0 \leq R[h] \leq 1$. In this case we say that *the hypothesis space $\mathcal{H}$ is too rich* and thus we are unable to give any guarantees about the learned function. As an example, if for all m and all training samples $z \in \mathcal{Z}^m$ there exists one hypothesis $h \in \mathcal{H}$ which achieves zero training error $R_{\text{emp}}[h, z]$, then the hypothesis space was much to rich.

2. In the general VC case the upper bound is of order $\mathcal{O}(\sqrt{\ln\left(\mathcal{N}_{\mathcal{H}}(2m)\right)/m})$ whereas in the zero training error case it grows as $\mathcal{O}(\ln(\mathcal{N}_{\mathcal{H}}(2m))/m)$ due to the exponent of ε of one in equation (4.12). Thus, it seems that we can tighten bounds by magnitudes if we can achieve zero training error. In fact, one can show that the exponent of ε in equation (4.11) smoothly decreases from the 2 to 1 as a function of the minimum expected risk $R[h^*]$. For specific conditions on the hypothesis space $\mathcal{H}$ one can show that, even in the general case, the exponent of ε is 1.

3. If the cardinality of $\mathcal{H}$ is finite we always know that $\mathcal{N}_{\mathcal{H}}(m) \leq |\mathcal{H}|$ for all m. As a consequence, in the case of finite cardinality of the hypothesis space we obtain our result (4.8) as a special case (with less favorable constants). A potential application of this result is to obtain upper bounds on the generalization error for decision tree learning. As the size of decision trees often grows exponentially in m, techniques like *pruning* effectively limit the number $|\mathcal{H}_m|$ and thus guarantee a small generalization error.

Remark 4.8 (Race for constants) *The proof of Theorem 4.7 does not provide the best constants possible. The best constants that can be achieved for the coefficients of the exponent in the exponential term are 2 and 1, respectively. We shall see in Subsection 4.3 that an improvement of these results* by orders of magnitude *can only be achieved if we give up the* a-priori *character of the bounds. Presently, the bounds are of the same value for all decision functions that achieve the same training error $R_{\text{emp}}[h, z]$. On the one hand, this characteristic is advantageous as it gives us a general warranty however malicious the distribution $\mathbf{P}_Z$ is. On the other hand, it only justifies the empirical risk minimization method as this is the only* data dependent *term entering the bound.*

4.2.2 Growth Function and VC Dimension

In the previous subsection we used the function $\mathcal{N}_{\mathcal{H}}$ which characterizes the *worst case diversity* of the hypothesis space $\mathcal{H}$ as a function of the training sample size. Moreover, due to the exponential term for the deviation of two means, all that matters for bounds on the generalization error is the logarithm of this function. More formally, this function is defined as follows.

Definition 4.9 (Covering number and growth function) *Let $\mathcal{H} \subseteq \mathcal{Y}^{\mathcal{X}}$ be a hypothesis space. Then the function $\mathcal{N}_{\mathcal{H}} : \mathbb{N} \to \mathbb{N}$ is defined as*

$$\mathcal{N}_{\mathcal{H}}(m) \stackrel{\text{def}}{=} \max_{z \in \mathcal{Z}^m} \left|\left\{\left(l_{0-1}\left(h\left(x_1\right), y_1\right), \cdots, l_{0-1}\left(h\left(x_m\right), y_m\right)\right) \mid h \in \mathcal{H}\right\}\right| , \qquad (4.16)$$

that is, the maximum number of different equivalence classes of functions w.r.t. the zero-one loss l_{0-1} on a sample of size m. This is called the covering number *of $\mathcal{H}$ w.r.t. zero-one loss l_{0-1}. The logarithm of this function is called the* growth function *and is denoted by $\mathcal{G}_{\mathcal{H}}$, i.e.,*

$$\mathcal{G}_{\mathcal{H}}(m) \stackrel{\text{def}}{=} \ln\left(\mathcal{N}_{\mathcal{H}}(m)\right) .$$

Clearly, the growth function depends neither on the sample nor on the unknown distribution $\mathbf{P}_Z$ but only on the sample size m and the hypothesis space $\mathcal{H}$. Ideally, this function would be calculated *before* learning and, as a consequence, we would be able to calculate the second term of the confidence intervals (4.14) and (4.15). Unfortunately, it is generally not possible to determine the exact value of the function $\mathcal{G}_{\mathcal{H}}$ for an arbitrary hypothesis space $\mathcal{H}$ and any m. Therefore one major interest in the VC and PAC community is to obtain tight upper bounds on the growth function. One of the first such bounds is given by the following results whose proof can be found in Appendix C.2.

Theorem 4.10 (Growth function bound and VC dimension) *For any hypothesis space $\mathcal{H}$, the growth function $\mathcal{G}_{\mathcal{H}}$ either*

1. *satisfies the equality*

$$\forall m \in \mathbb{N}: \qquad \mathcal{G}_{\mathcal{H}}(m) = \ln(2) \cdot m\,,$$

2. *or, there exists a natural number $\vartheta_{\mathcal{H}} \in \mathbb{N}$ such that*

$$\mathcal{G}_{\mathcal{H}}(m) \begin{cases} = \ln(2) \cdot m & \text{if } m \leq \vartheta_{\mathcal{H}} \\ \leq \ln\left(\sum_{i=0}^{\vartheta_{\mathcal{H}}} \binom{m}{i}\right) & \text{if } m > \vartheta_{\mathcal{H}} \end{cases}. \tag{4.17}$$

The number[4] $\vartheta_{\mathcal{H}} \in \mathbb{N}$ *is called the* VC dimension *of the hypothesis space $\mathcal{H}$ and is defined by*

$$\vartheta_{\mathcal{H}} \stackrel{\text{def}}{=} \max\left\{m \in \mathbb{N} \mid \mathcal{N}_{\mathcal{H}}(m) = 2^m\right\}. \tag{4.18}$$

This result is fundamental as it shows that we can upper bound the richness $\mathcal{N}_{\mathcal{H}}$ of the hypothesis space by an integer summary—the VC dimension. A lot of research has been done to obtain tight upper bounds on the VC dimension which has, by definition, the following combinatorial interpretation: If $\mathfrak{A}_{\mathcal{H}} = \{\{(x, y) \in \mathcal{Z} \mid l_{0-1}(h(x), y) = 1\} \mid h \in \mathcal{H}\}$ is the induced set of events that a hypothesis $h \in \mathcal{H}$ labels $(x, y) \in \mathcal{Z}$ incorrectly, then the VC dimension ϑ of $\mathfrak{A}_{\mathcal{H}}$ is the largest natural number ϑ such that there exists a sample $z \in \mathcal{Z}^{\vartheta}$ of size ϑ which can be subdivided in all 2^{ϑ} different ways by (set) intersection with $\mathfrak{A}_{\mathcal{H}}$. Then we say that $\mathfrak{A}_{\mathcal{H}}$ *shatters* z. If no such number exists we say that the VC dimension of $\mathfrak{A}_{\mathcal{H}}$ or $\mathcal{H}$ is infinite. Sometimes the VC dimension is also called the *shatter coefficient*.

In order to relate the above bound on the growth function in terms of the VC dimension to the confidence intervals (4.14) and (4.15) we make use of the inequality given in Theorem A.105 which states that for all $m > \vartheta$

$$\sum_{i=0}^{\vartheta} \binom{m}{i} < \left(\frac{em}{\vartheta}\right)^{\vartheta}. \tag{4.19}$$

4 We shall omit the subscript of $\vartheta_{\mathcal{H}}$ whenever the hypothesis space $\mathcal{H}$ is clear from context.

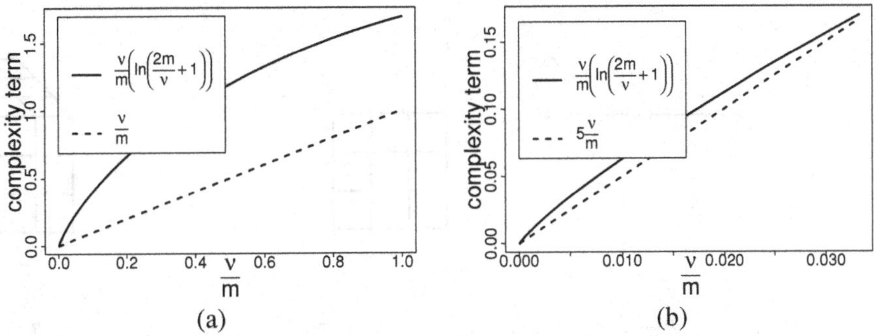

Figure 4.2 Growth of the complexity term $\frac{\vartheta}{m}\left(\ln\left(\frac{2m}{\vartheta}\right)+1\right)$ in the VC confidence interval (4.14) as a function of $\frac{\vartheta}{m}$. **(a)** On the whole interval [0, 1] the increase is clearly sub-linear. **(b)** For very small values of $\frac{\vartheta}{m} < \frac{1}{30}$ the growth is almost linear.

Therefore for all training sample sizes $m > \vartheta$, the growth function $\mathcal{G}_{\mathcal{H}}(m) \le \vartheta\left(\ln\left(\frac{m}{\vartheta}\right)+1\right)$ is sub-linear in ϑ due to the $\ln\left(\frac{m}{\vartheta}\right)$ term.

Remark 4.11 (Sufficient training sample size) *Using the upper bound (4.19) of the upper bound (4.17) for the growth function $\mathcal{G}_{\mathcal{H}}$ we obtain for the confidence interval (4.14) the following expression*

$$\forall 2m > \vartheta : \qquad R[h] \le R_{\mathrm{emp}}[h, z] + \sqrt{8\left(\frac{\ln\left(\frac{4}{\delta}\right)}{m} + \frac{\vartheta}{m}\left(\ln\left(\frac{2m}{\vartheta}\right)+1\right)\right)},$$

Neglecting the term $\ln(4/\delta)/m$ *(which decreases very quickly to zero for increasing m) we plot the value of* $\frac{\vartheta}{m}\left(\ln\left(\frac{2m}{\vartheta}\right)+1\right)$ *as a function of* $\frac{\vartheta}{m}$ *in Figure 4.2. Clearly, for* $\frac{m}{\vartheta} > 30$ *the contribution of the VC term is less than* 0.15 *and thus, by the constant factor of* 8*, we will have nontrivial results in these regimes. Vapnik suggested this as a rule of thumb for the practicability of his bound. By the plots in Figure 4.2 it is justifiable to say that,* for $\frac{m}{\vartheta} > 30$, *the training sample size is sufficiently large to guarantee a small generalization error of the empirical risk minimization algorithm.*

Remark 4.12 (Data dependent hypothesis spaces) *Another consequence of the reasoning given above is that the hypothesis space $\mathcal{H}$ must be independent of the training sample z. As we have seen in Chapter 2 there are two different viewpoints*

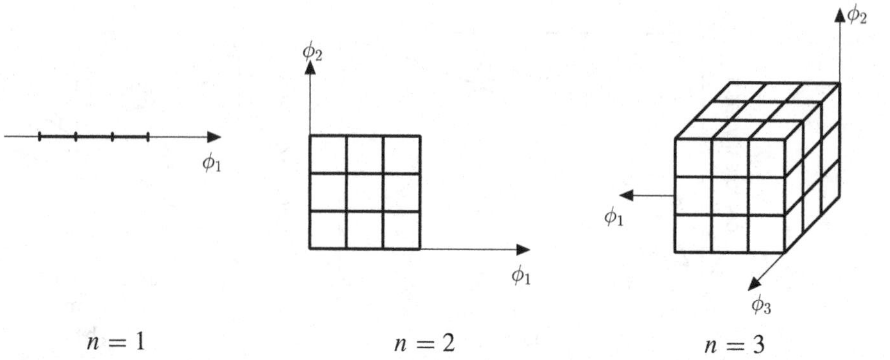

Figure 4.3 Curse of dimensionality. In order to reliably estimate a density in $\mathbb{R}^n$ we subdivide the n–dimensional space into cells and estimate their probability by the frequency that an example $x \in \boldsymbol{x}$ falls into it. Increasing the number of cells would increase the precision of this estimate. For a fixed precision, however, the number of cells depends *exponentially* on the number n of dimensions.

of margin maximization. First, having the norm of each normal vector $\mathbf{w}$ *fixed, margin maximization aims to minimize the margin loss* l_{margin} *given by equation (2.42). Second, defining the hypothesis space* $\mathcal{H}$ *to achieve a minimum real-valued output of one at each training point, this makes* $\mathcal{H}$ *data dependent and, thus, inappropriate for theoretical studies. Nevertheless this formulation of the problem is algorithmically advantageous.*

An important property of the VC dimension is that it does not necessarily coincide with the number of parameters used. This feature is the key to seeing that, by studying the convergence of expected risks, we are able to overcome a problem which is known as *curse of dimensionality*: The number of examples needed to reliably estimate the density in an n–dimensional space $\mathcal{X}$ grows exponentially with n (see also Figure 4.3). In the following we will give three examples showing that the VC dimension can be less than, equal to or greater than the number of parameters. Note that these three examples are intended to illustrate the difference between number of parameters and the VC dimension rather than being practically useful.

Example 4.13 (VC dimension and parameters) *Let us use the following three examples to illustrate the difference between the dimensionality of parameter space and the VC dimension (see Section 4.5 for references containing rigorous proofs).*

1. *Consider $\mathcal{X} = \mathbb{R}$ and*

$$\mathcal{H} = \left\{ x \mapsto \operatorname{sign}\left(\sum_{i=1}^{n} \left| w_i x^i \right| \operatorname{sign}(x) + w_0 \right) \;\middle|\; (w_0, w_1, \ldots, w_n) \in \mathbb{R}^{n+1} \right\}.$$

Clearly, all functions in $\mathcal{H}$ are monotonically increasing and have exactly one zero. Thus the maximum size d of a training sample z that can be labeled in all 2^d different ways is one. This implies that the VC dimension of $\mathcal{H}$ is one. As this holds regardless of n the VC dimension can be much smaller than the number of parameters. It is worth mentioning that for all $n \in \mathbb{N}$ there exists a one-dimensional parameterization of $\mathcal{H}$—each $\mathbf{w} \in \mathbb{R}^{n+1}$ is represented by its zero—which, however, the difficulty is to find a-priori.

2. *Consider $\mathcal{X} = \mathbb{R}^n$ and*

$$\mathcal{H} = \left\{ x \mapsto \operatorname{sign}(\langle \mathbf{w}, \mathbf{x} \rangle) \;\middle|\; \mathbf{w} \in \mathbb{R}^n \right\},$$

where $\mathbf{x} \stackrel{\text{def}}{=} \boldsymbol{\phi}(x)$ for some fixed feature mapping $\boldsymbol{\phi} : \mathcal{X} \to \mathcal{K} \subseteq \ell_2^n$ (see Definition 2.2). Given a sample $x = (x_1, \ldots, x_m)$ of m objects we thus obtain the $m \times n$ data matrix $\mathbf{X} = \left(\mathbf{x}_1'; \ldots; \mathbf{x}_m'\right) \in \mathbb{R}^{m \times n}$. If the training sample size m is bigger than the number n of dimensions the matrix $\mathbf{X}$ has at most rank n, i.e., $\mathbf{X}\mathbf{w} = \mathbf{t}$ has, in general, no solution. It follows that the VC dimension can be at most n. In the case of $m = n$, by choosing the training sample $(x_1, \ldots, x_m)$ such that $\mathbf{x}_i = \mathbf{e}_i$, we see that $\mathbf{X}\mathbf{w} = \mathbf{I}\mathbf{w} = \mathbf{w}$, that is, for any labeling $\mathbf{y} \in \{-1, +1\}^m$, we will find a vector $\mathbf{w} \in \mathbb{R}^n$ that realizes the labeling. Therefore the VC dimension of linear classifiers equals the number n of parameters.

3. *Consider $\mathcal{X} = \mathbb{R}$ and*

$$\mathcal{H} = \{ x \mapsto \operatorname{sign}(\sin(wx)) \mid w \in \mathbb{R} \}.$$

Through w we can parameterize the frequency of the sine and thus, for uniformly spaced training samples $x \in \mathcal{X}^m$ of any size m, we will find 2^m (extremely high) values of w that label the m points in all 2^m different ways. As a consequence the VC dimension is infinite though we have only one *parameter.*

4.2.3 Structural Risk Minimization

The analysis presented in the previous subsection revealed that the VC dimension of $\mathcal{H}$ is the fundamental quantity that controls the uniform convergence of empirical risks to expected risks and, as such, the generalization error of an empirical risk minimization algorithm $\mathcal{A}_{\text{ERM}}$. Ideally, we would like to make the VC dimension itself a quantity that can be minimized by a learning algorithm; in particular, if we have too small a training sample $z \in \mathcal{Z}^m$ of size m for too rich a hypothesis space $\mathcal{H} \subseteq \mathcal{Y}^{\mathcal{X}}$ having VC dimension $\vartheta \gg m$. A minimization of the VC dimension in parallel to the training error is, however, theoretically not justified as the VC dimension is only characterizing the complexity of $\mathcal{H}$ of empirical risk minimization algorithms.

One possible method of overcoming this problem is to use the principle of *structural risk minimization (SRM)*. By a *structure* we mean a set $\mathcal{S} = \{\mathcal{H}_1, \ldots, \mathcal{H}_s\}$ of s hypothesis spaces. It is often assumed that $\mathcal{H}_1 \subset \cdots \subset \mathcal{H}_s$ and thus the relation $\mathcal{H}_{i-1} \subset \mathcal{H}_i$ implies $\vartheta_{\mathcal{H}_{i-1}} \leq \vartheta_{\mathcal{H}_i}$ for the VC dimensions of $\mathcal{H}_{i-1}$ and $\mathcal{H}_i$. Then the idea of SRM is to compute a set $\left\{\mathcal{A}_{\text{ERM},\mathcal{H}_i}(z) \in \mathcal{H}_i\right\}_{i=1}^{s}$ of hypotheses which minimize the training error $R_{\text{emp}}[\cdot, z]$ in the hypothesis space $\mathcal{H}_i$. This set is later used to tradeoff the resulting training error $R_{\text{emp}}\left[\mathcal{A}_{\text{ERM},\mathcal{H}_i}(z), z\right]$ versus the complexity (measured in terms of VC dimension $\vartheta_{\mathcal{H}_i}$) using the confidence interval (4.14) or (4.15). Clearly we cannot directly apply Theorems 4.7 because they assume a fixed hypothesis space. Further, we might have some prior hope that the minimizer of the expected risk is within equivalence class $\mathcal{H}_i$ which we express by a probability distribution $\mathbf{P}_{\mathsf{S}}$. In order to get a theoretically justified result we make use of the following lemma which is the basis of multiple testing[5].

Lemma 4.14 (Multiple testing) *Suppose we are given a set* $\{\Upsilon_1, \ldots \Upsilon_s\}$ *of* s *measurable logic formulas* $\Upsilon : \bigcup_{m=1}^{\infty} \mathcal{Z}^m \times \mathbb{N} \times (0, 1] \to \{\text{true}, \text{false}\}$ *and a discrete probability measure* $\mathbf{P}_{\mathsf{S}}$ *over the sample space* $\{1, \ldots, s\}$. *Let us assume that*

$$\forall i \in \{1, \ldots, s\} : \forall m \in \mathbb{N} : \forall \delta \in (0, 1] : \qquad \mathbf{P}_{\mathsf{Z}^m}\left(\Upsilon_i\left(\mathbf{Z}, m, \delta\right)\right) \geq 1 - \delta\,.$$

Then, for all $m \in \mathbb{N}$ *and* $\delta \in (0, 1]$,

$$\mathbf{P}_{\mathsf{Z}^m}\left(\Upsilon_1\left(\mathbf{Z}, m, \delta \mathbf{P}_{\mathsf{S}}(1)\right) \wedge \cdots \wedge \Upsilon_s\left(\mathbf{Z}, m, \delta \mathbf{P}_{\mathsf{S}}(s)\right)\right) \geq 1 - \delta\,.$$

Proof The proof is a simple union bound argument. By definition

$$\begin{aligned} &\mathbf{P}_{\mathsf{Z}^m}\left(\Upsilon_1\left(\mathbf{Z}, m, \delta \mathbf{P}_{\mathsf{S}}(1)\right) \wedge \cdots \wedge \Upsilon_s\left(\mathbf{Z}, m, \delta \mathbf{P}_{\mathsf{S}}(s)\right)\right) \\ &\quad = 1 - \mathbf{P}_{\mathsf{Z}^m}\left(\neg\Upsilon_1\left(\mathbf{Z}, m, \delta \mathbf{P}_{\mathsf{S}}(1)\right) \vee \cdots \vee \neg\Upsilon_s\left(\mathbf{Z}, m, \delta \mathbf{P}_{\mathsf{S}}(s)\right)\right) \\ &\quad \geq 1 - \sum_{i=1}^{s} \mathbf{P}_{\mathsf{Z}^m}\left(\neg\Upsilon_i\left(\mathbf{Z}, m, \delta \mathbf{P}_{\mathsf{S}}(i)\right)\right) \qquad \text{(by the union bound)} \end{aligned}$$

5 In the theory of multiple statistical tests, the resulting statistical procedure is often called a *Bonferroni* test.

$$> 1 - \sum_{i=1}^{s} \delta \mathbf{P}_{\mathsf{S}}(i) = 1 - \delta\,. \qquad \text{(by assumption)}$$

The lemma is proved. ■

This simple lemma is directly applicable to Theorem 4.7 by noticing that for each training sample size m and for all hypothesis space $\mathcal{H}_i$ in the structure $\mathcal{S}$ the corresponding logic formulas are given by

$$\Upsilon_i(z, m, \delta) \equiv \forall h \in \mathcal{H}_i : \left|R[h] - R_{\text{emp}}[h, z]\right| \leq \sqrt{\frac{8}{m}\left(\ln\left(\frac{4}{\delta}\right) + \mathcal{G}_{\mathcal{H}_i}(2m)\right)},$$

$$\Upsilon_i(z, m, \delta) \equiv \forall h \in \mathcal{H}_i : R_{\text{emp}}[h, z] \neq 0 \vee R[h] \leq \frac{4}{m}\left(\ln\left(\frac{2}{\delta}\right) + \mathcal{G}_{\mathcal{H}_i}(2m)\right),$$

where the first formula is for the VC bound and the second for the PAC bound. Thus, we know that, with probability at least $1-\delta$, simultaneously for all hypothesis spaces $\mathcal{H}_i \in \mathcal{S}$ and all hypotheses $h \in \mathcal{H}_i$

$$R[h] \leq R_{\text{emp}}[h, z] + \sqrt{\frac{8}{m}\left(\ln\left(\frac{4}{\delta}\right) + \ln\left(\frac{1}{\mathbf{P}_{\mathsf{S}}(\mathcal{H}_i)}\right) + \mathcal{G}_{\mathcal{H}_i}(2m)\right)}, \tag{4.20}$$

and simultaneously for all hypothesis spaces $\mathcal{H}_i \in \mathcal{S}$ and all hypotheses $h \in \mathcal{H}_i$ achieving zero training error $R_{\text{emp}}[h, z] = 0$

$$R[h] \leq \frac{4}{m}\left(\ln\left(\frac{2}{\delta}\right) + \ln\left(\frac{1}{\mathbf{P}_{\mathsf{S}}(\mathcal{H}_i)}\right) + \mathcal{G}_{\mathcal{H}_i}(2m)\right). \tag{4.21}$$

Apparently, we are able to trade the complexity expressed by $\mathcal{G}_{\mathcal{H}_i}(2m)$ against the training error $R_{\text{emp}}[h, z]$ (see also Figure 4.4) or we can simply stop increasing complexity as soon as we have found a hypothesis space $\mathcal{H}_i$ containing a hypothesis having zero training error at a price of $-\ln(\mathbf{P}_{\mathsf{S}}(\mathcal{H}_i))$. Thanks to the exponential decrease, this price is very small if the number s of hypothesis spaces in $\mathcal{S}$ is small. Note that the SRM principle is a curious one: In order to have an algorithm it is necessary to have a good theoretical bound on the generalization error of the empirical risk minimization method. Another view of the structural risk minimization principle is that it is an attempt to solve the model selection problem. In place of the ultimate quantity to be minimized—the expected risk of the learned function $\mathcal{A}_{\text{ERM},\mathcal{H}_i}(z)$—a (probabilistic) bound on the latter is used, automatically giving a performance guarantee of the model selection principle itself.

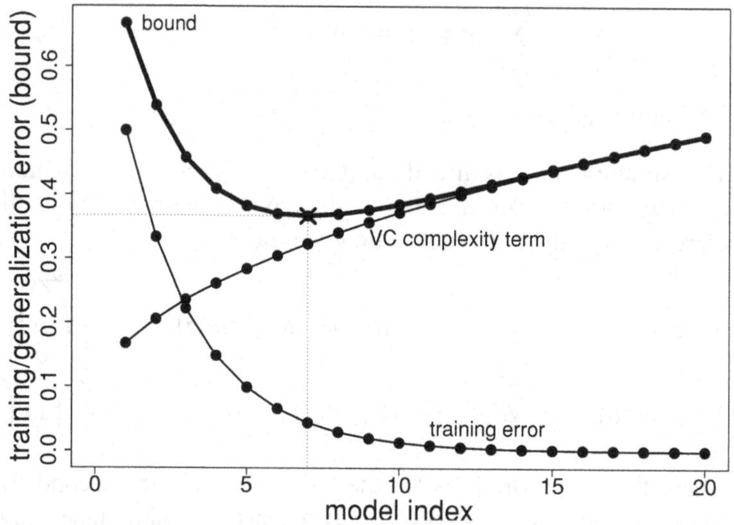

Figure 4.4 Structural risk minimization in action. Here we used hypothesis spaces $\mathcal{H}_i$ such that $\vartheta_{\mathcal{H}_i} = i$ and $\mathcal{H}_i \subseteq \mathcal{H}_{i+1}$. This implies that the training errors of the empirical risk minimizers can only be decreasing which leads to the typical situation depicted. Note that lines are used for visualization purposes because we consider only a finite set $\mathcal{S}$ of hypothesis spaces.

Remark 4.15 (The role of $\mathbf{P}_S$) *The role of the numbers $\mathbf{P}_S(\mathcal{H}_i)$ seems somewhat counterintuitive as we appear to be able to bias our estimate by adjusting these parameters. The belief $\mathbf{P}_S$ must, however, be specified* in advance *and represents some apportionment of our confidence to the different points where failure might occur. We recover the standard PAC and VC bound if $\mathbf{P}_S$ is peaked at exactly one hypothesis space. In the first work on SRM it was implicitly assumed that these numbers are $\frac{1}{s}$. Another interesting aspect of $\mathbf{P}_S$ is that, thanks to the exponential term in Theorem 4.7 using a uniform measure $\mathbf{P}_S$ we can consider up to $\mathcal{O}(e^m)$ different hypothesis spaces before deteriorating to trivial bounds.*

4.3 The Luckiness Framework

Using structural risk minimization we are able to make the complexity, as measured by the VC dimension of the hypothesis space, a variable of a model selection algorithm while still having guarantees for the expected risks. Nonetheless, we recall that the decomposition of the hypothesis space must be done *independently of the observed training sample* z. This rule certainly limits the applicability of structural risk minimization to an a-priori complexity penalization strategy. The resulting bounds effectively ignore the sample $z \in \mathcal{Z}^m$ except with regard to the training error $R_{\mathrm{emp}}[\mathcal{A}(z), z]$. A prominent example of the misuse of structural risk minimization was the first generalization error bounds for the support vector machine algorithm. It has become commonly accepted that the success of support vector machines can be explained through the structuring of the hypothesis space $\mathcal{H}$ of linear classifiers in terms of the geometrical margin $\gamma_z(\mathbf{w})$ of a linear classifier having normal vector $\mathbf{w}$ (see Definition 2.30). Obviously, however, the margin itself is a quantity that strongly depends on the sample z and thus a rigorous application of structural risk minimization is impossible! Nevertheless, we shall see in the following section that the margin is, in fact, a quantity which allows an algorithm to control its generalization error.

In order to overcome this limitation we will introduce the *luckiness framework*. The goals in the luckiness framework are to

1. Formalize under which conditions we can use the training sample $z \in \mathcal{Z}^m$ to decompose a given hypothesis space $\mathcal{H}$ and

2. Provide PAC or VC like results, namely, uniform bounds on the expected risks that *still do not depend* on the unknown probability measure $\mathbf{P_Z}$.

In contrast to the VC and PAC framework the new uniform bound on the expected risk $R[h]$ of all hypotheses $h \in \mathcal{H}$ is allowed to depend on the training sample z and the single hypothesis h considered[6].

Definition 4.16 (Luckiness generalization error bound) *Suppose we are given a hypothesis space* $\mathcal{H} \subseteq \mathcal{Y}^{\mathcal{X}}$ *and a loss function* $l : \mathcal{Y} \times \mathcal{Y} \to \mathbb{R}$. *Then the function* $\varepsilon_L : \mathbb{N} \times (0, 1] \times \cup_{m=1}^{\infty} \mathcal{Z}^m \times \mathcal{H} \to \mathbb{R}^+$ *is called a* luckiness generalization error bound *if, and only if, for all training sample sizes* $m \in \mathbb{N}$, *all* $\delta \in (0, 1]$ *and all* $\mathbf{P_Z}$

$$\mathbf{P}_{\mathbf{Z}^m}\left(\forall h \in \mathcal{H} : \; R[h] \leq \varepsilon_L(m, \delta, \mathbf{Z}, h)\right) \geq 1 - \delta .$$

6 Note that a VC and PAC generalization error bound is implicitly dependent on the training error $R_{\mathrm{emp}}[h, z]$.

Given such a result we have automatically obtained a bound for the algorithm which directly minimizes the $\varepsilon_L(|z|, \delta, z, h)$, i.e.,

$$\mathcal{A}_{\varepsilon_L}(z) \stackrel{\text{def}}{=} \operatorname*{argmin}_{h\in\mathcal{H}} \varepsilon_L(|z|, \delta, z, h) . \tag{4.22}$$

Note that at present only PAC results for the zero-one loss l_{0-1} are available. Hence we must assume that, for the training sample z, there exists at least one hypothesis $h \in \mathcal{H}$ such that $R_{\text{emp}}[h, z] = 0$.

The additional information we exploit in the case of sample based decompositions of the hypothesis space $\mathcal{H}$ is encapsulated in a luckiness function. The main idea is to fix in advance some assumption about the measure $\mathbf{P}_Z$, and encode this assumption in a real-valued function L defined on the space of training samples $z \in \mathcal{Z}^m$ and hypotheses $h \in \mathcal{H}$. The value of the function L indicates the extent to which the assumption is satisfied for the particular sample and hypothesis. More formally, this reads as follows.

Definition 4.17 (Luckiness function and level) *Let $\mathcal{H} \subseteq \mathcal{Y}^{\mathcal{X}}$ and $\mathcal{Z} = \mathcal{X} \times \mathcal{Y}$ be a given hypothesis and sample space, respectively. A* luckiness function *L is a permutation invariant function that maps each training sample z and hypothesis h to a real value, i.e.,*

$$L : \bigcup_{m=1}^{\infty} \mathcal{Z}^m \times \mathcal{H} \to \mathbb{R}.$$

Given a training sample $z = (\boldsymbol{x}, \boldsymbol{y})$, the level *$\ell_L$ of a function $h \in \mathcal{H}$ relative to L and z is defined by*

$$\ell_L(z, h) \stackrel{\text{def}}{=} \left|\left\{\left(l_{0-1}(g(x_1), y_1), \ldots, l_{0-1}(g(x_m), y_m)\right) \mid g \in H(h, z)\right\}\right| ,$$

where the set $H(h, z)$ is the subset of all hypotheses which are luckier on z, i.e.,

$$H(h, z) \stackrel{\text{def}}{=} \{g \in \mathcal{H} \mid L(z, g) \geq L(z, h)\} \subseteq \mathcal{H} .$$

The quantity ℓ_L plays the central role in what follows. Intuitively speaking, for a given training sample z and hypothesis h the level $\ell_L(z, h)$ counts the number of equivalence classes w.r.t. the zero-one loss l_{0-1} in $\mathcal{H}$ which contain functions $g \in \mathcal{H}$ that are luckier or at least as lucky as h. The main idea of the luckiness framework is to replace the coarse *worst case* argument—taking the covering number $\mathcal{N}_{\mathcal{H}}$ as the maximum number of equivalence classes with different losses for an application of the union bound—by an *actual sample* argument (see Subsection 4.2.1).

Thanks to the symmetrization by a ghost sample we only needed to show that for zero training error $R_{\mathrm{emp}}[h, \mathbf{z}] = 0$ on a sample of size m, the training error on the ghost sample $\tilde{\mathbf{z}}$ cannot exceed $\frac{\varepsilon}{2}$ with high probability and then use a union bound over all the equivalence classes. As we now want to make use of the luckiness $L(\mathbf{z}, h)$ for the estimation of the number of equivalence classes, we have to assume that also the luckiness (and thus the number of equivalence classes measured by ℓ_L) cannot increase too much. This is formally expressed in the following definition.

Definition 4.18 (Probable smoothness of luckiness functions) *A luckiness function L is* probably smooth with respect to the function $\omega : \mathbb{N} \times \mathbb{R} \times [0,1] \to \mathbb{N}$, *if for all $m \in \mathbb{N}$, all distributions $\mathbf{P}_{\mathsf{Z}}$ and all $\delta \in [0,1]$*

$$\mathbf{P}_{\mathsf{Z}^{2m}}\left(\exists h \in \mathcal{H} : \ell_L(\mathbf{Z}, h) > \omega\left(m, L\left(\left(\mathsf{Z}_1, \ldots, \mathsf{Z}_m\right), h\right), \delta\right)\right) \leq \delta .$$

The intuition behind this definition is that it captures when the luckiness can be estimated from the training sample $(z_1, \ldots, z_m) \in \mathcal{Z}^m$ with high probability. We have to make sure that with small probability (at most δ) over the random draw of a training and ghost sample there are more than $\omega(m, L((z_1, \ldots, z_m), h), \delta)$ equivalence classes that contain functions that are luckier than h on the training and ghost sample $(z_1, \ldots, z_m, z_{m+1}, \ldots, z_{2m})$. Now we are ready to give the main result in the luckiness framework.

Theorem 4.19 (Luckiness bound) *Suppose L is a luckiness function that is probably smooth w.r.t. the function ω. For any probability measure $\mathbf{P}_{\mathsf{Z}}$, any $d \in \mathbb{N}$ and any $\delta \in (0,1]$, with probability at least $1-\delta$ over the random draw of the training sample $\mathbf{z} \in \mathcal{Z}^m$ of size m, if $R_{\mathrm{emp}}[h, \mathbf{z}] = 0$ and $\omega\left(m, L(\mathbf{z}, h), \frac{\delta}{4}\right) \leq 2^d$ then*[7]

$$R[h] \leq \frac{2}{m}\left(d + \operatorname{ld}\left(\frac{4}{\delta}\right)\right) . \tag{4.23}$$

The lengthy proof is relegated to Appendix C.3. By the probable smoothness of L, the value of the function $\omega(m, L(\mathbf{z}, h), \delta/4)$ can never exceed 2^{2m} because, for the zero-one loss l_{0-1}, the maximum number $\ell_L(\mathbf{z}, h)$ of equivalence classes on a sample $\mathbf{z}$ of size maximally $2m$ is, for any $h \in \mathcal{H}$, at most this number. Hence we

7 Note that the symbol ld denotes the logarithm to base 2 (see also page 333).

can safely apply Lemma 4.14 using the following proposition

$$\forall h \in \mathcal{H} : R_{\text{emp}}[h, z] \neq 0 \vee \omega\left(m, L(z, h), \frac{\delta}{4}\right) > 2^i \vee R[h] \leq \frac{2}{m}\left(i + \text{ld}\left(\frac{4}{\delta}\right)\right),$$

which holds with probability at least $1 - \delta$ over the random draw of the training sample z. This means, simultaneously for all functions h which achieve zero training error $R_{\text{emp}}[h, z] = 0$ and $\omega(m, L(z, h), \delta p_d/4) \leq 2^d$, we know with probability at least $1 - \delta$ over the random draw of the training sample $z \in \mathcal{Z}^m$, that

$$R[h] \leq \frac{2}{m}\left(d + \text{ld}\left(\frac{4}{\delta p_d}\right)\right),$$

where the $2m$ numbers p_d must be positive and sum to one. This result is very impressive as it allows us to use the training sample $z \in \mathcal{Z}^m$ to decompose the hypothesis space $\mathcal{H}$. Such a decomposition is given by the *data-dependent structure* $\mathcal{S} = \{\mathcal{H}_1(z), \ldots, \mathcal{H}_{2m}(z)\}$ where $\mathcal{H}_i(z)$ is the set of all hypotheses which lead to a complexity value ω less than or equal to 2^i, i.e.,

$$\mathcal{H}_i(z) = \left\{h \in \mathcal{H} \;\middle|\; \omega\left(m, L(z, h), \frac{\delta}{4}\right) \leq 2^i\right\} \subseteq \mathcal{H}.$$

We refer to $\lceil \text{ld}(\omega(m, L(z, h), \cdot)) \rceil$ as an *effective complexity*—a complexity which depends on the data z and is not a-priori fixed. The price we pay for this generality is the *anytime applicability* of the bound: There is no guarantee *before* we have seen the training sample z that $\text{ld}(\omega(m, L(z, h), \cdot))$ will be small for any hypothesis h with zero training error $R_{\text{emp}}[h, z]$. As soon as we make use of $z \in \mathcal{Z}^m$ in the luckiness function L there will be a distribution $\mathbf{P}_Z$ which yields $\omega(m, L(z, h), \cdot) > 2^m$ for any consistent hypothesis $h \in V_{\mathcal{H}}(z)$ and thus we are unable to give *any* guarantee on the expected loss of these hypotheses. Such a distribution corresponds to the maximum violation of our belief in $\mathbf{P}_Z$ encoded a-priori by the choice of the luckiness function L.

Remark 4.20 (Conditional confidence intervals) *It is worth mentioning that the approach taken in the luckiness framework is far from new in classical statistics. The problem of* conditional confidence intervals *as a branch of classical test theory is very closely connected to the idea underlying luckiness. The main idea behind conditional confidence intervals is that although a confidence interval procedure* $\Phi : \mathcal{Z}^m \times [0, 1] \to \mathbb{R}$ *has the property that, for all measures* $\mathbf{P}_Z$,

$$\forall \delta \in [0, 1] : \qquad \mathbf{P}_{Z^m}(\forall h \in \mathcal{H} : R[h] \in \Phi(\mathbf{Z}, \delta)) \geq 1 - \delta,$$

there might exist a collection $\mathfrak{Z}$ *of training samples* $z \in \mathcal{Z}^m$ *such that, for all measures* $\mathbf{P}_\mathsf{Z}$,

$$\forall \delta \in [0,1] : \exists \kappa \in [0,1] : \quad \mathbf{P}_{\mathsf{Z}^m|\mathsf{Z}^m \in \mathfrak{Z}} \left(\forall h \in \mathcal{H} : R[h] \in \Phi(\mathbf{Z}, \delta)\right) \geq 1 - \delta - \kappa\,.$$

Such collections $\mathfrak{Z}$ *are called* positively biased relevant collections *and can effectively be used to tighten the confidence interval* Φ if the training sample z is witnessing the prior belief *expressed via positively biased relevant collections. Hence it is necessary to detect if a given training sample* z *falls into one of the preselected positively biased relevant collections. The function* ω *in Definition 4.18 can be considered to serve exactly this purpose.*

Before finishing this section we will give two examples of luckiness functions. For further examples the interested reader is referred to the literature mentioned in Section 4.5.

Example 4.21 (PAC luckiness) *In order to show that the luckiness framework is, in fact, a generalization of the PAC framework we consider the following luckiness function* $L(z,h) = -\vartheta_\mathcal{H}$ *where* $\vartheta_\mathcal{H}$ *is the VC dimension of* $\mathcal{H}$*. Then, by the upper bound given in Theorem A.105, we know that L is probably smooth w.r.t.*

$$\omega(m, L, \delta) = \left(\frac{2em}{-L}\right)^{-L},$$

because the number of equivalence classes on a sample of size $2m$ *can never exceed that number. If we set* $p_i = 1$ *if, and only if,* $i = \vartheta_\mathcal{H}$ *we see that, by the luckiness bound (4.23), simultaneously for all functions h that achieve zero training error* $R_{\text{emp}}[h, z] = 0$

$$R[h] \leq \frac{2}{m}\left(\vartheta_\mathcal{H}\,\text{ld}\left(\frac{2em}{\vartheta_\mathcal{H}}\right) + \text{ld}\left(\frac{4}{\delta}\right)\right),$$

which is, up to some constants, the same result as given by (4.15). Note that this luckiness function totally ignores the sample z *as mentioned in the context of the classical PAC framework.*

Example 4.22 (Empirical VC dimension luckiness) *Suppose we are given a training sample* z*. We define the* empirical VC dimension *as the largest natural number* $d = \vartheta_\mathcal{H}(z)$ *such that there exists a subset* $\{z_{i_1}, \ldots, z_{i_d}\} \subseteq \{z_1, \ldots, z_m\}$

on which the hypotheses $h \in \mathcal{H}$ incur all the 2^d loss patterns;

$$\vartheta_{\mathcal{H}}(z) \stackrel{\text{def}}{=} \max\left\{j \in \{1, \ldots, |z|\} \,\middle|\, \mathcal{N}_{\mathcal{H}}(z, j) = 2^j\right\},$$

$$\mathcal{N}_{\mathcal{H}}(z, j) \stackrel{\text{def}}{=} \max_{\tilde{z} \subseteq z : |\tilde{z}| = j} \left|\left\{\left(l_{0-1}\left(h\left(\tilde{x}_1\right), \tilde{y}_1\right), \ldots, l_{0-1}\left(h\left(\tilde{x}_j\right), \tilde{y}_j\right)\right) \mid h \in \mathcal{H}\right\}\right|.$$

Note that the classical VC dimension is obtained if z contains all points of the space $\mathcal{Z}$. Then we show in Appendix C.4 that $L(z, h) = -\vartheta_{\mathcal{H}}(z)$ is probably smooth w.r.t. the function

$$\omega(m, L, \delta) = \left(\frac{em}{-2L - 2\ln(\delta)}\right)^{-4L-4\ln(\delta)},$$

for all $\delta \in \left[0, \frac{1}{2}\right]$. This shows that we can replace the VC dimension $\vartheta_{\mathcal{H}}$ known before the training sample arrives with the empirical VC dimension $\vartheta_{\mathcal{H}}(z)$ *after having seen the data.*

Remark 4.23 (Vanilla luckiness) *The main luckiness result as presented in Theorem 4.19 is a simplified version of the original result. In the full version the notion of probable smoothness is complicated by allowing the possibility of exclusion of a data-dependent fraction of the double sample before bounding the number of equivalence classes of luckier functions $H(h, z)$. As a consequence the data-dependent fraction is added to the r.h.s. of equation (4.23). Using the more complicated luckiness result it can be shown that the margin $\gamma_z(\mathbf{w})$ of a linear classifier parameterized by $\mathbf{w}$ is a probably smooth luckiness function. However, in the next section we shall present an analysis for linear classifiers in terms of margins which yields better results than the results in the luckiness framework. It is worth mentioning that for some distributions the margin $\gamma_z(\mathbf{w})$ of any classifier $h_{\mathbf{w}}$ can be arbitrarily small and thus the bound can be worse than the a-priori bounds obtained in the classical PAC and VC frameworks.*

4.4 PAC and VC Frameworks for Real-Valued Classifiers

In Section 4.2 we introduced the growth function as a description of the complexity of a hypothesis space $\mathcal{H}$ when using the zero-one loss l_{0-1} and the empirical risk minimization principle. This bound is tight as, for each training sample size $m \in \mathbb{N}$, there exists a data distribution $\mathbf{P}_Z$ for which the number of equivalence classes equals the number given by the covering number $\mathcal{N}_{\mathcal{H}}$ (the exponentiated growth function). In fact, assuming that this number of equivalence classes is attained by the sample z_{worst}, this happens to be the case if $\mathbf{P}_{Z^m}(z_{\text{worst}}) = 1$.[8]

On the other hand, in the case of linear classifiers, i.e., $x \mapsto \langle \mathbf{x}, \mathbf{w} \rangle$ where $\mathbf{x} \stackrel{\text{def}}{=} \boldsymbol{\phi}(x)$ and $\boldsymbol{\phi} : \mathcal{X} \to \mathcal{K} \subseteq \ell_2^n$ (see also Definition 2.2), it seems plausible that the margin, that is, the minimal real-valued output *before* thresholding, provides confidence about the expected risk. Taking the geometrical picture given in Figure 2.1 on page 23 into account we see that, for a given training sample $z \in \mathcal{Z}^m$, the covering number $\mathcal{N}_{\mathcal{H}}$ on that particular sample is the number of different polyhedra on the surface of the unit hypersphere. Having attained a functional margin of $\tilde{\gamma}_z(\mathbf{w})$ (which equals $\gamma_z(\mathbf{w})$ if $\|\mathbf{w}\| = 1$) when using $h_{\mathbf{w}}(x) = \text{sign}(\langle \mathbf{x}, \mathbf{w} \rangle)$ for classification, we know that we can inscribe a ball of radius at least $\tilde{\gamma}_z(\mathbf{w})$ in one of the equivalence classes—the version space (see also Subsection 2.4.3). Intuitively we are led to ask "how many equivalence classes can maximally be achieved if we require the margin to be $\tilde{\gamma}_z(\mathbf{w})$ *beforehand*?". Ideally, we would like to use this number in place of the number $\mathcal{N}_{\mathcal{H}}$. The margin $\tilde{\gamma}_z(\mathbf{w})$ is best viewed as the scale at which we look on the hypothesis space $\mathcal{F}$ of real-valued functions. If the margin is at least γ then two functions are considered to be equivalent if their real-valued outputs differ by not more than γ on the given training sample z because they must correspond to the same classification which is carried out by thresholding the real-valued outputs. The scale sensitive version of the covering number $\mathcal{N}_{\mathcal{H}}$ when using real-valued functions $f \in \mathcal{F}$ for classification learning is defined as follows.

Definition 4.24 (Covering number of real-valued functions) *Let $\mathcal{F} \subseteq \mathbb{R}^{\mathcal{X}}$ be a set of real-valued functions mapping from $\mathcal{X}$ to $\mathbb{R}$. For a given sample $\boldsymbol{x} = (x_1, \ldots, x_m) \in \mathcal{X}^m$ and $\gamma > 0$ we define $\mathcal{N}_{\mathcal{F}}^{\infty}(\gamma, \boldsymbol{x})$ to be the smallest size of a* cover *$F_\gamma(\boldsymbol{x}) \subset \mathcal{F}$ such that, for every $f \in \mathcal{F}$, there exists a function $\hat{f}$ in the cover $F_\gamma(\boldsymbol{x})$ with*

$$\left\| \left(f(x_1) - \hat{f}(x_1), \ldots, f(x_m) - \hat{f}(x_m) \right) \right\|_\infty = \max_{i=1,\ldots,m} \left| f(x_i) - \hat{f}(x_i) \right| \le \gamma .$$

8 Since we already assumed that the training sample z_{worst} is iid w.r.t. a fixed distribution $\mathbf{P}_Z$, tightness of the growth function based bounds is only achieved if

$$\mathbf{P}_{Z^m}(z_{\text{worst}}) = 1 .$$

But, if there is only *one* training sample z_{worst} this is impossible due to the well known "concentration of measure phenomenon in product spaces" (see Talagrand (1996)).

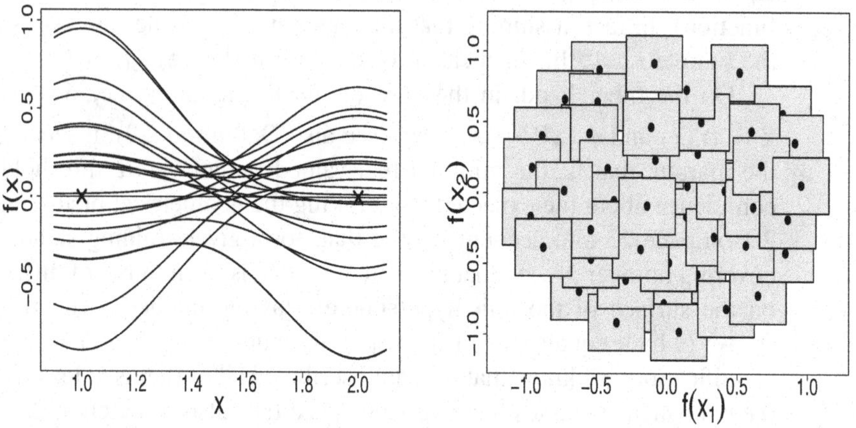

Figure 4.5 **(Left)** 20 real-valued function (solid lines) together with two training points $x_1, x_2 \in \mathbb{R}$ (crosses). The functions are given by $f(x) = \alpha_1 k(x_1, x) + \alpha_2 k(x_2, x)$ where $\boldsymbol{\alpha}$ is constrained to fulfill $\left\|\boldsymbol{\alpha}'\mathbf{G}\boldsymbol{\alpha}\right\|^2 \leq 1$ (see Definition 2.15) and k is given by the RBF kernel (see Table 2.1). **(Right)** A cover $F_\gamma((x_1, x_2))$ for the function class $\mathcal{F}$ (not the smallest). In the simple case of $m = 2$ each function $f \in \mathcal{F}$ is reduced to two scalars $f(x_1)$ and $f(x_2)$ and can therefore be represented as a point in the plane. Each big black dot corresponds to a function $\hat{f}$ in the cover $F_\gamma((x_1, x_2))$; all the gray dots in the box of side length 2γ correspond to the function covered.

The quantity $\mathcal{N}_{\mathcal{F}}^{\infty}(\gamma, \boldsymbol{x})$ *is called the* empirical covering number at scale γ. *We define the* covering number $\mathcal{N}_{\mathcal{F}}^{\infty}(\gamma, m)$ at scale γ by

$$\mathcal{N}_{\mathcal{F}}^{\infty}(\gamma, m) \stackrel{\text{def}}{=} \sup_{\boldsymbol{x} \in \mathcal{X}^m} \mathcal{N}_{\mathcal{F}}^{\infty}(\gamma, \boldsymbol{x}) \,.$$

Intuitively, the value $\mathcal{N}_{\mathcal{F}}^{\infty}(\gamma, \boldsymbol{x})$ measures how many "bricks" of side length 2γ we need to cover the cloud of points in $\mathbb{R}^m$ generated by $(f(x_1), \ldots, f(x_m))$ over the choice of $f \in \mathcal{F}$ (see Figure 4.5). By definition, for each $m \in \mathbb{N}$, the covering number is a function decreasing in γ. By increasing γ we allow the functions $f \in \mathcal{F}$ and $\hat{f} \in F_\gamma(\boldsymbol{x})$ to deviate by larger amounts and, thus, a smaller number of functions may well suffice to *cover* the set $\mathcal{F}$. Further, the covering number $\mathcal{N}_{\mathcal{F}}^{\infty}(\gamma, m)$ at scale γ *does not depend* on the sample but only on the sample size m. This allows us to proceed similarly to a classical PAC analysis. In order to use this refined covering number $\mathcal{N}_{\mathcal{F}}^{\infty}$ we now consider the following event:

There exists a function $f_{\mathbf{w}}$ that achieves zero training error $R_{\text{emp}}[h_{\mathbf{w}}, z]$ on the sample $z \in \mathcal{Z}^m$ and the covering number $\mathcal{N}_{\mathcal{F}}^{\infty}(\tilde{\gamma}_z(\mathbf{w})/2, 2m)$ at the measured scale $\tilde{\gamma}_z(\mathbf{w})/2$ is less than 2^d but the expected risk $R[h_{\mathbf{w}}]$ of $f_{\mathbf{w}}$ exceeds some pre-specified value ε.

At first glance, it may seem odd that we consider only the scale of half the observed margin $\tilde{\gamma}_z(\mathbf{w})$ and a covering number for a double sample of size $2m$. These are technical requirements which might be resolved using a different proving technique. Note that the covering number $\mathcal{N}_{\mathcal{F}}^{\infty}(\gamma, m)$ is independent of the sample $z \in \mathcal{Z}^m$ which allows us to define a function[9] $e : \mathbb{N} \to \mathbb{R}$ such that

$$e(d) \stackrel{\text{def}}{=} \min\left\{\gamma \in \mathbb{R}^+ \mid \mathcal{N}_{\mathcal{F}}^{\infty}(\gamma, 2m) \leq 2^d\right\} \quad \Rightarrow \quad \mathcal{N}_{\mathcal{F}}^{\infty}(e(d), 2m) \leq 2^d, \tag{4.24}$$

that is, $e(d)$ is the smallest margin which ensures that the covering number $\mathcal{N}_{\mathcal{F}}^{\infty}(e(d), 2m)$ is less than or equal to 2^d. Note that we must assume that the minimum $\gamma \in \mathbb{R}^+$ will be attained. Hence, the condition $\mathcal{N}_{\mathcal{F}}^{\infty}(\tilde{\gamma}_z(\mathbf{w})/2, 2m) \leq 2^d$ is equivalent to $\tilde{\gamma}_z(\mathbf{w}) \geq 2 \cdot e(d)$. Now, in order to bound the probability of the above mentioned event we proceed in a similar manner to the PAC analysis.

1. By the basic lemma C.2 we know that, for all $m\varepsilon > 2$,

$$\begin{aligned}\mathbf{P}_{\mathbf{Z}^m}\left(\exists f_{\mathbf{w}} \in \mathcal{F} : \left(R_{\text{emp}}\left[h_{\mathbf{w}}, \mathbf{Z}\right] = 0\right) \wedge \left(R\left[h_{\mathbf{w}}\right] > \varepsilon\right) \wedge \left(\tilde{\gamma}_{\mathbf{Z}}(\mathbf{w}) \geq 2 \cdot e(d)\right)\right) \\ < 2 \cdot \mathbf{P}_{\mathbf{Z}^{2m}}(J(\mathbf{Z}))\,,\end{aligned}$$

where the proposition $J(z\tilde{z})$ with $z, \tilde{z} \in \mathcal{Z}^m$ is given by

$$\exists f_{\mathbf{w}} \in \mathcal{F} : \left(R_{\text{emp}}[h_{\mathbf{w}}, z] = 0\right) \wedge \left(R_{\text{emp}}\left[h_{\mathbf{w}}, \tilde{z}\right] > \frac{\varepsilon}{2}\right) \wedge \left(\tilde{\gamma}_z(\mathbf{w}) \geq 2 \cdot e(d)\right).$$

2. Now we apply a technique known as *symmetrization by permutation* (see page 293 for more details). The core idea is to make use of the fact that the double sample $z \in \mathcal{Z}^{2m}$ is assumed to be an iid sample. Thus, deterministically swapping the ith pair $(x_i, y_i) \in (z_1, \ldots, z_m)$ with $(x_{i+m}, y_{i+m}) \in (z_{m+1}, \ldots, z_{2m})$ will not affect the probability of $J(\mathbf{Z})$. As a consequence we can consider the expected probability of $J(z)$ under the uniform distribution over all 2^m different swappings (represented as binary strings of length m) and then exchange the expectation over $\mathbf{P}_{\mathbf{Z}^{2m}}$ and the permutations. This allows us to *fix* the double sample $z \in \mathcal{Z}^{2m}$ and simply count the number of swappings that satisfy the condition stated by $J(\mathbf{Z})$.

3. For a fixed double sample $z = (\boldsymbol{x}, \boldsymbol{y}) \in (\mathcal{X} \times \mathcal{Y})^{2m}$ let us consider a cover $F_{e(d)}(\boldsymbol{x}) \subset \mathcal{F}$ at scale $e(d)$. So, for all functions $f \in \mathcal{F}$ there exists a real-valued

9 This function is also known as the *dyadic entropy number* (see also Appendix A.3.1).

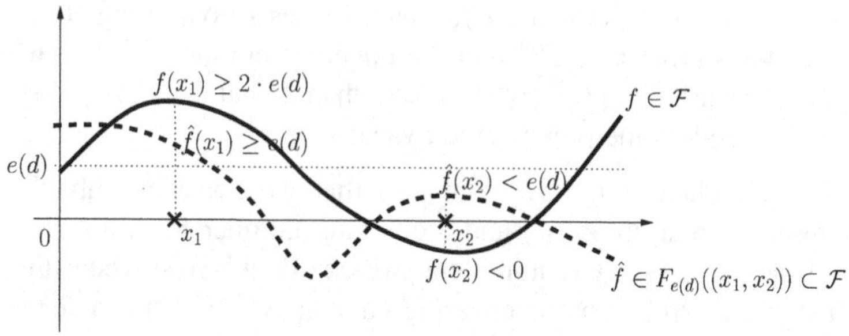

Figure 4.6 Relation between the real-valued output of a cover element $\hat{f} \in F_{e(d)}((x_1, x_2)) \subseteq \mathcal{F}$ and the real-valued output of the covered function $f \in \mathcal{F}$. For illustrative purposes we have simplified to the case of $m = 1$ and $z = \{(x_1, +1), (x_2, +1)\}$. Note that the distance of the functions is the maximum deviation on the real-valued output at the two points x_1 and x_2 only and thus at most $e(d)$. By assumption, f correctly classifies $(x_1, +1)$ with a margin greater than $2 \cdot e(d)$ and thus $\hat{f}(x_1) \geq e(d)$. Similarly, f incorrectly classifies $(x_2, +1)$ and thus $\hat{f}(x_2)$ must be strictly less than $e(d)$.

function $\hat{f} \in F_{e(d)}(\boldsymbol{x})$ whose real-valued output deviates by at most $e(d)$ from the real-valued output of f at the double sample $\boldsymbol{x} \in \mathcal{X}^{2m}$. By the margin condition $\tilde{\gamma}_{(z_1,\ldots,z_m)}(\mathbf{w}) \geq 2 \cdot e(d)$ we know that for all $f_{\mathbf{w}} \in \mathcal{F}$ which achieve zero training error, $R_{\text{emp}}[h_{\mathbf{w}}, (z_1, \ldots, z_m)] = 0$, the corresponding elements $\hat{f}_{\mathbf{w}}$ of the cover $F_{e(d)}(\boldsymbol{x})$ have a real-valued output $y_i \hat{f}_{\mathbf{w}}(x_i)$ on all objects $(x_1, \ldots, x_m)$ of at least $e(d)$. Similarly, for all $f_{\mathbf{w}} \in \mathcal{F}$ that misclassify points in $(z_{m+1}, \ldots, z_{2m})$ we know that their corresponding elements $\hat{f}_{\mathbf{w}}$ of the cover $F_{e(d)}(\boldsymbol{x})$ achieve real-valued outputs $y_i \hat{f}_{\mathbf{w}}(x_i)$ strictly less than $e(d)$ on these points since a misclassification corresponds to a negative output at these points (see Figure 4.6). As a consequence, the probability of $J(\boldsymbol{z})$ is upper bounded by the fraction of swapping permutations $\pi : \{1, \ldots, 2m\} \to \{1, \ldots, 2m\}$ such that

$$\exists \hat{f} \in F_{e(d)}(\boldsymbol{x}) : \left(\min_{i=1,\ldots,m} y_{\pi(i)} \hat{f}\left(x_{\pi(i)}\right) \geq e(d) \right) \wedge \tag{4.25}$$
$$\frac{1}{m} \left| \left\{ y_i \hat{f}(x_i) < e(d) \mid i \in \{\pi(m+1), \ldots, \pi(2m)\} \right\} \right| > \frac{\varepsilon}{2}.$$

4. Suppose there exists a swapping permutation satisfying the logical formula (4.25). Then the maximum number of points that can be swapped is $m - \frac{\varepsilon m}{2}$ because swapping any of the $\frac{\varepsilon m}{2}$ or more examples $(x_i, y_i) \in (z_{m+1}, \ldots, z_{2m})$ for which

$y_i \hat{f}(x_i) < e(d)$ into the first m examples would violate $\min_{i=1,\ldots,m} y_{\pi(i)} \hat{f}\left(x_{\pi(i)}\right) \geq e(d)$. Under the uniform distribution over all swappings this probability is less than $2^{-m} \cdot 2^{m-\frac{\varepsilon m}{2}} = 2^{-\frac{\varepsilon m}{2}}$. Further, the number of functions $\hat{f} \in F_{e(d)}(\boldsymbol{x})$ considered is less than or equal to $\mathcal{N}_{\mathcal{F}}^{\infty}(e(d), 2m)$ which by definition (4.24) is less than or equal to 2^d. Thus for a fixed sample this probability is less than $2^{d-\frac{\varepsilon m}{2}}$. It is worth noticing that this last step is the point where we use the observed margin $\tilde{\gamma}_z(\mathbf{w})$ to boil down the *worst case* number $\mathcal{N}_{\mathcal{H}}$ (when only considering the binary valued functions) to the number 2^d that needs to be witnessed by the observed margin $\tilde{\gamma}_z(\mathbf{w})$.

Using the fact that for all $d \in \mathbb{N}^+$, $2^{d-\frac{\varepsilon m}{2}} \geq 1$ whenever $m\varepsilon \leq 2$, we have shown the following theorem.

Theorem 4.25 (Covering number bound) *Let $\mathcal{F} \subseteq \mathbb{R}^{\mathcal{X}}$ be a set of real-valued functions parameterized by $\mathbf{w} \in \mathcal{W}$ whose associated classifications are $\mathcal{H} = \{x \mapsto \operatorname{sign}(f(x)) \mid f \in \mathcal{F}\}$. For the zero-one loss l_{0-1}, for all $d \in \mathbb{N}^+$ and $\varepsilon > 0$*

$$\mathbf{P}_{\mathbf{Z}^m}\left(\exists h_{\mathbf{w}} \in V_{\mathcal{H}}(\mathbf{Z}) : (R[h_{\mathbf{w}}] > \varepsilon) \wedge \left(\mathcal{N}_{\mathcal{F}}^{\infty}\left(\frac{\tilde{\gamma}_{\mathbf{Z}}(\mathbf{w})}{2}, 2m\right) \leq 2^d\right)\right) < 2^{d+1-\frac{\varepsilon m}{2}},$$

where the version space $V_{\mathcal{H}}(z)$ is defined in Definition 2.12.

An immediate consequence is, that with probability at least $1-\delta$ over the random draw of the training sample $z \in \mathcal{Z}^m$, the following statement $\Upsilon_i(z, m, \delta)$ is true

$$\forall h_{\mathbf{w}} \in V_{\mathcal{H}}(z) : \left(R[h_{\mathbf{w}}] \leq \frac{2}{m}\left(i + \operatorname{ld}\left(\frac{2}{\delta}\right)\right)\right) \vee \left(\mathcal{N}_{\mathcal{F}}^{\infty}\left(\frac{\tilde{\gamma}_z(\mathbf{w})}{2}, 2m\right) > 2^i\right).$$

Noticing that the bound becomes trivial for $i > \lceil m/2 \rceil$ (because the expected risk is at most one) we can safely apply the multiple testing lemma 4.14 with uniform $\mathbf{P}_{\mathbf{S}}$ over the natural numbers $i \in \{1, \ldots, \lceil m/2 \rceil\}$. Thus we have shown the following powerful corollary of Theorem 4.25.

Corollary 4.26 (Covering number bound) *Let $\mathcal{F} \subseteq \mathbb{R}^{\mathcal{X}}$ be a set of real-valued functions parameterized by $\mathbf{w} \in \mathcal{W}$ whose associated classifications are $\mathcal{H} = \{x \mapsto \operatorname{sign}(f(x)) \mid f \in \mathcal{F}\}$. For the zero-one loss l_{0-1}, for any $\delta \in (0, 1]$, with probability at least $1-\delta$ over the random draw of the training sample $z \in \mathcal{Z}^m$, for all hypotheses $h_{\mathbf{w}}$ that achieve zero training error $R_{\text{emp}}[h_{\mathbf{w}}, z] = 0$ and whose margin satisfies $\mathcal{N}_{\mathcal{F}}^{\infty}(\tilde{\gamma}_z(\mathbf{w})/2, 2m) \leq 2^{\frac{m}{2}}$ the expected risk $R[h_{\mathbf{w}}]$ is bounded* *from above by*

$$R[h_{\mathbf{w}}] \leq \frac{2}{m}\left(\left\lceil \operatorname{ld}\left(\mathcal{N}_{\mathcal{F}}^{\infty}\left(\frac{\tilde{\gamma}_{\mathbf{z}}(\mathbf{w})}{2}, 2m\right)\right)\right\rceil + \operatorname{ld}(m) + \operatorname{ld}\left(\frac{1}{\delta}\right)\right). \tag{4.26}$$

Although this result cannot immediately be used to uniformly bound the expected risk of $h_{\mathbf{w}}$ we see that maximizing the margin $\tilde{\gamma}_{\mathbf{z}}(\mathbf{w})$ will minimize the upper bound on the expected error $R[h_{\mathbf{w}}]$. Thus it justifies the class of large margin algorithms introduced in Chapter 2.

Remark 4.27 (Bounds using the empirical covering number) *By a more careful analysis it is possible to show that we can use the empirical covering number $\mathcal{N}_{\mathcal{F}}^{\infty}(\tilde{\gamma}_{\mathbf{z}}(\mathbf{w})/2, \mathbf{x})$ in place of the worst case covering number $\mathcal{N}_{\mathcal{F}}^{\infty}(\tilde{\gamma}_{\mathbf{z}}(\mathbf{w})/2, 2m)$ where $\mathbf{x} \in \mathcal{X}^m$ is the observed sample of m inputs. This, however, can only be achieved at the price of less favorable constants in the bound because we do not observe a ghost sample and therefore must use the training sample $z \in \mathcal{Z}^m$ to estimate $\mathcal{N}_{\mathcal{F}}^{\infty}(\tilde{\gamma}_{\mathbf{z}}(\mathbf{w})/2, 2m)$. Further, for practical application of the result, it still remains to characterize the empirical covering number $\mathcal{N}_{\mathcal{F}}^{\infty}(\tilde{\gamma}_{\mathbf{z}}(\mathbf{w})/2, \mathbf{x})$ by an easy-to-compute quantity of the sample $z \in \mathcal{Z}^m$.*

4.4.1 VC Dimensions for Real-Valued Function Classes

It would be desirable to make practical use of equation (4.26) for bounds similar to those given by Theorem 4.7. This is not immediately possible, the problem being determining $\mathcal{N}_{\mathcal{F}}^{\infty}$ for the observed margin. This problem is addressed using a one integer summary which, of course, is now allowed to vary for the different scales γ. Therefore, this summary is known as generalization of the VC dimension for real-valued functions.

Definition 4.28 (VC Dimension of real-valued function classes) *Let $\mathcal{F} \subseteq \mathbb{R}^{\mathcal{X}}$ be a set of real-valued functions from the space $\mathcal{X}$ to $\mathbb{R}$. We say that a sample of m points $\mathbf{x} = (x_1, \ldots, x_m) \in \mathcal{X}^m$ is γ–*shattered by* $\mathcal{F}$ if there are m real numbers $r_1, \ldots, r_m$ such that for all 2^m different binary vectors $\mathbf{y} \in \{-1, +1\}^m$ there is a function $f_{\mathbf{y}} \in \mathcal{F}$ satisfying*

$$f_{\mathbf{y}}(x_i) \begin{cases} \geq r_i + \gamma & \text{if } y_i = +1 \\ \leq r_i - \gamma & \text{if } y_i = -1 \end{cases}.$$

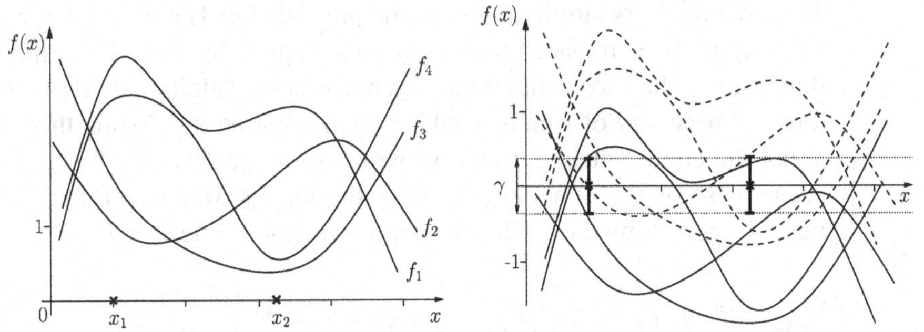

Figure 4.7 **(Left)** Two points x_1 and x_2 on the real line. The set $\mathcal{F}$ is depicted by the functions $\mathcal{F} = \{f_1, \ldots, f_4\}$. **(Right)** The maximum $\gamma \approx 0.37$ (vertical bar) we can consider for γ-shattering is quite large as we can shift the functions $\mathcal{F}$ by different values r_1 and r_2 for x_1 and x_2, respectively. The shifted set $\mathcal{F} - r_2$ for x_2 is shown by dashed lines. Note that $f_1 - r_i$, $f_2 - r_i$, $f_3 - r_i$ and $f_4 - r_i$ realize $\mathbf{y} = (-1, -1)$, $\mathbf{y} = (-1, +1)$, $\mathbf{y} = (+1, -1)$ and $\mathbf{y} = (+1, +1)$, respectively.

The fat shattering dimension $\mathrm{fat}_{\mathcal{F}} : \mathbb{R}^+ \to \mathbb{N}$ *maps a value* $\gamma \in \mathbb{R}^+$ *to the size of the largest* γ*–shattered set, if this is finite, or infinity otherwise.*

In order to see that the fat shattering dimension is clearly a generalization of the VC dimension we note that, for $\gamma \to 0$, the fat shattering dimension $\lim_{\gamma \to 0} \mathrm{fat}_{\mathcal{F}}(\gamma)$ equals the VC dimension $\vartheta_{\mathcal{H}}$ of the thresholded set $\mathcal{H} = \{\mathrm{sign}(f) \mid f \in \mathcal{F}\}$ of binary classifiers. By using the scale parameter $\gamma \in \mathbb{R}^+$ we are able to study the complexity of a set of real-valued functions proposed for binary classification at a much finer scale (see also Figure 4.7). Another advantage of this dimension is that, similarly to the VC and PAC theory presented in Section 4.2, we can use it to bound the only quantity entering the bound (4.26)—the log-covering number $\mathrm{ld}\left(\mathcal{N}_{\mathcal{F}}^{\infty}(\tilde{\gamma}_z(\mathbf{w})/2, 2m)\right)$. In 1997, Alon et al. proved the following lemma as a byproduct of a more general result regarding the characterization of Glivenko-Cantelli classes.

Lemma 4.29 (Bound on the covering number) *Let* $\mathcal{F} \subseteq \mathbb{R}^{\mathcal{X}}$ *be a set of functions from* $\mathcal{X}$ *to the closed interval* $[a, b]$. *For all* $m \in \mathbb{N}$ *and any* $\gamma \in (a, b)$ *such that* $d = \mathrm{fat}_{\mathcal{F}}\left(\frac{\gamma}{4}\right) \le m$,

$$\mathrm{ld}\left(\mathcal{N}_{\mathcal{F}}^{\infty}(\gamma, m)\right) \le 1 + d \cdot \mathrm{ld}\left(\frac{2em(b-a)}{d\gamma}\right) \mathrm{ld}\left(\frac{4m(b-a)^2}{\gamma^2}\right).$$

This bound is very similar to the bound presented in Theorem 4.10. The VC dimension $\vartheta_{\mathcal{H}}$ has been replaced by the corresponding value $\text{fat}_{\mathcal{F}}(\gamma)$ of the fat shattering dimension. The most important difference is the additional $\text{ld}\left(4m(b-a)^2/\gamma^2\right)$ term the necessity of which is still an open question in learning theory. The lemma is not directly applicable to the general case of real-valued functions $f \in \mathcal{F}$ because these may be unbounded. Thus the idea is to *truncate* the functions into a range $[-\tau, +\tau]$ by the application of a *truncation operator* T_τ, i.e.,

$$T_\tau(\mathcal{F}) \stackrel{\text{def}}{=} \{T_\tau(f) \mid f \in \mathcal{F}\}, \quad T_\tau(f)(x) \stackrel{\text{def}}{=} \begin{cases} \tau & \text{if } f(x) > \tau \\ f(x) & \text{if } -\tau \le f(x) \le \tau \\ -\tau & \text{if } f(x) < -\tau \end{cases} .$$

Obviously, for all possible scales $\gamma \in \mathbb{R}^+$ we know that the fat shattering dimension $\text{fat}_{T_\tau(\mathcal{F})}(\gamma)$ of the truncated set of functions is less than or equal to the fat shattering dimension $\text{fat}_{\mathcal{F}}(\gamma)$ of the non-truncated set $\mathcal{F}$ since every sample that is γ–shattered by $T_\tau(\mathcal{F})$ can be γ–shattered by $\mathcal{F}$, trivially, using the same but nontruncated functions. As a consequence we know that, for any value $\tau \in \mathbb{R}^+$ we might use for truncation, it holds that the log-covering number of the truncated set $T_\tau(\mathcal{F})$ of functions can be bounded in terms of the fat shattering dimension of $\mathcal{F}$ and the value of τ

$$\text{ld}\left(\mathcal{N}^\infty_{T_\tau(\mathcal{F})}(\gamma, m)\right) \le 1 + \text{fat}_{\mathcal{F}}\left(\frac{\gamma}{4}\right) \text{ld}\left(\frac{4em\tau}{\text{fat}_{\mathcal{F}}\left(\frac{\gamma}{4}\right) \cdot \gamma}\right) \text{ld}\left(\frac{16m\tau^2}{\gamma^2}\right) .$$

In addition we know that, regardless of the value of $\tau \in \mathbb{R}^+$, the function $T_\tau(f)$ performs the same classification as f, i.e., for any training sample $z \in \mathcal{Z}^m$ and all functions $f \in \mathcal{F}$

$$R\left[\text{sign}(f)\right] = R\left[\text{sign}(T_\tau(f))\right], \quad R_{\text{emp}}\left[\text{sign}(f), z\right] = R_{\text{emp}}\left[\text{sign}(T_\tau(f)), z\right].$$

Using these two facts we aim to replace the log-covering number of the function class $\mathcal{F}$ by the log-covering number $\text{ld}(\mathcal{N}^\infty_{T_\tau(\mathcal{F})}(\tilde{\gamma}_z(\mathbf{w})/2, 2m))$ of the set $T_\tau(\mathcal{F})$ of truncated real-valued functions. Note that $\tau \in \mathbb{R}^+$ must be chosen independently of the training sample $z \in \mathcal{Z}^m$. In order to achieve this we consider the following well defined function $\tilde{e} : \mathbb{N} \to \mathbb{R}$

$$\tilde{e}(d) \stackrel{\text{def}}{=} \min\left\{\gamma \in \mathbb{R}^+ \;\middle|\; \mathcal{N}^\infty_{T_\gamma(\mathcal{F})}(\gamma, 2m) \le 2^d\right\} \Rightarrow \mathcal{N}_{T_{\tilde{e}(d)}(\mathcal{F})}(\tilde{e}(d), 2m) \le 2^d ,$$

in place of the dyadic entropy number considered given in equation (4.24). By definition, whenever $\mathcal{N}^\infty_{T_{\tilde{e}(d)}(\mathcal{F})}(\tilde{\gamma}_z(\mathbf{w})/2, 2m) \le 2^d$ it must follow that $\tilde{\gamma}_z(\mathbf{w}) \ge 2 \cdot \tilde{e}(d)$ which, together with Lemma 4.29, implies that the log-covering number

$\mathrm{ld}(\mathcal{N}^{\infty}_{T_{\tilde{e}(d)}(\mathcal{F})}(\tilde{\gamma}_z(\mathbf{w})/2, 2m))$ cannot exceed

$$1 + \mathrm{fat}_{\mathcal{F}}\left(\frac{\tilde{\gamma}_z(\mathbf{w})}{8}\right) \mathrm{ld}\left(\frac{8em \cdot \tilde{e}(d)}{\mathrm{fat}_{\mathcal{F}}\left(\frac{\tilde{\gamma}_z(\mathbf{w})}{8}\right) \cdot \frac{\tilde{\gamma}_z(\mathbf{w})}{2}}\right) \mathrm{ld}\left(\frac{32m \cdot (\tilde{e}(d))^2}{\left(\frac{\tilde{\gamma}_z(\mathbf{w})}{2}\right)^2}\right)$$
$$\leq \underbrace{1 + \mathrm{fat}_{\mathcal{F}}\left(\frac{\tilde{\gamma}_z(\mathbf{w})}{8}\right) \mathrm{ld}\left(\frac{8em}{\mathrm{fat}_{\mathcal{F}}(\tilde{\gamma}_z(\mathbf{w})/8)}\right) \mathrm{ld}(32m)}_{b(\tilde{\gamma}_z(\mathbf{w}))} .$$

In other words, by Lemma 4.29 we know that whenever the training sample $z \in \mathcal{Z}^m$ and the weight vector $\mathbf{w} \in \mathcal{K}$ under consideration satisfy $b(\tilde{\gamma}_z(\mathbf{w})) \leq d$ then the log-covering number $\mathrm{ld}(\mathcal{N}^{\infty}_{T_{\tilde{e}(d)}(\mathcal{F})}(\tilde{\gamma}_z(\mathbf{w})/2, 2m))$ is upper bounded by d. By Theorem 4.25 it follows that, with probability at least $1-\delta$ over the random draw of the training sample $z \in \mathcal{Z}^m$, the statement

$$\Upsilon_i(z, m, \delta) \equiv \forall h_{\mathbf{w}} \in V_{\mathcal{H}}(z) : (b(\tilde{\gamma}_z(\mathbf{w})) > i) \vee \left(R[h_{\mathbf{w}}] \leq \frac{2}{m}\left(i + \mathrm{ld}\left(\frac{2}{\delta}\right)\right)\right)$$

is true. As a consequence, stratifying over the $\lceil \frac{m}{2} \rceil$ different natural numbers i using the multiple testing lemma 4.14 and a uniform $\mathbf{P}_S$ gives Theorem 4.30. Notice that by the assumptions of Lemma 4.29 the margin $\tilde{\gamma}_z(\mathbf{w})$ must be such that $\mathrm{fat}_{\mathcal{F}}(\tilde{\gamma}_z(\mathbf{w})/8)$ is less than or equal to $2m$.

Theorem 4.30 (Fat shattering bound) *Let $\mathcal{F} \subseteq \mathbb{R}^{\mathcal{X}}$ be a set of real-valued functions parameterized by $\mathbf{w} \in \mathcal{W}$ whose associated classifications are $\mathcal{H} = \{x \mapsto \mathrm{sign}(f(x)) \mid f \in \mathcal{F}\}$. For the zero-one loss l_{0-1}, for any $\delta \in (0, 1]$, with probability at least $1-\delta$ over the random draw of the training sample $z \in \mathcal{Z}^m$, for all hypotheses $h_{\mathbf{w}}$ that achieve zero training error $R_{\mathrm{emp}}[h_{\mathbf{w}}, z] = 0$ and whose margin $\tilde{\gamma}_z(\mathbf{w})$ satisfies $\vartheta_{\mathrm{eff}} = \mathrm{fat}_{\mathcal{F}}(\tilde{\gamma}_z(\mathbf{w})/8) \leq 2m$ the expected risk $R[h_{\mathbf{w}}]$ is bounded from above by*

$$R[h_{\mathbf{w}}] \leq \frac{2}{m}\left(\left\lceil \vartheta_{\mathrm{eff}} \mathrm{ld}\left(\frac{8em}{\vartheta_{\mathrm{eff}}}\right) \mathrm{ld}(32m) \right\rceil + \mathrm{ld}(m) + \mathrm{ld}\left(\frac{2}{\delta}\right)\right) . \tag{4.27}$$

Ignoring constants, it is worth noticing that compared to the original PAC bound given by equation (4.15) we have an additional $\mathrm{ld}(32m)$ factor in the complexity term of equation (4.27) which is due to the extra term in Lemma 4.29. Note that in contrast to the classical PAC result, we do not know *beforehand* that the margin—

whose fat shattering dimension replaces the VC dimension—will be large. As such, we call this bound an *a-posteriori bound.*

4.4.2 The PAC Margin Bound

Using Lemma 4.29 we reduced the problem of bounding the covering number $\mathcal{N}_{\mathcal{F}}^{\infty}$ to the problem of bounding the fat shattering dimension. If we restrict ourselves to linear classifiers in a feature space $\mathcal{K}$ we have the following result on the fat shattering dimension.

Lemma 4.31 (Fat shattering bound for linear classifiers) *Suppose that* $X = \{\mathbf{x} \in \mathcal{K} \mid \|\mathbf{x}\| \leq \varsigma\}$ *is a ball of radius* ς *in an inner product space* $\mathcal{K}$ *and consider the linear classifiers*

$$\mathcal{F} = \{\mathbf{x} \mapsto \langle \mathbf{w}, \mathbf{x} \rangle \mid \|\mathbf{w}\| \leq B\,,\ \mathbf{x} \in X\}$$

with norm bounded by B. *Then*

$$\mathrm{fat}_{\mathcal{F}}(\gamma) \leq \left(\frac{B\varsigma}{\gamma}\right)^2 . \tag{4.28}$$

The proof can be found in Appendix C.5. In terms of Figure 2.6 we see that (4.28) has an intuitive interpretation: The complexity measured by $\mathrm{fat}_{\mathcal{F}}$ at scale γ must be viewed with respect to the total extent of the data. If the margin has a small absolute value, its *effective* incurred complexity is large only if the extent of the data is large. Thus, for linear classifiers, the geometrical margin[10] $\gamma_{\mathbf{z}}(\mathbf{w})$ itself does not provide any measure of the complexity without considering the total extent of the data. Combining Lemma 4.31 with the bound given in Theorem 4.30 we obtain a practically useful result for the expected risk of linear classifiers in terms of the observed margin. Note that we must ensure that $\mathrm{fat}_{\mathcal{F}}(\gamma_{\mathbf{z}}(\mathbf{w})/8)$ is at most $2m$.

Theorem 4.32 (PAC Margin bound) *Suppose* $\mathcal{K}$ *is a given feature space. For all probability measures* $\mathbf{P}_{\mathsf{Z}}$ *such that* $\mathbf{P}_{\mathsf{X}}(\{x \mid \|\boldsymbol{\phi}(x)\| \leq \varsigma\}) = 1$, *for any* $\delta \in (0, 1]$, *with probability at least* $1-\delta$ *over the random draw of the training sample* $\mathbf{z} \in \mathcal{Z}^m$, *if we succeed in correctly classifying* m *samples* $\mathbf{z}$ *with a linear classifier* $f_{\mathbf{w}}$ *having a geometrical margin* $\gamma_{\mathbf{z}}(\mathbf{w})$ *of at least* $\sqrt{32/m}\,\varsigma$, *then the expected risk* $R[h_{\mathbf{w}}]$ *of*

10 Note that for $\|\mathbf{w}\| = 1$ functional margin $\tilde{\gamma}_{\mathbf{z}}(\mathbf{w})$ and geometrical margin $\gamma_{\mathbf{z}}(\mathbf{w})$ coincide.

$h_{\mathbf{w}}$ *w.r.t. the zero-one loss* l_{0-1} *is bounded from above by*

$$\frac{2}{m}\left(\left\lceil \frac{64\varsigma^2}{(\gamma_z(\mathbf{w}))^2}\operatorname{ld}\left(\frac{(\gamma_z(\mathbf{w}))^2 em}{8\varsigma^2}\right)\operatorname{ld}(32m)\right\rceil + \operatorname{ld}\left(\frac{2m}{\delta}\right)\right). \tag{4.29}$$

This result is the theoretical basis of the class of large margin algorithms as it *directly* allows us to make use of the attained geometrical margin $\gamma_z(\mathbf{w})$ for giving bounds on the expected risk $R[h_{\mathbf{w}}]$ of a linear classifiers. An appealing feature of the result is the subsequent capability of obtaining nontrivial bounds on the expected risk even when the number n of dimensions of feature space is much larger than the number m of training examples. Whilst this is impossible to achieve in the parametric statistics approach we see that by *directly* studying the expected risk we are able to defy the curse of dimensionality.

Remark 4.33 (Sufficient training sample size) *At first glance the bound (4.29) might represent progress. We must recall, however, that the theorem requires that the attained margin* $\gamma_z(\mathbf{w})$ *satisfies* $m(\gamma_z(\mathbf{w}))^2/\varsigma^2 \geq 32$. *Noticing that* $(\varsigma/\gamma_z(\mathbf{w}))^2$ *can be viewed as an* effective VC dimension ϑ_{eff} *we see that this is equivalent to assuming that* $\frac{m}{d_{\text{eff}}} \geq 32$*—the rule of thumb already given by Vapnik! However, calculating the minimum training sample size* m *for a given margin complexity* $\vartheta_{\text{eff}} = (\varsigma/\gamma_z(\mathbf{w}))^2$, *we see that equation (4.29) becomes nontrivial, i.e., less than one, only for astronomically large values of* m, *e.g.,* $m > 34\,816$ *for* $\vartheta_{\text{eff}} = 1$ *(see Figure 4.8). Thus it can be argued that Theorem 4.32 is more a qualitative justification of large margin algorithms than a practically useful result. We shall see in Section 5.1 that a conceptually different analysis leads to a similar bound for linear classifiers which is much more practically useful.*

4.4.3 Robust Margin Bounds

A major drawback of the margin bound given by Theorem 4.32 is its sensitivity to a few training examples $(x_i, y_i) \in z \in \mathcal{Z}^m$ for which the margin $\gamma_i(\mathbf{w})$ of a linear classifier $h_{\mathbf{w}}$ may be small. In the extreme case we can imagine a situation in which the first $m-1$ training examples from z are correctly classified with a maximum margin of $\gamma_i(\mathbf{w}) = \varsigma$ but the last observation has $\gamma_m(\mathbf{w}) = 0$. It does not seem plausible that this single point has such a large impact on the expected risk of $h_{\mathbf{w}}$ that we are unable to give *any* guarantee on the expected risk $R[h_{\mathbf{w}}]$. Algorithmically we have already seen that this difficulty can easily be overcome by the introduction of soft margins (see Subsection 2.4.2). As a consequence, Shawe-

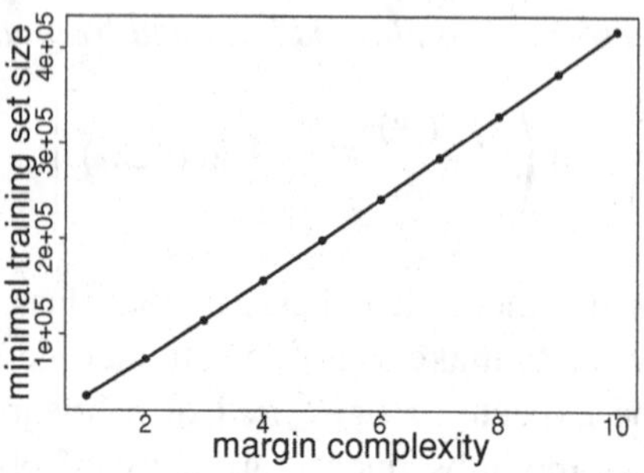

Figure 4.8 Minimal training sample size as a function of the margin complexity ς^2/γ^2 such that equation (4.29) becomes less than the one (ignoring the $\mathrm{ld}\,(2/\delta)$ term due to the astronomically large values of m).

Taylor and Cristianini called the existing margin bound "nonrobust". The core idea involved in making the margin bound (4.29) "robust" is to construct an inner product space $\widetilde{\mathcal{K}}$ from a given feature space $\mathcal{K} \subseteq \ell_2^n$ such that, for a linear classifier $h_{\mathbf{w}}$ that fails to achieve only positive margins $\gamma_i(\mathbf{w})$ on the training sample z, we can find a corresponding linear classifier $h_{\tilde{\mathbf{w}}}$ in the inner product space $\widetilde{\mathcal{K}}$ achieving a positive margin $\gamma_z(\widetilde{\mathbf{w}})$ on the mapped training sample whilst yielding the same classification as $h_{\mathbf{w}}$ for all unseen test objects. One way to achieve this is as follows:

1. Based on the given input space $\mathcal{X}$ and the feature space $\mathcal{K}$ with the associated mapping $\boldsymbol{\phi} : \mathcal{X} \to \mathcal{K}$ for each training sample size m we set up a new inner product space

$$\widetilde{\mathcal{K}} \stackrel{\text{def}}{=} \mathcal{K} \times \left\{ \sum_{i=1}^{j} \mathbf{I}_{x_i} \;\middle|\; j \in \{1, \ldots, m\}, \, \left(x_1, \ldots, x_j\right) \in \mathcal{X}^j \right\}$$

endowed with the following inner product[11]

$$\langle (\mathbf{w}, f), (\mathbf{x}, g) \rangle_{\widetilde{\mathcal{K}}} \stackrel{\text{def}}{=} \langle \mathbf{w}, \mathbf{x} \rangle_{\mathcal{K}} + \int f(x)\, g(x)\, dx\,, \tag{4.30}$$

where the second term on the r.h.s. of (4.30) is well defined because we only consider functions that are non-zero on finitely many (at most m) points. The inner product space $\widetilde{\mathcal{K}}$ can be set up *independently* of a training sample z. Given a positive value $\Delta > 0$, each point $x_i \in \boldsymbol{x}$ is mapped to $\widetilde{\mathcal{K}}$ by $\boldsymbol{\tau}_\Delta(x_i) \stackrel{\text{def}}{=} \left(\mathbf{x}_i, \Delta \mathbf{I}_{x_i}\right)$.

11 For the sake of clarity, we use a subscript on inner products $\langle \cdot, \cdot \rangle_{\mathcal{K}}$ in this subsection.

2. For a given linear classifier parameterized via its normal vector $\mathbf{w} \in \mathcal{K}$ we define a mapping $\boldsymbol{\omega}_{\Delta,\gamma} : \mathcal{K} \to \widetilde{\mathcal{K}}$ such that the minimum real-valued output (the functional margin) is at least $\gamma \in \mathbb{R}^+$, i.e.,

$$\min_{i=1,\dots,m} y_i \left\langle \boldsymbol{\omega}_{\Delta,\gamma}(\mathbf{w}), \boldsymbol{\tau}_\Delta(x_i) \right\rangle_{\widetilde{\mathcal{K}}} \geq \gamma > 0 .$$

This can be achieved by the following mapping

$$\boldsymbol{\omega}_{\Delta,\gamma}(\mathbf{w}) \stackrel{\text{def}}{=} \left(\mathbf{w}, \frac{1}{\Delta} \sum_{(x_i,y_i)\in z} y_i \cdot d\left((x_i, y_i), \mathbf{w}, \gamma\right) \cdot \mathbf{l}_{x_i} \right),$$

$$d\left((x, y), \mathbf{w}, \gamma\right) \stackrel{\text{def}}{=} \max\left\{0, \gamma - y \left\langle \mathbf{w}, \mathbf{x} \right\rangle_{\mathcal{K}}\right\},$$

where $d\left((x, y), \mathbf{w}, \gamma\right)$ measures how much $\mathbf{w}$ fails at $(x, y) \in \mathcal{Z}$ to achieve a *functional margin* of γ. Using equation (4.30) for each point $\left(x_j, y_j\right) \in z$ in the training sample it follows that the real-valued output in the new inner product space $\widetilde{\mathcal{K}}$ is at least γ

$$\begin{aligned} y_j \left\langle \boldsymbol{\omega}_{\Delta,\gamma}(\mathbf{w}), \boldsymbol{\tau}_\Delta\left(x_j\right) \right\rangle_{\widetilde{\mathcal{K}}} &= y_j \left\langle \mathbf{w}, \mathbf{x}_j \right\rangle_{\mathcal{K}} + y_j \sum_{(x_i,y_i)\in z} y_i \cdot d\left((x_i, y_i), \mathbf{w}, \gamma\right) \cdot \mathbf{l}_{x_i} \mathbf{l}_{x_j} \\ &= y_j \left\langle \mathbf{w}, \mathbf{x}_j \right\rangle_{\mathcal{K}} + d\left(\left(x_j, y_j\right), \mathbf{w}, \gamma\right) \\ &\geq y_j \left\langle \mathbf{w}, \mathbf{x}_j \right\rangle_{\mathcal{K}} + \gamma - y_j \left\langle \mathbf{w}, \mathbf{x}_j \right\rangle_{\mathcal{K}} = \gamma . \end{aligned}$$

Further, for each example $(x, y) \notin z$ not contained in the training sample we see that the real-valued output of the classifier $\boldsymbol{\omega}_{\Delta,\gamma}(\mathbf{w})$ equals the real-valued output of the unmodified weight vector $\mathbf{w}$, i.e.,

$$\begin{aligned} y \left\langle \boldsymbol{\omega}_{\Delta,\gamma}(\mathbf{w}), \boldsymbol{\tau}_\Delta(x) \right\rangle_{\widetilde{\mathcal{K}}} &= y \left\langle \mathbf{w}, \mathbf{x} \right\rangle_{\mathcal{K}} + y \sum_{(x_i,y_i)\in z} y_i \cdot d\left((x_i, y_i), \mathbf{w}, \gamma\right) \cdot \mathbf{l}_{x_i} \mathbf{l}_{x} \\ &= y \left\langle \mathbf{w}, \mathbf{x} \right\rangle_{\mathcal{K}} . \end{aligned}$$

Hence we can use $\boldsymbol{\omega}_{\Delta,\gamma}(\mathbf{w})$ to characterize the expected risk of $\mathbf{w}$ but at the same time exploit the fact that $\boldsymbol{\omega}_{\Delta,\gamma}(\mathbf{w})$ achieves margin of at least γ in the inner product space.

3. Let us assume that $\mathbf{P}_\mathsf{Z}$ is such that $\mathbf{P}_\mathsf{X}\left(\left\{x \in \mathcal{X} \mid \|\mathbf{x}\|_{\mathcal{K}} \leq \varsigma\right\}\right) = 1$. In order to apply Theorem 4.32 for $\boldsymbol{\omega}_{\Delta,\gamma}(\mathbf{w})$ and the set $\left\{\boldsymbol{\tau}_\Delta(x) \mid x \in \mathcal{X}\right\}$ we notice that, for a given value of γ and Δ,

(a) the geometrical margin of $\boldsymbol{\omega}_{\Delta,\gamma}(\mathbf{w})$ is at least

$$\frac{\left\langle \boldsymbol{\omega}_{\Delta,\gamma}(\mathbf{w}), \boldsymbol{\tau}_{\Delta}(x_j)\right\rangle_{\tilde{\mathcal{K}}}}{\left\|\boldsymbol{\omega}_{\Delta,\gamma}(\mathbf{w})\right\|_{\tilde{\mathcal{K}}}} \geq \frac{\gamma}{\sqrt{\|\mathbf{w}\|_{\mathcal{K}}^2 + \left(\frac{D(z,\mathbf{w},\gamma)}{\Delta}\right)^2}},$$

where

$$D(z,\mathbf{w},\gamma) \stackrel{\text{def}}{=} \sqrt{\sum_{(x_i,y_i)\in z} \left(d\left((x_i,y_i),\mathbf{w},\gamma\right)\right)^2}. \tag{4.31}$$

Note that $(D(z,\mathbf{w},1))^2$ exactly captures the squared sum of the slack variables in the soft margin support vector machine algorithm given by (2.49).

(b) all mapped points are contained in a ball of radius $\sqrt{\varsigma^2+\Delta^2}$ because

$$\forall x \in \mathcal{X}: \qquad \|\boldsymbol{\tau}_{\Delta}(x)\|_{\tilde{\mathcal{K}}}^2 = \|\mathbf{x}\|_{\mathcal{K}}^2 + \Delta^2 \leq \varsigma^2 + \Delta^2.$$

Thus by an application of Lemma 4.31 to a classifier $\boldsymbol{\omega}_{\Delta,\gamma}(\mathbf{w})$ we have shown the following lemma[12].

Lemma 4.34 (Margin distribution) *Suppose $\mathcal{K}$ is a given feature space. For all $\Delta > 0$, for all probability measures $\mathbf{P}_\mathsf{Z}$ such that $\mathbf{P}_\mathsf{X}(\{x \in \mathcal{X} \mid \|\mathbf{x}\|_{\mathcal{K}} \leq \varsigma\}) = 1$, for any $\delta \in (0,1]$, with probability at least $1-\delta$ over the random draw of the training sample $z \in \mathcal{Z}^m$, for all $\gamma \in (0,\varsigma]$ the expected risk $R[h_\mathbf{w}]$ of a linear classifier $h_\mathbf{w}$ w.r.t. the zero-one loss l_{0-1} is bounded from above by*

$$R[h_\mathbf{w}] \leq \frac{2}{m}\left(\left\lceil d_{\text{eff}}(\Delta)\,\text{ld}\left(\frac{8em}{d_{\text{eff}}(\Delta)}\right)\text{ld}(32m)\right\rceil + \text{ld}\left(\frac{2m}{\delta}\right)\right),$$

where

$$d_{\text{eff}}(\Delta) = \frac{64\left(\|\mathbf{w}\|_{\mathcal{K}}^2 + \left(\frac{D(z,\mathbf{w},\gamma)}{\Delta}\right)^2\right)\left(\varsigma^2+\Delta^2\right)}{\gamma^2} \tag{4.32}$$

must obey $d_{\text{eff}}(\Delta) \leq 2m$.

Note that the term $D(z,\mathbf{w},\gamma)$ given in equation (4.31) is not invariant under rescaling of $\mathbf{w}$. For a fixed value of γ increasing the norm $\|\mathbf{w}\|_{\mathcal{K}}$ of $\mathbf{w}$ can only lead to a decrease in the term $D(z,\mathbf{w},\gamma)$. Thus, without loss of generality, we will fix $\|\mathbf{w}\|_{\mathcal{K}} = 1$ in the following exposition.

12 With a slight lack of rigor we omitted the condition that there is no discrete probability $\mathbf{P}_\mathsf{Z}$ on misclassified training examples because $\boldsymbol{\omega}_{\Delta,\gamma}(\mathbf{w})$ characterizes $\mathbf{w}$ only at non-training examples.

Unfortunately, Lemma 4.34 is not directly applicable to obtaining a useful bound on the expected risk in terms of the margin distribution (measured by $D(z, \mathbf{w}, \gamma)$) as we are required to fix Δ in advance. The way to overcome this problem is to apply Lemma 4.14 for different values of Δ. By Lemma 4.34 we know that, with probability at least $1-\delta$ over the random draw of the training sample $z \in \mathcal{Z}^m$, the following statement is true

$$\Upsilon_i(z, m, \delta) \equiv \forall \mathbf{w} \in \mathcal{K} : (d_{\mathrm{eff}}(\Delta_i) > 2m) \vee \left(R[h_{\mathbf{w}}] \leq \frac{2}{m}\left(\left\lceil d_{\mathrm{eff}}(\Delta_i)\,\mathrm{ld}\left(\frac{8em}{d_{\mathrm{eff}}(\Delta_i)}\right)\mathrm{ld}(32m)\right\rceil + \mathrm{ld}\left(\frac{2m}{\delta}\right)\right)\right).$$

In Appendix C.6 we give an explicit sequence of Δ_i values which proves the final margin distribution bound.

Theorem 4.35 (Robust margin bound) *Suppose $\mathcal{K} \subseteq \ell_2^n$ is a given feature space. For all probability measures $\mathbf{P}_\mathsf{Z}$ such that $\mathbf{P}_\mathsf{X}(\{x \in \mathcal{X} \mid \|\mathbf{x}\|_{\mathcal{K}} \leq \varsigma\}) = 1$, for any $\delta \in (0, 1]$, with probability at least $1-\delta$ over the random draw of the training sample $z \in \mathcal{Z}^m$, for all $\gamma \in (0, \varsigma]$ the expected risk $R[h_{\mathbf{w}}]$ w.r.t. the zero-one loss l_{0-1} of a linear classifier $h_{\mathbf{w}}$ with $\|\mathbf{w}\|_{\mathcal{K}} = 1$ is bounded from above by*

$$R[h_{\mathbf{w}}] \leq \frac{2}{m}\left(\left\lceil d_{\mathrm{eff}}\,\mathrm{ld}\left(\frac{8em}{d_{\mathrm{eff}}}\right)\mathrm{ld}(32m)\right\rceil + \mathrm{ld}\left(\frac{(16+\mathrm{ld}(m))\,m}{\delta}\right)\right), \tag{4.33}$$

where

$$d_{\mathrm{eff}} = \frac{65\left(\varsigma + 3D(z, \mathbf{w}, \gamma)\right)^2}{\gamma^2}$$

must obey $d_{\mathrm{eff}} \leq 2m$.

Note that, by application of Lemma 4.14, we only gain an additional summand of $3 + \mathrm{ld}\left(\mathrm{ld}\left(\sqrt{m}\right)\right)$ in the numerator of equation (4.33). Coming back to our initial example we see that, in the case of $m-1$ examples correctly classified with a (maximum) geometrical margin of $\gamma_i(\mathbf{w}) = \varsigma$ and the mth example misclassified by a geometrical margin of 0, Theorem 4.35 gives us an effective dimensionality d_{eff} of $65 \cdot 16 = 1040$ and thus, for sufficiently large training sample size m, we will get a nontrivial bound on the expected risk $R[h_{\mathbf{w}}]$ of $h_{\mathbf{w}}$ although $h_{\mathbf{w}}$ admits training errors. Note, however, that the result is again more a qualitative justification of soft margins as introduced in Subsection 2.4.2 rather than being practically useful (see also Remark 4.33). This, however, is merely due to the fact that we set up the "robustness" trick on top of the fat shattering bound given in Theorem 4.30.

Remark 4.36 (Justification of soft margin support vector machines) *One of the motivations for studying robust margin bounds is to show that the soft margin heuristic introduced for support vector machines has a firm theoretical basis. In order to see this we note that in the soft margin case the norm $\|\mathbf{w}\|_{\mathcal{K}}$ of the resulting classifier is not of unit length as we fixed the functional margin to be one. Therefore, we consider the case of $\gamma = \frac{1}{\|\mathbf{w}\|_{\mathcal{K}}}$ and $\mathbf{w}_{\text{norm}} = \frac{\mathbf{w}}{\|\mathbf{w}\|_{\mathcal{K}}}$ which gives*

$$\begin{aligned}
\left(D\left(z, \mathbf{w}_{\text{norm}}, \frac{1}{\|\mathbf{w}\|_{\mathcal{K}}}\right)\right)^2 &= \sum_{i=1}^{m}\left(\max\left\{0, \frac{1}{\|\mathbf{w}\|_{\mathcal{K}}} - y_i\left\langle\frac{\mathbf{w}}{\|\mathbf{w}\|_{\mathcal{K}}}, \mathbf{x}_i\right\rangle_{\mathcal{K}}\right\}\right)^2 \\
&= \frac{1}{\|\mathbf{w}\|_{\mathcal{K}}^2}\sum_{i=1}^{m}\left(\max\left\{0, \left(1 - y_i\left\langle\mathbf{w}, \mathbf{x}_i\right\rangle_{\mathcal{K}}\right)\right\}\right)^2 \\
&= \frac{1}{\|\mathbf{w}\|_{\mathcal{K}}^2}\sum_{i=1}^{m} l_{\text{quad}}\left(\left\langle\mathbf{w}, \mathbf{x}_i\right\rangle_{\mathcal{K}}, y_i\right) = \frac{1}{\|\mathbf{w}\|_{\mathcal{K}}^2}\sum_{i=1}^{m}\xi_i^2,
\end{aligned}$$

according to the slack variables ξ_i introduced in equation (2.48) and (2.49). For the effective dimensionality d_{eff} it follows

$$\begin{aligned}
d_{\text{eff}} &= 65\,\|\mathbf{w}\|_{\mathcal{K}}^2\left(\varsigma + \frac{3}{\|\mathbf{w}\|_{\mathcal{K}}}\sqrt{\sum_{i=1}^{m}\xi_i^2}\right)^2 = 65\left(\varsigma\,\|\mathbf{w}\|_{\mathcal{K}} + 3\,\|\boldsymbol{\xi}\|_2\right)^2 && (4.34) \\
&\leq 65\left(\varsigma\,\|\mathbf{w}\|_{\mathcal{K}} + 3\,\|\boldsymbol{\xi}\|_1\right)^2, && (4.35)
\end{aligned}$$

where we use the fact that $\|\boldsymbol{\xi}\|_2 \leq \|\boldsymbol{\xi}\|_1$. Since by the assumption that $\xi_i > 0$ we know $\|\boldsymbol{\xi}\|_1 = \sum_{i=1}^{m}\xi_i$ and, thus, equation (4.35) and (4.34) are somewhat similar to the objective function minimized by the optimization problems (2.48) and (2.49).

Application to Adaptive Margin Machines

In Section 2.5 we have introduced adaptive margin machines as a fairly robust learning algorithm. In this subsection we show that a straightforward application of the margin distribution bound (4.33) reveals that the algorithm aims to minimize effective complexity although no *direct* margin maximization appears to be included in the objective function (2.57). The key fact we exploit is that, due to the constraints (2.58), we know, for each feasible solution $\boldsymbol{\alpha}$ and $\boldsymbol{\xi}$,

$$\forall i \in \{1,\ldots,m\}: \quad \underbrace{y_i \sum_{j=1}^{m} \alpha_j y_j \left\langle \mathbf{x}_j, \mathbf{x}_i \right\rangle}_{\langle \mathbf{w}, \mathbf{x}_i \rangle} \geq 1 - \xi_i + \lambda \alpha_i k\left(x_i, x_i\right)$$

which readily implies

$$\begin{aligned}
\forall i \in \{1,\ldots,m\}: \quad 1 - \langle \mathbf{w}, \mathbf{x}_i \rangle &\leq \xi_i - \lambda \alpha_i k\left(x_i, x_i\right), \\
\forall i \in \{1,\ldots,m\}: \quad \max\{0, 1 - \langle \mathbf{w}, \mathbf{x}_i \rangle\} &\leq \max\{0, \xi_i - \lambda \alpha_i k\left(x_i, x_i\right)\}. \quad (4.36)
\end{aligned}$$

Now for any linear classifier parameterized by $\mathbf{w}$ let us apply Theorem 4.35 with $\mathbf{w}_{\text{norm}} = \frac{\mathbf{w}}{\|\mathbf{w}\|}$ and $\gamma = \frac{1}{\|\mathbf{w}\|}$. The resulting effective complexity measured by d_{eff} is then given by

$$\begin{aligned}
d_{\text{eff}} &= 65 \|\mathbf{w}\|^2 \left(\varsigma + 3 \sqrt{\sum_{i=1}^{m} \left(\max\left\{0, \frac{1}{\|\mathbf{w}\|} - y_i \left\langle \frac{\mathbf{w}}{\|\mathbf{w}\|}, \mathbf{x}_i \right\rangle \right\}\right)^2} \right)^2 \\
&= 65 \left(\varsigma \|\mathbf{w}\| + 3 \sqrt{\sum_{i=1}^{m} \left(\max\left\{0, 1 - y_i \left\langle \mathbf{w}, \mathbf{x}_i \right\rangle\right\}\right)^2} \right)^2. \quad (4.37)
\end{aligned}$$

Combining equation (4.36) and (4.37) we have shown the following theorem for adaptive margin machines.

Theorem 4.37 (Adaptive margin machines bound) *Suppose $\mathcal{K} \subseteq \ell_2^n$ is a given feature space. For all probability measures $\mathbf{P}_\mathsf{Z}$ such that $\mathbf{P}_\mathsf{X}\left(\|\boldsymbol{\phi}(\mathsf{X})\| \leq \varsigma\right) = 1$, for any $\delta \in (0, 1]$, with probability at least $1 - \delta$ over the random draw of the training sample z, for all feasible solutions $\boldsymbol{\alpha} \geq \mathbf{0}$ and $\boldsymbol{\xi} \geq \mathbf{0}$ of the linear program (2.57)–(2.58) the expected risk $R[h_\mathbf{w}]$ w.r.t. the zero-one loss l_{0-1} of the corresponding linear classifier $\mathbf{w} = \sum_{i=1}^{m} \alpha_i y_i \mathbf{x}_i$ is bounded from above by*

$$R\left[h_\mathbf{w}\right] \leq \frac{2}{m}\left(\left\lceil d_{\text{eff}} \operatorname{ld}\left(\frac{8em}{d_{\text{eff}}}\right) \operatorname{ld}(32m) \right\rceil + \operatorname{ld}\left(\frac{(16 + \operatorname{ld}(m))\, m}{\delta}\right)\right),$$

where $d_{\text{eff}} \leq 2m$ with

$$d_{\text{eff}} = 65 \left(\varsigma \|\mathbf{w}\| + 3 \sum_{i=1}^{m} \max\left\{0, \xi_i - \lambda \alpha_i k\left(x_i, x_i\right)\right\} \right)^2. \quad (4.38)$$

Proof The proof is an immediate consequence of Theorem 4.35, equation (4.36) and equation (4.37) using the fact that the max function in the inner sum always returns positive numbers c_i and hence

$$\sqrt{\sum_{i=1}^{m} c_i^2} \leq \sqrt{\left(\sum_{i=1}^{m} c_i\right)^2} = \sum_{i=1}^{m} c_i \,.$$

The theorem is proved. ■

From this theorem we can get the following insight: As both the vector $\boldsymbol{\alpha}$ of the expansion coefficients and the vector $\boldsymbol{\xi}$ of the slack variables must be positive, the effective dimensionality d_{eff} is minimized whenever $\xi_i < \lambda\alpha_i k(x_i, x_i)$. Let us consider a fixed value of λ and a fixed linear classifier parameterized by $\boldsymbol{\alpha}$. Then the algorithm given by equations (2.57)–(2.58) aims to minimize the sum of the ξ_i's which, by equation (4.38), will minimize the resulting effective complexity of $\boldsymbol{\alpha}$. The amount by which this will influence d_{eff} is controlled via λ, i.e., for small values of λ (no regularization) the impact is very large whereas for $\lambda \to \infty$ (total regularization) the minimization of $\sum_{i=1}^{m} \xi_i$ has no further impact on the effective complexity.

4.5 Bibliographical Remarks

This chapter reviewed different mathematical models for learning. We demonstrated that classical statistical analysis is not suited for the purpose of learning because it studies the convergence of probability measures (see Billingsley (1968), Pollard (1984) and Amari (1985)) and thus leads to observations such as the "curse of dimensionality" (Bellman 1961). Further, classical statistical results often have to assume the "correctness" of the probabilistic model which is essential for the maximum likelihood method to provide good convergence results (see Devroye et al. (1996, Chapters 15, 16) for a discussion with some pessimistic results). In contrast, it has been suggested that studying convergence of risks directly is preferable (see Vapnik and Chervonenkis (1971), Vapnik (1982), Kearns and Vazirani (1994), Devroye et al. (1996), Vidyasagar (1997), Anthony (1997), Vapnik (1998) and Anthony and Bartlett (1999)). In the case of empirical risk minimization algorithms this has resulted in the so-called VC and PAC framework. The PAC framework was introduced 1984 in the seminal paper of Valiant (1984) in which he specializes the general question of convergence of expected risks to the problem of learning logic formulas assuming that the hypothesis space $\mathcal{H}$ contains the target formula. Hence all uncertainty is due to the unknown input distribution[13] $\mathbf{P}_X$. The restriction to logic formulas also simplified the matter because the number of hypotheses then becomes finite even though it grows exponentially in the number of binary features. Since then a number of generalizations have been proposed by dropping the assumption of finite hypothesis spaces and *realizability*, i.e., the "oracle" draws its target hypothesis h^* from the hypothesis space $\mathcal{H}$ which we use for learning (see Blumer et al. (1989) and Anthony (1997) for a comprehensive overview). The latter generalization became known as the *agnostic PAC framework* (Kearns et al. 1992). Though we have ignored computational complexity and computability aspects, the PAC model in its pure form is also concerned with these questions.

Apart from these developments, V. Vapnik and A. Chervonenkis already studied the general convergence question in the late 1960s. In honor of them, their framework is now known as the VC (Vapnik-Chervonenkis) framework. They showed that the convergence of expected risks is equivalent to the uniform convergence of frequencies to probabilities over a fixed set of events (Vapnik and Chervonenkis 1991) (see Vapnik (1998, Chapter 16) for a definition of "nontrivial" hypothesis spaces and Bartlett et al. (1996) for a constructive example). This equivalence is known as the *key theorem in learning theory*. The answer to a particular case of this problem was already available through the Glivenko-Cantelli lemma (Glivenko 1933; Cantelli 1933) which says that the empirical distribution function of a one dimensional random variable converges uniformly to the true distribution function in probability. The rate of convergence was proven for the first time in Kolmogorov (1933). Vapnik and Chervonenkis generalized the problem and asked themselves which property a set of events must share such that this convergence still takes place. As a consequence, these sets of events are known as Glivenko-Cantelli classes. In 1987, M. Talagrand obtained the general answer to the problem of identifying Glivenko-Cantelli classes (Talagrand 1987). Ten years later this result was independently rediscovered by Alon et al. (1997). It is worth mentioning that most of the results in the PAC framework are particular cases of more general results already obtained by Vapnik and coworkers two decades before.

The main VC and PAC bounds given in equations (4.11) and (4.12) were first proven in Vapnik and Chervonenkis (1974) and effectively differ by the exponent at the deviation of ε. In Vapnik (1982, Theorem 6.8) it is shown that this exponent continously varies from 2 to 1 w.r.t. the smallest achievable expected risk

13 In the original work of Valiant he used the term *oracle* to refer to the $\mathbf{P}_X$.

$\inf_{h\in\mathcal{H}} R[h]$ (see also Lee et al. (1998) for tighter results in the special case of convex hypothesis spaces). The VC and PAC analysis revealed that, for the case of learning, the growth function of a hypothesis space is an appropriate a-priori measure of its complexity. As the growth function is very difficult to compute, it is often characterized by a one-integer summary known as VC dimension (see Theorem 4.10 and Sontag (1998) for an excellent survey of the VC dimension). The first proof of this theorem is due to Vapnik and Chervonenkis (1971) and was discovered independently in Sauer (1972) and Shelah (1972); the former credits Erdös with posing it as a conjecture. In order to make the VC dimension a variable of the learning algorithm itself two conceptually different approaches were presented: By defining an a-priori structuring of the hypothesis space—sometimes also referred to as a *decomposition* of the hypothesis space $\mathcal{H}$ (Shawe-Taylor et al. 1998)—it is possible to provide guarantees for the generalization error with high confidence by sharing the confidence among the different hypothesis spaces. This principle, known as structural risk minimization, is due to Vapnik and Chervonenkis (1974). A more promising approach is to define an effective complexity via a luckiness function which encodes some prior hope about the learning problem given by the unknown $\mathbf{P}_\mathsf{Z}$. This framework, also termed the luckiness framework is due to Shawe-Taylor et al. (1998). For more details on the related problem of conditional confidence intervals the interested reader is referred to Brownie and Kiefer (1977), Casella (1988), Berger (1985) and Kiefer (1977). All examples given in Section 4.3 are taken from Shawe-Taylor et al. (1998). The luckiness framework is most advantageous if we refine what is required from a learning algorithm: A learning algorithm $\mathcal{A}$ is given a training sample $z \in \mathcal{Z}^m$ *and* a confidence $\delta \in (0, 1]$, and is then required to return a hypothesis $\mathcal{A}(z) \in \mathcal{H}$ together with an accuracy ε such that in at least $1 - \delta$ of the learning trials the expected risk of $\mathcal{A}(z)$ is less than or equal to the given ε. Y. Freund called such learning algorithms *self bounding learning algorithms* (Freund 1998). Although, without making explicit assumptions on $\mathbf{P}_\mathsf{Z}$, all learning algorithms might be equally good, a self bounding learning algorithm is able to tell the practitioner when its implicit assumptions are met. Obviously, a self bounding learning algorithm can only be constructed having a theoretically justified generalization error bound available.

In the last section of this chapter we presented a PAC analysis for the particular hypothesis space of linear classifiers making extensive use of the margin as a *data dependent complexity* measure. In Theorem 4.25 we showed that the margin, that is, the minimum real-valued output of a linear classifier before thresholding, allows us to replace the coarse application of the union bound over the worst case diversity of the binary-valued function class by a union bound over the number of equivalence classes witnessed by the observed margin. The proof of this result can also be found in Shawe-Taylor and Cristianini (1998, Theorem 6.8) and Bartlett (1998, Lemma 4). Using a scale sensitive version of the VC dimension known as the fat shattering dimension (Kearns and Schapire 1994) we obtained bounds on the expected risk of a linear classifier which can be directly evaluated *after learning*. An important tool was Lemma 4.29 which can be found in Alon et al. (1997). The final step was an application of Lemma 4.31 which was proven in Gurvits (1997) and later simplified in Bartlett and Shawe-Taylor (1999). It should be noted, however, that the application of Alon's result yields bounds which are practically irrelevant as they require the training sample size to be of order 10^5 in order to be nontrivial. Reinterpreting the margin we demonstrated that this margin bound directly gives a bound on the expected risk involving a function of the margin distribution. This study closely followed the original papers Shawe-Taylor and Cristianini (1998) and Shawe-Taylor and Cristianini (2000). A further application of this idea showed that although not containing any margin complexity, adaptive margin machines effectively minimize the complexity of the resulting classification functions. Recently it has been demonstrated that a functional analytic viewpoint offers ways to get much tighter bounds on the covering number at the scale of the observed margin (see Williamson et al. (2000), Shawe-Taylor and Williamson (1999), Schölkopf et al. (1999) and Smola et al. (2000)).

5 Bounds for Specific Algorithms

This chapter presents a theoretical study of the generalization error of specific algorithms as opposed to uniform guarantees about the expected risks over the whole hypothesis space. It starts with a PAC type or frequentist analysis for Bayesian learning algorithms. The main PAC-Bayesian generalization error bound measures the complexity of a posterior belief by its evidence. Using a summarization property of hypothesis spaces known as *Bayes admissibility*, it is possible to apply the main results to single hypotheses. For the particular case of linear classifiers we obtain a bound on the expected risk in terms of a normalized margin on the training sample. In contrast to the classical PAC margin bound, the new bound is an exponential improvement in terms of the achieved margin. A drawback of the new bound is its dependence on the number of dimensions of feature space.

In order to study more conventional machine learning algorithms the chapter introduces the compression framework. The main idea here is to take advantage of the fact that, for certain learning algorithms, we can remove training examples without changing its behavior. It will be shown that the intuitive notion of compression coefficients, that is, the fraction of necessary training examples in the whole training sample, can be justified by rigorous generalization error bounds. As an application of this framework we derive a generalization error bound for the perceptron learning algorithm which is controlled by the margin a support vector machine would have achieved on the same training sample. Finally, the chapter presents a generalization error bound for learning algorithms that exploits the robustness of a given learning algorithm. In the current context, robustness is defined as the property that a single extra training example has a limited influence on the hypothesis learned, measured in terms of its expected risk. This analysis allows us to show that the leave-one-out error is a good estimator of the generalization error, putting the common practice of performing model selection on the basis of the leave-one-out error on a sound theoretical basis.

5.1 The PAC-Bayesian Framework

Up to this point we have investigated the question of bounds on the expected risk that hold uniformly over a hypothesis space. This was done due to the assumption that the selection of a single hypothesis on the basis of the training sample $z \in \mathcal{Z}^m$ is the ultimate goal of learning. In contrast, a Bayesian algorithm results in (posterior) beliefs $\mathbf{P}_{\mathsf{H}|\mathsf{Z}^m=z}$ over all hypotheses. Based on the posterior measure $\mathbf{P}_{\mathsf{H}|\mathsf{Z}^m=z}$ different classification strategies are conceivable (see Subsection 3.1.1 for details). The power of a Bayesian learning algorithm is in the possibility of incorporating prior knowledge about the learning task at hand via the prior measure $\mathbf{P}_{\mathsf{H}}$. Recently D. McAllester presented some so-called PAC-Bayesian theorems which bound the expected risk of Bayesian classifiers while avoiding the use of the growth function and related quantities altogether. Unlike classical Bayesian analysis—where we make the implicit assumption that the unknown measure $\mathbf{P}_{\mathsf{Z}}$ of the data can be computed from the prior $\mathbf{P}_{\mathsf{H}}$ and the likelihood $\mathbf{P}_{\mathsf{Z}|\mathsf{H}=h}$ by $\mathbf{E}_{\mathsf{H}}\left[\mathbf{P}_{\mathsf{Z}|\mathsf{H}=h}\right]$—these results hold for *any* distribution $\mathbf{P}_{\mathsf{Z}}$ of the training data and thus fulfill the basic desiderata of PAC learning theory. The key idea to obtain such results is to take the concept of structural risk minimization to its extreme—where each hypothesis space contains *exactly* one hypothesis. A direct application of the multiple testing lemma 4.14 yields bounds on the expected risk for single hypotheses, which justify the use of the MAP strategy as one possible learning method in a Bayesian framework. Applying a similar idea to subsets of the hypothesis space $\mathcal{H}$ then results in uniform bounds for average classifications as carried out by the Gibbs classification strategy. Finally, the use of a simple inequality between the expected risk of the Gibbs and Bayes classification strategies completes the list of generalization error bounds for Bayesian algorithms. It is worth mentioning that we have already used prior beliefs in the application of structural risk minimization (see Subsection 4.2.3).

5.1.1 PAC-Bayesian Bounds for Bayesian Algorithms

In this section we present generalization error bounds for the three Bayesian classification strategies presented in Subsection 3.1.1. We shall confine ourselves to the PAC likelihood defined in Definition 3.3 which, in a strict Bayesian treatment, corresponds to the assumption that the loss is given by the zero-one loss l_{0-1}. Note, however, that the main ideas of the PAC-Bayesian framework carry over far beyond this simple model (see Section 5.4 for further references).

A Bound for the MAP Estimator

Let us consider *any* prior measure $\mathbf{P}_{\mathsf{H}}$ on a hypothesis space $\mathcal{H} = \{h_i\}_{i=1}^{\infty}$. Then, by the binomial tail bound given in Theorem A.116, we know that, for all $\varepsilon > 0$,

$$\forall h_i \in \mathcal{H}: \qquad \mathbf{P}_{\mathsf{Z}^m}\left(\left(R_{\text{emp}}\left[h_i, \mathbf{Z}\right] = 0\right) \wedge \left(R\left[h_i\right] > \varepsilon\right)\right) < \exp\left(-m\varepsilon\right),$$

that is, the probability that a fixed hypothesis commits no errors on a sample of size m, although its expected risk is greater than some prespecified ε, decays exponentially in ε. This is clearly equivalent to the the following statement

$$\Upsilon_i\left(z, m, \delta\right) \equiv \left(R_{\text{emp}}\left[h_i, z\right] \neq 0\right) \vee \left(R\left[h_i\right] \leq \frac{\ln\left(\frac{1}{\delta}\right)}{m}\right), \tag{5.1}$$

which holds with probability at least $1 - \delta$ over the random draw of the training sample $z \in \mathcal{Z}^m$. Hence, applying Lemma 4.14 with $\mathbf{P}_{\mathsf{S}} = \mathbf{P}_{\mathsf{H}}$ we have proven our first PAC-Bayesian result.

Theorem 5.1 (Bound for single hypotheses) *For any measure* $\mathbf{P}_{\mathsf{H}}$ *and any measure* $\mathbf{P}_{\mathsf{Z}}$, *for any* $\delta \in (0, 1]$, *with probability at least* $1 - \delta$ *over the random draw of the training sample* $z \in \mathcal{Z}^m$ *for all hypotheses* $h \in V_{\mathcal{H}}(z)$ *that achieve zero training error* $R_{\text{emp}}[h, z] = 0$ *and have* $\mathbf{P}_{\mathsf{H}}(h) > 0$, *the expected risk* $R[h]$ *is bounded from above by*

$$R\left[h\right] \leq \frac{1}{m}\left(\ln\left(\frac{1}{\mathbf{P}_{\mathsf{H}}\left(h\right)}\right) + \ln\left(\frac{1}{\delta}\right)\right). \tag{5.2}$$

This bound justifies the MAP estimation procedure because, by assumption of the PAC likelihood for each hypothesis h not in version space $V_{\mathcal{H}}(z)$, the posterior measure $\mathbf{P}_{\mathsf{H}|\mathsf{Z}^m=z}(h)$ vanishes due to the likelihood term. Thus, the posterior measure $\mathbf{P}_{\mathsf{H}|\mathsf{Z}^m=z}$ is merely a rescaled version of the prior measure $\mathbf{P}_{\mathsf{H}}$, only positive inside version space $V_{\mathcal{H}}(z)$. Hence, the maximizer $\mathcal{A}_{\text{MAP}}(z)$ of the posterior measure $\mathbf{P}_{\mathsf{H}|\mathsf{Z}^m=z}$ must be the hypothesis with maximal prior measure $\mathbf{P}_{\mathsf{H}}$ which is, at the same time, the minimizer of equation (5.2).

A Bound for the Gibbs Classification Strategy

Considering the Gibbs classification strategy given in Definition 3.8 we see that, due to the non-deterministic classification function, the expected risk of $Gibbs_z$

based on $\mathbf{P}_{\mathsf{H}|\mathsf{Z}^m=z}$ can be written as

$$R\left[Gibbs_z\right] = \mathbf{E}_{\mathsf{XY}}\left[\mathbf{E}_{\mathsf{H}|\mathsf{Z}^m=z}\left[l_{0-1}\left(\mathsf{H}\left(\mathsf{X}\right),\mathsf{Y}\right)\right]\right] = \mathbf{E}_{\mathsf{H}|\mathsf{Z}^m=z}\left[\mathbf{E}_{\mathsf{XY}}\left[l_{0-1}\left(\mathsf{H}\left(\mathsf{X}\right),\mathsf{Y}\right)\right]\right].$$

In case of the PAC likelihood we know that, for a given training sample $z \in \mathcal{Z}^m$, the posterior probability can only be positive for hypotheses h within version space $V_{\mathcal{H}}(z)$. Let us study the more general case of a Gibbs classification strategy $Gibbs_{H(z)}$ over a subset $H(z) \subseteq V_{\mathcal{H}}(z)$ of version space (the original Gibbs classification strategy $Gibbs_z$ is retained by setting $H(z) = V_{\mathcal{H}}(z)$), i.e.,

$$Gibbs_{H(z)}(x) = h(x)\,, \qquad h \sim \mathbf{P}_{\mathsf{H}|\mathsf{H}\in H(z)}\,. \tag{5.3}$$

The expected risk of this generalized classification strategy can then be written as

$$R\left[Gibbs_{H(z)}\right] = \mathbf{E}_{\mathsf{H}|\mathsf{H}\in H(z)}\left[\mathbf{E}_{\mathsf{XY}}\left[l_{0-1}\left(\mathsf{H}\left(\mathsf{X}\right),\mathsf{Y}\right)\right]\right] = \mathbf{E}_{\mathsf{H}|\mathsf{H}\in H(z)}\left[R\left[\mathsf{H}\right]\right]. \tag{5.4}$$

The main idea involved in obtaining a bound for this classification strategy is to split up the expectation value in equation (5.4) at some point $\varepsilon \in (0,1]$ and to use the fact that by the zero-one loss l_{0-1}, for all hypotheses $R[h] \le 1$,

$$R\left[Gibbs_{H(z)}\right] \le \varepsilon \cdot \mathbf{P}_{\mathsf{H}|\mathsf{H}\in H(z)}\left[R\left[\mathsf{H}\right] \le \varepsilon\right] + 1 \cdot \mathbf{P}_{\mathsf{H}|\mathsf{H}\in H(z)}\left[R\left[\mathsf{H}\right] > \varepsilon\right].$$

Thus, it is necessary to obtain an upper bound on $\mathbf{P}_{\mathsf{H}|\mathsf{H}\in H(z)}\left[R\left[\mathsf{H}\right] > \varepsilon\right]$ over the random draw of the training sample $z \in \mathcal{Z}^m$. Fully exploiting our knowledge about the probability of drawing a training sample z such that a hypothesis h in version space $V_{\mathcal{H}}(z)$ has an expected risk $R[h]$ larger than ε, we use equation (5.1) together with the quantifier reversal lemma (see Lemma C.10 in Appendix C.7). This yields that, for all $\beta \in (0,1)$, with probability at least $1-\delta$ over the random draw of the training sample z,

$$\forall \alpha \in (0,1]: \qquad \mathbf{P}_{\mathsf{H}}\left(\left(\mathsf{H} \in V_{\mathcal{H}}(z)\right) \wedge \left(R\left[\mathsf{H}\right] > \underbrace{\frac{1}{(1-\beta)}\frac{\ln\left(\frac{1}{\alpha\beta\delta}\right)}{m}}_{\varepsilon}\right)\right) < \alpha\,,$$

where we replace $R_{\mathrm{emp}}\left[\mathsf{H}, z\right] = 0$ by $\mathsf{H} \in V_{\mathcal{H}}(z)$ which is true by definition. Note that we exploit the fact that $\mathbf{P}_{\mathsf{Z}|\mathsf{H}=h} = \mathbf{P}_{\mathsf{Z}}$ which should not be confused with the purely Bayesian approach *to modeling* the data distribution $\mathbf{P}_{\mathsf{Z}}$ (see Chapter 3). In the current context, however, we consider the *unknown* true distribution $\mathbf{P}_{\mathsf{Z}}$ which is *not* influenced by the (algorithmical) model $h \in \mathcal{H}$ chosen. As by assumption $H(z) \subseteq V_{\mathcal{H}}(z)$ it easily follows that

$$\mathbf{P}_{\mathsf{H}|\mathsf{H}\in H(z)}\left(R\left[\mathsf{H}\right]>\varepsilon\right) = \frac{\mathbf{P}_{\mathsf{H}}\left(\left(\mathsf{H}\in H\left(z\right)\right)\wedge\left(R\left[\mathsf{H}\right]>\varepsilon\right)\right)}{\mathbf{P}_{\mathsf{H}}\left(H\left(z\right)\right)} < \frac{\alpha}{\mathbf{P}_{\mathsf{H}}\left(H\left(z\right)\right)}.$$

Finally, choosing $\alpha = \mathbf{P}_{\mathsf{H}}\left(H\left(z\right)\right)/m$ and $\beta = 1/m$, as well as exploiting the fact that the function $\mathbf{P}_{\mathsf{H}|\mathsf{H}\in H(z)}\left[R\left[\mathsf{H}\right]>\varepsilon\right]$ is monotonically increasing in ε, it is readily verified that, with probability at least $1-\delta$ over the random draw of the training sample $z\in\mathcal{Z}^m$,

$$\begin{aligned} R\left[Gibbs_{H(z)}\right] &\leq \varepsilon\cdot\left(1-\frac{1}{m}\right)+\frac{1}{m} \\ &= \frac{1}{m}\left(\ln\left(\frac{1}{\mathbf{P}_{\mathsf{H}}\left(H\left(z\right)\right)}\right)+2\ln\left(m\right)+\ln\left(\frac{1}{\delta}\right)+1\right). \end{aligned}$$

Thus we have shown our second PAC-Bayesian result.

Theorem 5.2 (Bound for subsets of hypotheses) *For any measure $\mathbf{P}_{\mathsf{H}}$ and any measure $\mathbf{P}_{\mathsf{Z}}$, for any $\delta\in(0,1]$, with probability at least $1-\delta$ over the random draw of the training sample $z\in\mathcal{Z}^m$ for all subsets $H\left(z\right)\subseteq V_{\mathcal{H}}\left(z\right)$ such that $\mathbf{P}_{\mathsf{H}}\left(H\left(z\right)\right)>0$, the expected risk of the associated Gibbs classification strategy $Gibbs_{H(z)}$ is bounded from above by*

$$R\left[Gibbs_{H(z)}\right]\leq\frac{1}{m}\left(\ln\left(\frac{1}{\mathbf{P}_{\mathsf{H}}\left(H\left(z\right)\right)}\right)+2\ln\left(m\right)+\ln\left(\frac{1}{\delta}\right)+1\right). \tag{5.5}$$

As expected, the Gibbs classification strategy $Gibbs_z$ given in Definition 3.8 minimizes the r.h.s. of equation (5.5). Remarkably, however, the bound on the expected risk for the Gibbs classification strategy is always smaller than or equal to the bound value for any single hypothesis. This is seemingly in contrast to a classical PAC analysis which views the learning process as a selection among hypotheses based on the training sample $z\in\mathcal{Z}^m$.

The Gibbs-Bayes Lemma

Finally, in order to obtain a PAC-Bayesian bound on the expected risk of the Bayes classification strategy given in Definition 3.7 we make use of the following simple lemma.

Lemma 5.3 (Gibbs-Bayes lemma) *For any measure $\mathbf{P}_{\mathsf{H}|\mathsf{Z}^m=z}$ over hypothesis space $\mathcal{H} \subseteq \mathcal{Y}^{\mathcal{X}}$ and any measure $\mathbf{P}_{\mathsf{XY}}$ over data space $\mathcal{X} \times \mathcal{Y} = \mathcal{Z}$, for all training samples $z \in \mathcal{Z}^m$ and the zero-one loss l_{0-1}*

$$R\left[Bayes_z\right] \leq |\mathcal{Y}| \cdot R\left[Gibbs_z\right] . \tag{5.6}$$

Proof For any training sample $z \in \mathcal{Z}^m$ and associated measure $\mathbf{P}_{\mathsf{H}|\mathsf{Z}^m=z}$ consider the set

$$Z_z = \left\{(x, y) \in \mathcal{Z} \mid l_{0-1}\left(Bayes_z\left(x\right), y\right) = 1\right\} .$$

For all points $(x, y) \notin Z_z$ in the complement, the r.h.s. of equation (5.6) is zero and thus the bound holds. For all points $(x, y) \in Z_z$ the expectation value $\mathbf{E}_{\mathsf{H}|\mathsf{Z}^m=z}\left[l_{0-1}\left(\mathsf{H}\left(x\right), y\right)\right]$ (as considered for the Gibbs classification strategy) will be at least $\frac{1}{|\mathcal{Y}|}$ because $Bayes_z\left(x\right)$ makes, by definition, the same classification as the majority of the h's weighted by $\mathbf{P}_{\mathsf{H}|\mathsf{Z}^m=z}$. As there are $|\mathcal{Y}|$ different classes the majority has to have a measure of at least $\frac{1}{|\mathcal{Y}|}$. Thus, multiplying this value by $|\mathcal{Y}|$ upper bounds the loss of one incurred on the l.h.s. by $Bayes_z$. The lemma is proved. ■

A direct application of this lemma to Theorem 5.2 finally yields our third PAC-Bayesian result.

Theorem 5.4 (Bound for the Bayes classification strategy) *For any measure $\mathbf{P}_{\mathsf{H}}$ and any measure $\mathbf{P}_{\mathsf{Z}}$, for any $\delta \in (0, 1]$, with probability at least $1 - \delta$ over the random draw of the training sample $z \in \mathcal{Z}^m$, for all subsets $H(z) \subseteq V_{\mathcal{H}}(z)$ such that $\mathbf{P}_{\mathsf{H}}\left(H\left(z\right)\right) > 0$ the expected risk of the generalized Bayes classification strategy $Bayes_{H(z)}$ given by*

$$Bayes_{H(z)}\left(x\right) \stackrel{\text{def}}{=} \underset{y \in \mathcal{Y}}{\operatorname{argmax}}\ \mathbf{P}_{\mathsf{H}|\mathsf{H} \in H(z)}\left(\left\{h \in \mathcal{H} \mid h\left(x\right) = y\right\}\right)$$

is bounded from above by

$$R\left[Bayes_{H(z)}\right] \leq \frac{|\mathcal{Y}|}{m}\left(\ln\left(\frac{1}{\mathbf{P}_{\mathsf{H}}\left(H\left(z\right)\right)}\right) + 2\ln\left(m\right) + \ln\left(\frac{1}{\delta}\right) + 1\right) . \tag{5.7}$$

Again, $H(z) = V_{\mathcal{H}}(z)$ minimizes the bound (5.7) and, as such, theoretically justifies the Bayes optimal decision using the whole of version space without assuming the "correctness" of the prior. Note, however, that the bound becomes trivial as soon as $\mathbf{P}_{\mathsf{H}}\left(V\left(z\right)\right) \leq \exp\left(-m/\left|\mathcal{Y}\right|\right)$. An appealing feature of these bounds is given by the fact that their complexity $\mathbf{P}_{\mathsf{H}}(V_{\mathcal{H}}(z))$ vanishes in the most "lucky" case of observing a training sample z such that all hypotheses are consistent with it.

If we have chosen too "small" a hypothesis space beforehand there might not even exist a single hypothesis consistent with the training sample; if, on the other hand, the hypothesis space $\mathcal{H}$ contains many different hypothesis the prior probability of single hypotheses is exponentially small. We have already seen this dilemma in the study of the structural risk minimization framework (see Subsection 4.2.3).

Remark 5.5 (Evidence and PAC-Bayesian complexity) *If we consider the PAC-likelihood* $\mathbf{P}_{\mathsf{Y}|\mathsf{X}=x,\mathsf{H}=h}(y) = \mathbf{I}_{h(x)=y}$ *we see that the posterior belief* $\mathbf{P}_{\mathsf{H}|\mathsf{Z}^m=z}$ *is a rescaled version of the prior belief* $\mathbf{P}_{\mathsf{H}|\mathsf{Z}^m=z}$*. More interestingly, the evidence* $\mathbf{E}_{\mathsf{H}}\left[\mathbf{P}_{\mathsf{Z}^m|\mathsf{H}=h}\right]$ *equals the prior probability of version space* $\mathbf{P}_{\mathsf{H}}(V_{\mathcal{H}}(z))$*. Thus, in the final bound (5.7) the effective complexity is the negated log-evidence, i.e., maximizing the log-evidence over a small number of different models is theoretically justified by a PAC-Bayesian bound (together with Lemma 4.14)* for any data distribution $\mathbf{P}_{\mathsf{Z}}$*. This result puts the heuristic model selection procedure of evidence maximization on a sound basis and furthermore removes the necessity of "correct priors".*

Bounds with Training Errors

It is worth mentioning that the three results presented above are based on the assertion given in equation (5.1). This (probabilistic) bound on the expected risk of hypotheses consistent with the training sample $z \in \mathcal{Z}^m$ is based on the binomial tail bound. If we replace this starting point with the corresponding assertion obtained from Hoeffding's inequality, i.e.,

$$\Upsilon_i(z, m, \delta) \equiv R[h_i] - R_{\mathrm{emp}}[h_i, z] \leq \sqrt{\frac{\ln\left(\frac{1}{\delta}\right)}{2m}}$$

and perform the same steps as before then we obtain bounds that hold uniformly over the hypothesis space (Theorem 5.1) or for all measurable subsets $H \subseteq \mathcal{H}$ of hypothesis space (Theorems 5.2 and 5.4). More formally, we obtain the following.

Theorem 5.6 (PAC-Bayesian bounds with training errors) *For any measure* $\mathbf{P}_{\mathsf{H}}$ *and any measure* $\mathbf{P}_{\mathsf{Z}}$*, for any* $\delta \in (0, 1]$*, with probability at least* $1 - \delta$ *over the* *random draw of the training sample $z \in \mathcal{Z}^m$, for all hypotheses $h \in \mathcal{H}$ such that $\mathbf{P}_{\mathsf{H}}(h) > 0$,*

$$R[h] \le R_{\mathrm{emp}}[h, z] + \sqrt{\frac{1}{2m}\left(\ln\left(\frac{1}{\mathbf{P}_{\mathsf{H}}(h)}\right) + \ln\left(\frac{1}{\delta}\right)\right)}.$$

Moreover, for all subsets $H(z) \subseteq \mathcal{H}$ such that $\mathbf{P}_{\mathsf{H}}(H(z)) > 0$ the expected risk $R\left[Gibbs_{H(z)}\right]$ of the Gibbs classification strategy $Gibbs_{H(z)}$ is bounded from above by

$$R_{\mathrm{emp}}[H(z), z] + \sqrt{\frac{1}{2m}\left(\ln\left(\frac{1}{\mathbf{P}_{\mathsf{H}}(H(z))}\right) + 2\ln(m) + \ln\left(\frac{1}{\delta}\right)\right)} + \frac{1}{m}, \qquad (5.8)$$

where $R_{\mathrm{emp}}[H(z), z] \stackrel{\mathrm{def}}{=} \mathbf{E}_{\mathsf{H}|\mathsf{H} \in H(z)}\left[R_{\mathrm{emp}}\left[\mathsf{H}, z\right]\right]$ is the average training error over all hypotheses in $H(z)$.

Clearly, even in the case of considering hypotheses which incur training errors, it holds that the bound is smaller for the Gibbs classification strategy than for any single hypothesis found by the MAP procedure. Moreover, the result on the expected risk of the Gibbs classification strategy (or the Bayes classification strategy when using Lemma 5.3) given in equation (5.8) defines an algorithm which selects a subset $H(z) \subseteq \mathcal{H}$ of hypothesis space $\mathcal{H}$ so as to minimize the bound. Note that by the selection of a subset this procedure automatically defines a principle for inferring a distribution $\mathbf{P}_{\mathsf{H}|\mathsf{H} \in H(z)}$ over the hypothesis space which is therefore called the *PAC-Bayesian posterior*.

Remark 5.7 (PAC-Bayesian posterior) *The ideas outlined can be taken one step further when considering not only subsets $H(z) \subseteq \mathcal{H}$ of a hypothesis space but whole measures[1] $\mathbf{Q}_{\mathsf{H}|\mathsf{Z}^m=z}$. In this case, for each test object $x \in \mathcal{X}$ we must consider a (Gibbs) classification strategy $Gibbs_{\mathbf{Q}_{\mathsf{H}|\mathsf{Z}^m=z}}$ that draws a hypothesis $h \in \mathcal{H}$ according to the measure $\mathbf{Q}_{\mathsf{H}|\mathsf{Z}^m=z}$ and uses it for classification. Then, it is possible to prove a result which bounds the expected risk of this Gibbs classification strategy $Gibbs_{\mathbf{Q}_{\mathsf{H}|\mathsf{Z}^m=z}}$ uniformly over all possible $\mathbf{Q}_{\mathsf{H}|\mathsf{Z}^m=z}$ by*

$$\mathbf{E}_{\mathbf{Q}_{\mathsf{H}|\mathsf{Z}^m=z}}\left[R_{\mathrm{emp}}\left[\mathsf{H}, z\right]\right] + \sqrt{\frac{D\left(\mathbf{Q}_{\mathsf{H}|\mathsf{Z}^m=z} \| \mathbf{P}_{\mathsf{H}}\right) + \ln(m) + \ln\left(\frac{1}{\delta}\right) + 2}{2m - 1}}, \qquad (5.9)$$

1 With a slight abuse of notation, in this remark we use $\mathbf{Q}_{\mathsf{H}|\mathsf{Z}^m=z}$ and $\mathbf{q}_{\mathsf{H}|\mathsf{Z}^m=z}$ to denote any measure and density over the hypothesis space based on the training sample $z \in \mathcal{Z}^m$.

where[2]

$$D\left(\mathbf{Q}_{\mathsf{H}|\mathsf{Z}^m=z}\|\mathbf{P}_{\mathsf{H}}\right)=\mathbf{E}_{\mathbf{Q}_{\mathsf{H}|\mathsf{Z}^m=z}}\left[\ln\left(\frac{\mathbf{q}_{\mathsf{H}|\mathsf{Z}^m=z}(\mathsf{H})}{\mathbf{f}_{\mathsf{H}}(\mathsf{H})}\right)\right]$$

is known as the Kullback-Leibler divergence *between* $\mathbf{Q}_{\mathsf{H}|\mathsf{Z}^m=z}$ *and* $\mathbf{P}_{\mathsf{H}}$. *Disregarding the square root and setting* $2m-1$ *to* m *(both are due to the application of Hoeffding's inequality) we therefore have that the PAC-Bayesian posterior is approximately given by the measure* $\mathbf{Q}_{\mathsf{H}|\mathsf{Z}^m=z}$ *which minimizes*

$$\mathbf{E}_{\mathbf{Q}_{\mathsf{H}|\mathsf{Z}^m=z}}\left[R_{\text{emp}}\left[\mathsf{H},z\right]\right]+\frac{D\left(\mathbf{Q}_{\mathsf{H}|\mathsf{Z}^m=z}\|\mathbf{P}_{\mathsf{H}}\right)+\ln(m)+\ln\left(\frac{1}{\delta}\right)+2}{m}. \tag{5.10}$$

Whenever we consider the negative log-likelihood as a loss function,

$$R_{\text{emp}}[h,z]=-\frac{1}{m}\sum_{i=1}^{m}\ln\left(\mathbf{P}_{\mathsf{Z}|\mathsf{H}=h}\left((x_i,y_i)\right)\right)=-\frac{1}{m}\ln\left(\mathbf{P}_{\mathsf{Z}^m|\mathsf{H}=h}(z)\right),$$

this minimizer equals the Bayesian posterior due to the following argument:

- *For all training sample sizes* $m\in\mathbb{N}$ *we have that*

$$\mathbf{E}_{\mathbf{Q}_{\mathsf{H}|\mathsf{Z}^m=z}}\left[R_{\text{emp}}\left[\mathsf{H},z\right]\right]=-\frac{1}{m}\mathbf{E}_{\mathbf{Q}_{\mathsf{H}|\mathsf{Z}^m=z}}\left[\ln\left(\mathbf{P}_{\mathsf{Z}^m|\mathsf{H}=h}(z)\right)\right].$$

- *Dropping all terms which do not depend on* $\mathbf{Q}_{\mathsf{H}|\mathsf{Z}^m=z}$, *equation (5.10) can be written as*

$$\begin{aligned}
&\frac{1}{m}\left(\mathbf{E}_{\mathbf{Q}_{\mathsf{H}|\mathsf{Z}^m=z}}\left[\ln\left(\frac{1}{\mathbf{P}_{\mathsf{Z}^m|\mathsf{H}=h}(z)}\right)\right]+\mathbf{E}_{\mathbf{Q}_{\mathsf{H}|\mathsf{Z}^m=z}}\left[\ln\left(\frac{\mathbf{q}_{\mathsf{H}|\mathsf{Z}^m=z}(\mathsf{H})}{\mathbf{f}_{\mathsf{H}}(\mathsf{H})}\right)\right]\right)\\
&=\frac{1}{m}\left(\mathbf{E}_{\mathbf{Q}_{\mathsf{H}|\mathsf{Z}^m=z}}\left[\ln\left(\frac{\mathbf{q}_{\mathsf{H}|\mathsf{Z}^m=z}(\mathsf{H})}{\mathbf{P}_{\mathsf{Z}^m|\mathsf{H}=h}(z)\,\mathbf{f}_{\mathsf{H}}(\mathsf{H})}\right)\right]\right)\\
&=\frac{1}{m}\left(\mathbf{E}_{\mathbf{Q}_{\mathsf{H}|\mathsf{Z}^m=z}}\left[\ln\left(\frac{\mathbf{q}_{\mathsf{H}|\mathsf{Z}^m=z}(\mathsf{H})}{\mathbf{f}_{\mathsf{H}|\mathsf{Z}^m=z}(\mathsf{H})\,\mathbf{P}_{\mathsf{Z}^m}(z)}\right)\right]\right)\\
&=\frac{1}{m}\left(\mathbf{E}_{\mathbf{Q}_{\mathsf{H}|\mathsf{Z}^m=z}}\left[\ln\left(\frac{\mathbf{q}_{\mathsf{H}|\mathsf{Z}^m=z}(\mathsf{H})}{\mathbf{f}_{\mathsf{H}|\mathsf{Z}^m=z}(\mathsf{H})}\right)-\ln\left(\mathbf{P}_{\mathsf{Z}^m}(z)\right)\right]\right).
\end{aligned}$$

This term is minimized if and only if $\mathbf{q}_{\mathsf{H}|\mathsf{Z}^m=z}(h)=\mathbf{f}_{\mathsf{H}|\mathsf{Z}^m=z}(h)$ *for all hypotheses* $h\in\mathcal{H}$. *Thus, the PAC-Bayesian framework provides a theoretical justification for the use of Bayes' rule in the Bayesian approach to learning as well as a*

2 Note that $\mathbf{q}$ and $\mathbf{f}$ denote the densities of the measures $\mathbf{Q}$ and $\mathbf{P}$, respectively (see also page 333).

quantification of the "correctness" of the prior choice, i.e., evaluating equation (5.9) for the Bayesian posterior $\mathbf{P}_{\mathsf{H}|\mathsf{Z}^m=z}$ provides us with a theoretical guarantee about the expected risk of the resulting Bayes classification strategy.

5.1.2 A PAC-Bayesian Margin Bound

Apart from building a theoretical basis for the Bayesian approach to learning, the PAC-Bayesian results presented can also be used to obtain (training) data-dependent bounds on the expected risk of single hypotheses $h \in \mathcal{H}$. One motivation for doing so is their tightness, i.e., the complexity term $-\ln(\mathbf{P}_{\mathsf{H}}(H(z)))$ is vanishing in maximally "lucky" situations. We shall use the Bayes classification strategy as yet another expression of the classification carried out by a single hypothesis $h \in \mathcal{H}$. Clearly, this can be done as soon as we are sure that, for a given subset $H(h) \subseteq \mathcal{H}$, $Bayes_{H(h)}$ behaves exactly the same as a single hypothesis $h \in \mathcal{H}$ on the whole space $\mathcal{Z}$ w.r.t. the loss function considered. More formally, this is captured by the following definition.

Definition 5.8 (Bayes admissibility) *Given a hypothesis space $\mathcal{H} \subseteq \mathcal{Y}^{\mathcal{X}}$ and a prior measure $\mathbf{P}_{\mathsf{H}}$ over $\mathcal{H}$ we call a subset $H(h) \subseteq \mathcal{H}$* Bayes admissible w.r.t. h and $\mathbf{P}_{\mathsf{H}}$ *if, and only if,*

$$\forall (x, y) \in \mathcal{Z}: \qquad l_{0-1}(h(x), y) = l_{0-1}\left(Bayes_{H(h)}(x), y\right).$$

For general hypothesis spaces $\mathcal{H}$ and prior measures $\mathbf{P}_{\mathsf{H}}$ it is difficult to verify the Bayes admissibility of a hypothesis. Nevertheless, for linear classifiers in some feature space $\mathcal{K}$, i.e., $x \mapsto \operatorname{sign}(\langle \mathbf{x}, \mathbf{w}\rangle)$ where $\mathbf{x} \stackrel{\text{def}}{=} \boldsymbol{\phi}(x)$ and $\boldsymbol{\phi} : \mathcal{X} \to \mathcal{K} \subseteq \ell_2^n$ (see also Definition 2.2), we have the following geometrically plausible lemma.

Lemma 5.9 (Bayes admissibility for linear classifiers in feature space) *For the uniform measure $\mathbf{P}_{\mathsf{W}}$ over the unit hypersphere $\mathcal{W} \subset \mathcal{K} \subseteq \ell_2^n$ each ball $\mathcal{B}_\tau(\mathbf{w}) = \{\mathbf{v} \in \mathcal{W} \mid \|\mathbf{w} - \mathbf{v}\| < \tau\} \subseteq \mathcal{W}$ is Bayes admissible w.r.t. to its center*

$$\mathbf{c} = \frac{\mathbf{E}_{\mathsf{W}|\mathsf{W} \in \mathcal{B}_r(\mathbf{w})}\left[\mathsf{W}\right]}{\left\|\mathbf{E}_{\mathsf{W}|\mathsf{W} \in \mathcal{B}_r(\mathbf{w})}\left[\mathsf{W}\right]\right\|}.$$

Proof The proof follows from the simple observation that the center of a ball is always in the bigger half when bisected by a hyperplane. ■

Remarkably, in using a ball $\mathcal{B}_\tau(\mathbf{w})$ rather than $\mathbf{w}$ to get a bound on the expected risk $R[h_\mathbf{w}]$ of $h_\mathbf{w}$ we make use of the fact that $h_\mathbf{w}$ *summarizes* all its neighboring classifiers $h_\mathbf{v} \in V_\mathcal{H}(z)$, $\mathbf{v} \in \mathcal{B}_\tau(\mathbf{w})$. This is somewhat related to the idea of a covering already exploited in the course of the proof of Theorem 4.25: The cover element $\hat{f} \in F_\gamma(x)$ carries all information about the training error of all the covered functions via its real-valued output referred to as the margin (see page 144 for more details).

In this section we apply the idea of Bayes admissibility w.r.t. the uniform measure $\mathbf{P}_\mathsf{W}$ to linear classifiers, that is, we express a linear classifier $x \mapsto \text{sign}(\langle \mathbf{x}, \mathbf{w}\rangle)$ as a Bayes classification strategy $Bayes_{\mathcal{B}_\tau(\mathbf{w})}$ over a subset $\mathcal{B}_\tau(\mathbf{w})$ of version space $V(z)$ such that $\mathbf{P}_\mathsf{W}(\mathcal{B}_\tau(\mathbf{W}))$ can be lower bounded solely in terms of the margin. As already seen in the geometrical picture on page 57 we need to *normalize* the geometrical margin $\gamma_i(\mathbf{w})$ of a linear classifier $h_\mathbf{w}$ by the length $\|\mathbf{x}_i\|$ of the ith training point in order to ensure that a ball of the resulting margin is fully within version space $V(z)$. Such a refined margin quantity $\Gamma_z(\mathbf{w})$ offers the advantage that no assumption about finite support of the input distribution $\mathbf{P}_\mathsf{X}$ needs to be made.

Theorem 5.10 (PAC-Bayesian margin bound) *Suppose $\mathcal{K} \subseteq \ell_2^n$ is a given feature space of dimensionality n. For all probability measures $\mathbf{P}_\mathsf{Z}$, for any $\delta \in (0,1]$, with probability at least $1-\delta$ over the random draw of the training sample $z \in \mathcal{Z}^m$, if we succeed in correctly classifying m samples z with a linear classifier $f_\mathbf{w}$ achieving a positive* normalized margin $\Gamma_z(\mathbf{w})$,

$$\Gamma_z(\mathbf{w}) \stackrel{\text{def}}{=} \min_{i=1,\dots,m} \frac{y_i \langle \mathbf{x}_i, \mathbf{w}\rangle}{\|\mathbf{w}\| \cdot \|\mathbf{x}_i\|} > 0\,, \tag{5.11}$$

then the generalization error of $h_\mathbf{w}$ is bounded from above by

$$R[h_\mathbf{w}] \le \frac{2}{m}\left(d \ln\left(\frac{1}{1-\sqrt{1-\Gamma_z^2(\mathbf{w})}}\right) + 2\ln(m) + \ln\left(\frac{1}{\delta}\right) + 2\right). \tag{5.12}$$

where $d = \min(m, n)$.

The proof is given in Appendix C.8. The most appealing feature of this new margin bound is, of course, that in the case of maximally large margins, i.e., $\Gamma_z(\mathbf{w}) = 1$, the first term vanishes and the bound reduces to

$$\frac{2}{m}\left(2\ln(m) + \ln\left(\frac{1}{\delta}\right) + 2\right).$$

Here, the numerator grows logarithmically whilst the denominator grows linearly hence giving a rapid decay to zero. Moreover, in the case of

$$\Gamma_z(\mathbf{w}) > \sqrt{2\exp\left(-\frac{1}{2}\right) - \exp(-1)} \approx 0.91$$

we enter a regime where $-\ln(1 - \sqrt{1 - \Gamma_z^2(\mathbf{w})}) < \frac{1}{2}$ and thus the troublesome situation of $d = m$ is compensated for by a large observed margin. The situation $d = m$ occurs if we use kernels which map the data into a high dimensional space as with the RBF kernel (see Table (2.1)).

Example 5.11 (Normalizing data in feature space) *Theorem 5.10 suggests the following learning algorithm: Given a version space $V(z)$ find the classifier $\mathbf{w}$ that maximizes $\Gamma_z(\mathbf{w})$. This algorithm, however, is given by the support vector machine* only if *the training data in feature space $\mathcal{K}$ are normalized. In Figure 5.1 we plotted the expected risks of support vector machine solutions (estimated over 100 different splits of the datasets*[3] `thyroid` *($m = 140$, $m_{\text{test}} = 75$) and* `sonar` *($m = 124$, $m_{\text{test}} = 60$)) with (dashed line) and without normalization (solid line) as a function of the polynomial degree p of a complete polynomial kernel (see Table 2.1). As suggested by Theorem 5.10 in almost all cases the normalization improved the performance of the support vector machine solution at a statistically significant level.*

Remark 5.12 (Sufficient training sample size) *It may seem that this bound on the expected risk of linear hypotheses in terms of the margin is much tighter than the PAC margin bound presented in Theorem 4.32 because its scaling behavior as a function of the margin is exponentially better. Nevertheless, the current result depends heavily on the dimensionality $n \in \mathbb{N}$ of the feature space $\mathcal{K} \subseteq \ell_2^n$ whereas the result in Theorem 4.32 is independent of this number. This makes the current result a practically relevant bound* if the number n of dimensions of feature space $\mathcal{K}$ is much smaller than the training sample size. *A challenging problem is to use the idea of structural risk minimization. If we can map the training sample $z \in \mathcal{Z}^m$ in a low dimensional space and quantify the change in the margin solely in terms of the number n of dimensions used and a training sample independent quantity, then we can use the margin plus an effective small dimensionality of feature space to tighten the bound on the expected risk of a single classifier.*

---

3 These datasets are taken from the UCI Benchmark Repository found at `http://www.ics.uci.edu/~mlearn`.

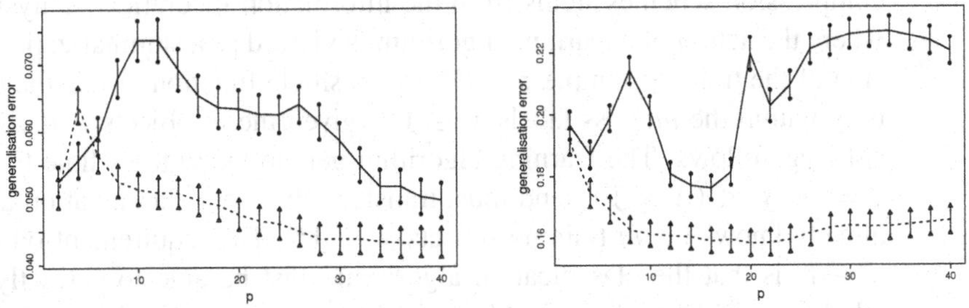

Figure 5.1 Expected risks of classifiers learned by a support vector machine with (dashed line) and without (solid line) normalization of the feature vectors $\mathbf{x}_i$. The error bars indicate one standard deviation over 100 random splits of the datasets. The plots are obtained on the `thyroid` dataset (left) and the `sonar` dataset (right).

Remark 5.13 ("Risky" bounds) *The way we incorporated prior knowledge into this bound was minimal. In fact, by making the assumption of a uniform measure $\mathbf{P}_{\mathsf{W}}$ on the surface of a sphere we have chosen the most uninformative prior possible. Therefore our result is solution independent; it is meaningless where (on the unit sphere) the margin $\Gamma_z(\mathbf{w})$ is observed. Remarkably, the PAC-Bayesian view offers ways to construct "risky" bounds by putting much more prior probability on a certain region of the hypotheses space $\mathcal{H}$. Moreover, we can incorporate unlabeled data much more easily by carefully adjusting our prior $\mathbf{P}_{\mathsf{W}}$.*

5.2 Compression Bounds

So far we have have studied uniform bounds only; in the classical PAC and VC framework we bounded the uniform convergence of training errors to expected risks (see Section 4.2.1). In the luckiness framework we bounded the expected risk uniformly over the (random) version space (see Theorem 4.19). In the PAC Bayesian framework we studied bounds on the expected risk of the Gibbs classification strategy uniformly over all subsets of hypothesis (version) space (Theorem 5.2 and 5.6), or possible posterior measures (equation (5.9)). We must recall, however, that these results are more than is needed. Ultimately we would like to bound the generalization error of a given algorithm rather than proving uniform bounds on the expected risk. In this section we will present such an analysis for algorithms that can be expressed as so-called compression schemes. The idea behind compression schemes stems from the information theoretical analysis of learning where the action of a learning algorithm is viewed as a summarization or compression of the training sample $z \in \mathcal{Z}^m$ into a single function. Since the uncertainty is only within the m class labels $\boldsymbol{y} \in \mathcal{Y}^m$ (given the m objects $\boldsymbol{x} \in \mathcal{X}^m$) the protocol is as follows: The learning algorithm gets to know the whole training sample $z = (\boldsymbol{x}, \boldsymbol{y}) \in (\mathcal{X} \times \mathcal{Y})^m$ and must transfer d bits to a classification algorithm that already knows the m training objects $\boldsymbol{x} \in \mathcal{X}^m$. The requirement on the choice of $d \in \mathbb{N}$ is that the classification algorithm must be able to correctly classify the whole training sample by just knowing the d bits and the objects $\boldsymbol{x}$. If this is possible then the sequence $\boldsymbol{y}$ of class labels must contain some redundancies w.r.t. the classification algorithm's ability to reproduce class labels, i.e., the hypothesis space $\mathcal{H} \subseteq \mathcal{Y}^{\mathcal{X}}$ chosen. Intuitively, a small compression coefficient d/m should imply a small expected risk of the classification strategy parameterized by the d bits. This will be shown in the next subsection. In the subsequent subsection we apply the resulting compression bound to the perceptron learning algorithm to prove the seemingly paradoxical result that there exists an upper bound on its generalization error driven by the margin a support vector machine would achieve on the same training sample. This should be understood as an example of the practical power of the compression framework rather than a negative result on the margin as a measure of the effective complexity of single (real-valued) hypotheses.

5.2.1 Compression Schemes and Generalization Error

In order to use the notion of compression schemes for bounds on the generalization error $R[\mathcal{A}, z]$ of a fixed learning algorithm $\mathcal{A} : \cup_{m=1}^{\infty} \mathcal{Z}^m \to \mathcal{H} \subseteq \mathcal{Y}^{\mathcal{X}}$ we are required to formally cast the latter into a compression framework. The learning algorithm $\mathcal{A}$ must be expressed as the composition of a compression and reconstruction function. More formally this reads as follows:

Definition 5.14 (Compression scheme) *Let the set $I_{d,m} \subset \{1, \ldots, m\}^d$ comprise all index vectors of size exactly $d \in \mathbb{N}$,*

$$I_{d,m} = \left\{(i_1, \ldots, i_d) \in \{1, \ldots, m\}^d\right\} .$$

Given a training sample $z \in \mathcal{Z}^m$ and an index vector $\mathbf{i} \in I_{d,m}$, let $z_{\mathbf{i}}$ be the subsequence indexed by $\mathbf{i}$,

$$z_{\mathbf{i}} \stackrel{\text{def}}{=} \left(z_{i_1}, \ldots, z_{i_d}\right) .$$

The algorithm $\mathcal{A} : \cup_{m=1}^{\infty} \mathcal{Z}^m \to \mathcal{H}$ *is called a* compression scheme of size d *if, and only if, there exist a* compression function $\mathcal{C}_d : \cup_{i=1}^{\infty} \mathcal{Z}^i \to I_{d,m}$ *and a* reconstruction function $\mathcal{R}_d : \mathcal{Z}^d \to \mathcal{Y}^{\mathcal{X}}$ *whose composition yields the same hypothesis as* $\mathcal{A}(\mathbf{z})$*, i.e.,*

$$\forall \mathbf{z} \in \mathcal{Z}^m : \qquad \mathcal{A}(\mathbf{z}) = \mathcal{R}_d\left(\mathbf{z}_{\mathcal{C}_d(\mathbf{z})}\right) . \tag{5.13}$$

The compression scheme is called permutation and repetition invariant *if, and only if, the reconstruction function* $\mathcal{R}_d$ *is invariant under permutation and repetition.*

Before we proceed to present a generalization error bound for compression schemes we will try to shed some light on this formal definition by casting a few of the algorithms presented in this book into this definition.

Example 5.15 (Perceptron learning algorithm) *In the case of the perceptron learning algorithm given in Algorithm 1 we see that the removal of all training examples* $(x_i, y_i) \in \mathbf{z}$ *that are never used to update the weight vector would not change the algorithm's solution because the algorithm decides on an update using only the current weight vector* $\mathbf{w}_t$ *and the current example* $(x_i, y_i) \in \mathbf{z}$*. Hence we could run the perceptron learning algorithm to track only the indices* $\mathbf{i}$ *of all those training examples used in an update step (compression function* $\mathcal{C}_{|\mathbf{i}|}$*). Afterwards we run the perceptron learning algorithm again on the subsample* $\mathbf{z}_{\mathbf{i}}$ *(reconstruction function* $\mathcal{R}_{|\mathbf{i}|}$*) which would give the same solution as running the algorithm on the full training sample* $\mathbf{z} \in \mathcal{Z}^m$*. Thus, by virtue of equation (5.13) the perceptron learning algorithm is a compression scheme.*

Example 5.16 (Support vector learning) *In order to see that support vector learning fits into the compression framework we notice that, due to the stationary conditions, at the solutions* $\hat{\boldsymbol{\alpha}} \in \mathbb{R}^m$, $\hat{\boldsymbol{\xi}} \in \mathbb{R}^m$ *to the mathematical programs presented in Section B.5*

$$\forall i \in \{1, \ldots, m\} : \qquad \hat{\alpha}_i \left(y_i \left\langle \mathbf{x}_i, \hat{\mathbf{w}} \right\rangle - 1 + \hat{\xi}_i \right) = 0 . \tag{5.14}$$

Now imagine we ran the support vector algorithm and found all training samples indices $\mathbf{i}$ *such that* $y_i \left\langle \mathbf{x}_i, \hat{\mathbf{w}} \right\rangle = 1 - \hat{\xi}_i$ *where* $(x_i, y_i) \in \mathbf{z}$ *(compression function* $\mathcal{C}_{|\mathbf{i}|}$*), that is, all patterns that lie directly on the hyperplanes* $\left\{ \mathbf{x} \in \mathcal{K} \mid \left\langle \mathbf{x}, \hat{\mathbf{w}} \right\rangle = \pm 1 \right\}$ *(if* $\hat{\xi}_i = 0$*) and within the margin or even on the wrong side of the hyperplane (if* $\hat{\xi}_i > 0$*). If we now reran the support vector learning algorithm on* $\mathbf{z}_{\mathbf{i}}$ *we would know that we obtain the same weight vector* $\hat{\mathbf{w}} = \sum_{i=1}^{m} \hat{\alpha}_i y_i \mathbf{x}_i$ *because, by* *virtue of equation (5.14), the left-out training examples must have had expansion coefficients of zero. Further, the ordering of $\mathbf{z_i}$ is irrelevant. As a consequence, the support vector learning algorithm is a permutation and repetition invariant compression scheme.*

It is interesting to note that the relevance vector machine algorithm (see Section 3.3) is not expressible as a compression scheme. Consider that we conduct a first run to select the training examples which have non-zero expansion coefficients in the final expansion. A rerun on this smaller subset of the training sample would not obtain the same classifier because the computation of the few nonzero expansion coefficients α_i uses all the m class labels $\boldsymbol{y} \in \mathcal{Y}^m$ and examples $\boldsymbol{x} \in \mathcal{X}^m$ given (see Algorithm 7).

In the following we confine ourselves to the zero-one loss $l_{0-1}(\hat{y}, y) = \mathbf{I}_{\hat{y} \neq y}$. As mentioned earlier this is not a severe restriction and can be overcome by using different large deviation bounds (see Subsection A.5.2). Let us start with the simple PAC case, that is, we assume that there exists a hypothesis $h^* \in \mathcal{Y}^\mathcal{X}$ such that $\mathbf{P}_{\mathsf{Y}|\mathsf{X}=x}(y) = \mathbf{I}_{h^*(x)=y}$. Then, for a given compression scheme of size $d \leq m$ we will bound the probability of having training samples $\boldsymbol{z} \in \mathcal{Z}^m$ such that the training error $R_{\text{emp}}[\mathcal{R}_d(\boldsymbol{z}_{\mathcal{C}_d(\boldsymbol{z})}), \boldsymbol{z}] = 0$ but the expected risk $R[\mathcal{R}_d(\boldsymbol{z}_{\mathcal{C}_d(\boldsymbol{z})})]$ of the function learned is greater than ε. This probability can be upper bounded by the probabilities that the reconstruction function $\mathcal{R}(\boldsymbol{z}_{\mathbf{i}})$ returns a hypothesis with this property summed over the choice of $\mathbf{i} \in I_{d,m}$, i.e.,

$$\begin{aligned}
&\mathbf{P}_{\mathsf{Z}^m}\left(\left(R_{\text{emp}}\left[\mathcal{R}_d\left(\mathbf{Z}_{\mathcal{C}_d(\mathbf{Z})}\right), \mathbf{Z}\right] = 0\right) \wedge \left(R\left[\mathcal{R}_d\left(\mathbf{Z}_{\mathcal{C}_d(\mathbf{Z})}\right)\right] > \varepsilon\right)\right) \\
&\quad \leq \mathbf{P}_{\mathsf{Z}^m}\left(\exists \mathbf{i} \in I_{d,m} : \left(R_{\text{emp}}\left[\mathcal{R}_d\left(\mathbf{Z}_{\mathbf{i}}\right), \mathbf{Z}\right] = 0\right) \wedge \left(R\left[\mathcal{R}_d\left(\mathbf{Z}_{\mathbf{i}}\right)\right] > \varepsilon\right)\right) \\
&\quad \leq \sum_{\mathbf{i} \in I_{d,m}} \mathbf{P}_{\mathsf{Z}^m}\left(\left(R_{\text{emp}}\left[\mathcal{R}_d\left(\mathbf{Z}_{\mathbf{i}}\right), \mathbf{Z}\right] = 0\right) \wedge \left(R\left[\mathcal{R}_d\left(\mathbf{Z}_{\mathbf{i}}\right)\right] > \varepsilon\right)\right). \qquad (5.15)
\end{aligned}$$

Clearly, for any $\mathbf{i} \in I_{d,m}$, a correct classification of the whole training sample $\boldsymbol{z} \in \mathcal{Z}^m$ implies a correct classification of the subset $\left(\boldsymbol{z} \setminus \left(z_{i_1}, \ldots, z_{i_d}\right)\right) \in \mathcal{Z}^{m-d}$ of training samples not used. Moreover, using the fact that $\mathbf{P}_{\mathsf{Z}^m}$ is a product measure, the single summands in (5.15) are upper bounded by

$$\mathbf{E}_{\mathsf{Z}^d}\left[\mathbf{P}_{\mathsf{Z}^{m-d}|\mathsf{Z}^d=z}\left(\left(R_{\text{emp}}\left[\mathcal{R}_d(\boldsymbol{z}), \mathbf{Z}\right] = 0\right) \wedge \left(R\left[\mathcal{R}_d(\boldsymbol{z})\right] > \varepsilon\right)\right)\right].$$

Note that in this expression the symbol $\mathbf{Z}$ denotes the $m-d$ random training examples whereas the symbol $\boldsymbol{z} \in \mathcal{Z}^d$ denotes the d training examples used to reconstruct the hypothesis. Since all the $m-d$ training examples $\mathbf{Z}$ are assumed to be drawn iid from $\mathbf{P}_\mathsf{Z}$ we know that the innermost probability cannot exceed

$(1-\varepsilon)^{m-d}$ due to the binomial tail bound. Further, we know that the number of different index vectors $\mathbf{i} \in I_{d,m}$ equals[4] m^d which finally gives that the probability in (5.15) is strictly less than $m^d (1-\varepsilon)^{m-d}$. This statement is equivalent to the following assertion $\Upsilon_i(z, m, \delta)$ that holds with probability at least $1-\delta$ over the random draw of the training sample $z \in \mathcal{Z}^m$ for all compression schemes $(\mathcal{C}_i, \mathcal{R}_i)$ of size i

$$\left(R_{\text{emp}}\left[\mathcal{R}_i\left(z, \mathcal{C}_i\left(z\right)\right), z\right] = 0\right) \Rightarrow \left(R\left[\mathcal{R}_i\left(z, \mathcal{C}_i\left(z\right)\right)\right] \le \frac{\ln\left(m^i\right) + \ln\left(\frac{1}{\delta}\right)}{m-i}\right).$$

Using Lemma 4.14 with uniform $\mathbf{P}_S$ over the numbers $i \in \{1, \ldots, m\}$ we have proven the following theorem.

Theorem 5.17 (PAC compression bound) *Suppose we are given a fixed learning algorithm $\mathcal{A} : \cup_{m=1}^{\infty} \mathcal{Z}^m \to \mathcal{H} \subseteq \mathcal{Y}^{\mathcal{X}}$ which is a compression scheme. For any probability measure $\mathbf{P}_Z$ and any $\delta \in (0, 1]$, with probability at least $1-\delta$ over the random draw of the training sample $z \in \mathcal{Z}^m$, if $R_{\text{emp}}[\mathcal{A}(z), z] = 0$ and $\mathcal{A}(z)$ corresponds to a compression scheme of size d, the expected risk $R[\mathcal{A}(z)]$ of the function $\mathcal{A}(z) \in \mathcal{H}$ is bounded from above by*

$$R\left[\mathcal{A}\left(z\right)\right] \le \frac{1}{m-d}\left(\ln\left(m^d\right) + \ln\left(m\right) + \ln\left(\frac{1}{\delta}\right)\right).$$

Furthermore, if $\mathcal{A}$ is a permutation and repetition invariant compression scheme, then

$$R\left[\mathcal{A}\left(z\right)\right] \le \frac{1}{m-d}\left(\ln\left(\binom{m}{d}\right) + \ln\left(m\right) + \ln\left(\frac{1}{\delta}\right)\right). \quad (5.16)$$

In order to understand the full power of this theorem we note that according to Theorem A.105 for all $d \in \{1, \ldots, m\}$, $\binom{m}{d} < \sum_{i=0}^{d} \binom{m}{i} < \left(\frac{em}{d}\right)^d$ which shows that for permutation and repetition invariant compression schemes the generalization error bound (5.16) can be written as[5]

$$R\left[\mathcal{A}\left(z\right)\right] \le \frac{2}{m}\left(d\ln\left(\frac{em}{d}\right) + \ln\left(m\right) + \ln\left(\frac{1}{\delta}\right)\right).$$

4 Note that in the case of permutation and repetition invariant compression schemes there are only $\binom{m}{d}$ different index vectors.

5 Note that this result is trivially true for $d > m/2$; in the other case we used $1/(m-d) \le 2/m$.

Disregarding the improved constants, this is the same bound as obtained in the PAC framework (see equation (4.21) and (4.19)) with the important difference that the number d of examples used is not known a-priori but depends on the training sample $z \in \mathcal{Z}^m$ and learning algorithm $\mathcal{A}$. Since we no longer consider the empirical risk minimization algorithm we see that it is possible to obtain guarantees on the generalization error $R[\mathcal{A}]$ even if the hypothesis space $\mathcal{H}$ has infinite VC dimension $\vartheta_{\mathcal{H}}$. It is worth mentioning that the result as it stands has an intuitive interpretation: If we view d/m as a (data dependent) *compression coefficient* then Theorem 5.17 justifies the statement that a small compression coefficient guarantees a small expected risk of the function learned.

From this derivation we see that the procedure can readily be generalized to the case of a *lossy compression scheme* of size d, that is, the hypothesis reconstructed by $\mathcal{R}_d(z_{\mathcal{C}_d(z)}) \in \mathcal{H}$ still commits some training errors on the given training sample z. If we fix the maximum number of training errors committed to $q \in \{1, \ldots, m\}$ we are interested in bounding the probability of having training samples $z \in \mathcal{Z}^m$ such that the training error $R_{\text{emp}}[\mathcal{R}_d(z_{\mathcal{C}_d(z)}), z] \le \frac{q}{m}$ but with the expected risk $R[\mathcal{R}_d(z_{\mathcal{C}_d(z)})]$ of the function learned greater than ε. Using the same technique as in the PAC case we obtain

$$\begin{aligned}
&\mathbf{P}_{\mathsf{Z}^m}\left(\left(R_{\text{emp}}\left[\mathcal{R}_d\left(\mathbf{Z}_{\mathcal{C}_d(\mathbf{Z})}\right), \mathbf{Z}\right] \le \frac{q}{m}\right) \wedge \left(R\left[\mathcal{R}_d\left(\mathbf{Z}_{\mathcal{C}_d(\mathbf{Z})}\right)\right] > \varepsilon\right)\right) \\
&\quad \le \sum_{\mathbf{i} \in I_{d,m}} \mathbf{P}_{\mathsf{Z}^m}\left(\left(R_{\text{emp}}\left[\mathcal{R}_d\left(\mathbf{Z}_{\mathbf{i}}\right), \mathbf{Z}\right] \le \frac{q}{m}\right) \wedge \left(R\left[\mathcal{R}_d\left(\mathbf{Z}_{\mathbf{i}}\right)\right] > \varepsilon\right)\right).
\end{aligned}$$

Again, for any $\mathbf{i} \in I_{d,m}$ we know that if $\mathcal{R}_d(z_{\mathbf{i}})$ commits no more than q errors on z, then the number of errors committed on the subset $(z \setminus z_{\mathbf{i}}) \in \mathcal{Z}^{m-d}$ cannot exceed q. Hence, any summand in the last expression is upper bounded by

$$\mathbf{E}_{\mathsf{Z}^d}\left[\mathbf{P}_{\mathsf{Z}^{m-d}|\mathsf{Z}^d=z}\left(\left(R_{\text{emp}}\left[\mathcal{R}_d(z), \mathbf{Z}\right] \le \frac{q}{m-d}\right) \wedge \left(R\left[\mathcal{R}_d(z)\right] > \varepsilon\right)\right)\right].$$

Using Hoeffding's inequality for any fixed sample $z \in \mathcal{Z}^d$ we know that the innermost probability cannot exceed $\exp\left(-2(m-d)(\varepsilon - q/(m-d))^2\right)$. By an application of the union bound over all the m^d different index vectors $\mathbf{i} \in I_{d,m}$ we conclude that the following statement $\Upsilon_{i,q}(z, m, \delta)$ holds, with probability at least $1-\delta$ over the random draw of the training sample $z \in \mathcal{Z}^m$, for all lossy compression schemes of size i and maximal number of training errors q

$$\left(R_{\text{emp}}[h_z, z] \le \frac{q}{m}\right) \Rightarrow \left(R[h_z] \le \frac{q}{m-d} + \sqrt{\frac{\ln(m^d) + \ln\left(\frac{1}{\delta}\right)}{2(m-d)}}\right),$$

where we used the shorthand notation $h_z \stackrel{\text{def}}{=} \mathcal{R}_i(z_{\mathbf{e}_i(z)})$. Combining the m^2 different statements for all the possible values of $i \in \{1, \ldots, m\}$ and $q \in \{1, \ldots, m\}$ and using Lemma 4.14 with uniform $\mathbf{P}_S$ we have proven the following theorem.

Theorem 5.18 (Lossy compression bound) *Suppose we are given a fixed learning algorithm $\mathcal{A} : \cup_{m=1}^{\infty} \mathcal{Z}^m \to \mathcal{H} \subseteq \mathcal{Y}^{\mathcal{X}}$ which is a compression scheme. For any probability measure $\mathbf{P}_Z$ and any $\delta \in (0, 1]$, with probability at least $1 - \delta$ over the random draw of the training sample $z \in \mathcal{Z}^m$, if $\mathcal{A}(z)$ corresponds to a compression scheme of size d, the expected risk $R[\mathcal{A}(z)]$ of the function $\mathcal{A}(z) \in \mathcal{H}$ is bounded from above by*

$$R[\mathcal{A}(z)] \le \frac{m}{m-d} R_{\text{emp}}[\mathcal{A}(z), z] + \sqrt{\frac{\ln(m^d) + 2\ln(m) + \ln\left(\frac{1}{\delta}\right)}{2(m-d)}}.$$

Furthermore, if $\mathcal{A}$ is a permutation and repetition invariant compression scheme, then

$$R[\mathcal{A}(z)] \le \frac{m}{m-d} R_{\text{emp}}[\mathcal{A}(z), z] + \sqrt{\frac{\ln\left(\binom{m}{d}\right) + 2\ln(m) + \ln\left(\frac{1}{\delta}\right)}{2(m-d)}}.$$

This result and Theorem 5.17 constitute the basic results of the compression framework. One of the most intriguing features of these inequalities is that, regardless of any a-priori complexity measure (e.g., VC dimension $\vartheta_{\mathcal{H}}$ or the size $|\mathcal{H}|$ of the hypothesis space $\mathcal{H}$), they will always attain nontrivial values, provided that the number d of training examples used is at least as small as half the training sample size. To some extent, this is similar reasoning to that used in the luckiness framework. The difference, however, is that in the compression framework we are considering what we are actually interested in—the expected risk $R[\mathcal{A}(z)]$ of the hypothesis $\mathcal{A}(z) \in \mathcal{H}$ learned—rather than providing uniform bounds over version space $V_{\mathcal{H}}(z)$ which introduce additional technical difficulties such as probable smoothness (see Definition 4.18).

Remark 5.19 (Ghost sample) *There exists an interesting relationship between the technique of symmetrization by a ghost sample (see page 124) used in the PAC/VC framework and the compression framework. Since we consider* only *the expected risk of the hypothesis learned by a fixed learning algorithm and assume that this hypothesis can be reconstructed from $d \ll m$ training examples, the remaining $m - d$ training examples constitute a ghost sample on which the hypothesis succeeds (lossless compression) or commits a small number q of errors (lossy compression). Hence, by exploiting the high compressibility of the training sample, there is no need for an extra ghost sample. In contrast, in the PAC/VC framework we cannot exploit the high compression coefficient of the hypothesis learned since we consider all consistent hypotheses uniformly. Furthermore, in this case the analysis is irrespective of the learning algorithm used.*

5.2.2 On-line Learning and Compression Schemes

One of the most interesting applications of the compression framework is in the area of on-line learning algorithms. Broadly speaking, an on-line algorithm is a learning algorithm that proceeds in trials. In each trial the algorithm is presented an unlabeled example $x_j \in \mathbf{x}$ and produces a prediction $h_j(x_j)$ using the current hypothesis $h_j \in \mathcal{H}$. It then receives a class label $y_j \in \mathbf{y}$ for the example $x_j \in \mathbf{x}$ and incurs a *mistake* if the label differs from the current hypothesis' prediction. After each revealed class label y_j the algorithm is allowed to change the current hypothesis h_j. More formally this reads as follows.

Definition 5.20 (On-line learning algorithm) *Given an input space $\mathcal{X}$, a finite output space $\mathcal{Y}$ and a hypothesis space $\mathcal{H} \subseteq \mathcal{Y}^{\mathcal{X}}$,* an on-line algorithm $\mathcal{A}_{\mathcal{U}}$ for *$\mathcal{H}$ can be written as*

$$\mathcal{A}_{\mathcal{U}}(z) \stackrel{\text{def}}{=} \mathcal{U}\left(y_{j_{|\mathbf{j}|}}, x_{j_{|\mathbf{j}|}}, \mathcal{U}\left(\cdots \mathcal{U}\left(y_{j_2}, x_{j_2}, \mathcal{U}\left(y_{j_1}, x_{j_1}, h_0\left(x_{j_1}\right)\right)\left(x_{j_2}\right)\right)\right)\left(x_{j_{|\mathbf{j}|}}\right)\right),$$

where $\mathcal{U} : \mathcal{Y} \times \mathcal{X} \times \mathcal{H} \to \mathcal{H}$ is an update function which maps the current class label $y_j \in \mathcal{Y}$, the current object $x_j \in \mathcal{X}$ and the current hypothesis $h_j \in \mathcal{H}$ to a (potentially) new hypothesis h_{j+1}. The index vector $\mathbf{j} = (j_1, j_2, \ldots) \in \bigcup_{i=1}^{\infty} \{1, \ldots, m\}^i$ determines the (deterministic) order of the training examples. Note that it is possible to present the same training example $(x_i, y_i) \in z$ several times.

An example of an on-line learning algorithm is the perceptron learning algorithm; starting at the hypothesis $h_0 : x \mapsto \text{sign}(\langle \mathbf{x}, \mathbf{0} \rangle)$, in each step the algorithm checks whether the current hypothesis correctly classifies the new training object. The current hypothesis is only changed if a mistake occurs. This class of algorithms deserves special attention for our current analysis.

Definition 5.21 (Mistake-driven algorithm) *An on-line learning algorithm $\mathcal{A}_\mathcal{U}$ is* mistake-driven *if the update function only changes the hypothesis following mistakes, i.e.,*

$$\forall x \in \mathcal{X} : \forall y \in \mathcal{Y} : \forall h \in \mathcal{H} : \qquad (y = h(x)) \Rightarrow \mathcal{U}(y, x, h) = h .$$

In the study of on-line learning algorithms performance is typically measured by the number of steps until convergence.

Definition 5.22 (Mistake bound) *Given a hypothesis space $\mathcal{H} \subseteq \mathcal{Y}^\mathcal{X}$ and an input sequence $\boldsymbol{x} \in \mathcal{X}^m$ let us assume that the sequence $\boldsymbol{y} \in \mathcal{Y}^m$ of class labels is obtained by $y_i = h(x_i)$ for some hypothesis $h \in \mathcal{H}$ (also called the target concept). The function $M_\mathcal{A} : \mathcal{Z}^m \to \mathbb{N}$ is called a* mistake bound for the on-line learning algorithm *$\mathcal{A}$ if it bounds from above the number of mistakes $\mathcal{A}$ incurs on $z = (\boldsymbol{x}, \boldsymbol{y}) \in \mathcal{Z}^m$ for any ordering $\mathbf{j} \in \cup_{i=1}^{\infty} \{1, \ldots, m\}^i$.*

Since a mistake-driven on-line learning algorithm $\mathcal{A}$ effectively disregards the training examples on which it never makes a mistake we are able to cast it into a compression framework. In fact, if we imagine running the mistake-driven algorithm $\mathcal{A}$ on the training sample $z \in \mathcal{Z}^m$, only tracking the indices $\mathbf{i}$ on which it makes a mistake (compression function $\mathcal{C}_{|\mathbf{i}|}$) and re-run the on-line learning algorithm on the reduced training sample[6] $z_\mathbf{i}$ (reconstruction function $\mathcal{R}_{|\mathbf{i}|}$) we obtain by definition the same final hypothesis. Thus we have the following theorem.

Theorem 5.23 (Mistake bounds into generalization error bounds) *Suppose we are given a mistake-driven on-line learning algorithm $\mathcal{A}$ for $\mathcal{H} \subseteq \mathcal{Y}^\mathcal{X}$ together with a mistake bound $M_\mathcal{A} : \mathcal{Z}^m \to \mathbb{N}$. For any probability measure $\mathbf{P}_\mathsf{Z}$ and any $\delta \in (0, 1]$, with probability at least $1 - \delta$ over the random draw of the training sample $z = (\boldsymbol{x}, \boldsymbol{y}) \in \mathcal{Z}^m$, if there exists a hypothesis $h \in \mathcal{H}$ such that $y_i = h(x_i)$*

6 Here we assume that, in a given ordering, all indices to removed examples have been dropped.

then the expected risk $R[\mathcal{A}(z)]$ *of the function* $\mathcal{A}(z)$ *is bounded from above by*

$$R[\mathcal{A}(z)] \leq \frac{2}{m}\left((M_{\mathcal{A}}(z)+1)\cdot \ln(m) + \ln\left(\frac{1}{\delta}\right)\right). \qquad (5.17)$$

We present two applications of Theorem 5.23 which demonstrate the power of this simple consideration by reproducing results already obtained (with much more effort) in the VC framework.

Example 5.24 (Perceptron learning algorithm) *Let us consider again the perceptron learning algorithm given on page 323. This algorithm is by definition a mistake-driven algorithm with a mistake bound*

$$M_{\mathcal{A}}(z) = \max_{\mathbf{w}\in\mathcal{W}} \left(\frac{\max_{x_i\in \boldsymbol{x}} \|\boldsymbol{\phi}(x_i)\|}{\gamma_z(\mathbf{w})}\right) = \left(\frac{\max_{x_i\in \boldsymbol{x}} \|\boldsymbol{\phi}(x_i)\|}{\gamma_z(\mathbf{w}_{\mathrm{SVM}})}\right)^2$$

as given in Theorem 2.31. Here, $\boldsymbol{\phi} : \mathcal{X} \to \mathcal{K} \subseteq \ell_2^n$ *is some mapping of the objects* $x \in \mathcal{X}$ *into a feature space* $\mathcal{K}$ *(see also Definition 2.2). Remarkably, this mistake bound is dominated by the margin a support vector machine would achieve on the same training sample* z*. Substituting this result directly into equation (5.17) shows that we can give a tighter generalization error bound for the perceptron learning algorithm by studying its properties than for the support vector machine algorithm when using the uniform bounds presented in the previous chapter (see Section 4.4 and Theorem 4.32).*

Example 5.25 (Halving algorithm) *For finite hypothesis spaces* $\mathcal{H}$*, there exists a mistake-driven learning algorithm which achieves a minimal mistake bound. This on-line learning algorithm is called the* halving algorithm *and proceeds as follows:*

1. *Initially, all hypotheses* $h \in \mathcal{H}$ *are stored in the set* $C = \mathcal{H}$ *of consistent classifiers.*

2. *Given a new training object* $x_i \in \boldsymbol{x}$ *the class* $\hat{y} \in \mathcal{Y}$ *which receives the majority of votes from all consistent classifiers* $h \in C$ *is predicted, that is,*

$$\hat{y} = \operatorname*{argmax}_{y\in\mathcal{Y}} |\{h \in C \mid h(x) = y\}| . \qquad (5.18)$$

3. *In the case of a mistake, i.e.,* $y_i \neq \hat{y}$ *all hypotheses in* C *which are inconsistent are removed, so,* $C \leftarrow C \setminus \{h \in C \mid h(x_i) \neq y_i\}$.

4. *If all training examples are correctly classified, it outputs C and classifies according to equation (5.18).*

Clearly, this is a mistake-driven procedure. Further, if $\mathcal{Y}$ has only two classes the maximum number of mistakes this algorithm incurs is $\operatorname{ld}(|\mathcal{H}|)$ *because, at each mistake, the set C is at least halved (if not, then (5.18) would not have incurred a mistake). Plugging* $\operatorname{ld}(|\mathcal{H}|)$ *for* $M_{\mathcal{A}}(z)$ *into equation (5.17) we see that we have recovered the basic VC bound for finite hypothesis spaces (see Theorem 4.6).*

5.3 Algorithmic Stability Bounds

In this last section we present a very recently developed method for studying the generalization error of learning algorithms. In contrast to the compression framework we now do not need to enforce the existence of compression and reconstruction functions. Instead, we take advantage of the robustness of a learning algorithm. The robustness of a learning algorithm $\mathcal{A}$ is a measure of the influence of an additional training example $(\tilde{x}, \tilde{y}) \in \mathcal{Z}$ on the learned hypothesis $\mathcal{A}(z) \in \mathcal{H}$. Here, the influence is quantified in terms of the loss achieved at any (potential) test object $x \in \mathcal{X}$. We observe that a robust learning algorithm guarantees that both the difference in expected risks and empirical risks of the function learned is bounded even if we replace one training example by its worst counterpart. This observation is of great help when using McDiarmid's inequality given in Theorem A.120—a large deviation result perfectly suited for the current purpose. This inequality bounds the probability that a function of the training sample $z \in \mathcal{Z}^m$ (the difference $R[\mathcal{A}(z)] - R_{\text{emp}}[\mathcal{A}(z), z]$ of the expected and empirical risk of the function learned from the training sample z) deviates from its expected value in terms of the maximum deviation between the function's value before and after one example is changed. In fact, the definition of robustness of a learning algorithm is mainly chosen so as to be able to apply this powerful inequality to our current problem.

5.3.1 Algorithmic Stability for Regression

Because of its simplicity we shall start with the regression estimation case, that is, we consider a training sample $z = (\boldsymbol{x}, \boldsymbol{t}) \in (\mathcal{X} \times \mathbb{R})^m$ drawn iid from an unknown distribution $\mathbf{P}_{\mathsf{Z}} = \mathbf{P}_{\mathsf{T}|\mathsf{X}}\mathbf{P}_{\mathsf{X}}$. In this case the hypotheses are given by real-valued functions $f \in \mathcal{F}$ where $\mathcal{F} \subseteq \mathbb{R}^{\mathcal{X}}$. Further, the loss function $l : \mathbb{R} \times \mathbb{R} \to \mathbb{R}$ becomes a function of predicted real values $\hat{t}$ and observed real values t (see, for example the squared loss defined on page 82). Before proceeding we introduce some abbreviations for the sake of notational simplicity. Given a sample $z \in \mathcal{Z}^m$, a natural number $i \in \{1, \ldots, m\}$ and an example $z \in \mathcal{Z}$ let

$$\begin{aligned} z_{\setminus i} &\stackrel{\text{def}}{=} (z_1, \ldots, z_{i-1}, z_{i+1}, \ldots, z_m) \in \mathcal{Z}^{m-1}, \\ z_{i \leftrightarrow z} &\stackrel{\text{def}}{=} (z_1, \ldots, z_{i-1}, z, z_{i+1}, \ldots, z_m) \in \mathcal{Z}^m, \end{aligned}$$

be the sample with the ith element deleted or the ith element replaced by z, respectively. Whenever the learning algorithm is clear from context, we use $f_z \stackrel{\text{def}}{=} \mathcal{A}(z)$. Then the notion of robustness of a learning algorithm is formally defined as follows.

Definition 5.26 (Uniform stability) *A learning algorithm* $\mathcal{A} : \cup_{m=1}^{\infty} \mathcal{Z}^m \to \mathcal{F}$ *is said to be* β_m–stable w.r.t. the loss function $l : \mathbb{R} \times \mathbb{R} \to \mathbb{R}$ *if the following holds for all* $i \in \{1, \ldots, m\}$

$$\forall z \in \mathcal{Z}^m : \forall (x, t) \in \mathcal{Z} : \qquad \left| l(f_z(x), t) - l\left(f_{z_{\setminus i}}(x), t\right) \right| \le \beta_m .$$

It is worth pointing out that β_m–stability of a learning algorithm $\mathcal{A}$ implies robustness in the more usual sense of measuring the influence of an *extra* training example $(\tilde{x}, \tilde{t}) \in \mathcal{Z}$. This is formally expressed in the following theorem.

Theorem 5.27 (Robustness of β_m–stable algorithms) *Suppose we are given a* β_m*–stable learning algorithm* $\mathcal{A} : \cup_{m=1}^{\infty} \mathcal{Z}^m \to \mathcal{F}$ *w.r.t. the loss function* $l : \mathbb{R} \times \mathbb{R} \to \mathbb{R}$*. Then, for any training sample* $z \in \mathcal{Z}^m$*, any* $\tilde{z} \in \mathcal{Z}$*, any* $(x, t) \in \mathcal{Z}$ *and all* $i \in \{1, \ldots, m\}$

$$\left| l(f_z(x), t) - l\left(f_{z_{i \leftrightarrow \tilde{z}}}(x), t\right) \right| \le 2\beta_m .$$

Proof First, we notice that that $l(f_z(x), t) - l\left(f_{z_{i \leftrightarrow \tilde{z}}}(x), t\right)$ equals

$$\underbrace{\left(l(f_z(x), t) - l\left(f_{z_{\setminus i}}(x), t\right)\right)}_{a} + \underbrace{\left(l\left(f_{z_{\setminus i}}(x), t\right) - l\left(f_{z_{i \leftrightarrow \tilde{z}}}(x), t\right)\right)}_{b} .$$

From this, the result follows by the triangle inequality applied to a and b and the fact that the absolute value of a and b is by definition upper bounded by β_m. ■

Note that the value of β_m depends on the training sample size m, so, for larger training samples the influence of a single example $(x, t) \in \mathcal{Z}$ should be decreasing toward zero. We will call an algorithm "stable" if the decrease in β_m is of order one, $\lim_{m\to\infty} \beta_m \cdot m^{-1} = 0$. In order to compute values of β_m for a rather large class of learning algorithms it is useful to introduce the following concept.

Definition 5.28 (Lipschitz continuous loss function) *A loss function $l : \mathbb{R}\times\mathbb{R} \to \mathbb{R}$ is said to be* Lipschitz continuous (in its first argument) *if*

$$\forall \hat{t} \in \mathbb{R} : \forall \tilde{t} \in \mathbb{R} : \forall t \in \mathbb{R} : \quad \left|l\left(\hat{t}, t\right) - l\left(\tilde{t}, t\right)\right| \leq C_l \cdot \left|\hat{t} - \tilde{t}\right| .$$

The value $C_l \in \mathbb{R}^+$ is called the Lipschitz constant *of the loss function l.*

Thus, whenever we are given a Lipschitz continuous loss function we are able to use the difference $\left|f_z(x) - f_{z_{\setminus i}}(x)\right|$ to bound the difference of the losses incurred by two functions $f_z \in \mathcal{F}$ and $f_{z_{\setminus i}} \in \mathcal{F}$ at any test object $x \in \mathcal{X}$. Let us give a few examples of Lipschitz continuous loss functions which we have already used in the consideration of learning algorithms for the regression estimation problem in Part I of this book.

Example 5.29 (Soft margin loss) *If we consider the linear soft margin loss function given in equation (2.47), namely $l_{\text{lin}}\left(\hat{t}, y\right) = \max\left\{1 - y\hat{t}, 0\right\}$ where $y \in \{-1, +1\}$, we see that*

$$\left|l_{\text{lin}}\left(\hat{t}, y\right) - l_{\text{lin}}\left(\tilde{t}, y\right)\right| \leq \left|y\tilde{t} - y\hat{t}\right| = \left|y\left(\tilde{t} - \hat{t}\right)\right| = \left|\hat{t} - \tilde{t}\right| .$$

This shows that l_{lin} is Lipschitz continuous with the Lipschitz constant $C_{l_{\text{lin}}} = 1$.

Example 5.30 (ε–insensitive loss) *A closer inspection of the ε–insensitive loss function (2.51), i.e., $l_\varepsilon\left(\hat{t}, t\right) = \max\left(\left|t - \hat{t}\right| - \varepsilon, 0\right)$, which is used for regression estimation with support vector machines, shows that this loss function is Lipschitz continuous with the Lipschitz constant $C_{l_\varepsilon} = 1$ because*

$$\left|l_\varepsilon\left(\hat{t}, t\right) - l_\varepsilon\left(\tilde{t}, t\right)\right| \leq \left|\left|t - \hat{t}\right| - \left|t - \tilde{t}\right|\right| \leq \left|\tilde{t} - \hat{t}\right| .$$

Using the concept of Lipschitz continuous loss functions we can upper bound the value of β_m for a rather large class of learning algorithms using the following theorem (see also Subsection 2.2.2).

Theorem 5.31 (Stability of regularized risk minimization algorithms) *Let $l : \mathbb{R} \times \mathbb{R} \to \mathbb{R}$ be a convex Lipschitz continuous function in its first argument with Lipschitz constant C_l. Given a reproducing kernel Hilbert space $\mathcal{F} \subseteq \mathbb{R}^{\mathcal{X}}$ with* *kernel $k : \mathcal{X} \times \mathcal{X} \to \mathbb{R}$, any algorithm $\mathcal{A} : \cup_{m=1}^{\infty} \mathcal{Z}^m \to \mathcal{F}$ which can be written as*

$$\mathcal{A}(z) \stackrel{\text{def}}{=} \underset{f \in \mathcal{F}}{\operatorname{argmin}} \frac{1}{m} \sum_{(x_i, t_i) \in z} l(f(x_i), t_i) + \lambda \|f\|^2 , \tag{5.19}$$

where $\lambda > 0$ is β_m–stable with respect to l with

$$\beta_m \leq \frac{C_l^2 \kappa^2}{2\lambda m} ,$$

where $\kappa = \sup_{x \in \mathcal{X}} k(x, x)$. Note that, in this formulation, the value m is fixed for any training sample z.

The proof of this result is given in Appendix C.9. By the generality of expression (5.19) it is possible to cast most of the learning algorithms presented in Part I of this book into this framework. Now, in order to obtain generalization error bounds for β_m–stable learning algorithms $\mathcal{A}$ we proceed as follows.

1. Since we aim to use McDiarmid's inequality we define a random variable $g(\mathbf{Z})$ which measures the difference of the expected risk $R[f_z]$ of the function f_z and some observable empirical quantity such as the training error $R_{\text{emp}}[f_z, z]$ or the leave-one-out error $R_{\text{loo}}[\mathcal{A}, z]$ (see Definition 2.35). An example of $g(\mathbf{Z})$ might be $g(\mathbf{Z}) = R[f_{\mathbf{Z}}] - R_{\text{emp}}\left[f_{\mathbf{Z}}, \mathbf{Z}\right]$.
2. We then need to upper bound the expectation of g over the random draw of training samples $z \in \mathcal{Z}^m$. This is because we are only interested in the probability that $g(\mathbf{Z})$ will be larger than some prespecified ε.
3. Another consequence of the usage of McDiarmid's inequality is that we need an upper bound on

$$\sup_{z \in \mathcal{Z}^m, \tilde{z} \in \mathcal{Z}} |g(z) - g(z_{i \leftrightarrow \tilde{z}})| ,$$

which should preferably not depend on $i \in \{1, \ldots, m\}$.

In Appendix C.9 we have carried out these steps to obtain generalization error bounds both in terms of the training error as well as of the leave-one-out error. This is summarized in the following theorem.

Theorem 5.32 (Algorithmic stability bound for regression estimation) *Suppose we are given a β_m–stable learning algorithm $\mathcal{A}$ w.r.t. a loss function $l : \mathbb{R} \times \mathbb{R} \to \mathbb{R}$.*

For all probability measures $\mathbf{P}_\mathsf{Z} = \mathbf{P}_\mathsf{XT}$ *such that*

$$\mathbf{P}_{\mathsf{Z}^{m+1}}\left(l\left(f_{(\mathsf{Z}_1,\ldots,\mathsf{Z}_m)}\left(\mathsf{X}_{m+1}\right),\mathsf{T}_{m+1}\right)\in[0,b]\right)=1\,,$$

for any $\varepsilon > 0$ *we have*

$$\mathbf{P}_{\mathsf{Z}^m}\left(R\left[f_\mathbf{Z}\right] > R_{\mathrm{emp}}\left[f_\mathbf{Z},\mathbf{Z}\right]+\varepsilon+2\beta_m\right) < \exp\left(-\frac{m\varepsilon^2}{2\left(4m\beta_m+b\right)^2}\right),$$

$$\mathbf{P}_{\mathsf{Z}^m}\left(R\left[f_\mathbf{Z}\right] > R_{\mathrm{loo}}\left[\mathcal{A},\mathbf{Z}\right]+\varepsilon+\beta_m\right) < \exp\left(-\frac{m\varepsilon^2}{2\left(2m\left(\beta_m+\beta_{m-1}\right)+b\right)^2}\right).$$

At first we note that these two bounds are essentially the same, i.e., the additive correction is $\approx \beta_m$ and the decay of the probability is $\mathcal{O}(\exp(-\varepsilon^2/m\beta_m^2))$. This comes as a slight surprise as VC theory appears to indicate that the training error R_{emp} is only a good indicator of the generalization error of an algorithm when the hypothesis space is of small VC dimension (see Theorem 4.7). In contrast the leave-one-out error disregards VC dimension and is an almost unbiased estimator of the expected generalization error of an algorithm (see Theorem 2.36). We must recall, however, that VC theory is used in the study of empirical risk minimization algorithms which *only* consider the training error as the cost function to be minimized. In contrast, in the current formulation we have to guarantee a certain stability of the learning algorithm. In particular, when considering the result of Theorem 5.31 we see that, in the case of $\lambda \to 0$, that is, the learning algorithm minimizes the empirical risk only, we can no longer guarantee a finite stability. In light of this fact, let us consider β_m–stable algorithms $\mathcal{A}$ such that $\beta_m \le \eta m^{-1}$, i.e., the influence of a single new training example is inversely proportional to the training sample size m with a decay of $\eta \in \mathbb{R}^+$. With this the first inequality in Theorem 5.32 states that, with probability at least $1-\delta$ over the random draw of the training sample $z \in \mathcal{Z}^m$,

$$R\left[\mathcal{A}(z)\right] \le R_{\mathrm{emp}}\left[\mathcal{A}(z),z\right]+\frac{2\eta}{m}+\sqrt{\frac{2\left(4\eta+b\right)^2\ln\left(\frac{1}{\delta}\right)}{m}}\,.$$

This is an amazingly tight generalization error bound whenever $\eta \ll \sqrt{m}$ because the expression is dominated by the second term. Moreover, this result provides us with practical guidelines on the possible values of the trade-off parameter λ. Since for regularized risk minimization algorithms of the form (5.19) we know that $\eta \le \frac{C_l^2\kappa^2}{2\lambda}$, it follows that $\lambda \ge \frac{C_l^2\kappa^2}{bm}$ because otherwise the bound would be trivial (as large as b) regardless of the empirical term $R_{\text{emp}}[\mathcal{A}(z), z]$. Before we proceed to the classification learning case we show an application of this new generalization error bound for a stable regression estimation algorithm presented in Part I.

Example 5.33 (Support vector regression) *In the case of linear functions $f_{\mathbf{w}} \in \mathbb{R}^{\mathcal{X}}$ of the form $f_{\mathbf{w}} = \langle \mathbf{w}, \mathbf{x} \rangle$, where $\mathbf{x} \stackrel{\text{def}}{=} \boldsymbol{\phi}(x)$ and $\boldsymbol{\phi} : \mathcal{X} \to \mathcal{K} \subseteq \ell_2^n$ is some mapping of the objects $x \in \mathcal{X}$ into a feature space $\mathcal{K}$ (see also Definition 2.2), we define $\|f_{\mathbf{w}}\|^2$ as $\|\mathbf{w}\|^2$. Then, if we consider the ε–insensitive loss as given by equation (2.51) we retain the* support vector regression algorithm

$$\mathcal{A}_{\text{SVR}}(z) = f_{\hat{\mathbf{w}}} \in \mathbb{R}^{\mathcal{X}} \quad \textit{such that} \quad \hat{\mathbf{w}} = \underset{\mathbf{w} \in \mathcal{K}}{\operatorname{argmin}} \; \frac{1}{m} \sum_{i=1}^{m} l_{\varepsilon}(\langle \mathbf{w}, \mathbf{x}_i \rangle, t_i) + \lambda \|\mathbf{w}\|^2 .$$

Introducing $2m$ positive slack variables $\xi_i \in \mathbb{R}^+$ that capture the deviation of $\langle \mathbf{w}, \mathbf{x}_i \rangle$ from the observed value t_i this learning algorithm can also be expressed in terms of the following mathematical program

$$\begin{array}{lll} \textit{minimize} & \frac{1}{m}\boldsymbol{\xi}'\mathbf{1} + \lambda \|\mathbf{w}\|^2 & \\ \textit{subject to} & t_i - \langle \mathbf{w}, \mathbf{x}_i \rangle \le \varepsilon + \xi_i , & i \in \{1, \ldots, m\} , \\ & \langle \mathbf{w}, \mathbf{x}_i \rangle - t_i \le \varepsilon + \xi_{i+m} , & i \in \{1, \ldots, m\} , \\ & \boldsymbol{\xi} \ge \mathbf{0} . & \end{array}$$

If we combine the Lipschitz continuity of the ε–insensitive loss given in Example 5.30 with Theorems 5.31 and 5.32 we see that the support vector regression *algorithm has a generalization error bound of*

$$R[\mathcal{A}_{\text{SVR}}(z)] \le \frac{1}{m}\left(\hat{\boldsymbol{\xi}}'\mathbf{1} + \frac{\kappa^2}{\lambda}\right) + \sqrt{\frac{2\left(2\frac{\kappa^2}{\lambda} + b\right)^2 \ln\left(\frac{1}{\delta}\right)}{m}} ,$$

where $\hat{\boldsymbol{\xi}} \in \mathbb{R}^{2m}$ is the value of the slack variables at the minimum, $\kappa = \sup_{x \in \mathcal{X}} k(x, x)$ and $b \in \mathbb{R}^+$ is a known upper bound on the values of the $t_i \in \mathbb{R}$. Note that $R[\mathcal{A}_{\text{SVR}}(z)]$ is the expected ε–insensitive loss of the learned function $f_{\hat{\mathbf{w}}}$. Besides providing a practically relevant generalization error bound the result also has the intuitive interpretation that, for smaller values of λ, the term $\hat{\boldsymbol{\xi}}'\mathbf{1}$ is non-increasing and competes with the increasing term $\frac{\kappa^2}{\lambda}$.

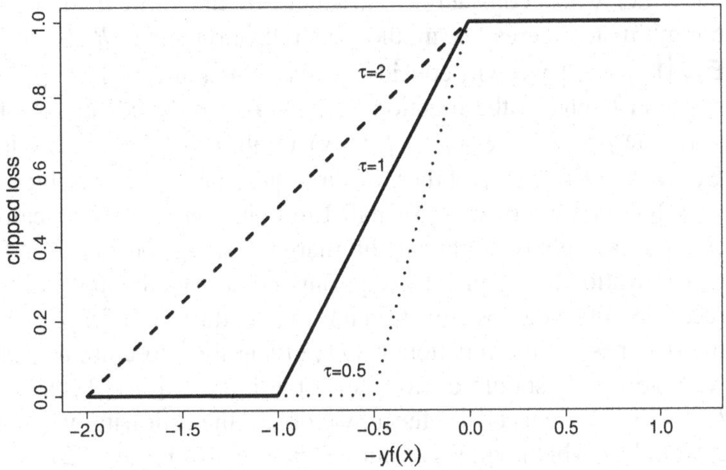

Figure 5.2 The *clipped linear soft margin loss* l_τ for various values of $\tau > 0$. Note that for $\tau \to 0$ the loss function approaches the zero-one loss $\mathbf{I}_{-yf(x)\geq 0}$.

5.3.2 Algorithmic Stability for Classification

In classification learning we are given a training sample $z = (\boldsymbol{x}, \boldsymbol{y}) \in (\mathcal{X} \times \mathcal{Y})^m$ together with a hypothesis space $\mathcal{H} \subseteq \mathcal{Y}^{\mathcal{X}}$ of classifiers h mapping objects $x \in \mathcal{X}$ to classes $y \in \mathcal{Y}$. We confine ourselves to the zero-one loss $l_{0-1}(\hat{y}, y) = \mathbf{I}_{\hat{y}\neq y}$ although the following reasoning also applies to any loss that takes only a finite set of values. Similarly to the results presented in the last subsection we would like to determine the β_m–stability of a given classification learning algorithm $\mathcal{A} : \cup_{m=1}^{\infty} \mathcal{Z}^m \to \mathcal{H}$. It turns out, however, that the only two possible values of β_m are 0 and 1. The former case occurs if, for all training samples $z \in \mathcal{Z}^m$ and all test examples $(x, y) \in \mathcal{Z}$,

$$\left|\mathbf{I}_{\mathcal{A}(z)(x)\neq y} - \mathbf{I}_{\mathcal{A}(z_{\setminus i})(x)\neq y}\right| = 0\,,$$

which is only possible if $\mathcal{H}$ only contains one hypothesis. If we exclude this trivial case from our considerations then we see that Theorem 5.32 only gives trivial results for classification learning algorithms. This is mainly due to the coarseness of the loss function l_{0-1}.

In order to circumvent this problem we shall exploit the real-valued output $f(x)$ when considering classifiers of the form $h(\cdot) = \operatorname{sign}(f(\cdot))$. Since our ultimate interest is in the generalization error $R[h] = \mathbf{E}_{\mathsf{XY}}\left[\mathbf{I}_{h(\mathsf{X})\neq\mathsf{Y}}\right] = \mathbf{E}_{\mathsf{XY}}\left[\mathbf{I}_{\mathsf{Y}\cdot f(\mathsf{X})\leq 0}\right]$ we will consider a loss function $l_\tau : \mathbb{R} \times \mathcal{Y} \to [0,1]$ which is an upper bound of the function $\mathbf{I}_{yf(x)\leq 0}$. To see the advantage of such a loss function note that $l_{0-1}(\hat{y}, y) \leq l_\tau(t, y)$ implies that $\mathbf{E}_{\mathsf{XY}}\left[l_{0-1}(\operatorname{sign}(f(\mathsf{X})), \mathsf{Y})\right] \leq \mathbf{E}_{\mathsf{XY}}\left[l_\tau(f(\mathsf{X}), \mathsf{Y})\right]$. Another useful requirement on the refined loss function l_τ is Lipschitz continuity with a small Lipschitz constant. This can be achieved by a slight refinement of the linear soft margin loss l_{lin} considered in Example 5.29. The generalization is obtained by requiring a real-valued output of at least τ on the correct side. Since the loss function has to pass through 1 for $f(x) = 0$ it follows that the steepness of the function is $1/\tau$, giving the Lipschitz constant as $1/\tau$. Finally we note that l_τ should always be in the interval $[0,1]$ because the zero-one loss l_{0-1} will never exceed 1. Hence, we obtain the following version of the linear soft margin loss which will serve our needs (see also Figure 5.2)

$$l_\tau(t, y) = \begin{cases} 0 & \text{if } yt > 1 \\ 1 - \frac{yt}{\tau} & \text{if } yt \in [0, \tau] \\ 1 & \text{if } yt < 0 \end{cases} . \tag{5.20}$$

A direct application of Theorem 5.32 to the expected and empirical risks using the loss function l_τ yields an algorithmic stability result for classification learning algorithms which use a thresholded real-valued function for classification.

Theorem 5.34 (Algorithmic stability for classification) *Let $\mathcal{F} \subseteq \mathbb{R}^{\mathcal{X}}$ be a set of real-valued functions and $\mathcal{A} : \cup_{m=1}^{\infty} \mathcal{Z}^m \to \mathcal{F}$ be a given learning algorithm such that the associated classifications are $\mathcal{H} = \{x \mapsto \operatorname{sign}(f(x)) \mid f \in \mathcal{F}\}$. For the zero-one loss l_{0-1}, for all probability measures $\mathbf{P}_{\mathsf{Z}}$ such that $\mathbf{P}_{\mathsf{X}}(k(\mathsf{X}, \mathsf{X}) \leq \kappa) = 1$, for any $\tau \in \mathbb{R}^+$ and any $\delta \in (0,1]$, with probability at least $1-\delta$ over the random draw of the training sample $z \in \mathcal{Z}^m$, the expected risk $R\left[\operatorname{sign}(\mathcal{A}(z))\right]$ of the classifier $\mathcal{A}(z) \in \mathcal{F}$ is bounded from above by*

$$R\left[\operatorname{sign}(\mathcal{A}(z))\right] \leq R_{\text{emp}}^{\tau}\left[\mathcal{A}(z), z\right] + \frac{\kappa^2}{\lambda m \tau^2} + \sqrt{\frac{2\left(2\frac{\kappa^2}{\lambda\tau^2} + 1\right)^2 \ln\left(\frac{1}{\delta}\right)}{m}} .$$

Note that the quantity $R_{\text{emp}}^{\tau}[f, z]$ is given by $R_{\text{emp}}^{\tau}[f, z] = \frac{1}{m}\sum_{i=1}^{m} l_\tau(f(x_i), y_i)$.

Again, we have the intuitive interpretation that, for larger values of τ, the term $R^{\tau}_{\text{emp}}[f, z] = \frac{1}{m}\sum_{i=1}^{m} l_{\tau}(f(x_i), y_i)$ is provably non-increasing whereas the term $\frac{\kappa^2}{\lambda m \tau^2}$ is always increasing. It is worth considering this theorem for the special case of linear soft margin support vector machines for classification learning (see Subsection 2.4.2). Without loss of generality let us assume that $\kappa^2 = 1$ as for RBF kernels and normalized kernels (see Table 2.1). Noticing that the sum $\sum_{i=1}^{m} \hat{\xi}_i$ of the slacks $\hat{\boldsymbol{\xi}} \in \mathbb{R}^m$ at the solution upper bounds $m \cdot R^{1}_{\text{emp}}[\mathcal{A}(z), z]$ we see that the linear soft margin algorithm $\mathcal{A}_{\text{SVC}}$ presented in Subsection 2.4.2 has a generalization error bound w.r.t. the zero-one loss l_{0-1} of

$$R\left[\text{sign}\left(\mathcal{A}_{\text{SVC}}(z)\right)\right] \le \frac{1}{m}\left(\hat{\boldsymbol{\xi}}'\mathbf{1} + \frac{1}{\lambda}\right) + 2\sqrt{\frac{(1+\lambda)^2 \ln\left(\frac{1}{\delta}\right)}{\lambda^2 m}}\,.$$

This bound provides an interesting model selection criterion for linear soft margin support vector machines. The model selection problem we considered here is the selection of the appropriate value of λ—the assumed noise level. In contrast to the results of Subsection 4.4.3 this bound *only holds for the linear soft margin support vector machine* and can thus be considered practically useful. This, however, remains to be shown empirically. The results in this section are so recent that no empirical studies have yet been carried out.

Remark 5.35 (Leave-one-out bounds) *In the current derivation we have only presented the application of the training error variant of Theorem 5.32. We omitted to show the application of the leave-one-out variant because the resulting bound would involve the leave-one-out error w.r.t. the clipped loss l_τ rather than the zero-one loss l_{0-1}. Although there exist a plethora of bounds on the leave-one-out error of most of the algorithms presented (e.g. Theorem 2.37) a computation of the leave-one-out error w.r.t. l_τ requires the invocation of the learning algorithm m times which is computationally infeasible. An interesting area for further research regards obtaining bounds on this quantity rather than on the usual leave-one-out error w.r.t. the zero-one loss l_{0-1}.*

5.4 Bibliographical Remarks

In this chapter we presented several frameworks for studying the generalization error of specific learning algorithms. We started with a framework seemingly combining the best of two worlds: By studying Bayesian algorithms we have the power of incorporating prior knowledge into the learning task via an explicit prior $\mathbf{P}_{\mathsf{H}}$ while we can still give PAC guarantees for the generalization error of Bayesian classification strategies. This framework, also known as the PAC-Bayesian framework, was introduced for the first time in Shawe-Taylor and Williamson (1997, p. 4) where the authors cast a Bayesian algorithm in the luckiness framework. Remarkably, they concede that "... a Bayesian might say that luckiness is just a complicated way of encoding a prior. The sole justification for our particular way of encoding is that it allows us to get the PAC like results we sought...". In contrast to their results—which hold for single classifiers drawn according to the posterior measure—McAllester (1998) considered classification *strategies* which allowed him to tighten the results and ease their proofs. Theorems 5.1, 5.2 and 5.6 can be found in this paper; the more general result given in equation (5.9) together with some remarks on how to generalize the framework to arbitrary loss functions can be found in McAllester (1999). The simple relationship between the expected risk of the Gibbs and the Bayes classification strategies (Theorem 5.7) is taken from Herbrich and Graepel (2001b). The full power of the bound for the Bayesian classifier can be exploited by making use of the fact that for "benign" hypothesis spaces the expected risk of one classifier can be expressed as the generalization error of a subset of classifiers. This analysis, together with the final PAC-Bayesian margin bound (Theorem 5.10) can be found in Herbrich and Graepel (2001b). Recently, it has been shown that not only the evidence can be justified in a distribution free framework, but also the estimated posterior probability $\mathbf{P}_{\mathsf{H}|\mathsf{Z}^m=z}(\mathsf{H}(x)=y)$ leads to a decrease in expected risk when used as a rejection criterion (see Freund et al. (2000)). In contrast to the bounds in the PAC-Bayesian framework, this paper studies only the generalization error of their (pseudo)-Bayesian prediction method which results in remarkably tight bounds. A work preceeding Shawe-Taylor and Williamson (1997) is by Haussler et al. (1994) where it was assumed that $\mathbf{P}_{\mathsf{H}}$ is known to the learning algorithm and corresponds to the probability of target concepts. Rather than studying the performance of Bayesian classification strategies for a fixed, but unknown, data distribution $\mathbf{P}_{\mathsf{Z}}$ it was assumed that the prior belief $\mathbf{P}_{\mathsf{H}}$ is used to govern $\mathbf{P}_{\mathsf{Y}|\mathsf{X}=x}$. It was shown that the *average* generalization error of classification strategies over $\mathbf{P}_{\mathsf{H}}$ can be arbitrarily bad without assuming that the learning algorithm uses the same $\mathbf{P}_{\mathsf{H}}$. It should be noted, however, that this quantity does not satisfy the PAC desiderata of not knowing the data distribution.

In the following section we introduced the notion of compression schemes. One of the earliest works in that area is by Littlestone and Warmuth (1986) which was summarized and extended to on-line learning algorithms in Floyd and Warmuth (1995). Theorem 5.17 is taken from this paper; the lossy compression scheme bound (Theorem 5.18) was proven in Graepel et al. (2000); see also Marchand and Shawe-Taylor (2001) for a result that avoids the exponent two at the deviation ε. Interestingly, all these results can be extended further by allowing the learning algorithm to save an additional b bits which would only incur an additional summand of $\frac{b}{m}$ in the resulting generalization error bound. An interesting combination of large margins of the linear classifier learned by an algorithm and sparsity w.r.t. the expansion coefficients is presented in Herbrich et al. (2000). The subsection on the combination of compression schemes and mistake bounds for mistake-driven on-line learning algorithms is taken from Floyd and Warmuth (1995). Example 5.24 is discussed in greater length in Graepel et al. (2001). The notion of on-line learning algorithms is due to Littlestone (1988). This paper also introduced the halving algorithm together with its mistake bound (see Example 5.25). An interesting question emerging from the analysis in the compression framework is the following: Given a learning algorithm which maps into a hypothesis space of VC dimension $\vartheta_{\mathcal{H}}$, is it always possible to find a compression scheme of size not more than $\vartheta_{\mathcal{H}}$ that will be consistent, provided some target concept from $\mathcal{H}$ is used to label the data? This is still an open problem; for first attempts to solve it the interested reader is referred to Floyd and Warmuth (1995).

Finally, we demonstrated that we can study the generalization error of learning algorithms by considering their robustness. The notion of robustness of a learning algorithm is far from new but was mainly considered in the analysis of the leave-one-out model selection procedure (see Devroye and Wagner (1979) and Kearns and Ron (1999)). The results presented in Section 5.3 are mainly taken from Bousquet and Elisseeff (2000) and Bousquet and Elisseeff (2001). The interested reader is referred to their work for further details.

III Appendices

A Theoretical Background and Basic Inequalities

The purpose of this appendix is twofold: On the one hand, it should serve as a reference for the case that we need more exactness in the reasoning. On the other hand, it gives brief introductions to probability theory, functional analysis and ill-posed problems. The section on probability theory is based on Feller (1966, Chapter 4) and Kockelkorn (2000). The following section about functional analysis is compiled from Barner and Flohr (1989), Cristianini and Shawe-Taylor (2000) and Debnath and Mikusinski (1998). The section about ill-posed problems is taken from Tikhonov and Arsenin (1977). Finally, we present a set of inequalities needed for the derivation of some of the results in the book.

A.1 Notation

In addition to the special notation introduced in the following sections, it was my objective to make things clearer by consistency. Thus, the general ideas underlying the notation are: Parentheses are used for the evaluation of a function, e.g., $f(x)$, whereas brackets should indicate the application of a functional, e.g., $R[f]$; the concept of bold face is to denote composed objects like tuples, vectors, matrices or vector valued functions[1], e.g., $\boldsymbol{x}$, $\mathbf{x}$, $\mathbf{X}$ or $\boldsymbol{\phi}$; calligraphic letters specify spaces or specific sets, e.g., $\mathcal{K}$; fraktur letters should stand for collection of sets and algebras, e.g., $\mathfrak{A}$; sans-serif letters indicate that the specific value of the object is subject to chance, e.g., X. Deviations from these broad guidelines are indicated to avoid too complicated a notation[2].

1 Sometimes, the symbol $\vec{x}$ is also used for vectors. This will always be indicated in order to avoid confusion.

2 Due to the lack of available symbols we will use $\mathcal{O}$ to denote the order of a term and $\mathfrak{B}$ to denote Borel sets. Furthermore, we use the special symbols E, P, v, f, F and I to denote the expectation value, the probability measure, the empirical probability measure, the density, the distribution function and the indicator function.

A.2 Probability Theory

In general, sets are denoted by roman upper capital letters, e.g., X, whilst elements are denoted by roman lower capital letters, e.g., x. For sets the indicator function $\mathbf{I}_X$ is defined by

$$\mathbf{I}_X(x) \stackrel{\text{def}}{=} \begin{cases} 0 & \text{if } x \notin X \\ 1 & \text{if } x \in X \end{cases} .$$

If $\Upsilon : \mathcal{X} \to \{\text{true}, \text{false}\}$ is a logical formula then $\mathbf{I}_{\Upsilon(x)}$ is shorthand notation for $\mathbf{I}_{\{z \in \mathcal{X} \mid \Upsilon(z)=\text{true}\}}(x)$.

Definition A.1 (σ–algebra) *Given a set $\mathcal{X}$, a collection $\mathfrak{X}$ of sets $X \subseteq \mathcal{X}$ is called a σ–*algebra *over $\mathcal{X}$ if and only if*

1. *If a set $X \in \mathfrak{X}$ so is its complement $X^c = \mathcal{X} \setminus X$.*
2. *If $X_i \in \mathfrak{X}$, $i = 1, \ldots, \infty$ is any countable collection of sets in $\mathfrak{X}$, then also their union $\cup_{i=1}^{\infty} X_i \in \mathfrak{X}$ and intersection $\cap_{i=1}^{\infty} X_i \in \mathfrak{X}$ belong to $\mathfrak{X}$.*

In short, any σ–algebra $\mathfrak{X}$ is closed under complementation and the formation of countable unions and intersections.

Definition A.2 (Borel sets) *Given $\mathcal{X} = \mathbb{R}^n$, the* Borel sets *$\mathfrak{B}_n$ are the smallest σ–algebra that contains all open intervals*

$$\{(x_1, \ldots, x_n) \in \mathbb{R}^n \mid \forall i \in \{1, \ldots, n\} : x_i \in (a_i, b_i)\}$$

for all $a_i, b_i \in \mathbb{R}$. Note that $\mathfrak{B}_n$ contains an uncountable number of sets.

Definition A.3 (Measurable and probability space) *A* measurable space *is defined by the tuple $(\mathcal{X}, \mathfrak{X})$. Here $\mathcal{X}$ is called the* sample space *and $\mathfrak{X}$ is a σ–algebra over $\mathcal{X}$. A* probability space *is defined by the triple $(\mathcal{X}, \mathfrak{X}, \mathbf{P})$ where $\mathbf{P}$ is a* probability measure *on $\mathcal{X}$, i.e., $\mathbf{P} : \mathfrak{X} \to [0, 1]$ such that $\mathbf{P}(\mathcal{X}) = 1$ and for all countable collections of non-overlapping sets $X_i \in \mathfrak{X}$, $i = 1, \ldots, \infty$*

$$\mathbf{P}\left(\bigcup_{i=1}^{\infty} X_i\right) = \sum_{i=1}^{\infty} \mathbf{P}(X_i) .$$

In most circumstances, the measurable space is clear from context. In order to avoid ambiguities about the used probability measure P we shall use a sans serif letter as a subscript. Thus, if Υ is a measurable logical formula over $x \in \mathcal{X}$, i.e., $\Upsilon : \mathcal{X} \to \{\text{true}, \text{false}\}$ and $\{x \in \mathcal{X} \mid \Upsilon(x) = \text{true}\} \in \mathfrak{X}$,

$$\mathsf{P}_\mathsf{X}(\Upsilon(\mathsf{X})) \stackrel{\text{def}}{=} \mathsf{P}(\{x \in \mathcal{X} \mid \Upsilon(x) = \text{true}\})$$

denotes the probability of $\Upsilon(x)$ when x is selected according to P.

Definition A.4 (Measurability) *Given a measurable space* $(\mathcal{X}, \mathfrak{X})$*, the real-valued function* $g : \mathcal{X} \to \mathbb{R}$ *is called* $\mathfrak{X}$–measurable *(or simply measurable) if and only if*

$$\forall z \in \mathbb{R} : \qquad \{x \in \mathcal{X} \mid g(x) \le z\} \in \mathfrak{X} .$$

Definition A.5 (Random variable) *Given a measurable space* $(\mathcal{X}, \mathfrak{X})$*, a* random variable *is a* $\mathfrak{X}$*–measurable real-valued function* $f : \mathcal{X} \to \mathbb{R}$.

In order to distinguish random variables from ordinary functions we also use sans serif letters to denote them, e.g., $\mathsf{Y} = f(\mathsf{X})$. Thus a random variable $\mathsf{Y} = f(\mathsf{X})$ induces a measure P_Y which acts on the real line, i.e., $\mathcal{Y} = \mathbb{R}$ and for which the σ–algebra $\mathfrak{Y}$ contains at least the intervals $\{(-\infty, z] \mid z \in \mathbb{R}\}$. The measure P_Y is induced by the measure P_X and f, i.e.,

$$\forall Y \in \mathfrak{B}_1 : \qquad \mathsf{P}_\mathsf{Y}(Y) \stackrel{\text{def}}{=} \mathsf{P}_\mathsf{X}(\{x \in \mathcal{X} \mid f(x) \in Y\}) .$$

Definition A.6 (Distribution function and density) *For a random variable* X *the function* $\mathsf{F}_\mathsf{X} : \mathbb{R} \to [0, 1]$ *defined by*

$$\mathsf{F}_\mathsf{X}(x) \stackrel{\text{def}}{=} \mathsf{P}_\mathsf{X}(\mathsf{X} \le x)$$

is called the distribution function *of* X. *The function* $\mathsf{f}_\mathsf{X} : \mathbb{R} \to \mathbb{R}$ *is called the* density *if*

$$\forall z \in \mathbb{R} : \qquad \mathsf{F}_\mathsf{X}(z) = \int_{x \le z} \mathsf{f}_\mathsf{X}(x)\, dx .$$

In the study of learning as well as statistics the expectation of a random variable is of particular importance.

Definition A.7 (Expectation) *Let $f : \mathcal{X} \to \mathbb{R}$ be a measurable function. The* expectation $\mathbf{E}_{\mathsf{X}}\left[f(\mathsf{X})\right]$ *of f over the random draw of x is defined by*

$$\mathbf{E}_{\mathsf{X}}\left[f(\mathsf{X})\right] \stackrel{\text{def}}{=} \int_{\mathbb{R}} f(x)\, d\mathbf{F}_{\mathsf{X}}(x)\,.$$

The expectation value is only defined if $\int_{\mathbb{R}} |f(x)|\, d\mathbf{F}_{\mathsf{X}}(x) < \infty$.

Definition A.8 (Variance) *The* variance $\mathrm{Var}(\mathsf{X})$ *of a random variable* X *is defined by*

$$\mathrm{Var}(\mathsf{X}) \stackrel{\text{def}}{=} \mathbf{E}_{\mathsf{X}}\left[(\mathsf{X}-\mu)^2\right] = \mathbf{E}_{\mathsf{X}}\left[\mathsf{X}^2\right] - \mu^2\,,$$

where $\mu = \mathbf{E}_{\mathsf{X}}\left[\mathsf{X}\right]$ is the expectation of the random variable X.

Definition A.9 (Product space) *Given two measurable spaces $(\mathcal{X}, \mathfrak{X})$ and $(\mathcal{Y}, \mathfrak{Y})$ we define the* product space *by $(\mathcal{X} \times \mathcal{Y}, \mathfrak{X} \times \mathfrak{Y})$. Here $\mathfrak{X} \times \mathfrak{Y}$ denotes the smallest σ–algebra which contains the sets $\{X \times Y \mid X \in \mathfrak{X}, Y \in \mathfrak{Y}\}$.*

Definition A.10 (Marginal and conditional measure) *Given the joint probability space $(\mathcal{X} \times \mathcal{Y}, \mathfrak{X} \times \mathfrak{Y}, \mathbf{P}_{\mathsf{XY}})$, the* marginal probability measure $\mathbf{P}_{\mathsf{X}}$ *is defined by*

$$\forall X \in \mathfrak{X}: \qquad \mathbf{P}_{\mathsf{X}}(X) \stackrel{\text{def}}{=} \mathbf{P}_{\mathsf{XY}}(X \times \mathcal{Y})\,.$$

Given $Y \in \mathfrak{Y}$, $\mathbf{P}_{\mathsf{Y}}(Y) > 0$, the conditional probability measure $\mathbf{P}_{\mathsf{X}|\mathsf{Y}\in Y}$ *is given by*

$$\forall X \in \mathfrak{X}: \qquad \mathbf{P}_{\mathsf{X}|\mathsf{Y}\in Y}(X) \stackrel{\text{def}}{=} \frac{\mathbf{P}_{\mathsf{XY}}(X \times Y)}{\mathbf{P}_{\mathsf{Y}}(Y)}\,.$$

($\mathbf{P}_{\mathsf{Y}}$ and $\mathbf{P}_{\mathsf{Y}|\mathsf{X}\in X}$ are given in the same way).

Definition A.11 (Independence) *We call the random variables* X *and* Y independent *(w.r.t. the measure $\mathbf{P}_{\mathsf{XY}}$), if and only if*

$$\forall X \in \mathfrak{X}: \forall Y \in \mathfrak{Y}: \qquad \mathbf{P}_{\mathsf{XY}}(X \times Y) = \mathbf{P}_{\mathsf{X}}(X)\,\mathbf{P}_{\mathsf{Y}}(Y)\,.$$

In this case, the marginal distributions suffice to define the whole product measure. If $(\mathcal{X}, \mathfrak{X})$ equals $(\mathcal{Y}, \mathfrak{Y})$ we shall write $\mathbf{P}_{\mathsf{X}^2}$ as an abbreviation for $\mathbf{P}_{\mathsf{XX}}$.

Whenever we deal with a sequence of n random variables $\mathsf{X}_1, \ldots, \mathsf{X}_n$ we denote the whole sequence by $\mathbf{X}$. Such a sequence can either be a column or row vector, which should be clear from the context. A particular element of the sample space $\mathcal{X}^n$ is then denoted by the n–tuple $\boldsymbol{x}$. Given an n–tuple $\boldsymbol{x} = (x_1, \ldots, x_n)$, the abbreviation $x \in \boldsymbol{x}$ should be understood as $\exists i \in \{1, \ldots, n\} : x_i = x$.

Definition A.12 (Expectation of a n–dimensional random variable) *Given n random variables* $\mathbf{X} = (\mathsf{X}_1, \ldots, \mathsf{X}_n)$ *with a joint measure* $\mathbf{P}_{\mathbf{X}}$*, the* expectation $\mathbf{E}_{\mathbf{X}}[\mathbf{X}]$ *is defined by the n–tuple*

$$\mathbf{E}_{\mathbf{X}}[\mathbf{X}] \stackrel{\text{def}}{=} \left(\mathbf{E}_{\mathsf{X}_1}[\mathsf{X}_1], \ldots, \mathbf{E}_{\mathsf{X}_n}[\mathsf{X}_n]\right) .$$

Definition A.13 (Covariance and covariance matrix) *Given two random variables* X *and* Y *with a joint measure* $\mathbf{P}_{\mathsf{XY}}$*, the* covariance $\operatorname{Cov}(\mathsf{X}, \mathsf{Y})$ *is defined by*

$$\operatorname{Cov}(\mathsf{X}, \mathsf{Y}) \stackrel{\text{def}}{=} \mathbf{E}_{\mathsf{XY}}\left[(\mathsf{X} - \mu)(\mathsf{Y} - \nu)\right] ,$$

where $\mu = \mathbf{E}_{\mathsf{X}}[\mathsf{X}]$ *and* $\nu = \mathbf{E}_{\mathsf{Y}}[\mathsf{Y}]$*. Note that* $\operatorname{Cov}(\mathsf{X}, \mathsf{X}) = \operatorname{Var}(\mathsf{X})$*. Given n random variables* $\mathbf{X} = (\mathsf{X}_1, \ldots, \mathsf{X}_n)$ *and m random variables* $\mathbf{Y} = (\mathsf{Y}_1, \ldots, \mathsf{Y}_m)$ *having a joint measure* $\mathbf{P}_{\mathbf{XY}}$*, the* $n \times m$ covariance matrix $\mathbf{Cov}(\mathbf{X}, \mathbf{Y})$ *is defined by*

$$\mathbf{Cov}(\mathbf{X}, \mathbf{Y}) \stackrel{\text{def}}{=} \begin{pmatrix} \operatorname{Cov}(\mathsf{X}_1, \mathsf{Y}_1) & \cdots & \operatorname{Cov}(\mathsf{X}_1, \mathsf{Y}_m) \\ \vdots & \ddots & \vdots \\ \operatorname{Cov}(\mathsf{X}_n, \mathsf{Y}_1) & \cdots & \operatorname{Cov}(\mathsf{X}_n, \mathsf{Y}_m) \end{pmatrix} .$$

If $\mathbf{X} = \mathbf{Y}$ *we abbreviate* $\mathbf{Cov}(\mathbf{X}, \mathbf{X}) \stackrel{\text{def}}{=} \mathbf{Cov}(\mathbf{X})$.

Definition A.14 (Empirical measure) *Given a measurable space* $(\mathcal{X}, \mathfrak{X})$ *and a sequence* $\boldsymbol{x} \in \mathcal{X}^n$ *we call* $\mathbf{v}_{\boldsymbol{x}}$ *the* empirical measure *defined by*

$$\forall A \in \mathfrak{X} : \qquad \mathbf{v}_{\boldsymbol{x}}(A) \stackrel{\text{def}}{=} \frac{|\{i \in \{1, \ldots, n\} \mid x_i \in A\}|}{n} .$$

A.2.1 Some Results for Random Variables

In this subsection we will present some results for the expectation and variance of sums and products of random variables. These will prove to be useful for most of Chapter 3.

Theorem A.15 (Expectation of sum and products) *Given two independent random variables* X *and* Y

$$\mathbf{E}_{\mathsf{XY}}\left[\mathsf{X}\cdot\mathsf{Y}\right] = \mathbf{E}_{\mathsf{X}}\left[\mathsf{X}\right]\cdot\mathbf{E}_{\mathsf{Y}}\left[\mathsf{Y}\right], \quad (A.1)$$
$$\mathbf{E}_{\mathsf{XY}}\left[\mathsf{X}+\mathsf{Y}\right] = \mathbf{E}_{\mathsf{X}}\left[\mathsf{X}\right]+\mathbf{E}_{\mathsf{Y}}\left[\mathsf{Y}\right]. \quad (A.2)$$

whenever the two terms on the r.h.s. exist. Note that statement (A.2) is also true if X *and* Y *are not independent.*

Corollary A.16 (Linearity of the expectation) *For any n–dimensional random variable* $\mathbf{X}$*, any matrix* $\mathbf{A} \in \mathbb{R}^{m\times n}$ *and any fixed vector* $\mathbf{b} \in \mathbb{R}^m$ *we have* $\mathbf{E}_{\mathbf{X}}\left[\mathbf{A}\mathbf{X}+\mathbf{b}\right] = \mathbf{A}\mathbf{E}_{\mathbf{X}}\left[\mathbf{X}\right]+\mathbf{b}$.

Theorem A.17 (Variance decomposition) *Given two independent random variables* X *and* Y *we have*

$$\operatorname{Var}(\mathsf{X}+\mathsf{Y}) = \operatorname{Var}(\mathsf{X})+\operatorname{Var}(\mathsf{Y}).$$

Proof Put $\mu = \mathbf{E}\left[\mathsf{X}\right]$ and $\nu = \mathbf{E}_{\mathsf{Y}}\left[\mathsf{Y}\right]$. Exploiting Definition A.8 we know that the variance $\operatorname{Var}(\mathsf{X}+\mathsf{Y})$ is given by

$$\begin{aligned}
\mathbf{E}_{\mathsf{XY}}\left[(\mathsf{X}+\mathsf{Y}-\mathbf{E}_{\mathsf{XY}}\left[\mathsf{X}+\mathsf{Y}\right])^2\right] &= \mathbf{E}_{\mathsf{XY}}\left[((\mathsf{X}-\mu)+(\mathsf{Y}-\nu))^2\right] \\
&= \mathbf{E}_{\mathsf{XY}}\left[\left((\mathsf{X}-\mu)^2+2(\mathsf{X}-\mu)(\mathsf{Y}-\nu)+(\mathsf{Y}-\nu)^2\right)\right] \\
&= \mathbf{E}_{\mathsf{X}}\left[(\mathsf{X}-\mu)^2\right]+2\mathbf{E}_{\mathsf{XY}}\left[(\mathsf{X}-\mu)(\mathsf{Y}-\nu)\right]+\mathbf{E}_{\mathsf{Y}}\left[(\mathsf{Y}-\nu)^2\right] \\
&= \mathbf{E}_{\mathsf{X}}\left[(\mathsf{X}-\mu)^2\right]+2\underbrace{\mathbf{E}_{\mathsf{X}}\left[\mathsf{X}-\mu\right]}_{=0}\underbrace{\mathbf{E}_{\mathsf{Y}}\left[\mathsf{Y}-\mu\right]}_{=0}+\mathbf{E}_{\mathsf{Y}}\left[(\mathsf{Y}-\nu)^2\right] \\
&= \operatorname{Var}(\mathsf{X})+\operatorname{Var}(\mathsf{Y}),
\end{aligned}$$

where the second line follows from Theorem A.15 and the fifth line from the assumed independence and Theorem A.15. ■

Theorem A.18 (Covariance decomposition) *For any pair of random variables* X *and* Y *with a joint measure* $\mathbf{P}_{\mathsf{XY}}$ *and any numbers* $a, b, c, d \in \mathbb{R}$,

$$\begin{aligned}
\operatorname{Cov}(\mathsf{X},\mathsf{Y}) &= \mathbf{E}_{\mathsf{XY}}\left[\mathsf{XY}\right]-\mathbf{E}_{\mathsf{X}}\left[\mathsf{X}\right]\mathbf{E}_{\mathsf{Y}}\left[\mathsf{Y}\right], \\
\operatorname{Cov}(a+b\mathsf{X}, c+d\mathsf{Y}) &= bd\cdot\operatorname{Cov}(\mathsf{X},\mathsf{Y}).
\end{aligned}$$

Proof The first assertion follows directly from Definition A.13 and Theorem A.15. For the second assertion let $\mu = \mathbf{E}_{\mathsf{X}}\left[\mathsf{X}\right]$ and $\nu = \mathbf{E}_{\mathsf{Y}}\left[\mathsf{Y}\right]$. Then we have

$$\begin{aligned}\mathrm{Cov}\,(a + b\mathsf{X}, c + d\mathsf{Y}) &= \mathbf{E}_{\mathsf{XY}}\left[(a + b\mathsf{X} - (a + b\mu))\,(c + d\mathsf{Y} - (c + d\nu))\right] \\ &= \mathbf{E}_{\mathsf{XY}}\left[bd \cdot (\mathsf{X} - \mu)\,(\mathsf{Y} - \nu)\right] = bd \cdot \mathrm{Cov}\,(\mathsf{X}, \mathsf{Y})\ ,\end{aligned}$$

where we the second line uses Theorem A.15 and Definition A.13. ■

Corollary A.19 (Variance scaling) *For any random variable* X *and any* $c \in \mathbb{R}$ *we have* $\mathrm{Var}\,(c\mathsf{X}) = c^2 \cdot \mathrm{Var}\,(\mathsf{X})$.

Corollary A.20 (Variance of sums of independent variables) *Given n independent identically distributed random variables* $\mathsf{X}_1, \ldots, \mathsf{X}_n$ *we have*

$$\mathrm{Var}\left(\frac{1}{n}\sum_{i=1}^{n}\mathsf{X}_i\right) = \frac{1}{n}\mathrm{Var}\,(\mathsf{X}_i)\ .$$

Corollary A.21 (Covariances of linear transformations) *For any n–dimensional random variable* $\mathbf{X}$, *any m–dimensional random variable* $\mathbf{Y}$, *any* $r \times n$ *matrix* $\mathbf{A}$, $s \times m$ *matrix* $\mathbf{B}$, $r \times 1$ *vector* $\mathbf{a}$ *and* $s \times 1$ *vector* $\mathbf{b}$,

$$\mathbf{Cov}\,(\mathbf{AX} + \mathbf{a}, \mathbf{BY} + \mathbf{b}) = \mathbf{A} \cdot \mathbf{Cov}\,(\mathbf{X}, \mathbf{Y}) \cdot \mathbf{B}'\ .$$

From the definition of conditional and marginal measures, we have the following important theorem.

Theorem A.22 (Bayes' theorem (Bayes 1763)) *Given the joint probability space* $(\mathcal{X} \times \mathcal{Y}, \mathfrak{X} \times \mathfrak{Y}, \mathbf{P}_{\mathsf{XY}})$ *then, for all* $X \in \mathfrak{X}$, $\mathbf{P}_{\mathsf{X}}(X) > 0$ *and* $Y \in \mathfrak{Y}$, $\mathbf{P}_{\mathsf{Y}}(Y) > 0$

$$\mathbf{P}_{\mathsf{X}|\mathsf{Y}\in Y}(X) = \frac{\mathbf{P}_{\mathsf{Y}|\mathsf{X}\in X}(Y)\,\mathbf{P}_{\mathsf{X}}(X)}{\mathbf{P}_{\mathsf{Y}}(Y)}\,.$$

If both X *and* Y *posses densities* $\mathbf{f}_{\mathsf{X}}$ *and* $\mathbf{f}_{\mathsf{Y}}$ *the theorem reads as follows*

$$\forall y \in \mathbb{R} : \forall x \in \mathbb{R} : \quad \mathbf{f}_{\mathsf{X}|\mathsf{Y}=y}(x) = \frac{\mathbf{f}_{\mathsf{Y}|\mathsf{X}=x}(y)\,\mathbf{f}_{\mathsf{X}}(x)}{\mathbf{f}_{\mathsf{Y}}(y)}\,.$$

Another important theorem we need is the following as found in Scheffé (1947).

Theorem A.23 (Scheffé's theorem) *For all densities* $\mathbf{f_X}$ *and* $\mathbf{f_Y}$ *on the measurable space* $(\mathbb{R}^n, \mathfrak{B}_n)$

$$\int_{\mathbb{R}^n} \left|\mathbf{f_X}(x) - \mathbf{f_Y}(x)\right| dx = 2 \sup_{A \in \mathfrak{B}_n} \left|\mathbf{P_X}(A) - \mathbf{P_Y}(A)\right| . \tag{A.3}$$

Proof Choose $C = \left\{x \in \mathbb{R}^n \mid \mathbf{f_X}(x) > \mathbf{f_Y}(x)\right\} \in \mathfrak{B}_n$ and $C^c = \mathbb{R}^n \setminus C \in \mathfrak{B}_n$. Then, for the ℓ_1 distance between $\mathbf{f_X}$ and $\mathbf{f_Y}$,

$$\begin{aligned} &\int_{\mathbb{R}^n} \left|\mathbf{f_X}(x) - \mathbf{f_Y}(x)\right| dx \\ &\quad = \int_C \left|\mathbf{f_X}(x) - \mathbf{f_Y}(x)\right| dx + \int_{C^c} \left|\mathbf{f_X}(x) - \mathbf{f_Y}(x)\right| dx \\ &\quad = \int_C \left(\mathbf{f_X}(x) - \mathbf{f_Y}(x)\right) dx + \int_{C^c} \left(\mathbf{f_Y}(x) - \mathbf{f_X}(x)\right) dx \\ &\quad = \mathbf{P_X}(C) - \mathbf{P_Y}(C) + (1 - \mathbf{P_Y}(C)) - (1 - \mathbf{P_X}(C)) \\ &\quad = 2\left(\mathbf{P_X}(C) - \mathbf{P_Y}(C)\right) . \end{aligned} \tag{A.4}$$

For a geometrical argument see Figure A.1. Now, for all $A \in \mathfrak{B}_n$

$$\begin{aligned} \left|\mathbf{P_X}(A) - \mathbf{P_Y}(A)\right| &= \left|\int_{A \cap C} \left(\mathbf{f_X}(x) - \mathbf{f_Y}(x)\right) dx + \int_{A \cap C^c} \left(\mathbf{f_X}(x) - \mathbf{f_Y}(x)\right) dx\right| \\ &= \left|\int_{A \cap C} \underbrace{\mathbf{f_X}(x) - \mathbf{f_Y}(x)}_{\geq 0} dx - \int_{A \cap C^c} \underbrace{\mathbf{f_Y}(x) - \mathbf{f_X}(x)}_{\geq 0} dx\right| \\ &\leq \max\left(\int_{A \cap C} \mathbf{f_X}(x) - \mathbf{f_Y}(x)\, dx, \int_{A \cap C^c} \mathbf{f_Y}(x) - \mathbf{f_X}(x)\, dx\right) \\ &\leq \max\left(\int_C \mathbf{f_X}(x) - \mathbf{f_Y}(x)\, dx, \int_{C^c} \mathbf{f_Y}(x) - \mathbf{f_X}(x)\, dx\right) \\ &= \mathbf{P_X}(C) - \mathbf{P_Y}(C) , \end{aligned}$$

where the second line follows by definition of C and the third line is always true because $\forall a > 0, b > 0 : |a - b| \leq \max(a, b)$. We have shown that the supremum in (A.3) is attained at $C \in \mathfrak{B}_n$ and thus equation (A.4) proves the theorem. ∎

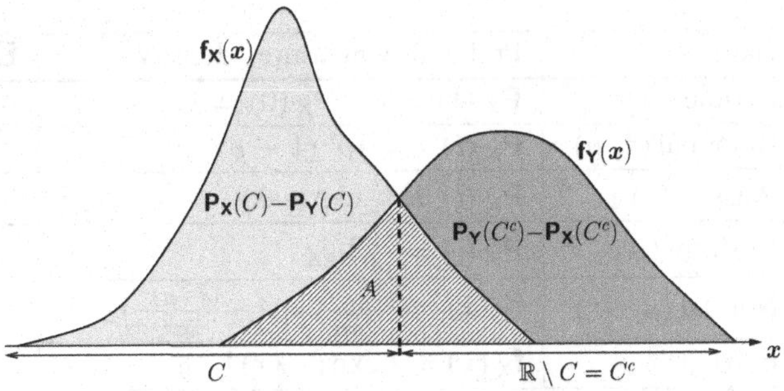

Figure A.1 Geometrical proof of Scheffé's theorem for $\mathbb{R}^1$. The quantity $\int_{\mathbb{R}^n} \left|\mathbf{f_X}(x) - \mathbf{f_Y}(x)\right| dx$ is given by the sum of the two shaded areas excluding the striped area A. Given the set $C = \left\{x \in \mathbb{R} \mid \mathbf{f_X}(x) > \mathbf{f_Y}(x)\right\}$ the quantity $\mathbf{P_X}(C) - \mathbf{P_Y}(C)$ is given by the light shaded area only. Since the area under both curves $\mathbf{f_X}$ and $\mathbf{f_Y}$ is exactly one it must hold that $\mathbf{P_X}(C) - \mathbf{P_Y}(C) = \mathbf{P_Y}(C^c) - \mathbf{P_X}(C^c)$ because we subtract A from both curves. This proves Scheffé's theorem.

A.2.2 Families of Probability Measures

In this subsection we present commonly used probability measures together with their expectation value and variance. We show that most of the distributions belong to the rather large class of measures in the exponential family which has many useful properties, e.g., canonical parameters and natural statistics (see Lindsey (1996) and Amari (1985)).

Probability Measures over the Natural Numbers $\mathbb{N}$

For the following measures we assume that the sample space $\mathcal{X}$ is the set of all natural numbers (including 0) and the σ–algebra is the collection of all subsets of $\mathbb{N}$. In Table A.1 we have summarized the most commonly used probability measures on natural numbers. Note that, for the binomial distribution, we assumed that $\binom{n}{i} = 0$ whenever $i > n$.

The *Bernoulli distribution* is used to model the outcome of a coin toss with a chance of p for "heads"; 1 is used to indicate "head". The *binomial distribution* models the outcome of i "heads" in n independent tosses of a coin with a chance of p for "heads". The *Poisson distribution* is the limiting case of the Binomial distribution if the number of tosses tend to infinity but the expectation value $np = \lambda$ remains constant.

Name	Probability measure / density	$\mathbf{E}_X[X]$	$\text{Var}(X)$
Bernoulli (p)	$\mathbf{P}_X(1) = 1 - \mathbf{P}_X(0) = p$	p	$p(1-p)$
Binomial (n, p)	$\mathbf{P}_X(i) = \binom{n}{i} p^i (1-p)^{n-i}$	np	$np(1-p)$
Poisson (λ)	$\mathbf{P}_X(i) = \frac{\lambda^i}{i!} \exp(-\lambda)$	λ	λ
Uniform (A)	$\mathbf{P}_X(i) = \frac{1}{\lvert A\rvert} \mathbf{I}_{i\in A}$	$\overline{A}$	$\overline{A^2} - \left(\overline{A}\right)^2$
Normal $\left(\mu, \sigma^2\right)$	$\mathbf{f}_X(x) = \frac{1}{\sqrt{2\pi}\sigma} \exp\left(-\frac{(x-\mu)^2}{2\sigma^2}\right)$	μ	σ^2
Exp (λ)	$\mathbf{f}_X(x) = \lambda \exp(-\lambda x) \mathbf{I}_{x\geq 0}$	$\frac{1}{\lambda}$	$\frac{1}{\lambda^2}$
Gamma (α, β)	$\mathbf{f}_X(x) = \frac{x^{\alpha-1}}{\beta^\alpha \Gamma(\alpha)} \exp\left(-\frac{x}{\beta}\right) \mathbf{I}_{x>0}$	$\alpha\beta$	$\alpha\beta^2$
Beta (α, β)	$\mathbf{f}_X(x) = \frac{\Gamma(\alpha+\beta)x^{\alpha-1}(1-x)^{\beta-1}}{\Gamma(\alpha)\Gamma(\beta)} \mathbf{I}_{x\in[0,1]}$	$\frac{\alpha}{\alpha+\beta}$	$\frac{\alpha\beta}{(\alpha+\beta)^2(\alpha+\beta+1)}$
Uniform $([a, b])$	$\mathbf{f}_X(x) = \frac{1}{b-a} \mathbf{I}_{x\in[a,b]}$	$\frac{a+b}{2}$	$\frac{(b-a)^2}{12}$

Table A.1 Summary of measures over the natural numbers $\mathbb{N}$ (first four rows) and the real line $\mathbb{R}^1$ (last five rows). Note that $\Gamma(\alpha) = \int_0^\infty t^{\alpha-1} \exp(-t)\, dt$ denotes the Gamma function. For plots of these distributions see page 209 and 210. Furthermore, the symbols $\overline{A}$ and $\overline{A^2}$ denote $\frac{1}{\lvert A\rvert} \sum_{a_i\in A} a_i$ and $\frac{1}{\lvert A\rvert} \sum_{a_i\in A} a_i^2$, respectively.

Probability Measures on the Real Line $\mathbb{R}^1$

For the following measures we assume that the sample space $\mathcal{X}$ is the real line $\mathbb{R}$ and the σ–algebra is the Borel sets $\mathfrak{B}_1$ (see Definition A.2). In Table A.1 we summarized commonly used probability measures on $\mathbb{R}^1$ by specifying their density function. For a comprehensive overview of measures on $\mathbb{R}^1$ see (Johnson et al. 1994).

Note that the *exponential distribution* $\text{Exp}(\lambda)$ is a special case of the *Gamma distribution* because $\text{Gamma}(1, \beta) = \text{Exp}\left(\beta^{-1}\right)$. The *Beta distribution* is the conjugate prior distribution of the success probability in a Binomial measure (see also Section 3.1). Finally, the *normal* or *Gaussian distribution* owes its importance to the well known central limit theorem.

Theorem A.24 (Central limit theorem) *Let* $X_1, X_2, \ldots$ *be mutually independent random variables with a common distribution* $\mathbf{F}_X$ *that satisfies*

$$\forall i \in \mathbb{N}: \qquad \left(\mathbf{E}_X\left[X_i\right] = 0\right) \wedge \left(\text{Var}(X_i) = 1\right). \tag{A.5}$$

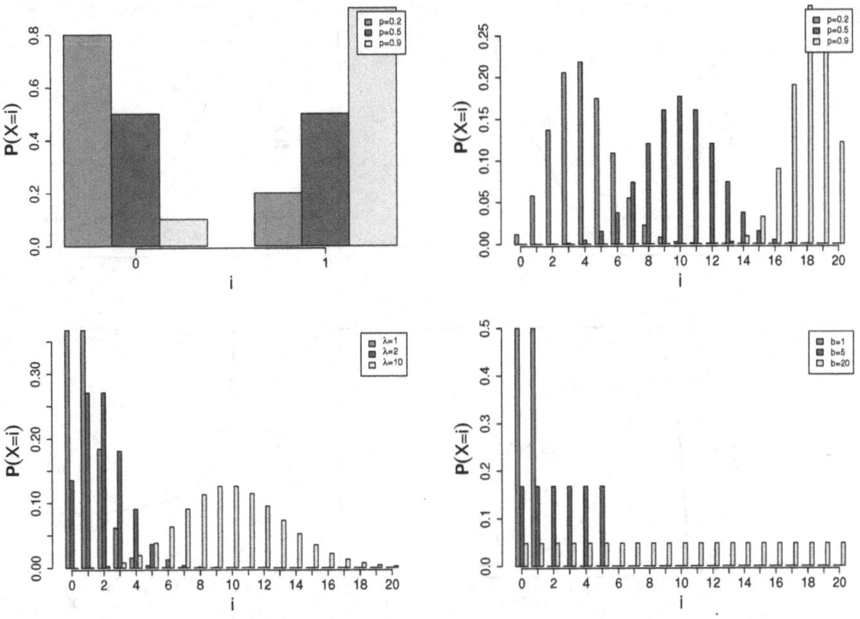

Figure A.2 The probability mass function $\mathsf{P_X}$ for the measures in Table A.1. **(Left)** Bernoulli and Poisson measure. **(Right)** Binomial and uniform measure. In the uniform measure plot, we consider the sets $A_b = \{0, \ldots, b\}$.

Then, for all such probability measures $\mathsf{P_X}$,

$$\forall x \in \mathbb{R}: \qquad \lim_{n\to\infty} \mathsf{P}_{\mathsf{X}^n}\left(\frac{\sum_{i=1}^{n} \mathsf{X}_i}{\sqrt{n}} \leq x\right) = \int_{-\infty}^{x} \frac{1}{\sqrt{2\pi}} \exp\left(-\frac{t^2}{2}\right) dt\,,$$

that is, the distribution function of the normalized sum of identically and independently distributed random variables that fulfill (A.5) approaches pointwise the normal distribution function with increasing sample size n.

Probability Measure on $\mathbb{R}^n$

The only multidimensional probability measure we consider is the n–dimensional normal distribution defined over the sample space $\mathcal{X} = \mathbb{R}^n$ and the σ–algebra $\mathfrak{B}_n$ (see Figure A.4).

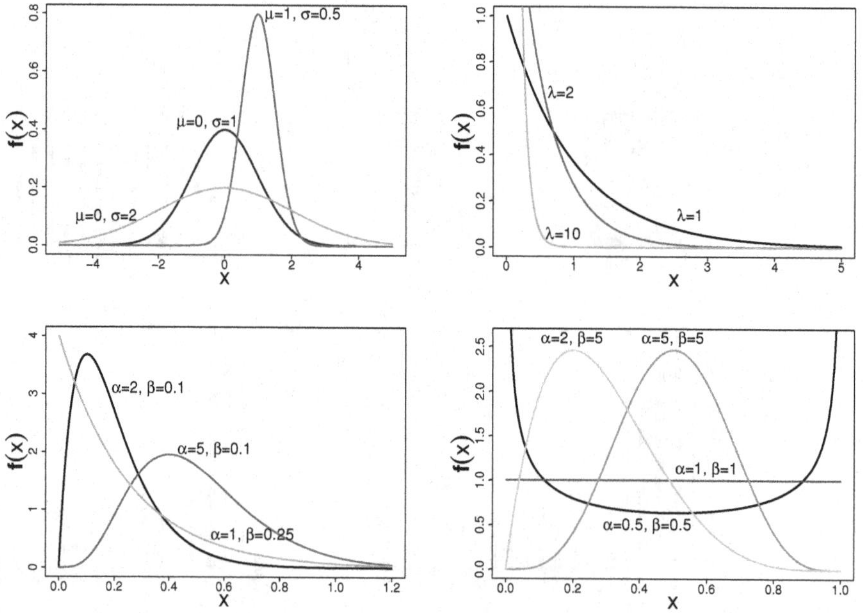

Figure A.3 The densities $\mathbf{f_X}$ for the measures in Table A.1. **(Left)** Densities of the Gaussian/normal and the Gamma measure. **(Right)** Densities of the exponential and Beta measure.

Definition A.25 (Multidimensional Gaussian measure) *Suppose we are given a vector* $\boldsymbol{\mu} \in \mathbb{R}^n$ *and a deterministic matrix* $\mathbf{A} \in \mathbb{R}^{n \times m}$. *Let* $\mathbf{Y} = (\mathsf{Y}_1, \ldots, \mathsf{Y}_m)$ *be a sequence of m independent normally random variables* Y_i *with mean zero and unit variance, i.e.,* $\mathsf{Y}_i \sim \text{Normal}(0, 1)$. *Then* $\mathbf{X} = \mathbf{AY} + \boldsymbol{\mu}$ *is said to be* normally *or* Gaussian distributed *with mean* $\mathbf{E_X}[\mathbf{X}] = \boldsymbol{\mu}$ *and covariance matrix* $\text{Cov}(\mathbf{X}) = \boldsymbol{\Sigma} = \mathbf{AA}'$. *Since the measure* $\mathbf{P_X}$ *is uniquely determined by these two quantities we also write* $\mathbf{Y} \sim \text{Normal}(\boldsymbol{\mu}, \boldsymbol{\Sigma})$.

Theorem A.26 (Density of a Gaussian measure) *If* $\mathbf{X} \sim \text{Normal}(\boldsymbol{\mu}, \boldsymbol{\Sigma})$, *then* $\mathbf{X}$ *possess a density* $\mathbf{f_X}$ *if and only if* $\boldsymbol{\Sigma}$ *is positive definite (see Definition A.57). The density* $\mathbf{f_X}$ *is given by*

$$\mathbf{f_X}(x) = \frac{1}{(2\pi)^{\frac{n}{2}} |\boldsymbol{\Sigma}|^{\frac{1}{2}}} \exp\left(-\frac{1}{2}(x - \boldsymbol{\mu})' \boldsymbol{\Sigma}^{-1} (x - \boldsymbol{\mu})\right). \tag{A.6}$$

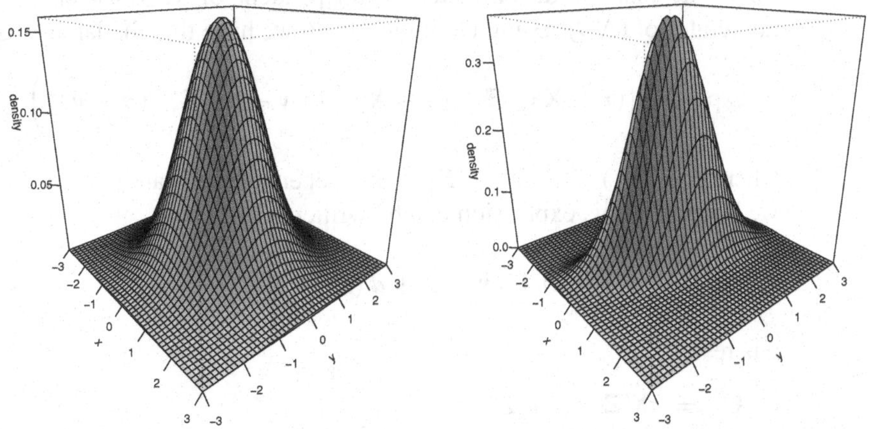

Figure A.4 Density of the multidimensional normal distribution. **(Left)** Here, we used $\boldsymbol{\Sigma} = \mathbf{I}$ and $\boldsymbol{\mu} = \mathbf{0}$. **(Right)** Density obtained from a transformation of the left density such that $\mathrm{Cov}(\mathsf{X}, \mathsf{Y}) = 0.5$ and $\boldsymbol{\mu} = \mathbf{0}$.

Theorem A.27 (Linear transformation of multidimensional Gaussian measures) *Let* $\mathbf{X} \sim \mathrm{Normal}(\boldsymbol{\mu}, \boldsymbol{\Sigma})$ *be an n–dimensional normally distributed random variable, let* $\mathbf{A} \in \mathbb{R}^{m\times n}$ *be a fixed matrix and let* $\mathbf{b} \in \mathbb{R}^m$ *be a fixed vector. Then, the random variable* $\mathbf{Y} = \mathbf{AX} + \mathbf{b}$ *is* $\mathbf{Y} \sim \mathrm{Normal}\left(\mathbf{A}\boldsymbol{\mu} + \mathbf{b}, \mathbf{A}\boldsymbol{\Sigma}\mathbf{A}'\right)$.

Proof The theorem follows directly from Corollary A.16 and A.21. ■

Theorem A.28 (Convolutions of Gaussian measures) *Let us assume that* $\mathbf{P}_{\mathsf{X}|\mathsf{Y}=y} = \mathrm{Normal}(\mathbf{X}y, \boldsymbol{\Xi})$ *is a Gaussian measure, where* $\mathbf{X} \in \mathbb{R}^{m\times n}$ *and* $\boldsymbol{\Xi} \in \mathbb{R}^{m\times m}$ *are fixed matrices for all values of* $y \in \mathbb{R}^n$. *If* $\mathbf{P}_{\mathsf{Y}} = \mathrm{Normal}(\boldsymbol{\mu}, \boldsymbol{\Sigma})$ *is a Gaussian measure then*

$$\mathbf{P}_{\mathsf{Y}|\mathsf{X}=x} = \mathrm{Normal}\left(\boldsymbol{\Psi}\left(\mathbf{X}'\boldsymbol{\Xi}^{-1}x + \boldsymbol{\Sigma}^{-1}\boldsymbol{\mu}\right), \boldsymbol{\Psi}\right). \tag{A.7}$$

$$\mathbf{P}_{\mathsf{X}} = \mathrm{Normal}\left(\mathbf{X}\boldsymbol{\mu}, \boldsymbol{\Xi} + \mathbf{X}\boldsymbol{\Sigma}\mathbf{X}'\right), \tag{A.8}$$

where $\boldsymbol{\Psi} = \left(\mathbf{X}'\boldsymbol{\Xi}^{-1}\mathbf{X} + \boldsymbol{\Sigma}^{-1}\right)^{-1}$.

Proof By Theorem A.22 we know that

$$\mathbf{f}_{\mathsf{Y}|\mathsf{X}=x}(y) = \frac{\mathbf{f}_{\mathsf{X}|\mathsf{Y}=y}(x)\,\mathbf{f}_{\mathsf{Y}}(y)}{\int_{\mathbb{R}^n} \mathbf{f}_{\mathsf{X}|\mathsf{Y}=\tilde{y}}(x)\,\mathbf{f}_{\mathsf{Y}}(\tilde{y})\,d\tilde{y}} = \frac{\mathbf{f}_{\mathsf{X}|\mathsf{Y}=y}(x)\,\mathbf{f}_{\mathsf{Y}}(y)}{\mathbf{f}_{\mathsf{X}}(x)}. \tag{A.9}$$

First note that the denominator is independent of y. Thus let us start with the numerator of (A.9). Using Definition A.26 we have that the latter is given by

$$c \cdot \exp\left(-\frac{1}{2}\left((x - \mathbf{X}y)' \, \Xi^{-1} (x - \mathbf{X}y) + (y - \mu)' \, \Sigma^{-1} (y - \mu)\right)\right),$$

where $c = (2\pi)^{-\frac{m+n}{2}} |\Xi|^{-\frac{1}{2}} |\Sigma|^{-\frac{1}{2}}$ is independent of x and y. From Theorem A.86 we know that this expression can be written as

$$c \cdot \exp\left(-\frac{1}{2}\left((y - \mathbf{c})' \, \mathbf{C} (y - \mathbf{c}) + d(x)\right)\right),$$

where

$$\begin{aligned}
\mathbf{C} &= \mathbf{X}'\Xi^{-1}\mathbf{X} + \Sigma^{-1}, \\
\mathbf{C}\mathbf{c} &= \mathbf{X}'\Xi^{-1}x + \Sigma^{-1}\mu, \\
d(x) &= (x - \mathbf{X}\mu)' \left(\Xi + \mathbf{X}\Sigma\mathbf{X}'\right)^{-1} (x - \mathbf{X}\mu).
\end{aligned}$$

Since $d(x)$ is not a function of y the term $\exp\left(-\frac{1}{2}d(x)\right)$ can be incorporated in the normalization constant c and, thus, equation (A.7) follows by equating $\Psi \stackrel{\text{def}}{=} \mathbf{C}^{-1}$. In order to show the second assertion we use the definition of $\mathbf{f_X}(x)$, i.e.,

$$\begin{aligned}
\mathbf{f_X}(x) &= \int_{\mathbb{R}^n} c \cdot \exp\left(-\frac{1}{2}\left((\tilde{y} - \mathbf{c})' \mathbf{C} (\tilde{y} - \mathbf{c}) + d(x)\right)\right) d\tilde{y} \\
&= c \cdot \exp\left(-\frac{1}{2}d(x)\right) \cdot \int_{\mathbb{R}^n} \exp\left(-\frac{1}{2}\left((\tilde{y} - \mathbf{c})' \mathbf{C} (\tilde{y} - \mathbf{c})\right)\right) d\tilde{y} \\
&= c \cdot \exp\left(-\frac{1}{2}d(x)\right) \cdot (2\pi)^{\frac{n}{2}} |\mathbf{C}|^{\frac{1}{2}} = \tilde{c} \cdot \exp\left(-\frac{1}{2}d(x)\right) \\
&= \tilde{c} \cdot \exp\left(-\frac{1}{2}(x - \mathbf{X}\mu)' \left(\Xi + \mathbf{X}\Sigma\mathbf{X}'\right)^{-1} (x - \mathbf{X}\mu)\right),
\end{aligned}$$

where the third line follows from Definition A.26 and the fact that probability densities always integrate to one. This proves equation (A.8). ■

Theorem A.29 (Marginal and conditional measures) *Let* $\mathbf{X} \sim \text{Normal}(\mu, \Sigma)$ *be an n–dimensional normally distributed random variable with* $\Sigma > 0$. *Let* $\mathbf{X} = (\mathbf{U}, \mathbf{V})$ *be partitioned into an r–dimensional random variable* $\mathbf{U}$ *and an s–dimensional random variable* $\mathbf{V}$ *where* $n = r + s$. *Then for all* $v \in \mathbb{R}^s$ *and* $u \in \mathbb{R}^r$

$$\mathbf{P_U} = \text{Normal}\left(\mu_U, \Sigma_{UU}\right), \tag{A.10}$$

$$\mathsf{P_V} = \text{Normal}\left(\boldsymbol{\mu}_V, \boldsymbol{\Sigma}_{VV}\right), \tag{A.11}$$

$$\mathsf{P_{U|V=\mathit{v}}} = \text{Normal}\left(\boldsymbol{\mu}_U + \boldsymbol{\Sigma}_{UV}\boldsymbol{\Sigma}_{VV}^{-1}\left(\boldsymbol{v} - \boldsymbol{\mu}_V\right), \boldsymbol{\Sigma}_{UU} - \boldsymbol{\Sigma}_{UV}\boldsymbol{\Sigma}_{VV}^{-1}\boldsymbol{\Sigma}_{VU}\right), \tag{A.12}$$

$$\mathsf{P_{V|U=\mathit{u}}} = \text{Normal}\left(\boldsymbol{\mu}_V + \boldsymbol{\Sigma}_{VU}\boldsymbol{\Sigma}_{UU}^{-1}\left(\boldsymbol{u} - \boldsymbol{\mu}_U\right), \boldsymbol{\Sigma}_{VV} - \boldsymbol{\Sigma}_{VU}\boldsymbol{\Sigma}_{UU}^{-1}\boldsymbol{\Sigma}_{UV}\right), \tag{A.13}$$

where

$$\boldsymbol{\mu} = \begin{pmatrix} \boldsymbol{\mu}_U \\ \boldsymbol{\mu}_V \end{pmatrix}, \qquad \boldsymbol{\Sigma} = \begin{pmatrix} \boldsymbol{\Sigma}_{UU} & \boldsymbol{\Sigma}_{UV} \\ \boldsymbol{\Sigma}_{VU} & \boldsymbol{\Sigma}_{VV} \end{pmatrix}.$$

Proof The assertions (A.10) and (A.11) follow directly from Theorem A.27 considering that

$$\mathsf{U} = \begin{pmatrix} \mathbf{I}_r & \mathbf{0} \\ \mathbf{0} & \mathbf{0} \end{pmatrix}\mathsf{X}, \quad \mathsf{V} = \begin{pmatrix} \mathbf{0} & \mathbf{0} \\ \mathbf{0} & \mathbf{I}_s \end{pmatrix}\mathsf{X}.$$

We shall prove equation (A.12) for the special case of $\boldsymbol{\mu} = \mathbf{0}$ only—the full result follows from Theorem A.27. First we exploit the fact that

$$\mathsf{f_{U|V=\mathit{v}}}\left(\boldsymbol{u}\right) = \frac{\mathsf{f_X}\left(\left(\boldsymbol{u}; \boldsymbol{v}\right)\right)}{\mathsf{f_V}\left(\boldsymbol{v}\right)}. \tag{A.14}$$

Since we know the density $\mathsf{f_V}$ already let us consider the joint density $\mathsf{f_X}$ as a function of $\boldsymbol{u}$ and $\boldsymbol{v}$. To this end we use equation (A.27) of Theorem A.80 to obtain a partitioned expression for the inverse $\boldsymbol{\Sigma}^{-1}$ of the covariance matrix $\boldsymbol{\Sigma}$, i.e.,

$$\boldsymbol{\Sigma}^{-1} = \begin{pmatrix} \mathbf{A} & \mathbf{B} \\ \mathbf{B}' & \mathbf{D} \end{pmatrix},$$

where the matrices $\mathbf{A}$, $\mathbf{B}$ and $\mathbf{D}$ are given by

$$\mathbf{A} = \left(\boldsymbol{\Sigma}_{UU} - \boldsymbol{\Sigma}_{UV}\boldsymbol{\Sigma}_{VV}^{-1}\boldsymbol{\Sigma}_{VU}\right)^{-1},$$

$$\mathbf{B} = -\mathbf{A}\boldsymbol{\Sigma}_{UV}\boldsymbol{\Sigma}_{VV}^{-1},$$

$$\mathbf{D} = \boldsymbol{\Sigma}_{VV}^{-1} + \boldsymbol{\Sigma}_{VV}^{-1}\boldsymbol{\Sigma}_{VU}\mathbf{A}\boldsymbol{\Sigma}_{UV}\boldsymbol{\Sigma}_{VV}^{-1}.$$

Now we can write the joint density $\mathsf{f_X}\left(\left(\boldsymbol{u}; \boldsymbol{v}\right)\right)$ as a function of $\boldsymbol{u}$ and $\boldsymbol{v}$

$$c \cdot \exp\left(-\frac{1}{2}\left(\boldsymbol{u}', \boldsymbol{v}'\right)\boldsymbol{\Sigma}^{-1}\left(\boldsymbol{u}; \boldsymbol{v}\right)\right) = c \cdot \exp\left(-\frac{1}{2}\left(\boldsymbol{u}'\mathbf{A}\boldsymbol{u} + 2\boldsymbol{u}'\mathbf{B}\boldsymbol{v} + \boldsymbol{v}'\mathbf{D}\boldsymbol{v}\right)\right)$$

$$= c \cdot \exp\left(-\frac{1}{2}\left(\left(\boldsymbol{u} + \mathbf{A}^{-1}\mathbf{B}\boldsymbol{v}\right)'\mathbf{A}\left(\boldsymbol{u} + \mathbf{A}^{-1}\mathbf{B}\boldsymbol{v}\right) + \boldsymbol{v}'\left(\mathbf{D} - \mathbf{B}'\mathbf{A}^{-1}\mathbf{B}\right)\boldsymbol{v}\right)\right),$$

using the constant $c = (2\pi)^{-\frac{n}{2}} |\boldsymbol{\Sigma}|^{-\frac{1}{2}}$. The last line can be proven by expanding it and making a term-wise comparison with the second line. Note that $\mathbf{D} - \mathbf{B}'\mathbf{A}^{-1}\mathbf{B} = \boldsymbol{\Sigma}_{VV}^{-1}$, which follows from applying equation (A.27) to $\boldsymbol{\Sigma}^{-1}$. Finally, using (A.14) shows that the conditional density of $\mathbf{U}$ given $\boldsymbol{v} \in \mathbb{R}^s$ is again normal with mean $-\mathbf{A}^{-1}\mathbf{B}\boldsymbol{v} = \boldsymbol{\Sigma}_{UV}\boldsymbol{\Sigma}_{VV}^{-1}\boldsymbol{v}$ and covariance matrix $\mathbf{A}^{-1} = \boldsymbol{\Sigma}_{UU} - \boldsymbol{\Sigma}_{UV}\boldsymbol{\Sigma}_{VV}^{-1}\boldsymbol{\Sigma}_{VU}$. The proof of equation (A.13) is analogous. ■

Exponential Family

All of the above measures belong to the class of measures in the exponential family. Let us start by defining formally the exponential family.

Definition A.30 (Exponential family) *A probability measure* $\mathbf{P_X}$ *is said to have an* exponential representation *if its density* $\mathbf{f_X}(\boldsymbol{x})$ *(continuous measures) or probability mass* $\mathbf{P_X}(\boldsymbol{x})$ *(discrete measures) at* $\boldsymbol{x} \in \mathcal{X}$ *can be written*

$$p(\boldsymbol{x}) = a_0(\boldsymbol{\theta})\, \tau_0(\boldsymbol{x}) \exp\left(\boldsymbol{\theta}'(\boldsymbol{\tau}(\boldsymbol{x}))\right),$$

for some $\boldsymbol{\theta} \in \mathcal{Q} \subseteq \mathbb{R}^n$, $\tau_0 : \mathcal{X} \to \mathbb{R}$, $\boldsymbol{\tau} : \mathcal{X} \to \mathbb{R}^n$. *The normalizing constant* $a_0(\boldsymbol{\theta})$ *is given by*

$$a_0(\boldsymbol{\theta}) \stackrel{\text{def}}{=} \left(\int_{\mathcal{X}} \tau_0(\boldsymbol{x}) \exp\left(\boldsymbol{\theta}'(\boldsymbol{\tau}(\boldsymbol{x}))\right) d\boldsymbol{x}\right)^{-1} \tag{A.15}$$

and is assumed to be finite. The set of all probability measures $\mathbf{P_X}$ *that have an exponential representation are defined as the* exponential family.

In Table A.2 we have given the functions τ_0 and $\boldsymbol{\tau}$ together with the normalization constant $a_0(\boldsymbol{\theta})$ for all the one-dimensional measures introduced. In the case of $\mathbf{X} \sim \text{Normal}(\boldsymbol{\mu}, \boldsymbol{\Sigma})$ where $\boldsymbol{\mu} \in \mathbb{R}^n$, a straightforward manipulation of the definition given in equation (A.6) shows that

$$\begin{aligned}
\boldsymbol{\theta} &= \left(\boldsymbol{\Sigma}^{-1}\boldsymbol{\mu}; -\frac{\Sigma_{11}^{-1}}{2}; -\Sigma_{12}^{-1}; \ldots; -\frac{\Sigma_{22}^{-1}}{2}; -\Sigma_{23}^{-1}; \ldots; -\frac{\Sigma_{nn}^{-1}}{2}\right), \qquad \text{(A.16)}\\
\boldsymbol{\tau}(\boldsymbol{x}) &= \left(\boldsymbol{x}; x_1^2; x_1x_2; \ldots; x_1x_n; x_2^2; x_2x_3; \ldots; x_n^2\right),\\
\tau_0(\boldsymbol{x}) &= 1,
\end{aligned}$$

Name	$\tau_0(\mathbf{x})$	$\boldsymbol{\theta}$	$\boldsymbol{\tau}(\mathbf{x})$	$a_0(\boldsymbol{\theta})$
Bernoulli (p)	1	$\ln\left(\frac{p}{1-p}\right)$	x	$(1+\exp(\theta))^{-1}$
Binomial (n, p)	$\binom{n}{x}$	$\ln\left(\frac{p}{1-p}\right)$	x	$(1+\exp(\theta))^{-n}$
Poisson (λ)	$\frac{1}{x!}$	$\ln(\lambda)$	x	$\exp(-\exp(\theta))$
Uniform (A)	1	—	—	$(\lvert A\rvert)^{-1}$
Normal (μ, σ^2)	1	$\left(\frac{\mu}{\sigma^2}; -\frac{1}{2\sigma^2}\right)$	$(x; x^2)$	$\sqrt{-\frac{\theta_2}{\pi}} \exp\left(-\frac{\theta_1}{2}\right)$
Exp (λ)	1	$-\lambda$	x	$-\theta$
Gamma (α, β)	x^{-1}	$\left(\alpha; -\frac{1}{\beta}\right)$	$(\ln(x); x)$	$-\theta_2^{\theta_1} \cdot \frac{1}{\Gamma(\theta_1)}$
Beta (α, β)	$x^{-1}(1-x)^{-1}$	$(\alpha; \beta)$	$(\ln(x); \ln(1-x))$	$\frac{\Gamma(\theta_1+\theta_2)}{\Gamma(\theta_1)\Gamma(\theta_2)}$
Uniform $([a, b])$	1	—	—	$(b-a)^{-1}$

Table A.2 Canonical parameterization of the measures given in Table A.1. Note that $\Gamma(\alpha) = \int_0^\infty t^{\alpha-1} \exp(-t)\, dt$ denotes the Gamma function.

is the parameterization of the multidimensional Gaussian in the exponential family. The value of $a_0(\boldsymbol{\theta})$ is calculated according to equation (A.15) and given by

$$a_0(\boldsymbol{\theta}) = (2\pi)^{-\frac{n}{2}} \lvert\boldsymbol{\Sigma}\rvert^{-\frac{1}{2}} \exp\left(-\frac{1}{2}\boldsymbol{\mu}'\boldsymbol{\Sigma}^{-1}\boldsymbol{\mu}\right). \tag{A.17}$$

A.3 Functional Analysis and Linear Algebra

In this section we introduce the basic terms of functional analysis together with some examples. This section is followed by a more detailed subsection about matrix algebra together with some useful matrix identities. For a more detailed treatment of matrices the interested reader is referred to (Harville 1997; Lütkepohl 1996).

Definition A.31 (Vector space) *A set*[3] $\mathcal{X}$ *is a* vector space *if addition and multiplication by scalar are defined such that, for* $\mathbf{x}, \mathbf{y} \in \mathcal{X}$, *and* $c \in \mathbb{R}$,

$$\mathbf{x}+\mathbf{y} \in \mathcal{X}, \quad c\mathbf{x} \in \mathcal{X}, \quad 1\mathbf{x} = \mathbf{x}, \quad 0\mathbf{x} = \mathbf{0}.$$

3 The notational similarity of $\mathcal{X}$ as a vector space as well as the sample space (in probability theory) is intended to indicate their similar roles in the two fields.

Here the addition operation $\mathbf{x}+\mathbf{y}$ *has to satisfy that, for all* $\mathbf{x}, \mathbf{y}, \mathbf{z} \in \mathcal{X}$,

$$\begin{aligned}
\mathbf{x}+\mathbf{y} &= \mathbf{y}+\mathbf{x}\,, \\
(\mathbf{x}+\mathbf{y})+\mathbf{z} &= \mathbf{x}+(\mathbf{y}+\mathbf{z})\ , \\
\exists \mathbf{0} \in \mathcal{X}: & \quad \mathbf{x}+\mathbf{0}=\mathbf{x}\,, \\
\exists -\mathbf{x} \in \mathcal{X}: & \quad \mathbf{x}+(-\mathbf{x})=\mathbf{0}\,,
\end{aligned}$$

as well as the distributive laws for scalar multiplication,

$$c\,(\mathbf{x}+\mathbf{y}) = c\mathbf{x}+c\mathbf{y}\,, \quad (c+d)\,\mathbf{x} = c\mathbf{x}+d\mathbf{x}\,.$$

Definition A.32 (Metric space) *Suppose* $\mathcal{X}$ *is a vector space. A* metric space $\mathcal{X}$ *is defined by the tuple* $(\mathcal{X}, \rho)$ *where* $\rho : \mathcal{X} \times \mathcal{X} \to \mathbb{R}^+$ *is called a* metric, *i.e., for all* $\mathbf{x}, \mathbf{y}, \mathbf{z} \in \mathcal{X}$,

$$\begin{aligned}
\rho\,(\mathbf{x}, \mathbf{y}) &\geq 0 \text{ and } \rho\,(\mathbf{x}, \mathbf{y}) = 0 \Leftrightarrow \mathbf{x} = \mathbf{y}\,, \\
\rho\,(\mathbf{x}, \mathbf{y}) &= \rho\,(\mathbf{y}, \mathbf{x})\ , \\
\rho\,(\mathbf{x}, \mathbf{y}) &\leq \rho\,(\mathbf{x}, \mathbf{z}) + \rho\,(\mathbf{z}, \mathbf{y})\ .
\end{aligned}$$

Definition A.33 (Normed space) *Suppose* $\mathcal{X}$ *is a vector space. A* normed space $\mathcal{X}$ *is defined by the tuple* $(\mathcal{X}, \|\cdot\|)$ *where* $\|\cdot\| : \mathcal{X} \to \mathbb{R}^+$ *is called a* norm, *i.e., for all* $\mathbf{x}, \mathbf{y} \in \mathcal{X}$ *and* $c \in \mathbb{R}$,

$$\begin{aligned}
\|\mathbf{x}\| &\geq 0 \text{ and } \|\mathbf{x}\| = 0 \Leftrightarrow \mathbf{x} = \mathbf{0}\,, \\
\|c\mathbf{x}\| &= |c| \cdot \|\mathbf{x}\|\ , \\
\|\mathbf{x}+\mathbf{y}\| &\leq \|\mathbf{x}\| + \|\mathbf{y}\|\ . \qquad \text{(A.18)}
\end{aligned}$$

This clearly induces a metric ρ *on* $\mathcal{X}$ *by* $\rho\,(\mathbf{x}, \mathbf{y}) = \|\mathbf{x}-\mathbf{y}\|$. *Note that equation (A.18) is known as the* triangle inequality.

Definition A.34 (ℓ_p^n and L_p) *Given a subset* $X \subseteq \mathcal{X}$, *the space* $L_p\,(X)$ *is the space of all functions* $f : X \to \mathbb{R}$ *such that*

$$\begin{aligned}
\int_X |f\,(\mathbf{x})|^p \, d\mathbf{x} < \infty \qquad & \text{if} \quad p < \infty\,, \\
\sup_{\mathbf{x} \in X} |f\,(\mathbf{x})| < \infty \qquad & \text{if} \quad p = \infty\,.
\end{aligned}$$

Endowing this space with the norm

$$\|f\|_p \stackrel{\text{def}}{=} \begin{cases} \left(\int_X |f(\mathbf{x})|^p \, d\mathbf{x}\right)^{\frac{1}{p}} & \text{if } p < \infty \\ \sup_{\mathbf{x}\in X} |f(\mathbf{x})| & \text{if } p = \infty \end{cases}$$

makes $L_p(X)$ a normed space (by Minkowski's inequality). The space ℓ_p^n of sequences of length n is defined by

$$\ell_p^n \stackrel{\text{def}}{=} \left\{ (x_1, \ldots, x_n) \in \mathbb{R}^n \;\middle|\; \begin{array}{ll} \sum_{i=1}^n |x_i|^p < \infty & \text{if } 0 < p < \infty \\ \max_{i=1,\ldots,n} |x_i| < \infty & \text{if } p = \infty \end{array} \right\}.$$

Definition A.35 (ℓ_p–norms) *Given $\mathbf{x} \in \ell_p^n$ we define the ℓ_p–*norm $\|\mathbf{x}\|_p$ *by*

$$\|\mathbf{x}\|_p \stackrel{\text{def}}{=} \begin{cases} \sum_{i=1}^n \mathbf{I}_{x_i \neq 0} & \text{if } p = 0 \\ \left(\sum_{i=1}^n |x_i|^p\right)^{1/p} & \text{if } 0 < p < \infty \\ \max_{i=1,\ldots,n} |x_i| & \text{if } p = \infty \end{cases}.$$

Definition A.36 (Balls in normed spaces) *Given a normed space $\mathcal{X}$, the* open ball *$\mathcal{B}_\tau(\mathbf{x}) \subseteq \mathcal{X}$ of radius τ around $\mathbf{x} \in \mathcal{X}$ is defined by*

$$\mathcal{B}_\tau(\mathbf{x}) \stackrel{\text{def}}{=} \{\mathbf{y} \in \mathcal{X} \mid \|\mathbf{x} - \mathbf{y}\| < \tau\}.$$

Equivalently, the closed ball *$\overline{\mathcal{B}}_\tau(\mathbf{x}) \subseteq \mathcal{X}$ is defined by*

$$\overline{\mathcal{B}}_\tau(\mathbf{x}) \stackrel{\text{def}}{=} \{\mathbf{y} \in \mathcal{X} \mid \|\mathbf{x} - \mathbf{y}\| \leq \tau\}.$$

Definition A.37 (Inner product space) *Suppose we are given a vector space $\mathcal{X}$. An* inner product space *$\mathcal{X}$ (or* pre-Hilbert space*) is defined by the tuple $(\mathcal{X}, \langle\cdot,\cdot\rangle)$, where $\langle\cdot,\cdot\rangle : \mathcal{X} \times \mathcal{X} \to \mathbb{R}$ is called an* inner product *and satisfies the following properties: For all $\mathbf{x}, \mathbf{y}, \mathbf{z} \in \mathcal{X}$ and $c, d \in \mathbb{R}$,*

$$\langle\mathbf{x},\mathbf{x}\rangle \geq 0 \tag{A.19}$$

$$\langle\mathbf{x},\mathbf{x}\rangle = 0 \quad \Leftrightarrow \quad \mathbf{x} = \mathbf{0}, \tag{A.20}$$

$$\langle c\mathbf{x} + d\mathbf{y}, \mathbf{z}\rangle = c\langle\mathbf{x},\mathbf{z}\rangle + d\langle\mathbf{y},\mathbf{z}\rangle, \tag{A.21}$$

$$\langle\mathbf{x},\mathbf{y}\rangle = \langle\mathbf{y},\mathbf{x}\rangle. \tag{A.22}$$

Clearly, each inner product space is a normed space when defining $\|\mathbf{x}\| \stackrel{\text{def}}{=} \sqrt{\langle\mathbf{x},\mathbf{x}\rangle}$. The function $\langle\cdot,\cdot\rangle : \mathcal{X} \times \mathcal{X} \to \mathbb{R}$ is called generalized inner product *if it only satisfies equation (A.20)–(A.22).*

Definition A.38 (Euclidean inner product) *If* $\mathcal{X} = \ell_2^n$ *we define the* Euclidean inner product *between* $\mathbf{x}, \mathbf{y} \in \mathcal{X}$ *by*

$$\langle \mathbf{x}, \mathbf{y} \rangle \stackrel{\text{def}}{=} \mathbf{x}'\mathbf{y} = \sum_{i=1}^{n} x_i y_i \,. \tag{A.23}$$

Example A.39 (ℓ_2^n and L_2) *Defining an inner product* $\langle \cdot, \cdot \rangle$ *in* ℓ_2^n *and* $L_2(X)$ *by (A.23) and*

$$\langle f, g \rangle = \int_X f(\mathbf{x})\, g(\mathbf{x})\, d\mathbf{x} \tag{A.24}$$

makes these two spaces inner product spaces because

1. $\langle \mathbf{x}, \mathbf{x} \rangle = \sum_{i=1}^{n} x_i^2 \geq 0$ *and* $\langle f, f \rangle = \int_X (f(\mathbf{x}))^2\, d\mathbf{x} \geq 0$.
2. $\langle \mathbf{x}, \mathbf{x} \rangle = \sum_{i=1}^{n} x_i^2 = 0$ *if and only if* $\mathbf{x} = \mathbf{0}$. *Similarly,* $\langle f, f \rangle = \int_X (f(\mathbf{x}))^2\, d\mathbf{x} = 0$ *if and only if* $f(\mathbf{x}) = 0$ *almost everywhere.*
3. *For the* ℓ_2^n *case we have*

$$\begin{aligned} \langle c\mathbf{x} + d\mathbf{y}, \mathbf{z} \rangle &= \sum_{i=1}^{n} (cx_i + dy_i)\, z_i = c \sum_{i=1}^{n} x_i z_i + d \sum_{i=1}^{n} y_i z_i \\ &= c \langle \mathbf{x}, \mathbf{z} \rangle + d \langle \mathbf{y}, \mathbf{z} \rangle \,. \end{aligned}$$

Similarly,

$$\begin{aligned} \langle af + bg, h \rangle &= \int_X (af(\mathbf{x}) + bg(\mathbf{x}))\, h(\mathbf{x})\, d\mathbf{x} \\ &= a \int_X f(\mathbf{x})\, h(\mathbf{x})\, d\mathbf{x} + b \int_X g(\mathbf{x})\, h(\mathbf{x})\, d\mathbf{x} \\ &= a \langle f, h \rangle + b \langle g, h \rangle \,. \end{aligned}$$

4. *The symmetry follows trivially from definition (A.23) and (A.24).*

Definition A.40 (Positive (semi)definiteness) *Given a vector space* $\mathcal{X}$*, a function* $f : \mathcal{X} \times \mathcal{X} \to \mathbb{R}$ *is said to be* positive definite *(*positive semidefinite*) if, and only if, for all* $n \in \mathbb{N}$*, all* $\mathbf{x}_1, \ldots, \mathbf{x}_n \in \mathcal{X}$ *and all* $\mathbf{a} \in \mathbb{R}^n$, $\mathbf{a} \neq \mathbf{0}$*, it satisfies*

$$\sum_{i=1}^{n} \sum_{j=1}^{n} a_i a_j f(\mathbf{x}_i, \mathbf{x}_j) > 0 \,. \quad \left(\sum_{i=1}^{n} \sum_{j=1}^{n} a_i a_j f(\mathbf{x}_i, \mathbf{x}_j) \geq 0 \right) .$$

Example A.41 (Positive semidefiniteness) *Consider any inner product* $\langle \cdot, \cdot \rangle = f(\cdot, \cdot)$ *on a vector space* $\mathcal{X}$*. Then, for all* $n \in \mathbb{N}$*, all* $\mathbf{a} \in \mathbb{R}^n$*,* $\mathbf{a} \neq \mathbf{0}$ *and any sequence* $\mathbf{x}_1, \ldots, \mathbf{x}_n \in \mathcal{X}$*,*

$$\begin{aligned}\sum_{i=1}^{n}\sum_{j=1}^{n} a_i a_j \langle \mathbf{x}_i, \mathbf{x}_j \rangle &= \sum_{i=1}^{n} a_i \sum_{j=1}^{n} a_j \langle \mathbf{x}_i, \mathbf{x}_j \rangle = \sum_{i=1}^{n} a_i \left\langle \mathbf{x}_i, \sum_{j=1}^{n} a_j \mathbf{x}_j \right\rangle \\ &= \left\langle \sum_{i=1}^{n} a_i \mathbf{x}_i, \sum_{j=1}^{n} a_j \mathbf{x}_j \right\rangle = \left\| \sum_{i=1}^{n} a_i \mathbf{x}_i \right\|^2 \geq 0\,,\end{aligned}$$

where the second step follows from equation (A.21) and the last step is a direct consequence of equation (A.19). Thus, the inner product is a positive semidefinite function by definition.

Definition A.42 (Cauchy sequence) *A sequence* $(\mathbf{x}_i)_{i \in \mathbb{N}}$ *in a normed space is said to be a* Cauchy sequence *if* $\lim_{n \to \infty} \sup_{m \geq n} \|\mathbf{x}_n - \mathbf{x}_m\| = 0$*. Note that all convergent sequences are Cauchy sequences but the converse is not true in general.*

Definition A.43 (Hilbert space) *A* Hilbert space $\mathcal{X}$ *is a complete inner product space. A space is called* complete *if every Cauchy sequence converges.*

Definition A.44 (Linear operator) *Given two Hilbert spaces* $\mathcal{H}$ *and* $\mathcal{F}$*, a mapping* $T : \mathcal{H} \to \mathcal{F}$ *is called* linear operator *if and only if*

1. *For all* $\mathbf{x} \in \mathcal{H}$ *and* $\mathbf{y} \in \mathcal{H}$*,* $T(\mathbf{x} + \mathbf{y}) = T\mathbf{x} + T\mathbf{y}$*.*
2. *For all* $\mathbf{x} \in \mathcal{H}$ *and all* $c \in \mathbb{R}$*,* $T(c\mathbf{x}) = c \cdot T\mathbf{x}$*.*

Definition A.45 (Eigenvalue and eigenvector) *Let* $T : \mathcal{H} \to \mathcal{H}$ *be a linear operator on a Hilbert space* $\mathcal{H}$*. If there is a vector* $\mathbf{x} \in \mathcal{H}$*,* $\mathbf{x} \neq \mathbf{0}$*, such that* $T\mathbf{x} = \lambda\mathbf{x}$ *for some scalar* λ*, then* λ *is an* eigenvalue *of* T *with the corresponding* eigenvector $\mathbf{x}$.

Definition A.46 (Self-adjoint operators) *A linear operator* $T : \mathcal{H} \to \mathcal{H}$ *on a Hilbert space* $\mathcal{H}$ *is* self-adjoint*, if, for all* $\mathbf{x}, \mathbf{y} \in \mathcal{H}$*,*

$$\langle T\mathbf{x}, \mathbf{y} \rangle = \langle \mathbf{x}, T\mathbf{y} \rangle\,.$$

A.3.1 Covering, Packing and Entropy Numbers

In this section we recall the notion of covering and packing numbers as well as entropy numbers. We present an elementary relation for covering and packing numbers; for further information the interested reader is referred to Kolmogorov and Fomin (1957), Carl and Stephani (1990) and Vidyasagar (1997).

Definition A.47 (ε–cover and ε–packing) *Let $(\mathcal{X}, \rho)$ be a metric space, let $A \subseteq \mathcal{X}$ and $\varepsilon > 0$. A set $B \subseteq \mathcal{X}$ is an ε–*cover for *A if for every $a \in A$ there exists $b \in B$ such that $\rho(a, b) \leq \varepsilon$, i.e.,*

$$A \subseteq \bigcup_{b \in B} \overline{\mathcal{B}}_\varepsilon(b) .$$

The cover B is said to be proper *if, and only if, $B \subseteq A$. The set $B \subseteq A$ is an* ε–packing of *A if, for all distinct $b, c \in B$, $d(b, c) > \varepsilon$.*

Definition A.48 (Covering and packing number) *Let $(\mathcal{X}, \rho)$ be a metric space, let $A \subseteq \mathcal{X}$ and $\varepsilon > 0$. The* covering number $\mathcal{N}_A^\rho(\varepsilon)$ *is the minimal cardinality of an ε–cover for A; if there is no such finite cover then it is defined to be ∞. The* packing number $\mathcal{M}_A^\rho(\varepsilon)$ *is the maximal cardinality of an ε–packing of A; if there is no such finite packing then it is defined to be ∞.*

In order to enhance understanding we have shown an ε–cover as well as an ε–packing in Figure A.5. There exists an elementary relationship between packing and covering numbers first proven in Kolmogorov and Tihomirov (1961); the current proof is taken from Anthony and Bartlett (1999).

Theorem A.49 (Packing and covering numbers) *Let $(\mathcal{X}, \rho)$ be a metric space. Then, for all $\varepsilon > 0$ and for every subset $A \subseteq \mathcal{X}$, the packing and covering numbers satisfy the following relation:*

$$\mathcal{M}_A^\rho(2\varepsilon) \leq \mathcal{N}_A^\rho(\varepsilon) \leq \mathcal{M}_A^\rho(\varepsilon) .$$

Proof Let us begin with the leftmost inequality. Suppose that $C \subseteq \mathcal{X}$ is an ε–cover of A and that $P \subseteq A$ is a 2ε–packing of A of maximum cardinality $\mathcal{M}_A^\rho(2\varepsilon)$. We need to show that $|P| \leq |C|$ which will be done by contradiction. Let us assume that $|P| > |C|$. Since C is an ε–cover of A we know that, for every $p \in P$, there

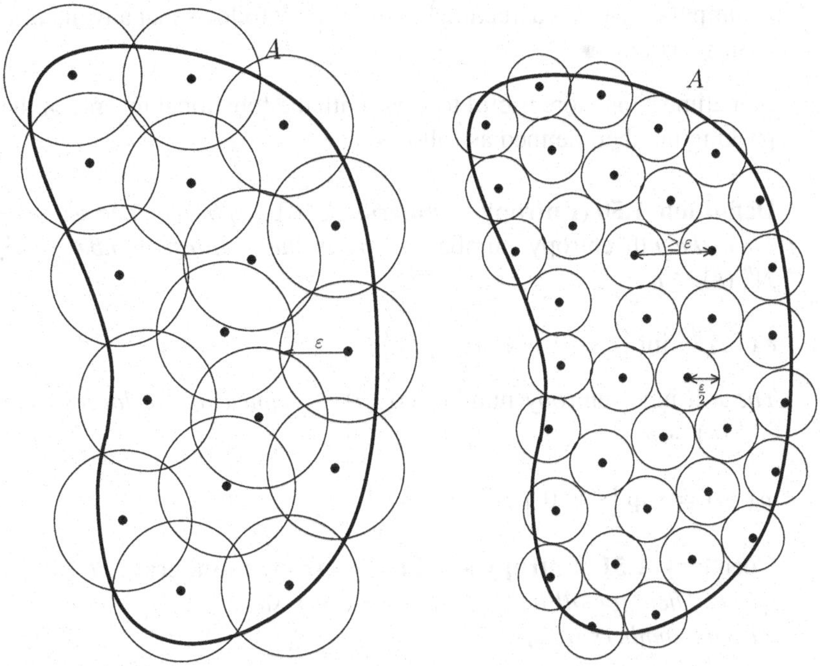

Figure A.5 **(Left)** ε–covering of the set $A \subset \mathbb{R}^2$ using the Euclidean metric. The black dots represent the ε–cover. **(Right)** ε–packing of the same set $A \subset \mathbb{R}^2$. Note that by definition we can place balls of radius $\frac{\varepsilon}{2}$ around the ε–packing and obtain a set of balls which have an empty intersection with each other.

exists a $c \in C$ such that $\rho(p, c) \leq \varepsilon$. By the "pigeonhole[4] principle" there must be some $c \in C$ such that for two points $p_1 \neq p_2$ in P, $\rho(p_1, c) \leq \varepsilon$ and $\rho(p_2, c) \leq \varepsilon$. Since ρ is a metric (see Definition A.32) we know that

$$\rho(p_1, p_2) \leq \rho(p_1, c) + \rho(p_2, c) \leq 2\varepsilon\,,$$

which contradicts the assumption that P is a 2ε–packing of A. Hence, $|P| \leq |C|$ as desired.

To prove the rightmost inequality, suppose that P is an ε–packing of maximum cardinality $\mathcal{M}_A^\rho(\varepsilon)$. Then, for any $a \in A$, there must exist a $p \in P$ with $\rho(p, a) \leq \varepsilon$ because otherwise we could form the packing $P \cup \{a\}$ which contradicts the

4 The pigeonhole principle states that if n pigeons are distributed over fewer than n pigeonholes, some pigeonholes must contain more than one pigeon (for Trybulec (1990) for a rigorous proof).

assumption that P is a maximal ε–packing. It follows that any maximum ε–packing is an ε–cover. ■

Sometimes it is more useful to work with the functional inverse of the covering and packing number, defined as follows.

Definition A.50 (Entropy numbers) *Let $(\mathcal{X}, \rho)$ be a metric space and let $A \subseteq \mathcal{X}$. Then the* nth entropy number $\epsilon_A(n)$ *is the smallest number $\varepsilon \geq 0$ such that $\mathcal{N}_A^\rho(\varepsilon) \leq n$,*

$$\epsilon_A(n) \stackrel{\text{def}}{=} \inf\left\{\varepsilon > 0 \;\middle|\; \mathcal{N}_A^\rho(\varepsilon) \leq n\right\}.$$

The nth inner entropy number $\varphi_A(n)$ *is defined as the largest $\varepsilon > 0$ such that $\mathcal{M}_A^\rho(\varepsilon) > n$,*

$$\varphi_A(n) \stackrel{\text{def}}{=} \sup\left\{\varepsilon > 0 \;\middle|\; \mathcal{M}_A^\rho(\varepsilon) \geq n\right\}.$$

Corollary A.51 (Entropy and inner entropy numbers) *Let $(\mathcal{X}, \rho)$ be a metric space. Then, for all $n \in \mathbb{N}^+$ and for every subset $A \subseteq \mathcal{X}$, the entropy and inner entropy numbers satisfy*

$$\varphi_A(n) \leq \epsilon_A(n) \leq 2 \cdot \varphi_A(n).$$

Proof The result follows directly from Theorem A.49 noticing that $\mathcal{N}_A^\rho(\varepsilon)$ and $\mathcal{M}_A^\rho(\varepsilon)$ are non-increasing functions for increasing ε, that is, we know that there exists a smallest $\Delta \geq 0$ such that

$$\mathcal{M}_A^\rho\underbrace{(2\epsilon_A(n) + \Delta)}_{\varphi_A(n)} = \mathcal{N}_A^\rho(\epsilon_A(n)) = n.$$

This shows the rightmost inequality. The leftmost inequality can be shown in an analogous way. ■

A.3.2 Matrix Algebra

Vectors, which are column vectors by definition, and matrices are denoted in bold face[5], e.g., $\mathbf{x}$ or $\mathbf{X}$. Vector components are denoted by subscripts omitting bold

5 This should not be confused with the special symbols E, P, v, f, F and I which denote the expectation value, the probability measure, the empirical probability measure, the density, the distribution function and the indicator function, respectively. Whenever the symbol $\mathbf{x}$ is already in use, we use $\vec{x}$ to denote a vector to avoid confusion.

face, i.e., x_i. Note that for matrices we *do not* omit the bold face, i.e., $\mathbf{X}_{ij}$ is the element of $\mathbf{X}$ in the ith row and jth column. We have for the $n \times 1$ vector $\mathbf{x}$ that $\mathbf{x} = (x_1, \ldots, x_n)' = (x_1; \ldots; x_n)$, i.e., a comma-separated list creates a row vector whereas a semicolon-separated list denotes a column vector. The $n \times n$ *identity matrix* is denoted by $\mathbf{I}_n$. We omit the index n whenever the size of the matrix is clear from the context. The vector $\mathbf{e}_i$ denotes the ith *unit vector*, i.e., all components are zero except the ith component which is one. The vector $\mathbf{1}$ is defined by $\sum_i \mathbf{e}_i = (1; \ldots; 1)$. The main importance of matrix algebra stems from the following theorem which builds the link between linear operators and matrices.

Theorem A.52 (Linear operators in finite dimensional spaces) *All linear operators $\boldsymbol{\phi} : \mathbb{R}^n \to \mathbb{R}^m$ for finite $n, m \in \mathbb{N}$ admit a representation of the form*

$$\boldsymbol{\phi}(\mathbf{x}) = \mathbf{A}\mathbf{x},$$

where $\mathbf{A} \in \mathbb{R}^{m \times n}$ is called the parameter matrix.

Proof Put $\mathbf{x} = \sum_{i=1}^n x_i \mathbf{e}_i$. By the two properties of linear operators

$$\boldsymbol{\phi}(\mathbf{x}) = \boldsymbol{\phi}\left(\sum_{i=1}^n x_i \mathbf{e}_i\right) = \sum_{i=1}^n x_i \boldsymbol{\phi}(\mathbf{e}_i) = \underbrace{(\boldsymbol{\phi}(\mathbf{e}_1), \ldots, \boldsymbol{\phi}(\mathbf{e}_n))}_{\mathbf{A}} \mathbf{x},$$

that is, the columns of the matrix $\mathbf{A}$ are the images of the n unit vectors $\mathbf{e}_i \in \mathbb{R}^n$. ∎

Types of Matrices

Definition A.53 (Square matrix) *A matrix $\mathbf{A} \in \mathbb{R}^{n \times m}$ is called a* square matrix *if, and only if, $m = n$.*

Definition A.54 (Symmetric matrix) *A square matrix $\mathbf{A}$ is called a* symmetric matrix *if, and only if, $\mathbf{A}' = \mathbf{A}$.*

Definition A.55 (Lower and upper triangular matrix) *A square matrix $\mathbf{A}$ is a called* lower (upper) triangular matrix *if, and only if, $\mathbf{A}_{ij} = 0 \Leftarrow i < j$ $(i > j)$.*

Definition A.56 (Diagonal matrix) *A square matrix $\mathbf{A}$ is called a* diagonal matrix *if, and only if, $\mathbf{A}_{ij} = 0$ for all $i \neq j$. They are denoted by* $\mathrm{diag}(a_1, \ldots, a_n)$.

Definition A.57 (Positive (semi)definite matrix) *A symmetric $n \times n$ matrix $\mathbf{A}$ is called* positive definite, *i.e.,* $\mathbf{A} > 0$, *if, and only if,*

$$\forall \mathbf{c} \in \mathbb{R}^n, \mathbf{c} \neq \mathbf{0}: \qquad \mathbf{c}'\mathbf{A}\mathbf{c} > 0\,.$$

If the inequality only holds with $\geq$ then $\mathbf{A}$ is called positive semidefinite. *This is denoted by $\mathbf{A} \geq 0$.*

Definition A.58 (Orthogonal matrix) *A square matrix $\mathbf{A}$ is called an* orthogonal matrix *if, and only if,* $\mathbf{A}'\mathbf{A} = \mathbf{I}$.

Definition A.59 (Singular matrix) *A square matrix $\mathbf{A}$ is* singular *if, and only if,* $|\mathbf{A}| = 0$; *otherwise the matrix is called a* non-singular *matrix.*

Transpose

Definition A.60 (Transpose of a matrix) *For any $n \times m$ matrix $\mathbf{A}$ the* transpose $\mathbf{A}'$ *is an $m \times n$ matrix defined by* $\mathbf{A}'_{ij} \stackrel{\text{def}}{=} \mathbf{A}_{ji}$.

Theorem A.61 (Transpose of matrix product) *For any $n \times m$ matrix $\mathbf{A}$ and $m \times r$ matrix $\mathbf{B}$,*

$$(\mathbf{A}\mathbf{B})' = \mathbf{B}'\mathbf{A}'\,.$$

Proof Follows trivially by comparing individual elements of both matrix products. ■

Rank

Definition A.62 (Rank of a matrix) *Given an $m \times n$ matrix $\mathbf{A}$ the rank* $\operatorname{rk}(\mathbf{A})$ *is the maximum number of columns which are linearly independent.*

Theorem A.63 (Rank of the transpose) *For any $m \times n$ matrix $\mathbf{A}$ we know that* $\operatorname{rk}(\mathbf{A}) = \operatorname{rk}(\mathbf{A}') \leq \min\{m, n\}$.

Determinant

Definition A.64 (Determinant of a matrix) *The* determinant $|\mathbf{A}|$ *of an* $n \times n$ *matrix* $\mathbf{A}$ *is defined by*

$$|\mathbf{A}| \stackrel{\text{def}}{=} \mathbf{A}, \qquad \text{if } n = 1,$$

$$|\mathbf{A}| \stackrel{\text{def}}{=} \begin{cases} \sum_{i=1}^{n} \mathbf{A}_{ij} \cdot \left|\mathbf{A}_{[ij]}\right| \cdot (-1)^{i+j} & \text{for any } j \in \{1,\ldots,n\} \\ \sum_{j=1}^{n} \mathbf{A}_{ij} \cdot \left|\mathbf{A}_{[ij]}\right| \cdot (-1)^{i+j} & \text{for any } i \in \{1,\ldots,n\} \end{cases}, \qquad \text{if } n > 1.$$

The $(n-1) \times (n-1)$ *matrix* $\mathbf{A}_{[ij]}$ *is obtained by deleting the* i*th row and* j*th column from* $\mathbf{A}$.

Theorem A.65 (Determinants of the transpose) *For any* $n \times n$ *matrix* $\mathbf{A}$ *we have* $|\mathbf{A}| = \left|\mathbf{A}'\right|$.

Proof The result is trivially true for $n = 1$. Let us assume the assertion is true of $n \in \mathbb{N}$. Then, for any $(n+1) \times (n+1)$ matrix $\mathbf{A}$, by definition

$$\begin{aligned} |\mathbf{A}| &= \sum_{j=1}^{n+1} \mathbf{A}_{1j} \cdot \left|\mathbf{A}_{[1j]}\right| \cdot (-1)^{1+j} = \sum_{j=1}^{n+1} \mathbf{A}_{j1} \cdot \left|\mathbf{A}_{[j1]}\right| \cdot (-1)^{1+j} \\ &= \sum_{j=1}^{n+1} \mathbf{A}'_{1j} \cdot \left|\mathbf{A}'_{[1j]}\right| \cdot (-1)^{1+j} = \left|\mathbf{A}'\right|, \end{aligned}$$

where the second line follows by assumption and the definition of the transpose. ∎

Theorem A.66 (Determinants of triangular matrices) *The determinant* $|\mathbf{A}|$ *of a lower (upper) triangular* $n \times n$ *matrix* $\mathbf{A}$ *is given by the product of the diagonal of* $\mathbf{A}$, *i.e.,*

$$|\mathbf{A}| = \prod_{i=1}^{n} \mathbf{A}_{ii}.$$

Proof Let us assume that $\mathbf{A}$ is lower triangular. The result follows by induction. The case $n = 1$ is covered by the Definition A.64. Let us assume the assertion is true for $n \in \mathbb{N}$. Then, for any $(n+1) \times (n+1)$ matrix $\mathbf{A}$, by definition

$$|\mathbf{A}| = \sum_{j=1}^{n+1} \mathbf{A}_{1j} \cdot \left|\mathbf{A}_{[1j]}\right| \cdot (-1)^{1+j} = \mathbf{A}_{11} \cdot \left|\mathbf{A}_{[11]}\right| = \mathbf{A}_{11} \cdot \prod_{i=1}^{n} \mathbf{A}_{i+1,i+1} ,$$

because, according to Definition A.55, all $\mathbf{A}_{1j}$ for $j > 1$ are zero. The last step follows from the fact that $\left|\mathbf{A}_{[11]}\right|$ is the determinant of the $n \times n$ lower triangular sub-matrix of $\mathbf{A}$ obtained by deletion of the first row and column. The case of $\mathbf{A}$ being upper triangular follows by an application of Theorem A.65. ■

Due to their lengths, the following three theorems are given without proof. The interested reader is referred to Mardia et al. (1979) and Harville (1997).

Theorem A.67 (Products of determinant) *For any two $n \times n$ matrices $\mathbf{A}$ and $\mathbf{B}$,*

$$|\mathbf{AB}| = |\mathbf{A}| \cdot |\mathbf{B}| .$$

Theorem A.68 (Determinant of triangular partitioned matrix) *Let $\mathbf{M}$ be a partitioned $n \times n$ matrix*

$$\mathbf{M} = \begin{pmatrix} \mathbf{A} & \mathbf{B} \\ \mathbf{C} & \mathbf{D} \end{pmatrix} ,$$

where $\mathbf{A} \in \mathbb{R}^{s \times s}$, $\mathbf{B} \in \mathbb{R}^{s \times r}$, $\mathbf{C} \in \mathbb{R}^{r \times s}$, $\mathbf{D} \in \mathbb{R}^{r \times r}$ and $n = r + s$. If either $\mathbf{B} = \mathbf{0}$ or $\mathbf{C} = \mathbf{0}$ we have

$$|\mathbf{M}| = |\mathbf{A}| \cdot |\mathbf{D}| .$$

Theorem A.69 (Determinant of linear combinations) *For any $n \times n$ matrix $\mathbf{A} = (\mathbf{a}_1, \ldots, \mathbf{a}_n)$, any $i, j \in \{1, \ldots, n\}$ and any $\lambda \in \mathbb{R}$*

$$\left|(\mathbf{a}_1, \ldots, \mathbf{a}_{j-1}, \mathbf{a}_j + \lambda \mathbf{a}_i, \mathbf{a}_{j+1}, \ldots, \mathbf{a}_n)\right| = |\mathbf{A}| .$$

Theorem A.70 (Determinant and rank) *For any $n \times n$ matrix $\mathbf{A}$ with $\text{rk}(\mathbf{A}) < n$ we have that $|\mathbf{A}| = 0$.*

Proof Since $\text{rk}(\mathbf{A}) < n$ we know that there exists a column $\mathbf{a}_i$ of $\mathbf{A}$ which can be linearly combined from the remaining $n-1$ columns. Without loss of generality suppose that this is the first column $\mathbf{a}_1$, i.e., $\mathbf{a}_1 = \sum_{j=1}^{n-1} \lambda_j \mathbf{a}_{j+1}$. According to

Theorem A.69 we know that

$$|\mathbf{A}| = \left| \left(\mathbf{a}_1 - \sum_{j=1}^{n-1} \lambda_j \mathbf{a}_{j+1}, \mathbf{a}_2, \ldots, \mathbf{a}_n \right) \right| = |(\mathbf{0}, \mathbf{a}_2, \ldots, \mathbf{a}_n)| = 0 .$$

where we used Definition A.64 with the first column of zeros. ■

Theorem A.71 (Scaling of determinant) *For any $n \times n$ matrix $\mathbf{A} = (\mathbf{a}_1, \ldots, \mathbf{a}_n)$ and any vector $\boldsymbol{\lambda} \in \mathbb{R}^n$*

$$|(\lambda_1 \mathbf{a}_1, \ldots, \lambda_n \mathbf{a}_n)| = |\mathbf{A}| \cdot \prod_{i=1}^{n} \lambda_i .$$

Proof Noticing that

$$(\lambda_1 \mathbf{a}_1, \ldots, \lambda_n \mathbf{a}_n) = \mathbf{A} \cdot \operatorname{diag}(\lambda_1, \ldots, \lambda_n) ,$$

the result follows from Theorems A.66 and A.67. ■

Theorem A.72 (Determinant of a partitioned matrix) *Let $\mathbf{M}$ be a partitioned $n \times n$ matrix*

$$\mathbf{M} = \begin{pmatrix} \mathbf{A} & \mathbf{B} \\ \mathbf{C} & \mathbf{D} \end{pmatrix} ,$$

where $\mathbf{A} \in \mathbb{R}^{s \times s}$, $\mathbf{B} \in \mathbb{R}^{s \times r}$, $\mathbf{C} \in \mathbb{R}^{r \times s}$, $\mathbf{D} \in \mathbb{R}^{r \times r}$ and $n = r + s$. If $\mathbf{A}^{-1}$ and $\mathbf{D}^{-1}$ exist then

$$|\mathbf{M}| = \begin{vmatrix} \mathbf{A} & \mathbf{B} \\ \mathbf{C} & \mathbf{D} \end{vmatrix} = |\mathbf{A}| \cdot \left| \mathbf{D} - \mathbf{C}\mathbf{A}^{-1}\mathbf{B} \right| = |\mathbf{D}| \cdot \left| \mathbf{A} - \mathbf{B}\mathbf{D}^{-1}\mathbf{C} \right| .$$

Proof In order to prove the assertion we use the fact that $\mathbf{M}$ can be written as the product of two partitioned block-triangular matrices, i.e.,

$$\begin{pmatrix} \mathbf{I}_s & \mathbf{0} \\ \mathbf{C}\mathbf{A}^{-1} & \mathbf{D} - \mathbf{C}\mathbf{A}^{-1}\mathbf{B} \end{pmatrix} \begin{pmatrix} \mathbf{A} & \mathbf{B} \\ \mathbf{0} & \mathbf{I}_r \end{pmatrix} = \begin{pmatrix} \mathbf{A} - \mathbf{B}\mathbf{D}^{-1}\mathbf{C} & \mathbf{B}\mathbf{D}^{-1} \\ \mathbf{0} & \mathbf{I}_r \end{pmatrix} \begin{pmatrix} \mathbf{I}_s & \mathbf{0} \\ \mathbf{C} & \mathbf{D} \end{pmatrix} .$$

Applying Theorems A.67 and A.68 proves the result. ■

Trace

Definition A.73 (Trace of a matrix) *The* trace $\mathrm{tr}(\mathbf{A})$ *of a square* $n \times n$ *matrix* $\mathbf{A}$ *is defined by*

$$\mathrm{tr}(\mathbf{A}) \stackrel{\text{def}}{=} \sum_{i=1}^{n} \mathbf{A}_{ii} .$$

Theorem A.74 (Trace of matrix products) *For any* $n \times m$ *matrix* $\mathbf{A}$ *and* $m \times n$ *matrix* $\mathbf{B}$,

$$\mathrm{tr}(\mathbf{AB}) = \mathrm{tr}(\mathbf{BA}) .$$

Proof By definition we know that

$$\mathrm{tr}(\mathbf{AB}) = \sum_{i=1}^{n} \left(\sum_{j=1}^{m} \mathbf{A}_{ij} \mathbf{B}_{ji} \right) = \sum_{j=1}^{m} \left(\sum_{i=1}^{n} \mathbf{B}_{ji} \mathbf{A}_{ij} \right) = \mathrm{tr}(\mathbf{BA}) .$$

The theorem is proved. ■

Inverse

Definition A.75 (Inverse of a matrix) *The square matrix* $\mathbf{A}^{-1}$ *is called the* inverse *of* $\mathbf{A} \in \mathbb{R}^{n \times n}$ *if, and only if,*

$$\mathbf{A}^{-1}\mathbf{A} = \mathbf{A}\mathbf{A}^{-1} = \mathbf{I}_n .$$

The inverse exists if, and only if, $\mathbf{A}$ *is non-singular, i.e.,* $|\mathbf{A}| \neq 0$.

Theorem A.76 (Inverse of square matrix) *If* $\mathbf{A}$ *and* $\mathbf{B}$ *are any two* $n \times n$ *matrices and* $\mathbf{AB} = \mathbf{I}_n$ *then* $\mathbf{B} = \mathbf{A}^{-1}$.

Proof From Theorem A.67 we know that $|\mathbf{A}| \cdot |\mathbf{B}| = |\mathbf{I}_n| = 1$. Hence both $\mathbf{A}^{-1}$ and $\mathbf{B}^{-1}$ exists because $|\mathbf{A}| \neq 0$ and $|\mathbf{B}| \neq 0$. As a consequence $\mathbf{A}^{-1} \cdot (\mathbf{AB}) = \mathbf{A}^{-1} \cdot \mathbf{I}_n \Leftrightarrow \mathbf{B} = \mathbf{A}^{-1}$ which proves the theorem. ■

Theorem A.77 (Product and transpose of inverses) *If the two square matrices* $\mathbf{A}$ *and* $\mathbf{B}$ *are invertible then*

$$(\mathbf{AB})^{-1} = \mathbf{B}^{-1}\mathbf{A}^{-1}, \qquad (\mathbf{A}')^{-1} = (\mathbf{A}^{-1})'.$$

Proof To prove the first assertion we have to show that $(\mathbf{B}^{-1}\mathbf{A}^{-1})(\mathbf{AB}) = \mathbf{I}$ which follows from Definition A.75. The second assertion follows from $(\mathbf{A}')^{-1}\mathbf{A}' = (\mathbf{A}^{-1})'\mathbf{A}' = (\mathbf{AA}^{-1})' = \mathbf{I}' = \mathbf{I}$ by virtue of Theorem A.61. ∎

Theorem A.78 (Inverse and determinant) *Let* $\mathbf{A}$ *be an invertible symmetric* $n \times n$ *matrix. Then the inverse* $\mathbf{A}^{-1}$ *can be computed as*

$$\mathbf{A}^{-1} = \frac{1}{|\mathbf{A}|}\begin{pmatrix} (-1)^{1+1}\cdot\left|\mathbf{A}_{[11]}\right| & \cdots & (-1)^{1+n}\cdot\left|\mathbf{A}_{[1n]}\right| \\ \vdots & \ddots & \vdots \\ (-1)^{n+1}\cdot\left|\mathbf{A}_{[n1]}\right| & \cdots & (-1)^{n+n}\cdot\left|\mathbf{A}_{[nn]}\right| \end{pmatrix}'.$$

Proof In order to proof the theorem we need to show that $\mathbf{A}^{-1}\mathbf{A} = \mathbf{I}_n$. For the i, j–th element of $\mathbf{A}^{-1}\mathbf{A}$ we have

$$\left(\mathbf{A}^{-1}\mathbf{A}\right)_{ij} = \frac{1}{|\mathbf{A}|}\cdot\sum_{l=1}^{n}(-1)^{i+l}\cdot\left|\mathbf{A}_{[il]}\right|\cdot\mathbf{A}_{lj} = \frac{1}{|\mathbf{A}|}\cdot\underbrace{\sum_{l=1}^{n}(-1)^{i+l}\cdot\left|\mathbf{A}_{[il]}\right|\cdot\mathbf{A}_{jl}}_{q_{ij}}.$$

By Definition A.64 for $i = j$ we see that $q_{ij} = |\mathbf{A}|$. In the case of $i \neq j$, q_{ij} can be viewed as the determinant of the matrix $\tilde{\mathbf{A}}$ obtained from $\mathbf{A}$ by replacing the jth column with the ith column. Hence $\mathrm{rk}(\tilde{\mathbf{A}}) < n$ and therefore, by Theorem A.70, we know that $q_{ij} = 0$ which proves the theorem. ∎

Theorem A.79 (Woodbury formula) *Let* $\mathbf{C}$ *be an invertible* $n \times n$ *matrix. Then, for any matrix* $\mathbf{A} \in \mathbb{R}^{n\times m}$ *and* $\mathbf{B} \in \mathbb{R}^{m\times n}$,

$$(\mathbf{C} + \mathbf{AB})^{-1} = \mathbf{C}^{-1} - \mathbf{C}^{-1}\mathbf{A}\left(\mathbf{I} + \mathbf{BC}^{-1}\mathbf{A}\right)^{-1}\mathbf{BC}^{-1}. \tag{A.25}$$

The r.h.s. exists if and only if the l.h.s. exists.

Proof Put $\mathbf{D} = \mathbf{I} + \mathbf{B}\mathbf{C}^{-1}\mathbf{A}$. First we show that the r.h.s. of equation (A.25) has the property that its product with $(\mathbf{C} + \mathbf{A}\mathbf{B})$ equals $\mathbf{I}$, i.e.,

$$\begin{aligned}
&\left(\mathbf{C}^{-1} - \mathbf{C}^{-1}\mathbf{A}\left(\mathbf{I} + \mathbf{B}\mathbf{C}^{-1}\mathbf{A}\right)^{-1}\mathbf{B}\mathbf{C}^{-1}\right)(\mathbf{C} + \mathbf{A}\mathbf{B}) \\
&\quad = \left(\mathbf{C}^{-1} - \mathbf{C}^{-1}\mathbf{A}\mathbf{D}^{-1}\mathbf{B}\mathbf{C}^{-1}\right)(\mathbf{C} + \mathbf{A}\mathbf{B}) \\
&\quad = \mathbf{I} + \mathbf{C}^{-1}\mathbf{A}\mathbf{B} - \mathbf{C}^{-1}\mathbf{A}\mathbf{D}^{-1}\mathbf{B} - \mathbf{C}^{-1}\mathbf{A}\mathbf{D}^{-1}\mathbf{B}\mathbf{C}^{-1}\mathbf{A}\mathbf{B} \\
&\quad = \mathbf{I} + \mathbf{C}^{-1}\mathbf{A}\left(\mathbf{I} - \mathbf{D}^{-1} - \mathbf{D}^{-1}\mathbf{B}\mathbf{C}^{-1}\mathbf{A}\right)\mathbf{B} \\
&\quad = \mathbf{I} + \mathbf{C}^{-1}\mathbf{A}\left(\mathbf{I} - \mathbf{D}^{-1}\underbrace{\left(\mathbf{I} + \mathbf{B}\mathbf{C}^{-1}\mathbf{A}\right)}_{\mathbf{D}}\right)\mathbf{B} = \mathbf{I}.
\end{aligned}$$

Since both the l.h.s. and r.h.s. of equation (A.25) are square matrices the result follows from Theorem A.76. ■

Theorem A.80 (Partitioned inverse of a matrix) *Let* $\mathbf{M}$ *be a partitioned invertible* $n \times n$ *matrix*

$$\mathbf{M} = \begin{pmatrix} \mathbf{A} & \mathbf{B} \\ \mathbf{C} & \mathbf{D} \end{pmatrix},$$

where $\mathbf{A} \in \mathbb{R}^{s\times s}$, $\mathbf{B} \in \mathbb{R}^{s\times r}$, $\mathbf{C} \in \mathbb{R}^{r\times s}$, $\mathbf{D} \in \mathbb{R}^{r\times r}$ *and* $n = r + s$. *If* $\mathbf{A}^{-1}$ *exists then* $\mathbf{E} = \left(\mathbf{D} - \mathbf{C}\mathbf{A}^{-1}\mathbf{B}\right)^{-1}$ *also exists and*

$$\mathbf{M}^{-1} = \begin{pmatrix} \mathbf{A}^{-1} + \mathbf{A}^{-1}\mathbf{B}\mathbf{E}\mathbf{C}\mathbf{A}^{-1} & -\mathbf{A}^{-1}\mathbf{B}\mathbf{E} \\ -\mathbf{E}\mathbf{C}\mathbf{A}^{-1} & \mathbf{E} \end{pmatrix}. \tag{A.26}$$

Further, if $\mathbf{D}^{-1}$ *exists then* $\mathbf{F} = \left(\mathbf{A} - \mathbf{B}\mathbf{D}^{-1}\mathbf{C}\right)^{-1}$ *also exists and*

$$\mathbf{M}^{-1} = \begin{pmatrix} \mathbf{F} & -\mathbf{F}\mathbf{B}\mathbf{D}^{-1} \\ -\mathbf{D}^{-1}\mathbf{C}\mathbf{F} & \mathbf{D}^{-1} + \mathbf{D}^{-1}\mathbf{C}\mathbf{F}\mathbf{B}\mathbf{D}^{-1} \end{pmatrix}. \tag{A.27}$$

Proof In order to prove equation (A.26) put

$$\mathbf{N} = \begin{pmatrix} \mathbf{A}^{-1} & \mathbf{0} \\ -\mathbf{C}\mathbf{A}^{-1} & \mathbf{I}_r \end{pmatrix}.$$

According to Theorem A.76

$$\mathbf{NM} = \begin{pmatrix} \mathbf{I}_s & \mathbf{A}^{-1}\mathbf{B} \\ \mathbf{0} & \mathbf{D} - \mathbf{CA}^{-1}\mathbf{B} \end{pmatrix}$$

is invertible because **N** and **M** are square matrices and, by assumption, invertible. Hence the rows of $\mathbf{D} - \mathbf{CA}^{-1}\mathbf{B}$ are linearly independent and therefore **E** exists. It remains to show that $\mathbf{MM}^{-1} = \mathbf{I}_n$ which follows from

$$\begin{aligned} \mathbf{A}\left(\mathbf{A}^{-1} + \mathbf{A}^{-1}\mathbf{BECA}^{-1}\right) - \mathbf{BECA}^{-1} &= \mathbf{I}_s + \mathbf{BECA}^{-1} - \mathbf{BECA}^{-1} = \mathbf{I}_s\,, \\ \mathbf{C}\left(\mathbf{A}^{-1} + \mathbf{A}^{-1}\mathbf{BECA}^{-1}\right) - \mathbf{DECA}^{-1} &= \left(\mathbf{C} + \mathbf{CA}^{-1}\mathbf{BEC} - \mathbf{DEC}\right)\mathbf{A}^{-1} \\ &= \left(\mathbf{E}^{-1} + \mathbf{CA}^{-1}\mathbf{B} - \mathbf{D}\right)\mathbf{ECA}^{-1} = \mathbf{0}\,, \\ -\mathbf{AA}^{-1}\mathbf{BE} + \mathbf{BE} &= \mathbf{0}\,, \\ -\mathbf{CA}^{-1}\mathbf{BE} + \mathbf{DE} &= \left(\mathbf{D} - \mathbf{CA}^{-1}\mathbf{B}\right)\mathbf{E} = \mathbf{I}_r\,. \end{aligned}$$

The proof of equation (A.27) follows by applying equation (A.26) to $\mathbf{M}'$ and noticing that $\mathbf{M}^{-1} = ((\mathbf{M}')^{-1})'$ due to Theorem A.77. ■

Spectral Decomposition

Definition A.81 (Eigenvector and eigenvalue) *Let* **A** *be an* $n \times n$ *matrix. Then the vector* $\mathbf{u} \in \mathbb{R}^n$, $\mathbf{u} \neq \mathbf{0}$ *is called an* eigenvector of **A** *with the* eigenvalue λ *if*

$$\mathbf{Au} = \lambda\mathbf{u}\,. \tag{A.28}$$

Since each eigenvector $\mathbf{u} \neq \mathbf{0}$ must obey $\mathbf{Au} = \lambda\mathbf{u}$ we know that each eigenvalue λ is a non-trivial solution of $(\mathbf{A} - \lambda\mathbf{I})\,\mathbf{u} = \mathbf{0}$. This, however, requires that $|\mathbf{A} - \lambda\mathbf{I}| = 0$.

Definition A.82 (Characteristic polynomial) *Given an* $n \times n$ *matrix* **A**, *the* characteristic polynomial $\Phi_{\mathbf{A}} : \mathbb{R} \to \mathbb{R}$ of **A** *is defined by*

$$\Phi_{\mathbf{A}}(\lambda) \stackrel{\text{def}}{=} |\mathbf{A} - \lambda\mathbf{I}|\,.$$

Note that the characteristic polynomial is a nth degree polynomial.

If **A** is not only square but also symmetric, it can be shown that all roots of $\Phi_{\mathbf{A}}$ are real. Using this result we can prove the following powerful theorem.

Theorem A.83 (Spectral decomposition theorem) *Any symmetric $n \times n$ matrix $\mathbf{A}$ can be written as*

$$\mathbf{A} = \mathbf{U}\boldsymbol{\Lambda}\mathbf{U}', \tag{A.29}$$

where $\mathbf{U}'\mathbf{U} = \mathbf{I}$ and $\boldsymbol{\Lambda} = \operatorname{diag}(\lambda_1, \ldots, \lambda_n)$.

Proof If we consider any two eigenvectors $\mathbf{u}_i$ and $\mathbf{u}_j$ then we know that

$$0 = \mathbf{u}_i' \left(\mathbf{A}\mathbf{u}_j\right) - \left(\mathbf{A}\mathbf{u}_i\right)' \mathbf{u}_j = \mathbf{u}_i'\mathbf{A}\mathbf{u}_j - \mathbf{u}_j'\mathbf{A}\mathbf{u}_i = \lambda_j\mathbf{u}_i'\mathbf{u}_j - \lambda_i\mathbf{u}_j'\mathbf{u}_i = \left(\lambda_j - \lambda_i\right)\mathbf{u}_i'\mathbf{u}_j\,,$$

where we exploit the symmetry of $\mathbf{A}$ and equation (A.28). Thus any two eigenvectors $\mathbf{u}_i, \mathbf{u}_j$ with different eigenvalues λ_i, λ_j are orthogonal. If $\mathbf{u}_{i_1}, \ldots, \mathbf{u}_{i_l}$ are l eigenvectors with the same eigenvalue λ then $\sum_{j=1}^{l} \alpha_l \mathbf{u}_{i_j}$ is also an eigenvector with the eigenvalue λ for any $\alpha_1, \ldots, \alpha_l$. This allows us to apply the Gram-Schmidt orthogonalization to all eigenvectors $\mathbf{u}_i$ with equal eigenvalues. Hence we can assume that all eigenvectors are orthogonal. Moreover, if $\mathbf{u}_i$ is an eigenvector then $\beta\mathbf{u}_i$ is also an eigenvector with the same eigenvalue. Thus, without loss of generality, we assume that $\|\mathbf{u}_i\| = 1$ for all i. Let us arrange all n eigenvectors of unit length columnwise in an $n \times n$ matrix $\mathbf{U} = (\mathbf{u}_1, \ldots, \mathbf{u}_n)$ in order of increasing eigenvalues λ_i. By construction this matrix has the property that $\mathbf{U}'\mathbf{U} = \mathbf{I}$. By virtue of equation (A.28) we have

$$\mathbf{A}\mathbf{U} = \mathbf{U}\boldsymbol{\Lambda}\,, \tag{A.30}$$

where $\boldsymbol{\Lambda} = \operatorname{diag}(\lambda_1, \ldots, \lambda_n)$. Since $\mathbf{U}$ is a square matrix Theorem A.76 shows that $\mathbf{U}\mathbf{U}' = \mathbf{I}$. Multiplying equation (A.30) by $\mathbf{U}'$ from the right results in $\mathbf{A} = \mathbf{U}\boldsymbol{\Lambda}\mathbf{U}'$ which proves the theorem. ■

Theorem A.84 (Trace and Determinant) *For any symmetric $n \times n$ matrix $\mathbf{A}$ with eigenvalues $\lambda_1, \ldots, \lambda_n$,*

$$|\mathbf{A}| = \prod_{i=1}^{n} \lambda_i\,, \qquad \operatorname{tr}(\mathbf{A}) = \sum_{i=1}^{n} \lambda_i\,.$$

Proof Consider the spectral decomposition of $\mathbf{A}$, i.e., $\mathbf{A} = \mathbf{U}\boldsymbol{\Lambda}\mathbf{U}'$. Using Theorem A.67 and $\mathbf{U}'\mathbf{U} = \mathbf{I}$ gives

$$|\mathbf{A}| = \left|\mathbf{U}\boldsymbol{\Lambda}\mathbf{U}'\right| = |\mathbf{U}| \cdot |\boldsymbol{\Lambda}| \cdot \left|\mathbf{U}'\right| = \left|\mathbf{U}'\right| \cdot |\mathbf{U}| \cdot |\boldsymbol{\Lambda}| = \left|\mathbf{U}'\mathbf{U}\right| \cdot |\boldsymbol{\Lambda}| = |\boldsymbol{\Lambda}|\,.$$

The first results follows by $|\mathbf{A}| = |\mathrm{diag}(\lambda_1, \ldots, \lambda_n)| = \prod_{i=1}^{n} \lambda_i$. The second result follows from the following argument

$$\mathrm{tr}(\mathbf{A}) = \mathrm{tr}\left(\mathbf{U}\boldsymbol{\Lambda}\mathbf{U}'\right) = \mathrm{tr}\left(\boldsymbol{\Lambda}\mathbf{U}'\mathbf{U}\right) = \mathrm{tr}(\boldsymbol{\Lambda}) = \sum_{i=1}^{n} \lambda_i ,$$

where we use Theorem A.74 in the second step. ■

Theorem A.85 (Eigenvalues and positive semidefiniteness) *A symmetric $n \times n$ matrix $\mathbf{A}$ is positive definite (positive semidefinite) if and only if all n eigenvalues λ_i of $\mathbf{A}$ are strictly positive (non-negative).*

Proof Let us assume the matrix $\mathbf{A}$ is positive definite, that is, for all $\mathbf{c} \in \mathbb{R}^n$, $\mathbf{c} \neq \mathbf{0}$ we know that $\mathbf{c}'\mathbf{A}\mathbf{c} > 0$. By Theorem A.83 we have $\mathbf{A} = \mathbf{U}\boldsymbol{\Lambda}\mathbf{U}'$ for $\mathbf{U} = (\mathbf{u}_1, \ldots, \mathbf{u}_n)$, $\mathbf{U}'\mathbf{U} = \mathbf{U}\mathbf{U}' = \mathbf{I}$ and $\boldsymbol{\Lambda} = \mathrm{diag}(\lambda_1, \ldots, \lambda_n)$. Using $\mathbf{c} = \mathbf{u}_i$ we obtain $\mathbf{u}_i'\mathbf{U}\boldsymbol{\Lambda}\mathbf{U}'\mathbf{u}_i = \lambda_i \|\mathbf{u}_i\|^2 = \lambda_i > 0$ for all $i \in \{1, \ldots, n\}$.

Now let us assume that all n eigenvalues λ_i are strictly positive. Then, for all vectors $\mathbf{c} \in \mathbb{R}^n$, $\mathbf{c} \neq \mathbf{0}$,

$$\mathbf{c}'\mathbf{A}\mathbf{c} = \mathbf{c}'\mathbf{U}\boldsymbol{\Lambda}\mathbf{U}'\mathbf{c} = \boldsymbol{\alpha}'\boldsymbol{\Lambda}\boldsymbol{\alpha} = \sum_{i=1}^{n} \lambda_i \alpha_i^2 > 0 .$$

Note that $\mathbf{U}'\mathbf{c} = \mathbf{0} \Leftrightarrow \mathbf{c} = \mathbf{0}$ because $\left\|\mathbf{U}'\mathbf{c}\right\|^2 = \mathbf{c}'\mathbf{U}\mathbf{U}'\mathbf{c} = \|\mathbf{c}\|^2$. The proof for the case of positive semidefiniteness follows from the same argument. ■

Quadratic forms

Theorem A.86 (Sum of quadratic forms) *Let $\mathbf{A} \in \mathbb{R}^{n\times n}$ and $\mathbf{B} \in \mathbb{R}^{m\times m}$ be two symmetric, positive semidefinite matrices. Then, for any matrix $\mathbf{X} \in \mathbb{R}^{n\times r}$, $\mathbf{Y} \in \mathbb{R}^{m\times r}$, $\mathbf{a} \in \mathbb{R}^n$ and $\mathbf{b} \in \mathbb{R}^m$, we have that*

$$D(\boldsymbol{\mu}) = (\mathbf{a} - \mathbf{X}\boldsymbol{\mu})'\mathbf{A}(\mathbf{a} - \mathbf{X}\boldsymbol{\mu}) + (\mathbf{b} - \mathbf{Y}\boldsymbol{\mu})'\mathbf{B}(\mathbf{b} - \mathbf{Y}\boldsymbol{\mu}) , \tag{A.31}$$

can be written as

$$D(\boldsymbol{\mu}) = (\boldsymbol{\mu} - \mathbf{c})'\mathbf{C}(\boldsymbol{\mu} - \mathbf{c}) + d \tag{A.32}$$

where

$$\mathbf{C} = \mathbf{X}'\mathbf{A}\mathbf{X} + \mathbf{Y}'\mathbf{B}\mathbf{Y} , \qquad d = \mathbf{a}'\mathbf{A}\mathbf{a} + \mathbf{b}'\mathbf{B}\mathbf{b} - \mathbf{c}'\mathbf{C}\mathbf{c} ,$$

and $\mathbf{c} \in \mathbb{R}^r$ *satisfies*

$$\mathbf{Cc} = \mathbf{X}'\mathbf{Aa} + \mathbf{Y}'\mathbf{Bb}\,.$$

In the special case of $\mathbf{C} > 0$ *and* $\mathbf{Y} = \mathbf{I}$ *we can write* $d \in \mathbb{R}$ *as*

$$d = (\mathbf{a} - \mathbf{Xb})' \left(\mathbf{A}^{-1} + \mathbf{XB}^{-1}\mathbf{X}'\right)^{-1} (\mathbf{a} - \mathbf{Xb})\,. \tag{A.33}$$

Proof The lengthy proof of the existence of $\mathbf{c} \in \mathbb{R}^r$ has been omitted and can be found in Kockelkorn (2000). Let us start by proving equation (A.32). Expanding (A.31) we obtain

$$\begin{aligned}
D(\boldsymbol{\mu}) &= \mathbf{a}'\mathbf{Aa} - 2\mathbf{a}'\mathbf{AX}\boldsymbol{\mu} + \boldsymbol{\mu}'\mathbf{X}'\mathbf{AX}\boldsymbol{\mu} + \boldsymbol{\mu}'\mathbf{Y}'\mathbf{BY}\boldsymbol{\mu} - 2\mathbf{b}'\mathbf{BY}\boldsymbol{\mu} + \mathbf{b}'\mathbf{Yb} \\
&= \mathbf{a}'\mathbf{Aa} - 2\boldsymbol{\mu}'\left(\mathbf{X}'\mathbf{Aa} + \mathbf{Y}'\mathbf{Bb}\right) + \boldsymbol{\mu}'\left(\mathbf{X}'\mathbf{AX} + \mathbf{Y}'\mathbf{BY}\right)\boldsymbol{\mu} + \mathbf{b}'\mathbf{Bb} \\
&= \mathbf{a}'\mathbf{Aa} - 2\boldsymbol{\mu}'\mathbf{Cc} + \boldsymbol{\mu}'\mathbf{C}\boldsymbol{\mu} + \mathbf{b}'\mathbf{Bb} \\
&= (\boldsymbol{\mu} - \mathbf{c})'\mathbf{C}(\boldsymbol{\mu} - \mathbf{c}) - \mathbf{c}'\mathbf{Cc} + \mathbf{a}'\mathbf{Aa} + \mathbf{b}'\mathbf{Bb}\,,
\end{aligned}$$

where we used the symmetry of $\mathbf{A}$ and $\mathbf{B}$ several times. This shows equation (A.32). In the special case of $\mathbf{Y} = \mathbf{I}$ we obtain

$$\mathbf{C} = \mathbf{X}'\mathbf{AX} + \mathbf{B}\,. \tag{A.34}$$

Let us introduce the following abbreviation $\mathbf{u} \overset{\text{def}}{=} \mathbf{a} - \mathbf{Xb} \Leftrightarrow \mathbf{a} = \mathbf{u} + \mathbf{Xb}$. Then we know

$$\mathbf{Cc} = \mathbf{X}'\mathbf{Aa} + \mathbf{Bb} = \mathbf{X}'\mathbf{A}(\mathbf{u} + \mathbf{Xb}) + \mathbf{Bb} = \mathbf{X}'\mathbf{Au} + \mathbf{Cb}\,,$$

where we have used equation (A.34). Since $\mathbf{C} > 0$ it follows that

$$\begin{aligned}
\mathbf{c}'\mathbf{Cc} &= \mathbf{c}'\mathbf{CC}^{-1}\mathbf{Cc} = \left(\mathbf{X}'\mathbf{Au} + \mathbf{Cb}\right)'\mathbf{C}^{-1}\left(\mathbf{X}'\mathbf{Au} + \mathbf{Cb}\right) \\
&= \mathbf{u}'\mathbf{AXC}^{-1}\mathbf{X}'\mathbf{Au} + 2\mathbf{u}'\mathbf{AXb} + \mathbf{b}'\mathbf{Cb}\,.
\end{aligned} \tag{A.35}$$

Further, we have

$$\mathbf{a}'\mathbf{Aa} = (\mathbf{u} + \mathbf{Xb})'\mathbf{A}(\mathbf{u} + \mathbf{Xb}) = \mathbf{u}'\mathbf{Au} + 2\mathbf{u}'\mathbf{AXb} + \mathbf{b}'\mathbf{X}'\mathbf{AXb}\,. \tag{A.36}$$

Combining equations (A.36), (A.35) and (A.34) thus yields

$$\begin{aligned}
\mathbf{a}'\mathbf{Aa} + \mathbf{b}'\mathbf{Bb} - \mathbf{c}'\mathbf{Cc} &= \mathbf{u}'\mathbf{Au} - \mathbf{u}'\mathbf{AXC}^{-1}\mathbf{X}'\mathbf{Au} + \mathbf{b}'\mathbf{X}'\mathbf{AXb} + \mathbf{b}'\mathbf{Bb} - \mathbf{b}'\mathbf{Cb} \\
&= \mathbf{u}'\mathbf{Au} - \mathbf{u}'\mathbf{AXC}^{-1}\mathbf{X}'\mathbf{Au} + \mathbf{b}'\left(\mathbf{X}'\mathbf{AX} + \mathbf{B}\right)\mathbf{b} - \mathbf{b}'\mathbf{Cb} \\
&= \mathbf{u}'\left(\mathbf{A} - \mathbf{AXC}^{-1}\mathbf{X}'\mathbf{A}\right)\mathbf{u}\,.
\end{aligned}$$

Finally, using the Woodbury formula given in Theorem A.79 we can write $\mathbf{A} - \mathbf{A}\mathbf{X}\mathbf{C}^{-1}\mathbf{X}'\mathbf{A} = \left(\left(\mathbf{A} - \mathbf{A}\mathbf{X}\mathbf{C}^{-1}\mathbf{X}'\mathbf{A}\right)^{-1}\right)^{-1}$ as

$$\begin{aligned}\left(\mathbf{A} - (\mathbf{A}\mathbf{X})\left(\mathbf{C}^{-1}\mathbf{X}'\mathbf{A}\right)\right)^{-1} &= \mathbf{A}^{-1} + \mathbf{X}\left(\mathbf{I} - \mathbf{C}^{-1}\mathbf{X}'\mathbf{A}\mathbf{X}\right)^{-1}\mathbf{C}^{-1}\mathbf{X}' \\ &= \mathbf{A}^{-1} + \mathbf{X}\left(\mathbf{C} - \mathbf{X}'\mathbf{A}\mathbf{X}\right)^{-1}\mathbf{X}' = \mathbf{A}^{-1} + \mathbf{X}\mathbf{B}^{-1}\mathbf{X}'.\end{aligned}$$

Putting all these results together proves equation (A.33). ■

Theorem A.87 (Rayleigh coefficient) *Let* $\mathbf{A} \in \mathbb{R}^{n\times n}$ *be a symmetric, positive semidefinite matrix with eigenvalues* $\lambda_1 \geq \cdots \geq \lambda_n \geq 0$. *Then, for all* $\mathbf{x} \in \mathbb{R}^n$,

$$\lambda_n \leq \frac{\mathbf{x}'\mathbf{A}\mathbf{x}}{\mathbf{x}'\mathbf{x}} \leq \lambda_1,$$

where the λ_i *are the eigenvalues of* $\mathbf{A}$ *sorted in decreasing order. Further, the right hand side becomes an equality if* $\mathbf{x}$ *is the eigenvector* $\mathbf{u}_1$ *of* $\mathbf{A}$ *corresponding to the largest eigenvalue* λ_1.

Proof According to Theorem A.83 we know that each symmetric $\mathbf{A}$ can be written as $\mathbf{A} = \mathbf{U}\mathbf{\Lambda}\mathbf{U}'$ where $\mathbf{U}'\mathbf{U} = \mathbf{U}\mathbf{U}' = \mathbf{I}$ and $\mathbf{\Lambda} = \operatorname{diag}(\lambda_1, \ldots, \lambda_n)$. For a given $\mathbf{x} \in \mathbb{R}^n$ let us consider $\mathbf{y} = \mathbf{U}'\mathbf{x}$. Then we know that

$$\frac{\mathbf{x}'\mathbf{A}\mathbf{x}}{\mathbf{x}'\mathbf{x}} = \frac{\mathbf{x}'\mathbf{U}\mathbf{\Lambda}\mathbf{U}'\mathbf{x}}{\mathbf{x}'\mathbf{U}\mathbf{U}'\mathbf{x}} = \frac{\mathbf{y}'\mathbf{\Lambda}\mathbf{y}}{\mathbf{y}'\mathbf{y}} = \frac{\sum_{i=1}^{n}\lambda_i y_i^2}{\sum y_i^2}. \tag{A.37}$$

Since $\lambda_n \leq \lambda_i$ and $\lambda_i \leq \lambda_1$ for all $i \in \{1, \ldots, n\}$ we know that

$$\sum_{i=1}^{n}\lambda_n y_i^2 \leq \sum_{i=1}^{n}\lambda_i y_i^2 \leq \sum_{i=1}^{n}\lambda_1 y_i^2. \tag{A.38}$$

The results follows directly from equation (A.37). Moreover, if $y_1 = 1$ and $y_i = 0$ for all $i \in \{2, \ldots, n\}$ then we attain an equality in (A.38). This is the case only for $\mathbf{x}$ being the first column of $\mathbf{U}$, i.e., the eigenvector $\mathbf{u}_1$ corresponding to the largest eigenvalue λ_1. ■

Theorem A.88 (Generalized Rayleigh coefficient) *Let* $\mathbf{A} \in \mathbb{R}^{n\times n}$ *be a symmetric, positive semidefinite matrix and* $\mathbf{B} = \mathbf{C}'\mathbf{C}$ *be a positive definite* $n \times n$ *matrix.*

Then, for all $\mathbf{x} \in \mathbb{R}^n$,

$$\lambda_n \leq \frac{\mathbf{x}'\mathbf{A}\mathbf{x}}{\mathbf{x}'\mathbf{B}\mathbf{x}} \leq \lambda_1 , \tag{A.39}$$

where the λ_i *are the eigenvalues of* $(\mathbf{C}^{-1})'\mathbf{A}\mathbf{C}^{-1}$ *sorted in decreasing order. Further, the right hand side becomes an equality if* $\mathbf{x} = \mathbf{C}^{-1}\mathbf{u}_1$ *where* $\mathbf{u}_1$ *is the eigenvector of* $(\mathbf{C}^{-1})'\mathbf{A}\mathbf{C}^{-1}$ *corresponding to the largest eigenvalue* λ_1*. In the special case of* $\mathbf{A} = \mathbf{a}\mathbf{a}'$ *we know that* $\lambda_1 = \mathbf{a}'\mathbf{B}^{-1}\mathbf{a}$ *and that the maximizer of (A.39) is given by* $\mathbf{x} = \mathbf{B}^{-1}\mathbf{a}$.

Proof Put $\mathbf{z} = \mathbf{C}\mathbf{x}$. Then for all $\mathbf{x} \in \mathbb{R}^n$

$$\frac{\mathbf{x}'\mathbf{A}\mathbf{x}}{\mathbf{x}'\mathbf{B}\mathbf{x}} = \frac{\mathbf{x}'\mathbf{A}\mathbf{x}}{\mathbf{x}'\mathbf{C}'\mathbf{C}\mathbf{x}} = \frac{\mathbf{z}'\left(\mathbf{C}^{-1}\right)'\mathbf{A}\mathbf{C}^{-1}\mathbf{z}}{\mathbf{z}'\mathbf{z}} ,$$

and therefore the first part follows from Theorem A.87. In the special case of $\mathbf{A} = \mathbf{a}\mathbf{a}'$ we obtain $(\mathbf{C}^{-1})'\mathbf{A}\mathbf{C}^{-1} = (\mathbf{C}^{-1})'\mathbf{a}\mathbf{a}'\mathbf{C}^{-1} = \mathbf{v}\mathbf{v}'$ where $\mathbf{v} = (\mathbf{C}^{-1})'\mathbf{a}$. The matrix $\mathbf{v}\mathbf{v}'$ has exactly one eigenvector $\mathbf{v}$ to the eigenvalue $\|\mathbf{v}\|^2$ because $(\mathbf{v}\mathbf{v}')\mathbf{v} = \mathbf{v}(\mathbf{v}'\mathbf{v}) = \|\mathbf{v}\|^2 \cdot \mathbf{v}$. Since $\|\mathbf{v}\|^2 = \mathbf{a}'\mathbf{C}^{-1}(\mathbf{C}^{-1})'\mathbf{a} = \mathbf{a}'(\mathbf{C}'\mathbf{C})^{-1}\mathbf{a} = \mathbf{a}'\mathbf{B}^{-1}\mathbf{a}$ and $\mathbf{x} = \mathbf{C}^{-1}\mathbf{v} = \mathbf{C}^{-1}(\mathbf{C}^{-1})'\mathbf{a} = (\mathbf{C}'\mathbf{C})^{-1}\mathbf{a} = \mathbf{B}^{-1}\mathbf{a}$ the special case is proved. ∎

Kronecker Product

Definition A.89 (Kronecker product) *Given an* $n \times m$ *and* $q \times r$ *matrix* $\mathbf{A}$ *and* $\mathbf{B}$*, respectively, the* Kronecker product $\mathbf{A} \otimes \mathbf{B}$ *is the* $nq \times mr$ *matrix*

$$\mathbf{A} \otimes \mathbf{B} \stackrel{\text{def}}{=} \begin{pmatrix} a_{11}\mathbf{B} & \cdots & a_{1m}\mathbf{B} \\ \vdots & \ddots & \vdots \\ a_{n1}\mathbf{B} & \cdots & a_{nm}\mathbf{B} \end{pmatrix} .$$

Theorem A.90 (Matrix product of Kronecker products) *For all* $m, n, q, r, s, t \in \mathbb{N}$ *and any* $n \times m$ *matrix* $\mathbf{A}$*,* $r \times q$ *matrix* $\mathbf{B}$*,* $m \times s$ *matrix* $\mathbf{C}$ *and* $q \times t$ *matrix* $\mathbf{D}$*,*

$$(\mathbf{A} \otimes \mathbf{B})(\mathbf{C} \otimes \mathbf{D}) = (\mathbf{A}\mathbf{C}) \otimes (\mathbf{B}\mathbf{D}) .$$

Proof Let us represent the matrices $\mathbf{A}$ and $\mathbf{B}$ in terms of their rows and $\mathbf{C}$ and $\mathbf{D}$ in terms of their columns,

$$\begin{aligned} \mathbf{A} &= \left(\mathbf{a}_1'; \ldots; \mathbf{a}_n'\right), \quad \mathbf{a}_i \in \mathbb{R}^m, \quad & \mathbf{B} &= \left(\mathbf{b}_1'; \ldots; \mathbf{b}_r'\right), \quad \mathbf{b}_j \in \mathbb{R}^q, \\ \mathbf{C} &= \left(\mathbf{c}_1, \ldots, \mathbf{c}_s\right), \quad \mathbf{c}_u \in \mathbb{R}^m, \quad & \mathbf{D} &= \left(\mathbf{d}_1, \ldots, \mathbf{d}_t\right), \quad \mathbf{d}_v \in \mathbb{R}^q . \end{aligned}$$

and $i \in \{1, \ldots, n\}$, $j \in \{1, \ldots, r\}$, $u \in \{1, \ldots, s\}$ and $v \in \{1, \ldots, t\}$. Let $i * j \stackrel{\text{def}}{=} (i-1) \cdot r + j$ and $u * v \stackrel{\text{def}}{=} (u-1) \cdot t + v$. Consider the element in the $i * j$–th row and $u * v$–th column of $(\mathbf{A} \otimes \mathbf{B})(\mathbf{C} \otimes \mathbf{D})$

$$\begin{aligned}
((\mathbf{A} \otimes \mathbf{B})(\mathbf{C} \otimes \mathbf{D}))_{i*j,u*v} &= \left(a_{i1}\mathbf{b}'_j, \ldots, a_{im}\mathbf{b}'_j\right)\left(c_{1u}\mathbf{d}'_v, \ldots, c_{mu}\mathbf{d}'_v\right)' \\
&= \sum_{l=1}^{m} a_{il}c_{lu}\mathbf{b}'_j\mathbf{d}_v \\
&= \mathbf{a}'_i\mathbf{c}_u \cdot \mathbf{b}'_j\mathbf{d}_v \\
&= (\mathbf{AC})_{iu} \cdot (\mathbf{BD})_{jv} \\
&= ((\mathbf{AC}) \otimes (\mathbf{BD}))_{i*j,u*v} ,
\end{aligned}$$

where the last step follows from Definition A.89. ■

Theorem A.91 (Eigenvalues of Kronecker products) *Let* $\mathbf{A}$ *and* $\mathbf{B}$ *be symmetric* $n \times n$ *and* $m \times m$ *matrices, respectively. Then the eigenvalues of the matrix* $\mathbf{A} \otimes \mathbf{B}$ *are all products of pairs of eigenvalues of* $\mathbf{A}$ *and* $\mathbf{B}$.

Proof Let $\{(\mathbf{u}_1, \lambda_1), \ldots, (\mathbf{u}_n, \lambda_n)\}$ and $\{(\mathbf{v}_1, \omega_1), \ldots, (\mathbf{v}_m, \omega_m)\}$ be the eigensystems of $\mathbf{A}$ and $\mathbf{B}$ where we take the liberty of having a few λ_i and ω_i zero (see Theorem A.83). Then, for all $i \in \{1, \ldots, n\}$ and $j \in \{1, \ldots, m\}$

$$\begin{aligned}
(\mathbf{A} \otimes \mathbf{B})\left(\mathbf{u}_i \otimes \mathbf{v}_j\right) &= (\mathbf{A}\mathbf{u}_i) \otimes \left(\mathbf{B}\mathbf{v}_j\right) = (\lambda_i\mathbf{u}_i) \otimes \left(\omega_j\mathbf{v}_j\right) \\
&= \left(\lambda_i\omega_j\right)\left(\mathbf{u}_i \otimes \mathbf{v}_j\right) ,
\end{aligned}$$

where we used Theorem A.90. Further,

$$\left\|\mathbf{u}_i \otimes \mathbf{v}_j\right\|^2 = \left(\mathbf{u}_i \otimes \mathbf{v}_j\right)'\left(\mathbf{u}_i \otimes \mathbf{v}_j\right) = \|\mathbf{u}_i\|^2 \cdot \left\|\mathbf{v}_j\right\|^2 = 1$$

which shows that $\mathbf{A} \otimes \mathbf{B}$ has at least mn eigenvectors with eigenvalues given by the product of all pairs of eigenvalues of $\mathbf{A}$ and $\mathbf{B}$. Since all eigenvectors are orthogonal to each other $\mathbf{A} \otimes \mathbf{B} \in \mathbb{R}^{mn \times mn}$ has at most mn eigenvectors. ■

Corollary A.92 (Positive definiteness of Kronecker products) *Let* $\mathbf{A}$ *and* $\mathbf{B}$ *be two positive definite (positive semidefinite) matrices. Then* $\mathbf{A} \otimes \mathbf{B}$ *is positive definite (positive semidefinite).*

Proof If $\mathbf{A}$ and $\mathbf{B}$ are positive definite then all eigenvalues of $\mathbf{A}$ and $\mathbf{B}$ are strictly positive (see Theorem A.85). Hence, by Theorem A.91 all eigenvalues of $\mathbf{A} \otimes \mathbf{B}$

are strictly positive and thus $\mathbf{A} \otimes \mathbf{B}$ is positive definite by Theorem A.85. The case of positive semidefinite matrices proceeds similarly. ■

Derivatives of Matrices

Definition A.93 (Derivative of a vector-valued function) *Let $\boldsymbol{\phi} : \mathbb{R}^m \to \mathbb{R}^n$ be a fixed function. Then the $m \times n$ matrix $\frac{\partial \boldsymbol{\phi}(\mathbf{x})}{\partial \mathbf{x}}$ of derivatives is defined by*

$$\frac{\partial \boldsymbol{\phi}(\mathbf{x})}{\partial \mathbf{x}} \stackrel{\text{def}}{=} \left(\frac{\partial \phi_j(\mathbf{x})}{\partial x_i} \right)_{i,j=1}^{m,n} = \begin{pmatrix} \frac{\partial \phi_1(\mathbf{x})}{\partial x_1} & \cdots & \frac{\partial \phi_n(\mathbf{x})}{\partial x_1} \\ \vdots & \ddots & \vdots \\ \frac{\partial \phi_1(\mathbf{x})}{\partial x_m} & \cdots & \frac{\partial \phi_n(\mathbf{x})}{\partial x_m} \end{pmatrix}.$$

Theorem A.94 (Derivative of a linear function) *Let $\boldsymbol{\phi} : \mathbb{R}^m \to \mathbb{R}^n$ be a linear function, i.e., $\boldsymbol{\phi}(\mathbf{x}) = \mathbf{A}\mathbf{x} + \mathbf{b}$ for a fixed matrix $\mathbf{A} \in \mathbb{R}^{n \times m}$ and vector $\mathbf{b} \in \mathbb{R}^n$. Then*

$$\frac{\partial \boldsymbol{\phi}(\mathbf{x})}{\partial \mathbf{x}} = \mathbf{A}'.$$

Proof For any $i \in \{1, \ldots, m\}$ and $j \in \{1, \ldots, n\}$ let us consider the i, j–th element of $\frac{\partial \boldsymbol{\phi}(\mathbf{x})}{\partial \mathbf{x}}$. We have $\frac{\partial \phi_j(\mathbf{x})}{\partial x_i} = \frac{\sum_{l=1}^{m} \mathbf{A}_{jl} x_l}{\partial x_i} = \mathbf{A}_{ji}$ which proves the theorem. ■

Theorem A.95 (Derivative of a quadratic form) *Let $\phi : \mathbb{R}^n \to \mathbb{R}$ be a quadratic form, i.e., $\phi(\mathbf{x}) = \mathbf{x}'\mathbf{A}\mathbf{x}$ for a fixed symmetric matrix $\mathbf{A} \in \mathbb{R}^{n \times n}$. Then*

$$\frac{\partial \phi(\mathbf{x})}{\partial \mathbf{x}} = 2\mathbf{A}\mathbf{x}.$$

Proof For any $i \in \{1, \ldots, n\}$ let us consider the ith element of $\frac{\partial \phi(\mathbf{x})}{\partial \mathbf{x}}$. We have

$$\frac{\partial \phi(\mathbf{x})}{\partial x_i} = \frac{\sum_{r=1}^{n} \sum_{s=1}^{n} x_r \mathbf{A}_{rs} x_s}{\partial x_i} = \sum_{\substack{s=1 \\ s \neq i}}^{n} \mathbf{A}_{is} x_s + \sum_{\substack{r=1 \\ r \neq i}}^{n} \mathbf{A}_{ri} x_r + 2 x_i \mathbf{A}_{ii} = \mathbf{A}\mathbf{x},$$

where the last equality follows from the symmetry of $\mathbf{A}$. ■

Theorem A.96 (Derivative of the inverse) *Let* $\mathbf{A}: \mathbb{R} \to \mathbb{R}^{n\times n}$ *be a matrix-valued function. Then*

$$\frac{\partial (\mathbf{A}(x))^{-1}}{\partial x} = -(\mathbf{A}(x))^{-1} \frac{\partial \mathbf{A}(x)}{\partial x} (\mathbf{A}(x))^{-1} .$$

Proof First note that, for all $x \in \mathbb{R}$, by definition $\mathbf{A}(x)(\mathbf{A}(x))^{-1} = \mathbf{I}$. Since $\mathbf{I}$ does not depend on x we have

$$\mathbf{0} = \frac{\partial \mathbf{I}}{\partial x} = \frac{\partial \mathbf{A}(x)(\mathbf{A}(x))^{-1}}{\partial x} = \frac{\partial \mathbf{A}(x)}{\partial x}(\mathbf{A}(x))^{-1} + \mathbf{A}(x)\frac{\partial (\mathbf{A}(x))^{-1}}{\partial x},$$

where the second part follows by component-wise application of the product rule of differentiation. The result follows by rearranging the terms. ∎

Theorem A.97 (Derivative of the log-determinant) *For any symmetric* $n \times n$ *matrix* $\mathbf{A}$,

$$\frac{\partial \ln(|\mathbf{A}|)}{\partial \mathbf{A}} = \mathbf{A}^{-1} .$$

Proof Let us consider the i, j–th element of the $n \times n$ matrix of derivatives, i.e., $\partial \ln(|\mathbf{A}|)/\partial \mathbf{A}_{ij}$. By the chain rule of differentiation and Definition A.64 we know

$$\begin{aligned} \frac{\partial \ln(|\mathbf{A}|)}{\partial \mathbf{A}_{ij}} &= \frac{d \ln(|\mathbf{A}|)}{d|\mathbf{A}|} \cdot \frac{\partial |\mathbf{A}|}{\partial \mathbf{A}_{ij}} = \frac{1}{|\mathbf{A}|} \cdot \frac{\partial \left(\sum_{l=1}^{n} \mathbf{A}_{lj} \cdot \left|\mathbf{A}_{[lj]}\right| \cdot (-1)^{l+j}\right)}{\partial \mathbf{A}_{ij}} \\ &= \frac{1}{|\mathbf{A}|} \cdot \left|\mathbf{A}_{[ij]}\right| \cdot (-1)^{i+j} , \end{aligned}$$

because all the $\left|\mathbf{A}_{[lj]}\right|$ involve determinants of matrices which do not contain $\mathbf{A}_{ij}$. Exploiting the symmetry of $\mathbf{A}$ and Theorem A.78 proves the theorem. ∎

The following theorem is given without proof; the interested reader is referred to Magnus and Neudecker (1999).

Theorem A.98 (Derivative of a quadratic form) *For any non-singular* $n \times n$ *matrix* $\mathbf{A}$ *and* $\mathbf{a}, \mathbf{b} \in \mathbb{R}^n$,

$$\frac{\partial \mathbf{a}'\mathbf{A}^{-1}\mathbf{b}}{\partial \mathbf{A}} = -\left(\mathbf{A}^{-1}\right)' \mathbf{a}\mathbf{b}' \left(\mathbf{A}^{-1}\right)' .$$

A.4 Ill-Posed Problems

The concept of well and ill-posed problems was introduced in Hadamard (1902) in an attempt to clarify what types of boundary conditions are most natural for various types of differential equations. The solution to any quantitative problem usually ends in finding the "solution" $\mathbf{y}$ from given "initial data" $\mathbf{x}$,

$$\mathbf{y} = S(\mathbf{x}) \,. \tag{A.40}$$

We shall consider $\mathbf{x}$ and $\mathbf{y}$ as elements of metric spaces $\mathcal{X}$ and $\mathcal{Y}$ with the metrics $\rho_{\mathcal{X}}$ and $\rho_{\mathcal{Y}}$. The metric is usually determined by the formulation of the problem. Suppose that the concept of solution is defined by equation (A.40).

Definition A.99 (Stable solution) *The problem of determining the solution* $\mathbf{y} = S(\mathbf{x})$ *in the space of* $\mathcal{Y}$ *from the initial data* $\mathbf{x} \in \mathcal{X}$ *is said to be* stable on the spaces $(\mathcal{Y}, \mathcal{X})$ *if, for every* $\varepsilon > 0$, *there exists a positive number* $\delta(\varepsilon) > 0$ *such that*

$$\forall \mathbf{x}_1, \mathbf{x}_2 \in \mathcal{X}: \qquad \rho_{\mathcal{X}}(\mathbf{x}_1, \mathbf{x}_2) \leq \delta(\varepsilon) \Rightarrow \rho_{\mathcal{Y}}(S(\mathbf{x}_1), S(\mathbf{x}_2)) \leq \varepsilon \,.$$

Definition A.100 (Well-posed and ill-posed problems) *The problem of determining the solution* $\mathbf{y} = S(\mathbf{x})$ *in the space of* $\mathcal{Y}$ *from the initial data* $\mathbf{x} \in \mathcal{X}$ *is said to be* well-posed on the spaces $(\mathcal{Y}, \mathcal{X})$ *if*

1. *for every element* $\mathbf{x} \in \mathcal{X}$ *there exists a solution* $\mathbf{y}$ *in the space* $\mathcal{Y}$.
2. *the solution* $\mathbf{y} = S(\mathbf{x})$ *is unique.*
3. *the problem is stable on the spaces* $(\mathcal{Y}, \mathcal{X})$.

Problems that do not satisfy these conditions are said to be ill-posed.

A.5 Basic Inequalities

A.5.1 General (In)equalities

This section collects some general results which are frequently used in the main body. Each theorem is followed by its proof.

Theorem A.101 (Lower bound for the exponential) *For all $x \in \mathbb{R}$ we have*

$$1 + x \leq \exp(x) ,$$

with equality if and only if $x = 0$.

Proof Consider the function $f(x) = 1 + x - \exp(x)$. The first and second derivatives of this function are $\frac{df(x)}{dx} = 1 - \exp(x)$ and $\frac{d^2 f(x)}{dx^2} = -\exp(x)$. Hence this function has a maximum at $x^* = 0$ which implies that $f(x) \leq f(0) = 0 \Leftrightarrow 1 + x \leq \exp(x)$. ■

Theorem A.102 (Euler's inequality) *For all $x > 0$ and all $a \in \mathbb{R}$, $a \geq 0$*

$$\left(1 + \frac{a}{x}\right)^x < \exp(a) .$$

Proof From Theorem A.101 we know that $1 + a/x < \exp(a/x)$, because, by assumption, $a \neq 0$. Since $x > 0$ this implies $(1 + a/x)^x < (\exp(a/x))^x = \exp(a)$ which proves the theorem. ■

Theorem A.103 (Binomial theorem) *For all $x \in \mathbb{R}$ and all $d \in \mathbb{N}$ we have*

$$(1 + x)^d = \sum_{i=0}^{d} \binom{d}{i} x^i .$$

Proof We proof the theorem by induction over d. The theorem is trivially true for all $d = 0$ and all $x \in \mathbb{R}$. Suppose the theorem is true for some $d \in \mathbb{N}$. Then

$$\begin{aligned}
(1 + x)^{d+1} &= (1 + x) \sum_{i=0}^{d} \binom{d}{i} x^i = \sum_{i=0}^{d} \binom{d}{i} x^i + \sum_{i=1}^{d+1} \binom{d}{i-1} x^i \\
&= \binom{d}{0} x^0 + \sum_{i=1}^{d} \left(\binom{d}{i} + \binom{d}{i-1} \right) x^i + \binom{d}{d} x^{d+1} \\
&= \binom{d+1}{0} x^0 + \sum_{i=1}^{d} \binom{d+1}{i} x^i + \binom{d+1}{d+1} x^{d+1} \\
&= \sum_{i=0}^{d+1} \binom{d+1}{i} x^i ,
\end{aligned}$$

where we have used

$$\binom{d}{i} + \binom{d}{i-1} = \binom{d+1}{i} \tag{A.41}$$

in the third line. ∎

Corollary A.104 (Binomial coefficients) *For all $a, b \in \mathbb{R}$ and all $d \in \mathbb{N}$ we have*

$$(a+b)^d = \sum_{i=0}^{d} \binom{d}{i} a^i \cdot b^{d-i} .$$

Proof Using Theorem A.103 with the factorization $(a+b)^d = (b\,(a/b+1))^d$ proves the corollary. ∎

Theorem A.105 (Upper bound for the sum of binomials) *For any $m \in \mathbb{N}$ and $d \in \{1, \ldots, m\}$ we have*

$$\sum_{i=0}^{d} \binom{m}{i} < \left(\frac{em}{d}\right)^d .$$

Proof The result follows from Theorems A.103 and A.102. Noticing $\left(\frac{m}{d}\right)^{d-i} \geq 1$ for all $i \in \{0, \ldots, d\}$ we see that

$$\begin{aligned}
\sum_{i=0}^{d} \binom{m}{i} &\leq \sum_{i=0}^{d} \binom{m}{i} \left(\frac{m}{d}\right)^{d-i} = \left(\frac{m}{d}\right)^d \sum_{i=0}^{d} \binom{m}{i} \left(\frac{d}{m}\right)^i \\
&\leq \left(\frac{m}{d}\right)^d \sum_{i=0}^{m} \binom{m}{i} \left(\frac{d}{m}\right)^i = \left(\frac{m}{d}\right)^d \left(1 + \frac{d}{m}\right)^m \\
&< \left(\frac{m}{d}\right)^d \exp(d) = \left(\frac{em}{d}\right)^d .
\end{aligned}$$

The theorem is proven. ∎

Theorem A.106 (Cauchy-Schwarz inequality (Cauchy 1821)) *For any two elements $\mathbf{x}$ and $\mathbf{y}$ of an inner product space $\mathcal{X}$ we have*

$$|\langle \mathbf{x}, \mathbf{y} \rangle| \leq \|\mathbf{x}\| \cdot \|\mathbf{y}\| .$$

Proof If $\mathbf{y} = \mathbf{0}$ then the inequality is true because both sides are zero. Assume then $\mathbf{y} \neq \mathbf{0}$. For any $c \in \mathbb{R}$ we have

$$0 \leq \langle \mathbf{x} + c\mathbf{y}, \mathbf{x} + c\mathbf{y} \rangle = \|\mathbf{x}\|^2 + 2c \langle \mathbf{x}, \mathbf{y} \rangle + c^2 \|\mathbf{y}\|^2 .$$

Now put $c = -\frac{\langle \mathbf{x}, \mathbf{y} \rangle}{\|\mathbf{y}\|^2}$ to obtain

$$0 \leq \|\mathbf{x}\|^2 - \frac{\langle \mathbf{x}, \mathbf{y} \rangle}{\|\mathbf{y}\|^2} \langle \mathbf{x}, \mathbf{y} \rangle \quad \Leftrightarrow \quad |\langle \mathbf{x}, \mathbf{y} \rangle| \leq \|\mathbf{x}\| \cdot \|\mathbf{y}\| ,$$

as $\|\mathbf{y}\|^2 > 0$ by assumption. ■

Note that the Cauchy-Schwarz inequality remains valid even if equation (A.20) is replaced by $\mathbf{y} = \mathbf{0} \Rightarrow \|\mathbf{y}\| = \mathbf{0}$.

Theorem A.107 (Union bound) *Let $X_1, \ldots, X_n \in \mathfrak{X}$ be a finite number of sets from the σ–algebra $\mathfrak{X}$. Then, for any measure $\mathbf{P}_\mathsf{X}$,*

$$\mathbf{P}_\mathsf{X}(X_1 \cup \cdots \cup X_n) \leq \sum_{i=1}^{n} \mathbf{P}_\mathsf{X}(X_i) .$$

Proof Consider two arbitrary sets $A \in \mathfrak{X}$ and $B \in \mathfrak{X}$. By definition

$$\mathbf{P}_\mathsf{X}(A \cup B) = \mathbf{P}_\mathsf{X}(A) + \mathbf{P}_\mathsf{X}(B) - \mathbf{P}_\mathsf{X}(A \cap B) \leq \mathbf{P}_\mathsf{X}(A) + \mathbf{P}_\mathsf{X}(B) .$$

Hence

$$\mathbf{P}_\mathsf{X}(X_1 \cup \cdots \cup X_n) \leq \mathbf{P}_\mathsf{X}(X_1) + \mathbf{P}_\mathsf{X}(X_2 \cup \cdots \cup X_n) \leq \cdots \leq \sum_{i=1}^{n} \mathbf{P}_\mathsf{X}(X_i) ,$$

which proves the theorem. ■

A.5.2 Large Deviation Bounds

In this subsection we present a series of theorems which aim to bound the probability that a random variable X is far from its expected value $\mathbf{E}_\mathsf{X}[\mathsf{X}]$. We will only scratch the surface of the theory of large deviation bounds; the interested reader is referred to Devroye et al. (1996), Feller (1950), Feller (1966) and Devroye and Lugosi (2001) for further details.

The following important theorem shows that, in the limit of an infinitely large sample, there is no variation in the mean of the sample. The mean value of a sequence of random variable is no longer random but is precisely given by the expectation value of each single random variable.

Theorem A.108 (Law of large numbers) *For any random variable* X *with finite expectation* $\mu = \mathbf{E}_{\mathsf{X}}\left[\mathsf{X}\right]$ *and variance* $\mathrm{Var}\left(\mathsf{X}\right)$ *we have*

$$\forall \varepsilon > 0: \qquad \lim_{n\to\infty} \mathbf{P}_{\mathsf{X}^n}\left(\left|\frac{1}{n}\sum_{i=1}^{n} \mathsf{X}_i - \mu\right| > \varepsilon\right) = 0 \tag{A.42}$$

We shall prove this theorem shortly. Now, the problem of *large deviations* is to determine how fast the convergence (A.42) happens to be. We would like to know how likely it is that a mean of n independently identically distributed (*iid*) numbers deviates from their common expectation by more than $\varepsilon > 0$. Let us start with a simple theorem bounding the tail of any positive random variable.

Theorem A.109 (Markov's inequality (Markov 1912)) *If the random variable* X *fulfills* $\mathbf{F}_{\mathsf{X}}\left(0\right) = 0$ *then, for all* $\lambda > 0$,

$$\mathbf{P}_{\mathsf{X}}\left(\mathsf{X} > \lambda \mathbf{E}_{\mathsf{X}}\left[\mathsf{X}\right]\right) < \frac{1}{\lambda}.$$

Proof By Definition A.7 we know that

$$\begin{aligned}
\mathbf{E}_{\mathsf{X}}\left[\mathsf{X}\right] &= \int_0^\infty x \, d\mathbf{F}_{\mathsf{X}}\left(x\right) > \int_{\lambda \mathbf{E}_{\mathsf{X}}\left[\mathsf{X}\right]}^\infty x \, d\mathbf{F}_{\mathsf{X}}\left(x\right) \\
&\geq \lambda \mathbf{E}_{\mathsf{X}}\left[\mathsf{X}\right] \int_{\lambda \mathbf{E}_{\mathsf{X}}\left[\mathsf{X}\right]}^\infty d\mathbf{F}_{\mathsf{X}}\left(x\right) \geq \lambda \mathbf{E}_{\mathsf{X}}\left[\mathsf{X}\right] \mathbf{P}_{\mathsf{X}}\left(\mathsf{X} > \lambda \mathbf{E}_{\mathsf{X}}\left[\mathsf{X}\right]\right).
\end{aligned}$$

Dividing both sides by $\lambda \mathbf{E}_{\mathsf{X}}\left[\mathsf{X}\right]$ (which is always positive by $\mathbf{F}_{\mathsf{X}}\left(0\right) = 0$ and the choice of λ) gives the desired result. ■

A direct consequence of this theorem is Chebyshev's inequality.

Theorem A.110 (Chebyshev's inequality (Tschebyscheff 1936)) *If* $\mathbf{E}_{\mathsf{X}}\left[\mathsf{X}^2\right]$ *exists, then for all* $\varepsilon > 0$

$$\mathbf{P}_{\mathsf{X}}\left(\left|\mathsf{X}\right| > \varepsilon\right) < \frac{\mathbf{E}_{\mathsf{X}}\left[\mathsf{X}^2\right]}{\varepsilon^2}. \tag{A.43}$$

In particular, we have for all $\varepsilon > 0$

$$\mathbf{P}_{\mathsf{X}}\left(\left|\mathsf{X} - \mathbf{E}_{\mathsf{X}}\left[\mathsf{X}\right]\right| > \varepsilon\right) < \frac{\mathrm{Var}\left(\mathsf{X}\right)}{\varepsilon^2}\,.$$

Proof Define a new random variable $\mathsf{Y} = \mathsf{X}^2$. Then $\mathbf{F}_{\mathsf{Y}}\left(0\right) = 0$, $\varepsilon^2 > 0$ and

$$\mathbf{P}_{\mathsf{X}}\left(\left|\mathsf{X}\right| > \varepsilon\right) = \mathbf{P}_{\mathsf{Y}}\left(\mathsf{Y} > \varepsilon^2\right) < \frac{\mathbf{E}_{\mathsf{Y}}\left[\mathsf{Y}\right]}{\varepsilon^2} = \frac{\mathbf{E}_{\mathsf{X}}\left[\mathsf{X}^2\right]}{\varepsilon^2}\,,$$

where the inequality follows from Theorem A.109.

Proof of Theorem A.108. Let us denote $\mu = \mathbf{E}_{\mathsf{X}}\left[\mathsf{X}\right]$. Then, by Chebyshev's inequality , for all $\varepsilon > 0$,

$$\begin{aligned}\mathbf{P}_{\mathsf{X}^n}\left(\left|\frac{1}{n}\sum_{i=1}^{n}\mathsf{X}_i - \mu\right| > \varepsilon\right) &= \mathbf{P}_{\mathsf{X}^n}\left(\left|\frac{1}{n}\sum_{i=1}^{n}\mathsf{X}_i - \mathbf{E}_{\mathsf{X}^n}\left[\frac{1}{n}\sum_{i=1}^{n}\mathsf{X}_i\right]\right| > \varepsilon\right)\\ &\leq \frac{\mathrm{Var}\left(n^{-1}\sum_{i=1}^{n}\mathsf{X}_i\right)}{\varepsilon^2}\,.\end{aligned}$$

By Corollary A.20 we know that, for n iid variables X_i, $\mathrm{Var}\left(n^{-1}\sum_{i=1}^{n}\mathsf{X}_i\right) = \frac{1}{n}\mathrm{Var}\left(\mathsf{X}\right)$ and thus, for all $\varepsilon > 0$, $\lim_{n\to\infty}\mathrm{Var}\left(n^{-1}\sum_{i=1}^{n}\mathsf{X}_i\right)\cdot\varepsilon^{-2} = 0$ whenever $\mathrm{Var}\left(\mathsf{X}\right)$ is finite. The law of large numbers is proved. ■

Although the general applicability of Chebyshev's inequality is an appealing feature the bound is, in general, very loose (see also Devroye and Lugosi (2001)). A key to obtaining tighter bounds comes through a more clever use of Markov's inequality—a technique known as *Chernoff's bounding method.* The idea is very simple: By Markov's inequality and the monotonicity of $f\left(z\right) = \exp\left(sz\right)$, for all $s > 0$, we know that, for all $\varepsilon > 0$,

$$\begin{aligned}&\mathbf{P}_{\mathsf{X}^n}\left(\frac{1}{n}\sum_{i=1}^{n}\mathsf{X}_i - \mathbf{E}_{\mathsf{X}}\left[\mathsf{X}\right] > \varepsilon\right)\\ &\quad= \mathbf{P}_{\mathsf{X}^n}\left(\exp\left(\frac{s}{n}\sum_{i=1}^{n}\left(\mathsf{X}_i - \mathbf{E}_{\mathsf{X}}\left[\mathsf{X}\right]\right)\right) > \exp\left(s\varepsilon\right)\right)\\ &\quad< \frac{\mathbf{E}_{\mathsf{X}^n}\left[\exp\left(\frac{s}{n}\sum_{i=1}^{n}\left(\mathsf{X}_i - \mathbf{E}_{\mathsf{X}}\left[\mathsf{X}\right]\right)\right)\right]}{\exp\left(s\varepsilon\right)}\end{aligned}$$

$$= \frac{\prod_{i=1}^{n} \mathbf{E}_{\mathsf{X}_i}\left[\exp\left(\frac{s}{n}\left(\mathsf{X}_i - \mathbf{E}_{\mathsf{X}}\left[\mathsf{X}\right]\right)\right)\right]}{\exp\left(s\varepsilon\right)}, \tag{A.44}$$

where the third line follows from Theorem A.109 and the last line follows from the independence of the X_i and Theorem A.15. Now the problem of finding tight bounds for large deviations reduces to the problem of bounding the function $\exp\left(sn^{-1}\left(\mathsf{X} - \mathbf{E}_{\mathsf{X}}\left[\mathsf{X}\right]\right)\right)$ which is also called the *moment generating function* (see Feller (1966)).For random variables with finite support the most elegant bound is due to Hoeffding (1963)[6].

Lemma A.111 *Let* X *be a random variable with* $\mathbf{E}_{\mathsf{X}}\left[\mathsf{X}\right] = 0$, $\mathbf{P}_{\mathsf{X}}\left(\mathsf{X} \in [a, b]\right) = 1$. *Then, for all* $s > 0$,

$$\mathbf{E}_{\mathsf{X}}\left[\exp\left(s\mathsf{X}\right)\right] \leq \exp\left(\frac{s^2\left(b-a\right)^2}{8}\right).$$

Proof By the convexity of the exponential function

$$\forall x \in [a, b]: \qquad \exp\left(sx\right) \leq \frac{x-a}{b-a}\exp\left(sb\right) + \frac{b-x}{b-a}\exp\left(sa\right).$$

Exploiting $\mathbf{E}_{\mathsf{X}}\left[\mathsf{X}\right] = 0$, and introducing the notation $p \stackrel{\text{def}}{=} -\frac{a}{b-a}$ we have that $\exp\left(ps\left(b-a\right)\right) = \exp\left(-sa\right)$. Thus, we get

$$\begin{aligned}
\mathbf{E}_{\mathsf{X}}\left[\exp\left(s\mathsf{X}\right)\right] &\leq p\exp\left(sb\right) + \left(1-p\right)\exp\left(sa\right) \\
&= \frac{p\exp\left(sb\right)\exp\left(ps\left(b-a\right)\right)}{\exp\left(ps\left(b-a\right)\right)} + \frac{\left(1-p\right)\exp\left(sa\right)\exp\left(ps\left(b-a\right)\right)}{\exp\left(ps\left(b-a\right)\right)} \\
&= \frac{1-p+p\exp\left(s\left(b-a\right)\right)}{\exp\left(ps\left(b-a\right)\right)} \\
&= \exp\left(g\left(u\right)\right),
\end{aligned}$$

where

$$u \stackrel{\text{def}}{=} s\left(b-a\right) \geq 0, \quad g\left(u\right) \stackrel{\text{def}}{=} -pu + \ln\left(1-p+p\exp\left(u\right)\right).$$

By a straightforward calculation we see that the derivative of g is

$$\frac{dg\left(u\right)}{du} = -p + \frac{p\exp\left(u\right)}{1-p+p\exp\left(u\right)},$$

6 The proof presented can be found in Devroye et al. (1996).

therefore $g(0) = \left.\frac{dg(u)}{du}\right|_{u=0} = 0$. Moreover,

$$\begin{aligned}\frac{d^2g(u)}{du^2} &= \frac{p\exp(u)(1-p+p\exp(u)) - p\exp(u)\,p\exp(u)}{(1-p+p\exp(u))^2}\\ &= \frac{(1-p)\,p\exp(u)}{(1-p+p\exp(u))^2},\end{aligned}$$

and the maximum of $\frac{d^2g(u)}{du^2}$ is attained for $u = 0$. Hence $\frac{d^2g(u)}{du^2} \le (1-p)\,p \le \frac{1}{4}$. Thus, by Taylor series expansion with remainder, for some $u_0 \in [0, u]$,

$$g(u) = g(0) + u \cdot \left.\frac{dg(u)}{du}\right|_{u=0} + \frac{u^2}{2} \cdot \left.\frac{d^2g(u)}{du^2}\right|_{u=u_0} \le \frac{u^2}{8} = \frac{s^2(b-a)^2}{8}.$$

The lemma is proved. ■

Using this lemma we can now prove Chernoff's inequality (Chernoff 1952; Okamoto 1958) which was later generalized by Hoeffding (1963).

Theorem A.112 (Hoeffding's inequality) *Let* $\mathsf{X}_1, \ldots, \mathsf{X}_n$ *be independent bounded random variables such that, for all* $i \in \{1, \ldots, n\}$, $\mathbf{P}_{\mathsf{X}_i}(\mathsf{X}_i \in [a, b]) = 1$ *and* $\mathbf{E}_{\mathsf{X}_i}[\mathsf{X}_i] = \mu$. *Then, for all* $\varepsilon > 0$,

$$\mathbf{P}_{\mathsf{X}^n}\left(\frac{1}{n}\sum_{i=1}^{n}\mathsf{X}_i - \mu > \varepsilon\right) < \exp\left(-\frac{2n\varepsilon^2}{(b-a)^2}\right) \tag{A.45}$$

and

$$\mathbf{P}_{\mathsf{X}^n}\left(\left|\frac{1}{n}\sum_{i=1}^{n}\mathsf{X}_i - \mu\right| > \varepsilon\right) < 2\exp\left(-\frac{2n\varepsilon^2}{(b-a)^2}\right). \tag{A.46}$$

Proof Noting that $\mathbf{E}_{\mathsf{X}}[\mathsf{X} - \mu] = 0$ we can apply Lemma A.111 together with equation (A.44) to obtain

$$\mathbf{P}_{\mathsf{X}^n}\left(\frac{1}{n}\sum_{i=1}^{n}\mathsf{X}_i - \mu > \varepsilon\right) < \frac{\prod_{i=1}^{n}\exp\left(\frac{s^2(b-a)^2}{8n^2}\right)}{\exp(s\varepsilon)} = \exp\left(\frac{s^2}{8n}(b-a)^2 - s\varepsilon\right).$$

Minimization of this expression w.r.t. s gives $s = 4n\varepsilon/(b-a)^2$. Hence we have

$$\mathbf{P}_{\mathsf{X}^n}\left(\frac{1}{n}\sum_{i=1}^{n}\mathsf{X}_i - \mu > \varepsilon\right) < \exp\left(\frac{s^2}{8n}(b-a)^2 - s\varepsilon\right) = \exp\left(-\frac{2n\varepsilon^2}{(b-a)^2}\right).$$

This proves equation (A.45). By using $\mathsf{Y}_i = -\mathsf{X}_i$ we see

$$\begin{aligned}\mathbf{P}_{\mathsf{Y}^n}\left(\frac{1}{n}\sum_{i=1}^{n}\mathsf{Y}_i - \mathbf{E}_{\mathsf{Y}}\left[\mathsf{Y}\right] > \varepsilon\right) &= \mathbf{P}_{\mathsf{X}^n}\left(\mu - \frac{1}{n}\sum_{i=1}^{n}\mathsf{X}_i > \varepsilon\right) \\ &< \exp\left(-\frac{2n\varepsilon^2}{(b-a)^2}\right).\end{aligned}$$

Thus, using Theorem A.107 we obtain equation (A.46). ■

This inequality is appropriate if we have only knowledge of the support of $\mathbf{P}_{\mathsf{X}}$. However, this bound does not take into account the variance of the random variable X. We shall provide a bound on the moment generating function taking into account *both* support and variance.

Lemma A.113 *Let* X *be a random variable with* $\mathbf{E}_{\mathsf{X}}\left[\mathsf{X}\right] = 0$, $\mathbf{P}_{\mathsf{X}}\left(|\mathsf{X}| \le c\right) = 1$ *and* $\sigma^2 = \mathrm{Var}\left(\mathsf{X}\right) = \mathbf{E}_{\mathsf{X}}\left[\mathsf{X}^2\right]$. *Then, for all* $s > 0$,

$$\mathbf{E}_{\mathsf{X}}\left[\exp\left(s\mathsf{X}\right)\right] \le \exp\left(\frac{\sigma^2}{c^2}\left(\exp\left(sc\right) - 1 - sc\right)\right).$$

Proof First we note that, for all $j \in \{2, \ldots, \infty\}$,

$$\mathbf{E}_{\mathsf{X}}\left[\mathsf{X}^j\right] = \mathbf{E}_{\mathsf{X}}\left[\mathsf{X}^{j-2}\mathsf{X}^2\right] \le \mathbf{E}_{\mathsf{X}}\left[c^{j-2}\mathsf{X}^2\right] = c^{j-2}\sigma^2,$$

because, by assumption, the random variable is bounded by c. Exploiting the fact that $\exp(x) = \sum_{j=0}^{\infty}\frac{x^j}{j!}$ we therefore obtain

$$\begin{aligned}\mathbf{E}_{\mathsf{X}}\left[\exp\left(s\mathsf{X}\right)\right] &= \mathbf{E}_{\mathsf{X}}\left[1 + s\mathsf{X} + \sum_{j=2}^{\infty}\frac{s^j\mathsf{X}^j}{j!}\right] = 1 + \sum_{j=2}^{\infty}\frac{s^j}{j!}\mathbf{E}_{\mathsf{X}}\left[\mathsf{X}^j\right] \\ &\le 1 + \sum_{j=2}^{\infty}\frac{s^j}{j!}c^{j-2}\sigma^2\end{aligned}$$

$$
\begin{aligned}
&= 1 + \frac{\sigma^2}{c^2} \sum_{j=2}^{\infty} \frac{s^j c^j}{j!} \\
&= 1 + \frac{\sigma^2}{c^2} \left(\exp(sc) - 1 - sc\right) .
\end{aligned}
$$

Finally, using Theorem A.101 proves the lemma. ■

Theorem A.114 (Bennett (1962)) *Let* $\mathsf{X}_1, \ldots, \mathsf{X}_n$ *be independent random variables such that, for all* $i \in \{1, \ldots, n\}$, $\mathbf{P}_{\mathsf{X}_i}(|\mathsf{X}_i| \le c) = 1$ *and* $\mathbf{E}_{\mathsf{X}_i}\left[\mathsf{X}_i\right] = 0$. *Then, for any* $\varepsilon > 0$,

$$
\mathbf{P}_{\mathsf{X}^n}\left(\sum_{i=1}^{n} \mathsf{X}_i > \varepsilon\right) < \exp\left(-\frac{\varepsilon}{c}\left(\left(1 + \frac{n\sigma^2}{\varepsilon c}\right) \ln\left(1 + \frac{\varepsilon c}{n\sigma^2}\right) - 1\right)\right) ,
$$

where $\sigma^2 = \mathbf{E}_{\mathsf{X}}\left[\mathsf{X}^2\right] = \mathrm{Var}(\mathsf{X})$.

Proof Using equation (A.44) and the Lemma A.113 yields

$$
\mathbf{P}_{\mathsf{X}^n}\left(\sum_{i=1}^{n} \mathsf{X}_i > \varepsilon\right) < \exp\left(\frac{n\sigma^2}{c^2}\left(\exp(sc) - 1 - sc\right) - s\varepsilon\right) , \qquad \text{(A.47)}
$$

which needs to be minimized w.r.t. s. Setting the first derivative of the logarithm of equation (A.47) to zero gives

$$
\frac{n\sigma^2}{c^2}\left(c\exp(sc) - c\right) - \varepsilon = 0 ,
$$

which implies that the minimum is at $s = \frac{1}{c}\ln\left(1 + \frac{\varepsilon c}{n\sigma^2}\right)$. Resubstituting this value in equation (A.47) results in the following bound

$$
\begin{aligned}
&\exp\left(\frac{n\sigma^2}{c^2}\left(\left(1 + \frac{\varepsilon c}{n\sigma^2}\right) - 1 - \ln\left(1 + \frac{\varepsilon c}{n\sigma^2}\right)\right) - \frac{\varepsilon}{c}\ln\left(1 + \frac{\varepsilon c}{n\sigma^2}\right)\right) \\
&= \exp\left(\frac{\varepsilon}{c} - \frac{n\sigma^2}{c^2}\ln\left(1 + \frac{\varepsilon c}{n\sigma^2}\right) - \frac{\varepsilon}{c}\ln\left(1 + \frac{\varepsilon c}{n\sigma^2}\right)\right) \\
&= \exp\left(-\frac{\varepsilon}{c}\left(\left(1 + \frac{n\sigma^2}{\varepsilon c}\right)\ln\left(1 + \frac{\varepsilon c}{n\sigma^2}\right) - 1\right)\right)
\end{aligned}
$$

The theorem is proved. ■

The full power of this theorem becomes apparent if we bound $\left(1+\frac{1}{x}\right)\ln(1+x)$ even further.

Theorem A.115 (Bernstein (1946)) *Suppose we are given n independent random variables* $\mathsf{X}_1,\ldots,\mathsf{X}_n$ *such that for all* $i \in \{1,\ldots,n\}$, $\mathbf{P}_{\mathsf{X}_i}(|\mathsf{X}_i| \le c) = 1$ *and* $\mathbf{E}_{\mathsf{X}_i}[\mathsf{X}_i] = 0$. *Then, for any* $\varepsilon > 0$,

$$\mathbf{P}_{\mathsf{X}^n}\left(\frac{1}{n}\sum_{i=1}^{n}\mathsf{X}_i > \varepsilon\right) < \exp\left(-\frac{n\varepsilon^2}{2\sigma^2 + c\varepsilon}\right),$$

where $\sigma^2 = \mathbf{E}_{\mathsf{X}}\left[\mathsf{X}^2\right] = \mathrm{Var}(\mathsf{X})$.

Proof First we show that $\ln(1+x) \ge 2x/(2+x)$ which follows from considering the function $f(x) = \ln(1+x) - 2x/(2+x)$. The function f has the derivative $1/(1+x) - 4/\left((2+x)^2\right)$ whose only positive zero is at $x = 0$. Since $f(1) = \ln(2) - 2/3 > 0$ and $f(0) = 0$ it follows that, for all positive $x \in \mathbb{R}$, $f(x) \ge 0 \Leftrightarrow \ln(1+x) \ge 2x/(2+x)$. Using $x = \frac{\varepsilon c}{n\sigma^2}$ in Theorem A.114 shows that, for all $\lambda > 0$,

$$\begin{aligned}
\mathbf{P}_{\mathsf{X}^n}\left(\sum_{i=1}^{n}\mathsf{X}_i > \lambda\right) &< \exp\left(-\frac{\lambda}{c}\left(\left(1+\frac{n\sigma^2}{\lambda c}\right)\frac{2\frac{\lambda c}{n\sigma^2}}{2+\frac{\lambda c}{n\sigma^2}} - 1\right)\right) \\
&= \exp\left(-\frac{\lambda}{c}\left(\frac{\frac{2\lambda c}{n\sigma^2}+2}{2+\frac{\lambda c}{n\sigma^2}} - 1\right)\right) \\
&= \exp\left(-\frac{2\lambda^2 c + 2\lambda n\sigma^2}{2cn\sigma^2 + \lambda c^2} + \frac{\lambda}{c}\right) \\
&= \exp\left(-\frac{\lambda^2}{2n\sigma^2 + \lambda c}\right).
\end{aligned}$$

Substituting $\lambda = n\varepsilon$ proves the theorem. ∎

If all we need is a bound on the probability that $\mathsf{X}_1 + \cdots + \mathsf{X}_n = 0$ we can eliminate the exponent 2 on ε as opposed to Hoeffding's and Bernstein's inequality.

Theorem A.116 (Binomial tail bound) *Let* $\mathsf{X}_1,\ldots,\mathsf{X}_n$ *be independent random variables such that, for all* $i \in \{1,\ldots,n\}$, $\mathbf{P}_{\mathsf{X}_i}(\mathsf{X}_i = 1) = 1 - \mathbf{P}_{\mathsf{X}_i}(\mathsf{X}_i = 0) =$

$\mathbf{E}_{\mathsf{X}_i}\left[\mathsf{X}_i\right] = \mu$. *Then, for all* $\varepsilon \in (0, \mu)$,

$$\mathbf{P}_{\mathsf{X}^n}\left(\frac{1}{n}\sum_{i=1}^{n}\mathsf{X}_i = 0\right) < \exp\left(-n\varepsilon\right) .$$

Proof By the independence of the X_i we have

$$\mathbf{P}_{\mathsf{X}^n}\left(\frac{1}{n}\sum_{i=1}^{n}\mathsf{X}_i = 0\right) = (1-\mu)^n \leq \exp\left(-n\mu\right) < \exp\left(-n\varepsilon\right) ,$$

where the second step follows from Theorem A.102. ■

Theorem A.117 (Binomial mean deviation bound) *Let* $\mathsf{X}_1, \ldots, \mathsf{X}_n$ *be independent random variables such that, for all* $i \in \{1, \ldots, n\}$, $\mathbf{P}_{\mathsf{X}_i}\left(\mathsf{X}_i = 1\right) = 1 - \mathbf{P}_{\mathsf{X}_i}\left(\mathsf{X}_i = 0\right) = \mathbf{E}_{\mathsf{X}_i}\left[\mathsf{X}_i\right] = \mu$. *Then, for all* $\alpha \in [0, 1]$ *and for all* $\lambda \in \mathbb{N}$ *we have*

$$\mathbf{P}_{\mathsf{X}^n}\left(\frac{1}{n}\sum_{i=1}^{n}\mathsf{X}_i \geq \alpha\mu\right) > \frac{\lambda-1}{\lambda} ,$$

provided that $n\mu \geq \lambda\left(1-\alpha\right)^{-2}$.

Proof First note that the statement in the theorem is equivalent to

$$\mathbf{P}_{\mathsf{X}^n}\left(\sum_{i=1}^{n}\mathsf{X}_i \geq \alpha n\mu\right) > \frac{\lambda-1}{\lambda} .$$

By Theorem A.110 we know that

$$\mathbf{P}_{\mathsf{X}^n}\left(\sum_{i=1}^{n}\mathsf{X}_i \geq n\mu - \sqrt{\lambda n\mu\left(1-\mu\right)}\right) > \frac{\lambda-1}{\lambda} ,$$

because $\mathrm{Var}\left(\sum_i \mathsf{X}_i\right) = n\mu\left(1-\mu\right)$ by the independence assumption and Theorem A.17. Thus, it suffices to show that $n\mu - \sqrt{\lambda n\mu\left(1-\mu\right)} \geq \alpha n\mu$ given that $n\mu \geq \lambda\left(1-\alpha\right)^{-2}$. However, by definition $\mu \in [0, 1]$ and thus

$$n\mu \;\geq\; \frac{\lambda}{(1-\alpha)^2}\left(1-\mu\right) ,$$

$$\sqrt{n\mu} \geq \sqrt{\frac{\lambda}{(1-\alpha)^2}(1-\mu)},$$
$$(1-\alpha)\,n\mu \geq \sqrt{\lambda n\mu(1-\mu)}.$$

The theorem is proven. ■

Large Deviations of Functions of Random Variables

Finally, there exists a further generalization of large deviation bounds when considering any function $f : \mathcal{X}^n \to \mathbb{R}$ of n random variables $\mathsf{X}_1, \ldots, \mathsf{X}_n$. Again, we aim to bound the probability that $f(\mathsf{X}_1, \ldots, \mathsf{X}_n)$ deviates from $\mathbf{E}_{\mathsf{X}^n}\left[f(\mathsf{X}_1, \ldots, \mathsf{X}_n)\right]$. Before we start we need some additional quantities.

Definition A.118 (Martingale and martingale difference) *A sequence of random variables* $\mathsf{Y}_1, \ldots, \mathsf{Y}_n$ *is called a* martingale *w.r.t. another sequence* $\mathsf{X}_1, \ldots, \mathsf{X}_n$ *if for every* $i \in \{1, \ldots, n\}$, $\mathsf{Y}_i = g(\mathsf{X}_1, \ldots, \mathsf{X}_i)$ *is a function of* $\mathsf{X}_1, \ldots, \mathsf{X}_i$ *and*

$$\mathbf{P}_{\mathsf{X}^i}\left(\mathbf{E}_{\mathsf{X}_{i+1}|\mathsf{X}^i=x}\left[g((x, \mathsf{X}_{i+1}))\right] \neq g(\mathbf{X})\right) = 0.$$

A sequence of random variables $\mathsf{V}_1, \ldots, \mathsf{V}_n$ *is called a* martingale difference sequence *w.r.t. another sequence* $\mathsf{X}_1, \ldots, \mathsf{X}_n$ *if, for every* $i \in \{1, \ldots, n\}$, $\mathsf{V}_i = g(\mathsf{X}_1, \ldots, \mathsf{X}_i)$ *is a function of* $\mathsf{X}_1, \ldots, \mathsf{X}_i$ *and*

$$\mathbf{P}_{\mathsf{X}^i}\left(\mathbf{E}_{\mathsf{X}_{i+1}|\mathsf{X}^i=x}\left[g((x, \mathsf{X}_{i+1}))\right] \neq 0\right) = 0.$$

In order to tackle this problem we use a slight modification of equation (A.44) already noticed in Hoeffding (1963): Whenever $\mathsf{V}_1, \ldots, \mathsf{V}_n$ forms a martingale difference sequence w.r.t. $\mathsf{X}_1, \ldots, \mathsf{X}_n$ then, for all $s > 0$,

$$\mathbf{P}_{\mathsf{X}^n}\left(\sum_{i=1}^{n} \mathsf{V}_i > \varepsilon\right) < \frac{\mathbf{E}_{\mathsf{X}^n}\left[\exp\left(s \sum_{i=1}^{n} \mathsf{V}_i\right)\right]}{\exp\{s\varepsilon\}}$$
$$= \frac{\prod_{i=1}^{n} \mathbf{E}_{\mathsf{X}_i|\mathsf{X}^{i-1}=x}\left[\exp(s\mathsf{V}_i)\right]}{\exp\{s\varepsilon\}}. \tag{A.48}$$

However, the significance of this simple extension was not recognized until 1989 when it triggered a revolution in certain applications (McDiarmid 1989). In the current case of interest we note that

$$\mathsf{V}_i \stackrel{\text{def}}{=} \mathbf{E}_{\mathsf{X}^{n-i}|\mathsf{X}^i=(\boldsymbol{x},x)}\left[f\left((\boldsymbol{x},x,\mathbf{X})\right)\right] - \mathbf{E}_{\mathsf{X}^{n-i+1}|\mathsf{X}^{i-1}=\boldsymbol{x}}\left[f\left((\boldsymbol{x},\mathbf{X})\right)\right] \tag{A.49}$$

forms a martingale difference sequence w.r.t. $\mathsf{X}_1, \ldots, \mathsf{X}_n$ which implies that all we need is an upper bound on $\mathbf{E}_{\mathsf{X}_i|\mathsf{X}^{i-1}=\boldsymbol{x}}\left[\exp\left(s\mathsf{V}_i\right)\right]$. We shall use the following lemma.

Lemma A.119 *For any function $f : \mathcal{X}^n \to \mathbb{R}$ such that for all $i \in \{1, \ldots n\}$*

$$\sup_{\boldsymbol{x}\in\mathcal{X}^n, \tilde{x}\in\mathcal{X}} \left|f\left(x_1, \ldots, x_n\right) - f\left(x_1, \ldots, x_{i-1}, \tilde{x}, x_{i+1}, \ldots x_n\right)\right| \le c_i \tag{A.50}$$

we know that, for all measures P_X, all $\boldsymbol{x} \in \mathcal{X}^{i-1}$, all $x \in \mathcal{X}$ and $i \in \{1, \ldots, n\}$,

$$\left|\mathbf{E}_{\mathsf{X}^{n-i}|\mathsf{X}^i=(\boldsymbol{x},x)}\left[f\left(\boldsymbol{x},x,\mathbf{X}\right)\right] - \mathbf{E}_{\mathsf{X}^{n-i+1}|\mathsf{X}^{i-1}=\boldsymbol{x}}\left[f\left(\boldsymbol{x},\mathbf{X}\right)\right]\right| \le |c_i| .$$

Proof By definition we know that

$$\begin{aligned}
&\left|\mathbf{E}_{\mathsf{X}^{n-i}|\mathsf{X}^i=(\boldsymbol{x},x)}\left[f\left(\boldsymbol{x},x,\mathbf{X}\right)\right] - \mathbf{E}_{\mathsf{X}^{n-i+1}|\mathsf{X}^{i-1}=\boldsymbol{x}}\left[f\left(\boldsymbol{x},\mathbf{X}\right)\right]\right| \\
&\quad = \left|\mathbf{E}_{\mathsf{X}^{n-i}|\mathsf{X}^i=(\boldsymbol{x},x)}\left[\mathbf{E}_{\mathsf{X}_{i+1}}\left[f\left(\boldsymbol{x},x,\mathbf{X}\right) - f\left(\boldsymbol{x},\mathsf{X}_i,\mathbf{X}\right)\right]\right]\right| \\
&\quad \le \mathbf{E}_{\mathsf{X}^{n-i}|\mathsf{X}^i=(\boldsymbol{x},x)}\left[\mathbf{E}_{\mathsf{X}_{i+1}}\left[\underbrace{\left|f\left(\boldsymbol{x},x,\mathbf{X}\right) - f\left(\boldsymbol{x},\mathsf{X}_i,\mathbf{X}\right)\right|}_{\le |c_i|}\right]\right] \le |c_i| ,
\end{aligned}$$

where the third line follows by the triangle inequality and from equation (A.50). ■

Theorem A.120 (McDiarmid's inequality (McDiarmid 1989)) *For any function $f : \mathcal{X}^n \to \mathbb{R}$ such that (A.50) holds we know that for all measures P_X*

$$\mathsf{P}_{\mathsf{X}^n}\left(f\left(\mathbf{X}\right) - \mathbf{E}_{\mathsf{X}^n}\left[f\left(\mathbf{X}\right)\right] > \varepsilon\right) < \exp\left(-\frac{\varepsilon^2}{2\sum_{i=1}^n c_i^2}\right)$$

Proof First we combine Lemma A.119 with Lemma A.111 to obtain

$$\mathbf{E}_{\mathsf{X}_i|\mathsf{X}^{i-1}=\boldsymbol{x}}\left[\exp\left(s\mathsf{V}_i\right)\right] \le \exp\left(-\frac{s^2c_i^2}{2}\right)$$

Using equation (A.48) this implies that

$$\mathsf{P}_{\mathsf{X}^n}\left(f\left(\mathbf{X}\right) - \mathbf{E}_{\mathsf{X}^n}\left[f\left(\mathbf{X}\right)\right] > \varepsilon\right) < \exp\left(\frac{s^2\sum_{i=1}^n c_i^2}{2} - s\varepsilon\right) .$$

Minimizing w.r.t. s results in $s = \varepsilon / \left(\sum_{i=1}^{n} c_i^2\right)$. Resubstituted into the latter expression proves the theorem. ■

Note that the original result in McDiarmid (1989) contains a slightly better constant of 2 rather than $\frac{1}{2}$ in the exponential term which is proven using the same technique. As an example of the power of this theorem consider the simple function $f(x_1, \ldots, x_n) = \frac{1}{n} \sum_{i=1}^{n} x_i$ where $x_i \in [a, b]$. Noticing that $c_i = \frac{a-b}{n}$ we see that Hoeffding's inequality can easily be proven using McDiarmid's inequality.

B Proofs and Derivations—Part I

This appendix gives all proofs and derivations of Part I in detail. If necessary the theorems are restated before proving them. This appendix is not as self-contained as the chapters in the main body of this book; it is probably best to read it in conjunction with the corresponding chapter.

B.1 Functions of Kernels

In this section we present the proofs of Theorem 2.20 and Corollary 2.21.

Proof of Theorem 2.20. For all $r \in \mathbb{N}$ and all sequences $(x_1, \ldots, x_r) \in \mathcal{X}^r$ let $\mathbf{K}_1, \mathbf{K}_2, \mathbf{K}_+, \mathbf{K}_c, \mathbf{K}_{+c}, \mathbf{K}_*$ and $\mathbf{K}_f$ be the $r \times r$ matrices whose i, j–th element is given by $k_1(x_i, x_j), k_2(x_i, x_j), k_1(x_i, x_j)+k_2(x_i, x_j), c \cdot k_1(x_i, x_j), k_1(x_i, x_j)+c$, $k_1(x_i, x_j) \cdot k_2(x_i, x_j)$ and $f(x_i) \cdot f(x_j)$, respectively. We need to show that $\mathbf{K}_+, \mathbf{K}_c$, $\mathbf{K}_{+c}$, $\mathbf{K}_*$ and $\mathbf{K}_f$ are positive semidefinite using only that $\mathbf{K}_1$ and $\mathbf{K}_2$ are positive semidefinite, i.e., for all $\boldsymbol{\alpha} \in \mathbb{R}^r$, $\boldsymbol{\alpha}'\mathbf{K}_1\boldsymbol{\alpha} \geq 0$ and $\boldsymbol{\alpha}'\mathbf{K}_2\boldsymbol{\alpha} \geq 0$.

1. $\boldsymbol{\alpha}'\mathbf{K}_+\boldsymbol{\alpha} = \boldsymbol{\alpha}'(\mathbf{K}_1 + \mathbf{K}_2)\boldsymbol{\alpha} = \boldsymbol{\alpha}'\mathbf{K}_1\boldsymbol{\alpha} + \boldsymbol{\alpha}'\mathbf{K}_2\boldsymbol{\alpha} \geq 0$.
2. $\boldsymbol{\alpha}'\mathbf{K}_c\boldsymbol{\alpha} = c \cdot \boldsymbol{\alpha}'\mathbf{K}_1\boldsymbol{\alpha} \geq 0$.
3. $\boldsymbol{\alpha}'\mathbf{K}_{+c}\boldsymbol{\alpha} = \boldsymbol{\alpha}'\left(\mathbf{K}_1 + c\mathbf{1}\mathbf{1}'\right)\boldsymbol{\alpha} = \boldsymbol{\alpha}'\mathbf{K}_1\boldsymbol{\alpha} + c\left\|\mathbf{1}'\boldsymbol{\alpha}\right\|^2 \geq 0$.
4. According to Corollary A.92 the $r^2 \times r^2$ matrix $\mathbf{H} = \mathbf{K}_1 \otimes \mathbf{K}_2$ is positive definite, that is, for all $\mathbf{a} \in \mathbb{R}^{r^2}$, $\mathbf{a}'\mathbf{H}\mathbf{a} \geq 0$. Given any $\boldsymbol{\alpha} \in \mathbb{R}^r$, let us consider $\mathbf{a} = \left(\alpha_1\mathbf{e}_1'; \ldots; \alpha_r\mathbf{e}_r'\right) \in \mathbb{R}^{r^2}$. Then,

$$\mathbf{a}'\mathbf{H}\mathbf{a} = \sum_{i=1}^{r^2}\sum_{j=1}^{r^2} a_i a_j \mathbf{H}_{ij} = \sum_{i=1}^{r}\sum_{j=1}^{r} \alpha_i\alpha_j \mathbf{H}_{i+(i-1)r, j+(j-1)r}$$

$$= \sum_{i=1}^{r}\sum_{j=1}^{r}\alpha_i\alpha_j k_1\left(x_i, x_j\right) k_2\left(x_i, x_j\right) = \boldsymbol{\alpha}'\mathbf{K}_*\boldsymbol{\alpha} \geq 0\,.$$

5. For any function $f : \mathcal{X} \to \mathbb{R}$ we know that

$$\boldsymbol{\alpha}'\mathbf{K}_f\boldsymbol{\alpha} = \sum_{i=1}^{r}\sum_{j=1}^{r}\alpha_i\alpha_j f\left(x_i\right) f\left(x_j\right) = \left(\sum_{i=1}^{r} a_i f\left(x_i\right)\right)^2 \geq 0\,.$$

Proof of Corollary 2.21. The first assertion follows directly from propositions 3 and 4 of Theorem 2.20. For the proof of the second assertion note that

$$\exp\left(\frac{k_1\left(x, \tilde{x}\right)}{\sigma^2}\right) = \sum_{i=0}^{\infty}\frac{1}{\sigma^{2i} i!}k_1^i\left(x, \tilde{x}\right) = 1 + \sum_{i=1}^{\infty}\frac{1}{\sigma^{2i} i!}k_1^i\left(x, \tilde{x}\right)\,.$$

Hence, by propositions 1, 2 and 3 of Theorem 2.20 the second assertion is proved. In order to prove the third assertion note that

$$\exp\left(-\frac{k_1\left(x, x\right) - 2k_1\left(x, \tilde{x}\right) + k_1\left(\tilde{x}, \tilde{x}\right)}{2\sigma^2}\right)$$
$$= \underbrace{\exp\left(-\frac{k_1\left(x, x\right)}{2\sigma^2}\right)}_{f(x)} \cdot \underbrace{\exp\left(-\frac{k_1\left(\tilde{x}, \tilde{x}\right)}{2\sigma^2}\right)}_{f(\tilde{x})} \cdot \exp\left(\frac{k_1\left(x, \tilde{x}\right)}{\sigma^2}\right)\,.$$

Now using propositions 4 and 5 of Theorem 2.20 and the second assertion of this corollary proves the third assertion. The last assertion follows directly from proposition 4 and 5 of Theorem 2.20 as

$$k\left(x, \tilde{x}\right) = \frac{k_1\left(x, \tilde{x}\right)}{\sqrt{k_1\left(x, x\right) \cdot k_1\left(\tilde{x}, \tilde{x}\right)}} = \underbrace{\sqrt{\frac{1}{k_1\left(x, x\right)}}}_{f(x)} \cdot \underbrace{\sqrt{\frac{1}{k_1\left(\tilde{x}, \tilde{x}\right)}}}_{f(\tilde{x})} \cdot k_1\left(x, \tilde{x}\right)\,.$$

The corollary is proved. ■

B.2 Efficient Computation of String Kernels

In this section we prove that the recursions given in equations (2.26)–(2.27) and (2.29)–(2.30) compute the kernel functions (2.25) and (2.28), respectively.

B.2.1 Efficient Computation of the Substring Kernel

In order to compute the kernel (2.25) efficiently we note that, in the outer sum over $\boldsymbol{b} \in \Sigma^s$, it suffices to consider all possible substrings of length s that are contained in $\boldsymbol{u}$. Hence we can rewrite the kernel k_r by

$$\begin{aligned}
k_r(\boldsymbol{u}, \boldsymbol{v}) &= \sum_{s=1}^{r} \sum_{i=1}^{|\boldsymbol{u}|-s+1} \sum_{j=1}^{|\boldsymbol{v}|-s+1} \lambda^{2s} \mathbf{I}_{\boldsymbol{u}[i:(i+s-1)]=\boldsymbol{v}[j:(j+s-1)]} \\
&= \sum_{i=1}^{|\boldsymbol{u}|} \sum_{j=1}^{|\boldsymbol{v}|} \lambda^2 \mathbf{I}_{u_i=v_j} + \sum_{i=1}^{|\boldsymbol{u}|-1} \sum_{j=1}^{|\boldsymbol{v}|-1} \lambda^4 \mathbf{I}_{\boldsymbol{u}[i:(i+1)]=\boldsymbol{v}[j:(j+1)]} + \cdots \\
&= \sum_{i=1}^{|\boldsymbol{u}|} \sum_{j=1}^{|\boldsymbol{v}|} \lambda^2 \left(\mathbf{I}_{u_i=v_j} + \lambda^2 \left(\mathbf{I}_{\boldsymbol{u}[i:(i+1)]=\boldsymbol{v}[j:(j+1)]} + \lambda^2 (\cdots) \right) \right).
\end{aligned}$$

The innermost nested sum can be evaluated recursively when we take advantage of the fact that $\boldsymbol{u}[i:(i+s)] \neq \boldsymbol{v}[j:(j+s)]$ implies that $\boldsymbol{u}[i:(i+s+t)] \neq \boldsymbol{v}[j:(j+s+t)]$ for all $t \in \mathbb{N}$. This proves equations (2.26)–(2.27).

B.2.2 Efficient Computation of the Subsequence Kernel

The proof that the recursions given in equation (2.29)–(2.30) compute the kernel given in equation (2.28) proceeds in two stages:

1. First, we establish that (2.30) computes

$$k_r'(\boldsymbol{u}, \boldsymbol{v}) = \begin{cases} 1 & \text{if } r = 0 \\ \sum_{\boldsymbol{b}\in\Sigma^r} \sum_{\{\mathbf{i} \mid \boldsymbol{b}=\boldsymbol{u}[\mathbf{i}]\}} \sum_{\{\mathbf{j} \mid \boldsymbol{b}=\boldsymbol{v}[\mathbf{j}]\}} \lambda^{|\boldsymbol{u}|+|\boldsymbol{v}|-i_1-j_1+2} & \text{otherwise} \end{cases}. \qquad \text{(B.1)}$$

2. Second, we directly show that (2.29) holds.

In order to prove equation (B.1) we analyze three cases:

1. If either $|\boldsymbol{u}| < r$ or $|\boldsymbol{v}| < r$ we know that one of the sums in equation (B.1) is zero because $\boldsymbol{u}$ or $\boldsymbol{v}$ cannot contain a subsequence longer than the strings themselves. This justifies the first part of (2.30).
2. If $r = 0$ then the second part of (2.30) is equivalent to the first part of equation (B.1).

3. For a given character $u \in \Sigma$ and a given string $\boldsymbol{v} \in \Sigma^*$ consider $M_u = \{\boldsymbol{b} \in \Sigma^r \mid b_r = u\}$ and $J_u = \left\{\mathbf{j} \in \{1, \ldots, |\boldsymbol{v}|\}^r \mid v_{j_r} = u\right\}$, i.e., all subsequences of length r such that the last character in $\boldsymbol{b}$ equals u and all index vectors over $\boldsymbol{v}$ such that the last indexed character equals u. Then we know that

$$\sum_{\boldsymbol{b}\in\Sigma^r} \sum_{\{\mathbf{i}|\boldsymbol{b}=(\boldsymbol{u}u_s)[\mathbf{i}]\}} \sum_{\{\mathbf{j}|\boldsymbol{b}=\boldsymbol{v}[\mathbf{j}]\}} \lambda^{|\boldsymbol{u}u_s|+|\boldsymbol{v}|-i_1-j_1+2}$$

$$= \sum_{\boldsymbol{b}\in M_{u_s}} \sum_{\{\mathbf{i}|\boldsymbol{b}=(\boldsymbol{u}u_s)[\mathbf{i}]\}} \left(\sum_{\mathbf{j}\in J_{u_s}} \lambda^{|\boldsymbol{u}u_s|+|\boldsymbol{v}|-i_1-j_1+2} + \sum_{\{\mathbf{j}|\boldsymbol{b}=\boldsymbol{v}[\mathbf{j}]\}\setminus J_{u_s}} \lambda^{|\boldsymbol{u}u_s|+|\boldsymbol{v}|-i_1-j_1+2} \right)$$
$$+ \sum_{\boldsymbol{b}\in\Sigma^r\setminus M_{u_s}} \sum_{\{\mathbf{i}|\boldsymbol{b}=(\boldsymbol{u}u_s)[\mathbf{i}]\}} \sum_{\{\mathbf{j}|\boldsymbol{b}=\boldsymbol{v}[\mathbf{j}]\}} \lambda^{|\boldsymbol{u}u_s|+|\boldsymbol{v}|-i_1-j_1+2}.$$

Now the first term can be rewritten as

$$\sum_{\boldsymbol{b}\in M_{u_s}} \sum_{\{\mathbf{i}|\boldsymbol{b}=(\boldsymbol{u}u_s)[\mathbf{i}]\}} \sum_{\mathbf{j}\in J_{u_s}} \lambda^{|\boldsymbol{u}u_s|+|\boldsymbol{v}|-i_1-j_1+2}$$
$$= \sum_{\boldsymbol{b}\in\Sigma^{r-1}} \sum_{\{\mathbf{i}|\boldsymbol{b}=\boldsymbol{u}[\mathbf{i}]\}} \sum_{\{t|v_t=u_s\}} \sum_{\{\mathbf{j}|\boldsymbol{b}=(\boldsymbol{v}[1:(t-1)])[\mathbf{j}]\}} \lambda^{|\boldsymbol{u}u_s|+|\boldsymbol{v}|-i_1-j_1+2}$$
$$= \sum_{\{t|v_t=u_s\}} \lambda^{|\boldsymbol{v}|-t+2} \underbrace{\sum_{\boldsymbol{b}\in\Sigma^{r-1}} \sum_{\{\mathbf{i}|\boldsymbol{b}=\boldsymbol{u}[\mathbf{i}]\}} \sum_{\{\mathbf{j}|\boldsymbol{b}=(\boldsymbol{v}[1:(t-1)])[\mathbf{j}]\}} \lambda^{|\boldsymbol{u}|+(t-1)-i_1-j_1+2}}_{k'_{r-1}(\boldsymbol{u},\boldsymbol{v}[1:(t-1)])}.$$

Since for all remaining subsequences $\boldsymbol{b} \in \Sigma^r$ the last character does not match with u_s we can summarize the remaining terms by

$$\lambda \cdot \underbrace{\sum_{\boldsymbol{b}\in\Sigma^r} \sum_{\{\mathbf{i}|\boldsymbol{b}=\boldsymbol{u}[\mathbf{i}]\}} \sum_{\{\mathbf{j}|\boldsymbol{b}=\boldsymbol{v}[\mathbf{j}]\}} \lambda^{|\boldsymbol{u}|+|\boldsymbol{v}|-i_1-j_1+2}}_{k'_r(\boldsymbol{u},\boldsymbol{v})}.$$

Thus, we have shown the third part of (2.30).

It remains to prove that (2.29) is true. Again, we analyze the two different cases:

1. If either $|\boldsymbol{u}| < r$ or $|\boldsymbol{v}| < r$ we know that one of the sums in equation (2.28) is zero because $\boldsymbol{u}$ or $\boldsymbol{v}$ cannot contain a subsequence longer than the strings themselves. This justifies the first part of (2.29).

2. Let M_u and J_u be defined as in the previous analysis. Then we know

$$\begin{aligned}
k_r(\boldsymbol{u}u_s, \boldsymbol{v}) &= \sum_{\boldsymbol{b}\in M_{u_s}} \sum_{\{\mathbf{i}|\boldsymbol{b}=(\boldsymbol{u}u_s)[\mathbf{i}]\}} \sum_{\mathbf{j}\in J_{u_s}} \lambda^{l(\mathbf{i})+l(\mathbf{j})} \\
&\quad + \sum_{\boldsymbol{b}\in M_{u_s}} \sum_{\{\mathbf{i}|\boldsymbol{b}=(\boldsymbol{u}u_s)[\mathbf{i}]\}} \sum_{\{\mathbf{j}|\boldsymbol{b}=\boldsymbol{v}[\mathbf{j}]\}\setminus J_{u_s}} \lambda^{l(\mathbf{i})+l(\mathbf{j})} \\
&\quad + \sum_{\boldsymbol{b}\in \Sigma^r\setminus M_{u_s}} \sum_{\{\mathbf{i}|\boldsymbol{b}=(\boldsymbol{u}u_s)[\mathbf{i}]\}} \sum_{\{\mathbf{j}|\boldsymbol{b}=\boldsymbol{v}[\mathbf{j}]\}} \lambda^{l(\mathbf{i})+l(\mathbf{j})} .
\end{aligned}$$

Using Definition 2.24 the first term can be written

$$\begin{aligned}
\sum_{\boldsymbol{b}\in M_{u_s}} \sum_{\{\mathbf{i}|\boldsymbol{b}=(\boldsymbol{u}u_s)[\mathbf{i}]\}} \sum_{\mathbf{j}\in J_{u_s}} \lambda^{l(\mathbf{i})+l(\mathbf{j})} &= \sum_{\boldsymbol{b}\in M_{u_s}} \sum_{\{\mathbf{i}|\boldsymbol{b}=(\boldsymbol{u}u_s)[\mathbf{i}]\}} \sum_{\mathbf{j}\in J_{u_s}} \lambda^{i_r+j_r-i_1-j_1+2} \\
&= \sum_{\boldsymbol{b}\in \Sigma^{r-1}} \sum_{\{\mathbf{i}|\boldsymbol{b}=\boldsymbol{u}[\mathbf{i}]\}} \sum_{\{t|v_t=u_s\}} \sum_{\{\mathbf{j}|\boldsymbol{b}=(\boldsymbol{v}[1:(t-1)])[\mathbf{j}]\}} \lambda^{|\boldsymbol{u}|+1+(t-1)+1-i_1-j_1+2} \\
&= \lambda^2 \cdot \sum_{\{t|v_t=u_s\}} \underbrace{\sum_{\boldsymbol{b}\in \Sigma^{r-1}} \sum_{\{\mathbf{i}|\boldsymbol{b}=\boldsymbol{u}[\mathbf{i}]\}} \sum_{\{\mathbf{j}|\boldsymbol{b}=(\boldsymbol{v}[1:(t-1)])[\mathbf{j}]\}} \lambda^{|\boldsymbol{u}|+(t-1)+2}}_{k'_{r-1}(\boldsymbol{u},\boldsymbol{v}[1:(t-1)])} .
\end{aligned}$$

Since the remaining sums run over all $\boldsymbol{b} \in \Sigma^r$ where b_r is not equal to u_s (or to any symbol in $\boldsymbol{v}$ if it matches with u_s) they can be computed by $k_r(\boldsymbol{u}, \boldsymbol{v})$. This completes the proof that the recursion given in equations (2.29)–(2.30) computes (2.28).

B.3 Representer Theorem

In this section we present the proof of Theorem 2.29 also found in Schölkopf et al. (2001).

Proof Let us introduce the mapping $\Phi : \mathcal{X} \to \mathcal{F}$ defined by

$$\Phi(x) = k(x, \cdot) .$$

Since k is a reproducing kernel, by equation (2.36) we know that

$$\forall x, \tilde{x} \in \mathcal{X} : \qquad (\Phi(x))(\tilde{x}) = k(x, \tilde{x}) = \langle \Phi(x), \Phi(\tilde{x}) \rangle . \tag{B.2}$$

Now, given $\boldsymbol{x} = (x_1, \ldots, x_m)$, any $f \in \mathcal{F}$ can be decomposed into a part that exists in the span of the $\Phi(x_i)$ and a part which is orthogonal to it,

$$f = \sum_{i=1}^{m} \alpha_i \Phi(x_i) + v$$

for some $\boldsymbol{\alpha} \in \mathbb{R}^m$ and $v \in \mathcal{F}$ satisfying that $\forall x_i \in \boldsymbol{x} : \langle v, \Phi(x_i) \rangle = 0$. Using equation (B.2), the application of f to any arbitrary training point $x_j \in \boldsymbol{x}$ yields

$$\begin{aligned} f(x_j) &= \left\langle \sum_{i=1}^{m} \alpha_i \Phi(x_i) + v, \Phi(x_j) \right\rangle = \sum_{i=1}^{m} \alpha_i \langle \Phi(x_i), \Phi(x_j) \rangle \\ &= \sum_{i=1}^{m} \alpha_i k(x_i, x_j) , \end{aligned}$$

independent of v. Hence, the first term in equation (2.38) is independent of v. As for the second term, since v is orthogonal to $\sum_{i=1}^{m} \alpha_i \Phi(x_i)$ and g_{reg} is strictly monotonic we get

$$\begin{aligned} g_{\text{reg}}(\|f\|) &= g\left(\left\| \sum_{i=1}^{m} \alpha_i \Phi(x_i) + v \right\|\right) \\ &= g\left(\sqrt{\left\| \sum_{i=1}^{m} \alpha_i \Phi(x_i) \right\|^2 + \|v\|^2}\right) \\ &\geq g\left(\left\| \sum_{i=1}^{m} \alpha_i \Phi(x_i) \right\|\right) , \end{aligned}$$

with equality occurring if, and only if, $v = 0$. Hence, setting $v = 0$ does not affect the first term in equation (2.38) while strictly reducing the second term—hence any minimizer must have $v = 0$. As a consequence, any minimizer takes the form $f = \sum_{i=1}^{m} \alpha_i \Phi(x_i)$, so, using equation (B.2)

$$f(\cdot) = \sum_{i=1}^{m} \alpha_i k(x_i, \cdot) .$$

The theorem is proved. ■

B.4 Convergence of the Perceptron

In this section we present the proof of Novikoff's perceptron convergence theorem (see Theorem 2.31) which makes extensive use of the geometry in a feature space $\mathcal{K}$. This elegant proof is the heart of many mistake bounds for linear classifiers.

Proof Suppose $\mathbf{w}_t$ is the final solution vector after t mistakes. Then, by the algorithm in Section D.1 on page 323 the last update step reads

$$\mathbf{w}_t = \mathbf{w}_{t-1} + y_i \mathbf{x}_i \,.$$

Hence the inner product with the vector $\mathbf{w}^*$ satisfies

$$\begin{aligned} \langle \mathbf{w}^*, \mathbf{w}_t \rangle &= \langle \mathbf{w}^*, \mathbf{w}_{t-1} \rangle + y_i \langle \mathbf{w}^*, \mathbf{x}_i \rangle \\ &\geq \langle \mathbf{w}^*, \mathbf{w}_{t-1} \rangle + \gamma_z (\mathbf{w}^*) \geq \cdots \geq t \gamma_z (\mathbf{w}^*) \,, \end{aligned}$$

where the last step follows from repeated applications up to step $t = 0$ where by assumption $\mathbf{w}_0 = \mathbf{0}$. Similarly, by definition of the algorithm,

$$\begin{aligned} \|\mathbf{w}_t\|^2 &= \|\mathbf{w}_{t-1}\|^2 + \underbrace{2 y_i \langle \mathbf{w}_{t-1}, \mathbf{x}_i \rangle}_{\leq 0} + \|\mathbf{x}_i\|^2 \\ &\leq \|\mathbf{w}_{t-1}\|^2 + \varsigma^2 \leq \cdots \leq t \varsigma^2 \,. \end{aligned}$$

Using the Cauchy-Schwarz inequality (see Theorem A.106) we thus have

$$t \gamma_z (\mathbf{w}^*) \leq \langle \mathbf{w}^*, \mathbf{w}_t \rangle \leq \|\mathbf{w}^*\| \cdot \|\mathbf{w}_t\| \leq \sqrt{t} \varsigma \,.$$

This is clearly equivalent to

$$t \leq \left(\frac{\varsigma}{\gamma_z (\mathbf{w}^*)} \right)^2 .$$

The theorem is proved. ■

B.5 Convex Optimization Problems of Support Vector Machines

Here, we give a derivation of the dual optimization problems of SVMs. For the sake of understandability we denote by $\mathbf{Y} \stackrel{\text{def}}{=} \operatorname{diag}(y_1, \ldots, y_m)$ the $m \times m$ diagonal matrix of class labels (-1 and $+1$) and by $\mathbf{G} \stackrel{\text{def}}{=} \left(\langle \mathbf{x}_i, \mathbf{x}_j \rangle \right)_{i,j=1}^{m,m}$ the $m \times m$ Gram matrix.

B.5.1 Hard Margin SVM

Consider the optimization problem given by equation (2.45). Written in terms of the primal Lagrangian, the solution $\hat{\mathbf{w}}$ can be expressed by[1]

$$\begin{aligned}
\left(\hat{\mathbf{w}}, \hat{\boldsymbol{\alpha}}\right) &= \operatorname*{argmin}_{\mathbf{w}\in\mathcal{K}} \operatorname*{argmax}_{\mathbf{0}\le\boldsymbol{\alpha}} L\left(\mathbf{w}, \boldsymbol{\alpha}\right), \\
L\left(\mathbf{w}, \boldsymbol{\alpha}\right) &= \frac{1}{2}\left\|\mathbf{w}\right\|^2 - \sum_{i=1}^{m} \alpha_i y_i \left\langle \mathbf{x}_i, \mathbf{w}\right\rangle + \boldsymbol{\alpha}'\mathbf{1}.
\end{aligned}$$

Taking the derivative w.r.t. the primal variable $\mathbf{w}$ we obtain

$$\left.\frac{\partial L\left(\mathbf{w}, \boldsymbol{\alpha}\right)}{\partial \mathbf{w}}\right|_{\mathbf{w}=\hat{\mathbf{w}}} = \hat{\mathbf{w}} - \sum_{i=1}^{m} \alpha_i y_i \mathbf{x}_i = \mathbf{0} \quad \Leftrightarrow \quad \hat{\mathbf{w}} = \sum_{i=1}^{m} \alpha_i y_i \mathbf{x}_i .$$

Substitution into the primal Lagrangian yields the Wolfe dual, that is,

$$\begin{aligned}
\hat{\boldsymbol{\alpha}} &= \operatorname*{argmax}_{\mathbf{0}\le\boldsymbol{\alpha}} W\left(\boldsymbol{\alpha}\right) \\
W\left(\boldsymbol{\alpha}\right) &= \frac{1}{2}\boldsymbol{\alpha}'\mathbf{YGY}\boldsymbol{\alpha} - \boldsymbol{\alpha}'\mathbf{YGY}\boldsymbol{\alpha} + \boldsymbol{\alpha}'\mathbf{1} = \boldsymbol{\alpha}'\mathbf{1} - \frac{1}{2}\boldsymbol{\alpha}'\mathbf{YGY}\boldsymbol{\alpha}.
\end{aligned}$$

B.5.2 Linear Soft Margin Loss SVM

Now consider the case involving the linear soft margin loss (see equation (2.48)). First, let us multiply the objective function by the constant $C = \frac{1}{2\lambda m}$ which would not change the solution but render the derivation much easier. Expressed in terms of the primal Lagrangian the solution $\hat{\mathbf{w}}$ can be written as

$$\begin{aligned}
\left(\hat{\mathbf{w}}, \hat{\boldsymbol{\xi}}, \hat{\boldsymbol{\alpha}}, \hat{\boldsymbol{\beta}}\right) &= \operatorname*{argmin}_{\mathbf{w}\in\mathcal{K}, \mathbf{0}\le\boldsymbol{\xi}} \operatorname*{argmax}_{\mathbf{0}\le\boldsymbol{\alpha}, \mathbf{0}\le\boldsymbol{\beta}} L\left(\mathbf{w}, \boldsymbol{\xi}, \boldsymbol{\alpha}, \boldsymbol{\beta}\right), \\
L\left(\mathbf{w}, \boldsymbol{\xi}, \boldsymbol{\alpha}, \boldsymbol{\beta}\right) &= \frac{1}{2}\left\|\mathbf{w}\right\|^2 + C\boldsymbol{\xi}'\mathbf{1} - \sum_{i=1}^{m} \alpha_i y_i \left\langle \mathbf{x}_i, \mathbf{w}\right\rangle + \boldsymbol{\alpha}'\mathbf{1} - \boldsymbol{\alpha}'\boldsymbol{\xi} - \boldsymbol{\beta}'\boldsymbol{\xi} \\
&= \frac{1}{2}\left\|\mathbf{w}\right\|^2 - \sum_{i=1}^{m} \alpha_i y_i \left\langle \mathbf{x}_i, \mathbf{w}\right\rangle + \boldsymbol{\alpha}'\mathbf{1} + \boldsymbol{\xi}'\left(C\mathbf{1} - \boldsymbol{\alpha} - \boldsymbol{\beta}\right).
\end{aligned}$$

1 Note that the constant positive factor of $\frac{1}{2}$ does not change the minimum.

The corresponding dual is found by differentiation w.r.t. the primal variables $\mathbf{w}$ and $\boldsymbol{\xi}$, that is,

$$\begin{aligned}\left.\frac{\partial L(\mathbf{w},\boldsymbol{\xi},\boldsymbol{\alpha},\boldsymbol{\beta})}{\partial\mathbf{w}}\right|_{\mathbf{w}=\hat{\mathbf{w}}} &= \hat{\mathbf{w}}-\sum_{i=1}^{m}\alpha_i y_i\mathbf{x}_i=\mathbf{0} \quad\Leftrightarrow\quad \hat{\mathbf{w}}=\sum_{i=1}^{m}\alpha_i y_i\mathbf{x}_i\,,\\ \left.\frac{\partial L(\mathbf{w},\boldsymbol{\xi},\boldsymbol{\alpha},\boldsymbol{\beta})}{\partial\boldsymbol{\xi}}\right|_{\boldsymbol{\xi}=\hat{\boldsymbol{\xi}}} &= C\mathbf{1}-\boldsymbol{\alpha}-\boldsymbol{\beta}=\mathbf{0} \quad\Leftrightarrow\quad \boldsymbol{\alpha}=C\mathbf{1}-\boldsymbol{\beta}\,.\end{aligned} \tag{B.3}$$

Substituting these stationarity conditions into the primal Lagrangian we obtain the following dual objective function

$$\begin{aligned}\left(\hat{\boldsymbol{\alpha}},\hat{\boldsymbol{\beta}}\right) &= \operatorname*{argmax}_{\mathbf{0}\le\boldsymbol{\alpha},\mathbf{0}\le\boldsymbol{\beta}} W(\boldsymbol{\alpha},\boldsymbol{\beta})\,,\\ W(\boldsymbol{\alpha},\boldsymbol{\beta}) &= \frac{1}{2}\boldsymbol{\alpha}'\mathbf{YGY}\boldsymbol{\alpha}-\boldsymbol{\alpha}'\mathbf{YGY}\boldsymbol{\alpha}+\boldsymbol{\alpha}'\mathbf{1}=\boldsymbol{\alpha}'\mathbf{1}-\frac{1}{2}\boldsymbol{\alpha}'\mathbf{YGY}\boldsymbol{\alpha}\,.\end{aligned}$$

Since $\boldsymbol{\beta}\ge\mathbf{0}$, the second stationarity condition (B.3) restricts each α_i to be less than or equal to C. As a consequence the final Wolfe dual is given by

$$\begin{aligned}\hat{\boldsymbol{\alpha}} &= \operatorname*{argmax}_{\mathbf{0}\le\boldsymbol{\alpha}\le C\mathbf{1}} W(\boldsymbol{\alpha})\,,\\ W(\boldsymbol{\alpha}) &= \boldsymbol{\alpha}'\mathbf{1}-\frac{1}{2}\boldsymbol{\alpha}'\mathbf{YGY}\boldsymbol{\alpha}\,.\end{aligned}$$

B.5.3 Quadratic Soft Margin Loss SVM

Consider the quadratic soft margin loss given by equation (2.49). Again, let us multiply the objective function by the constant $\frac{1}{2\lambda m}$. Expressed in terms of the primal Lagrangian the solution $\hat{\mathbf{w}}$ can be written as

$$\begin{aligned}\left(\hat{\mathbf{w}},\hat{\boldsymbol{\xi}},\hat{\boldsymbol{\alpha}},\hat{\boldsymbol{\beta}}\right) &= \operatorname*{argmin}_{\mathbf{w}\in\mathcal{K},\mathbf{0}\le\boldsymbol{\xi}}\ \operatorname*{argmax}_{\mathbf{0}\le\boldsymbol{\alpha},\mathbf{0}\le\boldsymbol{\beta}} L(\mathbf{w},\boldsymbol{\xi},\boldsymbol{\alpha},\boldsymbol{\beta})\,,\\ L(\mathbf{w},\boldsymbol{\xi},\boldsymbol{\alpha},\boldsymbol{\beta}) &= \frac{1}{2}\|\mathbf{w}\|^2+\frac{1}{2\lambda m}\boldsymbol{\xi}'\boldsymbol{\xi}-\sum_{i=1}^{m}\alpha_i y_i\langle\mathbf{x}_i,\mathbf{w}\rangle+\boldsymbol{\alpha}'\mathbf{1}-\boldsymbol{\alpha}'\boldsymbol{\xi}-\boldsymbol{\beta}'\boldsymbol{\xi}\\ &= \frac{1}{2}\|\mathbf{w}\|^2-\sum_{i=1}^{m}\alpha_i y_i\langle\mathbf{x}_i,\mathbf{w}\rangle+\boldsymbol{\alpha}'\mathbf{1}+\boldsymbol{\xi}'\left(\frac{1}{2\lambda m}\boldsymbol{\xi}-\boldsymbol{\alpha}-\boldsymbol{\beta}\right).\end{aligned}$$

The corresponding dual is found by differentiation w.r.t. the primal variables $\mathbf{w}$ and $\boldsymbol{\xi}$, that is,

$$\left.\frac{\partial L(\mathbf{w},\boldsymbol{\xi},\boldsymbol{\alpha},\boldsymbol{\beta})}{\partial \mathbf{w}}\right|_{\mathbf{w}=\hat{\mathbf{w}}} = \hat{\mathbf{w}} - \sum_{i=1}^{m}\alpha_i y_i \mathbf{x}_i = \mathbf{0} \quad\Leftrightarrow\quad \hat{\mathbf{w}} = \sum_{i=1}^{m}\alpha_i y_i \mathbf{x}_i\,,$$
$$\left.\frac{\partial L(\mathbf{w},\boldsymbol{\xi},\boldsymbol{\alpha},\boldsymbol{\beta})}{\partial \boldsymbol{\xi}}\right|_{\boldsymbol{\xi}=\hat{\boldsymbol{\xi}}} = \frac{1}{\lambda m}\hat{\boldsymbol{\xi}} - \boldsymbol{\alpha} - \boldsymbol{\beta} = \mathbf{0} \quad\Leftrightarrow\quad \hat{\boldsymbol{\xi}} = \lambda m(\boldsymbol{\alpha}+\boldsymbol{\beta})\,.$$

Substituting the stationarity conditions into the primal we obtain

$$\left(\hat{\boldsymbol{\alpha}},\hat{\boldsymbol{\beta}}\right) = \underset{\mathbf{0}\le\boldsymbol{\alpha},\mathbf{0}\le\boldsymbol{\beta}}{\operatorname{argmax}}\, W(\boldsymbol{\alpha},\boldsymbol{\beta})\,,$$
$$\begin{aligned} W(\boldsymbol{\alpha},\boldsymbol{\beta}) &= \frac{1}{2}\boldsymbol{\alpha}'\mathbf{YGY}\boldsymbol{\alpha} - \boldsymbol{\alpha}'\mathbf{YGY}\boldsymbol{\alpha} + \boldsymbol{\alpha}'\mathbf{1} + \lambda m(\boldsymbol{\alpha}+\boldsymbol{\beta})'\left(\frac{1}{2}(\boldsymbol{\alpha}+\boldsymbol{\beta}) - \boldsymbol{\alpha} - \boldsymbol{\beta}\right) \\ &= \frac{1}{2}\boldsymbol{\alpha}'\mathbf{YGY}\boldsymbol{\alpha} - \boldsymbol{\alpha}'\mathbf{YGY}\boldsymbol{\alpha} + \boldsymbol{\alpha}'\mathbf{1} + \lambda m(\boldsymbol{\alpha}+\boldsymbol{\beta})'\left(-\frac{1}{2}(\boldsymbol{\alpha}+\boldsymbol{\beta})\right) \\ &= \boldsymbol{\alpha}'\mathbf{1} - \frac{1}{2}\boldsymbol{\alpha}'\mathbf{YGY}\boldsymbol{\alpha} - \frac{\lambda m}{2}\|\boldsymbol{\alpha}+\boldsymbol{\beta}\|^2\,. \end{aligned}$$

Noticing that decreasing $\boldsymbol{\beta}$ will always lead to an increase in $W(\boldsymbol{\alpha},\boldsymbol{\beta})$, we simply set $\hat{\boldsymbol{\beta}} = \mathbf{0}$. Hence, the final Wolfe dual is given by

$$\hat{\boldsymbol{\alpha}} = \underset{\mathbf{0}\le\boldsymbol{\alpha}}{\operatorname{argmax}}\, W(\boldsymbol{\alpha})\,,$$
$$W(\boldsymbol{\alpha}) = \boldsymbol{\alpha}'\mathbf{1} - \frac{1}{2}\boldsymbol{\alpha}'\mathbf{YGY}\boldsymbol{\alpha} - \frac{\lambda m}{2}\boldsymbol{\alpha}'\boldsymbol{\alpha}\,.$$

B.5.4 ν–Linear Margin Loss SVM

Now consider the case involving the linear soft margin loss and the reparameterization by $\nu\in[0,1]$ (see equation (2.52)). Expressed in terms of the primal Lagrangian the solution $\mathbf{w}^*$ can be written as

$$\left(\hat{\mathbf{w}},\hat{\boldsymbol{\xi}},\hat{\rho},\hat{\boldsymbol{\alpha}},\hat{\boldsymbol{\beta}},\hat{\delta}\right) = \underset{\mathbf{w}\in\mathcal{K},\mathbf{0}\le\boldsymbol{\xi},0\le\rho}{\operatorname{argmin}}\ \underset{\mathbf{0}\le\boldsymbol{\alpha},\mathbf{0}\le\boldsymbol{\beta},0\le\delta}{\operatorname{argmax}}\ L(\mathbf{w},\boldsymbol{\xi},\rho,\boldsymbol{\alpha},\boldsymbol{\beta},\delta)\,,$$
$$L(\mathbf{w},\boldsymbol{\xi},\rho,\boldsymbol{\alpha},\boldsymbol{\beta},\delta) = \frac{1}{2}\|\mathbf{w}\|^2 + \rho\left(\boldsymbol{\alpha}'\mathbf{1} - \nu - \delta\right) + \boldsymbol{\xi}'\left(\frac{1}{m}\mathbf{1} - \boldsymbol{\alpha} - \boldsymbol{\beta}\right)$$

$$-\sum_{i=1}^{m} \alpha_i y_i \langle \mathbf{x}_i, \mathbf{w} \rangle .$$

The corresponding dual is found by differentiation w.r.t. the primal variables $\mathbf{w}$, $\boldsymbol{\xi}$ and ρ, that is,

$$\begin{aligned}
\left.\frac{\partial L(\mathbf{w}, \boldsymbol{\xi}, \rho, \boldsymbol{\alpha}, \boldsymbol{\beta}, \delta)}{\partial \mathbf{w}}\right|_{\mathbf{w}=\hat{\mathbf{w}}} &= \hat{\mathbf{w}} - \sum_{i=1}^{m} \alpha_i y_i \mathbf{x}_i = \mathbf{0} \Leftrightarrow \hat{\mathbf{w}} = \sum_{i=1}^{m} \alpha_i y_i \mathbf{x}_i , \\
\left.\frac{\partial L(\mathbf{w}, \boldsymbol{\xi}, \rho, \boldsymbol{\alpha}, \boldsymbol{\beta}, \delta)}{\partial \boldsymbol{\xi}}\right|_{\boldsymbol{\xi}=\hat{\boldsymbol{\xi}}} &= \frac{1}{m}\mathbf{1} - \boldsymbol{\alpha} - \boldsymbol{\beta} = \mathbf{0} \quad \Leftrightarrow \quad \boldsymbol{\alpha} = \frac{1}{m}\mathbf{1} - \boldsymbol{\beta} , \qquad \text{(B.4)} \\
\left.\frac{\partial L(\mathbf{w}, \boldsymbol{\xi}, \rho, \boldsymbol{\alpha}, \boldsymbol{\beta}, \delta)}{\partial \rho}\right|_{\rho=\hat{\rho}} &= \boldsymbol{\alpha}'\mathbf{1} - \nu - \delta = 0 \quad \Leftrightarrow \quad \boldsymbol{\alpha}'\mathbf{1} = \nu + \delta . \qquad \text{(B.5)}
\end{aligned}$$

Resubstituting these stationarity conditions into the primal Lagrangian we obtain the following dual objective function

$$\begin{aligned}
\left(\hat{\boldsymbol{\alpha}}, \hat{\boldsymbol{\beta}}, \hat{\delta}\right) &= \underset{\mathbf{0} \le \boldsymbol{\alpha}, \mathbf{0} \le \boldsymbol{\beta}, 0 \le \delta}{\operatorname{argmax}} \; W(\boldsymbol{\alpha}, \boldsymbol{\beta}, \delta) , \\
W(\boldsymbol{\alpha}, \boldsymbol{\beta}, \delta) &= \frac{1}{2}\boldsymbol{\alpha}'\mathbf{YGY}\boldsymbol{\alpha} - \boldsymbol{\alpha}'\mathbf{YGY}\boldsymbol{\alpha} + \hat{\rho}\left(\boldsymbol{\alpha}'\mathbf{1} - \nu - \delta\right) + \hat{\boldsymbol{\xi}}'\left(\frac{1}{m}\mathbf{1} - \boldsymbol{\alpha} - \boldsymbol{\beta}\right) \\
&= -\frac{1}{2}\boldsymbol{\alpha}'\mathbf{YGY}\boldsymbol{\alpha} .
\end{aligned}$$

Since $\boldsymbol{\beta} \ge \mathbf{0}$, the second stationarity condition (B.4) restricts each α_i to be less than or equal to $\frac{1}{m}$. Since $\delta \ge 0$ the third stationarity condition (B.5) is equivalent to $\boldsymbol{\alpha}'\mathbf{1}$ to be greater or equal to ν. Hence, the final Wolfe dual is given by

$$\begin{aligned}
\hat{\boldsymbol{\alpha}} &= \underset{\mathbf{0} \le \boldsymbol{\alpha} \le \frac{1}{m}\mathbf{1}, \boldsymbol{\alpha}'\mathbf{1} \ge \nu}{\operatorname{argmax}} \; W(\boldsymbol{\alpha}) , \\
W(\boldsymbol{\alpha}) &= -\frac{1}{2}\boldsymbol{\alpha}'\mathbf{YGY}\boldsymbol{\alpha} .
\end{aligned}$$

B.6 Leave-One-Out Bound for Kernel Classifiers

Here we give the proof of Theorem 2.37. The proof is adapted from the original proof given in Jaakkola and Haussler (1999b); we do not have to enforce convexity of the potential function J and have dropped the assumption that $\alpha_i \in [0, 1]$.

Proof of Theorem 2.37. The basic idea of this proof is to find an expression of the leave-one-out error of an algorithm using only the coefficients $\hat{\boldsymbol{\alpha}}$ obtained by learning on the whole training sample. Thus we try to relate a leave-one-our error at the tth example with the coefficients obtained by joint maximization of the function W given by

$$W(\boldsymbol{\alpha}) = -\frac{1}{2}\sum_{i=1}^{m}\sum_{j=1}^{m}\alpha_i\alpha_j y_i y_j k\left(x_i, x_j\right) + \sum_{i=1}^{m} J\left(\alpha_i\right).$$

Some notational comments are in order: Subscripts on W refer to the left out example, the subscript on α to the value of the particular component, and the superscripts on $\boldsymbol{\alpha}$ to the maximizer for the corresponding functions W.

Leaving out the tth example we know that the remaining α's are obtained by the maximization of

$$W_t(\boldsymbol{\alpha}) = -\frac{1}{2}\sum_{\substack{i=1\\i\neq t}}^{m}\sum_{\substack{j=1\\j\neq t}}^{m}\alpha_i\alpha_j y_i y_j k\left(x_i, x_j\right) + \sum_{\substack{i=1\\i\neq t}}^{m} J\left(\alpha_i\right).$$

Let the learning algorithm $\mathcal{A}_W$ result in $\boldsymbol{\alpha}^t \in \mathbb{R}^m$, i.e.,

$$\boldsymbol{\alpha}^t = \underset{\mathbf{0}\leq\boldsymbol{\alpha}\leq\mathbf{u}}{\operatorname{argmax}}\; W_t(\boldsymbol{\alpha}).$$

Naturally, $\boldsymbol{\alpha}^t$ is different from $\hat{\boldsymbol{\alpha}}$ because the latter is jointly optimized with α_t in the objective function. In order to relate the decision function (2.54) based on $\boldsymbol{\alpha}^t$ with the decision function (2.54) based on $\hat{\boldsymbol{\alpha}}$ obtained by joint optimization we aim to find a function $\widehat{W}: \mathbb{R}^m \to \mathbb{R}$

- whose maximum is attained at $\hat{\boldsymbol{\alpha}}$ and
- which involves W_t.

In order to achieve this we construct W from W_t by adding the missed summands and fixing α_t to its *optimal* value $\hat{\alpha}_t$. This gives

$$\begin{aligned}\widehat{W}(\boldsymbol{\alpha}) &= W_t(\boldsymbol{\alpha}) - \frac{1}{2}\sum_{\substack{i=1\\i\neq t}}^{m}\alpha_i\hat{\alpha}_t y_i y_t k\left(x_i, x_t\right) - \frac{1}{2}\sum_{j=1}^{m}\hat{\alpha}_t\alpha_j y_t y_j k\left(x_t, x_j\right) + J\left(\hat{\alpha}_t\right)\\ &= W_t(\boldsymbol{\alpha}) - \hat{\alpha}_t y_t\sum_{\substack{i=1\\i\neq t}}^{m}\alpha_i y_i k\left(x_i, x_t\right) - \frac{1}{2}\hat{\alpha}_t\hat{\alpha}_t k\left(x_t, x_t\right) + J\left(\hat{\alpha}_t\right),\end{aligned}\qquad\text{(B.6)}$$

where we used the symmetry of the Mercer kernel k. Note that the last two terms in (B.6) do not change the maximum because they only depend on the fixed value $\hat{\alpha}_t$. As a consequence we shall omit them in the following argument. Since $\hat{\boldsymbol{\alpha}}$ maximizes $\widehat{W}$ we know that

$$\widehat{W}\left(\hat{\boldsymbol{\alpha}}\right) \geq \widehat{W}\left(\boldsymbol{\alpha}^t\right),$$

$$W_t\left(\hat{\boldsymbol{\alpha}}\right) - \hat{\alpha}_t y_t \sum_{\substack{i=1\\ i\neq t}}^{m} \hat{\alpha}_i y_i k\left(x_i, x_t\right) \geq W_t\left(\boldsymbol{\alpha}^t\right) - \hat{\alpha}_t y_t \sum_{\substack{i=1\\ i\neq t}}^{m} \alpha_i^t y_i k\left(x_i, x_t\right),$$

$$-\hat{\alpha}_t y_t \sum_{\substack{i=1\\ i\neq t}}^{m} \alpha_i^t y_i k\left(x_i, x_t\right) \leq -\hat{\alpha}_t y_t \sum_{\substack{i=1\\ i\neq t}}^{m} \hat{\alpha}_i y_i k\left(x_i, x_t\right) - \left(W_t\left(\boldsymbol{\alpha}^t\right) - W_t\left(\hat{\boldsymbol{\alpha}}\right)\right).$$

As by definition $\boldsymbol{\alpha}^t$ maximizes W_t we have

$$W_t\left(\boldsymbol{\alpha}^t\right) \geq W_t\left(\hat{\boldsymbol{\alpha}}\right) \quad \Leftrightarrow \quad W_t\left(\boldsymbol{\alpha}^t\right) - W_t\left(\hat{\boldsymbol{\alpha}}\right) \geq 0,$$

which shows that

$$-\hat{\alpha}_t y_t \sum_{\substack{i=1\\ i\neq t}}^{m} \alpha_i^t y_i k\left(x_i, x_t\right) \leq -\hat{\alpha}_t y_t \sum_{\substack{i=1\\ i\neq t}}^{m} \hat{\alpha}_i y_i k\left(x_i, x_t\right)$$

$$-y_t \underbrace{\sum_{\substack{i=1\\ i\neq t}}^{m} \alpha_i^t y_i k\left(x_i, x_t\right)}_{\mathcal{A}_W\left(\left(z_1,\ldots,z_{t-1},z_{t+1},\ldots,z_m\right)\right)\left(x_t\right)} \leq -y_t \sum_{\substack{i=1\\ i\neq t}}^{m} \hat{\alpha}_i y_i k\left(x_i, x_t\right),$$

because, by assumption, $\hat{\alpha}_t$ is positive. A leave-one-out error at the tth example occurs if, and only if, the l.h.s. of the inequality is positive. This is as the braced term is exactly the real-valued output at x_t when the tth example is left out during learning. Thus the sum of step functions of the r.h.s. bounds the leave-one-out error from above. The theorem is proved. ■

B.7 Laplace Approximation for Gaussian Processes

In this section we derive a method to compute the vector $\boldsymbol{\mu} = \left(\hat{\mathbf{t}}, \hat{t}\right) \in \mathbb{R}^{m+1}$ which maximizes the expression (3.18). As a byproduct we will also give the explicit form of the covariance matrix $\boldsymbol{\Sigma}$ of the Laplace approximation defined in equation (3.19). Finally, we derive a stable algorithm for computing the expansion coefficients $\boldsymbol{\alpha} \in \mathbb{R}^m$ for classification using Gaussian processes.

B.7.1 Maximization of $\mathbf{f}_{\mathsf{T}^{m+1}|\mathsf{X}=x,\mathsf{Z}^m=z}$

In order to find the maximum of the density $\mathbf{f}_{\mathsf{T}^{m+1}|\mathsf{X}=x,\mathsf{Z}^m=z}$ we use Bayes' theorem

$$\begin{aligned}\mathbf{f}_{\mathsf{T}^{m+1}|\mathsf{X}=x,\mathsf{Z}^m=z}\left((\boldsymbol{t},t)\right) &= \mathbf{f}_{\mathsf{T}^{m+1}|\mathsf{X}=x,\mathsf{X}^m=\boldsymbol{x},\mathsf{Y}^m=\boldsymbol{y}}\left((\boldsymbol{t},t)\right)\\ &= \frac{\mathbf{P}_{\mathsf{Y}^m|\mathsf{T}^{m+1}=(\boldsymbol{t},t),\mathsf{X}^m=\boldsymbol{x},\mathsf{X}=x}(\boldsymbol{y})\,\mathbf{f}_{\mathsf{T}^{m+1}|\mathsf{X}^m=\boldsymbol{x},\mathsf{X}=x}\left((\boldsymbol{t},t)\right)}{\mathbf{P}_{\mathsf{Y}^m|\mathsf{X}^m=\boldsymbol{x},\mathsf{X}=x}(\boldsymbol{y})}\\ &= \frac{\mathbf{P}_{\mathsf{Y}^m|\mathsf{T}^m=\boldsymbol{t},\mathsf{X}^m=\boldsymbol{x}}(\boldsymbol{y})\,\mathbf{f}_{\mathsf{T}^{m+1}|\mathsf{X}^m=\boldsymbol{x},\mathsf{X}=x}\left((\boldsymbol{t},t)\right)}{\mathbf{P}_{\mathsf{Y}^m|\mathsf{X}^m=\boldsymbol{x}}(\boldsymbol{y})}\,,\end{aligned}$$

where we use the fact that the test object $x \in \mathcal{X}$ and its associated latent variable T have no influence on the generation of the class labels $\boldsymbol{y}$ at the training objects $\boldsymbol{x}$. Now, taking the logarithm will not change the maximum but will render optimization much easier. Hence, we look for the vector $(\hat{\boldsymbol{t}}, \hat{t})$ which maximizes

$$J(\boldsymbol{t},t) = \underbrace{\ln\left(\mathbf{P}_{\mathsf{Y}^m|\mathsf{T}^m=\boldsymbol{t},\mathsf{X}^m=\boldsymbol{x}}(\boldsymbol{y})\right)}_{Q_1(\boldsymbol{t})} + \underbrace{\ln\left(\mathbf{f}_{\mathsf{T}^{m+1}|\mathsf{X}^m=\boldsymbol{x},\mathsf{X}=x}\left((\boldsymbol{t},t)\right)\right)}_{Q_2(\boldsymbol{t},t)} - \ln\left(\mathbf{P}_{\mathsf{Y}^m|\mathsf{X}^m=\boldsymbol{x}}(\boldsymbol{y})\right).$$

Note that the last term is a normalization constant which does not depend on $(\boldsymbol{t}, t)$ and can thus be omitted from the optimization. Let us start by considering the second term $Q_2(\boldsymbol{t}, t)$ which effectively builds the link between Gaussian processes for regression and for classification. By assumption[2] $\mathbf{P}_{\mathsf{T}^{m+1}|\mathsf{X}^m=\boldsymbol{x},\mathsf{X}=x} = \text{Normal}(\mathbf{0}, \mathbf{G}_{m+1})$ and thus, according to Definition A.26, this term is given by

$$Q_2(\boldsymbol{t},t) = -\frac{1}{2}\left((m+1)\ln(2\pi) + \ln(|\mathbf{G}_{m+1}|) + (\boldsymbol{t}',t)\,\mathbf{G}_{m+1}^{-1}\begin{pmatrix}\boldsymbol{t}\\ t\end{pmatrix}\right), \qquad \text{(B.7)}$$

where

$$\mathbf{G}_{m+1} = \begin{pmatrix}\mathbf{XX}' & \mathbf{Xx}\\ \mathbf{x}'\mathbf{X}' & \mathbf{x}'\mathbf{x}\end{pmatrix} = \begin{pmatrix}\mathbf{G}_m & \mathbf{Xx}\\ \mathbf{x}'\mathbf{X}' & \mathbf{x}'\mathbf{x}\end{pmatrix} \quad \text{and} \quad \mathbf{G}_{m+1}^{-1} = \begin{pmatrix}\mathbf{M} & \mathbf{m}\\ \mathbf{m}' & \kappa\end{pmatrix} \qquad \text{(B.8)}$$

are the $(m+1) \times (m+1)$ Gram matrix and its inverse of the training and test object(s). Using Theorem A.80 for the inverse of a partitioned matrix $\mathbf{G}_{m+1}$ we

2 For the sake of understandability we consider a regression model without any variance σ_t^2. Note, however, that we can always incorporate the variance afterwards by changing the kernel according to equation (3.15) (see Remark 3.10). This is particularly important if $\mathbf{G}_{m+1}$ is not of full rank.

know that $\mathbf{G}_{m+1}^{-1}$ can be written as in equation (B.8) where

$$\mathbf{M} = \mathbf{G}_m^{-1} + \frac{1}{\kappa}\mathbf{mm}', \quad \mathbf{m} = -\kappa \mathbf{G}_m^{-1}\mathbf{Xx}, \quad \kappa = \left(\mathbf{x}'\mathbf{x} - \mathbf{x}'\mathbf{X}'\mathbf{G}_m^{-1}\mathbf{Xx}\right)^{-1}. \tag{B.9}$$

Hence it follows that (B.7) can be written as

$$Q_2(\mathbf{t}, t) = -\frac{1}{2}\left(\mathbf{t}'\mathbf{M}\mathbf{t} + 2t\mathbf{t}'\mathbf{m} + t^2\kappa\right) + c, \tag{B.10}$$

where we summarize all terms independent of $\mathbf{t}$ and t in $c \in \mathbb{R}$. We note that $Q_1(\mathbf{t})$ does not depend on t and thus, for any value of $\mathbf{t} \in \mathbb{R}^m$, we can analytically derive the optimal value $\hat{t}$ of t by maximizing $Q_2(\mathbf{t}, \cdot)$. Taking the derivative of (B.10) w.r.t. t and setting this function to zero gives

$$\left.\frac{\partial Q_2(\mathbf{t}, t)}{\partial t}\right|_{t=\hat{t}} = 2\mathbf{t}'\mathbf{m} + 2\hat{t}\kappa \quad \Leftrightarrow \quad \hat{t} = -\frac{\mathbf{t}'\mathbf{m}}{\kappa} = \mathbf{t}'\mathbf{G}_m^{-1}\mathbf{Xx}. \tag{B.11}$$

Substituting this expression into (B.10) shows that this term equals

$$Q_2(\mathbf{t}) = -\frac{1}{2}\left(\mathbf{t}'\mathbf{M}\mathbf{t} - \frac{2}{\kappa}\mathbf{t}'\mathbf{mm}'\mathbf{t} + \frac{1}{\kappa}\mathbf{t}'\mathbf{mm}'\mathbf{t}\right) + c = -\frac{1}{2}\mathbf{t}'\mathbf{G}_m^{-1}\mathbf{t} + c. \tag{B.12}$$

Let us turn our attention to the first term $Q_1(\mathbf{t})$ of $J(\mathbf{t}, t)$. If we define $\pi(t) = \exp\left(\beta^{-1}\cdot t\right) / \left(1 + \exp\left(\beta^{-1}\cdot t\right)\right)$ then the likelihood model (3.16) can be written as

$$\mathbf{P}_{\mathsf{Y}|\mathsf{T}=t}(y) = \pi(t)^{\frac{y+1}{2}}(1-\pi(t))^{\frac{1-y}{2}},$$

where we use that $y \in \{-1, +1\}$. By exploiting the independence of the Y_i given the value of $\mathsf{T}_i = t_i$ we can rewrite $Q_1(\mathbf{t})$ in the following form

$$\begin{aligned}
Q_1(\mathbf{t}) &= \sum_{i=1}^{m} \ln\left(\mathbf{P}_{\mathsf{Y}_i|\mathsf{T}=t_i}(y_i)\right) \\
&= \frac{1}{2}\sum_{i=1}^{m}\left((y_i+1)\ln(\pi(t_i)) + (1-y_i)\ln(1-\pi(t_i))\right) \\
&= \frac{1}{2}\sum_{i=1}^{m}\left((y_i+1)\beta^{-1}t_i - 2\ln\left(1+\exp\left(\beta^{-1}\cdot t_i\right)\right)\right) \\
&= \frac{1}{2\beta}(\mathbf{y}+\mathbf{1})'\mathbf{t} - \sum_{i=1}^{m}\ln\left(1+\exp\left(\beta^{-1}\cdot t_i\right)\right).
\end{aligned} \tag{B.13}$$

Combining equations (B.12) and (B.13) we obtain the following revised objective function $J(\boldsymbol{t})$ to be maximized over $\boldsymbol{t} \in \mathbb{R}^m$

$$J(\boldsymbol{t}) = \frac{1}{2\beta}(\boldsymbol{y}+\mathbf{1})'\boldsymbol{t} - \sum_{i=1}^{m} \ln\left(1+\exp\left(\beta^{-1}\cdot t_i\right)\right) - \frac{1}{2}\boldsymbol{t}'\mathbf{G}_m^{-1}\boldsymbol{t} + c\,. \tag{B.14}$$

A straightforward calculation reveals that the gradient vector is given by

$$\left.\frac{\partial J(\boldsymbol{t})}{\partial \boldsymbol{t}}\right|_{\boldsymbol{t}=\hat{\boldsymbol{t}}} = \frac{1}{2\beta}(\boldsymbol{y}+\mathbf{1}) - \frac{1}{\beta}\boldsymbol{\pi}(\hat{\boldsymbol{t}}) - \mathbf{G}_m^{-1}\hat{\boldsymbol{t}}\,, \tag{B.15}$$

where $\boldsymbol{\pi}(\hat{\boldsymbol{t}}) = (\pi(\hat{t}_1), \ldots, \pi(\hat{t}_m))'$. As can be seen from this expression, due to the term $\boldsymbol{\pi}(\hat{\boldsymbol{t}})$, it is not possible to compute the roots $\hat{\boldsymbol{t}}$ of this equation in a closed form. We use the *Newton-Raphson method*,

$$\boldsymbol{t}_{i+1} = \boldsymbol{t}_i - \eta\cdot\mathbf{H}_{\boldsymbol{t}_i}^{-1}\cdot\left.\frac{\partial J(\boldsymbol{t})}{\partial \boldsymbol{t}}\right|_{\boldsymbol{t}=\boldsymbol{t}_i}\,,$$

where the $m \times m$ *Hessian* matrix $\mathbf{H}_{\hat{\boldsymbol{t}}}$ is given by

$$\mathbf{H}_{\hat{\boldsymbol{t}}} = \begin{pmatrix} \left.\frac{\partial J(\boldsymbol{t})}{\partial t_1 \partial t_1}\right|_{t_1=\hat{t}_1} & \cdots & \left.\frac{\partial J(\boldsymbol{t})}{\partial t_1 \partial t_m}\right|_{t_1=\hat{t}_1, t_m=\hat{t}_m} \\ \vdots & \ddots & \vdots \\ \left.\frac{\partial J(\boldsymbol{t})}{\partial t_m \partial t_1}\right|_{t_m=\hat{t}_m, t_1=\hat{t}_1} & \cdots & \left.\frac{\partial J(\boldsymbol{t})}{\partial t_m \partial t_m}\right|_{t_m=\hat{t}_m} \end{pmatrix} = -\mathbf{P} - \mathbf{G}_m^{-1}\,.$$

The diagonal matrix $\mathbf{P}$ in the definition of $\mathbf{H}_{\boldsymbol{t}}$ is given by

$$\mathbf{P} = \frac{1}{\beta}\cdot\operatorname{diag}\left(a(\hat{t}_1), \ldots, a(\hat{t}_m)\right)\,, \tag{B.16}$$

$$a(\hat{t}_i) \stackrel{\text{def}}{=} \left.\frac{d\pi(t)}{dt}\right|_{t=\hat{t}_i} = \frac{1}{\beta}\frac{\exp\left(\beta^{-1}\cdot\hat{t}_i\right)}{\left(1+\exp\left(\beta^{-1}\cdot\hat{t}_i\right)\right)^2} = \frac{1}{\beta}\pi(\hat{t}_i)\left(1-\pi(\hat{t}_i)\right)\,. \tag{B.17}$$

Thus the update step of the Newton-Raphson method is given by

$$\boldsymbol{t}_{i+1} = \boldsymbol{t}_i + \eta\cdot\left(\mathbf{G}_m^{-1}+\mathbf{P}\right)^{-1}\left(\frac{1}{2\beta}(\boldsymbol{y}+\mathbf{1}) - \frac{1}{\beta}\boldsymbol{\pi}(\boldsymbol{t}_i) - \mathbf{G}_m^{-1}\boldsymbol{t}_i\right)\,,$$

where $\eta \in \mathbb{R}^+$ has to be chosen such that $J(\boldsymbol{t}_{i+1}) > J(\boldsymbol{t}_i)$. Once this procedure has converged to $\hat{\boldsymbol{t}} \in \mathbb{R}^m$ (which must provably happen because the negative Hessian is always positive-definite) we can compute $\hat{t} \in \mathbb{R}$ by equation (B.11).

B.7.2 Computation of $\boldsymbol{\Sigma}$

In order to find the covariance matrix $\boldsymbol{\Sigma}$ of the Laplace approximation we exploit equations (B.10) and (B.9). A direct calculation reveals that inverse covariance matrix $\boldsymbol{\Sigma}^{-1}$ is given by

$$\boldsymbol{\Sigma}^{-1} = \begin{pmatrix} \mathbf{M}+\mathbf{P} & \mathbf{m} \\ \mathbf{m}' & \kappa \end{pmatrix},$$

where $\mathbf{M} \in \mathbb{R}^{m\times m}$, $\mathbf{m} \in \mathbb{R}^m$ and $\kappa \in \mathbb{R}$ are defined in equation (B.8) and $\mathbf{P} \in \mathbb{R}^{m\times m}$ is given in equation (B.16). Applying the second statement of Theorem A.80 we can directly compute the covariance matrix $\boldsymbol{\Sigma}$ for the Laplace approximation, i.e.,

$$\boldsymbol{\Sigma} = \begin{pmatrix} \left(\mathbf{G}_m^{-1}+\mathbf{P}\right)^{-1} & -\kappa^{-1}\left(\mathbf{G}_m^{-1}+\mathbf{P}\right)^{-1}\mathbf{m} \\ -\kappa^{-1}\mathbf{m}'\left(\mathbf{G}_m^{-1}+\mathbf{P}\right)^{-1} & \kappa^{-1}+\kappa^{-2}\mathbf{m}'\left(\mathbf{G}_m^{-1}+\mathbf{P}\right)^{-1}\mathbf{m} \end{pmatrix}.$$

This expression can be further simplified by noticing that $\left(\mathbf{G}_m^{-1}+\mathbf{P}\right)^{-1} = (\mathbf{I}+\mathbf{G}_m\mathbf{P})^{-1}\mathbf{G}_m$. Hence, using the definitions in equation (B.8) we obtain that

$$\begin{aligned}
-\kappa^{-1}\left(\mathbf{G}_m^{-1}+\mathbf{P}\right)^{-1}\mathbf{m} &= (\mathbf{I}+\mathbf{G}_m\mathbf{P})^{-1}\mathbf{X}\mathbf{x}, \\
\kappa^{-1}+\kappa^{-2}\mathbf{m}'\left(\mathbf{G}_m^{-1}+\mathbf{P}\right)^{-1}\mathbf{m} &= \mathbf{x}'\mathbf{x}-\mathbf{x}'\mathbf{X}'\mathbf{G}_m^{-1}\mathbf{X}\mathbf{x}+\mathbf{x}'\mathbf{X}'\mathbf{G}_m^{-1}(\mathbf{I}+\mathbf{G}_m\mathbf{P})^{-1}\mathbf{X}\mathbf{x} \\
&= \mathbf{x}'\mathbf{x}-\mathbf{x}'\mathbf{X}'\mathbf{G}_m^{-1}\left(\mathbf{I}-(\mathbf{I}+\mathbf{G}_m\mathbf{P})^{-1}\right)\mathbf{X}\mathbf{x} \\
&= \mathbf{x}'\mathbf{x}-\mathbf{x}'\mathbf{X}'\mathbf{G}_m^{-1}\left(\mathbf{I}-\mathbf{I}+\mathbf{G}_m(\mathbf{I}+\mathbf{P}\mathbf{G}_m)^{-1}\mathbf{P}\right)\mathbf{X}\mathbf{x} \\
&= \mathbf{x}'\mathbf{x}-\mathbf{x}'\mathbf{X}'(\mathbf{I}+\mathbf{P}\mathbf{G}_m)^{-1}\mathbf{P}\mathbf{X}\mathbf{x},
\end{aligned}$$

where the fourth line follows from the Woodbury formula (see Theorem A.79). In summary,

$$\boldsymbol{\Sigma} = \begin{pmatrix} (\mathbf{I}+\mathbf{G}_m\mathbf{P})^{-1}\mathbf{G}_m & (\mathbf{I}+\mathbf{G}_m\mathbf{P})^{-1}\mathbf{X}\mathbf{x} \\ \mathbf{x}'\mathbf{X}'(\mathbf{I}+\mathbf{G}_m\mathbf{P})^{-1} & \mathbf{x}'\mathbf{x}-\mathbf{x}'\mathbf{X}'(\mathbf{I}+\mathbf{P}\mathbf{G}_m)^{-1}\mathbf{P}\mathbf{X}\mathbf{x} \end{pmatrix}.$$

B.7.3 Stabilized Gaussian Process Classification

If we are only concerned with the classification of a new test object $x \in \mathcal{X}$ we exploit the fact that $\operatorname{sign}(\hat{t})$ always equals the class label $y \in \{-1,+1\}$ with the larger probability $\mathbf{P}_{\mathsf{Y}|\mathsf{X}=x,\mathsf{Z}^m=z}(y)$ (see equation (3.21) for a definition of this term). Let us show that $\hat{t}=0$ implies $\mathbf{P}_{\mathsf{Y}|\mathsf{X}=x,\mathsf{Z}^m=z}(+1) = \mathbf{P}_{\mathsf{Y}|\mathsf{X}=x,\mathsf{Z}^m=z}(-1) = \frac{1}{2}$; the result follows by the monotonicity of $\mathbf{P}_{\mathsf{Y}|\mathsf{T}=t}$ as a function of t. At first we note that $\pi(t) =$

$1-\pi(-t)$ where $\pi(t) = \mathbf{P}_{\mathsf{Y}|\mathsf{T}=t}(+1) = \exp\left(\beta^{-1}\cdot t\right) / \left(1+\exp\left(\beta^{-1}\cdot t\right)\right)$. Using this relation we have

$$\begin{aligned}
\mathbf{P}_{\mathsf{Y}|\mathsf{X}=x,\mathsf{Z}^m=z}(+1) &= \int_{\mathbb{R}} \underbrace{\mathbf{P}_{\mathsf{Y}|\mathsf{T}=t}(+1)}_{\pi(t)} \cdot \frac{1}{\sqrt{2\pi}\sigma}\exp\left(-\frac{t^2}{2\sigma^2}\right) dt \\
&= \int_{\mathbb{R}} (1-\pi(-t)) \cdot \frac{1}{\sqrt{2\pi}\sigma}\exp\left(-\frac{t^2}{2\sigma^2}\right) dt \\
&= \int_{\mathbb{R}} \underbrace{\mathbf{P}_{\mathsf{Y}|\mathsf{T}=s}(-1)}_{1-\pi(s)} \cdot \frac{1}{\sqrt{2\pi}\sigma}\exp\left(-\frac{s^2}{2\sigma^2}\right) ds \\
&= \mathbf{P}_{\mathsf{Y}|\mathsf{X}=x,\mathsf{Z}^m=z}(-1)\,,
\end{aligned}$$

where the third line follows by $s=-t$ and the assumption that $\hat{t}=0$. Since $\hat{t} = \hat{\boldsymbol{t}}'\mathbf{G}_m^{-1}\mathbf{X}\mathbf{x}$ we know that the Gaussian process classification function is given by

$$h_{\mathrm{GPC}}(x) = \operatorname{sign}\left(\sum_{i=1}^{m} \alpha_i \langle \mathbf{x}_i, \mathbf{x}\rangle\right), \qquad \boldsymbol{\alpha} = \mathbf{G}_m^{-1}\hat{\boldsymbol{t}}\,.$$

In order to avoid unnecessary inversions of the Gram matrix $\mathbf{G}_m$—which is an ill-posed problem if $\mathbf{G}_m$ is almost singular—we shall reformulate the Newton-Raphson method in terms of $\boldsymbol{\alpha} \in \mathbb{R}^m$ using $\boldsymbol{t} = \mathbf{G}_m\boldsymbol{\alpha}$. Let the Gram matrix $\mathbf{G}_m = \left(\mathbf{g}_1'; \ldots; \mathbf{g}_m'\right)$ be given by its m rows $\mathbf{g}_1, \ldots, \mathbf{g}_m \in \mathbb{R}^m$. Then equation (B.14) can be rewritten as

$$J(\boldsymbol{\alpha}) = \frac{1}{2\beta}(\boldsymbol{y}+\mathbf{1})'\mathbf{G}_m\boldsymbol{\alpha} - \sum_{i=1}^{m} \ln\left(1+\exp\left(\beta^{-1}\cdot \mathbf{g}_i'\boldsymbol{\alpha}\right)\right) - \frac{1}{2}\boldsymbol{\alpha}'\mathbf{G}_m\boldsymbol{\alpha}\,.$$

As a consequence the gradient and Hessian are given by

$$\begin{aligned}
\left.\frac{\partial J(\boldsymbol{\alpha})}{\partial \boldsymbol{\alpha}}\right|_{\boldsymbol{\alpha}=\boldsymbol{\alpha}} &= \frac{1}{2\beta}\mathbf{G}_m(\boldsymbol{y}+\mathbf{1}) - \frac{1}{\beta}\mathbf{G}_m'\boldsymbol{\pi}(\mathbf{G}_m\boldsymbol{\alpha}) - \mathbf{G}_m\boldsymbol{\alpha}\,, \\
\mathbf{H}_{\boldsymbol{\alpha}} &= -\mathbf{G}_m'\mathbf{P}\mathbf{G}_m - \mathbf{G}_m = -\mathbf{G}_m(\mathbf{P}\mathbf{G}_m + \mathbf{I})\,,
\end{aligned}$$

where $\boldsymbol{\pi}(\mathbf{G}_m\boldsymbol{\alpha}) = \left(\pi\left(\mathbf{g}_1'\boldsymbol{\alpha}\right), \ldots, \pi\left(\mathbf{g}_m'\boldsymbol{\alpha}\right)\right)'$ and

$$\mathbf{P} = \frac{1}{\beta}\cdot \operatorname{diag}\left(a\left(\mathbf{g}_1'\boldsymbol{\alpha}\right), \ldots, a\left(\mathbf{g}_m'\boldsymbol{\alpha}\right)\right).$$

The Newton-Raphson algorithm computes $\boldsymbol{\alpha}_{i+1}$ from $\boldsymbol{\alpha}_i$ by

$$\begin{aligned}\boldsymbol{\alpha}_{i+1} &= \boldsymbol{\alpha}_i + \eta \cdot \mathbf{G}_m^{-1} \left(\mathbf{P}\mathbf{G}_m + \mathbf{I}\right)^{-1} \mathbf{G}_m \left(\frac{1}{2\beta} (\mathbf{y} + \mathbf{1}) - \frac{1}{\beta} \boldsymbol{\pi} \left(\mathbf{G}_m \boldsymbol{\alpha}_i\right) - \boldsymbol{\alpha}_i \right) \\ &= \boldsymbol{\alpha}_i + \eta \cdot \left(\mathbf{P}\mathbf{G}_m + \mathbf{I}\right)^{-1} \left(\frac{1}{\beta} \left(\frac{\mathbf{y} + \mathbf{1}}{2} - \boldsymbol{\pi} \left(\mathbf{G}_m \boldsymbol{\alpha}_i\right) \right) - \boldsymbol{\alpha}_i \right).\end{aligned}$$

The adaptation of the parameter η is done by incrementally choosing η from the sequence $\left(2^{-i}\right)_{i \in \mathbb{N}}$. As soon as $J\left(\boldsymbol{\alpha}_{i+1}\right) \geq J\left(\boldsymbol{\alpha}_i\right)$ we update $\boldsymbol{\alpha}_i$ and re-compute $\mathbf{P}$ and $\boldsymbol{\pi}\left(\mathbf{G}_m \boldsymbol{\alpha}_i\right)$ making sure that i never exceeds a certain value[3].

B.8 Relevance Vector Machines

In this section we derive an explicit update rule for computing the parameter vector $\hat{\boldsymbol{\theta}}$ and $\hat{\sigma}_t^2$ which locally maximizes the evidence $\mathbf{f}_{\mathsf{T}^m|\mathsf{X}^m=x}(\boldsymbol{t})$. In order to ease the optimization we consider the log-evidence given by

$$E\left(\boldsymbol{\theta}, \sigma_t^2\right) = -\frac{1}{2} \left(m \ln(2\pi) + \underbrace{\ln\left(\left|\sigma_t^2 \mathbf{I}_m + \mathbf{X}\boldsymbol{\Theta}\mathbf{X}'\right|\right)}_{Q_1(\boldsymbol{\theta}, \sigma_t^2)} + \underbrace{\boldsymbol{t}'\left(\sigma_t^2 \mathbf{I}_m + \mathbf{X}\boldsymbol{\Theta}\mathbf{X}'\right)^{-1} \boldsymbol{t}}_{Q_2(\boldsymbol{\theta}, \sigma_t^2)} \right).$$

Due to its length we have divided the derivation into several parts. Afterwards, we derive the relevance vector machine algorithm for classification using ideas already outlined in Section B.7. We shall compute the weight vector $\boldsymbol{\mu} \in \mathbb{R}^n$ which maximizes $\mathbf{f}_{\mathsf{W}|\mathsf{Z}^m=z}$ together with the covariance matrix $\boldsymbol{\Sigma} \in \mathbb{R}^{n \times n}$ defined in equation (3.27).

B.8.1 Derivative of the Evidence w.r.t. $\boldsymbol{\theta}$

As our goal is to maximize E over the choice of $\boldsymbol{\theta} \in \mathbb{R}^n$ we aim to compute the derivative w.r.t. $\boldsymbol{\theta}$. At first we have that

$$\frac{\partial E\left(\boldsymbol{\theta}, \sigma_t^2\right)}{\partial \boldsymbol{\theta}} = -\frac{1}{2} \left(\frac{\partial Q_1\left(\boldsymbol{\theta}, \sigma_t^2\right)}{\partial \boldsymbol{\theta}} + \frac{\partial Q_2\left(\boldsymbol{\theta}, \sigma_t^2\right)}{\partial \boldsymbol{\theta}} \right).$$

3 We use $i_{\max} = 8$ in our implementation.

Let us start with $Q_1(\boldsymbol{\theta}, \sigma_t^2)$. According to Theorem A.72 we know

$$\left|\boldsymbol{\Theta}^{-1}\right| \cdot \left|\sigma_t^2 \mathbf{I}_m + \mathbf{X}\boldsymbol{\Theta}\mathbf{X}'\right| = \left|\sigma_t^2 \mathbf{I}_m\right| \cdot \left|\boldsymbol{\Theta}^{-1} + \sigma_t^{-2}\mathbf{X}'\mathbf{X}\right| ,$$

which implies

$$\begin{aligned} Q_1(\boldsymbol{\theta}, \sigma_t^2) &= \ln\left(\left|\sigma_t^2 \mathbf{I}_m\right|\right) + \ln\left(\left|\boldsymbol{\Theta}^{-1} + \sigma_t^{-2}\mathbf{X}'\mathbf{X}\right|\right) - \ln\left(\left|\boldsymbol{\Theta}^{-1}\right|\right) \\ &= m \ln\left(\sigma_t^2\right) + \ln\left(\left|\boldsymbol{\Sigma}^{-1}\right|\right) + \sum_{i=1}^{n} \ln\left(\theta_i\right) . \end{aligned} \tag{B.18}$$

Here we use equation (3.24) for the definition of $\boldsymbol{\Sigma} = \left(\boldsymbol{\Theta}^{-1} + \sigma_t^{-2}\mathbf{X}'\mathbf{X}\right)^{-1}$. For the sake of understandability we compute the derivative of Q_1 component-wise, that is, we compute $\partial Q_1(\boldsymbol{\theta}, \sigma_t^2) / \partial \theta_j$. By Theorem A.97 we know

$$\begin{aligned} \frac{\partial Q_1(\boldsymbol{\theta}, \sigma_t^2)}{\partial \theta_j} &= \frac{\partial \ln\left(\left|\boldsymbol{\Sigma}^{-1}\right|\right)}{\partial \theta_j} + \frac{1}{\theta_j} = \sum_{r=1}^{n}\sum_{s=1}^{n} \frac{\partial \ln\left(\left|\boldsymbol{\Sigma}^{-1}\right|\right)}{\partial\left(\boldsymbol{\Sigma}^{-1}\right)_{rs}} \cdot \frac{\partial\left(\boldsymbol{\Sigma}^{-1}\right)_{rs}}{\partial \theta_j} + \frac{1}{\theta_j} \\ &= \sum_{r=1}^{n}\sum_{s=1}^{n} \boldsymbol{\Sigma}_{rs} \cdot \frac{\partial\left(\boldsymbol{\Theta}^{-1} + \sigma_t^{-2}\mathbf{X}'\mathbf{X}\right)_{rs}}{\partial \theta_j} + \frac{1}{\theta_j} \\ &= \frac{1}{\theta_j} - \frac{1}{\theta_j^2}\boldsymbol{\Sigma}_{jj} . \end{aligned}$$

Now, let us consider the second term $Q_2(\boldsymbol{\theta}, \sigma_t^2)$. First, we use the Woodbury formula (see Theorem A.79) to obtain

$$\begin{aligned} \left(\sigma_t^2 \mathbf{I}_m + \mathbf{X}\boldsymbol{\Theta}\mathbf{X}'\right)^{-1} &= \sigma_t^{-2}\mathbf{I}_m - \sigma_t^{-4}\mathbf{X}\left(\mathbf{I}_n + \sigma_t^{-2}\boldsymbol{\Theta}\mathbf{X}'\mathbf{X}\right)^{-1}\boldsymbol{\Theta}\mathbf{X}' \\ &= \sigma_t^{-2}\mathbf{I}_m - \sigma_t^{-4}\mathbf{X}\left(\boldsymbol{\Theta}\left(\boldsymbol{\Theta}^{-1} + \sigma_t^{-2}\mathbf{X}'\mathbf{X}\right)\right)^{-1}\boldsymbol{\Theta}\mathbf{X}' \\ &= \sigma_t^{-2}\mathbf{I}_m - \sigma_t^{-4}\mathbf{X}\left(\boldsymbol{\Theta}^{-1} + \sigma_t^{-2}\mathbf{X}'\mathbf{X}\right)^{-1}\mathbf{X}' \\ &= \sigma_t^{-2}\left(\mathbf{I}_m - \sigma_t^{-2}\mathbf{X}\boldsymbol{\Sigma}\mathbf{X}'\right) , \end{aligned} \tag{B.19}$$

by exploiting the definition of $\boldsymbol{\Sigma}$, as given in equation (3.24). Using the fact that $\boldsymbol{\mu} = \sigma_t^{-2}\boldsymbol{\Sigma}\mathbf{X}'\boldsymbol{t} = \boldsymbol{\Sigma}\boldsymbol{\tau}$ and the abbreviation $\boldsymbol{\tau} = \sigma_t^{-2}\mathbf{X}'\boldsymbol{t}$ we can rewrite Q_2 by

$$Q_2(\boldsymbol{\theta}, \sigma_t^2) = \boldsymbol{t}'\left(\sigma_t^2 \mathbf{I}_m + \mathbf{X}\boldsymbol{\Theta}\mathbf{X}'\right)^{-1}\boldsymbol{t} = \sigma_t^{-2}\boldsymbol{t}'\left(\boldsymbol{t} - \mathbf{X}\boldsymbol{\mu}\right) = \sigma_t^{-2}\boldsymbol{t}'\boldsymbol{t} - \boldsymbol{\tau}'\boldsymbol{\mu} .$$

Then the derivative of Q_2 w.r.t. to θ_j is given by

$$\frac{\partial Q_2(\boldsymbol{\theta}, \sigma_t^2)}{\partial \theta_j} = \frac{\partial\left(\sigma_t^{-2}\boldsymbol{t}'\boldsymbol{t} - \boldsymbol{\tau}'\boldsymbol{\mu}\right)}{\partial \theta_j} = -\boldsymbol{\tau}'\frac{\partial \boldsymbol{\mu}}{\partial \theta_j} ,$$

because $\boldsymbol{\mu}$ is the only term that depends on θ_j. Using Theorem A.96 we know

$$\frac{\partial \boldsymbol{\mu}}{\partial \theta_j} = \frac{\partial \boldsymbol{\Sigma}\boldsymbol{\tau}}{\partial \theta_j} = \frac{\partial \boldsymbol{\Sigma}}{\partial \theta_j}\boldsymbol{\tau} = \frac{\partial \left(\boldsymbol{\Sigma}^{-1}\right)^{-1}}{\partial \theta_j}\boldsymbol{\tau} = -\boldsymbol{\Sigma}\frac{\partial \boldsymbol{\Sigma}^{-1}}{\partial \theta_j}\boldsymbol{\Sigma}\boldsymbol{\tau} = -\boldsymbol{\Sigma}\left(-\frac{1}{\theta_j^2}\mathbf{1}_{jj}\right)\boldsymbol{\Sigma}\boldsymbol{\tau},$$

where $\mathbf{1}_{jj} \in \mathbb{R}^{n\times n}$ is used to denote a matrix of zeros except for the j, j–th element which is one. As a consequence,

$$\frac{\partial Q_2\left(\boldsymbol{\theta}, \sigma_t^2\right)}{\theta_j} = -\boldsymbol{\tau}'\frac{\partial \boldsymbol{\mu}}{\partial \theta_j} = -\boldsymbol{\tau}'\boldsymbol{\Sigma}\left(\frac{1}{\theta_j^2}\mathbf{1}_{jj}\right)\boldsymbol{\Sigma}\boldsymbol{\tau} = -\boldsymbol{\mu}'\left(\frac{1}{\theta_j^2}\mathbf{1}_{jj}\right)\boldsymbol{\mu} = -\frac{\mu_j^2}{\theta_j^2},$$

where we use the symmetry of $\boldsymbol{\Sigma} \in \mathbb{R}^{n\times n}$. Combining these results,

$$\frac{\partial E\left(\boldsymbol{\theta}, \sigma_t^2\right)}{\partial \boldsymbol{\theta}} = -\frac{1}{2}\left(\frac{1}{\theta_1} - \frac{\Sigma_{11} + \mu_1^2}{\theta_1^2}, \ldots, \frac{1}{\theta_n} - \frac{\Sigma_{nn} + \mu_n^2}{\theta_n^2}\right)'. \tag{B.20}$$

B.8.2 Derivative of the Evidence w.r.t. σ_t^2

In order to compute the derivative w.r.t. σ_t^2 we again consider Q_1 and Q_2 separately. Using Theorem A.97 we obtain

$$\begin{aligned}
\frac{\partial Q_1\left(\boldsymbol{\theta}, \sigma_t^2\right)}{\partial \sigma_t^2} &= \frac{\partial \ln\left(\left|\sigma_t^2\mathbf{I}_m + \mathbf{X}\boldsymbol{\Theta}\mathbf{X}'\right|\right)}{\partial \sigma_t^2} \\
&= \sum_{r=1}^{m}\sum_{s=1}^{m} \frac{\partial \ln\left(\left|\sigma_t^2\mathbf{I}_m + \mathbf{X}\boldsymbol{\Theta}\mathbf{X}'\right|\right)}{\partial\left(\sigma_t^2\mathbf{I}_m + \mathbf{X}\boldsymbol{\Theta}\mathbf{X}'\right)_{rs}} \cdot \frac{\partial\left(\sigma_t^2\mathbf{I}_m + \mathbf{X}\boldsymbol{\Theta}\mathbf{X}'\right)_{rs}}{\partial \sigma_t^2} \\
&= \sum_{r=1}^{m}\left(\sigma_t^2\mathbf{I}_m + \mathbf{X}\boldsymbol{\Theta}\mathbf{X}'\right)_{rr}^{-1} = \operatorname{tr}\left(\left(\sigma_t^2\mathbf{I}_m + \mathbf{X}\boldsymbol{\Theta}\mathbf{X}'\right)^{-1}\right).
\end{aligned}$$

This expression can further be simplified exploiting equation (B.19), i.e.,

$$\frac{\partial Q_1\left(\boldsymbol{\theta}, \sigma_t^2\right)}{\partial \sigma_t^2} = \operatorname{tr}\left(\sigma_t^{-2}\left(\mathbf{I}_m - \sigma_t^{-2}\mathbf{X}\boldsymbol{\Sigma}\mathbf{X}'\right)\right) = m \cdot \sigma_t^{-2} - \sigma_t^{-4} \cdot \operatorname{tr}\left(\boldsymbol{\Sigma}\mathbf{X}'\mathbf{X}\right),$$

where we used Theorem A.74 and $\boldsymbol{\Sigma} = \left(\boldsymbol{\Theta}^{-1} + \sigma_t^{-2}\mathbf{X}'\mathbf{X}\right)^{-1}$ as given in equation (3.24). Finally, we see that

$$\boldsymbol{\Sigma}\mathbf{X}\mathbf{X}' = \sigma_t^2\boldsymbol{\Sigma}\left(\sigma_t^{-2}\mathbf{X}\mathbf{X}' + \boldsymbol{\Theta}^{-1} - \boldsymbol{\Theta}^{-1}\right) = \sigma_t^2\left(\mathbf{I}_n - \boldsymbol{\Sigma}\boldsymbol{\Theta}^{-1}\right)$$

from which it follows that

$$\frac{\partial Q_1\left(\boldsymbol{\theta},\sigma_t^2\right)}{\partial \sigma_t^2}=\frac{m-\sum\limits_{i=1}^{n}\left(1-\frac{\boldsymbol{\Sigma}_{ii}}{\theta_i}\right)}{\sigma_t^2}\,.$$

In order to compute Q_2 we apply Theorem A.96 and obtain

$$\begin{aligned}\frac{\partial Q_2\left(\boldsymbol{\theta},\sigma_t^2\right)}{\partial \sigma_t^2} &= \frac{\partial\left(\boldsymbol{t}'\left(\sigma_t^2\mathbf{I}_m+\mathbf{X}\boldsymbol{\Theta}\mathbf{X}'\right)^{-1}\boldsymbol{t}\right)}{\partial \sigma_t^2}\\ &= \boldsymbol{t}'\left(-\left(\sigma_t^2\mathbf{I}_m+\mathbf{X}\boldsymbol{\Theta}\mathbf{X}'\right)^{-1}\left(\sigma_t^2\mathbf{I}_m+\mathbf{X}\boldsymbol{\Theta}\mathbf{X}'\right)^{-1}\right)\boldsymbol{t}\,.\end{aligned}$$

Using equation (B.19) together with $\boldsymbol{\mu}=\sigma_t^{-2}\boldsymbol{\Sigma}\mathbf{X}'\boldsymbol{t}$ (see equation (3.24)) the innermost term in the latter expression can be rewritten as

$$\left(\sigma_t^2\mathbf{I}_m+\mathbf{X}\boldsymbol{\Theta}\mathbf{X}'\right)^{-1}\boldsymbol{t}=\sigma_t^{-2}\left(\mathbf{I}_m-\sigma_t^{-2}\mathbf{X}\boldsymbol{\Sigma}\mathbf{X}'\right)\boldsymbol{t}=\sigma_t^{-2}\left(\boldsymbol{t}-\mathbf{X}\boldsymbol{\mu}\right),$$

which then leads to

$$\frac{\partial Q_2\left(\boldsymbol{\theta},\sigma_t^2\right)}{\partial \sigma_t^2}=-\left(\left(\sigma_t^2\mathbf{I}_m+\mathbf{X}\boldsymbol{\Theta}\mathbf{X}'\right)^{-1}\boldsymbol{t}\right)'\left(\left(\sigma_t^2\mathbf{I}_m+\mathbf{X}\boldsymbol{\Theta}\mathbf{X}'\right)^{-1}\boldsymbol{t}\right)=-\frac{\|\boldsymbol{t}-\mathbf{X}\boldsymbol{\mu}\|^2}{\sigma_t^4}\,.$$

Putting both results finally gives the derivative of E w.r.t. σ_t^2

$$\frac{\partial E\left(\boldsymbol{\theta},\sigma_t^2\right)}{\partial \sigma_t^2}=-\frac{1}{2}\left(\frac{\sigma_t^2\left(m-\sum_{i=1}^{n}\left(1-\frac{\boldsymbol{\Sigma}_{ii}}{\theta_i}\right)\right)-\|\boldsymbol{t}-\mathbf{X}\boldsymbol{\mu}\|^2}{\sigma_t^4}\right)\,. \tag{B.21}$$

B.8.3 Update Algorithms for Maximizing the Evidence

Although we are able to compute the derivative of the evidence E w.r.t. its parameters $\boldsymbol{\theta}$ and σ_t^2 (see equations (B.20) and (B.21)) we see that we cannot explicitly compute their roots because the terms $\boldsymbol{\Sigma}_{ii}$ and μ_i involve the current solution $\boldsymbol{\theta}$ and σ_t^2. However, in order to maximize the evidence (or log-evidence) w.r.t. the parameters $\boldsymbol{\theta}\in\left(\mathbb{R}^+\right)^m$ and $\sigma_t^2\in\mathbb{R}^+$ we exploit the fact that any rearrangement of the gradient equation

$$\left.\frac{\partial E\left(\boldsymbol{\theta},\sigma_t^2\right)}{\partial \boldsymbol{\theta}}\right|_{\boldsymbol{\theta}=\hat{\boldsymbol{\theta}}}=\hat{\boldsymbol{\theta}}-\mathbf{g}\left(\hat{\boldsymbol{\theta}}\right),$$

allows us to use the update rule $\boldsymbol{\theta}_{\text{new}} = \mathbf{g}(\boldsymbol{\theta}_{\text{old}})$ to compute a (local) maximum of E, i.e., the fixpoint of $\mathbf{g} : \mathbb{R}^n \to \mathbb{R}^n$. A closer look at equation (B.20) shows that

$$\theta_i^{(\text{new})} = \boldsymbol{\Sigma}_{ii} + \mu_i^2 , \tag{B.22}$$

is a valid update rule. Introducing $\zeta_i = 1 - \theta_i^{-1}\Sigma_{ii}$ we see that another possible update rule is given by

$$\theta_i^{(\text{new})} = \frac{\mu_i^2}{\zeta_i} , \tag{B.23}$$

which follows from (B.22) as

$$\theta_i = \boldsymbol{\Sigma}_{ii} + \mu_i^2 , \quad \Leftrightarrow \quad \theta_i - \boldsymbol{\Sigma}_{ii} = \mu_i^2 , \quad \Leftrightarrow \quad \theta_i \zeta_i = \mu_i^2 .$$

In practice it has been observed that the update rule given in equation (B.23) leads to faster convergence although it does not benefit from the guarantee of convergence. According to equation (B.21) we see that

$$\left(\sigma_t^2\right)^{(\text{new})} = \frac{\|\boldsymbol{t} - \mathbf{X}\boldsymbol{\mu}\|^2}{m - \sum_{i=1}^n \zeta_i} ,$$

is an update rule which has shown excellent convergence properties in our experiments.

B.8.4 Computing the Log-Evidence

In the relevance vector machine algorithm it is necessary to compute the log-evidence $E\left(\boldsymbol{\theta}, \sigma_t^2\right)$ to monitor convergence. The crucial quantity for the computation of this quantity is the covariance matrix $\boldsymbol{\Sigma} \in \mathbb{R}^{n\times n}$ and its inverse $\boldsymbol{\Sigma}^{-1}$. In order to save computational time we use equation (B.18) to efficiently compute $Q_1\left(\boldsymbol{\theta}, \sigma_t^2\right)$,

$$Q_1\left(\boldsymbol{\theta}, \sigma_t^2\right) = m \ln\left(\sigma_t^2\right) + \ln\left(\left|\boldsymbol{\Sigma}^{-1}\right|\right) + \sum_{i=1}^n \ln\left(\theta_i\right) .$$

Since we already need to compute $\|\boldsymbol{t} - \mathbf{X}\boldsymbol{\mu}\|^2$ and $\boldsymbol{\mu}$ in each update step it is advantageous to rewrite the expression $Q_2\left(\boldsymbol{\theta}, \sigma_t^2\right)$ by

$$\begin{aligned} Q_2\left(\boldsymbol{\theta}, \sigma_t^2\right) &= \sigma_t^{-2}\boldsymbol{t}'\left(\boldsymbol{t} - \mathbf{X}\boldsymbol{\mu}\right) \\ &= \sigma_t^{-2}\|\boldsymbol{t} - \mathbf{X}\boldsymbol{\mu}\|^2 + \sigma_t^{-2}\boldsymbol{t}'\mathbf{X}\boldsymbol{\mu} - \sigma_t^{-2}\boldsymbol{\mu}'\mathbf{X}'\mathbf{X}\boldsymbol{\mu} \end{aligned}$$

$$= \sigma_t^{-2} \|t - \mathbf{X}\mu\|^2 + \mu'\Sigma^{-1}\mu - \sigma_t^{-2}\mu'\mathbf{X}'\mathbf{X}\mu$$
$$= \sigma_t^{-2} \|t - \mathbf{X}\mu\|^2 + \mu'\Theta^{-1}\mu\,,$$

where we use $\mu = \sigma^{-2}\Sigma\mathbf{X}'t$ and $\Sigma = \left(\Theta^{-1} + \sigma_t^{-2}\mathbf{X}'\mathbf{X}\right)^{-1} \Leftrightarrow \Theta^{-1} = \Sigma^{-1} - \sigma_t^{-2}\mathbf{X}'\mathbf{X}$ as given by equation (3.24).

B.8.5 Maximization of $\mathbf{f}_{\mathsf{W}|\mathsf{Z}^m=z}$

In order to find the maximum $\mu \in \mathbb{R}^n$ of the density $\mathbf{f}_{\mathsf{W}|\mathsf{Z}^m=z}$ we use Bayes' theorem

$$\mathbf{f}_{\mathsf{W}|\mathsf{Z}^m=z}(\mathbf{w}) = \mathbf{f}_{\mathsf{W}|\mathsf{X}^m=x,\mathsf{Y}^m=y}(\mathbf{w}) = \frac{\mathbf{P}_{\mathsf{Y}^m|\mathsf{W}=\mathbf{w},\mathsf{X}^m=x}(y)\,\mathbf{f}_{\mathsf{W}}(\mathbf{w})}{\mathbf{P}_{\mathsf{Y}^m|\mathsf{X}^m=x}(y)}\,,$$

where we exploit the fact that $\mathbf{f}_{\mathsf{W}|\mathsf{X}^m=x} = \mathbf{f}_{\mathsf{W}}$ as objects have no influence on weight vectors. Taking logarithms and dropping all terms which do not depend on $\mathbf{w}$ we end up looking for the maximizer $\mu \in \mathbb{R}^n$ of

$$J(\mathbf{w}) = \ln\left(\mathbf{P}_{\mathsf{Y}^m|\mathsf{W}=\mathbf{w},\mathsf{X}^m=x}(y)\right) + \ln\left(\mathbf{f}_{\mathsf{W}}(\mathbf{w})\right).$$

According to Section B.7 we know that the first term is given by $\frac{1}{2\beta}(y+\mathbf{1})'t - \sum_{i=1}^m \ln\left(1 + \exp\left(\beta^{-1}\cdot t_i\right)\right)$ where $t \in \mathbb{R}^m$ is the vector of latent activations at the m training objects x. By definition, however, $t = \mathbf{X}\mathbf{w}$ which completes the definition of the first term. For the second term we know that $\mathbf{P}_{\mathsf{W}} = \text{Normal}(\mathbf{0}, \Theta)$. Hence, representing $\mathbf{X} = \left(\mathbf{x}_1'; \ldots; \mathbf{x}_m'\right) \in \mathbb{R}^{m\times n}$ by its m rows $\mathbf{x}_i'$ yields

$$J(\mathbf{w}) = \frac{1}{2\beta}(y+\mathbf{1})'\mathbf{X}\mathbf{w} - \sum_{i=1}^m \ln\left(1 + \exp\left(\beta^{-1}\cdot \mathbf{x}_i'\mathbf{w}\right)\right) - \frac{1}{2}\mathbf{w}'\Theta^{-1}\mathbf{w} + c\,,$$

where $c = -\frac{1}{2}(m\cdot\ln(2\pi) + |\Theta|)$ does not depend on $\mathbf{w}$. Taking the derivative w.r.t. $\mathbf{w}$ we obtain

$$\left.\frac{\partial J(\mathbf{w})}{\partial \mathbf{w}}\right|_{\mathbf{w}=\mathbf{w}} = \frac{1}{2\beta}\mathbf{X}'(y+\mathbf{1}) - \frac{1}{\beta}\mathbf{X}'\boldsymbol{\pi}(\mathbf{X}\mathbf{w}) - \Theta^{-1}\mathbf{w}\,, \tag{B.24}$$

where $\boldsymbol{\pi}(t) = (\pi(t_1), \ldots, \pi(t_m))' \in \mathbb{R}^m$ and the function $\pi : \mathbb{R} \to [0,1]$ defined by $\pi(t) = \exp\left(\beta^{-1}\cdot t\right) / \left(1 + \exp\left(\beta^{-1}\cdot t\right)\right)$ is known as the sigmoid resulting from the likelihood model (3.16). Clearly, we cannot compute the root(s) of this gradient equation due to the non-linear term $\boldsymbol{\pi}(\mathbf{X}\mathbf{w})$. Let us use the Newton-Raphson method to find a local maximum μ iteratively. To this end we have to compute the Hessian $\mathbf{H}_{\mathbf{w}}$, that is, the $n \times n$ matrix of second derivatives of J

evaluated at $\mathbf{w}$. Using equation (B.24), the Hessian $\mathbf{H}_{\mathbf{w}}$ is given by

$$\mathbf{H}_{\mathbf{w}} = -\mathbf{X}'\mathbf{P}\mathbf{X} - \boldsymbol{\Theta}^{-1},$$

where $\mathbf{P} \in \mathbb{R}^{m \times m}$ is a diagonal matrix

$$\mathbf{P} = \frac{1}{\beta^2} \cdot \operatorname{diag}\left(\pi\left(\mathbf{x}_1'\mathbf{w}\right)\left(1 - \pi\left(\mathbf{x}_1'\mathbf{w}\right)\right), \ldots, \pi\left(\mathbf{x}_m'\mathbf{w}\right)\left(1 - \pi\left(\mathbf{x}_m'\mathbf{w}\right)\right)\right).$$

As a consequence, the Newton-Raphson algorithm performs the following update

$$\begin{aligned} \mathbf{w}_{i+1} &= \mathbf{w}_i - \eta \cdot \mathbf{H}_{\mathbf{w}_i}^{-1} \left.\frac{\partial J(\mathbf{w})}{\partial \mathbf{w}}\right|_{\mathbf{w}=\mathbf{w}_i} \\ &= \mathbf{w}_i + \eta\left(\mathbf{X}'\mathbf{P}\mathbf{X} + \boldsymbol{\Theta}^{-1}\right)^{-1}\left(\frac{1}{\beta}\mathbf{X}'\left(\frac{\mathbf{y}+\mathbf{1}}{2} - \pi(\mathbf{X}\mathbf{w})\right) - \boldsymbol{\Theta}^{-1}\mathbf{w}\right). \end{aligned}$$

The parameter $\eta \in \mathbb{R}^+$ is chosen from the sequence $\left(2^{-i}\right)_{i \in \mathbb{N}}$ in such a way that $J(\mathbf{w}_{i+1}) > J(\mathbf{w}_i)$. After convergence of this update rule (which must converge because the negative Hessian is positive definite) the solution $\mathbf{w}_i$ is provably the maximizer $\boldsymbol{\mu} \in \mathbb{R}^n$ of $\mathbf{f}_{\mathsf{W}|\mathsf{Z}^m=z}$. Note that that the inverse of the negated Hessian $\mathbf{H}_{\boldsymbol{\mu}}$ evaluated at the final solution $\boldsymbol{\mu}$ is the covariance matrix $\boldsymbol{\Sigma}$ defined in (3.27). We shall need this matrix to perform one update step on the (so far fixed) parameter $\boldsymbol{\theta}$.

B.9 A Derivation of the Operation $\oplus_\mu$

Let us derive the operation $\oplus_\mu : \mathcal{W} \times \mathcal{W} \rightarrow \mathcal{W}$ acting on vectors of unit length. This function has to have the following properties (see Section 3.4.1)

$$\left\|\mathbf{s} \oplus_\mu \mathbf{t}\right\|^2 = 1, \quad \text{(B.25)}$$

$$\left\|\mathbf{t} - \mathbf{s} \oplus_\mu \mathbf{t}\right\| = \mu \left\|\mathbf{t} - \mathbf{s}\right\|, \quad \text{(B.26)}$$

$$\mathbf{s} \oplus_\mu \mathbf{t} = \rho_1 \mathbf{s} + \rho_2 \mathbf{t}, \quad \text{(B.27)}$$

$$\rho_1 \geq 0, \quad \rho_2 \geq 0. \quad \text{(B.28)}$$

Here we assume that $\|\mathbf{s}\|^2 = \|\mathbf{t}\|^2 = 1$. Inserting equation (B.27) into (B.25) gives

$$\|\rho_1 \mathbf{s} + \rho_2 \mathbf{t}\|^2 = \rho_1^2 + \rho_2^2 + 2\rho_1\rho_2 \langle \mathbf{s}, \mathbf{t} \rangle = 1. \quad \text{(B.29)}$$

In a similar fashion combining equations (B.27) and (B.26) gives

$$\left\|\mathbf{t} - \mathbf{s} \oplus_\mu \mathbf{t}\right\|^2 = \mu^2 \|\mathbf{t} - \mathbf{s}\|^2$$

$$\begin{aligned}\|(1-\rho_2)\,\mathbf{t}-\rho_1\mathbf{s}\|^2 &= \mu^2\,\|\mathbf{t}-\mathbf{s}\|^2\\ (1-\rho_2)\,(1-\rho_2-2\rho_1\,\langle\mathbf{s},\mathbf{t}\rangle)+\rho_1^2 &= 2\mu^2\,(1-\langle\mathbf{s},\mathbf{t}\rangle)\ .\end{aligned} \tag{B.30}$$

Note that equation (B.29) is quadratic in ρ_2 and has the following solution

$$\rho_2 \;=\; \underbrace{-\rho_1\,\langle\mathbf{s},\mathbf{t}\rangle \pm\sqrt{\rho_1^2\,(\langle\mathbf{s},\mathbf{t}\rangle)^2-\rho_1^2+1}}_{A}\ . \tag{B.31}$$

Let us substitute equation (B.31) into the l.h.s. of equation (B.30). This gives the following quadratic equation in ρ_1

$$\begin{aligned}(1-A+\rho_1\,\langle\mathbf{s},\mathbf{t}\rangle)\,(1-A-\rho_1\,\langle\mathbf{s},\mathbf{t}\rangle)+\rho_1^2 &= 2\mu^2\,(1-\langle\mathbf{s},\mathbf{t}\rangle)\\ (1-A)^2-\rho_1^2\,(\langle\mathbf{s},\mathbf{t}\rangle)^2+\rho_1^2 &= 2\mu^2\,(1-\langle\mathbf{s},\mathbf{t}\rangle)\\ 1-A &= \mu^2\,(1-\langle\mathbf{s},\mathbf{t}\rangle)\\ \rho_1^2\left((\langle\mathbf{s},\mathbf{t}\rangle)^2-1\right)+1 &= \left(\mu^2\,(1-\langle\mathbf{s},\mathbf{t}\rangle)-1\right)^2,\end{aligned} \tag{B.32}$$

whose solution is given by

$$\rho_1=\mu\sqrt{-\frac{\mu^2-\mu^2\,\langle\mathbf{s},\mathbf{t}\rangle-2}{\langle\mathbf{s},\mathbf{t}\rangle+1}}\ .$$

Inserting this formula back into equation (B.31), and making use of the identity (B.32), we obtain for ρ_2

$$\rho_2=-\rho_1\,\langle\mathbf{s},\mathbf{t}\rangle\pm\sqrt{\rho_1^2\left((\langle\mathbf{s},\mathbf{t}\rangle)^2-1\right)+1}=-\rho_1\,\langle\mathbf{s},\mathbf{t}\rangle\pm\left(\mu^2\,(1-\langle\mathbf{s},\mathbf{t}\rangle)-1\right)\ .$$

B.10 Fisher Linear Discriminant

Given a training sample $z=(x,y)\in\mathcal{Z}^m$, let us compute the maximum likelihood estimates $\hat{\boldsymbol{\mu}}_y$ and $\hat{\boldsymbol{\Sigma}}$ of the mean vector $\boldsymbol{\mu}_y\in\mathbb{R}^n$ and the covariance $\boldsymbol{\Sigma}\in\mathbb{R}^{n\times n}$ of an n-dimensional Gaussian measure, respectively. Let us assume that $\mathbf{P}_{\mathsf{Y}}(+1)=\mathbf{P}_{\mathsf{Y}}(-1)=\frac{1}{2}$. Then the logarithm of the likelihood can be written as

$$L\left(\boldsymbol{\mu}_y,\boldsymbol{\Sigma}\right)\;=\;\ln\left(\prod_{i=1}^{m}(2\pi)^{-\frac{n}{2}}\,|\boldsymbol{\Sigma}|^{-\frac{1}{2}}\exp\left(-\frac{1}{2}\left(\mathbf{x}_i-\boldsymbol{\mu}_{y_i}\right)'\boldsymbol{\Sigma}^{-1}\left(\mathbf{x}_i-\boldsymbol{\mu}_{y_i}\right)\right)\right),$$

$$= -\sum_{i=1}^{m} \frac{1}{2} \left(n \ln (2\pi) + \ln (|\boldsymbol{\Sigma}|) + \left(\mathbf{x}_i - \boldsymbol{\mu}_{y_i} \right)' \boldsymbol{\Sigma}^{-1} \left(\mathbf{x}_i - \boldsymbol{\mu}_{y_i} \right) \right) .$$

Let us start with the maximizer w.r.t. the mean vectors $\boldsymbol{\mu}_y$. Setting the derivative to zero we obtain, for both classes $y \in \{-1, +1\}$,

$$\left. \frac{\partial L \left(\boldsymbol{\mu}_y, \boldsymbol{\Sigma} \right)}{\partial \boldsymbol{\mu}_y} \right|_{\boldsymbol{\mu}_y = \hat{\boldsymbol{\mu}}_y} = \sum_{(x_i, y) \in z} \left(\boldsymbol{\Sigma}^{-1} \mathbf{x}_i - \boldsymbol{\Sigma}^{-1} \hat{\boldsymbol{\mu}}_y \right) = \mathbf{0} ,$$

$$\hat{\boldsymbol{\mu}}_y = \frac{1}{m_y} \sum_{(x_i, y) \in z} \mathbf{x}_i , \tag{B.33}$$

where m_y equals the number of samples of class y in $z \in \mathcal{Z}^m$. Further, according to Theorems A.97 and A.98 we know

$$\left. \frac{\partial L \left(\boldsymbol{\mu}_y, \boldsymbol{\Sigma} \right)}{\partial \boldsymbol{\Sigma}} \right|_{\boldsymbol{\Sigma} = \hat{\boldsymbol{\Sigma}}} = -\frac{1}{2} \sum_{i=1}^{m} \left(\hat{\boldsymbol{\Sigma}}^{-1} - \hat{\boldsymbol{\Sigma}}^{-1} \left(\mathbf{x}_i - \boldsymbol{\mu}_{y_i} \right) \left(\mathbf{x}_i - \boldsymbol{\mu}_{y_i} \right)' \hat{\boldsymbol{\Sigma}}^{-1} \right) = \mathbf{0} ,$$

$$m \hat{\boldsymbol{\Sigma}}^{-1} = \hat{\boldsymbol{\Sigma}}^{-1} \left(\sum_{i=1}^{m} \left(\mathbf{x}_i - \boldsymbol{\mu}_{y_i} \right) \left(\mathbf{x}_i - \boldsymbol{\mu}_{y_i} \right)' \right) \hat{\boldsymbol{\Sigma}}^{-1}$$

$$\hat{\boldsymbol{\Sigma}} = \frac{1}{m} \sum_{y \in \{-1,+1\}} \sum_{(x_i, y) \in z} \left(\mathbf{x}_i - \boldsymbol{\mu}_y \right) \left(\mathbf{x}_i - \boldsymbol{\mu}_y \right)' .$$

If we substitute $\hat{\boldsymbol{\mu}}_y$ as given in equation (B.33) for $\boldsymbol{\mu}_y$ we obtain

$$\begin{aligned} \hat{\boldsymbol{\Sigma}} &= \frac{1}{m} \left(\sum_{y \in \{-1,+1\}} \sum_{(x_i, y) \in z} \left(\mathbf{x}_i - \hat{\boldsymbol{\mu}}_y \right) \left(\mathbf{x}_i - \hat{\boldsymbol{\mu}}_y \right)' \right) \\ &= \frac{1}{m} \left(\sum_{i=1}^{m} \mathbf{x}_i \mathbf{x}_i' - \sum_{y \in \{-1,+1\}} \left(2 \sum_{(x_i, y) \in z} \mathbf{x}_i \hat{\boldsymbol{\mu}}_y' - m_y \hat{\boldsymbol{\mu}}_y \hat{\boldsymbol{\mu}}_y' \right) \right) \\ &= \frac{1}{m} \left(\mathbf{X}'\mathbf{X} - \sum_{y \in \{-1,+1\}} m_y \hat{\boldsymbol{\mu}}_y \hat{\boldsymbol{\mu}}_y' \right) . \end{aligned}$$

C Proofs and Derivations—Part II

This appendix gives all proofs and derivations of Part II in detail. If necessary the theorems are restated before proving them. This appendix is not as self-contained as the chapters in the main body of this book; it is probably best to read it in conjunction with the corresponding chapter.

C.1 VC and PAC Generalization Error Bounds

In this section we present the proof of Theorem 4.7. It involves several lemmas which will also be of importance in other sections of this book. We shall therefore start by proving these lemmas before proceeding to the final proof. The version of the proof presented closely follows the original paper Vapnik and Chervonenkis (1971) and its polished version, found in Anthony and Bartlett (1999).

C.1.1 Basic Lemmas

In this section we prove three *basic lemmas*—the key ingredients required to obtain bounds on the generalization error in the VC, PAC and luckiness frameworks. The original proof of Lemma C.1 is due to Vapnik and Chervonenkis (1971). We shall present a simplified version of the proof, as found in Devroye et al. (1996, p. 193). The proof of Lemma C.3 is the solution to Problem 12.7 in Devroye et al. (1996, p. 209) and is only a special case of Lemma C.2 which uses essentially the same technique as the proof of Lemma C.1. In order to enhance readability we shall use the shorthand notation $z_{[i:j]} \stackrel{\text{def}}{=} (z_i, \ldots, z_j)$.

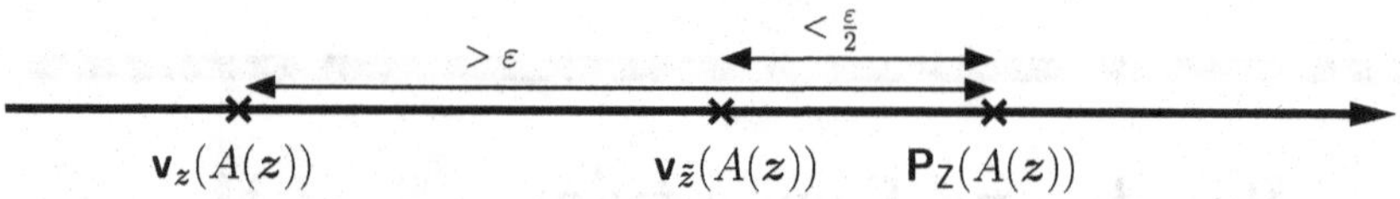

Figure C.1 Graphical illustration of the main step in the basic lemma. If $\mathbf{v}_z(A(z))$ deviates from $\mathbf{P}_Z(A(z))$ by at least ε but $\mathbf{v}_{\tilde{z}}(A(z))$ is $\frac{\varepsilon}{2}$-close to $\mathbf{P}_Z(A(z))$ then $\mathbf{v}_z(A(z))$ and $\mathbf{v}_{\tilde{z}}(A(z))$ deviate by at least $\frac{\varepsilon}{2}$.

Lemma C.1 (VC basic lemma) *For all probability measures* $\mathbf{P}_Z$ *and all subsets* $\mathfrak{A}$ *of the* σ*–algebra* $\mathfrak{Z}$ *over the sample space* $\mathcal{Z}$*, if* $m\varepsilon^2 > 2$ *we have*

$$\mathbf{P}_{Z^m}\left(\sup_{A\in\mathfrak{A}} |\mathbf{P}_Z(A) - \mathbf{v}_{\mathbf{Z}}(A)| > \varepsilon\right) < 2\mathbf{P}_{Z^{2m}}\left(\sup_{A\in\mathfrak{A}} \left|\mathbf{v}_{\mathbf{Z}_{[1:m]}}(A) - \mathbf{v}_{\mathbf{Z}_{[(m+1):2m]}}(A)\right| > \frac{\varepsilon}{2}\right).$$

Proof Given a sample $z \in \mathcal{Z}^m$, let $A(z) \in \mathfrak{A}$ be given by

$$A(z) = \operatorname*{argsup}_{A\in\mathfrak{A}} |\mathbf{P}_Z(A) - \mathbf{v}_z(A)| .$$

Clearly, whenever for $z, \tilde{z} \in \mathcal{Z}^m$

$$\underbrace{(|\mathbf{v}_z(A(z)) - \mathbf{P}_Z(A(z))| > \varepsilon)}_{Q_1(z)} \wedge \underbrace{\left(|\mathbf{v}_{\tilde{z}}(A(z)) - \mathbf{P}_Z(A(z))| < \frac{\varepsilon}{2}\right)}_{Q_2(z\tilde{z})}$$

it follows that the proposition

$$Q_3(z\tilde{z}) \equiv |\mathbf{v}_z(A(z)) - \mathbf{v}_{\tilde{z}}(A(z))| > \frac{\varepsilon}{2}$$

is true as well (see also Figure C.1). Henceforth, we know that

$$\begin{aligned}\mathbf{P}_{Z^{2m}}(Q_3(\mathbf{Z})) &\geq \mathbf{P}_{Z^{2m}}\left(Q_1\left(\mathbf{Z}_{[1:m]}\right) \wedge Q_2(\mathbf{Z})\right) \\ &= \mathbf{E}_{Z_1^m}\left[\mathbf{I}_{Q_1(\mathbf{Z}_1)}\mathbf{P}_{Z_2^m|Z_1^m=z_1}(Q_2(z_1\mathbf{Z}_2))\right].\end{aligned}$$

Now, $\mathbf{P}_{Z_2^m|Z_1^m=z_1}(Q_2(z_1\mathbf{Z}_2))$ is the probability that the mean of m random variables, taking values in $\{0, 1\}$, does not exceed a distance of $\frac{\varepsilon}{2}$ from their common expectation $\mathbf{P}_Z(A(z_1))$. The variance of such a random variable is given by $\frac{\mathbf{P}_Z(A(z_1))(1-\mathbf{P}_Z(A(z_1)))}{m} \leq \frac{1}{4m}$ and thus, by Chebyshev's inequality (see Theorem A.110) and the assumed independence of $\mathbf{Z}_2$ from $\mathbf{Z}_1$, it follows that

$$\mathbf{P}_{Z_2^m|Z_1^m=z_1}(Q_2(z_1\mathbf{Z}_2)) \geq 1 - \frac{\mathbf{P}_Z(A(z_1))(1-\mathbf{P}_Z(A(z_1)))}{m\left(\frac{\varepsilon}{2}\right)^2} \geq 1 - \frac{1}{m\varepsilon^2} > \frac{1}{2},$$

where the last inequality follows from $m\varepsilon^2 > 2$ by assumption. Furthermore, we know that whenever $Q_3(z)$ holds $\sup_{A\in\mathfrak{A}} |\mathbf{v}_z(A) - \mathbf{v}_{\tilde{z}}(A)| > \frac{\varepsilon}{2}$ because $A(z_1) \in \mathfrak{A}$. In summary

$$\begin{aligned}\mathbf{P}_{\mathsf{Z}^{2m}}\left(\sup_{A\in\mathfrak{A}} \left|\mathbf{v}_{\mathbf{Z}_{[1:m]}}(A) - \mathbf{v}_{\mathbf{Z}_{[(m+1):2m]}}(A)\right| > \frac{\varepsilon}{2}\right) &> \frac{1}{2}\mathbf{P}_{\mathsf{Z}^m}(Q_1(\mathbf{Z})) \\ &= \frac{1}{2}\mathbf{P}_{\mathsf{Z}^m}\left(\sup_{A\in\mathfrak{A}} |\mathbf{P}_{\mathsf{Z}}(A) - \mathbf{v}_{\mathbf{Z}}(A)| > \varepsilon\right).\end{aligned}$$

The lemma is proved. ■

Lemma C.2 (Luckiness basic lemma) *For all probability measures $\mathbf{P}_{\mathsf{Z}}$, all measurable logical formulas $\Upsilon : \bigcup_{m=1}^{\infty} \mathcal{Z}^m \rightarrow \{\text{true}, \text{false}\}$ and all subsets $\mathfrak{A}$ of the σ–algebra $\mathfrak{Z}$ over the sample space $\mathcal{Z}$, if $m\varepsilon > 8$ we have*

$$\begin{aligned}&\mathbf{P}_{\mathsf{Z}^m}\left(\exists A \in \mathfrak{A} : (\Upsilon(\mathbf{Z})) \wedge (\mathbf{v}_{\mathbf{Z}}(A) = 0) \wedge (\mathbf{P}_{\mathsf{Z}}(A) > \varepsilon)\right) < \\ &\quad 2\mathbf{P}_{\mathsf{Z}^{2m}}\left(\exists A \in \mathfrak{A} : \left(\Upsilon\left(\mathbf{Z}_{[1:m]}\right)\right) \wedge \left(\mathbf{v}_{\mathbf{Z}_{[1:m]}}(A) = 0\right) \wedge \left(\mathbf{v}_{\mathbf{Z}_{[(m+1):2m]}}(A) > \frac{\varepsilon}{2}\right)\right).\end{aligned}$$

Proof Given a sample $z \in \mathcal{Z}^m$, let $A(z) \in \mathfrak{A}$ be such that $\mathbf{P}_{\mathsf{Z}}(A(z)) > \varepsilon \wedge \mathbf{v}_z(A(z)) = 0$ if such a set exists or any set $A \in \mathfrak{A}$ otherwise. For any $z, \tilde{z} \in \mathcal{Z}^m$ let us define

$$\begin{aligned}Q_1(z\tilde{z}) &\equiv \mathbf{v}_{\tilde{z}}(A(z)) \geq \frac{\varepsilon}{2}, \quad Q_2(z) \equiv (\Upsilon(z)) \wedge (\mathbf{v}_z(A(z)) = 0), \\ Q_3(z) &\equiv \mathbf{P}_{\mathsf{Z}}(A(z)) > \varepsilon.\end{aligned}$$

First, it holds that

$$\begin{aligned}\mathbf{P}_{\mathsf{Z}^{2m}}\left(Q_1(\mathbf{Z}) \wedge Q_2\left(\mathbf{Z}_{[1:m]}\right)\right) &\geq \mathbf{P}_{\mathsf{Z}^{2m}}\left(Q_1(\mathbf{Z}) \wedge Q_2\left(\mathbf{Z}_{[1:m]}\right) \wedge Q_3\left(\mathbf{Z}_{[1:m]}\right)\right) \\ &= \mathbf{E}_{\mathsf{Z}_1^m}\left[\mathbf{I}_{Q_2(\mathbf{Z}_1)\wedge Q_3(\mathbf{Z}_1)}\mathbf{P}_{\mathsf{Z}_2^m|\mathsf{Z}_1^m=z_1}(Q_1(z_1\mathbf{Z}_2))\right].\end{aligned}$$

By the indicator event we know that $\mathbf{P}_{\mathsf{Z}}(A(z_1)) > \varepsilon$ whenever we need to evaluate $\mathbf{P}_{\mathsf{Z}_2^m|\mathsf{Z}_1^m=z_1}(Q_1(z_1\mathbf{Z}_2))$ which is the probability that a binomially distributed variable with expectation greater than ε exceeds a value of $\frac{m\varepsilon}{2}$ where by assumption of the lemma $m\varepsilon > 8$ and the sample $\mathbf{Z}_2$ is assumed to be independent of $\mathbf{Z}_1$. By the binomial mean deviation bound (see Theorem A.117 setting $\lambda = 2$ and $\alpha = \frac{1}{2}$) this probability is lower bounded by

$$\mathbf{P}_{\mathsf{Z}_2^m|\mathsf{Z}_1^m=z_1}(Q_1(z_1\mathbf{Z}_2)) \geq \frac{1}{2}.$$

In summary

$$\begin{aligned}\mathbf{P}_{\mathsf{Z}^{2m}}&\left(\exists A\in\mathfrak{A}:\left(\Upsilon\left(\mathbf{Z}_{[1:m]}\right)\right)\wedge\left(\mathbf{v}_{\mathbf{Z}_{[1:m]}}(A)=0\right)\wedge\left(\mathbf{v}_{\mathbf{Z}_{[(m+1):2m]}}(A)>\frac{\varepsilon}{2}\right)\right)\\&\geq\mathbf{P}_{\mathsf{Z}_1^m\mathsf{Z}_2^m}\left(Q_1(\mathbf{Z})\wedge Q_2\left(\mathbf{Z}_{[1:m]}\right)\right)>\frac{1}{2}\mathbf{P}_{\mathsf{Z}^m}\left(Q_2(\mathbf{Z})\wedge Q_3(\mathbf{Z})\right)\\&=\frac{1}{2}\mathbf{P}_{\mathsf{Z}^m}\left(\exists A\in\mathfrak{A}:\left(\Upsilon(\mathbf{Z})\right)\wedge\left(\mathbf{v}_{\mathbf{Z}}(A)=0\right)\wedge\left(\mathbf{P}_{\mathsf{Z}}(A)>\varepsilon\right)\right).\end{aligned}$$

The lemma is proved. ■

Lemma C.3 (PAC basic lemma) *For all probability measures $\mathbf{P}_{\mathsf{Z}}$ and all subsets $\mathfrak{A}$ of the σ–algebra $\mathfrak{Z}$ over the sample space $\mathcal{Z}$, if $m\varepsilon>8$ we have*

$$\begin{aligned}\mathbf{P}_{\mathsf{Z}^m}&\left(\exists A\in\mathfrak{A}:\left(\mathbf{v}_{\mathbf{Z}}(A)=0\right)\wedge\left(\mathbf{P}_{\mathsf{Z}}(A)>\varepsilon\right)\right)\\&<2\mathbf{P}_{\mathsf{Z}^{2m}}\left(\exists A\in\mathfrak{A}:\left(\mathbf{v}_{\mathbf{Z}_{[1:m]}}(A)=0\right)\wedge\left(\mathbf{v}_{\mathbf{Z}_{[(m+1):2m]}}(A)>\frac{\varepsilon}{2}\right)\right).\end{aligned}$$

Proof Using $\Upsilon(z)=\text{true}$ in Lemma C.2 proves the assertion. ■

C.1.2 Proof of Theorem 4.7

Proof Let us start by proving equation (4.11). First, we note that, due to Lemma C.1, it suffices to bound the probability[1]

$$\underbrace{\mathbf{P}_{\mathsf{Z}^{2m}}\left(\exists h\in\mathcal{H}:\left|R_{\text{emp}}\left[h,(\mathsf{Z}_1,\ldots,\mathsf{Z}_m)\right]-R_{\text{emp}}\left[h,(\mathsf{Z}_{m+1},\ldots,\mathsf{Z}_{2m})\right]\right|>\frac{\varepsilon}{2}\right)}_{J(\mathbf{Z})}.$$

Since all $2m$ samples Z_i are drawn iid from $\mathbf{P}_{\mathsf{Z}}$ we know that, for any permutation $\pi:\{1,\ldots,2m\}\to\{1,\ldots,2m\}$,

$$\mathbf{P}_{\mathsf{Z}^{2m}}\left(J(\mathbf{Z})\right)=\mathbf{P}_{\mathsf{Z}^{2m}}\left(J(\Pi(\mathbf{Z}))\right),$$

where we use the shorthand notation $\Pi(\mathbf{Z})$ to denote the action of π on the indices of $\mathbf{Z}=(\mathsf{Z}_1,\ldots,\mathsf{Z}_{2m})$, i.e., $\Pi((\mathsf{Z}_1,\ldots,\mathsf{Z}_{2m}))\stackrel{\text{def}}{=}\left(\mathsf{Z}_{\pi(1)},\ldots,\mathsf{Z}_{\pi(2m)}\right)$. Now consider all 2^m different swapping permutations $\Pi_{\mathbf{s}}$ indexed by $\mathbf{s}\in\{0,1\}^m$, i.e., $\Pi_{\mathbf{s}}(z)$ swaps z_i and z_{i+m} if, and only if, $s_i=1$. Using the uniform measure $\mathbf{P}_{\mathsf{S}^m}$

1 Note that in due course of the proof we use the symbol z (and $\mathbf{Z}$) to refer to a (random) training sample (drawn iid from $\mathbf{P}_{\mathsf{Z}}$) of size $2m$.

where $\mathbf{P}_{\mathsf{S}}(0) = \mathbf{P}_{\mathsf{S}}(1) = \frac{1}{2}$ we get

$$\mathbf{P}_{\mathsf{Z}^{2m}}(J(\mathbf{Z})) = \mathbf{E}_{\mathsf{S}^m}\left[\mathbf{P}_{\mathsf{Z}^{2m}|\mathsf{S}^m=\mathbf{s}}(J(\Pi_{\mathbf{s}}(\mathbf{Z})))\right] = \mathbf{E}_{\mathsf{Z}^{2m}}\left[\mathbf{P}_{\mathsf{S}^m|\mathsf{Z}^{2m}=z}(J(\Pi_{\mathsf{S}}(z)))\right],$$

Note that $\mathbf{P}_{\mathsf{Z}^{2m}\mathsf{S}^m} = \mathbf{P}_{\mathsf{Z}^{2m}}\mathbf{P}_{\mathsf{S}^m}$, hence the two measures are independent so that $\mathbf{P}_{\mathsf{S}^m|\mathsf{Z}^{2m}=z} = \mathbf{P}_{\mathsf{S}^m}$. The advantage of this formulation is that we only need to find the probability of $J(\Pi_{\mathsf{S}}(z))$ over the random choice of permutations S *for a fixed double sample* $z \in \mathcal{Z}^{2m}$. Since the double sample z is fixed, it follows that the number of hypotheses h considered in $J(\Pi_{\mathbf{s}}(z))$ must effectively be finite because, regardless of the permutation $\Pi_{\mathbf{s}}$, any two hypotheses $h \in \mathcal{H}$ and $\tilde{h} \in \mathcal{H}$ with the property

$$\forall i \in \{1, \ldots, 2m\}: \quad h(x_i) = \tilde{h}(x_i)$$

lead to the same difference in training errors on $(z_1, \ldots, z_m)$ and $(z_{m+1}, \ldots, z_{2m})$. Thus, let $\mathcal{N}_{\mathcal{H}}(z) \in \mathbb{N}$ be the number of equivalence classes w.r.t. the zero-one loss

$$\mathcal{N}_{\mathcal{H}}(z) \stackrel{\text{def}}{=} \left|\left\{\left(l_{0-1}(h(x_1), y_1), \ldots l_{0-1}\left(h\left(x_{|z|}\right), y_{|z|}\right)\right) \mid h \in \mathcal{H}\right\}\right| \leq 2^{|z|},$$

and let $\hat{h}_1, \ldots, \hat{h}_{\mathcal{N}_{\mathcal{H}}(z)} \in \mathcal{H}$ be the corresponding hypotheses realizing the $\mathcal{N}_{\mathcal{H}}(z)$ different loss patterns. By the union bound it follows that $\mathbf{P}_{\mathsf{S}^m|\mathsf{Z}^{2m}=z}(J(\Pi_{\mathsf{S}}(z)))$ is less than or equal to

$$\sum_{i=1}^{\mathcal{N}_{\mathcal{H}}(z)} \mathbf{P}_{\mathsf{S}^m|\mathsf{Z}^{2m}=z}\left(\left|\frac{1}{m}\sum_{j=1}^{m} \mathbf{I}_{\hat{h}_i\left(x_{\pi_{\mathsf{S}}(j)}\right)\neq y_{\pi_{\mathsf{S}}(j)}} - \frac{1}{m}\sum_{j=1}^{m} \mathbf{I}_{\hat{h}_i\left(x_{\pi_{\mathsf{S}}(j+m)}\right)\neq y_{\pi_{\mathsf{S}}(j+m)}}\right| > \frac{\varepsilon}{2}\right)$$

$$= \sum_{i=1}^{\mathcal{N}_{\mathcal{H}}(z)} \mathbf{P}_{\mathsf{S}^m|\mathsf{Z}^{2m}=z}\left(\left|\frac{1}{m}\sum_{j=1}^{m}\left(\mathbf{I}_{\hat{h}_i\left(x_{\pi_{\mathsf{S}}(j)}\right)\neq y_{\pi_{\mathsf{S}}(j)}} - \mathbf{I}_{\hat{h}_i\left(x_{\pi_{\mathsf{S}}(j+m)}\right)\neq y_{\pi_{\mathsf{S}}(j+m)}}\right)\right| > \frac{\varepsilon}{2}\right),$$

where we used the definition of $R_{\text{emp}}[h, (z_1, \ldots, z_m)]$ given in equation (2.11) and $z = ((x_1, y_1), \ldots, (x_{2m}, y_{2m}))$. Since we consider the uniform measure over swappings we know that each summand over $j \in \{1, \ldots, m\}$ is a uniformly distributed random variable with outcomes $\pm\left|\mathbf{I}_{\hat{h}_i\left(x_{\pi_{\mathsf{S}}(j)}\right)\neq y_{\pi_{\mathsf{S}}(j)}} - \mathbf{I}_{\hat{h}_i\left(x_{\pi_{\mathsf{S}}(j+m)}\right)\neq y_{\pi_{\mathsf{S}}(j+m)}}\right|$. As a consequence these random variables are always in the interval $[-1, +1]$ with expectation zero. Thus, a direct application of Hoeffding's inequality (see Theorem

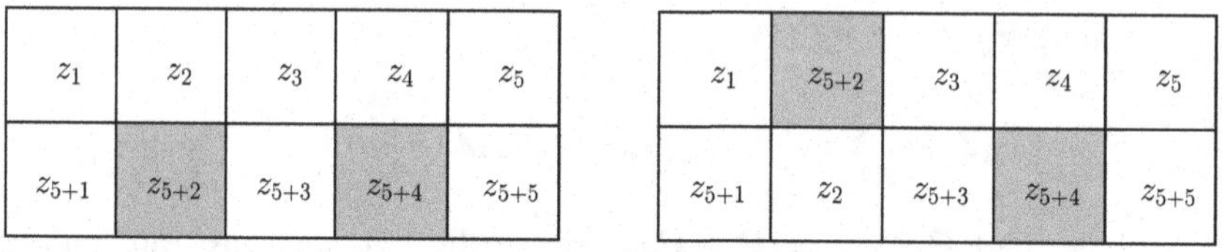

Figure C.2 Counting swappings that ensure $R_{\text{emp}}[\hat{h}_i, (z_1, \ldots, z_m)] = 0$ while $R_{\text{emp}}[\hat{h}_i, (z_{m+1}, \ldots, z_{2m})] > \varepsilon$ where $\hat{h}_i \in \mathcal{H}$. Each example $z_j \in (z_{m+1}, \ldots, z_{2m})$ where $l_{0-1}(\hat{h}_i(x_j), y_j) = 1$ is shown as a gray cell. We used $m = 5$ and $\varepsilon = \frac{2}{m}$. **(Left)** Clearly, whenever z_6, z_8 or z_{10} is swapped the training error in the first half remains zero. **(Right)** If we swap z_7 or z_9 into the first half we will violate the zero training error condition and therefore must not swap them.

A.112) yields

$$\mathbf{P}_{\mathsf{Z}^{2m}}\left(J\left(\mathbf{Z}\right)\right) < \mathbf{E}_{\mathsf{Z}^{2m}}\left(\sum_{i=1}^{\mathcal{N}_{\mathcal{H}}(\mathbf{Z})} 2\exp\left(-\frac{m\varepsilon^2}{8}\right)\right) = \mathbf{E}_{\mathsf{Z}^{2m}}\left[\mathcal{N}_{\mathcal{H}}\left(\mathbf{Z}\right)\right] \cdot 2\exp\left(-\frac{m\varepsilon^2}{8}\right).$$

Using the worst case quantity $\mathcal{N}_{\mathcal{H}}(2m) \stackrel{\text{def}}{=} \max_{z \in \mathcal{Z}^{2m}} \mathcal{N}_{\mathcal{H}}(z)$ completes the proof of assertion (4.11).

The second equation (4.12) is proven in a similar way. First, according to Lemma C.3 all we need to bound is the probability

$$\mathbf{P}_{\mathsf{Z}^{2m}}\underbrace{\left(\exists h \in \mathcal{H} : R_{\text{emp}}\left[h, (\mathsf{Z}_1, \ldots, \mathsf{Z}_m)\right] = 0 \wedge R_{\text{emp}}\left[h, (\mathsf{Z}_{m+1}, \ldots, \mathsf{Z}_{2m})\right] > \frac{\varepsilon}{2}\right)}_{J(\mathbf{Z})}.$$

If we again consider all 2^m swapping permutations π_s we see that this probability equals

$$\mathbf{E}_{\mathsf{Z}^{2m}}\left[\sum_{i=1}^{\mathcal{N}_{\mathcal{H}}(\mathbf{Z})} \mathbf{P}_{\mathsf{S}^m|\mathsf{Z}^{2m}=z}\left(Q_z\left(\hat{h}_i\right)\right)\right],$$

where the event $Q_z\left(\hat{h}_i\right) \subseteq \{0,1\}^m$ is the set of all swappings such that $\hat{h}_i$ incurs no training errors on the first m samples $(z_1, \ldots, z_m)$ but at least $\frac{m\varepsilon}{2}$ training errors on the second m samples $(z_{m+1},\ldots,z_{2m})$, i.e.,

$$Q_z\left(\hat{h}_i\right)=\left\{\mathbf{s}\,\middle|\left(\sum_{j=1}^{m}\mathbf{I}_{\hat{h}_i\left(x_{\pi_{\mathbf{s}}(j)}\right)=y_{\pi_{\mathbf{s}}(j)}}=0\right)\wedge\left(\sum_{j=1}^{m}\mathbf{I}_{\hat{h}_i\left(x_{\pi_{\mathbf{s}}(j+m)}\right)\neq y_{\pi_{\mathbf{s}}(j+m)}}>\frac{m\varepsilon}{2}\right)\right\}.$$

Here, the set $\hat{h}_1,\ldots\hat{h}_{\mathcal{N}_{\mathcal{H}}(z)}\in\mathcal{H}$ are again $\mathcal{N}_{\mathcal{H}}(z)$ different hypotheses w.r.t. the training errors on $z=(z_1,\ldots,z_{2m})$. In contrast to the previous case, the cardinality of $Q_z\left(\hat{h}_i\right)$ is easily upper bounded by $2^{m-\frac{m\varepsilon}{2}}$ because, whenever we swap any of the at least $\frac{m\varepsilon}{2}$ patterns $\left(x_{j+m},y_{j+m}\right)$ that incur a loss on the second m samples, we violate the assumption of zero training error on the first m samples (see also Figure C.2). Since we use the uniform measure $\mathbf{P}_{\mathsf{S}^m}$ it follows that

$$\mathbf{P}_{\mathsf{Z}^{2m}}\left(J\left(\mathbf{Z}\right)\right)\leq\mathbf{E}_{\mathsf{Z}^{2m}}\left[\sum_{i=1}^{\mathcal{N}_{\mathcal{H}}(\mathbf{Z})}2^{-m}\cdot2^{m-\frac{m\varepsilon}{2}}\right]=\mathbf{E}_{\mathsf{Z}^{2m}}\left[\mathcal{N}_{\mathcal{H}}\left(\mathbf{Z}\right)\right]\cdot2^{-\frac{m\varepsilon}{2}}.$$

Bounding the expectation $\mathbf{E}_{\mathsf{Z}^{2m}}\left[\mathcal{N}_{\mathcal{H}}\left(\mathbf{Z}\right)\right]$ by its maximum $\mathcal{N}_{\mathcal{H}}(2m)$ from above and using $2^{-x}=\exp\left(-x\cdot\ln\left(2\right)\right)\leq\exp\left(-\frac{x}{2}\right)$ for all $x\geq0$ proves equation (4.12). ■

C.2 Bound on the Growth Function

In this section we prove Theorem 4.10 using proof by contradiction. This elegant proof is due to E. Sontag and is taken from Sontag (1998). At first let us introduce the function $\Phi:\mathbb{N}\times\mathbb{N}\to\mathbb{N}$ defined by

$$\Phi\left(m,\vartheta\right)\stackrel{\text{def}}{=}\sum_{i=0}^{\vartheta}\binom{m}{i}.$$

Defining $\binom{m}{i}=0$ whenever $i>m$ we see that $\Phi\left(m,\vartheta\right)=2^m$ if $\vartheta\geq m$ because by Theorem A.103,

$$\Phi\left(m,m\right)=\sum_{i=0}^{m}\binom{m}{i}=\sum_{i=0}^{m}\binom{m}{i}\cdot1^i=\left(1+1\right)^m=2^m. \tag{C.1}$$

Let us start with a central lemma which essentially forms the heart of the proof.

Lemma C.4 *Let $m \in \mathbb{N}$, $\vartheta \in \{0, \ldots, m\}$ and $r > \Phi(m, \vartheta)$, and suppose that the matrix $\mathbf{A} \in \{0, 1\}^{m \times r}$ is such that all its r columns are distinct. Then, there is some $(\vartheta + 1) \times 2^{\vartheta+1}$ sub-matrix of $\mathbf{A}$ whose $2^{\vartheta+1}$ columns are distinct.*

Proof We proceed by induction over $m \in \mathbb{N}$. Note that the lemma is trivially true for $\vartheta = m$ because, according to equation (C.1), $\Phi(m, m) = 2^m$. But, each binary matrix with m rows has at most 2^m distinct columns; hence there exists no value of r. Let us start by proving the assertion for $m = 1$: We have just shown that we only need to consider $\vartheta = 0$. Then, the only possible value of r is 2 because $\Phi(1, 0) = 1$. For this value, however, the only $(\vartheta + 1) \times 2^{\vartheta+1} = 1 \times 2$ sub-matrix of the $m \times r = 1 \times 2$ matrix $\mathbf{A}$ is $\mathbf{A}$ itself which by assumption has 2 distinct columns.

We next assume the result is true for $m - 1$ and prove it for m. Let us consider any matrix $\mathbf{A} \in \{0, 1\}^{m \times r}$ with $r > \Phi(m, \vartheta)$ distinct columns. By interchanging columns, this matrix can always be transfered into the form

$$\left(\begin{pmatrix} 0 \cdots 0 \\ \mathbf{B} \end{pmatrix} \begin{pmatrix} 1 \cdots 1 \\ \mathbf{B} \end{pmatrix} \begin{pmatrix} * \cdots * \\ \mathbf{C} \end{pmatrix} \right),$$

where $\mathbf{B}$ and $\mathbf{C}$ are $(m - 1) \times r_1$ and $(m - 1) \times (r - 2r_1)$ matrices, respectively, and "$*$" is a placeholder for either 0 or 1. Let us consider two matrices $\mathbf{B}$ and $\mathbf{C}$ for the largest value of r_1 (number of columns of $\mathbf{B}$). Then, by assumption, all $r - r_1$ columns of $\begin{pmatrix} \mathbf{B} & \mathbf{C} \end{pmatrix}$ must be distinct because

- If $\mathbf{B}$ were to have two equal columns or $\mathbf{B}$ and $\mathbf{C}$ were to have a column in common then $\mathbf{A}$ would contain two equals columns which contradicts the assumption.
- If $\mathbf{C}$ were to have two equal columns then the corresponding first entries in $\mathbf{A}$ must be different and this contradicts the maximal choice of r_1.

Bearing in mind that we only need to show the lemma for $\vartheta \in \{0, \ldots, m - 1\}$ we now distinguish two cases:

1. $r - r_1 > \Phi(m - 1, \vartheta)$: In this case the inductive assumption applies to $\begin{pmatrix} \mathbf{B} & \mathbf{C} \end{pmatrix}$, i.e., this $(m - 1) \times (r - r_1)$ matrix already contains a $(\vartheta + 1) \times 2^{\vartheta+1}$ sub-matrix as desired to hold for $\mathbf{A}$.

2. $r - r_1 \leq \Phi(m-1, \vartheta)$: In this case the inductive assumption applies to $\mathbf{B}$ because $r_1 = r - (r - r_1) > \Phi(m, \vartheta) - \Phi(m-1, \vartheta) = \Phi(m-1, \vartheta - 1)$ where the last step follows from equation (A.41). Since we know that $\mathbf{B}$ contains a $\vartheta \times 2^\vartheta$ sub-matrix with 2^ϑ distinct columns it follows that

$$\left(\begin{pmatrix} 0 \cdots 0 \\ \\ \mathbf{B} \\ \\ \end{pmatrix} \begin{pmatrix} 1 \cdots 1 \\ \\ \mathbf{B} \\ \\ \end{pmatrix} \right)$$

contains a $(\vartheta + 1) \times 2^{\vartheta+1}$ sub-matrix with $2^{\vartheta+1}$ distinct columns.

The lemma is proved. ∎

We can now proceed to the main proof.

Proof of Theorem 4.10. Suppose that the VC dimension of $\mathcal{H}$ is ϑ. For all $m \geq \vartheta$ consider a training sample $z = (z_1, \ldots, z_m) \in \mathcal{Z}^m$ for which the maximum of equation (4.16) is attained. Let $\hat{h}_1, \ldots, \hat{h}_{\mathcal{N}_\mathcal{H}(m)} \in \mathcal{H}$ be the hypotheses realizing the $\mathcal{N}_\mathcal{H}(m)$ different zero-one loss patterns and arrange all these m–dimensional binary vectors in an $m \times \mathcal{N}_\mathcal{H}(m)$ matrix $\mathbf{A}$, i.e.,

$$\mathbf{A} = \begin{pmatrix} l_{0-1}\left(\hat{h}_1(x_1), y_1\right) & \cdots & l_{0-1}\left(\hat{h}_{\mathcal{N}_\mathcal{H}(m)}(x_1), y_1\right) \\ \vdots & \ddots & \vdots \\ l_{0-1}\left(\hat{h}_1(x_m), y_m\right) & \cdots & l_{0-1}\left(\hat{h}_{\mathcal{N}_\mathcal{H}(m)}(x_m), y_m\right) \end{pmatrix}.$$

If it were the case that $\mathcal{N}_\mathcal{H}(m) > \Phi(m, \vartheta)$ then Lemma C.4 states that there is a sub-matrix with $\vartheta + 1$ rows and all possible distinct $2^{\vartheta+1}$ columns, i.e., there exists a subsequence of z of length $\vartheta + 1$ which is shattered by $\mathcal{H}$. This is a contradiction to the maximal choice of the VC dimension ϑ (see equation (4.18)) Hence, $\mathcal{N}_\mathcal{H}(m) \leq \Phi(m, \vartheta)$ which proves Theorem 4.10. ∎

C.3 Luckiness Bound

In this section we prove Theorem 4.19 which is the main result in the luckiness framework. Note that this proof works "inversely", i.e., instead of upper bounding the probability that the expected risk is larger than ε by some term $\delta(\varepsilon)$ and later solving for ε, we show that our choice of ε guarantees that the above mentioned probability is less than δ. Let us restate the theorem.

Theorem C.5 *Suppose L is a luckiness function that is probably smooth w.r.t. the function ω. For any $\delta \in [0, 1]$, any probability measure $\mathbf{P}_\mathsf{Z}$ and any $d \in \mathbb{N}$,*

$$\mathbf{P}_{\mathsf{Z}^m}\left(\exists h \in \mathcal{H} : Q_1(\mathbf{Z}, h) \wedge Q_2(\mathbf{Z}, h) \wedge Q_3(h)\right) < \delta ,$$

where the propositions Q_1, Q_2 and Q_3 are given by

$$Q_1(z, h) \equiv R_{\text{emp}}[h, z] = 0 , \quad Q_2(z, h) \equiv \omega\left(L(z, h), \frac{\delta}{4}\right) \leq 2^d ,$$

$$Q_3(h) \equiv R[h] > \varepsilon(m, d, \delta) , \qquad \text{and } \varepsilon(m, d, \delta) = \frac{2}{m}\left(d + \operatorname{ld}\left(\frac{4}{\delta}\right)\right) .$$

The result (4.23) follows from the fact that the negation of the conjunction says that, for all hypotheses $h \in \mathcal{H}$, either $R_{\text{emp}}[h, z] \neq 0$ or $\omega(L(z, h), \delta/4) > 2^d$ or $R[h] \leq \varepsilon(m, d, \delta)$.

Proof Due to the length of the proof we have structured it into three steps. We will abbreviate $\varepsilon(m, d, \delta)$ by ε and will use the shorthand notation $z_{[i:j]} \stackrel{\text{def}}{=} \left(z_i, z_{i+1}, \ldots, z_j\right)$. If Q_i and Q_j are propositions, $Q_{ij} \stackrel{\text{def}}{=} Q_i \wedge Q_j$.

Symmetrization by a Ghost Sample

By Lemma C.2 we know that, for all $m \in \mathbb{N}$,

$$\mathbf{P}_{\mathsf{Z}^m}\left(\exists h \in \mathcal{H} : Q_{12}(\mathbf{Z}, h) \wedge Q_3(h)\right) \leq 2 \cdot \underbrace{\mathbf{P}_{\mathsf{Z}^{2m}}\left(\exists h \in \mathcal{H} : Q_{12}\left(\mathbf{Z}_{[1:m]}, h\right) \wedge Q_4\left(\mathbf{Z}_{[(m+1):2m]}, h\right)\right)}_{J(\mathbf{Z})} ,$$

where the proposition Q_4 is given by

$$Q_4(z, h) \equiv R_{\text{emp}}[h, z] > \frac{\varepsilon}{2} .$$

In order to see that we consider the following logical formula Υ and σ–algebra $\mathfrak{A}_\mathcal{H}$ induced by $\mathcal{H}$:

$$\Upsilon(z, h) \equiv Q_2(z, h) ,$$

$$\mathfrak{A}_\mathcal{H} = \left\{ A_h \stackrel{\text{def}}{=} \{(x, y) \in \mathcal{Z} \mid l_{0-1}(h(x), y) = 1\} \mid h \in \mathcal{H} \right\} .$$

Hence, $R[h] = \mathbf{P}_\mathsf{Z}(A_h)$, $R_{\text{emp}}[h,z] = \mathbf{v}_z(A_h)$ and, by the choice of ε we ensured that $m\varepsilon > 8$. Thus, it now suffices to show that $\mathbf{P}_{\mathsf{Z}^{2m}}(J(\mathbf{Z})) \le \frac{\delta}{2}$.

Upper bounding the probability of samples where the growth function increases too much

In order to make use of the probable smoothness of L we distinguish the event that the number of equivalence classes w.r.t. the zero-one loss l_{0-1} that contain functions luckier than h is larger than $\omega\left(m, L\left(z_{[1:m]}, h\right), d/4\right)$ and its negation. In order to accomplish this we define the proposition S by

$$S(z) \equiv \exists h \in \mathcal{H} : \ell_L(z,h) > \omega\left(L\left((z_1,\ldots,z_m), h\right), \delta/4\right) .$$

We see that, by the probable smoothness of the luckiness L given in Definition 4.18,

$$\begin{aligned}
\mathbf{P}_{\mathsf{Z}^{2m}}(J(\mathbf{Z})) &= \mathbf{P}_{\mathsf{Z}^{2m}}(J(\mathbf{Z}) \wedge S(\mathbf{Z})) + \mathbf{P}_{\mathsf{Z}^{2m}}(J(\mathbf{Z}) \wedge (\neg S(\mathbf{Z}))) \\
&\le \mathbf{P}_{\mathsf{Z}^{2m}}(S(\mathbf{Z})) + \mathbf{P}_{\mathsf{Z}^{2m}}(J(\mathbf{Z}) \wedge (\neg S(\mathbf{Z}))) \\
&\le \frac{\delta}{4} + \mathbf{P}_{\mathsf{Z}^{2m}}(J(\mathbf{Z}) \wedge (\neg S(\mathbf{Z}))) ,
\end{aligned}$$

Now we upper bound $\mathbf{P}_{\mathsf{Z}^{2m}}(J(\mathbf{Z}) \wedge (\neg S(\mathbf{Z})))$ by $\frac{\delta}{4}$.

Symmetrization by Permutation

By defining $Q_5(z,h) = Q_2\left(z_{[1:m]}, h\right) \wedge (\neg S(z))$, that is,

$$Q_5(z,h) \equiv \ell_L(z,h) \le 2^d ,$$

we see that the proposition $J(z) \wedge (\neg S(z))$ is given by

$$Q(z) \equiv \exists h \in \mathcal{H} : Q_1\left(z_{[1:m]}, h\right) \wedge Q_4\left(z_{[(m+1):2m]}, h\right) \wedge Q_5(z,h) .$$

Now we shall use a technique which is known as *symmetrization by permutation* and which is due to Kahane (1968) according to van der Vaart and Wellner (1996). Since all $2m$ samples $\mathbf{Z}_i$ are drawn iid from $\mathbf{P}_\mathsf{Z}$ we know that, for any permutation $\pi : \{1,\ldots,2m\} \to \{1,\ldots,2m\}$,

$$\mathbf{P}_{\mathsf{Z}^{2m}}(Q(\mathbf{Z})) = \mathbf{P}_{\mathsf{Z}^{2m}}(Q(\Pi(\mathbf{Z}))) ,$$

where we use the shorthand notation $\Pi(\mathbf{Z})$ to denote the action of π on the indices of $\mathbf{Z} = (\mathsf{Z}_1, \ldots, \mathsf{Z}_{2m})$, i.e., $\Pi((\mathsf{Z}_1, \ldots, \mathsf{Z}_{2m})) \stackrel{\text{def}}{=} (\mathsf{Z}_{\pi(1)}, \ldots, \mathsf{Z}_{\pi(2m)})$. Now consider all 2^m different swapping permutations $\Pi_{\mathbf{s}}$ indexed by $\mathbf{s} \in \{0,1\}^m$, i.e., $\Pi_{\mathbf{s}}(z)$ swaps z_i and z_{i+m} if, and only if, $s_i = 1$. It follows that

$$\mathbf{P}_{\mathsf{Z}^{2m}}(Q(\mathbf{Z})) = \mathbf{E}_{\mathsf{S}}\left[\mathbf{P}_{\mathsf{Z}^{2m}|\mathsf{S}=\mathbf{s}}(Q(\Pi_{\mathbf{s}}(\mathbf{Z})))\right] = \mathbf{E}_{\mathsf{Z}^{2m}}\left[\mathbf{P}_{\mathsf{S}|\mathsf{Z}^{2m}=z}(Q(\Pi_{\mathsf{S}}(z)))\right]$$

for any discrete measure $\mathbf{P}_{\mathsf{S}}$. Clearly, $\mathbf{P}_{\mathsf{Z}^{2m}\mathsf{S}} = \mathbf{P}_{\mathsf{Z}^{2m}}\mathbf{P}_{\mathsf{S}}$ which implies that $\mathbf{P}_{\mathsf{S}|\mathsf{Z}^{2m}=z} = \mathbf{P}_{\mathsf{S}}$. Hence, if we show that $\mathbf{P}_{\mathsf{S}}(Q(\Pi_{\mathsf{S}}(z)))$ is at most $\frac{\delta}{4}$ for each double sample $z \in \mathcal{Z}^{2m}$, we have proven the theorem. The appealing feature of the technique is that we can fix z in the further analysis. In our particular case we obtain that $\mathbf{P}_{\mathsf{S}}(Q(\Pi_{\mathsf{S}}(z)))$ is given by

$$\mathbf{P}_{\mathsf{S}}\left(\exists h \in \mathcal{H} : Q_1\left(\Pi_{\mathsf{S}}(z)_{[1:m]}, h\right) \wedge Q_4\left(\Pi_{\mathsf{S}}(z)_{[(m+1):2m]}, h\right) \wedge Q_5(z, h)\right), \quad \text{(C.2)}$$

where we used the fact that the luckiness function is permutation invariant. Since the double sample $z \in \mathcal{Z}^{2m}$ is fixed, we can arrange the hypotheses $h \in \mathcal{H}$ in decreasing order of their luckiness on the fixed double sample, i.e., $i > j \Rightarrow L(z, h_i) \leq L(z, h_j)$. Now let

$$c(i) \stackrel{\text{def}}{=} \left|\left\{\left(l_{0-1}\left(h_j(x_1), y_1\right), \ldots, l_{0-1}\left(h_j(x_{2m}), y_{2m}\right)\right) \mid j \in \{1, \ldots, i\}\right\}\right|$$

be the number of equivalence classes w.r.t. the zero-one loss incurred by the first i hypotheses. Finally, let i^* be such that $c(i^*) \leq 2^d$ but $c(i^*+1) > 2^d$. Then equation (C.2) can be rewritten as

$$\mathbf{P}_{\mathsf{S}}\left(\exists j \in \left\{1, \ldots, i^*\right\} : Q_1\left(\Pi_{\mathsf{S}}(z)_{[1:m]}, h_j\right) \wedge Q_4\left(\Pi_{\mathsf{S}}(z)_{[(m+1):2m]}, h_j\right)\right),$$

because by construction we know that $h_1, \ldots, h_{i^*+1}$ are the only hypotheses that are at least as lucky as h_{i^*+1} on z but $\ell_L(z, h_{i^*+1}) > 2^d$. Since $c(i^*) \leq 2^d$ there are not more than $q \leq 2^d$ hypotheses $\hat{h}_1, \ldots, \hat{h}_q \subseteq \{h_1, \ldots, h_{i^*}\}$ which realize the $c(i^*)$ different zero-one loss function patterns. Thus, by an application of the union bound we have that the probability in equation (C.2) is bounded from above by

$$\sum_{i=1}^{q} \mathbf{P}_{\mathsf{S}}\left(Q_1\left(\Pi_{\mathsf{S}}(z)_{[1:m]}, \hat{h}_i\right) \wedge Q_4\left(\Pi_{\mathsf{S}}(z)_{[(m+1):2m]}, \hat{h}_i\right)\right).$$

However, if we assume a uniform measure $\mathbf{P}_{\mathsf{S}}$ over the 2^m different swapping permutations each summand cannot be bigger than $2^{m-\frac{\varepsilon m}{2}} \cdot 2^{-m} = 2^{-\frac{\varepsilon m}{2}}$ because, whenever we swap one of the at least $\frac{\varepsilon m}{2}$ examples that incur a mistake on the second m examples (according to Q_4) into the first m examples, we violate Q_1 (see also Figure C.2). Thus we see that

$$\begin{aligned}\mathbf{P}_{\mathsf{Z}^{2m}}(J(\mathbf{Z}) \wedge (\neg S(\mathbf{Z}))) &\leq \mathbf{P}_{\mathsf{Z}^{2m}}(Q(\mathbf{Z})) \\ &\leq q \cdot 2^{-\frac{m}{2}\varepsilon} \leq 2^d \cdot 2^{-d-\mathrm{ld}\left(\frac{4}{\delta}\right)} = \frac{\delta}{4},\end{aligned}$$

which completes the proof. ∎

C.4 Empirical VC Dimension Luckiness

In this section we proof the probable smoothness of the empirical VC dimension (see Section 4.3). This proof is mainly taken from Shawe-Taylor et al. (1998).

Theorem C.6 (Probable smoothness of the empirical VC dimension luckiness) *Given a hypothesis space $\mathcal{H}$, for any $\delta \in \left[0, \frac{1}{2}\right]$ the unluckiness function $U(z, h) = \vartheta_{\mathcal{H}}(z)$ is probably smooth w.r.t. the function*

$$\omega(U, \delta) = \left(\frac{2em}{\tau(U,\delta) \cdot U}\right)^{\tau(U,\delta)\cdot U}, \quad \tau(U,\delta) = 4\left(1 + \frac{1}{U}\ln\left(\frac{1}{\delta}\right)\right).$$

Proof Given a double sample $z_1 z_2 \in \mathcal{Z}^{2m}$, $|z_1| = m$ we note that, according to Theorem 4.10 and A.105, $\omega(U, \delta) = \left(\frac{2em}{\tau U}\right)^{\tau U}$ is an upper bound on the number of equivalence classes w.r.t. the zero-one loss l_{0-1} on that double sample if $\vartheta_{\mathcal{H}}(z_1 z_2) \leq \tau U$. Thus it suffices to show that, for any $\delta \in [0, 1]$,

$$\mathbf{P}_{\mathsf{Z}^{2m}}\underbrace{\left(\tau\left(\vartheta_{\mathcal{H}}((\mathsf{Z}_1, \ldots, \mathsf{Z}_m)), \delta\right) \cdot \vartheta_{\mathcal{H}}((\mathsf{Z}_1, \ldots, \mathsf{Z}_m)) < \vartheta_{\mathcal{H}}(\mathbf{Z})\right)}_{Q(\mathbf{Z})} \leq \delta.$$

Since all $2m$ samples Z_i are drawn iid from $\mathbf{P}_\mathsf{Z}$ we know that, for any permutation $\pi : \{1, \ldots, 2m\} \to \{1, \ldots, 2m\}$,

$$\mathbf{P}_{\mathsf{Z}^{2m}}(Q(\mathbf{Z})) = \mathbf{P}_{\mathsf{Z}^{2m}}(Q(\Pi(\mathbf{Z}))),$$

where we use the shorthand notation $\Pi(\mathbf{Z})$ to denote the action of π on the indices of $\mathbf{Z} = (\mathsf{Z}_1, \ldots, \mathsf{Z}_{2m})$, i.e., $\Pi((\mathsf{Z}_1, \ldots, \mathsf{Z}_{2m})) \stackrel{\text{def}}{=} \left(\mathsf{Z}_{\pi(1)}, \ldots, \mathsf{Z}_{\pi(2m)}\right)$. Now consider all 2^m different swapping permutations $\Pi_\mathbf{s}$ indexed by $\mathbf{s} \in \{0, 1\}^m$, i.e.,

$\Pi_s(z)$ swaps z_i and z_{i+m} if, and only if, $s_i = 1$. It follows that

$$\mathbf{P}_{Z^{2m}}(Q(\mathbf{Z})) = \mathbf{E}_{\mathbf{S}}\left[\mathbf{P}_{Z^{2m}|\mathbf{S}=s}(Q(\Pi_s(\mathbf{Z})))\right] = \mathbf{E}_{Z^{2m}}\left[\mathbf{P}_{\mathbf{S}|Z^{2m}=z}(Q(\Pi_{\mathbf{S}}(z)))\right]$$

for any discrete measure $\mathbf{P}_{\mathbf{S}}$. Clearly, $\mathbf{P}_{Z^{2m}\mathbf{S}} = \mathbf{P}_{Z^{2m}}\mathbf{P}_{\mathbf{S}}$ which implies that $\mathbf{P}_{\mathbf{S}|Z^{2m}=z} = \mathbf{P}_{\mathbf{S}}$. Hence, if we show that $\mathbf{P}_{\mathbf{S}}(Q(\Pi_{\mathbf{S}}(z)))$ is at most δ for each double sample $z \in \mathcal{Z}^{2m}$ and the uniform measure $\mathbf{P}_{\mathbf{S}}$ on $\{0,1\}^m$, we have proven the theorem. Let $d = \vartheta_{\mathcal{H}}(z)$ be the empirical VC dimension on the fixed double sample. By definition, there must exists at least one subsequence $\tilde{z} = \left(z_{i_1}, \ldots, z_{i_d}\right) \subset z$ of length d that is shattered by $\mathcal{H}$. The important observation is that any subsequence of length $j \in \{1, \ldots, d\}$ of $\tilde{z}$ must also be shattered by $\mathcal{H}$ because, otherwise, $\tilde{z}$ is not shattered by $\mathcal{H}$. Let $j^* \in [0, m]$ be such that $\tau(j^*, \delta) \cdot j^* = d$;

$$j^* = \frac{d}{4} + \ln(\delta) . \qquad \text{(C.3)}$$

Whenever any swapping permutation π_s is such that more than $\lfloor j^* \rfloor$ examples of the subsequence $\tilde{z}$ are swapped into the first half, $Q(\Pi_s(z))$ cannot be true because the empirical VC dimension on the first half was at least $\lfloor j^* \rfloor + 1$ and τ is monotonically increasing in its first argument. Thus, $\mathbf{P}_{\mathbf{S}}(Q(\Pi_{\mathbf{S}}(z)))$ is bounded from above by

$$2^{-m} \cdot \sum_{j=0}^{\lfloor j^* \rfloor} S_{d,j} \le \sum_{j=0}^{\lfloor j^* \rfloor} \binom{d}{j} 2^{-d} < \frac{1}{2^d}\left(\frac{ed}{j^*}\right)^{j^*} < \frac{(e\tau(j^*, \delta))^{j^*}}{2^{\tau(j^*,\delta)\cdot j^*}} ,$$

where $S_{d,j}$ is the number of swappings that swap *exactly* j of the d examples into the first half. The second step follows directly from Lemma C.7 and the observation that $4j^* < d$ for all $\delta \in \left[0, \frac{1}{2}\right]$. The last step is a consequence of Theorem A.105 and equation (C.3). In order to complete the proof it suffices to show that $j^* \ln(e\tau(j^*, \delta)) - j^* \cdot \tau(j^*, \delta) \cdot \ln(2) < \ln(\delta)$. Using the definition of τ and Theorem A.101 we see that the latter term is given by

$$\begin{aligned} & j^*\left(1 + \ln\left(4\left(1 - \frac{1}{j^*}\ln(\delta)\right)\right) - 4\ln(2)\left(1 - \frac{1}{j^*}\ln(\delta)\right)\right) \\ & < j^*\left(1 + \ln(4) - \frac{1}{j^*}\ln(\delta) - 4\ln(2) + \frac{4\ln(2)}{j^*}\ln(\delta)\right) \\ & < (4\ln(2) - 1)\ln(\delta) < 2\ln(\delta) < \ln(\delta) , \end{aligned}$$

because $1 + \ln(4) - 4\ln(2) < 0$ and $\ln(\delta) < 0$ for all $\delta \in \left[0, \frac{1}{2}\right]$. The theorem is proved. ■

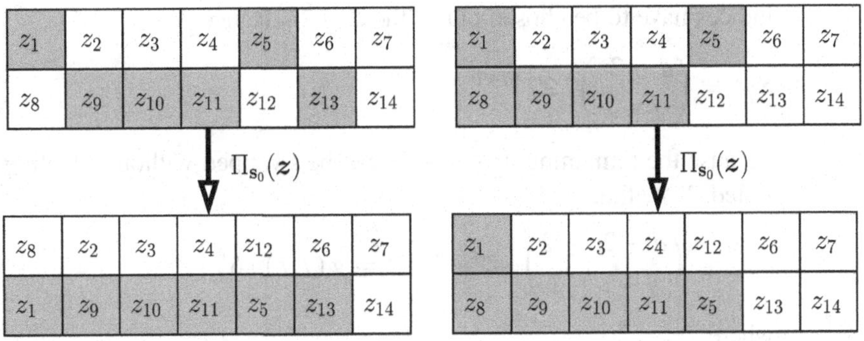

Figure C.3 Counting swappings such that exactly j of the $d = 6$ examples (gray background) are within the first $m = 7$ examples. **(Left)** Since no two of the d indices are the swapping counterpart to each other we can swap all gray examples into the second half and start counting. **(Right)** Since z_1 and z_8 are within the d examples there will always be $r = 1$ gray example in the first half.

Lemma C.7 *For any double sample* $z \in \mathcal{Z}^{2m}$*, for any* $d \leq m$*, for any subsample* $\tilde{z} = (z_{i_1}, \ldots, z_{i_d}) \subset z$ *and for any* $j < d/3$*, the number* $S_{d,j}$ *of swappings such that exactly* j *examples of* $\tilde{z}$ *are within the first* m *examples is bounded by*

$$S_{d,j} \leq \binom{d}{j} \cdot 2^{m-d} .$$

Proof First, let us assume that the subsample $\tilde{z}$ is such that no two indices i_p and i_q have the property that $|i_p - i_q| = m$ (Figure C.3 (left)). Then we observe that the number $S_{d,j}$ is exactly $\binom{d}{j}2^{m-d}$ due to the following argument: Since $d \leq m$ and no two indices are the swapping counterpart of each other, there must exists a swapping π_{s_0} such that all examples in $\tilde{z} \subset z$ are in the second half. In order to ensure that exactly j of the d examples are in the first half we have to swap them back into the first half (starting from $\Pi_{s_0}(z)$). Now there are $\binom{d}{j}$ many choices of distinct examples to swap. Further, swapping any of the $m - d$ examples not in $\tilde{z}$ that are in the second half of $\Pi_{s_0}(z)$ into the first half would not alter the event; hence the 2^{m-d} term.

Now let us assume that there are $r \in \{1, \ldots, j\}$ pairs of indices i_p and i_q such that $|i_p - i_q| = m$ and let $S^r_{d,j}$ be the number of swappings that satisfy the condition stated (Figure C.3 (right)). In this case, whatever the swapping, r examples of $\tilde{z}$ are in the first half, and to make up the number to j a further $j - r$

indices have to be chosen out of the $d-2r$. Hence

$$S^r_{d,j} = \binom{d-2r}{j-r} \cdot 2^{m-d+2r}$$

because the remaining $m-d-2r$ can be swapped without affecting the condition stated. Note that

$$S^{r+1}_{d,j} = \binom{d-2r-2}{j-r-1} \cdot 2^{m-d+2r+2} = g(j,r) \cdot S^r_{d,j},$$

where

$$g(j,r) = 4\frac{(j-r)(d-j-r)}{(d-2r)(d-2r-1)}.$$

It is easily verified that, for any $r \in \{1, \ldots, j\}$, the function g attains its maximum for $j = d/2$. However, as by assumption $j < d/3$ we know that

$$g(j,r) < \frac{4}{9}\frac{(d-3r)(2d-3r)}{(d-2r)(d-2r-1)}$$

in the possible range of j. Hence, the function $g(j,r)$ is strictly less than 1 if $d \geq 9$ because this implies that

$$d^2 - 9d + 18r > 0 \Rightarrow 4(d-3r)(2d-3r) < 9(d-2r)(d-2r-1).$$

As a consequence, for $d \geq 9$ the result is true because

$$S^r_{d,j} < S^0_{d,j} = S_{d,j} = \binom{d}{j} \cdot 2^{m-d}$$

for all $r \in \{1, \ldots, j\}$. For $d < 9$ the only possible cases are $j = 0$ (trivial), $j = 1$, $r = 1$ and $j = 2$, $r \in \{1, 2\}$ which can easily verified to be true. The theorem is proved. ■

C.5 Bound on the Fat Shattering Dimension

This elegant proof of Lemma 4.31 can be found in Bartlett and Shawe-Taylor (1999) and dates back to Gurvits (1997). We will restate the original proof using the shorthand notation $\sum A \stackrel{\text{def}}{=} \sum_{a_i \in A} a_i$.

Proof The proof involves two lemmas that make extensive use of the geometry in an inner product space $\mathcal{K}$. We show that if $S \subset X$ is γ–shattered by $\mathcal{F}$, then every subset $S_0 \subseteq S$ satisfies $\left\| \sum S_0 - \sum (S \setminus S_0) \right\| \geq \frac{|S|\gamma}{B}$. At the same time, for all $S \subset X$, some $S_0 \subseteq S$ satisfies $\left\| \sum S_0 - \sum (S \setminus S_0) \right\| \leq \sqrt{|S|}\varsigma$. Combining these two assertions yields

$$1 \geq \frac{|S|\gamma}{\sqrt{|S|}B\varsigma} = \sqrt{|S|}\frac{\gamma}{B\varsigma} \quad \Rightarrow \quad |S| \leq \left(\frac{B\varsigma}{\gamma}\right)^2 ,$$

for every γ–shattered set S. This proves the lemma.

Lemma C.8 *If $S \subset X$ is γ–shattered by $\mathcal{F}$, then every subset $S_0 \subseteq S$ satisfies*

$$\left\| \sum S_0 - \sum (S \setminus S_0) \right\| \geq \frac{|S|\gamma}{B} .$$

Proof Suppose $S = \{\mathbf{x}_1, \ldots, \mathbf{x}_m\}$ is γ–shattered by $\mathcal{F}$ witnessed by the m real numbers $r_1, \ldots, r_m$. Then, for all $\mathbf{y} = (y_1, \ldots, y_m) \in \{-1, +1\}^m$ there is a $\mathbf{w}_\mathbf{y}$ with $\|\mathbf{w}_\mathbf{y}\| \leq B$ such that, for all $i \in \{1, \ldots, m\}$, $y_i \left(\langle \mathbf{w}_\mathbf{y}, \mathbf{x}_i \rangle - r_i\right) \geq \gamma$. Fix a subset $S_0 \subseteq S$. We consider two cases: If

$$\sum \{r_i \mid \mathbf{x}_i \in S_0\} \geq \sum \{r_i \mid \mathbf{x}_i \in (S \setminus S_0)\} ,$$

then we consider $y_i = +1$ if, and only if, $\mathbf{x}_i \in S_0$. In this case we have $\langle \mathbf{w}_\mathbf{y}, \mathbf{x}_i \rangle \geq r_i + \gamma$ if $\mathbf{x}_i \in S_0$ and $-\langle \mathbf{w}_\mathbf{y}, \mathbf{x}_i \rangle \geq -r_i + \gamma$ if $\mathbf{x}_i \in (S \setminus S_0)$. If follows that

$$\begin{aligned} \left\langle \mathbf{w}_\mathbf{y}, \sum S_0 \right\rangle &\geq \sum \{r_i \mid \mathbf{x}_i \in S_0\} + |S_0|\gamma \\ -\left\langle \mathbf{w}_\mathbf{y}, \sum (S \setminus S_0) \right\rangle &\geq -\sum \{r_i \mid \mathbf{x}_i \in (S \setminus S_0)\} + |S \setminus S_0|\gamma , \end{aligned}$$

which, combined together, gives

$$\begin{aligned} \left\langle \mathbf{w}_\mathbf{y}, \sum S_0 - \sum (S \setminus S_0) \right\rangle &\geq \sum \{r_i \mid \mathbf{x}_i \in S_0\} - \sum \{r_i \mid \mathbf{x}_i \in (S \setminus S_0)\} + |S|\gamma \\ &\geq |S|\gamma . \end{aligned}$$

Using the Cauchy-Schwarz inequality (see Theorem A.106) and the assumption $\|\mathbf{w}_\mathbf{y}\| \leq B$, we know

$$\begin{aligned} B \left\| \sum S_0 - \sum (S \setminus S_0) \right\| &\geq \|\mathbf{w}_\mathbf{y}\| \cdot \left\| \sum S_0 - \sum (S \setminus S_0) \right\| \\ &\geq \left\langle \mathbf{w}_\mathbf{y}, \sum S_0 - \sum (S \setminus S_0) \right\rangle \geq |S|\gamma . \end{aligned}$$

In the other case, we consider $y_i = +1$ if, and only if, $\mathbf{x}_i \in (S \setminus S_0)$, and use an identical argument. ■

Lemma C.9 *For all $S \subset X$, some $S_0 \subseteq S$ satisfy*

$$\left\| \sum S_0 - \sum (S \setminus S_0) \right\| \leq \sqrt{|S|}\varsigma\,.$$

Proof The proof uses the probabilistic method (Alon et al. 1991). Suppose $S = \{\mathbf{x}_1, \ldots, \mathbf{x}_m\}$. We choose S_0 randomly by defining $\mathbf{x}_i \in S_0 \Leftrightarrow \mathsf{B}_i = +1$, where $\mathsf{B}_1, \ldots, \mathsf{B}_m$ are independent random variables with $\mathbf{P}_{\mathsf{B}_i}(+1) = \mathbf{P}_{\mathsf{B}_i}(-1) = \frac{1}{2}$. Then,

$$\begin{aligned}
\mathbf{E}_{\mathsf{B}^m}\left[\left\| \sum S_0 - \sum (S \setminus S_0) \right\|^2\right] &= \mathbf{E}_{\mathsf{B}^m}\left[\left\| \sum_{i=1}^m \mathsf{B}_i \mathbf{x}_i \right\|^2\right] \\
&= \mathbf{E}_{\mathsf{B}^m}\left[\left\langle \sum_{i=1}^m \mathsf{B}_i \mathbf{x}_i, \sum_{j=1}^m \mathsf{B}_j \mathbf{x}_j \right\rangle\right] \\
&= \sum_{i=1}^m \mathbf{E}_{\mathsf{B}^m}\left[\left\langle \mathsf{B}_i \mathbf{x}_i, \sum_{j=1}^m \mathsf{B}_j \mathbf{x}_j \right\rangle\right] \\
&= \sum_{i=1}^m \mathbf{E}_{\mathsf{B}^m}\left[\left\langle \mathsf{B}_i \mathbf{x}_i, \sum_{i \neq j} \mathsf{B}_j \mathbf{x}_j + \mathsf{B}_i \mathbf{x}_i \right\rangle\right] \\
&= \sum_{i=1}^m \left(\sum_{i \neq j} \mathbf{E}_{\mathsf{B}^m}\left[\mathsf{B}_i \cdot \mathsf{B}_j\right] \left\langle \mathbf{x}_i, \mathbf{x}_j \right\rangle + \mathbf{E}_{\mathsf{B}^m}\left[\|\mathsf{B}_i \mathbf{x}_i\|^2\right] \right) \\
&= \sum_{i=1}^m \mathbf{E}_{\mathsf{B}^m}\left[\|\mathsf{B}_i \mathbf{x}_i\|^2\right] \leq |S|\,\varsigma^2,
\end{aligned}$$

where the last line follows from the fact that the B_i have zero mean and are independent, i.e., $\mathbf{E}_{\mathsf{B}^m}\left[\mathsf{B}_i \cdot \mathsf{B}_j\right] = 0$ for $i \neq j$. Since the expectation is no more than $|S|\,\varsigma^2$, there must be a set S_0 for which $\left\| \sum S_0 - \sum (S \setminus S_0) \right\|^2$ is no more than $|S|\,\varsigma^2$. ■

C.6 Margin Distribution Bound

In course of the derivation of the sequence Δ_i we shall sometimes abbreviate $D(\mathbf{z}, \mathbf{w}, \gamma)$ by D. Let us consider the value of $d_{\text{eff}}(\Delta)$ given by equation (4.32) for a fixed value of γ and $\|\mathbf{w}\| = 1$, i.e.,

$$d_{\text{eff}}(\Delta) = \frac{64\left(1 + \left(\frac{D}{\Delta}\right)^2\right)(\varsigma^2 + \Delta^2)}{\gamma^2} = \frac{64}{\gamma^2}\underbrace{\left(\varsigma^2 + \Delta^2 + \frac{\varsigma^2 D^2}{\Delta^2} + D^2\right)}_{f(\Delta)}. \tag{C.4}$$

Given an observed margin distribution D we would like to replace Δ in equation (C.4) with the minimizing value $\Delta^*(D)$ of the term $d_{\text{eff}}(\Delta)$ which is equivalent to the minimizer of $f(\Delta)$. A straightforward calculation shows that this value has to be $\Delta^*(D) = \sqrt{\varsigma D}$ because

$$\left.\frac{df}{d\Delta}\right|_{\Delta^*} = 2\Delta^*(D) - \frac{2\varsigma^2 D^2}{(\Delta^*(D))^3} = 0, \quad \left.\frac{d^2 f}{d\Delta^2}\right|_{\Delta=\sqrt{\varsigma D}} = 2 + \frac{6}{\sqrt{\varsigma D}} > 0.$$

In this case the value of $f(\Delta^*(D))$ equals $\varsigma^2 + 2\varsigma D + D^2 = (\varsigma + D)^2$. First, note that the largest value of D is $2\varsigma\sqrt{m}$ because, in the worst case, $\mathbf{w}$ fails for all m points to achieve a functional margin of γ by at most 2ς (all points are assumed to be in a ball of radius less than or equal to ς) and, thus, $D^2 \le 4\varsigma^2 m \Leftrightarrow D \le 2\varsigma\sqrt{m}$. Hence we set up an arithmetic series $(\Delta_i)_{i=1,\ldots,s}$ of values *before having observed the data* such that $\Delta_1 = 2\varsigma\sqrt{m}$ and $\Delta_{i+1} = \frac{\Delta_i}{2}$ which ensures that, for all values of D, there will be a Δ_i such that

$$\frac{\Delta^*(D)}{2} = \frac{\sqrt{\varsigma D}}{2} \le \Delta_i \le \sqrt{\varsigma D} = \Delta^*(D).$$

Using the lower bound $\frac{\sqrt{\varsigma D}}{2}$ for Δ_i in equation (C.4) we see that, for all D,

$$\begin{aligned} f(\Delta^*(D)) &\le f(\Delta_i) \le f\left(\frac{\sqrt{\varsigma D}}{2}\right) = \varsigma^2 + \frac{1}{4}\varsigma D + 4\varsigma D + D^2 \le (\varsigma + 3D)^2 \\ &< \frac{65}{64}(\varsigma + 3D)^2. \end{aligned}$$

Finally note that it suffices to consider the series until $\frac{\varsigma}{64} < \Delta_s \leq \frac{\varsigma}{32}$ because, for all D such that $\Delta^*(D) = \sqrt{\varsigma D} < \frac{\varsigma}{32} \Leftrightarrow \sqrt{\frac{D}{\varsigma}} \leq \frac{1}{32}$, it is readily verified that

$$\begin{aligned} f\left(\Delta^*(D)\right) &= (\varsigma + D)^2 \\ &\leq f(\Delta_s) = \left(1 + \frac{D^2}{\Delta_s^2}\right)\left(\varsigma^2 + \Delta_s^2\right) \leq \left(1 + \frac{64^2 D^2}{\varsigma^2}\right)\left(\varsigma^2 + \frac{\varsigma^2}{32^2}\right) \\ &\leq \varsigma^2\left(1 + \frac{64^2}{32^4}\right)\left(1 + \frac{1}{1024}\right) \\ &< \frac{65}{64}\varsigma^2 < \frac{65}{64}(\varsigma + 3D)^2 . \end{aligned}$$

The number s is easily determined by making use of the definition $\Delta_s = 2\varsigma\sqrt{m} \cdot 2^{-s+1}$ and $\frac{\varsigma}{64} < \Delta_s$ which yields $s < 8 + \frac{1}{2}\operatorname{ld}(m)$.

C.7 The Quantifier Reversal Lemma

This section presents the quantifier reversal lemma due to David McAllester (see McAllester (1998)). This lemma is of particular importance in the derivation of generalization error bounds in the PAC-Bayesian framework (see Section 5.1). Broadly speaking, if a logical formula acts on two random variables and we have the formula true for *all* values of one of the random variables, then the quantifier reversal lemma allows us to move the all-quantifier over that random variable into a "all-but-a-fraction-of-δ" statement for a fixed value of the other random variable. Thus, it provides an upper bound on the conditional distribution of the random variable.

Lemma C.10 (Quantifier reversal lemma) *Let* X *and* Y *be random variables and let* δ *range over* $(0, 1]$. *Let* $\Upsilon : \mathcal{X} \times \mathcal{Y} \times \mathbb{R} \to \{\text{true}, \text{false}\}$ *be any measurable logical formula on the product space such that for any* $x \in \mathcal{X}$ *and* $y \in \mathcal{Y}$ *we have*

$$\{\delta \in (0, 1] \mid \Upsilon(x, y, \delta)\} = (0, \delta_{\max}]$$

for some $\delta_{\max}$. *If*

$$\forall x \in \mathcal{X} : \forall \delta \in (0, 1] : \qquad \mathbf{P}_{\mathsf{Y}|\mathsf{X}=x}\left(\Upsilon(x, \mathsf{Y}, \delta)\right) \geq 1 - \delta ,$$

then, for any $\beta \in (0, 1)$, *we have*

$$\forall \delta \in (0, 1] : \; \mathbf{P}_{\mathsf{Y}}\left(\forall \alpha \in (0, 1] : \mathbf{P}_{\mathsf{X}|\mathsf{Y}=y}\left(\Upsilon\left(\mathsf{X}, y, (\alpha\beta\delta)^{\frac{1}{1-\beta}}\right)\right) \geq 1 - \alpha\right) \geq 1 - \delta \, .$$

Let us start with a simple lemma we need for of the proof.

Lemma C.11 *Let* X *be a random variable such that* $\mathbf{P}_{\mathsf{X}}([0, 1]) = 1$ *and let* g *be any measurable, monotonically decreasing function from the interval* $[0, 1]$ *to the reals, i.e.,* $g : [0, 1] \to \mathbb{R}$ *is such that* $x \geq y$ *implies* $g(x) \leq g(y)$. *If*

$$\forall \delta \in [0, 1] : \qquad \mathbf{F}_{\mathsf{X}}(\delta) \leq \delta \, ,$$

then

$$\mathbf{E}_{\mathsf{X}}\left[g(\mathsf{X})\right] \leq \int_0^1 g(x) \, dx \, . \tag{C.5}$$

Proof By the definition of the expectation (Definition A.7) we know that

$$\begin{aligned}
\mathbf{E}_{\mathsf{X}}\left[g(\mathsf{X})\right] &= \int_0^1 g(x) \, d\mathbf{F}_{\mathsf{X}}(x) = -\int_0^1 \mathbf{F}_{\mathsf{X}}(x) \, d(g(x)) + \left[g(x) \cdot \mathbf{F}_{\mathsf{X}}(x)\right]_0^1 \\
&= \int_0^1 \mathbf{F}_{\mathsf{X}}(x) \, d(-g(x)) + g(1) \, ,
\end{aligned}$$

where the first line follows from partial integration and the second line uses the fact that $\mathbf{F}_{\mathsf{X}}(0) = 0$ and $\mathbf{F}_{\mathsf{X}}(1) = 1$. Since $-g(x)$ is, by assumption, a monotonically increasing function we know that any positive difference $g(x) - g(\tilde{x}) > 0$ implies that $x - \tilde{x} > 0$. Hence for the first integral we can use the upper bound on $\mathbf{F}_{\mathsf{X}}$ to obtain

$$\begin{aligned}
\mathbf{E}_{\mathsf{X}}\left[g(\mathsf{X})\right] &\leq \int_0^1 x \, d(-g(x)) + g(1) \\
&= \int_0^1 g(x) \, dx + \left[x \cdot (-g(x))\right]_0^1 + g(1) = \int_0^1 g(x) \, dx \, .
\end{aligned}$$

The lemma is proved. ■

Using this lemma we can now proceed to prove the quantifier reversal lemma.

Proof of Theorem C.10. Define $f : \mathcal{X} \times \mathcal{Y} \to \mathbb{R}$ in the following way

$$f(x, y) = \begin{cases} 0 & \text{if} \quad \{\delta \in (0,1] \mid \Upsilon(x, y, \delta)\} = (0, \delta_{\max}] = \emptyset \\ \delta_{\max} & \text{if} \quad \{\delta \in (0,1] \mid \Upsilon(x, y, \delta)\} = (0, \delta_{\max}] \neq \emptyset \end{cases} .$$

By definition, for any $x \in \mathcal{X}$, and $y \in \mathcal{Y}$ and $\delta \in (0, 1]$ we know that $\Upsilon(x, y, \delta) =$ true is equivalent to the fact that $f(x, y) \geq \delta$. For a given $x \in \mathcal{X}$ we define the new random variable $\mathsf{T} \stackrel{\text{def}}{=} f(x, \mathsf{Y})$. Then the assumption of the theorem implies that

$$\forall x \in \mathcal{X} : \forall \delta \in (0, 1] : \quad \mathbf{P}_{\mathsf{Y}|\mathsf{X}=x}(\Upsilon(x, \mathsf{Y}, \delta)) \geq 1 - \delta \Leftrightarrow \mathbf{F}_{\mathsf{T}}(\delta) \leq \delta .$$

Now, note that for $\beta \in (0, 1)$, $g(z) = z^{\beta-1}$ is an monotonically decreasing function since the exponent is strictly negative. From Lemma C.11 we conclude

$$\forall x \in \mathcal{X} : \forall \delta \in (0, 1] : \quad \mathbf{E}_{\mathsf{Y}|\mathsf{X}=x}\left[f^{\beta-1}(x, \mathsf{Y})\right] = \mathbf{E}_{\mathsf{T}}\left[\mathsf{T}^{\beta-1}\right] \leq \int_0^1 z^{\beta-1}\, dz = \frac{1}{\beta} .$$

Taking the expectation over $x \in \mathcal{X}$ gives

$$\forall \delta \in (0, 1] : \qquad \mathbf{E}_{\mathsf{X}}\left[\mathbf{E}_{\mathsf{Y}|\mathsf{X}=x}\left[f^{\beta-1}(x, \mathsf{Y})\right]\right] \leq \frac{1}{\beta} .$$

We can exchange the expectation values by the theorem of repeated integrals (see Feller (1966)). Thus, using Markov's inequality given in Theorem A.109 we obtain

$$\forall \delta \in (0, 1] : \quad \mathbf{P}_{\mathsf{Y}}\left(\mathbf{E}_{\mathsf{X}|\mathsf{Y}=y}\left[f^{\beta-1}(\mathsf{X}, y)\right] \leq \frac{1}{\beta\delta}\right) \geq 1 - \delta .$$

Applying Markov's inequality once again to the conditional expectation value $\mathbf{E}_{\mathsf{X}|\mathsf{Y}=y}\left[f^{\beta-1}(\mathsf{X}, y)\right]$ gives

$$\forall \delta \in (0, 1] : \mathbf{P}_{\mathsf{Y}}\left(\forall \alpha \in (0, 1] : \mathbf{P}_{\mathsf{X}|\mathsf{Y}=y}\left(f^{\beta-1}(\mathsf{X}, y) \leq \frac{1}{\alpha\beta\delta}\right) \geq 1 - \alpha\right) \geq 1 - \delta .$$

Finally, rearranging terms and using the fact that $\Upsilon(x, y, \delta) =$ true is equivalent to $f(x, y) \geq \delta$ we obtain

$$\forall \delta \in (0, 1] : \mathbf{P}_{\mathsf{Y}}\left(\forall \alpha \in (0, 1] : \mathbf{P}_{\mathsf{X}|\mathsf{Y}=y}\left(\Upsilon\left(\mathsf{X}, y, (\alpha\beta\delta)^{\frac{1}{1-\beta}}\right)\right) \geq 1 - \alpha\right) \geq 1 - \delta .$$

The theorem is proved. ■

C.8 A PAC-Bayesian Margin Bound

This section contains the proof of Theorem 5.10. In course of this proof we need several theorems and lemmas which have been delegated to separate subsections due to their length.

Proof of Theorem 5.10. Geometrically, the hypothesis space $\mathcal{H}$ is isomorphic the unit sphere $\mathcal{W}$ in $\mathbb{R}^n$ (see Figure 2.8). Let us assume that $\mathbf{P_W}$ is uniform on the unit sphere. Given the training sample $z \in \mathcal{Z}^m$ and a classifier having normal $\mathbf{w} \in \mathcal{W}$ we show in Theorem C.13 that the open ball

$$\mathcal{B}(\mathbf{w}) = \left\{ \mathbf{v} \in \mathcal{W} \;\middle|\; \langle \mathbf{w}, \mathbf{v} \rangle > \sqrt{1 - \Gamma_z^2(\mathbf{w})} \right\} \subseteq \mathcal{W} \tag{C.6}$$

is fully within the version space $V(z)$. Such a set $\mathcal{B}(\mathbf{w})$ is, by definition, point symmetric w.r.t. $\mathbf{w}$ and hence we can use $-\ln(\mathbf{P_W}(\mathcal{B}(\mathbf{w})))$ to bound the expected risk of $h_{\mathbf{w}}$. Since $\mathbf{P_W}$ is uniform on the unit sphere, the value $-\ln(\mathbf{P_W}(\mathcal{B}(\mathbf{w})))$ is simply the logarithm of the *volume ratio* of the surface of the unit sphere to the surface of all $\mathbf{v} \in \mathcal{W}$ satisfying equation (C.6). A combination of Theorem C.14 and C.15 shows that this ratio is given by

$$\begin{aligned} \ln\left(\frac{1}{\mathbf{P_W}(\mathcal{B}(\mathbf{w}))}\right) &= \ln\left(\frac{\int_0^\pi \sin^{n-2}(\theta)\, d\theta}{\int_0^{\arccos\left(\sqrt{1-(\Gamma_z(\mathbf{w}))^2}\right)} \sin^{n-2}(\theta)\, d\theta}\right) \\ &\le n \cdot \ln\left(\frac{1}{1 - \sqrt{1 - \Gamma_z^2(\mathbf{w})}}\right) + \ln(2)\,. \end{aligned}$$

Using Theorem 5.4 and Lemma 5.9 and bounding $\ln(2)$ by one from above we obtain the desired result. Note that m points $\{\mathbf{x}_1, \ldots, \mathbf{x}_m\}$ maximally span an m–dimensional space and, thus, we can marginalize over the remaining $n - m$ dimensions of feature space $\mathcal{K}$. This gives $d = \min(m, n)$. ■

C.8.1 Balls in Version Space

In this section we prove that the open ball

$$\mathcal{B}(\mathbf{w}) = \left\{ \mathbf{v} \in \mathcal{W} \;\middle|\; \langle \mathbf{w}, \mathbf{v} \rangle > \sqrt{1 - \Gamma_z^2(\mathbf{w})} \right\}$$

around a linear classifier having normal $\mathbf{w}$ of unit length contains classifiers within version space $V(z)$ only. Here, $\Gamma_z(\mathbf{w})$ is the margin of the hyperplane $\mathbf{w}$ on a set of points *normalized by the length* $\|\mathbf{x}_i\|$ *of the* $\mathbf{x}_i$ (see equation (5.11) for a formal definition). In order to prove this result we need the following lemma.

Lemma C.12 *Suppose $\mathcal{K} \subseteq \ell_2^n$ is a fixed feature space. Assume we are given two points $\mathbf{w} \in \mathcal{W}$ and $\mathbf{x} \in \mathcal{K}$ such that $\langle \mathbf{w}, \mathbf{x} \rangle = \gamma > 0$. Then, for all $\mathbf{v} \in \mathcal{W}$ with*

$$\langle \mathbf{w}, \mathbf{v} \rangle > \sqrt{1 - \frac{\gamma^2}{\|\mathbf{x}\|^2}} \tag{C.7}$$

it follows that $\langle \mathbf{v}, \mathbf{x} \rangle > 0$.

Proof Since we only evaluate the inner product of any admissible $\mathbf{v} \in \mathcal{W}$ with $\mathbf{w} \in \mathcal{W}$ and $\mathbf{x} \in \mathcal{K}$, we can make the following approach

$$\mathbf{v} = \lambda \frac{\mathbf{x}}{\|\mathbf{x}\|} + \tau \left(\mathbf{w} - \gamma \frac{\mathbf{x}}{\|\mathbf{x}\|^2} \right).$$

Note that the vectors $\frac{\mathbf{x}}{\|\mathbf{x}\|}$ and $\mathbf{w} - \gamma \frac{\mathbf{x}}{\|\mathbf{x}\|^2}$ are orthogonal by construction. Furthermore, the squared length of $\mathbf{w} - \gamma \frac{\mathbf{x}}{\|\mathbf{x}\|^2}$ is given by $1 - \gamma^2 / \|\mathbf{x}\|^2$. Therefore, the unit norm constraint on $\mathbf{v}$ implies that

$$\tau^2 = \frac{1 - \lambda^2}{1 - \frac{\gamma^2}{\|\mathbf{x}\|^2}}.$$

Furthermore, assumption (C.7) becomes

$$\begin{aligned}
\left\langle \lambda \frac{\mathbf{x}}{\|\mathbf{x}\|} + \tau \left(\mathbf{w} - \gamma \frac{\mathbf{x}}{\|\mathbf{x}\|^2} \right), \mathbf{w} \right\rangle &> \sqrt{1 - \frac{\gamma^2}{\|\mathbf{x}\|^2}} \\
\lambda \frac{\gamma}{\|\mathbf{x}\|} \pm \sqrt{\frac{1 - \lambda^2}{1 - \frac{\gamma^2}{\|\mathbf{x}\|^2}}} \left(1 - \frac{\gamma^2}{\|\mathbf{x}\|^2} \right) &> \sqrt{1 - \frac{\gamma^2}{\|\mathbf{x}\|^2}} \\
\underbrace{\lambda \frac{\gamma}{\|\mathbf{x}\|} - \sqrt{1 - \frac{\gamma^2}{\|\mathbf{x}\|^2}} \left(1 \pm \sqrt{1 - \lambda^2} \right)}_{f(\lambda)} &> 0 .
\end{aligned}$$

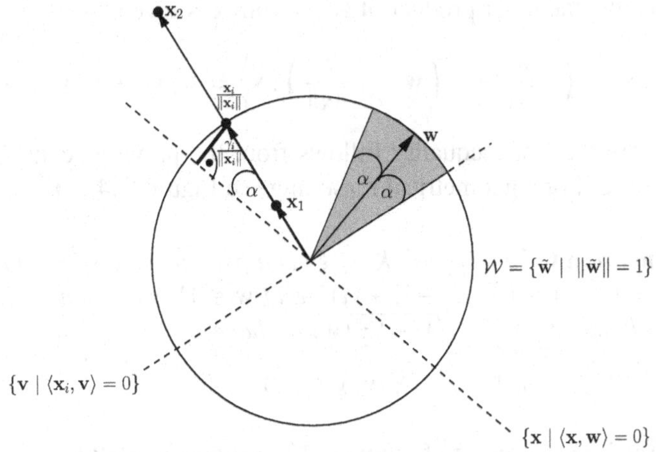

Figure C.4 Suppose the point $\mathbf{x}_1$ (or $\mathbf{x}_2$) is given. We must show that all classifiers having normal $\tilde{\mathbf{w}}$ of unit length and $\langle \mathbf{w}, \tilde{\mathbf{w}} \rangle > \sqrt{1 - \gamma_i^2 / \|\mathbf{x}_i\|^2}$ are on the same side of the hyperplane $\{\mathbf{v} \in \mathcal{K} \mid \langle \mathbf{x}_i, \mathbf{v} \rangle = 0\}$, i.e., $\langle \tilde{\mathbf{v}}, \mathbf{x}_i \rangle > 0$, where $\gamma_i = \langle \mathbf{x}_i, \mathbf{w} \rangle$. From the picture it is clear that, regardless of $\|\mathbf{x}_i\|$, $\sin(\alpha) = (\gamma_i / \|\mathbf{x}_i\|)$ or equivalently $\cos(\alpha) = \sqrt{1 - \sin^2(\alpha)} = \sqrt{1 - \gamma_i^2 / \|\mathbf{x}_i\|^2}$. Obviously, all vectors $\tilde{\mathbf{w}}$ of unit length which enclose an angle less than α with $\mathbf{w}$ are on the same side (the dark cone). As $\cos(\alpha)$ is monotonically decreasing for $\alpha \in \left(0, \frac{\pi}{2}\right)$, these classifiers must satisfy $\langle \mathbf{w}, \tilde{\mathbf{w}} \rangle = \cos\left(\sphericalangle\left(\mathbf{w}, \tilde{\mathbf{w}}\right)\right) > \sqrt{1 - \gamma_i^2 / \|\mathbf{x}_i\|^2}$.

In order to solve for λ we consider the l.h.s. as a function of λ and determine the range of values in which $f(\lambda)$ is positive. A straightforward calculation reveals that $[0, \lambda_{\max}]$ with

$$\lambda_{\max} = \frac{2\gamma}{\|\mathbf{x}\|}\sqrt{1 - \frac{\gamma^2}{\|\mathbf{x}\|^2}},$$

is the only range in which $f(\lambda)$ is positive. As a consequence, the assumption $\langle \mathbf{w}, \mathbf{v} \rangle > \sqrt{1 - \gamma^2 / \|\mathbf{x}\|^2}$ is equivalent to

$$0 < \lambda \|\mathbf{x}\| < 2\gamma\sqrt{1 - \frac{\gamma^2}{\|\mathbf{x}\|}}.$$

Finally, the inner product of any $\mathbf{v}$ with $\mathbf{x}$ is given by

$$\langle \mathbf{v}, \mathbf{x} \rangle = \left\langle \lambda \frac{\mathbf{x}}{\|\mathbf{x}\|} + \tau \left(\mathbf{w} - \gamma \frac{\mathbf{x}}{\|\mathbf{x}\|} \right), \mathbf{x} \right\rangle = \lambda \|\mathbf{x}\| + \tau (\gamma - \gamma) > 0 ,$$

where the last inequality follows from the previous consideration. The lemma is proved. For a geometrical reasoning see Figure C.4. ■

Theorem C.13 *Suppose $\mathcal{K} \subseteq \ell_2^n$ is a fixed feature space. Given a training sample $z = (x, y) \in (\mathcal{X} \times \{-1, +1\})^m$ and $\mathbf{w} \in \mathcal{W}$ such that $\Gamma_z(\mathbf{w}) > 0$, for all $\mathbf{v} \in \mathcal{W}$ such that $\langle \mathbf{w}, \mathbf{v} \rangle > \sqrt{1 - \Gamma_z^2(\mathbf{w})}$ we have*

$$\forall i \in \{1, \ldots, m\} : \qquad y_i \langle \mathbf{v}, \mathbf{x}_i \rangle > 0 .$$

Proof According to Lemma C.12 we know that all $\mathbf{v} \in B_i$ with

$$B_i = \left\{ \mathbf{v} \in \mathcal{W} \;\middle|\; \langle \mathbf{w}, \mathbf{v} \rangle > \sqrt{1 - \frac{(y_i \langle \mathbf{x}_i, \mathbf{w} \rangle)^2}{\|\mathbf{x}_i\|^2}} \right\} ,$$

parameterize classifiers consistent with the ith point $\mathbf{x}_i$. Clearly, the intersection of all B_i gives the classifiers $\mathbf{w}$ which jointly satisfy the constraints $y_i \langle \mathbf{w}, \mathbf{x}_i \rangle > 0$. Noticing that the size of B_i depends inversely on $y_i \langle \mathbf{x}_i, \mathbf{w} \rangle$ we see that all $\mathbf{v}$ such that $\langle \mathbf{w}, \mathbf{v} \rangle > \Gamma_z(\mathbf{w})$ jointly classify all points $\mathbf{x}_i$ correctly. The theorem is proved. ■

C.8.2 Volume Ratio Theorem

In this subsection we explicitly derive the volume ratio between the largest inscribable ball in version space and the whole parameter space for the special case of linear classifiers in $\mathbb{R}^n$. Given a point $\mathbf{w} \in \mathcal{W}$ and a positive number $\gamma > 0$ we can characterize the ball of radius γ in the parameter space by

$$\mathcal{B}_\gamma(\mathbf{w}) = \left\{ \mathbf{v} \in \mathcal{W} \;\middle|\; \|\mathbf{w} - \mathbf{v}\|^2 < \gamma^2 \right\} = \left\{ \mathbf{v} \in \mathcal{W} \;\middle|\; \langle \mathbf{w}, \mathbf{v} \rangle > 1 - \gamma^2/2 \right\} .$$

In the following we will calculate the exact value of the *volume ratio* $\frac{\text{vol}(\mathcal{W})}{\text{vol}(\mathcal{B}_\gamma(\mathbf{w}))}$ where $\mathbf{w}$ can be chosen arbitrarily (due to the symmetry of the sphere).

Theorem C.14 *Suppose we are given a fixed feature space $\mathcal{K} \subseteq \ell_2^n$. Then the fraction of the whole surface* $\text{vol}(\mathcal{W})$ *of the unit sphere to the surface* $\text{vol}(\mathcal{B}_\gamma(\mathbf{w}))$

with Euclidean distance less than γ from any point $\mathbf{w} \in \mathcal{W}$ is given by

$$\frac{\mathrm{vol}(\mathcal{W})}{\mathrm{vol}\left(\mathcal{B}_\gamma(\mathbf{w})\right)} = \frac{\int_0^\pi \sin^{n-2}(\theta)\, d\theta}{\int_0^{\arccos\left(1-\frac{\gamma^2}{2}\right)} \sin^{n-2}(\theta)\, d\theta}.$$

Proof As the derivation requires the calculation of surface integrals on the hypersphere in ℓ_2^n we define each admissible $\mathbf{w} \in \mathcal{W}$ by its polar coordinates and carry out the integration over the angles. Thus we specify the coordinate transformation $\boldsymbol{\tau} : \mathbb{R}^n \to \mathbb{R}^n$ from polar coordinates into Cartesian coordinates, i.e., every $\mathbf{w} \in \mathcal{W}$ is expressed via $n-2$ angles $\boldsymbol{\theta} = (\theta_1, \ldots, \theta_{n-2})'$ ranging from 0 to π, one angle $0 \le \varphi \le 2\pi$, and the radius function $r(\boldsymbol{\theta}, \varphi)$ which is in the case of a sphere of constant value r. This transformation reads

$$\begin{aligned}
\tau_1(r, \varphi, \boldsymbol{\theta}) &= r \cdot \sin(\varphi)\sin(\theta_1)\cdots\sin(\theta_{n-2}) && \text{(C.8)}\\
\tau_2(r, \varphi, \boldsymbol{\theta}) &= r \cdot \cos(\varphi)\sin(\theta_1)\cdots\sin(\theta_{n-2})\\
&\vdots\\
\tau_{n-1}(r, \varphi, \boldsymbol{\theta}) &= r \cdot \cos(\theta_{n-3})\sin(\theta_{n-2})\\
\tau_n(r, \varphi, \boldsymbol{\theta}) &= r \cdot \cos(\theta_{n-2}). && \text{(C.9)}
\end{aligned}$$

Without loss of generality we choose $\mathbf{w}$ to be $\tilde{\boldsymbol{\theta}} = \mathbf{0}$, $\tilde{\varphi} = 0$. Hence the ball $\mathcal{B}_\gamma(\tilde{\mathbf{w}})$ of radius γ is the following set of angles

$$\begin{aligned}
&\left\{\varphi \in [0, 2\pi], \boldsymbol{\theta} \in [0, \pi]^{n-2} \,\middle|\, \left\langle \boldsymbol{\tau}(1, \varphi, \boldsymbol{\theta}), \boldsymbol{\tau}\left(1, \tilde{\varphi}, \tilde{\boldsymbol{\theta}}\right)\right\rangle > 1 - \frac{\gamma^2}{2}\right\}\\
&\quad = \left\{\varphi \in [0, 2\pi], \boldsymbol{\theta} \in [0, \pi]^{n-2} \,\middle|\, \cos(\theta_{n-2}) > 1 - \frac{\gamma^2}{2}\right\}\\
&\quad = \left\{\varphi \in [0, 2\pi], \boldsymbol{\theta} \in [0, \pi]^{n-2} \,\middle|\, \theta_{n-2} < \arccos\left(1 - \frac{\gamma^2}{2}\right)\right\}.
\end{aligned}$$

As can be seen from this expression the margin γ characterizing the ball simply possesses a restriction on the angle θ_{n-2} in the integration. Thus, the quantity of interest is given by

$$\frac{\int_0^{2\pi}\int_0^\pi \cdots \int_0^\pi \left|J_n(r, \varphi, \theta_1, \ldots, \theta_{n-2})\right| d\theta_{n-2}\cdots d\theta_1\, d\varphi}{\int_0^{2\pi}\int_0^\pi \cdots \int_0^\Psi \left|J_n(r, \varphi, \theta_1, \ldots, \theta_{n-2})\right| d\theta_{n-2}\cdots d\theta_1\, d\varphi}, \tag{C.10}$$

where $\Psi = \arccos\left(1-\gamma^2/2\right)$ and J_n is the functional determinant of $\boldsymbol{\tau}$ given by equation (C.8)–(C.9),

$$J_n(r,\varphi,\theta_1,\ldots,\theta_{n-2}) = |\mathbf{J}_n| \;, \tag{C.11}$$

where the *Jacobian matrix* $\mathbf{J}_n$ is formally defined as

$$\mathbf{J}_n \stackrel{\text{def}}{=} \begin{pmatrix} \left.\frac{\partial\tau_1(r,\varphi,\boldsymbol{\theta})}{\partial r}\right|_r & \left.\frac{\partial\tau_1(r,\varphi,\boldsymbol{\theta})}{\partial\varphi}\right|_\varphi & \cdots & \left.\frac{\partial\tau_1(r,\varphi,\boldsymbol{\theta})}{\partial\theta_{n-2}}\right|_{\theta_{n-2}} \\ \vdots & \vdots & \ddots & \vdots \\ \left.\frac{\partial\tau_n(r,\varphi,\boldsymbol{\theta})}{\partial r}\right|_r & \left.\frac{\partial\tau_n(r,\varphi,\boldsymbol{\theta})}{\partial\varphi}\right|_\varphi & \cdots & \left.\frac{\partial\tau_n(r,\varphi,\boldsymbol{\theta})}{\partial\theta_{n-2}}\right|_{\theta_{n-2}} \end{pmatrix} .$$

If $\mathbf{J}_{n-1} = (\mathbf{j}_1,\ldots,\mathbf{j}_{n-1}) \in \mathbb{R}^{(n-1)\times(n-1)}$ is the Jacobian matrix for the mapping $\boldsymbol{\tau}$ when applied for points in $\mathbb{R}^{n-1}$ then we see that

$$\mathbf{J}_n = \begin{pmatrix} \sin(\theta_{n-2})\cdot\mathbf{J}_{n-1} & r\cdot\cos(\theta_{n-2})\cdot\mathbf{j}_1 \\ \begin{pmatrix}\cos(\theta_{n-2}) & 0 & \cdots & 0\end{pmatrix} & -r\cdot\sin(\theta_{n-2}) \end{pmatrix} . \tag{C.12}$$

Hence the nth row of this matrix contains only two non-zero elements

$$\left.\frac{\partial\tau_n(r,\varphi,\boldsymbol{\theta})}{\partial r}\right|_r = \cos(\theta_{n-2}) \;, \quad \left.\frac{\partial\tau_n(r,\varphi,\boldsymbol{\theta})}{\partial\theta_{n-2}}\right|_{\theta_{n-2}} = -r\cdot\sin(\theta_{n-2}) \;.$$

Now, using the Laplace expansion of (C.11) in the nth row (see Definition A.64) we obtain

$$|\mathbf{J}_n| = (-1)^{n+1}\cos(\theta_{n-2})\left|\mathbf{J}_{[n,1]}\right| - (-1)^{n+n}\cdot r\sin(\theta_{n-2})\left|\mathbf{J}_{[n,n]}\right| \;,$$

where $\mathbf{J}_{[i,j]}$ is the $(n-1)\times(n-1)$ sub-matrix obtained by deletion of the ith row and the jth column of $\mathbf{J}_n$. From equation (C.12) and Theorem A.71 it follows that $\left|\mathbf{J}_{[n,n]}\right| = \sin^{n-1}(\theta_{n-2})\cdot|\mathbf{J}_{n-1}|$. Further we know that

$$\begin{aligned} \left|\mathbf{J}_{[n,1]}\right| &= \left|(\sin(\theta_{n-2})\cdot\mathbf{j}_2,\ldots,\sin(\theta_{n-2})\cdot\mathbf{j}_{n-1}, r\cdot\cos(\theta_{n-2})\cdot\mathbf{j}_1)\right| \\ &= (-1)^{n-2}\cdot\left|(r\cdot\cos(\theta_{n-2})\cdot\mathbf{j}_1,\sin(\theta_{n-2})\cdot\mathbf{j}_2,\ldots,\sin(\theta_{n-2})\cdot\mathbf{j}_{n-1})\right| \\ &= (-1)^{n-2}\cdot r\cdot\cos(\theta_{n-2})\cdot\sin^{n-2}(\theta_{n-2})\cdot|\mathbf{J}_{n-1}| \;. \end{aligned}$$

Hence, $|\mathbf{J}_n|$ is given by

$$\begin{aligned} |\mathbf{J}_n| &= -\cos^2(\theta_{n-2})\cdot r\cdot\sin^{n-2}(\theta_{n-2})\cdot|\mathbf{J}_{n-1}| - r\cdot\sin^n(\theta_{n-2})\cdot|\mathbf{J}_{n-1}| \;, \\ &= -|\mathbf{J}_{n-1}|\cdot r\cdot\sin^{n-2}(\theta_{n-2})\left(\cos^2(\theta_{n-2})+\sin^2(\theta_{n-2})\right) \\ &= -|\mathbf{J}_{n-1}|\cdot r\cdot\sin^{n-2}(\theta_{n-2}) \;, \end{aligned}$$

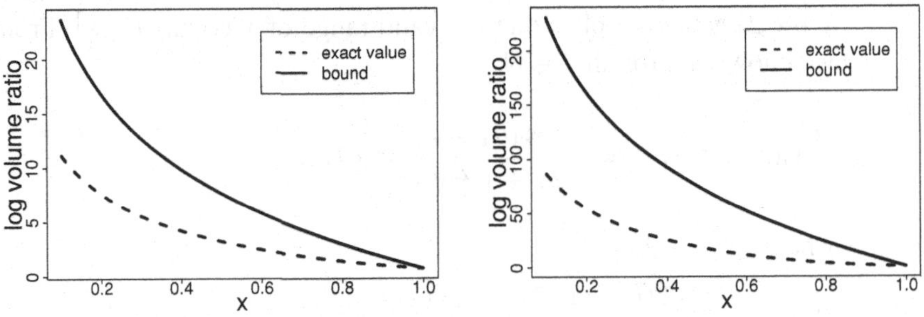

(a) (b)

Figure C.5 Comparison of the bound (C.14) (solid line) with the exact value (C.13) (dashed line) over the whole range of possible values of x for **(a)** $n = 10$ and **(b)** $n = 100$. Interestingly, in the relevant regime of large values of x the bound seems to be very tight regardless of the number of dimensions.

which, substituted into equation (C.10) gives

$$\frac{\mathrm{vol}\,(\mathcal{W})}{\mathrm{vol}\,(\mathcal{B}_\gamma\,(\mathbf{w}))} = \frac{\int_0^\pi \sin^{n-2}\,(\theta_{n-2})\;d\theta_{n-2}}{\int_0^\Psi \sin^{n-2}\,(\theta_{n-2})\;d\theta_{n-2}}\,, \tag{C.13}$$

where $\Psi = \arccos\left(1 - \gamma^2/2\right)$. The theorem is proved. ■

C.8.3 A Volume Ratio Bound

In this section we present a practically useful upper bound for the expression given in equation (C.13). In order to check the usefulness of this expression we have compared the exact value of (C.13) with the upper bound and found that in the interesting regime of large margins the bound seems to be within a factor of 2 from the exact value (see Figure C.5).

Theorem C.15 *For all $j \in \mathbb{N}$ and all $0 < x \leq 1$*

$$\ln\left(\frac{\int_0^\pi \sin^{2j+1}\,(\theta)\;d\theta}{\int_0^{\Psi(x)} \sin^{2j+1}\,(\theta)\;d\theta}\right) \leq \ln\left(\frac{1}{x}\right)^{2j+1} + \ln\,(2)\,, \tag{C.14}$$

where $\Psi\,(x) = \arccos\,(1 - x)$.

Proof Without loss of generality, we consider a transformation of the variable $x \mapsto 2x$ which implies that the valid range of x equals $\left(0, \frac{1}{2}\right]$. From Bois (1961) we know that, for all $j \in \mathbb{N}$,

$$\int \sin^{2j+1}(\theta)\, d\theta = -\frac{\cos(\theta)}{2j+1} \sum_{i=0}^{j} \sin^{2i}(\theta)\, B_{j,i}\,, \tag{C.15}$$

where

$$\begin{aligned} B_{j,i} &= \frac{2(i+1)\cdot 2(i+2)\cdot\dots\cdot 2j}{(2i+1)\cdot(2i+3)\cdot\dots\cdot(2j-1)} \\ &= \frac{2\cdot 4\cdots 2j}{1\cdot 3\cdots(2j-1)}\cdot\frac{1\cdot 3\cdots(2i-1)}{2\cdot 4\cdots(2i)} \\ &= \frac{4^j\,(j!)^2\,(2i)!}{(2j)!\,(i!)^2\,4^i} = \frac{4^j}{4^i}\frac{\binom{2i}{i}}{\binom{2j}{j}}\,. \end{aligned} \tag{C.16}$$

Let us introduce the abbreviation

$$S(j,x) = \int_0^{\arccos(1-2x)} \sin^{2j+1}(\theta)\; d\theta\,.$$

Then the numerator of (C.14) (after the transformation $x \mapsto 2x$) is given by $S(j, 1)$ whereas the denominator of (C.14) is simply $S(j, x)$. From equation (C.15) we see

$$\begin{aligned} S(j,x) &= -\frac{\cos(\theta)}{2j+1}\sum_{i=0}^{j}\sin^{2i}(\theta)\,B_{j,i}\Bigg|_0^{\arccos(1-2x)} \\ &= \frac{4^j}{(2j+1)\binom{2j}{j}}\left(1+(2x-1)\sum_{i=0}^{j}\binom{2i}{i}x^i(1-x)^i\right), \end{aligned}$$

where we have used (C.16) and

$$\sin^{2i}(\theta) = \left(\sin^2(\theta)\right)^i = \left(1-\cos^2(\theta)\right)^i = \left(1-(1-2x)^2\right)^i = \left(4x-4x^2\right)^i.$$

Expanding the first term of the sum we obtain for the logarithm of the fraction of integrals

$$\ln\left(\frac{S(j,1)}{S(j,x)}\right) = \ln\left(\frac{2}{2x+(2x-1)\sum_{i=1}^{j}\binom{2i}{i}x^i(1-x)^i}\right).$$

In Lemma C.20 we show that for any $j \in \mathbb{N}^+$ and $0 \leq x < \frac{1}{2}$

$$\sum_{i=1}^{j} \binom{2i}{i} x^i (1-x)^i \leq \frac{2x\left((2x)^{2j}-1\right)}{2x-1}.$$

Inserting this into the last expression and taking into account that $(2x-1) \leq 0$ in the relevant regime of x we obtain

$$\begin{aligned}
\ln\left(\frac{S(j,1)}{S(j,x)}\right) &\leq \ln\left(\frac{2}{2x + (2x-1)\frac{2x\left((2x)^{2j}-1\right)}{(2x-1)}}\right) = \ln\left(\frac{2}{(2x)^{2j+1}}\right) \\
&= -(2j+1)\ln(x) + \ln(2),
\end{aligned}$$

which proves the theorem. Note that in the case of $x = \frac{1}{2}$ the problem reduces to

$$\ln\left(\frac{S(j,1)}{S\left(j,\frac{1}{2}\right)}\right) = \underbrace{-(2j+1)\ln(2x)}_{0} + \ln(2),$$

which finalizes the proof. ■

C.8.4 Bollmann's Lemma

In the course of the proof of Theorem C.15 we needed a tight upper bound on the growth of $\sum_{i=1}^{j} \binom{2i}{i} x^i (1-x)^i$ as a function of x. In the following we present a series of lemmas resulting in a reasonably accurate upper bound called *Bollmann's lemma* (Lemma C.20).

Lemma C.16 *For all* $i \in \mathbb{N}^+$

$$\binom{2(i+1)}{i+1} = \binom{2i}{i}\left(4 - \frac{2}{i+1}\right).$$

Proof A straightforward calculation shows that

$$\begin{aligned}
\binom{2(i+1)}{i+1} &= \frac{2(i+1)(2i+1)}{(i+1)(i+1)}\binom{2i}{i} = \binom{2i}{i}\frac{4i+2}{i+1} \\
&= \binom{2i}{i}\left(4 - \frac{2}{i+1}\right).
\end{aligned}$$

The lemma is proved. ■

Lemma C.17 *For all $i \in \mathbb{N}^+$ and $j \in \mathbb{N}^+$*

$$\binom{2(j+1)}{j+1}\binom{2i}{i} \leq 2\binom{2(i+j)}{i+j}.$$

Proof We prove the lemma by induction over i. For $i = 1$ it follows that

$$\binom{2(j+1)}{j+1}\binom{2}{1} = 2\binom{2(j+1)}{j+1}.$$

Assume the assertion is true for $i \in \mathbb{N}^+$. Then

$$\begin{aligned}
\binom{2(j+1)}{j+1}\binom{2(i+1)}{i+1} &= \binom{2(j+1)}{j+1}\binom{2i}{i}\left(4 - \frac{2}{i+1}\right) \\
&\leq 2\binom{2(i+j)}{i+j}\left(4 - \frac{2}{i+1}\right) \\
&\leq 2\binom{2(i+j)}{i+j}\left(4 - \frac{2}{i+j+1}\right) \\
&= 2\binom{2(i+j+1)}{i+j+1},
\end{aligned}$$

where we used Lemma C.16 in the first and last lines. ■

Lemma C.18 *For all $0 \leq x < \frac{1}{2}$*

$$\sum_{i=1}^{\infty}\binom{2i}{i}x^i(1-x)^i = \frac{2x}{1-2x}.$$

Proof This can be seen by considering

$$\begin{aligned}
\arcsin(u) &= u + \sum_{i=1}^{\infty}\binom{2i}{i}\frac{1}{4^i}\frac{u^{2i+1}}{2i+1}, \\
\frac{d\arcsin(u)}{du} &= 1 + \sum_{i=1}^{\infty}\binom{2i}{i}\frac{1}{4^i}u^{2i} = \frac{1}{\sqrt{1-u^2}}.
\end{aligned}$$

Using $u = 2\sqrt{x(1-x)}$ we obtain the result, i.e.,

$$\sum_{i=1}^{\infty}\binom{2i}{i}\frac{1}{4^i}\left(2\sqrt{x(1-x)}\right)^{2i} = \frac{1}{\sqrt{1-4x(1-x)}} - 1$$

$$\sum_{i=1}^{\infty}\binom{2i}{i}x^i(1-x)^i = \frac{1-\sqrt{1-4x(1-x)}}{\sqrt{1-4x(1-x)}}$$
$$= \frac{1-\sqrt{(1-2x)^2}}{\sqrt{(1-2x)^2}}.$$

The lemma is proved. ■

Lemma C.19 *For all* $0 \le x < \frac{1}{2}$ *and* $j \in \mathbb{N}^+$

$$4x^2\sum_{i=1}^{\infty}\binom{2(i+j)}{i+j}x^{i+j}(1-x)^{i+j} \le \sum_{i=1}^{\infty}\binom{2(i+j+1)}{i+j+1}x^{i+j+1}(1-x)^{i+j+1}.$$

Proof Put $A(i,j,x) \stackrel{\text{def}}{=} \sum_{i=1}^{\infty}\binom{2(i+j)}{i+j}x^{i+j}(1-x)^{i+j}$. Then the result to be proven simply reads $4x^2 \cdot A(i,j,x) \le A(i,j+1,x)$. By Lemma C.17 we have

$$\sum_{i=1}^{\infty}\binom{2i}{i}\binom{2(j+1)}{j+1}x^{i+j}(1-x)^{i+j} \le 2 \cdot A(i,j,x).$$

Since $0 < 1-x \le 1+2x$, by Lemma C.18 it follows that

$$(1-x)\sum_{i=1}^{\infty}\binom{2i}{i}\binom{2(j+1)}{j+1}x^{i+j}(1-x)^{i+j} \le 2(1+2x)\cdot A(i,j,x),$$
$$(1-x)\binom{2(j+1)}{j+1}x^j(1-x)^j\frac{2x}{1-2x} \le 2(1+2x)\cdot A(i,j,x).$$

Multiplying both sides by $\frac{1-2x}{2}$ (which is, by assumption, positive) yields

$$\binom{2(j+1)}{j+1}x^{j+1}(1-x)^{j+1} \le \left(1-4x^2\right)\cdot A(i,j,x).$$

Rearranging terms gives

$$4x^2 \cdot A(i,j,x) \le A(i,j,x) - \binom{2(j+1)}{j+1}x^{j+1}(1-x)^{j+1} = A(i,j+1,x).$$

The lemma is proved. ■

Lemma C.20 *For any $j \in \mathbb{N}^+$ and $0 < x < \frac{1}{2}$*

$$\sum_{i=1}^{j} \binom{2i}{i} x^i (1-x)^i \leq \frac{2x\left((2x)^{2j}-1\right)}{2x-1} .$$

Proof The assertion can be transformed into

$$\begin{aligned}
\sum_{i=1}^{j} \binom{2i}{i} x^i (1-x)^i &\leq \frac{2x\left((2x)^{2j}-1\right)}{2x-1} \\
&= \frac{2x\left(1-(2x)^{2j}\right)}{1-2x} \\
&\leq \frac{2x}{1-2x} - \frac{(2x)^{2j+1}}{1-2x} \\
&\leq \sum_{i=1}^{\infty} \binom{2i}{i} x^i (1-x)^i - \frac{(2x)^{2j+1}}{1-2x} ,
\end{aligned}$$

which is equivalent to

$$(2x)^{2j+1} \leq (1-2x) \sum_{i=1}^{\infty} \binom{2(i+j)}{i+j} x^{i+j} (1-x)^{i+j} .$$

We prove this by induction over j. For $j = 1$ we have

$$\binom{2}{1} x (1-x) = 2x - 2x^2 \leq 2x + 4x^2 = \frac{8x^3 - 2x}{2x-1} = \frac{2x\left((2x)^2-1\right)}{2x-1} .$$

Assume the assertion is true for j. Then

$$\begin{aligned}
(2x)^{2(j+1)+1} &= 4x^2 (2x)^{2j+1} \\
&\leq 4x^2 \left((1-2x) \sum_{i=1}^{\infty} \binom{2(i+j)}{i+j} x^{i+j} (1-x)^{i+j} \right) \\
&\leq (1-2x) \sum_{i=1}^{\infty} \binom{2(i+j+1)}{i+j+1} x^{i+j+1} (1-x)^{i+j+1} ,
\end{aligned}$$

where the second line is assumed to be true and the third line follows from Lemma C.19. The lemma is proved. ■

C.9 Algorithmic Stability Bounds

In this section we present the proofs of the main theorems from Section 5.3. In order to enhance the readability of the proofs we use the same notation as introduced on page 186, that is, given a sample $z \in \mathcal{Z}^m$, a natural number $i \in \{1, \ldots, m\}$ and an example $z \in \mathcal{Z}$ let

$$z_{\setminus i} \stackrel{\text{def}}{=} (z_1, \ldots, z_{i-1}, z_{i+1}, \ldots, z_m) \in \mathcal{Z}^{m-1},$$

$$z_{i \leftrightarrow z} \stackrel{\text{def}}{=} (z_1, \ldots, z_{i-1}, z, z_{i+1}, \ldots, z_m) \in \mathcal{Z}^m,$$

be the sample with the ith element deleted or the ith element replaced by z, respectively. Whenever the learning algorithm is clear from the context, we use $f_z \stackrel{\text{def}}{=} \mathcal{A}(z)$ to denote the hypothesis learned by $\mathcal{A}$ given $z \in \mathcal{Z}^m$.

C.9.1 Uniform Stability of Functions Minimizing a Regularized Risk

This subsection proves Theorem 5.31. The proof is mainly taken from Bousquet and Elisseeff (2000).

Proof of Theorem 5.31. In course of the proof we shall often consider the difference between the functions $f_{z_{\setminus i}}$ and f_z obtained by learning on the reduced training sample $z_{\setminus i}$ and the full training sample z. Let us denote this difference by $\Delta f \stackrel{\text{def}}{=} \left(f_{z_{\setminus i}} - f_z\right)$. Then we must bound the difference $\left|l\left(f_{z_{\setminus i}}(x), t\right) - l\left(f_z(x), t\right)\right|$ for any $(x, t) \in \mathcal{Z}$. Using the Lipschitz continuity of l we know that

$$\left|l\left(f_{z_{\setminus i}}(x), t\right) - l\left(f_z(x), t\right)\right| \leq C_l \cdot \left|f_{z_{\setminus i}}(x) - f_z(x)\right| = C_l \cdot |\Delta f(x)| .$$

Since we consider a reproducing kernel Hilbert space $\mathcal{F}$ of real-valued functions $f \in \mathbb{R}^{\mathcal{X}}$ we know that (see also equations (2.36) and (2.37))

$$|\Delta f(x)| = |\langle \Delta f, k(x, \cdot)\rangle| \leq \|\Delta f\| \cdot k(x, x) . \tag{C.17}$$

Thus, it suffices to have an upper bound on $\|\Delta f\|$. We shall show shortly that $\|\Delta f\|^2 \leq \frac{C_l}{2\lambda m} |\Delta f(x_i)|$ which, together with the last inequality implies that

$$\|\Delta f\|^2 \leq \frac{C_l}{2\lambda m} |\Delta f(x_i)| \leq \frac{C_l}{2\lambda m} \|\Delta f\| \cdot k(x_i, x_i) \Leftrightarrow \|\Delta f\| \leq \frac{C_l}{2\lambda m} \cdot k(x_i, x_i) .$$

Resubstituting this expression into equation (C.17) gives

$$\left|l\left(f_{z_{\setminus i}}(x), t\right) - l\left(f_z(x), t\right)\right| \le C_l \cdot \|\Delta f\| \cdot k(x,x) \le \frac{C_l^2 \kappa^2}{2\lambda m},$$

where κ is defined by $\kappa = \sup_{x\in\mathcal{X}} k(x,x)$. It remains to prove the upper bound on the $\|\Delta f\|^2$. At first we exploit the fact that $f_{z_{\setminus i}}$ and f_z are the minimizers of equation (5.19) for the two different training samples $z_{\setminus i} \in \mathcal{Z}^{m-1}$ and $z \in \mathcal{Z}^m$, respectively. Formally this reads

$$R_{\text{reg}}[f_z, z] - R_{\text{reg}}[f_z + \eta\cdot\Delta f] \le 0\,, \quad R_{\text{reg}}\left[f_{z_{\setminus i}}, z_{\setminus i}\right] - R_{\text{reg}}\left[f_{z_{\setminus i}} - \eta\cdot\Delta f\right] \le 0,$$

where we assume $\eta \in (0,1)$ and R_{reg} is defined by

$$R_{\text{reg}}[f,z] = \underbrace{\frac{1}{m}\sum_{(x_i,t_i)\in z} l\left(f(x_i), t_i\right)}_{R_m[f,z]} + \lambda\|f\|^2\,.$$

Adding the above two inequalities and exploiting $R_{\text{reg}}[f,z] = R_{\text{reg}}\left[f, z_{\setminus i}\right] + \frac{1}{m} l\left(f(x_i), t_i\right)$ we obtain

$$\frac{1}{m}\left(l\left(f_z(x_i), t_i\right) - l\left(\left(f_z + \eta\cdot\Delta f\right)(x_i), t_i\right)\right) + \lambda\cdot A \le B\,, \tag{C.18}$$

where A and B are given by

$$A = \|f_z\|^2 + \left\|f_{z_{\setminus i}}\right\|^2 - \|f_z + \eta\cdot\Delta f\|^2 - \left\|f_{z_{\setminus i}} - \eta\cdot\Delta f\right\|^2,$$

$$B = R_m\left[f_z + \eta\Delta f, z_{\setminus i}\right] + R_m\left[f_{z_{\setminus i}} + \eta\Delta f, z_{\setminus i}\right] - R_m\left[f_z, z_{\setminus i}\right] - R_m\left[f_{z_{\setminus i}}, z_{\setminus i}\right].$$

Using the definition of Δf allows us to determine A directly

$$\begin{aligned} A &= 2\eta\left(-\langle f_z, \Delta f\rangle + \left\langle f_{z_{\setminus i}}, \Delta f\right\rangle - \eta\|\Delta f\|^2\right) \\ &= 2\eta\left(\left\langle f_{z_{\setminus i}} - f_z, \Delta f\right\rangle - \eta\|\Delta f\|^2\right) = 2\eta(1-\eta)\|\Delta f\|^2\,. \end{aligned}$$

Since the loss function l is assumed to be convex in its first argument we know that for all $(x,t)\in\mathcal{Z}$ and all $\eta\in(0,1)$

$$l\left(\left(f_z + \eta\cdot\Delta f\right)(x), t\right) - l\left(\left(f_z\right)(x), t\right) \le \eta\cdot\left(l\left(\left(f_{z_{\setminus i}}\right)(x), t\right) - l\left(\left(f_z\right)(x), t\right)\right).$$

This implies that the following two inequalities hold true

$$R_m\left[f_z + \eta\Delta f, z_{\setminus i}\right] - R_m\left[f_z, z_{\setminus i}\right] \le \eta\left(R_m\left[f_{z_{\setminus i}}, z_{\setminus i}\right] - R_m\left[f_z, z_{\setminus i}\right]\right),$$

$$R_m\left[f_{z_{\setminus i}} - \eta\Delta f, z_{\setminus i}\right] - R_m\left[f_{z_{\setminus i}}, z_{\setminus i}\right] \le \eta\left(R_m\left[f_z, z_{\setminus i}\right] - R_m\left[f_{z_{\setminus i}}, z_{\setminus i}\right]\right).$$

Adding these two inequalities shows that $B \le 0$. Using the Lipschitz continuity of the loss we see that equation (C.18) can be written as

$$\begin{aligned} \|\Delta f\|^2 &\le \frac{l\left(\left(f_z + \eta \cdot \Delta f\right)(x_i), t_i\right) - l\left(f_z(x_i), t_i\right)}{2\eta(1-\eta)\lambda m} \\ &\le \frac{C_l \cdot \left|\left(f_z + \eta \cdot \Delta f\right)(x_i) - f_z(x_i)\right|}{2\eta(1-\eta)\lambda m} = \frac{C_l}{2(1-\eta)\lambda m}\left|\Delta f(x_i)\right|. \end{aligned}$$

Taking the limit of the latter expression for $\eta \to 0$ shows that $\|\Delta f\|^2 \le \frac{C_l}{2\lambda m}\left|\Delta f(x_i)\right|$ which completes the proof. ■

C.9.2 Algorithmic Stability Bounds

In this subsection we prove Theorem 5.32. We start with some simple lemmas which help us to structure the main proof.

Lemma C.21 *Let $\mathcal{A} : \cup_{m=1}^{\infty} \mathcal{Z}^m \to \mathcal{F}$ be a β_m–stable learning algorithm w.r.t. a loss function $l : \mathbb{R} \times \mathbb{R} \to \mathbb{R}$. Then we have*

$$\mathbf{E}_{\mathbf{Z}^m}\left[R\left[f_{\mathbf{Z}}\right] - R_{\text{emp}}\left[f_{\mathbf{Z}}, \mathbf{Z}\right]\right] \le 2\beta_m, \qquad \mathbf{E}_{\mathbf{Z}^m}\left[R\left[f_{\mathbf{Z}}\right] - R_{\text{loo}}\left[\mathcal{A}, \mathbf{Z}\right]\right] \le \beta_m.$$

Proof By the independence of the training sample $z \in \mathcal{Z}^m$ from the test example $z = (x, t) \in \mathcal{Z}$ we note that the expectation $\mathbf{E}_{\mathbf{Z}^m}\left[R\left[f_{\mathbf{Z}}\right] - R_{\text{emp}}\left[f_{\mathbf{Z}}, \mathbf{Z}\right]\right]$ can be rewritten as

$$\frac{1}{m}\sum_{i=1}^{m}\int_{\mathcal{Z}^m}\int_{\mathcal{Z}} \underbrace{l\left(f_z(x), t\right) - l\left(f_{z_{i\leftrightarrow(x,t)}}(x), t\right)}_{q(z,(x,t))} d\mathbf{F}_{\mathbf{Z}}((x,t))\, d\mathbf{F}_{\mathbf{Z}^m}(z).$$

By virtue of Theorem 5.27, for any $i \in \{1, \ldots, m\}$ the integrand $q(z, (x, t))$ is upper bounded by $2\beta_m$ thanks to the β_m–stability of the learning algorithm $\mathcal{A}$. This proves the first assertion. Similarly, for the second assertion we know that $\mathbf{E}_{\mathbf{Z}^m}\left[R\left[f_{\mathbf{Z}}\right] - R_{\text{loo}}\left[\mathcal{A}, \mathbf{Z}\right]\right]$ can be written as

$$\frac{1}{m}\sum_{i=1}^{m}\int_{\mathcal{Z}^m}\int_{\mathcal{Z}} l\left(f_z(x), t\right) - l\left(f_{z_{\setminus i}}(x_i), t_i\right) d\mathbf{F}_{\mathbf{Z}}((x,t))\, d\mathbf{F}_{\mathbf{Z}^m}(z).$$

Since, for any $i \in \{1, \ldots, m\}$, the example $z_i = (x_i, t_i)$ is not used in finding $f_{z_{\setminus i}}$ but has the same distribution as $z = (x, t)$ the latter expression equals

$$\frac{1}{m}\sum_{i=1}^{m}\int_{\mathcal{Z}^m}\int_{\mathcal{Z}}\underbrace{l\left(f_z\left(x\right),t\right)-l\left(f_{z_{\setminus i}}\left(x\right),t\right)}_{q(z,(x,t))}\,d\mathbf{F}_{\mathsf{Z}}\left(\left(x,t\right)\right)\,d\mathbf{F}_{\mathsf{Z}^m}\left(z\right).$$

By assumption $\mathcal{A}$ is a β_m–stable algorithm w.r.t. l which implies that the integrand is bounded from above by β_m. The lemma is proved. ■

Lemma C.22 *Let $\mathcal{A} : \cup_{m=1}^{\infty}\mathcal{Z}^m \to \mathcal{F}$ be a β_m–stable learning algorithm w.r.t. a given loss function $l : \mathbb{R}\times\mathbb{R} \to [0, b]$. Then, for any $i \in \{1, \ldots, m\}$, we have*

$$\begin{aligned}\sup_{z\in\mathcal{Z}^m,\tilde{z}\in\mathcal{Z}}\left|R\left[f_z\right]-R\left[f_{z_{i\leftrightarrow\tilde{z}}}\right]\right| &\leq 2\beta_m\,,\\ \sup_{z\in\mathcal{Z}^m,\tilde{z}\in\mathcal{Z}}\left|R_{\text{emp}}\left[f_z,z\right]-R_{\text{emp}}\left[f_{z_{i\leftrightarrow\tilde{z}}},z_{i\leftrightarrow\tilde{z}}\right]\right| &\leq 2\beta_m+\frac{b}{m}\,,\\ \sup_{z\in\mathcal{Z}^m,\tilde{z}\in\mathcal{Z}}\left|R_{\text{loo}}\left[\mathcal{A},z\right]-R_{\text{loo}}\left[\mathcal{A},z_{i\leftrightarrow\tilde{z}}\right]\right| &\leq 2\beta_{m-1}+\frac{b}{m}\,.\end{aligned}$$

Proof The first assertion follows directly from Theorem 5.27 noticing that, by the β_m–stability of $\mathcal{A}$, for all $z \in \mathcal{Z}^m$, all $\tilde{z} \in \mathcal{Z}$ and all $i \in \{1, \ldots, m\}$

$$\left|R\left[f_z\right]-R\left[f_{z_{i\leftrightarrow\tilde{z}}}\right]\right| \leq \mathbf{E}_{\mathsf{XT}}\left[\left|l\left(f_z\left(\mathsf{X}\right),\mathsf{T}\right)-l\left(f_{z_{i\leftrightarrow\tilde{z}}}\left(\mathsf{X}\right),\mathsf{T}\right)\right|\right] \leq 2\beta_m\,.$$

In order to prove the second assertion we note that, for all $i \in \{1, \ldots, m\}$,

$$\begin{aligned}R_{\text{emp}}\left[f_z,z\right] &= \frac{m-1}{m}R_{\text{emp}}\left[f_z,z_{\setminus i}\right]+\frac{1}{m}l\left(f_z\left(x_i\right),t_i\right).\\ R_{\text{emp}}\left[f_{z_{i\leftrightarrow\tilde{z}}},z_{i\leftrightarrow\tilde{z}}\right] &= \frac{m-1}{m}R_{\text{emp}}\left[f_{z_{i\leftrightarrow\tilde{z}}},z_{\setminus i}\right]+\frac{1}{m}l\left(f_{z_{i\leftrightarrow\tilde{z}}}\left(\tilde{x}\right),\tilde{t}\right).\end{aligned}$$

As, by assumption, $\mathcal{A}$ is a β_m–stable algorithm, using Theorem 5.27 shows that $\left|R_{\text{emp}}\left[f_z,z_{\setminus i}\right]-R_{\text{emp}}\left[f_{z_{i\leftrightarrow\tilde{z}}},z_{\setminus i}\right]\right|$ cannot exceed $2\beta_m$. Further, by the finiteness of the loss function l it follows that

$$\left|R_{\text{emp}}\left[f_z,z\right]-R_{\text{emp}}\left[f_{z_{i\leftrightarrow\tilde{z}}},z_{i\leftrightarrow\tilde{z}}\right]\right| \leq 2\frac{m-1}{m}\beta_m+\frac{b}{m} < 2\beta_m+\frac{b}{m}\,.$$

The proof of the final assertion is analogous and exploiting that, for all $i \in \{1, \ldots, m\}$

$$R_{\text{loo}}[\mathcal{A}, z] = \frac{1}{m}\sum_{\substack{j=1\\j\neq i}}^{m} l\left(f_{z_{\setminus j}}(x_j), t_j\right) + \frac{1}{m} l\left(f_{z_{\setminus i}}(x_i), t_i\right),$$

$$R_{\text{loo}}[\mathcal{A}, z_{i\leftrightarrow\tilde{z}}] = \frac{1}{m}\sum_{\substack{j=1\\j\neq i}}^{m} l\left(f_{z_{(i\leftrightarrow\tilde{z})\setminus j}}(x_j), t_j\right) + \frac{1}{m} l\left(f_{z_{\setminus i}}(\tilde{x}), \tilde{t}\right).$$

Taking into account that $f_{z_{\setminus j}}$ is obtained by learning using a training sample of size $m-1$ the third statement of the lemma follows immediately. ■

Using these two lemmas allows us to present the proof of Theorem 5.32.

Proof of Theorem 5.32. Let us start with the first equation involving the training error $R_{\text{emp}}[f_z, z]$. To this end we define the function $g(\mathbf{Z}) = R[f_{\mathbf{Z}}] - R_{\text{emp}}[f_{\mathbf{Z}}, \mathbf{Z}]$ of the m random variables $\mathsf{Z}_1, \ldots, \mathsf{Z}_m$. By Lemma C.22 we know that for all $i \in \{1, \ldots, m\}$

$$\sup_{z\in\mathcal{Z}^m, \tilde{z}\in\mathcal{Z}} |g(z) - g(z_{i\leftrightarrow\tilde{z}})| \leq 4\beta_m + \frac{b}{m},$$

because the difference

$$|g(z) - g(z_{i\leftrightarrow\tilde{z}})| = \left|R[f_z] - R_{\text{emp}}[f_z, z] - \left(R\left[f_{z_{i\leftrightarrow\tilde{z}}}\right] - R_{\text{emp}}\left[f_{z_{i\leftrightarrow\tilde{z}}}, z_{i\leftrightarrow\tilde{z}}\right]\right)\right|$$

is bounded from above by the sum of the two terms $\left|R[f_z] - R\left[f_{z_{i\leftrightarrow\tilde{z}}}\right]\right|$ and $\left|R_{\text{emp}}[f_z, z] - R_{\text{emp}}\left[f_{z_{i\leftrightarrow\tilde{z}}}, z_{i\leftrightarrow\tilde{z}}\right]\right|$ due to the triangle inequality. Further, by Lemma C.21 we know

$$g(z) > \varepsilon + 2\beta_m \;\Rightarrow\; g(z) > \varepsilon + \mathbf{E}_{\mathbf{Z}^m}\left[g(\mathbf{Z})\right].$$

Thus, using McDiarmid's inequality given in Theorem A.120 shows that

$$\begin{aligned}\mathbf{P}_{\mathbf{Z}^m}\left(g(\mathbf{Z}) > \varepsilon + 2\beta_m\right) &\leq \mathbf{P}_{\mathbf{Z}^m}\left(g(\mathbf{Z}) - \mathbf{E}_{\mathbf{Z}^m}\left[g(\mathbf{Z})\right] > \varepsilon\right)\\ &< \exp\left(-\frac{m\varepsilon^2}{2(4m\beta_m + b)^2}\right).\end{aligned}$$

The proof for the case of the leave-one-out error $R_{\text{loo}}[\mathcal{A}, z]$ is analogous: If we define the function $g(\mathbf{Z}) = R[f_{\mathbf{Z}}] - R_{\text{loo}}\left[\mathcal{A}, \mathbf{Z}\right]$ of the m random variables

$\mathbf{Z}_1, \ldots, \mathbf{Z}_m$ then, by Lemma C.22, for all $i \in \{1, \ldots, m\}$,

$$\sup_{z \in \mathcal{Z}^m, \tilde{z} \in \mathcal{Z}} |g(z) - g(z_{i \leftrightarrow \tilde{z}})| \leq 2(\beta_m + \beta_{m-1}) + \frac{b}{m}.$$

In addition, by Lemma C.21 we have that

$$g(z) > \varepsilon + \beta_m \Rightarrow g(z) > \varepsilon + \mathbf{E}_{\mathbf{Z}^m}\left[g(\mathbf{Z})\right].$$

The result follows again by an application of McDiarmid's inequality to $g(\mathbf{Z})$. ■

D Pseudocodes

This section contains all the pseudocodes of the algorithms introduced in the book. A set of implementations in *R* (a publicly available version of *S-PLUS*) can be found at `http://www.kernel-machines.org/`.

D.1 Perceptron Algorithm

This section contains three different implementations of the classical perceptron

Algorithm 1 Perceptron learning algorithm (in primal variables).

Require: A feature mapping $\boldsymbol{\phi} : \mathcal{X} \to \mathcal{K} \subseteq \ell_2^n$
Ensure: A linearly separable training sample $z = ((x_1, y_1), \ldots, (x_m, y_m))$

```
  w_0 = 0; t = 0
  repeat
    for j = 1, ..., m do
      if y_j ⟨φ(x_j), w⟩ ≤ 0 then
        w_{t+1} = w_t + y_j φ(x_j)
        t ← t + 1
      end if
    end for
  until no mistakes have been made within the for loop
  return the final weight vector w_t
```

algorithm (see Rosenblatt (1958)) which differ by the representation used for the weight vector (Algorithms 1 and 2). The dual algorithm 2 can be sped up by caching the real-valued outputs of the temporary solutions (Algorithm 3).

Algorithm 2 Perceptron learning algorithm (in dual variables).

Require: A feature mapping $\boldsymbol{\phi} : \mathcal{X} \to \mathcal{K} \subseteq \ell_2^n$
Ensure: A linearly separable training sample $z = ((x_1, y_1), \ldots, (x_m, y_m))$
  $\boldsymbol{\alpha} = \mathbf{0}$
  repeat
    for $j = 1, \ldots, m$ **do**
      if $y_j \sum_{i=1}^{m} \alpha_i \left\langle \boldsymbol{\phi}(x_i), \boldsymbol{\phi}(x_j) \right\rangle \leq 0$ **then**
        $\alpha_j \leftarrow \alpha_j + y_j$
      end if
    end for
  until no mistakes have been made within the **for** loop
  return the vector $\boldsymbol{\alpha}$ of expansion coefficients

Algorithm 3 Kernel perceptron learning algorithm (optimized).

Require: A kernel function $k : \mathcal{X} \times \mathcal{X} \to \mathbb{R}$
Ensure: A linearly separable training sample $z = ((x_1, y_1), \ldots, (x_m, y_m))$
  $\mathbf{o} = \boldsymbol{\alpha} = \mathbf{0}$
  repeat
    for $j = 1, \ldots, m$ **do**
      if $y_j o_j \leq 0$ **then**
        $\alpha_j \leftarrow \alpha_j + y_j$
        for $i = 1, \ldots, m$ **do**
          $o_i \leftarrow o_i + y_j k\left(x_j, x_i\right)$
        end for
      end if
    end for
  until no mistakes have been made within the **for** loop
  return the vector $\boldsymbol{\alpha}$ of expansion coefficients

D.2 Support Vector and Adaptive Margin Machines

In the following subsections we give the pseudocode for support vector machines and adaptive margin machines. We assume access to a solver for the quadratic programming problem which computes the solution vector $\mathbf{x}^*$ to the following problem

$$\begin{aligned}
\text{minimize} \quad & \frac{1}{2}\mathbf{x}'\mathbf{H}\mathbf{x} + \mathbf{c}'\mathbf{x} \\
\text{subject to} \quad & \mathbf{A}_1\mathbf{x} = \mathbf{b}_1 . \\
& \mathbf{A}_2\mathbf{x} \leq \mathbf{b}_2 , \\
& \mathbf{l} \leq \mathbf{x} \leq \mathbf{u} .
\end{aligned} \tag{D.1}$$

Packages that aim to solving these type of problem are, for example MINOS (Murtagh and Saunders 1993), LOQO (Vanderbei 1994) or CPLEX (CPLEX Optimization Inc. 1994). An excellent introduction to the problem of mathematical programming is given in Hadley (1962), Hadley (1964) and Vanderbei (1997). We used the *PR LOQO* package[1] of A. Smola together with *R*, which is a publicly available version of *S-PLUS*, for all experiments.

D.2.1 Standard Support Vector Machines

For the standard SVM with box constraints $\mathbf{0} \leq \boldsymbol{\alpha} \leq \frac{1}{2\lambda}\mathbf{1}$ we set

$$\begin{aligned}
\mathbf{x} &= \boldsymbol{\alpha} , \\
\mathbf{H} &= \mathbf{YGY} \quad \Leftrightarrow \quad \mathbf{H}_{ij} = y_i y_j k\left(x_i, x_j\right) , \\
\mathbf{c} &= -\mathbf{1}_m , \\
\mathbf{l} &= \mathbf{0}_m , \\
\mathbf{u} &= \frac{1}{2\lambda m}\mathbf{1}_m .
\end{aligned}$$

We obtain hard margin SVMs for $\lambda \to 0$ (in practice we used $\lambda m = 10^{-20}$). In the case of quadratic margin loss we apply a hard margin SVM with the diagonal of $\mathbf{H}$ additively correct by $\lambda m \cdot \mathbf{1}$ (see Subsection 2.4.2).

1 Publicly available at `http://www.kernel-machines.org/`.

D.2.2 ν–Support Vector Machines

For the ν-SVMs we set

$$\begin{aligned}
\mathbf{x} &= \boldsymbol{\alpha}\,, \\
\mathbf{H} &= \mathbf{YGY} \quad \Leftrightarrow \quad \mathbf{H}_{ij} = y_i y_j k\left(x_i, x_j\right)\,, \\
\mathbf{c} &= \mathbf{0}_m\,, \\
\mathbf{A}_2 &= -\mathbf{1}_m'\,, \\
\mathbf{b}_2 &= -\nu\,, \\
\mathbf{l} &= \mathbf{0}_m\,, \\
\mathbf{u} &= \frac{1}{m}\mathbf{1}_m\,.
\end{aligned}$$

D.2.3 Adaptive Margin Machines

Finally, in the case of Adaptive Margin Machines we set the variables as follows:

$$\begin{aligned}
\mathbf{x} &= \begin{pmatrix} \boldsymbol{\alpha} \\ \boldsymbol{\xi} \end{pmatrix}, \quad \mathbf{c} = \begin{pmatrix} \mathbf{0}_m \\ \mathbf{1}_m \end{pmatrix}, \\
\mathbf{H} &= \mathbf{0}_{2m,2m}\,, \\
\mathbf{A}_2 &= \left(-\mathbf{Y}\widetilde{\mathbf{G}}\mathbf{Y}, -\mathbf{I}_m\right)\,, \\
\mathbf{b}_2 &= -\mathbf{1}_m\,, \\
\mathbf{l} &= \begin{pmatrix} \mathbf{0}_m \\ \mathbf{0}_m \end{pmatrix},
\end{aligned}$$

where the $m \times m$ matrix $\widetilde{\mathbf{G}}$ is given by

$$\widetilde{\mathbf{G}}_{ij} = \begin{cases} k\left(x_i, x_j\right) & \text{if } i \neq j \\ k\left(x_i, x_j\right) - \lambda & \text{if } i = j \end{cases}\,.$$

D.3 Gaussian Processes

In this section we give the pseudocode for both Bayesian linear regression (Algorithm 4) and Bayesian linear classification (Algorithm 5). These algorithms are also an implementation of Gaussian processes for regression and classification. Note that the classification algorithm is obtained by using a Laplace approximation to the true posterior density $\mathbf{f}_{\mathsf{T}_{m+1}|\mathsf{X}=x,\mathsf{Z}^m=z}$. For a Markov-Chain Monte-Carlo implementation see Neal (1997b).

Algorithm 4 Gaussian processes regression estimation.

Require: A variance on the outputs $\sigma_t^2 \in \mathbb{R}^+$
Require: A feature mapping $\boldsymbol{\phi} : \mathcal{X} \to \mathcal{K} \subseteq \ell_2^n$
Require: A training sample $z = ((x_1, t_1), \ldots, (x_m, t_m)) \in (\mathcal{X} \times \mathbb{R})^m$

$\mathbf{G} = \left(\left(\langle \boldsymbol{\phi}(x_i), \boldsymbol{\phi}(x_j) \rangle \right)_{i,j=1}^m + \sigma_t^2 \mathbf{I}_m \right) \in \mathbb{R}^{m \times m}$

$\boldsymbol{\alpha} = \mathbf{G}^{-1} \mathbf{t}$

return the vector $\boldsymbol{\alpha}$ of expansion coefficients

With respect to Algorithm 5, it is advantageous to solve the equation $\mathbf{H}\boldsymbol{\Delta} = \mathbf{g}$ for $\boldsymbol{\Delta}$ rather than explicitly computing the inverse $\mathbf{H}^{-1}$ and carrying out the matrix-vector product as shown in the inner loop in the pseudocode. Many software packages would provide numerically stable algorithms such as Gauss-Jordan decomposition for solving systems of linear equations. Further note that we use $\pi(t) = 1/(1 + \exp(-t))$ which equals (see Section B.7)

$$\pi(t) = \frac{\exp(t)}{1 + \exp(t)} = \frac{\exp(t) \cdot \exp(-t)}{(1 + \exp(t)) \cdot \exp(-t)} = \frac{1}{1 + \exp(-t)}$$

but whose computation is much more stable as $\exp(-t) \approx 0$ for moderately large values of t.

D.4 Relevance Vector Machines

In this section we give the pseudocode for relevance vector machines—both in the regression estimation (Algorithm 6) and classification scenario (Algorithm 7). In order to unburden the algorithms we use the notation $\mathbf{w}_{[\mathbf{n}]}$ to refer to the vector

Algorithm 5 Gaussian processes classification using the Laplace approximation.

Require: A variance on the latent variables $\sigma_t^2 \in \mathbb{R}^+$ and a noise level $\beta \in \mathbb{R}^+$
Require: A feature mapping $\boldsymbol{\phi} : \mathcal{X} \to \mathcal{K} \subseteq \ell_2^n$
Require: A training sample $z = ((x_1, y_1), \ldots, (x_m, y_m)) \in (\mathcal{X} \times \{-1, +1\})^m$
Require: A tolerance criterion TOL $\in (0, 1)$

$\mathbf{G} = \frac{1}{\beta} \cdot \left(\left(\langle \boldsymbol{\phi}(x_i), \boldsymbol{\phi}(x_j) \rangle \right)_{i,j=1}^m + \sigma_t^2 \mathbf{I}_m \right) \in \mathbb{R}^{m \times m}$
$\boldsymbol{\alpha} = \mathbf{0};\ \boldsymbol{t} = \mathbf{G}\boldsymbol{\alpha}$
$J = \frac{1}{2}(\boldsymbol{y} + \mathbf{1})'\boldsymbol{t} - \sum_{i=1}^m \ln(1 + \exp(t_i)) - \frac{1}{2}\boldsymbol{\alpha}'\mathbf{G}\boldsymbol{\alpha}$
repeat
  $\boldsymbol{\pi} = \left((1 + \exp(-t_1))^{-1}, \ldots, (1 + \exp(-t_m))^{-1} \right)'$
  $\mathbf{g} = \frac{1}{2}(\boldsymbol{y} + \mathbf{1}) - \boldsymbol{\pi} - \boldsymbol{\alpha}$
  $\mathbf{H} = -\left(\operatorname{diag}(\pi_1(1 - \pi_1), \ldots, \pi_m(1 - \pi_m))\, \mathbf{G} + \mathbf{I}\right)$
  $\boldsymbol{\Delta} = \mathbf{H}^{-1}\mathbf{g},\ \eta = 1$
  repeat
    $\tilde{\boldsymbol{\alpha}} = \boldsymbol{\alpha} - \eta\boldsymbol{\Delta};\ \tilde{\boldsymbol{t}} = \mathbf{G}\tilde{\boldsymbol{\alpha}}$
    $\tilde{J} = \frac{1}{2}(\boldsymbol{y} + \mathbf{1})'\tilde{\boldsymbol{t}} - \sum_{i=1}^m \ln\left(1 + \exp\left(\tilde{t}_i\right)\right) - \frac{1}{2}\tilde{\boldsymbol{\alpha}}'\mathbf{G}\tilde{\boldsymbol{\alpha}}$
    $\eta \leftarrow \frac{\eta}{2}$
  until $\tilde{J} > J$
  $\boldsymbol{\alpha} = \tilde{\boldsymbol{\alpha}},\ J = \tilde{J},\ \boldsymbol{t} = \tilde{\boldsymbol{t}}$
until $\frac{\|\mathbf{g}\|}{m} < \text{TOL}$
return the vector $\boldsymbol{\alpha}$ of expansion coefficients

$\left(w_{n_1}, \ldots, w_{n_{|\mathbf{n}|}}\right)$ obtained from $\mathbf{w}$ by arranging those components indexed by $\mathbf{n} = \left(n_1, \ldots, n_{|\mathbf{n}|}\right)$. As an example consider $\mathbf{w} = (w_1, \ldots, w_{10})$ and $\mathbf{n} = (1, 3, 6, 10)$ which gives $\mathbf{w}_{[\mathbf{n}]} = (w_1, w_3, w_6, w_{10})$. We have given the two algorithms in a form where we delete feature ϕ_i if the associated hyper-parameter θ_i falls below a prespecified tolerance, which should be close to the maximal precision of the computer used. This is necessary because, otherwise, the inversion of $\boldsymbol{\Sigma}$ would be an ill-posed problem and would lead to numerical instabilities. We can monitor convergence of the algorithm for classification learning by inspecting the value J which should only be increasing. In contrast, when considering the regression estimation case we should use the Cholesky decomposition of the matrix $\boldsymbol{\Sigma}^{-1}$ to efficiently compute the evidence. The *Cholesky decomposition* of the matrix $\boldsymbol{\Sigma}^{-1}$ is given by $\boldsymbol{\Sigma}^{-1} = \mathbf{R}'\mathbf{R}$ where $\mathbf{R}$ is an upper triangular matrix (see Definition A.55). The advantage of this decomposition is that $\boldsymbol{\Sigma} = \mathbf{R}^{-1}\left(\mathbf{R}^{-1}\right)'$ by virtue of Theorem A.77. Further, having such a decomposition simplifies the task of computing the determinant as (see Theorems A.15 and A.66)

$$\ln\left(\left|\boldsymbol{\Sigma}^{-1}\right|\right) = \ln\left(\left|\mathbf{R}'\mathbf{R}\right|\right) = \ln\left(\left|\mathbf{R}'\right|\right) + \ln\left(\left|\mathbf{R}\right|\right) = 2\sum_{i=1}^{n} \ln\left(\mathbf{R}_{ii}\right).$$

For a more detailed treatment of numerical issues in matrix algebra the interested reader is referred to Golub and van Loan (1989) and Press et al. (1992). These algorithms can also be applied to the expansion coefficients $\boldsymbol{\alpha} \in \mathbb{R}^m$ in a kernel classifier model $h_{\boldsymbol{\alpha}}$ (or kernel regression model $f_{\boldsymbol{\alpha}}$)

$$f_{\boldsymbol{\alpha}}(x) = \sum_{i=1}^{m} \alpha_i k(x_i, x), \qquad h_{\boldsymbol{\alpha}}(x) = \operatorname{sign}\left(\sum_{i=1}^{m} \alpha_i k(x_i, x)\right).$$

The only difference between the algorithms is that $\mathbf{w}$ must be replaced by $\boldsymbol{\alpha}$ and $\mathbf{X}$ needs to be replaced by $\mathbf{G} = \left(k\left(x_i, x_j\right)\right)_{i,j=1}^{m,m} \in \mathbb{R}^{m\times m}$. It is worth mentioning that, in principle, *any* function $k : \mathcal{X}\times\mathcal{X} \to \mathbb{R}$ could be used, that is, not only symmetric positive semidefinite functions corresponding to Mercer kernels are allowed.

Algorithm 6 Regression estimation with relevance vector machines.

Require: A data matrix $\mathbf{X} \in \mathbb{R}^{m\times n}$ and m real-valued outputs $\boldsymbol{t} \in \mathbb{R}^m$
Require: A vector $\boldsymbol{\theta} \in \left(\mathbb{R}^+\right)^n$ and a variance $\sigma_t^2 \in \mathbb{R}^+$
Require: The maximum number of iterations, $i_{\max}$; a tolerance for pruning TOL $\in \mathbb{R}^+$
  for $i = 1, \ldots, i_{\max}$ **do**
    $\mathbf{n} = \left(j \in \{1, \ldots, n\} \mid \theta_j > \text{TOL}\right)$ (all non-pruned indices)
    $\widetilde{\mathbf{X}} \in \mathbb{R}^{m\times|\mathbf{n}|}$ contains the $|\mathbf{n}|$ columns from $\mathbf{X}$ indexed by $\mathbf{n}$
    $\tilde{\boldsymbol{\theta}} = \boldsymbol{\theta}_{[\mathbf{n}]}$
    $\boldsymbol{\Sigma} = \left(\sigma_t^{-2}\widetilde{\mathbf{X}}'\widetilde{\mathbf{X}} + \operatorname{diag}\left(\tilde{\theta}_1^{-1}, \ldots, \tilde{\theta}_{|\mathbf{n}|}^{-1}\right)\right)^{-1}$
    $\mathbf{w}_{[\mathbf{n}]} = \sigma_t^{-2}\boldsymbol{\Sigma}\widetilde{\mathbf{X}}'\boldsymbol{t}$
    $\boldsymbol{\zeta} = \mathbf{1} - \left(\tilde{\theta}_1^{-1} \cdot \boldsymbol{\Sigma}_{11}, \ldots, \tilde{\theta}_{|\mathbf{n}|}^{-1} \cdot \boldsymbol{\Sigma}_{|\mathbf{n}|,|\mathbf{n}|}\right)'$
    $\theta_{n_j} = \frac{w_{n_j}^2}{\zeta_j}$ for all $j \in \{1, \ldots, |\mathbf{n}|\}$
    $\sigma_t^2 = \frac{\left\|\boldsymbol{t} - \widetilde{\mathbf{X}}\mathbf{w}_{[\mathbf{n}]}\right\|^2}{m - \boldsymbol{\zeta}'\mathbf{1}}$
  end for
  return the weight vector $\mathbf{w}$

Algorithm 7 Classification learning with relevance vector machines.

Require: A data matrix $\mathbf{X} \in \mathbb{R}^{m \times n}$ and m classes $\boldsymbol{y} \in \{-1, +1\}^m$
Require: A vector $\boldsymbol{\theta} \in \left(\mathbb{R}^+\right)^n$
Require: The maximum number of iterations, $i_{\max}$; a tolerance for pruning TOL $\in \mathbb{R}^+$
  $\mathbf{w} = \mathbf{0}$
  for $i = 1, \ldots, i_{\max}$ **do**
    $\mathbf{n} = \left(j \in \{1, \ldots, n\} \mid \theta_j > \text{TOL}\right)$ (all non-pruned indices)
    $\widetilde{\mathbf{X}} \in \mathbb{R}^{m \times |\mathbf{n}|}$ contains the $|\mathbf{n}|$ columns from $\mathbf{X}$ indexed by $\mathbf{n}$
    $\tilde{\boldsymbol{\theta}} = \boldsymbol{\theta}_{[\mathbf{n}]}$; $\boldsymbol{\Theta}^{-1} = \operatorname{diag}\left(\tilde{\theta}_1^{-1}, \ldots, \tilde{\theta}_{|\mathbf{n}|}^{-1}\right)$; $\boldsymbol{t} = \widetilde{\mathbf{X}}\mathbf{w}_{[\mathbf{n}]}$
    $J = \frac{1}{2}(\boldsymbol{y} + \mathbf{1})' \boldsymbol{t} - \sum_{i=1}^{m} \ln(1 + \exp(t_i)) - \frac{1}{2}\mathbf{w}'_{[\mathbf{n}]}\boldsymbol{\Theta}^{-1}\mathbf{w}_{[\mathbf{n}]}$
    repeat
      $\boldsymbol{\pi} = \left((1 + \exp(-t_1))^{-1}, \ldots, (1 + \exp(-t_m))^{-1}\right)'$
      $\mathbf{g} = \widetilde{\mathbf{X}}'\left(\frac{1}{2}(\boldsymbol{y} + \mathbf{1}) - \boldsymbol{\pi}\right) - \boldsymbol{\Theta}^{-1}\mathbf{w}_{[\mathbf{n}]}$
      $\mathbf{H} = -\left(\widetilde{\mathbf{X}}' \cdot \operatorname{diag}(\pi_1(1 - \pi_1), \ldots, \pi_m(1 - \pi_m)) \cdot \widetilde{\mathbf{X}} + \boldsymbol{\Theta}^{-1}\right)$
      $\boldsymbol{\Delta} = \mathbf{H}^{-1}\mathbf{g}$, $\eta = 1$
      repeat
        $\tilde{\mathbf{w}} = \mathbf{w}$; $\tilde{\mathbf{w}}_{[\mathbf{n}]} = \mathbf{w}_{[\mathbf{n}]} - \eta\boldsymbol{\Delta}$; $\tilde{\boldsymbol{t}} = \widetilde{\mathbf{X}}\tilde{\mathbf{w}}_{[\mathbf{n}]}$
        $\tilde{J} = \frac{1}{2}(\boldsymbol{y} + \mathbf{1})' \tilde{\boldsymbol{t}} - \sum_{i=1}^{m} \ln\left(1 + \exp\left(\tilde{t}_i\right)\right) - \frac{1}{2}\tilde{\mathbf{w}}'_{[\mathbf{n}]}\boldsymbol{\Theta}^{-1}\tilde{\mathbf{w}}_{[\mathbf{n}]}$
        $\eta \leftarrow \frac{\eta}{2}$
      until $\tilde{J} > J$
      $\mathbf{w} = \tilde{\mathbf{w}}$; $J = \tilde{J}$; $\boldsymbol{t} = \tilde{\boldsymbol{t}}$
    until $\frac{\|\mathbf{g}\|}{|\mathbf{n}|} < \text{TOL}$
    $\boldsymbol{\Sigma} = -\mathbf{H}^{-1}$
    $\boldsymbol{\zeta} = \mathbf{1} - \left(\tilde{\theta}_1^{-1} \cdot \boldsymbol{\Sigma}_{11}, \ldots, \tilde{\theta}_{|\mathbf{n}|}^{-1} \cdot \boldsymbol{\Sigma}_{|\mathbf{n}|,|\mathbf{n}|}\right)'$
    $\theta_{n_i} = \frac{w_{n_i}^2}{\zeta_i}$ for all $i \in \{1, \ldots, |\mathbf{n}|\}$
  end for
  return the weight vector $\mathbf{w}$

D.5 Fisher Discriminants

In this section we present the Fisher discriminant algorithm both in primal and dual variables (Algorithms 8 and 9). As mentioned earlier, when computing $\mathbf{w} = \hat{\boldsymbol{\Sigma}}^{-1}\left(\hat{\boldsymbol{\mu}}_{+1} - \hat{\boldsymbol{\mu}}_{-1}\right)$ it is advantageous to solve $\hat{\boldsymbol{\Sigma}}\mathbf{w} = \left(\hat{\boldsymbol{\mu}}_{+1} - \hat{\boldsymbol{\mu}}_{-1}\right)$ for $\mathbf{w}$ instead. Many software packages would provide numerically stable algorithms such as Gauss-Jordan decomposition for solving systems of linear equations. Note that we have included the estimated class probabilities $\mathbf{P}_{\mathsf{Y}}(y)$ in the construction of the offset b.

Algorithm 8 Fisher discriminant algorithm (in primal variables).

Require: A feature mapping $\boldsymbol{\phi} : \mathcal{X} \to \mathcal{K} \subseteq \ell_2^n$
Require: A training sample $z = ((x_1, y_1), \ldots, (x_m, y_m))$
Determine the numbers m_{+1} and m_{-1} of samples of class $+1$ and -1
$\hat{\boldsymbol{\mu}}_{+1} = \frac{1}{m_{+1}} \sum_{(x_i,+1)\in z} \boldsymbol{\phi}(x_i)$; $\hat{\boldsymbol{\mu}}_{-1} = \frac{1}{m_{-1}} \sum_{(x_i,-1)\in z} \boldsymbol{\phi}(x_i)$
$\hat{\boldsymbol{\Sigma}} = \frac{1}{m}\left(\sum_{i=1}^{m} \boldsymbol{\phi}(x_i)(\boldsymbol{\phi}(x_i))' - m_{+1}\hat{\boldsymbol{\mu}}_{+1}\hat{\boldsymbol{\mu}}_{+1}' - m_{-1}\hat{\boldsymbol{\mu}}_{-1}\hat{\boldsymbol{\mu}}_{-1}'\right)$
$\mathbf{w} = \hat{\boldsymbol{\Sigma}}^{-1}\left(\hat{\boldsymbol{\mu}}_{+1} - \hat{\boldsymbol{\mu}}_{-1}\right)$
$b = \frac{1}{2}\left(\hat{\boldsymbol{\mu}}_{-1}'\hat{\boldsymbol{\Sigma}}^{-1}\hat{\boldsymbol{\mu}}_{-1} - \hat{\boldsymbol{\mu}}_{+1}'\hat{\boldsymbol{\Sigma}}^{-1}\hat{\boldsymbol{\mu}}_{+1}\right) + \ln\left(\frac{m_{+1}}{m_{-1}}\right)$
return the weight vector $\mathbf{w} \in \mathbb{R}^n$ and the offset $b \in \mathbb{R}$

Algorithm 9 Fisher discriminant algorithm (in dual variables).

Require: A training sample $z = ((x_1, y_1), \ldots, (x_m, y_m))$
Require: A kernel function $k : \mathcal{X} \times \mathcal{X} \to \mathbb{R}$ and a regularization parameter $\lambda \in \mathbb{R}^+$
Determine the numbers m_{+1} and m_{-1} of samples of class $+1$ and -1
$\mathbf{G} = \left(k\left(x_i, x_j\right)\right)_{i,j=1}^{m,m} \in \mathbb{R}^{m\times m}$
$\mathbf{k}_{+1} = \frac{1}{m_{+1}}\mathbf{G}\left(\mathbf{I}_{y_1=+1}, \ldots, \mathbf{I}_{y_m=+1}\right)'$; $\mathbf{k}_{-1} = \frac{1}{m_{-1}}\mathbf{G}\left(\mathbf{I}_{y_1=-1}, \ldots, \mathbf{I}_{y_m=-1}\right)'$
$\mathbf{S} = \frac{1}{m}\left(\mathbf{G}\mathbf{G} - m_{+1}\mathbf{k}_{+1}\mathbf{k}_{+1}' - m_{-1}\mathbf{k}_{-1}\mathbf{k}_{-1}'\right) + \lambda\mathbf{I}_m$
$\boldsymbol{\alpha} = \mathbf{S}^{-1}\left(\mathbf{k}_{+1} - \mathbf{k}_{-1}\right)$
$b = \frac{1}{2}\left(\mathbf{k}_{-1}'\mathbf{S}^{-1}\mathbf{k}_{-1} - \mathbf{k}_{+1}'\mathbf{S}^{-1}\mathbf{k}_{+1}\right) + \ln\left(\frac{m_{+1}}{m_{-1}}\right)$
return the vector $\boldsymbol{\alpha}$ of expansion coefficients and the offset $b \in \mathbb{R}$

D.6 Bayes Point Machines

This section contains the pseudocode of the kernel billiard for computing the Bayes point (Algorithm 10). In the course of the algorithm's implementation we sometimes need normalized vectors $\boldsymbol{\beta}_{\text{norm}}$ of the vector $\boldsymbol{\beta}$ of expansion coefficients found by,

$$\boldsymbol{\beta}_{\text{norm}} = \frac{1}{\sum_{i=1}^{m}\sum_{j=1}^{m}\beta_i\beta_j k\left(x_i, x_j\right)}\boldsymbol{\beta}\,. \tag{D.2}$$

Algorithm 10 Kernel billiard algorithm (in dual variables).

Require: A tolerance criterion $\text{TOL} \in [0, 1]$ and $\tau_{\max} \in \mathbb{R}^+$
Require: A training sample $z = ((x_1, y_1), \ldots, (x_m, y_m)) \in (\mathcal{X} \times \{-1, +1\})^m$
Require: A kernel function $k : \mathcal{X} \times \mathcal{X} \to \mathbb{R}$
Ensure: for all $i \in \{1, \ldots, m\}$, $y_i \sum_{j=1}^{m} \gamma_j k\left(x_i, x_j\right) > 0$
  $\boldsymbol{\alpha} = \mathbf{0}$; $\boldsymbol{\beta}$ = random; normalize $\boldsymbol{\beta}$ using (D.2)
  $\Xi = \xi_{\max} = 0$; $p_{\min} = 1$
  while $\rho_2\left(p_{\min}, \Xi/\left(\Xi + \xi_{\max}\right)\right) > \text{TOL}$ **do**
    repeat
      for $i = 1, \ldots, m$ **do**
        $d_i = y_i \sum_{j=1}^{m} \gamma_j k\left(x_j, x_i\right)$; $\nu_i = y_i \sum_{j=1}^{m} \beta_j k\left(x_j, x_i\right)$; $\tau_i = -d_i/\nu_i$
      end for
      $c' = \operatorname{argmin}_{i:\tau_i > 0} \tau_i$
      if $\tau_{c'} \geq \tau_{\max}$ **then**
        $\boldsymbol{\beta}$ = random, but $y_c \sum_{j=1}^{m} \beta_j k\left(x_j, x_c\right) > 0$; normalize $\boldsymbol{\beta}$ using (D.2)
      else
        $c = c'$
      end if
    until $\tau_{c'} < \tau_{\max}$
    $\tilde{\boldsymbol{\gamma}} = \boldsymbol{\gamma} + \tau_c \boldsymbol{\beta}$; normalize $\tilde{\boldsymbol{\gamma}}$ using (D.2); $\beta_c = \beta_c - 2\nu_c y_c / k\left(x_c, x_c\right)$
    $\boldsymbol{\zeta} = \boldsymbol{\gamma} + \tilde{\boldsymbol{\gamma}}$; normalize $\boldsymbol{\zeta}$ using (D.2)
    $\xi = \sqrt{\sum_{i=1}^{m}\sum_{j=1}^{m}\left(\gamma_i - \tilde{\gamma}_i\right)\left(\gamma_j - \tilde{\gamma}_j\right) k\left(x_i, x_j\right)}$
    $p = \sum_{i=1}^{m}\sum_{j=1}^{m} \zeta_i \alpha_j k\left(x_i, x_j\right)$
    $\boldsymbol{\alpha} = \rho_1\left(p, \frac{\Xi}{\Xi+\xi}\right)\boldsymbol{\alpha} + \rho_2\left(p, \frac{\Xi}{\Xi+\xi}\right)\boldsymbol{\zeta}$
    $p_{\min} = \min\left(p, p_{\min}\right)$; $\xi_{\max} = \max\left(\xi, \xi_{\max}\right)$; $\Xi = \Xi + \xi$; $\boldsymbol{\gamma} = \tilde{\boldsymbol{\gamma}}$
  end while
  return the vector $\boldsymbol{\alpha}$ of expansion coefficients

List of Symbols

Whenever possible, the third column gives a pointer to the page of first occurrence or definition.

Symbol	meaning	page
$\langle \cdot, \cdot \rangle$	inner product	217
$\|\cdot\|_p$	ℓ_p–norm	216
$\|\mathbf{A}\|$	determinant of the matrix $\mathbf{A}$	225
$\mathbf{A}_{[ij]}$	matrix obtained from $\mathbf{A}$ by deletion of the ith row and jth column	225
$\otimes$	Kronecker product	236
$\stackrel{\text{def}}{=}$	the l.h.s. is defined by the r.h.s	
$\mathbf{0}$	vector of zeros	215
$\mathbf{1}$	vector of ones	215
$\wedge$	logical "and"	
$\vee$	logical "or"	
$\neg$	logical "not"	

A		
$\mathcal{A}$	learning algorithm	24
$\mathcal{A}_{\text{ERM}}$	empirical risk minimization algorithm	26
$\mathcal{A}_{\Omega}$	structural risk minimization algorithm	29
$\mathcal{A}_{\varepsilon}$	bound minimization learning algorithm	136
$\mathcal{A}_{\mathfrak{U}}$	on-line learning algorithm	182
$\boldsymbol{\alpha} \in \mathbb{R}^m$	linear expansion coefficients of the weight vector $\mathbf{w}$	32

B

$\mathfrak{B}_n$	Borel sets over $\mathbb{R}^n$	200
$\mathcal{B}_\tau(\mathbf{x})$	open ball of radius τ around $\mathbf{x}$	217
$\overline{\mathcal{B}}_\tau(\mathbf{x})$	closed ball of radius τ around $\mathbf{x}$	217
$Bayes_z$	Bayes classification strategy	80
$Bayes_{H(z)}$	generalized Bayes classification strategy	168

C

$\mathbf{C} \in \mathbb{R}^{2\times 2}$	cost matrix	22
$\mathrm{Cov}(\mathsf{X}, \mathsf{Y})$	covariance between X and Y	203
$\mathbf{Cov}(\mathbf{X}, \mathbf{Y})$	covariance matrix for $\mathbf{X}$ and $\mathbf{Y}$	203
$\mathcal{C}(z)$	compression function	176
χ	model parameter(s)	66

D

$\delta \in (0, 1]$	confidence level	
$\mathcal{D}$	model space	79

E

$\mathbf{E}_\mathsf{X}[\mathsf{X}]$	expectation of X	201
$\varepsilon \in \mathbb{R}$	deviation or generalization error bound	122
$\mathbf{e}_i$	ith unit vector	223
$\mathcal{E}(z)$	estimator for a probability measure $\mathbf{P}_\mathsf{Z}$ given the sample $z \in \mathcal{Z}^m$	117
$e(d)$	dyadic entropy number	143
$\epsilon_A(d)$	entropy number of A	222

F

$\phi_i : \mathcal{X} \to \mathbb{R}$	feature on $\mathcal{X}$	19
$\boldsymbol{\phi} : \mathcal{X} \to \mathcal{K}$	feature mapping	19
$\mathcal{F} \subseteq \mathbb{R}^{\mathcal{X}}$	real-valued function space	21
$f_{\mathbf{w}} : \mathcal{X} \to \mathbb{R}$	real-valued function	20
$f_z : \mathcal{X} \to \mathbb{R}$	real-valued function learned from $z \in \mathcal{Z}^m$	186
$f^* : \mathcal{X} \to \mathbb{R}$	optimal real-valued function	21
$\hat{f} : \mathcal{X} \to \mathbb{R}$	real-valued function in a cover $F_\gamma(\boldsymbol{x})$	141
$F_\gamma(\boldsymbol{x}) \subset \mathcal{F}$	cover of $\mathcal{F}$ given the sample $\boldsymbol{x}$	141
F_X	distribution function	201
$\mathbf{f}_{\boldsymbol{\theta}}$	Fisher score at $\boldsymbol{\theta}$	45
f_X	density of the random variable X	201
$\text{fat}_{\mathcal{F}}(\gamma)$	fat shattering dimension at scale γ	147
$\varphi_A(d)$	inner entropy number	222

G

$\mathbf{G} \in \mathbb{R}^{m \times m}$	Gram matrix	33
$\gamma_i(\mathbf{w})$	geometrical margin of $\mathbf{w}$ at z_i	50
$\gamma_z(\mathbf{w})$	geometrical margin of $\mathbf{w}$ on the training set z	50
$\tilde{\gamma}_i(\mathbf{w})$	functional margin of $\mathbf{w}$ at z_i	50
$\tilde{\gamma}_z(\mathbf{w})$	functional margin of $\mathbf{w}$ on the training set z	50
$Gibbs_z$	Gibbs classification strategy	81
$Gibbs_{H(z)}$	generalized Gibbs classification strategy	166

H

$\mathcal{H} \subseteq \mathcal{Y}^{\mathcal{X}}$	hypothesis space	19, 21
$h : \mathcal{X} \to \mathcal{Y}$	hypothesis	19
$h_{\mathbf{w}} : \mathcal{X} \to \mathcal{Y}$	binary hypothesis	20
$h_{\boldsymbol{\theta}} : \mathcal{X} \to \mathcal{Y}$	induced classifier for a given probability model $\mathbf{P}_{\mathsf{Z}\mid\mathbf{Q}=\boldsymbol{\theta}}$	116
$h^* : \mathcal{X} \to \mathcal{Y}$	optimal hypothesis	118

I

$\mathbf{I}$	indicator function	200
$\boldsymbol{I}$	Fisher information matrix	45
$\mathbf{i}$	index vector	38, 41
$I_{\boldsymbol{v},\boldsymbol{u}}$	set of index vectors for $\boldsymbol{v}$ in $\boldsymbol{u}$	41
$I_{d,m}$	set of index vectors	176

K

$\mathcal{K} \subseteq \ell_2^n$	feature (kernel) space	19
$k(x, \tilde{x})$	kernel value between $x, \tilde{x} \in \mathcal{X}$	32
$\mathbf{K} \in \mathbb{R}^{m \times m}$	kernel matrix	33

L

$\ell_2^n \subseteq \mathbb{R}^n$	space of square summable sequences of length n	218
$\ell_L(z, h)$	level of h given z	136
L_2	space of square integrable functions	218
$(\lambda_i)_{i \in \mathbb{N}}$	sequence of eigenvalues	35
$l(\hat{y}, y)$	loss between $\hat{y}$ and y	21
$l_{0-1}(\hat{y}, y)$	zero-one loss between $\hat{y}$ and y	22
$l_{\mathbf{C}}(\hat{y}, y)$	cost matrix loss between $\hat{y}$ and y	23
$l_{\text{margin}}(t)$	margin loss of t	52
$l_{\text{lin}}(\hat{t}, y)$	linear soft margin loss between $\hat{t}$ and y	54
$l_{\text{quad}}(\hat{t}, y)$	quadratic soft margin loss between $\hat{t}$ and y	54
$l_\varepsilon(\hat{t}, t)$	ε–insensitive loss between $\hat{t}$ and t	60
$l_2(\hat{t}, t)$	squared loss	82
$\mathcal{L}(\boldsymbol{\theta})$	likelihood of the parameter $\boldsymbol{\theta}$	75
$L(z, h)$	luckiness of h given z	136
$\ln(\cdot)$	natural logarithm	
$\text{ld}(\cdot)$	logarithm to base 2	

M

m	training sample size	18
$\mathcal{M} \subseteq \ell_2^n$	Mercer space	35
$\mathcal{M}_A^\rho(\varepsilon)$	packing number at scale ε	220
$M_{\mathcal{A}}(z)$	mistake bound for $\mathcal{A}$	183

N

$\mathbb{N}$	natural numbers	
n	dimension of feature space	19
N	dimension of input space	38
$\mathcal{N}_A^\rho(\varepsilon)$	covering number at scale ε	220
$\mathcal{N}_{\mathcal{H}}(z)$	empirical covering number at z for binary-valued functions	287
$\mathcal{N}_{\mathcal{H}}(m)$	worst case covering number for binary-valued functions	288
$\mathcal{N}_{\mathcal{F}}^\infty(\gamma, \boldsymbol{x})$	empirical covering number of $\mathcal{F}$ at scale γ	141
$\mathcal{N}_{\mathcal{F}}^\infty(\gamma, m)$	(worst case) covering number of $\mathcal{F}$ at scale γ	141
ν	fraction of margin errors	60

O

$\mathcal{O}(\cdot)$	order of a term	

P

$\mathbf{P}_{\mathsf{X}}$	probability measure on $\mathcal{X}$	200
$\mathcal{P}$	family of probability measures	214
π_s	swapping permutation	286

Q

$\mathbb{Q}$	rational numbers	
$\boldsymbol{\theta} \in \mathcal{Q}$	parameter vector	214
$\mathcal{Q}$	parameter space	214
$\mathbf{Q}$	the random variable of $\boldsymbol{\theta}$; in Remark 5.7 a measure such as $\mathbf{P}$	116, 170
$\hat{\boldsymbol{\theta}}_z$	estimator for the parameter of the probability measure $\mathbf{P}_\mathsf{Z}$ estimated using $\mathcal{E}$	117

R

$\mathbb{R}$	real numbers	
$R[f]$	expected risk of $f \in \mathcal{F}$	22
$R[h]$	expected risk of $h \in \mathcal{H}$	22
$R_{\boldsymbol{\theta}}[h]$	expected risk of $h \in \mathcal{H}$ under $\mathbf{P}_{\mathsf{Z}\mid\mathbf{Q}=\boldsymbol{\theta}}$	116
$R[\mathcal{A}, z]$	generalization error of $\mathcal{A}$ given $z \in \mathcal{Z}^m$	25
$R[\mathcal{A}, m]$	generalization error of $\mathcal{A}$ for training sample size m	61
$R_{\text{emp}}[f, z]$	empirical risk of $f \in \mathcal{F}$ given $z \in \mathcal{Z}^m$	25
$R_{\text{reg}}[f, z]$	regularized risk of $f \in \mathcal{F}$ given $z \in \mathcal{Z}^m$	29
$\mathcal{R}(z, \mathbf{i})$	reconstruction function	176
ρ	metric	216

S

sign	sign function, i.e., $\text{sign}(x) = 2 \cdot \mathbf{I}_{x \geq 0} - 1$	
Σ	alphabet	41
$\boldsymbol{\Sigma}$	covariance matrix	38
ς	radius of sphere enclosing training data	51

T

$\operatorname{tr}(\mathbf{A})$	trace of the matrix **A**	228
$\boldsymbol{t} \in \mathbb{R}^m$	sample of real-valued outputs	82

U

$\boldsymbol{u} \in \Sigma^r$	string	41
$\vec{u} \in \ell_2^N$	vector in input space	38
$\mathcal{U}(y, x, h)$	update algorithm	182

V

$\mathbf{v}_x$	empirical probability measure	18, 203
$V(z) \subseteq \mathcal{W}$	version space	26
$V_{\mathcal{H}}(z) \subseteq \mathcal{H}$	version space in $\mathcal{H}$	26
$\operatorname{Var}(\mathsf{X})$	variance of X	202
$\boldsymbol{v} \in \Sigma^r$	string	41
$\vec{v} \in \ell_2^N$	vector in input space	38
$\vartheta_{\mathcal{H}}$	VC dimension of $\mathcal{H}$	128
$\vartheta_{\mathcal{H}}(z)$	empirical VC dimension of $\mathcal{H}$	140

W

$\mathcal{W} \subset \mathcal{K}$	unit hyper-sphere in $\mathbb{R}^n$	21
$\mathcal{W}(z)$	canonical hyperplanes	52
$\mathbf{w} \in \mathcal{K}$	weight vector	20
$W_{\pm 1}(\mathbf{x})$	hemispheres in $\mathcal{W}$ induced by $\mathbf{x}$	24
$W_0(\mathbf{x})$	decision boundary induced by $\mathbf{x}$	24
W_z	equivalence classes of weight vectors	24
$W(\boldsymbol{\alpha})$	Wolfe dual	53
$\Omega[f]$	regularization functional of $f \in \mathcal{F}$	29

X

$\mathcal{X}$	input space	17
$\boldsymbol{x} \in \mathcal{X}^m$	sample of training objects	18
$x \in \mathcal{X}$	input point	
$x_i \in \boldsymbol{x}$	ith training point	18
$\vec{x} \in \mathcal{X}$	input vector if $\mathcal{X} \in \ell_2^N$	30
$(\vec{x})_i$	ith component of $\vec{x}$	30
$\mathbf{x} = \boldsymbol{\phi}(x)$	mapped input point x	19
$\mathbf{X} \in \mathbb{R}^{m \times n}$	data matrix of mapped input points	19
$X_{\pm 1}(\mathbf{w})$	decision regions induced by $\mathbf{w}$	24
$X_0(\mathbf{w}) \in \mathcal{K}$	decision boundary in feature space	24
$\widetilde{X}_0(\mathbf{w}) \in \mathcal{X}$	decision boundary in input space	24
$\mathfrak{X}$	σ–algebra over $\mathcal{X}$	200
$\boldsymbol{\xi}$	vector of margin slack variables	54

Y

$\mathcal{Y}$	output space (often $\{-1, +1\}$)	17
$\boldsymbol{y} \in \mathcal{Y}^m$	sample of training outputs	18
$y \in \mathcal{Y}$	output class	
$y_i \in \boldsymbol{y}$	class of ith training point	18
$\psi_i : \mathcal{X} \to \mathbb{R}$	Mercer feature on $\mathcal{X}$	34
$\boldsymbol{\psi} : \mathcal{X} \to \mathcal{K}$	Mercer feature mapping	35

Z

$\mathcal{Z} = \mathcal{X} \times \mathcal{Y}$	(labeled) data space	18
$z \in \mathcal{Z}^m$	(labeled) training sample	18
$z_{\setminus i} \in \mathcal{Z}^{m-1}$	training sample with the ith element deleted	186
$z_{i \leftrightarrow z} \in \mathcal{Z}^m$	training sample with the ith element replaced by $z \in \mathcal{Z}$	186
$z_{[i:j]}$	subsequence $(z_i, \ldots, z_j)$ of z	283
Z	random training sample	

References

Aizerman, M. A., É. M. Braverman, and L. I. Rozonoér (1964). Theoretical foundations of the potential function method in pattern recognition learning. *Automation and Remote Control 25*, 821–837.

Allwein, E. L., R. E. Schapire, and Y. Singer (2000). Reducing multiclass to binary: a unifying approach for margin classifiers. In P. Langley (Ed.), *Proceedings of the International Conference on Machine Learning*, San Francisco, California, pp. 9–16. Morgan Kaufmann Publishers.

Alon, N., S. Ben-David, N. Cesa-Bianchi, and D. Haussler (1997). Scale-sensitive dimensions, uniform convergence, and learnability. *Journal of the ACM 44*(4), 615–631.

Alon, N., J. H. Spencer, and P. Erdös (1991). *The Probabilsitic Method.* John Wiley and Sons.

Amari, S. (1985). *Differential-Geometrical Methods in Statistics.* Berlin: Springer.

Anlauf, J. K. and M. Biehl (1989). The AdaTron: an adaptive perceptron algorithm. *Europhysics Letters 10*, 687–692.

Anthony, M. (1997). Probabilistic analysis of learning in artificial neural networks: The PAC model and its variants. *Neural Computing Surveys 1*, 1–47.

Anthony, M. and P. Bartlett (1999). *A Theory of Learning in Artificial Neural Networks.* Cambridge University Press.

Baldi, P. and S. Brunak (1998). *Bioinformatics: The Machine Learning Approach.* MIT Press.

Barber, D. and C. K. I. Williams (1997). Gaussian processes for Bayesian classification via Hybrid Monte Carlo. In M. C. Mozer, M. I. Jordan, and T. Petsche (Eds.), *Advances in Neural Information Processing Systems 9*, pp. 340–346. MIT Press.

Barner, M. and F. Flohr (1989). *Analysis.* deGryter.

Bartlett, P., P. Long, and R. C. Williamson (1996). Fat-shattering and the learnability of real-valued functions. *Journal of Computer and System Sciences 52*(3), 434–452.

Bartlett, P. L. (1998). The sample complexity of pattern classification with neural networks: The size of the weights is more important than the size of the network. *IEEE Transactions on Information Theory 44*(2), 525–536.

Bartlett, P. L. and J. Shawe-Taylor (1999). Generalization performance of support vector machines and other pattern classifiers. In B. Schölkopf, C. J. C. Burges, and A. J. Smola (Eds.), *Advances in Kernel Methods—Support Vector Learning*, Cambridge, MA, pp. 43–54. MIT Press.

Baudat, G. and F. Anouar (2000). Generalized discriminant analysis using a kernel approach. *Neural Computation 12*, 2385–2404.

Bayes, T. (1763). An essay towards solving a problem in the doctrine of chances. *Philiosophical Transactions of the Royal Socienty 53*, 370–418.

Bellman, R. E. (1961). *Adaptive Control Processes*. Princeton, NJ: Princeton University Press.

Bennett, G. (1962). Probability inequalities for the sum of independent random variables. *Journal of the American Statistical Association 57*, 33–45.

Bennett, K. (1998). Combining support vector and mathematical programming methods for classification. In *Advances in Kernel Methods—Support Vector Learning*, pp. 307–326. MIT Press.

Berger, J. (1985). The frequentist viewpoint and conditioning. In *Proccedings of the Berkley Symposium*, pp. 15–44.

Bernardo, J. and A. Smith (1994). *Bayesian Theory*. Chichester: John Wiley and Sons.

Bernstein, S. (1946). *The Theory of Probabilities*. Moscow: Gastehizdat Publishing House.

Biehl, M. and M. Opper (1995). Perceptron learning: The largest version space. In *Proceedings of Workshop: Theory of Neural Networks: The Statistical Mechanics Perspective*.

Billingsley, P. (1968). *Convergence of Probability Measures*. John Wiley and Sons.

Bishop, C. M. (1995). *Neural Networks for Pattern Recognition*. Oxford: Clarendon Press.

Bishop, C. M. and M. E. Tipping (2000). Variational relevance vector machines. In *Proceedings of 16th Conference on Uncertainty in Artificial Intelligence UAI'2000*, pp. 46–53.

Block, H. D. (1962). The perceptron: A model for brain functioning. *Reviews of Modern Physics 34*, 123–135. Reprinted in *Neurocomputing* by Anderson and Rosenfeld.

Blumer, A., A. Ehrenfeucht, D. Haussler, and M. Warmuth (1989). Learnability and the Vapnik-Chervonenkis Dimension. *Journal of the ACM 36*(4), 929–965.

Bois, G. P. (1961). *Tables of Indefinite Integrals*. Dover Publications.

Boser, B. E., I. M. Guyon, and V. N. Vapnik (1992, July). A training algorithm for optimal margin classifiers. In D. Haussler (Ed.), *Proceedings of the Annual Conference on Computational Learning Theory*, Pittsburgh, PA, pp. 144–152. ACM Press.

Bousquet, O. and A. Elisseeff (2000). Stability and generalization. Technical report, Centre de Mathematiques Appliquees.

Bousquet, O. and A. Elisseeff (2001). Algorithmic stability and generalization performance. In T. K. Leen, T. G. Dietterich, and V. Tresp (Eds.), *Advances in Neural Information Processing Systems 13*, pp. 196–202. MIT Press.

Box, G. E. P. and G. C. Tiao (1973). *Bayesian Inference in Statistical Analysis*. Addison-Wesley.

Brown, M. P. S., W. N. Grundy, D. Lin, N. Cristianini, C. Sugnet, T. S. Furey, M. Ares, and D. Haussler (2000). Knowledge-based analysis of microarray gene expression data using support vector machines. *Proceedings of the National Academy of Sciences 97*(1), 262–267.

Brownie, C. and J. Kiefer (1977). The ideas of conditional confidence in the simplest setting. *Communications in Statistics—Theory and Methods 6*(8), 691–751.

Burges, C. J. C. (1998). A tutorial on support vector machines for pattern recognition. *Data Mining and Knowledge Discovery 2*(2), 121–167.

Cantelli, F. (1933). Sulla probabilita come limita della frequenza. *Rend. Accad. Lincei 26*(1), 39.

Carl, B. and I. Stephani (1990). *Entropy, compactness, and the approximation of operators*. Cambridge, UK: Cambridge University Press.

Casella, G. (1988). Conditionally acceptable frequentist solutions. In *Statistical Decision Theory*, Volume 1, pp. 73–84.

Cauchy, A. (1821). *Cours d'analyse de l'Ecole Royale Polytechnique: Analyse algebrique*. Paris: Debure freres.

Chernoff, H. (1952). A measure of asymptotic efficiency of tests of a hypothesis based on the sum of observations. *Annals of Mathematical Statistics 23*, 493–507.

Cortes, C. (1995). *Prediction of Generalization Ability in Learning Machines.* Ph. D. thesis, Department of Computer Science, University of Rochester.

Cortes, C. and V. Vapnik (1995). Support vector networks. *Machine Learning 20*, 273–297.

Cox, R. (1946). Probability, frequency, and reasonable expectations. *American Journal of Physics 14*, 1–13.

CPLEX Optimization Inc. (1994). Using the CPLEX callable library. Manual.

Cristianini, N. and J. Shawe-Taylor (1999). Bayesian voting schemes and large margin classifiers. In B. Schölkopf, C. J. C. Burges, and A. J. Smola (Eds.), *Advances in Kernel Methods—Support Vector Learning*, Cambridge, MA, pp. 55–68. MIT Press.

Cristianini, N. and J. Shawe-Taylor (2000). *An Introduction to Support Vector Machines.* Cambridge, UK: Cambridge University Press.

Debnath, L. and P. Mikusinski (1998). *Hilbert Spaces with Applications.* Academic Press.

Dempster, A. P., N. M. Laird, and D. B. Rubin (1977). Maximum Likelihood from Incomplete Data via the EM Algorithm. *Journal of the Royal Statistical Society B 39*(1), 1–22.

Devroye, L., L. Györfi, and G. Lugosi (1996). *A Probabilistic Theory of Pattern Recognition.* Number 31 in Applications of mathematics. New York: Springer.

Devroye, L. and G. Lugosi (2001). *Combinatorial Methods in Density Estimation.* Springer.

Devroye, L. P. and T. J. Wagner (1979). Distribution-free performance bounds for potential function rules. *IEEE Transactions on Information Theory 25*(5), 202–207.

Dietrich, R., M. Opper, and H. Sompolinsky (2000). Support vectors and statistical mechanics. In A. J. Smola, P. L. Bartlett, B. Schölkopf, and D. Schuurmans (Eds.), *Advances in Large Margin Classifiers*, Cambridge, MA, pp. 359–367. MIT Press.

Duda, R. O. and P. E. Hart (1973). *Pattern Classification and Scene Analysis.* New York: John Wiley and Sons.

Duda, R. O., P. E. Hart, and D. G. Stork (2001). *Pattern Classification and Scene Analysis.* New York: John Wiley and Sons. Second edition.

Feller, W. (1950). *An Introduction To Probability Theory and Its Application*, Volume 1. New York: John Wiley and Sons.

Feller, W. (1966). *An Introduction To Probability Theory and Its Application*, Volume 2. New York: John Wiley and Sons.

Fisher, R. A. (1936). The use of multiple measurements in taxonomic problems. *Annals of Eugenics 7*, 179–188.

Floyd, S. and M. Warmuth (1995). Sample compression, learnability, and the Vapnik Chervonenkis dimension. *Machine Learning 27*, 1–36.

Freund, Y. (1998). Self bounding learning algorithms. In *Proceedings of the Annual Conference on Computational Learning Theory*, Madison, Wisconsin, pp. 247–258.

Freund, Y., Y. Mansour, and R. E. Schapire (2000). Analysis of a pseudo-Bayesian prediction method. In *Proceedings of the Conference on Information Science and Systems*.

Gardner, E. (1988). The space of interactions in neural networks. *Journal of Physics A 21*, 257–270.

Gardner, E. and B. Derrida (1988). Optimal storage properties of neural network models. *Journal of Physics A 21*, 271–284.

Gentile, C. and M. K. Warmuth (1999). Linear hinge loss and average margin. In M. S. Kearns, S. A. Solla, and D. A. Cohn (Eds.), *Advances in Neural Information Processing Systems 11*, Cambridge, MA, pp. 225–231. MIT Press.

Gibbs, M. and D. J. C. Mackay (1997). Efficient implementation of Gaussian processes. Technical report, Cavendish Laboratory, Cambridge, UK.

Girosi, F. (1998). An equivalence between sparse approximation and support vector machines. *Neural Computation 10*(6), 1455–1480.

Glivenko, V. (1933). Sulla determinazione empirica delle leggi di probabilita. *Giornale dell'Istituta Italiano degli Attuari 4*, 92.

Golub, G. H. and C. F. van Loan (1989). *Matrix Computations*. John Hopkins University Press.

Graepel, T., R. Herbrich, and J. Shawe-Taylor (2000). Generalisation error bounds for sparse linear classifiers. In *Proceedings of the Annual Conference on Computational Learning Theory*, pp. 298–303.

Graepel, T., R. Herbrich, and R. C. Williamson (2001). From margin to sparsity. In T. K. Leen, T. G. Dietterich, and V. Tresp (Eds.), *Advances in Neural Information Processing Systems 13*, Cambridge, MA, pp. 210–216. MIT Press.

Guermeur, Y., A. Elisseeff, and H. Paugam-Moisy (2000). A new multi-class SVM based on a uniform convergence result. In *Proccedings of IJCNN 2000.*

Gurvits, L. (1997). A note on a scale-sensitive dimension of linear bounded functionals in Banach spaces. In M. Li and A. Maruoka (Eds.), *Proceedings of the International Conference on Algorithmic Learning Theory*, LNAI-1316, Berlin, pp. 352–363. Springer.

Guyon, I. and D. Storck (2000). Linear discriminant and support vector classifiers. In A. J. Smola, P. L. Bartlett, B. Schölkopf, and D. Schuurmans (Eds.), *Advances in Large Margin Classifiers*, Cambridge, MA, pp. 147–169. MIT Press.

Hadamard, J. (1902). Sur les problèmes aux dèrivèes partielles et leur signification physique. *Bullentin Princeton University 13*, 49–52.

Hadley, G. (1962). *Linear Programming*. London: Addison-Wesley.

Hadley, G. (1964). *Nonlinear and Dynamic Programming*. London: Addison-Wesley.

Harville, D. A. (1997). *Matrix Algebra From a Statistican's Perspective*. Springer.

Hastie, T. and R. Tibshirani (1998). Classification by pairwise coupling. In M. I. Jordan, M. J. Kearns, and S. A. Solla (Eds.), *Advances in Neural Information Processing Systems 10*, Cambridge, MA, pp. 507–513. MIT Press.

Haussler, D. (1999). Convolutional kernels on discrete structures. Technical Report UCSC-CRL-99-10, Computer Science Department, University of California at Santa Cruz.

Haussler, D., M. Kearns, and R. Schapire (1994). Bounds on the sample complexity of Bayesian learning using information theory and the VC dimension. *Machine Learning 14*, 88–113.

Herbrich, R. (2000). *Learning Linear Classifiers—Theory and Algorithms*. Ph. D. thesis, Technische Universität Berlin.

Herbrich, R. and T. Graepel (2001a). Large scale Bayes point machines. In T. K. Leen, T. G. Dietterich, and V. Tresp (Eds.), *Advances in Neural Information Processing Systems 13*, Cambridge, MA, pp. 528–534. MIT Press.

Herbrich, R. and T. Graepel (2001b). A PAC-Bayesian margin bound for linear classifiers: Why SVMs work. In T. K. Leen, T. G. Dietterich, and V. Tresp (Eds.), *Advances in Neural Information Processing Systems 13*, Cambridge, MA, pp. 224–230.

Herbrich, R., T. Graepel, and C. Campbell (2001). Bayes point machines. *Journal of Machine Learning Research 1*, 245–279.

Herbrich, R., T. Graepel, and J. Shawe-Taylor (2000). Sparsity vs. large margins for linear classifiers. In *Proceedings of the Annual Conference on Computational Learning Theory*, pp. 304–308.

Hoeffding, W. (1963). Probability inequalities for sums of bounded random variables. *Journal of the American Statistical Association 58*, 13–30.

Jaakkola, T., M. Meila, and T. Jebara (2000). Maximum entropy discrimination. In S. A. Solla, T. K. Leen, and K.-R. Müller (Eds.), *Advances in Neural Information Processing Systems 12*, Cambridge, MA, pp. 470–476. MIT Press.

Jaakkola, T. S., M. Diekhans, and D. Haussler (1999). Using the fisher kernel method to detect remote protein homologies. In *Proccedings of the International Conference on Intelligence Systems for Molecular Biology*, pp. 149–158. AAAI Press.

Jaakkola, T. S. and D. Haussler (1999a). Exploiting generative models in discriminative classifiers. In M. S. Kearns, S. A. Solla, and D. A. Cohn (Eds.), *Advances in Neural Information Processing Systems 11*, Cambridge, MA, pp. 487–493. MIT Press.

Jaakkola, T. S. and D. Haussler (1999b). Probabilistic kernel regression models. In *Proceedings of the 1999 Conference on AI and Statistics*.

Jaynes, E. T. (1968, September). Prior probabilities. *IEEE Transactions on Systems Science and Cybernetics SSC-4*(3), 227–241.

Jebara, T. and T. Jaakkola (2000). Feature selection and dualities in maximum entropy discrimination. In *Uncertainity In Artificial Intelligence*.

Jeffreys, H. (1946). An invariant form for the prior probability in estimation problems. *Proceedings of the Royal Statistical Society A 186*, 453–461.

Joachims, T. (1998). Text categorization with support vector machines: Learning with many relevant features. In *Proceedings of the European Conference on Machine Learning*, Berlin, pp. 137–142. Springer.

Joachims, T. (1999). Making large-scale SVM learning practical. In B. Schölkopf, C. J. C. Burges, and A. J. Smola (Eds.), *Advances in Kernel Methods—Support Vector Learning*, Cambridge, MA, pp. 169–184. MIT Press.

Johnson, N. L., S. Kotz, and N. Balakrishnan (1994). *Continuous Univariate Distributions. Volume 1 (Second Edition)*. John Wiley and Sons.

Kahane, J. P. (1968). *Some Random Series of Functions*. Cambridge University Press.

Karchin, R. (2000). Classifying g-protein coupled receptors with support vector machines. Master's thesis, University of California.

Kearns, M. and D. Ron (1999). Algorithmic stability and sanity-check bounds for leave-one-out cross-validation. *Neural Computation 11*(6), 1427–1453.

Kearns, M. J. and R. E. Schapire (1994). Efficient distribution-free learning of probabilistic concepts. *Journal of Computer and System Sciences 48*(3), 464–497.

Kearns, M. J., R. E. Schapire, and L. M. Sellie (1992). Toward efficient agnostic learning (extended abstract). In *Proceedings of the Annual Conference on Computational Learning Theory*, Pittsburgh, Pennsylvania, pp. 341–352. ACM Press.

Kearns, M. J. and U. V. Vazirani (1994). *An Introduction to Computational Learning Theory*. Cambridge, Massachusetts: MIT Press.

Keerthi, S. S., S. K. Shevade, C. Bhattacharyya, and K. R. K. Murthy (1999b). A fast iterative nearest point algorithm for support vector machine classifier design. Technical Report Technical Report TR-ISL-99-03, Indian Institute of Science, Bangalore. http://guppy.mpe.nus.edu.sg/~mpessk/npa_tr.ps.gz.

Keerthi, S. S., S. K. Shevade, C. Bhattacharyya, and K. R. K. Murthy (1999a). Improvements to Platt's SMO algorithm for SVM classifier design. Technical Report CD-99-14, Dept. of Mechanical and Production Engineering, Natl. Univ. Singapore, Singapore.

Kiefer, J. (1977). Conditional confidence statements and confidence estimators. *Journal of the American Statistical Association 72*, 789–807.

Kimeldorf, G. S. and G. Wahba (1970). A correspondence between Bayesian estimation on stochastic processes and smoothing by splines. *Annals of Mathematical Statistics 41*, 495–502.

Kivinen, J., M. K. Warmuth, and P. Auer (1997). The perceptron learning algorithm vs. winnow: Linear vs. logarithmic mistake bounds when few input variables are relevant. *Artificial Intelligence 97*(1–2), 325–343.

Kockelkorn, U. (2000). *Lineare statistische Methoden*. Oldenburg-Verlag.

Kolmogorov, A. (1933). Sulla determinazione empirica di una leggi di distribuzione. *Giornale dell'Istituta Italiano degli Attuari 4*, 33.

Kolmogorov, A. N. and S. V. Fomin (1957). *Functional Analysis*. Graylock Press.

Kolmogorov, A. N. and V. M. Tihomirov (1961). ε-entropy and ε-capacity of sets in functional spaces. *American Mathematical Society Translations, Series 2 17*(2), 277–364.

König, H. (1986). *Eigenvalue Distribution of Compact Operators*. Basel: Birkhäuser.

Krauth, W. and M. Mézard (1987). Learning algorithms with optimal stability in neural networks. *Journal of Physics A 20*, 745–752.

Lambert, P. F. (1969). Designing pattern categorizers with extremal paradigm information. In S. Watanabe (Ed.), *Methodologies of Pattern Recognition*, New York, pp. 359–391. Academic Press.

Lauritzen, S. L. (1981). Time series analysis in 1880, a discussion of contributions made by T. N. Thiele. *ISI Review 49*, 319–333.

Lee, W. S., P. L. Bartlett, and R. C. Williamson (1998). The importance of convexity in learning with squared loss. *IEEE Transactions on Information Theory 44*(5), 1974–1980.

Levin, R. D. and M. Tribus (1978). The maximum entropy formalism. In *Proceedings of the Maximum Entropy Formalism Conference*. MIT Press.

Lindsey, J. K. (1996). *Parametric Statistical Inference*. Clarendon Press.

Littlestone, N. (1988). Learning quickly when irrelevant attributes abound: A new linear-treshold algorithm. *Machine Learning 2*, 285–318.

Littlestone, N. and M. Warmuth (1986). Relating data compression and learnability. Technical report, University of California Santa Cruz.

Lodhi, H., J. Shawe-Taylor, N. Cristianini, and C. Watkins (2001). Text classification using kernels. In T. K. Leen, T. G. Dietterich, and V. Tresp (Eds.), *Advances in Neural Information Processing Systems 13*, Cambridge, MA, pp. 563–569. MIT Press.

Lunts, A. and V. Brailovsky (1969). On estimation of characters obtained in statistical procedure of recognition (in Russian). *Technicheskaya Kibernetica 3*.

Lütkepohl, H. (1996). *Handbook of Matrices*. Chichester: John Wiley and Sons.

MacKay, D. (1994). Bayesian non-linear modelling for the energy prediction competition. *ASHRAE Transcations 4*, 448–472.

MacKay, D. J. (1999). Information theory, probability and neural networks. available at http://wol.ra.phy.cam.ac.uk/mackay/itprnn.

MacKay, D. J. C. (1991). *Bayesian Methods for Adaptive Models*. Ph. D. thesis, Computation and Neural Systems, California Institute of Technology, Pasadena, CA.

MacKay, D. J. C. (1992). The evidence framework applied to classification networks. *Neural Computation 4*(5), 720–736.

MacKay, D. J. C. (1998). Introduction to Gaussian processes. In C. M. Bishop (Ed.), *Neural Networks and Machine Learning*, pp. 133–165. Berlin: Springer.

Magnus, J. R. and H. Neudecker (1999). *Matrix Differential Calculus with Applications in Statistics and Econometrics (Revised Edition)*. John Wiley and Sons.

Marchand, M. and J. Shawe-Taylor (2001). Learning with the set covering machine. In *Proceedings of the International Conference on Machine Learning*, San Francisco, California, pp. 345–352. Morgan Kaufmann Publishers.

Mardia, K. V., J. T. Kent, and J. M. Bibby (1979). *Multivariate Analysis*. Academic Press.

Markov, A. A. (1912). *Wahrscheinlichkeitsrechnung*. Leipzig: B.G. Teubner Verlag.

Matheron, G. (1963). Principles of geostatistics. *Economic Geology 58*, 1246–1266.

McAllester, D. A. (1998). Some PAC Bayesian theorems. In *Proceedings of the Annual Conference on Computational Learning Theory*, Madison, Wisconsin, pp. 230–234. ACM Press.

McAllester, D. A. (1999). PAC-Bayesian model averaging. In *Proceedings of the Annual Conference on Computational Learning Theory*, Santa Cruz, USA, pp. 164–170.

McDiarmid, C. (1989). On the method of bounded differences. In *Survey in Combinatorics*, pp. 148–188. Cambridge University Press.

Mercer, J. (1909). Functions of positive and negative type and their connection with the theory of integral equations. *Philosophical Transactions of the Royal Society, London A 209*, 415–446.

Mika, S., G. Rätsch, J. Weston, B. Schölkopf, and K.-R. Müller (1999). Fisher discriminant analysis with kernels. In Y.-H. Hu, J. Larsen, E. Wilson, and S. Douglas (Eds.), *Neural Networks for Signal Processing IX*, pp. 41–48. IEEE.

Minka, T. (2001). *Expectation Propagation for approximative Bayesian inference*. Ph. D. thesis, MIT Media Labs, Cambridge, USA.

Minsky, M. and S. Papert (1969). *Perceptrons: An Introduction To Computational Geometry*. Cambridge, MA: MIT Press.

Mitchell, T. M. (1977). Version spaces: a candidate elimination approach to rule learning. In *Proceedings of the International Joint Conference on Artificial Intelligence*, Cambridge, Massachusetts, pp. 305–310. IJCAI.

Mitchell, T. M. (1982). Generalization as search. *Artificial Intelligence 18*(2), 202–226.

Mitchell, T. M. (1997). *Machine Learning*. New York: McGraw-Hill.

Murtagh, B. A. and M. A. Saunders (1993). MINOS 5.4 user's guide. Technical Report SOL 83.20, Stanford University.

Neal, R. (1996). *Bayesian Learning in Neural Networks*. Springer.

Neal, R. M. (1997a). Markov chain Monte Carlo method based on 'slicing' the density function. Technical report, Department of Statistics, University of Toronto. TR-9722.

Neal, R. M. (1997b). Monte Carlo implementation of Gaussian process models for Bayesian regression and classification. Technical Report 9702, Dept. of Statistics.

Neal, R. M. (1998). Assessing relevance determination methods using delve. In *Neural Networks and Machine Learning*, pp. 97–129. Springer.

Novikoff, A. B. J. (1962). On convergence proofs on perceptrons. In *Proceedings of the Symposium on the Mathematical Theory of Automata*, Volume 12, pp. 615–622. Polytechnic Institute of Brooklyn.

Okamoto, M. (1958). Some inequalities relating to the partial sum of binomial probabilities. *Annals of the Institue of Statistical Mathematics 10*, 29–35.

Opper, M. and D. Haussler (1991). Generalization performance of Bayes optimal classification algorithms for learning a perceptron. *Physical Review Letters 66*, 2677.

Opper, M. and W. Kinzel (1995). *Statistical Mechanics of Generalisation*, pp. 151. Springer.

Opper, M., W. Kinzel, J. Kleinz, and R. Nehl (1990). On the ability of the optimal perceptron to generalize. *Journal of Physics A 23*, 581–586.

Opper, M. and O. Winther (2000). Gaussian processes for classification: Mean field algorithms. *Neural Computation 12*(11), 2655–2684.

Osuna, E., R. Freund, and F. Girosi (1997). An improved training algorithm for support vector machines. In J. Principe, L. Gile, N. Morgan, and E. Wilson (Eds.), *Neural Networks for Signal Processing VII—Proceedings of the 1997 IEEE Workshop*, New York, pp. 276–285. IEEE.

Platt, J. (1999). Fast training of support vector machines using sequential minimal optimization. In B. Schölkopf, C. J. C. Burges, and A. J. Smola (Eds.), *Advances in Kernel Methods—Support Vector Learning*, Cambridge, MA, pp. 185–208. MIT Press.

Platt, J. C., N. Cristianini, and J. Shawe-Taylor (2000). Large margin DAGs for multiclass classification. In S. A. Solla, T. K. Leen, and K.-R. Müller (Eds.), *Advances in Neural Information Processing Systems 12*, Cambridge, MA, pp. 547–553. MIT Press.

Poggio, T. (1975). On optimal nonlinear associative recall. *Biological Cybernetics 19*, 201–209.

Pollard, D. (1984). *Convergence of Stochastic Processess*. New York: Springer.

Press, W. H., S. A. Teukolsky, W. T. Vetterling, and B. P. Flannery (1992). *Numerical Recipes in C: The Art of Scientific Computing (2nd ed.)*. Cambridge: Cambridge University Press. ISBN 0-521-43108-5.

Robert, C. P. (1994). *The Bayesian choice: A decision theoretic motivation*. New York: Springer.

Rosenblatt, F. (1958). The perceptron: A probabilistic model for information storage and organization in the brain. *Psychological Review 65*(6), 386–408.

Rosenblatt, F. (1962). *Principles of neurodynamics: Perceptron and Theory of Brain Mechanisms*. Washington D.C.: Spartan-Books.

Roth, V. and V. Steinhage (2000). Nonlinear discriminant analysis using kernel functions. In S. A. Solla, T. K. Leen, and K.-R. Müller (Eds.), *Advances in Neural Information Processing Systems 12*, Cambridge, MA, pp. 568–574. MIT Press.

Ruján, P. (1993). A fast method for calculating the perceptron with maximal stability. *Journal de Physique I France 3*, 277–290.

Ruján, P. (1997). Playing billiards in version space. *Neural Computation 9*, 99–122.

Ruján, P. and M. Marchand (2000). Computing the Bayes kernel classifier. In A. J. Smola, P. L. Bartlett, B. Schölkopf, and D. Schuurmans (Eds.), *Advances in Large Margin Classifiers*, Cambridge, MA, pp. 329–347. MIT Press.

Rumelhart, D. E., G. E. Hinton, and R. J. Williams (1986). *Parallel Distributed Processing*. Cambridge, MA: MIT Press.

Rychetsky, M., J. Shawe-Taylor, and M. Glesner (2000). Direct Bayes point machines. In *Proceedings of the International Conference on Machine Learning*.

Salton, G. (1968). *Automatic Information Organization and Retrieval*. New York: McGraw-Hill.

Sauer, N. (1972). On the density of families of sets. *Journal of Combinatorial Theory 13*, 145–147.

Scheffé, H. (1947). A useful convergence theorem for probability distributions. *Annals of Mathematical Statistics 18*, 434–438.

Schölkopf, B., C. Burges, and V. Vapnik (1995). Extracting support data for a given task. In U. M. Fayyad and R. Uthurusamy (Eds.), *Proceedings, First International*

Conference on Knowledge Discovery & Data Mining, Menlo Park. AAAI Press.

Schölkopf, B., C. J. C. Burges, and A. J. Smola (1998). *Advances in Kernel Methods.* MIT Press.

Schölkopf, B., R. Herbrich, and A. J. Smola (2001). A generalized representer theorem. In *Proceedings of the Annual Conference on Computational Learning Theory.*

Schölkopf, B., J. Shawe-Taylor, A. J. Smola, and R. C. Williamson (1999). Kernel-dependent support vector error bounds. In *Ninth International Conference on Artificial Neural Networks*, Conference Publications No. 470, London, pp. 103–108. IEE.

Schölkopf, B., A. Smola, R. C. Williamson, and P. L. Bartlett (2000). New support vector algorithms. *Neural Computation 12*, 1207–1245.

Shawe-Taylor, J., P. L. Bartlett, R. C. Williamson, and M. Anthony (1998). Structural risk minimization over data-dependent hierarchies. *IEEE Transactions on Information Theory 44*(5), 1926–1940.

Shawe-Taylor, J. and N. Cristianini (1998). Robust bounds on generalization from the margin distribution. NeuroCOLT Technical Report NC-TR-1998-029, ESPRIT NeuroCOLT2 Working Group, http://www.neurocolt.com.

Shawe-Taylor, J. and N. Cristianini (2000). Margin distribution and soft margin. In A. J. Smola, P. L. Bartlett, B. Schölkopf, and D. Schuurmans (Eds.), *Advances in Large Margin Classifiers*, Cambridge, MA, pp. 349–358. MIT Press.

Shawe-Taylor, J. and R. C. Williamson (1997). A PAC analysis of a Bayesian estimator. Technical report, Royal Holloway, University of London. NC2-TR-1997-013.

Shawe-Taylor, J. and R. C. Williamson (1999). Generalization performance of classifiers in terms of observed covering numbers. In P. Fischer and H. U. Simon (Eds.), *Proceedings of the European Conference on Computational Learning Theory*, Volume 1572 of *LNAI*, Berlin, pp. 285–300. Springer.

Shelah, S. (1972). A combinatorial problem; stability and order for models and theories in infinitary languages. *Pacific Journal of Mathematics 41*, 247–261.

Shevade, S. K., S. S. Keerthi, C. Bhattacharyya, and K. R. K. Murthy (1999). Improvements to SMO algorithm for SVM regression. Technical Report CD-99-16, Dept. of Mechanical and Production Engineering, Natl. Univ. Singapore, Singapore.

Smola, A. and B. Schölkopf (1998). From regularization operators to support vector kernels. In M. I. Jordan, M. J. Kearns, and S. A. Solla (Eds.), *Advances in Neural Information Processing Systems 10*, Cambridge, MA, pp. 343–349. MIT Press.

Smola, A. and B. Schölkopf (2001). A tutorial on support vector regression. *Statistics and Computing*. Forthcoming.

Smola, A., B. Schölkopf, and K.-R. Müller (1998). The connection between regularization operators and support vector kernels. *Neural Networks 11*, 637–649.

Smola, A. J. (1996). Regression estimation with support vector learning machines. Diplomarbeit, Technische Universität München.

Smola, A. J. (1998). *Learning with Kernels*. Ph. D. thesis, Technische Universität Berlin. GMD Research Series No. 25.

Smola, A. J. and P. L. Bartlett (2001). Sparse greedy Gaussian process regression. In T. K. Leen, T. G. Dietterich, and V. Tresp (Eds.), *Advances in Neural Information Processing Systems 13*, pp. 619–625. MIT Press.

Smola, A. J., P. L. Bartlett, B. Schölkopf, and D. Schuurmans (2000). *Advances in Large Margin Classifiers*. Cambridge, MA: MIT Press.

Smola, A. J. and B. Schölkopf (1998). On a kernel-based method for pattern recognition, regression, approximation and operator inversion. *Algorithmica 22*, 211–231.

Smola, A. J., J. Shawe-Taylor, B. Schölkopf, and R. C. Williamson (2000). The entropy regularization information criterion. In S. A. Solla, T. K. Leen, and K.-R. Müller (Eds.), *Advances in Neural Information Processing Systems 12*, Cambridge, MA, pp. 342–348. MIT Press.

Sollich, P. (2000). Probabilistic methods for support vector machines. In S. A. Solla, T. K. Leen, and K.-R. Müller (Eds.), *Advances in Neural Information Processing Systems 12*, Cambridge, MA, pp. 349–355. MIT Press.

Sontag, E. D. (1998). VC dimension of neural networks. In C. M. Bishop (Ed.), *Neural Networks and Machine Learning*, pp. 69–94. Berlin: Springer.

Sutton, R. S. and A. G. Barto (1998). *Reinforcement Learning: An Introduction*. MIT Press.

Talagrand, M. (1987). The Glivenko-Cantelli problem. *Annals of Probability 15*, 837–870.

Talagrand, M. (1996). A new look at independence. *Annals of Probability 24*, 1–34.

Tikhonov, A. N. and V. Y. Arsenin (1977). *Solution of Ill-posed problems*. V.H. Winston and Sons.

Tipping, M. (2001). Sparse bayesian learning and the relevance vector machine. *Journal of Machine Learning Research 1*, 211–244.

Tipping, M. E. (2000). The relevance vector machine. In S. A. Solla, T. K. Leen, and K.-R. Müller (Eds.), *Advances in Neural Information Processing Systems 12*, Cambridge, MA, pp. 652–658. MIT Press.

Trecate, G. F., C. K. Williams, and M. Opper (1999). Finite-dimensional approximation of Gaussian processes. In M. S. Kearns, S. A. Solla, and D. A. Cohn (Eds.), *Advances in Neural Information Processing Systems 11*, Cambridge, MA, pp. 218–224. MIT Press.

Trybulec, W. A. (1990). Pigeon hole principle. *Journal of Formalized Mathematics 2*.

Tschebyscheff, P. L. (1936). *Wahrscheinlichkeitsrechnung (in Russian)*. Moskau: Akademie Verlag.

Valiant, L. G. (1984). A theory of the learnable. *Communications of the ACM 27*(11), 1134–1142.

van der Vaart, A. W. and J. A. Wellner (1996). *Weak Convergence and Empirical Processes*. Springer.

Vanderbei, R. J. (1994). LOQO: An interior point code for quadratic programming. TR SOR-94-15, Statistics and Operations Research, Princeton Univ., NJ.

Vanderbei, R. J. (1997). *Linear Programming: Foundations and Extensions*. Hingham: Kluwer Academic.

Vapnik, V. (1995). *The Nature of Statistical Learning Theory*. New York: Springer.

Vapnik, V. (1998). *Statistical Learning Theory*. New York: John Wiley and Sons.

Vapnik, V. and A. Chervonenkis (1974). *Theory of Pattern Recognition [in Russian]*. Moscow: Nauka. (German Translation: W. Wapnik & A. Tscherwonenkis, *Theorie der Zeichenerkennung*, Akademie-Verlag, Berlin, 1979).

Vapnik, V. and A. Lerner (1963). Pattern recognition using generalized portrait method. *Automation and Remote Control 24*, 774–780.

Vapnik, V. N. (1982). *Estimation of Dependences Based on Empirical Data*. Springer.

Vapnik, V. N. and A. Y. Chervonenkis (1971). On the uniform convergence of relative frequencies of events to their probabilities. *Theory of Probability and its Applications 16*(2), 264–281.

Vapnik, V. N. and A. Y. Chervonenkis (1991). The necessary and sufficient conditions for consistency in the empirical risk minimization method. *Pattern Recognition and Image Analysis 1*(3), 283–305.

Vapnik, V. N. and S. Mukherjee (2000). Support vector method for multivariate density estimation. In S. A. Solla, T. K. Leen, and K.-R. Müller (Eds.), *Advances in Neural Information Processing Systems 12*, Cambridge, MA, pp. 659–665. MIT Press.

Veropoulos, K., C. Campbell, and N. Cristianini (1999). Controlling the sensitivity of support vector machines. In *Proceedings of IJCAI Workshop Support Vector Machines*, pp. 55–60.

Vidyasagar, M. (1997). *A Theory of Learning and Generalization*. New York: Springer.

Wahba, G. (1990). *Spline Models for Observational Data*, Volume 59 of *CBMS-NSF Regional Conference Series in Applied Mathematics*. Philadelphia: SIAM.

Wahba, G. (1999). Support vector machines, reproducing kernel Hilbert spaces and the randomized GACV. In B. Schölkopf, C. J. C. Burges, and A. J. Smola (Eds.), *Advances in Kernel Methods—Support Vector Learning*, Cambridge, MA, pp. 69–88. MIT Press.

Watkin, T. (1993). Optimal learning with a neural network. *Europhysics Letters 21*, 871.

Watkins, C. (2000). Dynamic alignment kernels. In A. J. Smola, P. L. Bartlett, B. Schölkopf, and D. Schuurmans (Eds.), *Advances in Large Margin Classifiers*, Cambridge, MA, pp. 39–50. MIT Press.

Weston, J., A. Gammerman, M. Stitson, V. Vapnik, V. Vovk, and C. Watkins (1999). Support vector density estimation. In B. Schölkopf, C. J. C. Burges, and A. J. Smola (Eds.), *Advances in Kernel Methods—Support Vector Learning*, Cambridge, MA, pp. 293–306. MIT Press.

Weston, J. and R. Herbrich (2000). Adaptive margin support vector machines. In A. J. Smola, P. L. Bartlett, B. Schölkopf, and D. Schuurmans (Eds.), *Advances in Large Margin Classifiers*, Cambridge, MA, pp. 281–295. MIT Press.

Weston, J. and C. Watkins (1998). Multi-class support vector machines. Technical Report CSD-TR-98-04, Department of Computer Science, Royal Holloway, University of London, Egham, TW20 0EX, UK.

Williams, C. K. I. (1998). Prediction with Gaussian processes: From linear regression to linear prediction and beyond. In M. I. Jordan (Ed.), *Learning and Inference in Graphical Models*. Kluwer Academic.

Williams, C. K. I. and D. Barber (1998). Bayesian classification with Gaussian processes. *IEEE Transactions on Pattern Analysis and Machine Intelligence PAMI 20*(12), 1342–1351.

Williams, C. K. I. and M. Seeger (2001). Using the Nyström method to speed up kernel machines. In T. K. Leen, T. G. Dietterich, and V. Tresp (Eds.), *Advances in Neural Information Processing Systems 13*, Cambridge, MA, pp. 682–688. MIT Press.

Williamson, R. C., A. J. Smola, and B. Schölkopf (2000). Entropy numbers of linear function classes. In N. Cesa-Bianchi and S. Goldman (Eds.), *Proceedings of the Annual Conference on Computational Learning Theory*, San Francisco, pp. 309–319. Morgan Kaufmann Publishers.

Wolpert, D. H. (1995). *The Mathematics of Generalization*. Addison-Wesley.

Index

Printed in the United States
by Baker & Taylor Publisher Services

Printed in the United States
by Baker & Taylor Publisher Services